HUMAN SERVICES

HUMAN SERVICES

CONTEMPORARY ISSUES AND TRENDS

THIRD EDITION

Edited by

HOWARD S. HARRIS

Late, Bronx Community College

DAVID C. MALONEY

Fitchburg State College

FRANKLYN M. ROTHER

Brookdale Community College

PEARSON

ALLYN AND BACON

Boston • New York • San Francisco
Mexico City • Montreal • Toronto • London • Madrid • Munich • Paris
Hong Kong • Singapore • Tokyo • Cape Town • Sydney

Series Editor: Patricia Quinlin
Senior Editorial Assistant: Annemarie Kennedy
Composition and Prepress Buyer: Linda Cox
Manufacturing Buyer: JoAnne Sweeney
Cover Administrator: Kristina Mose-Libon
Editorial–Production Service: Matrix Productions Inc.
Electronic Composition: Omegatype Typography, Inc.

For related titles and support materials, visit our online catalog at www.ablongman.com.

Between the time Website information is gathered and then published, it is not unusual for some sites to have closed. Also, the transcription of URLs can result in unintended typographical errors. The publisher would appreciate notification where these errors occur so that they may be corrected in subsequent editions.

Library of Congress Cataloging–in–Publication Data

Human services : contemporary issues and trends / edited by Howard S. Harris,
 David C. Maloney, Franklyn M. Rother. —3rd ed.
     p. cm.
   Includes bibliographical references and index.
   ISBN 0-205-32770-2
     1. Human services. 2. Human services personnel. I. Harris, Howard S.,
 1942– II. Maloney, David C. III. Rother, Franklyn, M.

HV40.H784 2004
361—dc21

                                                                2003051943

Printed in the United States of America

DEDICATION

*The third edition of this collection of readings is dedicated
to the memory of Howard S. Harris, whose passing
was on April 22, 2000. This text is also dedicated to
his lovely wife of many years, Carol, and his son, Scott,
whom he held with immeasurable pride.*

*As a human service educator and administrator at his beloved
Bronx Community College, he was highly regarded and
formally recognized throughout his career.
As a person, he will be remembered always as a sensitive
and compassionate man who masterfully balanced
commitment and work ethic with an endearing
and caring acceptance of all those he met.*

*In all that he taught me, in all that he helped me with,
and in all that he overlooked in me, I am forever enriched
by his being a part of my life.*

David

CONTENTS

FOREWORD *Harold L. McPheeters* **xi**

PREFACE **xiii**

PART ONE
HUMAN SERVICES: ORIGINS, DEVELOPMENT, AND BASICS **1**

CHAPTER 1 **BASIC CONCEPTS AND DEFINITIONS OF HUMAN SERVICES**
Paul F. Cimmino **5**

SPECIAL FOCUS FEATURE
Letter to Paul Cimmino from Harold McPheeters **19**

CHAPTER 2 **HISTORICAL ROOTS OF HUMAN SERVICES** *Joel Diambra* **23**

CHAPTER 3 **HUMAN SERVICES AND WELFARE REFORM**

A. THE NEW AMERICAN CONTRACT WITH THE POOR
Frances Fox Piven **33**

**B. WELFARE REFORM'S IMPACT ON PEOPLE—CASE
EXAMPLES: IMPLICATIONS FOR HUMAN SERVICE WORK
AND HUMAN SERVICE WORKERS** *Michael Seliger* **37**

CHAPTER 4 **EMPOWERMENT: THEORY AND PRACTICE**

**A. EMPOWERMENT: TOWARD A NEW DEFINITION OF
SELF-HELP** *Audrey Cohen* **41**

**B. HOW ALUMNI PERCEIVE AND USE THE CONSTRUCTIVE
ACTION** *Shirley Conyard* **49**

Key Terms for Part One 59
Pivotal Issues for Discussion of Part One 59
Suggested Readings for Part One 60

PART TWO
HUMAN SERVICE PROFESSIONALS: SKILLS, VALUES, AND STANDARDS   61

SPECIAL FOCUS FEATURE
Welcome to Human Services: A Journey in Helping Others   *Margaret J. French*   63

CHAPTER 5   HUMAN SERVICES: NECESSARY SKILLS AND VALUES
Lorence A. Long and Maureen Doyle   67

CHAPTER 6   TECHNIQUES AND SKILLS IN INTERVIEWING: THE ROLE OF COMPETENCE-BASED LEARNING IN HUMAN SERVICE EDUCATION   *John Hancock*   77

SPECIAL FOCUS FEATURE
Using Short-Term Psychotherapy to Treat Post-Traumatic Stress Disorder (PTSD)
Lynne Schmelter-Davis   87

CHAPTER 7   HELPING SERVICES FOR GROUPS   *Barbara Somerville*   89

SPECIAL FOCUS FEATURE
Conflict Resolution: An Example of Using Skills in Working with Groups
Janet Hagen   105

CHAPTER 8   NATIONAL COMMUNITY SUPPORT SKILL STANDARDS PROJECT: IMPLICATIONS FOR HUMAN SERVICE EDUCATION
Mary Di Giovanni, Franklyn M. Rother, and David C. Maloney   111

SPECIAL FOCUS FEATURE
The Human Service Worker: A Generic Job Description   *A joint publication of NOHSE and CSHSE*   123

Key Terms for Part Two   127
Pivotal Issues for Discussion of Part Two   127
Suggested Readings for Part Two   127

PART THREE
HUMAN SERVICE WORK WITH FAMILIES AND CHILDREN   129

CHAPTER 9   DOMESTIC VIOLENCE, BATTERED WOMEN, AND DIMENSIONS OF THE PROBLEM   *Maria Munoz-Kantha*   131

CHAPTER 10   THE CHILD WELFARE DELIVERY SYSTEM
IN THE UNITED STATES   *David S. Liederman, Madelyn DeWoody,
and Megan C. Sylvester*   141

CHAPTER 11   CHILD MALTREATMENT AND ABUSE: THE PROBLEM
AND HUMAN SERVICES   *James Edell Lopez*   153

CHAPTER 12   YOUTH AND HUMAN SERVICES   *Walter de Oliveira and
Christopher R. Edginton*   167

SPECIAL FOCUS FEATURE
Pregnant Productions: A Vygotsky-Inspired Approach to Teens and Teen Pregnancy
Rafael Mendez   **181**

Key Terms for Part Three   193
Pivotal Issues for Discussion of Part Three   193
Suggested Readings for Part Three   194

PART FOUR
HUMAN SERVICE CLIENTS: SPECIAL POPULATIONS   195

CHAPTER 13   WORKING WITH PEOPLE WHO LIVE WITH HIV AND AIDS: THE
PROBLEM AND HUMAN SERVICES   *Wm. Lynn McKinney*   197

CHAPTER 14   HUMAN SERVICES FOR HOMELESS PEOPLE
Lorence A. Long   211

CHAPTER 15   HELPING FOR ALCOHOL AND DRUG ABUSE   *Marcel A. Duclos and
Marianne Gfroerer*   225

SPECIAL FOCUS FEATURE
A Social Norms Approach to Reduction of Alcohol and Drug Abuse among College Students
Franklyn M. Rother   **223**

CHAPTER 16   HELPING SERVICES FOR OLDER ADULTS   *Kathleen J. Niccum*   239

CHAPTER 17   HUMAN SERVICES AND CRIMINAL JUSTICE: PEOPLE AND THE
SYSTEM   *David C. Whelan*   249

SPECIAL FOCUS FEATURE
Architecture for Justice: Direct Supervision Management   *Anthony W. Pellicane*   **253**

Key Terms for Part Four   255
Pivotal Issues for Discussion of Part Four   255
Suggested Readings for Part Four   255

PART FIVE
CHANGING THE SYSTEM(S) IN HUMAN SERVICES   257

CHAPTER 18   POLICY, POLITICS, AND HUMAN SERVICES
Harold L. McPheeters   259

CHAPTER 19   COMMUNITY ORGANIZING AS HUMAN SERVICE
Lee Stuart   267

CHAPTER 20   HUMAN SERVICES IN THE MENTAL HEALTH ARENA: FROM
INSTITUTION TO COMMUNITY   *Joseph Mehr*   275

CHAPTER 21   AMERICANS WITH DISABILITIES: ADVOCACY, LAW,
AND HUMAN SERVICES   *Christine Lewis Shane*   287

Key Terms for Part Five   297
Pivotal Issues for Discussion of Part Five   297
Suggested Readings for Part Five   298

PART SIX
LAW, ETHICS, AND PROFESSIONAL ISSUES   299

CHAPTER 22   LEGAL FOUNDATIONS IN HUMAN SERVICES:
CONSIDERATIONS FOR CLIENTS AND WORKERS
David C. Maloney and Peter Clark   301

CHAPTER 23   LAW, ETHICS, AND THE HUMAN SERVICE WORKER
Naydean Blair   317

SPECIAL FOCUS FEATURE
Ethical Standards of Human Service Professionals   *National Organization for
Human Service Education*   329

CHAPTER 24   HUMAN SERVICES AS A CAREER: PERSONAL SURVIVAL
AND PROFESSIONAL GROWTH   *Miriam Clubok*   333

CHAPTER 25   BURNOUT: AVOIDING THE TRAP   *H. Frederick Sweitzer*   339

Key Terms for Part Six   354
Pivotal Issues for Discussion of Part Six   354
Suggested Readings for Part Six   354

PART SEVEN
EMERGING ISSUES AND TRENDS   357

CHAPTER 26   **TRENDS AND CHALLENGES OF CULTURAL DIVERSITY**
R. Donna Petrie   359

CHAPTER 27   **TECHNOLOGY AND HUMAN SERVICES**   *Stan Rosenzweig*   367

CHAPTER 28   **TECHNOLOGY AND SOCIALITY IN THE NEW MILLENNIUM:
CURRENT CHALLENGES FOR THE HUMAN SERVICE
GENERALIST**   *Eugene M. DeRobertis and Robert Saldarini*   375

SPECIAL FOCUS FEATURE
How Service-Learning Experiences Transform Students' Lives   *Linda Mass*   383

CHAPTER 29   **RESEARCH MODELS IN HUMAN SERVICES**   *Rod Underwood
and Michael Lee*   387

Key Terms for Part Seven   406
Pivotal Issues for Discussion of Part Seven   406
Suggested Readings for Part Seven   407

APPENDIX A   **MID-TERM INTERVIEW: OBSERVER RATING FORM**   **408**

APPENDIX B   **MID-TERM INTERVIEW: SELF-EVALUATION PAPER**   **410**

ABOUT THE EDITORS   **413**

ABOUT THE AUTHORS   **414**

INDEX   **421**

FOREWORD

The human service education movement began in response to the demands of the Great Society of the 1960s for workers who might be trained in a shorter time and for more comprehensive service to persons with biopsychosocial problems than traditional professionals had provided. Each of the established professions is based on a single theoretical concept of the nature and treatment of such problems, but experience teaches that human service problems almost always involve a complicated blend of biological, psychological, social, economic, and political factors. What was needed was not so much a team of highly specialized experts in each of these disciplines, but a generalist worker who could use the best of each discipline in a pragmatic relationship to help clients solve their problems and empower themselves to function more effectively.

The human service worker was not to be atheoretical or purely empirical, but rather a multidisciplinary practitioner who could draw from a basic knowledge of all the major disciplines to advocate for each client what seemed pragmatically best for the circumstances. The worker was not to be a specialist in any particular technology or theoretical orientation. If specialized skills in these areas were deemed necessary, the worker was to negotiate for them on behalf of the client.

The human service movement enjoyed remarkable success in its early years, and it has continued to evolve over the past thirty years. However, it has also encountered challenges resulting from retrenchment in human service funding and the expansion of educational programs in the traditional professions, particularly by their moving to practitioner-training programs at baccalaureate and master's degree levels that formerly would have been unacceptable to those professions. At the same time, there have been remarkable changes in society's values and perceptions about many aspects of human service problems and society's response to them, including the role and status of women, the role of minorities, the role of consensus, and more recently, reduced and capitation funding and managed care in both public and private human service agencies. And there have been new realities to address—the spread of AIDS, the aging of the population, and the ongoing widespread use and abuse of mind-altering substances, especially among younger persons.

More than one hundred years ago, James Russell Lowell wrote in "Once to Every Man and Nation":

New occasions teach new duties,
Time makes ancient good uncouth;
They must upward still and onward,
Who would keep abreast of truth.

And so it is today for human service educators! Educators and students must remain vigilant about changes in the field and be flexible to meet the new challenges with informed strategies.

This book contains a set of supplemental readings to address some of the changes facing the human services in 2003 and their inherent challenges for human service educators and practitioners. In a dynamically changing world, it is essential that such a book be issued every few years to assess and better respond to society's new occasions and new values.

Harold L. McPheeters, M.D.

PREFACE

The first edition of *Human Services: Contemporary Issues and Trends* was intended to define and identify the human service movement during its third decade of development. The contributing authors crafted their articles specifically for that book, thereby creating a new body of knowledge. The book received a favorable reception and appealed to a wide range of audiences. It was adopted for use in two-year, four-year, and graduate-level programs and in institutions where there were no human service programs. The distribution was in both urban and rural colleges within and outside the United States.

The challenge of the second edition was to reflect the developments of the preceding three years in the field of human services, and to do so in a volume the same size as the first edition. It was a difficult task to eliminate or *cut down* excellent articles so that new material could be included. The new volume had to encompass, for example, welfare reform and the implications of the National Community Support Skill Standards Project. Additionally, some articles required substantial revision due to important changes in areas such as the child welfare system or helping people who are living with HIV and AIDS.

The third edition of the book contains two new chapters that expand on the importance of technology and social change and research the effectiveness of the empowerment educational model. Additionally, new topic chapters include Historical Roots of Human Services; Techniques and Skills in Interviewing; and Legal Foundations in Human Services. Several new Special Focus Features introduce the reader to emerging issues and trends that affect human service education and practice: service-learning, social norms theory, architectural design and corrections supervision, and short-term therapy.

For this edition, the content is organized in seven parts. Part One presents an extended view of the conceptual framework of the field of human services, with historical references and contemporary reflections and research. In the lead chapter, Paul Cimmino discusses the many aspects of human services. Chapter 1 is followed by a commentary by Harold L. McPheeters. In Chapter 2, Joel Diambra presents the historical background necessary for understanding the human service movement. In Chapter 3, Frances Fox Piven discusses welfare reform from a political perspective, and Michael Seliger describes its impact with actual case studies. In Chapter 4, Audrey Cohen elaborates on the concept of empowerment within the context of the college's educational model, with a follow-up research study by Shirley Conyard on alumni perceptions and use of the "constructive action" process in human service practice.

Part Two focuses on the skills, values, and standards required in human service professional practice. It begins with an orientation to the field by Margaret J. French, who shares with the reader her many years of experience as a human service educator. Lorence Long and Maureen Doyle in Chapter 5 discuss the practical skills, knowledge, and values necessary for a successful human service worker. In Chapter 6, John Hancock discusses specific techniques and skills in interviewing, followed by a Special Focus Feature on short-term therapy by Lynne Schmelter-Davis. In Chapter 7, Barbara Somerville explores human service practice with groups, with a Special Focus Feature on conflict resolution by Janet Hagen. Mary DiGiovanni, Franklyn M. Rother, and David C. Maloney conclude Part Two with a descriptive list of the National Skill Standards for Human Services Practitioner Education and Training Programs in Chapter 8. These skills standards are used by the Council for Standards in Human Service Education to identify exemplary programs and to grant program approval. A generic job description for human service workers follows as a Special Focus Feature.

Part Three focuses on human service issues facing families and children. In Chapter 9, Maria Munoz-Kantha discusses family violence and helping battered women. David Liederman, Madelyn DeWoody, and Megan Sylvester describe the child welfare system and include extensive material on this subject area in Chapter 10. In Chapter 11, James Edell Lopez explores the problem of child abuse. A focus on youth services by Walter de Oliveira and Christopher Edginton in Chapter 12 is followed by a Special Focus Feature by Rafael Mendez describing a community-based teenage pregnancy prevention program.

Part Four continues the focus on human service clients in special populations. In Chapter 13, Wm. Lynn McKinney explores human services for people living with HIV and AIDS. Lorence Long, in Chapter 14, describes services for homeless people, with a follow-up concerning alcohol and drug treatment services in Chapter 15 by Marcel Duclos and Marianne Gfroerer. A new Special Focus Feature by Franklyn Rother introduces the reader to Social Norms theory and its application in a college setting. In Chapter 16, Kathleen Niccum describes services for older adults, and in Chapter 17 David Whelan discusses human services within the criminal justice system. Concluding Part Four, Anthony Pellicane describes how direct supervision of inmates is influenced by the architectural design of the facility.

Part Five looks at systems change in the human service field. Chapter 18, by Harold McPheeters, discusses political involvement in concrete terms. In Chapter 19, Lee Stuart describes change through community organizing, drawing on her experience with the Industrial Areas Foundation. In Chapter 20, John Mehr discusses the recent shift to community-based rather than institutional settings in delivering mental health services. Christine Lewis Shane in Chapter 21 describes the changes initiated by the Americans with Disabilities Act.

Part Six covers the topics of law, ethics, and professional issues. In Chapter 22, Peter Clark and David Maloney explore the legal foundations of the human service field. Chapter 23, by Naydean Blair, focuses on ethical and legal obligations of human service workers. This is followed by a Special Focus Feature on the Ethical Standards for Human Service Professionals. In Chapter 24, Miriam Clubok discusses surviving and growing in a human service career. H. Frederick Sweitzer, in Chapter 25, explores ways to avoid burnout.

Part Seven examines the emerging influences and trends in the human service profession. In Chapter 26, R. Donna Petrie considers cultural diversity challenges. The rapidly changing technology used for information and communication is explored by Stan Rosenzweig. Chapter 28, by Eugene DeRobertis and Robert Saldarini, describes the challenges posed by technology for human service workers and society as a whole. A new Special Focus Feature by Linda Mass highlights the importance of Service-Learning in human service education. Part Seven concludes with Chapter 29, in which

Rod Underwood and Michael Lee emphasize the importance of objective examination through research and evaluation.

The third edition of this book has been made possible by the enthusiasm and cooperation shown by these contributors in crafting articles for it. We acknowledge and appreciate their efforts. We recognize the support and assistance of the following Allyn & Bacon staff: Kevin Stone, Karen Hanson, Judy Fifer, Patricia Quinlin, and Annemarie Kennedy. We want to thank Carol Harris and the fine colleagues at Bronx Community College, Monty Gray and Regina Wingfall, who have assisted us during this difficult time in your own lives. Finally, we want to thank Howard Harris, whose contributions to our professional lives have enriched us throughout our careers and in whose memory we dedicate this edition of the book.

PART ONE

HUMAN SERVICES: ORIGINS, DEVELOPMENT, AND BASICS

Part One includes four chapters and two special focus features that will provide a foundation for your understanding of the field of human services. You will learn about the different meanings and contexts of the term "human services." You will also come to appreciate the evolution of contemporary human services as a way of responding to a wide array of social and personal problems. In these readings, you will see the dramatic effect that government, through legislation and policy implementation, can have on how human service needs are met. You will find that the terms and ideas introduced in these chapters will reappear throughout the book and be useful in your human service career.

In Chapter 1, Paul Cimmino discusses the basic concepts and definitions in the field of human services, making it clear that "human services" is a complex term and that the field is both broad and varied. Paul Cimmino presents a strong case for human services as a distinct profession and field of study within the helping professions and within social sciences. As you begin your study of the human service profession, you will understand that you are part of a movement that sees itself as one way that a just society expresses its concern for the worth and well-being of each person. You will better understand your future role as a human service worker as it compares with and differs from other professional careers in social work, psychology, psychiatry, and mental health counseling. Human services is an "eclectic" field, which means that it draws upon and uses aspects of other fields such as clinical psychology and social work. Many of your teachers, who are human service educators, have had their initial training and experience in these other fields.

After reading this first chapter, you will come to recognize the many different tasks undertaken by human service workers and to understand how these tasks change with different consumer, or client, populations. You will also become aware of a wide variety of human service work, which, regardless of how this work is applied or carried out, is always involved in solutions to human problems and social issues. With these ideas in mind, you will better appreciate the scope and range of human services and how these services attempt to change both individuals and society. Immediately following Chapter 1, as a Special Focus Feature, is a letter by Harold McPheeters that comments on aspects of the chapter. This letter will be of interest to you as you prepare for a career as a professional helper.

Chapter 2 will help to provide the foundations and historical references to the human service field and will, along with Chapter 1, provide the general backdrop for later chapters, each of which will contribute special and important elaboration of details and issues. Together, these chapters provide a continuous and comprehensive presentation of the professional field of human services.

In any first exposure to an academic discipline, professional field of work, or general subject matter, the introductory student will feel the need for a sense of "intellectual grounding," or an awareness of the origins of these ideas or bodies of knowledge and the ways in which the field developed to its present condition.

In Chapter 2, Joel Diambra provides a network of historical references, both remote and recent, that illustrate the breadth and depth of what is current and contemporary in the field. From the preceding chapter you gained a basic understanding of human services as a concept and how that concept is applied to the "helping" professions. This chapter traces the history of human services from early values in various traditions to the impact of recent social and political forces. This chapter will provide you with an understanding of how this field of professional work and training began, how it developed over time, and what have been its major influences.

In order to be an effective professional, one must stay current with events relevant to many aspects of human services, such as *welfare reform*. Chapter 3 is presented in two segments, which together should give you a comprehensive perspective on welfare reform. In Chapter 3a, Frances Fox Piven interprets the legislative changes (starting at the federal level) in welfare in its political context. In Chapter 3b, Michael Seliger shows the consequences of these changes for human services by presenting composite cases of actual people who have been affected by the reforms.

In Chapter 4a, Audrey Cohen introduces the concept of *empowerment* as the purpose of human services. A training model, focusing on "Purpose," is discussed and illustrated in terms of dimensions of eight performance areas. It will be interesting for you to compare the development and implementation of this model with the Skill Standards Project discussed in Chapter 8. As you grasp these basic concepts, you will need to know how the human service movement evolved to its present state and how these professional services emerged to their present-day form.

Shirley Conyard, in Chapter 4b, presents research findings that discuss how alumni perceive the usefulness of Constructive Action, a documentation of a student's implementation of a purpose change goal, and interpretive application of the theories and concepts learned in the classroom. Her discussion of the influence of this particular human service model on graduate practitioners provides us with considerations about all human service education.

After reading Chapters 1 through 4 and gaining a broader awareness of the origins and history of the concept of human services and the emergence of the human service worker, you will better grasp and appreciate the role of education in preparing people to enter the professional field of human services.

LEARNING OBJECTIVES FOR PART ONE: HUMAN SERVICES: ORIGINS, DEVELOPMENT, AND BASICS

After reading and studying Chapters 1, 2, 3a, 3b, 4a, and 4b,

- You will know the meaning of human services.
- You will be able to recognize the consumers/clients in human services.
- You will be able to describe a human service worker.
- You will understand the impact of welfare reform.
- You will understand purpose-centered education and the Constructive Action approach.

CHAPTER 1

BASIC CONCEPTS AND DEFINITIONS OF HUMAN SERVICES

PAUL F. CIMMINO

This chapter is dedicated to the development of basic definitions that describe and identify human services. However, any attempt to define human services in one sentence, or to use one description, is doomed to fail. According to Schmolling, Youkeles, and Burger, there is no generally accepted or "official" definition of human services (1993, p. 9). Human services is a multidisciplinary profession that reflects complex human interactions and a comprehensive social system. To understand human services, it is important to develop ideas that construct an organized perspective of the field. In this chapter, three general questions about human services are incorporated into the text. First, *"What is it, and what* isn't *it?"* Second, *"Who is helped and why?"* Third, *"How is help delivered and by whom?"* These fundamental questions tend to exemplify the basic concepts and definitions in human services. This chapter proceeds to introduce important terms, definitions, subconcepts, and concentration areas in human services, which are expounded upon by a host of authors who have contributed their expertise to create this book.

The professional field of human services can be reduced to three basic concepts: *intervention* (needs and services); *professionalism* (applied practice and credentialing); and *education* (academic training and research). Each basic concept comprises important aspects of the human service field and identifies primary areas of the profession. The supporting background that nourishes

intervention, professionalism, and *education* in human services is the history of the human service movement (Fullerton, 1990). The formal development of human services in society is located in the legislative, training, and service history of the field. This chapter attempts to offer a collective understanding of these important areas related to the professional development of human services. In this chapter, basic concepts and definitions converge to generate a comprehensive and theoretical notion of human services in forming an overview of the field. To further assist the reader in developing thoughts about the human service profession, and to avoid ambiguity in the field, a medley of contemporary definitions of human services is presented later in the chapter.

Finally, an important letter written by Dr. Harold McPheeters in 1992, which addresses the basic question of what comprises human services, is presented to close the chapter. McPheeters's letter was sent in response to a manuscript written by me in 1991. The paper proposes an idealistic model that defines human services in terms of its purpose and professional responsibility in society. Later in the chapter, the central ideas are summarized, providing an orientation to the thoughtful feedback from Harold McPheeters. In my view, his written response conveys landmark perspectives in development of the emerging human service field. Thus, the ideas stemming from my paper and McPheeters's response invite a judicious overview of this chapter for the reader's developing knowledge of human services.

THE BASIC CONCEPT OF PURPOSE IN HUMAN SERVICES

Human services is a term that reflects the need for society to help its members live adequate and rewarding lives (Eriksen, 1977). The human service field encompasses a variety of functions and characteristics. Human service activity is the act of people helping other people meet their needs in an organized social context. Thus, the human service function is a process of directed change taking place as the result of interaction between human service workers, clients, and organizations. Ideally, the changes human service workers attempt to facilitate are intended to assist clients in achieving optimum human potential. In order to help a variety of people in this fashion, the human service worker trains as a generalist and must be familiar with various approaches in the helping process (Schmolling, Youkeles, and Burger, 1993, p. 146).

The human service orientation to helping people recognizes that clients are an intricate part of their environment. Today, the need for human services in society is obvious. Human services has emerged in response to the increase of human problems in our modern world (Mehr, 1988). The complications of living in a rapidly changing society causes massive stress on human beings. Often people are unable to meet their own basic needs due to harsh social conditions and oppression (Ryan, 1976). Socialization for many individuals is deprived or detrimental relative to basic life needs. The problems people experience can be rooted in family backgrounds, education, economics, disease, disability, self-concepts, or legal matters. The human service model acknowledges these conditions as primary factors in human dysfunction but not necessarily predictors of a person's capacity. The human service ideology of helping people focuses on the immediate needs and presenting problems of the client. This approach does not prejudge clients and recognizes that any person in need of human services is a legitimate consumer of services. By the same token, human services practice attempts to relieve human suffering while promoting independence from the human service system.

The conceptual evolution of human services as a professional helping process stems from historical movements in the field. The history of the human service movement is addressed in a later chapter. However, it is useful to mention the significance of this history in the development of a functional human service concept. The predecessors of today's human service and social welfare systems were social reforms in England, which were particularly established in the Elizabethan Poor Laws of 1601. Prior to this legislation, the church assumed responsibility to relieve the poor and served in the capacity of a public agency (Woodside and McClam, 1994, pp. 38–43). Legislation stemming from the Elizabethan Poor Laws, and the Law of Settlement added sixty years later, initiated the idea of compulsory taxation to raise funds to help the needy and established eligibility requirements for recipients (Woodside and McClam, 1994, pp. 42–43). These early developments in English social reform and legislation more than 350 years ago are bridges to contemporary human services in the United States.

The impact of social and legislative changes during the 1950s, 1960s, and 1970s fostered the creation of human services as it exists today (Woodside and McClam, 1990, p. 41). The response to deinstitutionalization in the 1960s, coupled with influences of the civil rights movement along with a series of related legislation, resulted in the creation of a new "human service worker." Examples of important legislation in the development of contemporary services are the Manpower Development Training Act of 1962, the Mental Health Study Act of 1955, the Social Security Amendments of 1962, the Scheuer Subprofessional Career Act of 1966, and the Community Mental Health Centers Act of 1963. Such legislation promoted the human service movement of the 1960s and 1970s, whereby a process ensued creating opportunities for training programs and progressive development in human service education. Consequently, a blend of agency services, social policies, academic programs, professional practice development, and people working together for social change formulate the helping process called human services.

HUMAN SERVICE INTERVENTION

Human Services Intervention is defined as a broad field of human endeavor in which the professional acts as an agent to assist individuals, families, and communities to better cope with crisis, change and stress; to prevent and alleviate stress; and to function effectively in all areas of life and living. Human Services Practice is conducted in the broad spectrum of human services in a manner that is responsive to both current and future trends and needs for human resource development, and committed to humanitarian values (Montana State University–Billings: Catalog 1991–93, Sexton, R., 1987).

The preceding definition of human service intervention reflects the functional role of the field in society. The amount of public support for human service programs is determined by the state of the economy (Schmolling, Youkeles, and Burger, 1993, p. 24). Since sufficient funding for human service programs is inconsistent, fulfilling the mission of effective intervention in helping clients often fluctuates. Thus, the delivery capability of human services to the public is unpredictable and frequently inadequate in providing resources to sufficiently help clients. In spite of this condition, human service intervention remains committed to reflecting the values and priorities of society (Eriksen, 1977, p. 10).

Human service intervention is the bridge between people and various subsystems in society (Eriksen, 1977, p. 10). The intervention philosophy of human services reflects humanitarian values. Eriksen identified the following philosophical principles as fundamental to the delivery of human services:

1. Human services are the embodiment of our national commitment to building a just society based on respect for people's rights and needs.
2. Every individual in our society is entitled to services that will prevent his/her pain, maintain integrity, enable him/her with realities, stimulate personal growth, and promote a satisfying life.
3. Prevention of people's problems and discomforts is as important a part of human services as restitution and rehabilitation after the fact.
4. The integration of human services is crucial to their effectiveness.
5. Human services are accountable to the consumers.
6. Human services tasks and goals:

The paramount goal of human services is to enable people to live more satisfying, more autonomous, and more productive lives, through the utilization of society's knowledge, resources, and technological innovations. To that end, society's systems will be working for its people, putting people before paper (Eriksen, 1977, pp. 10, 11, 12).

The three primary models in the helping professions are the medical model, public health (social welfare) model, and human service model. Of these recognized interventions, the human service model is unique in its view of people, services, and the social environment as integrated entities. The medical model and public health models, on the other hand, have an individualistic orientation to causation relative to people's problems. For instance, the medical model concentrates on the individual, views clients as needing help because they are sick, and refers to people as patients. The medical model engendered the discipline of psychiatry at the end of the eighteenth century, and its history is closely related to the development of the human service profession. The public health model contends that individuals have problems that are also linked to social conditions and views disease as multicausal (Woodside and McClam, 1994, p. 89). Hypothetically, both these models are based on determinism, suggesting that disease and social problems are an individual's responsibility, not society's, and if controlled they would have less effect on the human condition. The human service model expects disease and social problems to always affect the lives of people and focuses on providing services to help individuals deal with problems stemming from these conditions. Similarly, by using these models to describe and approach the problem-solving process, the human service worker is able to expand resources and systems for service delivery and intervention.

THE GENERALIST ROLES OF THE HUMAN SERVICE WORKER

The basic roles human service professionals play in the helping process were initially developed by the Southern Regional Education Board (SREB) as part of an effort to produce functional comparisons to other established professions. The project also defined four levels of competence (discussed later in this chapter) to correlate with role functions. The SREB identified thirteen roles that human service workers perform that were derived by evaluating the needs of clients, families, and communities (SREB, 1969). These roles include the following:

1. *Outreach worker*—reaches out to detect people with problems and can make appropriate referrals for needed services.
2. *Broker*—helps people get to existing services and provides follow-up to ensure continued care.
3. *Advocate*—pleads and fights for services, policy, rules, regulations, and laws for client's behalf.
4. *Evaluator*—assesses client or community needs and problems, whether medical, psychiatric, social, or educational.
5. *Teacher-educator*—performs a range of instructional activities from simple coaching to teaching highly technical content directed to individuals and groups.
6. *Behavior changer*—carries out a range of activities planned primarily to change behavior, ranging from coaching and counseling to casework, psychotherapy, and behavior therapy.
7. *Mobilizer*—helps to get new resources for clients or communities.
8. *Consultant*—works with other professions and agencies regarding their handling of problems, needs, and programs.
9. *Community planner*—works with community boards, committees, and so on to ensure that community developments enhance self-actualization and minimize emotional stress on people.
10. *Caregiver*—provides services for persons who need ongoing support of some kind (i.e., financial assistance, day care, social support, twenty-four-hour care).
11. *Data manager*—performs all aspects of data handling, gathering, tabulating, analyzing, synthesizing, program evaluation, and planning.
12. *Administrator*—carries out activities that are primarily agency or institution oriented (e.g., budgeting, purchasing, and personnel activities).
13. *Assistant to specialist*—acts as assistant to specialist (e.g., psychiatrist, psychologist, or nurse), relieving them of burdensome tasks.

The framework of the helping process in human services is characterized by the role functions and structures listed above and not restricted to frontline workers who provide direct services; administrators and supervisors also facilitate service delivery.

THE SOCIAL IDEOLOGY OF HUMAN SERVICES

Eriksen's principles represent a social ideology about human services that parallels the needs of an individual living in society. Social policy advocates who hold humanitarian perspectives contend the previously mentioned conditions are individual rights that should be afforded to all people. Many of these scholars argue that an adequate standard of living is a constitutional right. However, the U.S. Constitution does not specify living standards for citizens. To a large extent, the life standards developed by humanitarian scholars are actually postulations drawn from language in the U.S. Constitution, the Declaration of Independence, the Bill of Rights, and a variety of subsequent federal and state civil rights legislation. For instance, the opening remarks (second paragraph) of the Declaration of Independence include this statement: "We hold these truths to be self-evident, that all men are created equal, that they are endowed by their Creator with certain inalienable rights, that among these are life, liberty and the pursuit of happiness." Similarly, the U.S. Constitution, Amendment XV, Section 1, states, "The right of citizens of the United States to vote shall not be denied or abridged by the United States or by any State on account of race, color, or previous condition of servitude."

One can see how expanding the meaning of this language from both documents can imply the right to be afforded a certain quality of life in American society. The degree of social obligation held by the government in promoting social equity or empowering people to become self-sufficient has been a controversial topic among social policy makers and scholars. To a large extent, the present model of social welfare and human service delivery systems is not functionally consistent with the idea of society taking responsibility for the problems of its members. However, the notion of society taking partial responsibility for its members' hardships parallels the professional ideologies promoted in this chapter (Schmolling, Youkeles, and Burger, 1993, p. 18). To date, social policy relative to human services remains guided by an ideology of individualism and community derived from traditional perspectives. Conservative American values continue to place emphasis on hard work, perseverance, and self-reliance. Thus emerges the concept of Americans as rugged individuals who can pull themselves up by their bootstraps, a concept that remains deeply embedded in our society. This attitude translates into a community model of social services that supports programs dealing only with immediate situations (human problems) and generally opposes programs that go beyond meeting basic survival needs (Schmolling, Youkeles, and Burger, 1993, pp. 18, 19).

Proactive Human Services

The concept of human services supports the empowerment of people to become self-sufficient and capable of meeting their own needs without assistance from human services. Therefore, human services aims to provide clients the kind of direct support that facilitates eventual emancipation and prevents a state of dependency on the system. This kind of assistance is referred to as the proactive approach to human services. This form of intervention utilizes strategies that invest in the prevention of problems and stabilization of client systems into the future. Ideally, planning beyond the problem to help the client become socially self-sufficient is the heart of the professional human service model. However, a crisis-oriented, pluralistic society that has recently come to recognize the concept of multicausality and the impact of psychosocial stress cannot be expected to change from traditional (reactive) perspectives on human problems to a prevention model or proactive perspective in a short period of time.

Human service intervention is based in theory on fundamental values about human life that are woven into the fabric of American heritage and more specifically identified in civil rights legislation. Professional perspectives of service delivery to clients recognize a standard of living for all people that promotes self-reliance, social perseverance, and a sense of personal gratification in social life. Linked to these values or life conditions are social values emphasizing certain essential human needs. Since the human service worker is an agent of society who advocates for the psychosocial advancement of the individual, it follows that the human service model is closely associated with civil rights legislation aimed at helping deprived population groups. Consequently, the identification of essential human needs is important for definitions of human service intervention and the development of basic problem-solving processes.

THE HUMAN SERVICE IDEOLOGY OF THE INDIVIDUAL

The general notion that problem behaviors are often the result of an individual's failure to satisfy basic human needs is a fundamental principle underlying human service practice. The human service model places a portion of responsibility on society for perpetuating social problems that reduce opportunities for people to be successful. The human service worker seeks to assist clients to adequately function in the same system that impairs them. A client may be in need of shelter, medical attention, transportation, education, food, emotional support, or legal services. Therefore, as an agent of a larger system (macrosocial system), the primary focus of the human service worker is fulfilling the needs of the individual client (microsocial system). In this sense, the human service worker becomes an *agent of change in the client system, placing the person first in the value system of the helping profession* (Cimmino, 1993).

The focus of human service intervention on *human needs* is an essential aspect of service delivery. There are numerous concepts in the literature that propose definitions of human needs. One concept, developed by Abraham Maslow (1968), is a self-actualization theory that outlines a hierarchy of human needs and is applicable to the human service model.

The hierarchy Maslow conceptualized consists of five levels. At the base are **physiological needs** for food, shelter, oxygen, water, and general survival. These conditions are fundamental to life. When people satisfy these basic survival needs, they are able to focus on **safety needs,** which involve the need for a secure and predictable environment. This may mean living in decent housing in a safe neighborhood. After safety needs have been fulfilled, the need for **belongingness and love** emerges. This includes intimacy and acceptance from others. When these three lower-level needs are partly satisfied, **esteem needs** develop in the context of the person's social environment. This level involves recognition by others that a person is competent or respected. Most people desire appreciation and positive reinforcement from others. At the top of the hierarchy exists the need for **self-actualization,** having to do with the fulfillment of a person's innate potential as a human being.

Maslow perceived self-actualized people as possessing attributes that are consistent with highly competent and successful individuals.

Although Maslow is considered a primary figure in humanistic psychology, there has been subsequent research to test the validity of his concepts. Follow-up research studies have produced mixed results; some results demonstrate support (Neher, 1991), while others refute the hypotheses (Schmolling, Youkeles, and Burger, 1993). Nevertheless, most people do live in a network of social relationships in which they seek external gratification in attending to their needs.

Another perspective on human needs is defined by Hansell's motivation theory (Schmolling, Youkeles, and Burger, 1993). This theory contends that people must achieve seven basic attachments in order to meet their needs. If a person is unsuccessful in achieving each attachment, ultimately a state of crisis and stress will result. Listed below are the seven basic attachments, accompanied with signs of failure of each one:

1. Food, water, and oxygen, along with informational supplies. Signs of failure: boredom, apathy, and physical disorder.
2. Intimacy, sex, closeness, and opportunity to exchange deep feelings. Signs of failure: loneliness, isolation, and lack of sexual satisfaction.
3. Belonging to a social peer group. Signs of failure: not feeling part of anything.
4. A clear, definite self-identity. Signs of failure: feeling doubtful and indecisive.
5. A social role that carries with it a sense of being a competent member of society. Signs of failure: depression and a sense of failure.
6. The need to be linked to a cash economy through a job, a spouse with income, social security benefits, or other ways. Sign of failure: lack of purchasing power, possibly an inability to purchase essentials.
7. A comprehensive system of meaning with clear priorities in life. Signs of failure: sense of drifting through life, detachment, and alienation.

Both Maslow's and Hansell's ideas about human needs provide a practical purpose for human service intervention. Essentially, human service workers attempt to find ways to help the client satisfy his or her unmet needs. The definition of the client situation or *presenting problem* generally involves evidence of failures indicated above. Similarly, the identification of problems such as poor housing, lack of food, fear of neighborhood, detrimental relationships, and low self-esteem suggests a physical, social, or psychological crisis that blocks the development of a person and the ability to function, as implied by Maslow's and Hansell's theories of self-actualization and motivation.

CRISIS INTERVENTION

When human service intervention is required as the result of a sudden disruption in the life of a client precipitated by a situational crisis or catastrophic event, *crisis intervention* is the consequence. Often, in these circumstances, even those people who do not expect to become consumers of the human service system suddenly find themselves clients. The practice of delivering crisis intervention services is supported by *crisis intervention theory*. Studies and research in crisis intervention theory and practice are primarily the domain of sociology, psychology, social psychology, social work, community psychiatry, and social welfare policy. The practice of crisis intervention in human services was developed by a variety of clinical practitioners in areas such as nursing, psychology, medicine, psychiatry, and clinical social work (Slaikeu, 1990). The application of crisis intervention methods is a recent development based on various human behavior theories, including those from Freud, Hartmann, Rado, Erickson, Lindemann, and Caplan (Aguilera and Messick, 1978; Slaikeu, 1990). Slaikeu (1990) cites the Coconut Grove fire on November 28, 1942, where 493 people perished when flames devoured the crowded nightclub. According to Slaikeu:

> *Lindemann and others from the Massachusetts General Hospital played an active role in helping survivors and those who had lost loved ones in the disaster. His clinical report (Lindemann, 1944) on the psychological symptoms of the survivors became the cornerstone for subsequent theorizing on the grief process, a series of stages through which a mourner progresses on the way toward accepting and resolving loss (p. 6).*

The evolution of community psychiatry and the suicide prevention movement of the 1960s marks an important historical development in crisis-intervention human services. An important figure in crisis theory and the associated approaches in service delivery was Gerald Caplan, a public health psychiatrist. Some of his contributions are discussed by Slaikeu (1990):

> *Building on the start given by Lindemann, Gerald Caplan, associated with Harvard School of Public Health, first formulated the significance of life crisis in an adult's psychopathology. Caplan's crisis theory was cast in the framework of Eriksen's developmental psychology. Caplan's interest was on how people negotiated the various transitions from one stage to another. He identified the importance of both personal and social resources in determining whether developmental crises (and situational or unexpected crises) would be worked out for better or for worse. Caplan's preventative psychiatry, with its focus on early intervention to promote positive growth and minimize the chance of psychological impairment, led to an emphasis on mental health consultation. Since many early crises could be identified and even predicted, it became important to train a wide range of community practitioners. The role of the mental health professional became one of assisting teachers, nurses, clergy, guidance counselors, and others in learning how to detect and deal with life crises in community settings (pp. 6–7).*

The formal emergence of community mental health programs in the United States became a way to implement recommendations from the U.S. Congress Joint Commission on Mental Illness and Health (1961). With strong support from the Kennedy Administration to provide mental health services in a community setting (not restricting them only to hospitals), crisis intervention programs and the outreach emergency services were established as an integral part of every comprehensive community mental health system and a prerequisite for federal funding.

A person who is experiencing a crisis faces a problem that cannot be resolved by using the coping mechanisms that have worked in the past (Aguilera and Messick, p. 1). According to Woodside and McClam (1990):

> *An individual's equilibrium is disrupted by pressures or upsets, which result in stress so severe that he or she is unable to find relief using coping skills that worked before. The crisis is the individual's emotional response to the threatening or hazardous situation, not the situation itself. Crises can be divided into two types: developmental and situational. A developmental crisis is an individual's response to a situation that is reasonably predictable in the life cycle. Situational or accidental crises do not occur with any regularity. The sudden and unpredictable nature of this type of crisis makes any preparation or individual control impossible. Examples are fire or other natural disasters, fatal illness, relocation, unplanned pregnancy, and rape. The skills and strategies that helpers use to provide immediate help for a person in crisis constitute crisis intervention (p. 217).*

People in crisis require immediate help and are in desperate situations. The human service philosophy (idealistically) is consistent with established crisis-intervention theory, which places the client's needs as a priority in the value system of the helping profession. For the human service worker, the value of putting people first is an important professional orientation, not just something that happens as the result of a crisis. In a crisis situation, the human service worker must quickly establish a working relationship and positive rapport with clients. The worker's knowledge and skills are important in supporting the client's sense of hope and eventual return to self-reliance (Woodside and McClam, 1990, p. 223). In most cases, there is more than one worker helping the client. Generally clients are involved in a social network of supportive programs that

involve different agencies and stem from an assortment of referrals. Collectively, the human service system coordinates efforts that are designed to return the client to a pre-crisis state of functioning. This objective is usually accomplished as the result of well-coordinated service delivery and effective problem-solving skills.

CLIENT SYSTEMS IN HUMAN SERVICE INTERVENTION

To continue discussions about the basic concept of human service intervention, it is important to understand the *total view* of the practice field. Much like social work, human services is directed toward the resolution of client problems that are part of a larger and dynamic social system. The nature of the service delivery system encompasses two distinct levels of interaction: providing direct services (face-to-face) and encompassing the acquisition of services from larger social systems. The *client system* is the immediate condition of the client's psychological and social life circumstances. Client systems comprise many components, such as family relationships, social and cultural attributes, economic status, age, gender, employment, physical and mental health, legal issues, education, living conditions, religion, and self-esteem. In short, the client system involves the immediate environment as the most significant influence on the client's life and behavior.

Micro- and Macrosocial Systems in Human Service Practice

The human service worker provides direct services to the client and is working simultaneously with the client system. For example, a worker who is assigned to an individual client may also work with the person's spouse, family members, other workers, and agencies in the client system. In this context, the human service worker is engaged in two distinct systems called micro- and macrosocial systems. A great deal has been written about the roles of micro- and macrosocial systems in the process of delivering human services. However, a brief review of the concept can help the reader understand the basis of human service intervention in the social environment.

Every client lives in both micro- and macrosocial systems. The human service worker is enmeshed in these two systems. Microsocial systems include individuals, small groups, families, and couples. Macrosocial systems involve large groups, organizations, communities, neighborhoods, and bureaucracies. Whittaker (1977) explains:

> The goals in macro intervention include changes within organizations, communities and societies, while micro intervention aims at enhancing social functioning or alleviation of social problems for a particular individual, family, or small group. Macro intervention relies heavily on theories of "big system" change (formal organization theory, community theory) drawn from sociology, economics and political science. Micro intervention tends to be based on theories of individual change drawn from psychology, small group sociology, and human development. Finally, we can distinguish differences in the strategies of macro and micro interventions. Macro intervention uses social action strategies, lobbying, coordination of functions, and canvassing; micro intervention typically relies on more circumscribed strategies directed at individual change: direct counseling, individual advocacy actions, and crisis intervention (p. 44).

Human service intervention is closely associated with micro- and macrosystems in relationship to the notion of *social treatment*. From a human service practice perspective, social treatment includes all those remedial efforts directed at the resolution of a client's problems within the context of the social environment (Whittaker, 1977). Theoretically, the client and worker move through micro- and macrosystems in a dynamic process, each bound by their social roles. By the same token, their relationship formulates a unique set of mutual needs and values as a result of the common objectives they share in problem solving and service delivery. In this sense, theoretical distinctions between macro- and microsystems are consistent for both worker and client. However, their circumstances in the social system are different in that one is in the "client system," while the worker functions in the "human service delivery system." Each operate and negotiate within the boundaries of micro- and macrosystems of society. For example, a client system may include family relationships, housing, legal issues, and behavioral problems, whereas the human service worker as a provider must meet the needs of both the client system and the human service system.

Acting in a formal capacity, the human service worker must adhere to employment conditions (job description), social policy, professional ethics, and administrative aspects of service delivery. Human service providers operate in a maze of agency dynamics and organizational structures. This level of activity in the human services is generally in the scope of *macropractice*. In this context, the worker also deals directly with the client. Human service workers are most often face-to-face with clients either interviewing, counseling, working with the family, or doing something else to help them. This kind of intervention is called *micropractice*. The client system and the workers' system together set up a situational framework for professional human service intervention at micro and macro levels. This dualistic nature of professional practice is fundamental to the working model in human services. Further, it underscores how comprehensive and complex human service work in contemporary society really is.

INTRODUCTION OF THE SOCIAL HEALTH GENERALIST CONCEPT

Today's human service worker must possess special knowledge of the human service delivery system as well as client systems and understand the impact of various environmental influences on human behavior and communities. Annexed to this knowledge base is the need for the worker to have competent communication skills so as to be effective with a variety of clients and to operate comfortably in different agency roles. Such demands upon the modern worker produce the notion of a *social health generalist* in contemporary welfare, mental health, and human service systems (Cimmino, 1993). Compared with the mental health generalist concept of the 1960s and 1970s (McPheeters and King, 1971), the social health generalist sharply reflects the need for the human service worker in modern society to be prepared for today's challenges, which stem from rapid social change and related programmatic influences on economic restructuring of human service delivery systems. To work effectively in any human service agency today, the worker must possess a functionally broader knowledge base of community resources, case management strategies, behavior, social policy, political influences, and human factors that affect the delivery of human services. Joseph Mehr (1988) elucidates the social health generalist notion when he discusses current conceptions of human service systems and bases his book on a *generic human services concept* (Mehr, 1988, p. 11). In contrast, the mental health generalists of the past were primarily trained to focus on microsocial systems by providing direct assistance in institutional or closed settings. The social health generalist's basic training and professional orientation must address a wider spectrum of client conditions and support human service systems that conceptually go beyond the immediate client and agency environment.

The generalist concept is historically rooted in mental health technology systems. However, modern life demands that the provision of human services reach beyond the mental health field. Therefore, the profession must expand the generalist concept to reflect what human service workers actually do in modern society. This condition was illustrated earlier in the discussion of *generalist roles the human service worker* performs in the formal helping process. The academic and practice training in recognized human service programs today are designed to prepare a different generalist worker from that of the past. According to Schmolling, Youkeles, and Burger (1993):

Many educators feel that the term 'paraprofessional,' widely accepted in the past, no longer accurately reflects the knowledge, abilities, skills, and training of graduates in recognized undergraduate human service programs of today. They feel graduates of such programs should be considered professional human service workers. The work roles and functions of generalist human service workers vary greatly. Generalist workers represent the largest number of workers and usually have the most contact with those in need. In some instances, the duties of the generalist workers are similar to those of professionals (p. 182).

The social health generalist human service worker is capable of adjusting to a variety of settings in the human service field. Similar to the mental health generalist, the primary focus remains helping "target persons," either directly or indirectly. These target groups can be individual clients, families, small groups, or a neighborhood or community (McPheeters, 1990). Target groups refer to identified persons (clients) in need of human service intervention. However, the expansion of the term *human services* to include a wider spectrum of social, health, and welfare systems is a significant distinction from past concepts of the mental health generalist. For example, human service workers in a mental health setting are required to understand other service-delivery systems and social dynamics outside the place where they are employed. This includes a knowledge base that integrates client needs with external and internal forces that influence service delivery, such as insurance requirements, diagnosis, and legal, community, or administrative complications. In today's human service industry, the frequency of worker contact with clients and their families, as well as interagency collaboration, is steadily increasing for a variety of reasons. The framework of practice today reflects the notion that all clients are consumers and have the right to access an empowering process by way of the human service system (Halley, Kopp, and Austin, 1992). Thus, the professional role of the contemporary human service worker scales the wall of institutional framework by comprehending conditions outside agency boundaries and must engender an enormous level of social awareness and professional skill. Consequently, the decision-making capacity of the generalist in today's human service field requires a working knowledge of micro- and macrosystems within the social treatment model (Whittaker, 1977).

McPheeters and King (1971) describe the generalist as possessing the following characteristics:

1. The generalist works with a limited number of clients or families (in consultation with other professionals) to provide "across the board" services as needed.
2. The generalist is able to work in a variety of agencies and organizations that provide mental health services.
3. The generalist is able to work cooperatively with any of the existing professions.
4. The generalist is familiar with a number of therapeutic services and techniques.
5. The generalist is a "beginning professional" who is expected to continue to learn and grow (McPheeters and King, 1971).

McPheeters's characteristics are generally applicable to the notion of the new social health generalist. However, several important modifications to his previous description of the generalist concept are proposed to effectively address contemporary frameworks of service delivery and justify the neologism *social health generalist*.

In his article, McPheeters (1990, p. 36) places emphasis on the differentiation between the generalist and the specialist. He asserts that it is not based simply on division of labor. Rather, the generalist is concerned with all the problems surrounding the client or family, whereas the specialist focuses on a particular skill or activity. McPheeters's characteristics describing the generalist can generally apply to the new social health generalist concept. However, there are some important adjustments necessary that offer theoretical criteria for consistency with the contemporary human service field. The first concern is that McPheeters's second characteristic, "agen-cies and organizations that provide mental health services," must expand to include a larger view of the human service system. Replacing the term "mental health services" with *human services* or *human services and related subsystems* seems more appropriate and fitting to today's human service worker. Similarly, his fourth characteristic states that "the generalist is familiar with a number of therapeutic services and techniques." The focus here reflects a limited perspective in comparison to the practice framework and related concepts of the modern human service worker. Recognition of the need for a broader knowledge base involving multidisciplinary services and other theoretical frameworks is essential for human services to effectively operate in modern society. A professional knowledge base to include social systems, personality theory, and social treatment intervention strategies can more accurately point to the scope of information that today's worker must possess. With these two modifications, the mental health generalist concept can continue to provide professional foundations for today's *social health generalist worker*.

Dr. Harold McPheeters Responds

At the 1992 National Organization for Human Services Education Conference in Alexandria, Virginia, I had the distinct privilege of hearing Dr. Harold McPheeters give the keynote address. At the conclusion of his presentation, I spoke with him about his views on human services. During our conversation, I asked if he would be interested in reading my manuscript and commenting on the ideas it developed (Cimmino, 1993). He agreed. Several weeks later, I received his four-page written response. I was very impressed with his articulation and depth of reaction to the content of my study. Dr. McPheeters's response to "Exactly What Is Human Services" offers an expansion of insight to contemporary thinking about this relatively new field from its most noted professional figure and pioneer.

REFERENCES

Aguilera, D. C. and J. M. Messick (1978). *Crisis intervention, theory and methodology.* Saint Louis: C. V. Mosby.

Cimmino, P. (1993). "Exactly What Is Human Services? The Evolution of a Profession: Academic Discipline and Social Science." Bronx, NY: *Council for Standards in Human Service Education Monograph Series.*

Eriksen, K. (1977). *Human Services Today.* Reston, VA: Reston Publishing Company.

Fullerton, S. (1990). "A Historical Perspective of the Baccalaureate-Level Professional Education in Human Services." *Journal of the National Organization for Human Services Education,* 9(1).

Halley, A., J. Kopp, and M. Austin (1992). *Delivering Human Services: A Learning Approach to Practice,* New York: Longman.

McPheeters, H. (1990). "Development of the Human Services Generalist Concept." *History of the Human Services Movement, CSHSE Monograph Series, 31,* 40.

McPheeters, H. L., and J. B. King (1971). *Plans for Teaching Mental Health Workers.* Atlanta, GA: Southern Regional Education Board.

Mehr, J. (1988). *Human Services, Concepts and Intervention Strategies,* 4th ed. Boston: Allyn and Bacon.

Neher, A. (1991). Maslow's theory of motivation: A critique. *Journal of Humanistic Psychology,* 31, 89–112.

Ryan, W. (1976). *Blaming the Victim.* New York: Vintage Books.

Schmolling, P., M. Youkeles, and W. R. Burger (1993). *Human Services in Contemporary America.* Pacific Grove, CA: Brooks/Cole.

Slaikeu, K. A. (1990). *Crisis Intervention: A Handbook for Practice and Research.* Boston, MA: Allyn and Bacon.

Whittaker, J. K. (1977). *Social Treatment: An Approach to Interpersonal Helping.* Chicago, IL: Aldine Publishing Company.

Woodside, M. R., and T. McClam (1990). "Problem Solving in the Human Service Curriculum." *Journal of the National Organization of Human Services Education,* 9(1).

Woodside, M. R., and T. McClam (1994). *An Introduction to Human Services.* Pacific Grove, CA: Brooks/Cole.

SUGGESTED FURTHER READING

Bernstein, G. S., and J. A. Halaszyn (1989). *"Human Services"?. . . That Must Be So Rewarding.* Baltimore, MD: P.H. Brookes.

Caputo, R. (1988). *Management and Information Systems in Human Services.* New York: Haworth Press, Inc.

Collins, R., J. Fischer, and P. Cimmino (1994). "Human Services Student Patterns: A Study of the Influence of Selected Psychodynamic Factors upon Career Choice." Bellingham, WA: *Journal of the National Organization for Human Service Education* 14(1).

Erdman, D. M., and R. J. Lundman (1979). *Corporate and Governmental Deviance.* New York: Harper and Row.

Erikson, Erik H. (1963). *Childhood and Society,* 2nd ed. New York: Norton.

Frederick, H. S., and J. S. Jones (1990). "Self-Understanding in Human Services Education: Goals and Methods." Kingston, RI: *Journal of the National Organization for Human Services Education* 9(1).

Fullerton, S., and D. Osher (1990). "History of the Human Services Movement." Knoxville, TN: *Council for Standards in Human Service Education Monograph Series.*

Fullerton, S. (1990). "Development of Baccalaureate-Level Professional Education in Human Services." Knoxville, TN: *Council for Standards in Human Services Education Monograph Series.*

Kuhn, T. S. (1975). *The Structure of Scientific Revolutions.* Chicago, IL: University of Chicago Press.

Lindemann, E. (1944). "Symptomatology and management of acute grief." *American Journal of Psychiatry,* 101:141–148.

Linzer, L. (1990). "Ethics and Human Services Practice." Kingston, RI: *Journal of the National Organization of Human Services Education* 9(1).

Macht, J. (1990). "A Historical Perspective." *History of the Human Services Movement, CSHSE Monograph Series* 9, 22.

Maslow, A. (1968). *Toward a Psychology of Being.* New York: John Wiley & Sons.

Nilsson, A. T. (1989). "Undergraduate Training for the Human Services: Many Routes to the Same Field." Kingston, RI: *Journal of the National Organization for Human Services Education* 9(1), 19–25.

Osher, D. (1990). "More than Needs and Services: Antecedent and Current Social Conditions That Influence the Human Services Movement." *History of the Human Services Movement, CSHSE Monograph Series,* 23–30.

Petrie, D. R. (1989). "Entry-Level Skills of Human Service Work." Kingston, RI: *Journal of the National Organization of Human Services Education* 9(1), 37–41.

Sherif, M., and C. Sherif (1969). *Social Psychology.* New York: Harper and Row.

Simon, E. (1990). "The Challenge of the Future: Towards the 21st Century: The History of the Human Services Movement." Knoxville, TN: *Council for Standards in Human Service Education Monograph Series,* 101:115.

Woodside, M. R. (1989). "Case Study Method: A Technique for Professional Development." *Journal of the National Organization of Human Services Education,* 8(1).

LETTER TO PAUL CIMMINO
FROM HAROLD McPHEETERS

435 Forest Valley Rd., NE
Atlanta, GA 30342–2354
October 23, 1992

Paul F. Cimmino, Ph.D., ACSW
Montana State University—Billings
Department of Counseling and Human Services
1500 N. 30th St.
Billings, MT 59101

Dear Dr. Cimmino,

Now that we are back from our trip that included my talk at the NOHSE Meeting, I am nearly caught up with unpaid bills and unanswered letters. I have also read your "Exactly What Is Human Services." I agree that there is a substantial need to provide a sharper conceptualization for Human Services, especially as it differs from Social Work, where there seems to be the greatest conflict with both sets of practitioners claiming the same turf. This has never been done well by either profession.

Most of the professions within the overall arena of Human Services rightfully claim a "humanitarian" base, but most are also premised upon some theoretical foundation regarding the nature of Human Service problems and possible solutions. Thus much of medicine and the health care field assumes a biomedical causation and biomedical remedies, while psychology assumes a psychological/behavioral causation and set of interventions. Social work is theoretically based on the notion of social causation and interventions, and the early social workers functioned in that way. However, social work, especially case-work, has drifted over into the psychological realm where many practitioners choose to practice what is much closer to psychological therapy than what most old-time social workers would have found appropriate. Perhaps this is because the scientific evidence for social causation and social interventions has been difficult to obtain and because the field has drifted to a strong "value oriented" base. Social work is based on a value system of beliefs far more than the other human service professions, which tend to have more firm evidence for their work.

At times, that value orientation causes social workers considerable internal conflict in practice. For example, they profess a belief in client self-determination, but in reality, they frequently find that the constraints of the fiscal/legal system in which they work do not allow the client to make his/her own decisions (e.g., the workers can't provide all the money the clients want or need; committed patients or prisoners cannot go home, even if they want to), and the workers find that they are actually the agents of social constraint. Another value of social work is its belief in democratic majority rule, but so many of their clients are in the minority. Then what?

My point is that there are inherent problems in making values (which often conflict with each other) the base upon which to build a profession, as social work has found. At the same time, there are severe limitations in building a profession on a single academic/knowledge base, because human service problems and their solutions require a broad biopsychosocial perspective. Worst of all is a profession based on a narrow technology (e.g., psychoanalysis, surgery, behavioral therapy), because then every client's problems are seen in terms of the need for that specific technology.

The early work we did in this field was in the area of mental health technology—not broad human services. I have felt a bit uneasy as the academicians moved to the broader terminology of "human services" without making much change in their academic programs. However, I still feel that the basic concept of the "generalist" worker, as we defined it in mental health, and as you seem to do in your paper, is the most appropriate orientation for the new field. In that formulation, the focus of concern of the worker is for the client and family and the totality of their problems/needs—not just one theoretical part of them. The worker is an advocate for that client, much as a family practitioner is the advocate for his client/family, doing what he can himself and making referrals to meet specialized needs, but even then keeping in touch and helping the specialist understand special needs and following up after the specialist has done his "thing." The worker helps the client with all the biopsychosocial aspects of his need, and needs a keen knowledge and appreciation of all of them. (In my judgment, many of the Human Services education programs have greatly devalued the biomedical aspects.)

The worker must be quite analytical about the client's needs to assure that the client does not fall into prolonged dependency. This may be a difficult point for workers who focus too much on "humanitarian" needs; it can lead to fostering dependency if the distinction is not clearly understood. I believe "advocacy" is desirable, but at this level (the client level), I see it related to helping the client get what he needs in a system that would not ordinarily serve him.

These are all concepts that apply at the level of the individual human service worker engaged with individual clients and families. At higher academic and organizational levels, I see Human Services working much more with the systems of services, creating new services, linking them more effectively and economically, and so on. The advocacy here is more related to systems (e.g., economic, organizational, political). We need much more research in these areas. I get impatient with advanced human service educational programs that focus on preparing "therapists" for individual clients (Why not just switch those students to psychology or social work?), or that provide rather stereotyped education about organizational theory and management with little research to determine its relevance to human service systems. I believe that management concepts developed from manufacturing and business are in some ways actually antithetical to human services, but we need much more research to be sure.

I tend to be cautious about blaming the larger system of society for its shortcomings in relation to the human services. In my judgment, we in the human services have not done a good job of defining those problems and needs and especially what would be both effective and cost-effective interventions. American society is far too committed to a philosophy of competition and winning. The sorriest part of it is that the losers are seen as "deficient" or "bad" and thus to blame for and deserving of their own plights. We teach these competitive concepts in school, on TV, in books, in newspapers (right now we have both the World Series and the presidential elections underway and winning or losing on our national mind every hour). We need a gentler philosophy that says that everyone is important and must be brought to his/her level of greatest contribution and participation in our society (not just the winners) and that everyone has a stake in bringing about that state of our nation.

At the same time, we in the human services must be sure that we know what we are doing in our interventions and that they are cost-effective. (A glaring example of such a current problem is the vast increases we have seen in recent years in institutional care for disturbed children/adolescents and alcoholics. They cannot be justified, and society is now saying so by establishing managed care organizations to control the "abuses." It is a discredit to the mental health establishment that it has allowed this to happen, but they "won" all those concessions to have those conditions "covered" by third-party payment programs.) We must not simply whine for more money and prestige for human services without assuring that we are making good use of our funds and talents. Human Services programs at advanced academic levels, with careful research, more refined program evaluation, and critical analysis (not just blind advocacy), could help us do better in those areas.

All this is a long way about to endorse your concept that human services puts the client/family at the center of concern and works to help in the totality of that person/family's biopsychosocial realities—not just some theoretical portion of it. One problem you will experience at the highest conceptual level is that all the other human service professions will say that they do exactly the same thing. A careful analysis of what they *really* do will show that they focus on only a theoretical part of it, but then I'm not so sure that human service workers, as presently trained, are as well prepared in some of the broad biopsychosocial aspects of the human need (the biomedical aspects and aspects having to do with antisocial behavior, corrections, and criminology) as they really should be.

What kind of reaction did you receive to this paper? We surely need more attention to this kind of effort to more clearly define just what we are. There is great reluctance from legislators, third-party payers, and so on to accept any "new" professions that will simply raise the costs of human services to the public and the taxpayers. It behooves any new group to firmly establish its rationale for being and to sharpen the distinctions between it and other closely related professions in language and concepts that are practical and make sense to the larger society. Fuzzy abstractions will not cut the mustard.

I hope this helps.

Cordially yours,

Harold L. McPheeters

CHAPTER 2

HISTORICAL ROOTS OF HUMAN SERVICES

JOEL F. DIAMBRA

Writing from Knoxville, Tennessee, home of the late Alex Haley, author of the epic novel and made-for-television mini-series, *Roots,* it seems only appropriate to begin this book by reviewing our professional roots. Indeed, it is prudent and necessary to review the recent history of human service work prior to propelling ourselves into prophetic speculation and prognostications of times to come. History and future are juxtaposed with the forever-fleeting present, sharing an ever-present boundary that quickly vanishes into the past. This makes the past and future unusual relatives: two stepsisters, both twins to a third sister, the present. Confounding and more dynamic than sisters, one becomes the other as cyclical time passes: future becomes present, present becomes past, and the past predicts the future. This chapter will review the twentieth-century historical roots of human services. The focus is a macro rather than micro review, enabling the reader to place into historical perspective the contents of the upcoming chapters.

The history of human services struggles to clearly identify a "big-bang" origin. Its inception is subject to more than one interpretation. However, human service history is clearly developmental in nature, with evolutionary roots. From inauspicious beginnings to its professionally tailored and internationally collaborating present, recent developments in human services will be briefly reviewed in this chapter.

So why does a book entitled *Human Services: Contemporary Issues and Trends,* which is clearly focused on present and future events in human services, include a chapter dedicated to a recent historical review? Students often complain and express their dislike of history. The traditional excuse that it has no relevance on the events of today may be heard echoing through the cinderblock halls of public and private institutions of higher learning. In these same halls, the vernacular may be more commonly stated as "Let's get on with it." You, too, may be internally voicing like sentiments.

But before you dive into the following chapters, remember that many of the upcoming projections for the field of human services will someday be historical events. They will not simply be bygone events to be quickly dismissed and discounted, but events that have shaped tomorrow's future of human service delivery—so read with renewed interest and appreciation. Accurate predictions will become the future, the future will become today, and today will become a past full of rich stories and events that once predicted and defined human services for tomorrow.

Before beginning to retrace the recent historical path of human services, an operational definition is required. Harris and Maloney (1996) broadly defined human services as "a process of negotiating social systems to respond in the best interest of people in need" (p. 13). Burger and Youkeles (2000) identified the common denominator of all human services as meeting people's needs. Specific to the human service worker, Woodside and McClam (1998) defined the professional as a generalist able to work side-by-side with a variety of other professionals. Neukrug

(2000) points out that human service professionals must be skillful at wearing many professional hats as they play a number of roles to encourage client growth and change. Simply put, human services is about facilitating clients' efforts to grow and change while also effectively negotiating the service system in order to meet their needs.

A BLEND OF PROFESSIONS

Human services, as a bona fide profession with a defining mission and distinctive history, emerged from a blend of disciplines. The fields of social services, psychology, and counseling have provided the preeminent material to form a new hybrid species: human services. It may be more accurate to say that the human service profession borrowed from many of its sister professions and eclectically broadened its perspective by inclusion rather than exclusion. Social services provided a sense of mission and genuine compassion from its earliest roots. Furthermore, contemporary policy has been strongly influenced by social services. The disciplines of psychology and mental health contributed a theoretical and scientific component to the profession. Later, vocational and school counseling furnished human services with a contemporary perspective full of practical tools and helping strategies. Let us review these perspectives to see specifically how each influenced the development of human services as we know it today.

Social Service Roots

The human service literature is replete with historical accounts written from a social service perspective. A few significant historical events pertinent to social services highlight the genuinely humane response to the plight of others displayed by early social service workers.

The 1890s brought a more devastating depression than that felt during the 1870s. Social unrest caused by unemployment and racial tensions stimulated the need for social services. These early social and human service workers, through exposure to the conditions of their "clients," began to understand that poverty was a complex problem and more difficult to resolve than they had been led to believe. Effective assistance required dedicated, paid professionals trained to remain objective and perform a variety of skills in systematic fashion.

One of the most significant developments of this period was the settlement house movement. Settlement social workers, out of their genuine concern and compassion, saw themselves more as neighbors than as professionals. This posture allowed them to empathize with the daily struggles of the people to whom they provided assistance. The English and American settlement house movements had many similarities, but they had a few distinct traits as well. American social workers' religious orientation was subtler than that of their British counterparts, and the British movement had more men involved than did the American movement. Women, usually young, college-aged women, were predominant figures in the settlement house movement within the United States. Two of these remarkable young women, Jane Addams and Ellen Gates Starr, started the most famous American settlement house: Chicago's Hull House. Prejudice was also a typical profile common to both sets of social workers. Driven by a strong desire to help others, many remained ignorant of their own personal biases and consequently accepted popular stereotypes.

Forced by overwhelming client needs, social workers began to look beyond themselves and their immediate neighborhoods. Determined to create a more efficient and effective organizational system, social workers initiated a plan to improve the lives of women and children on a broader level. These efforts resulted in a national Children's Bureau headed by Julia Lathrop from Chicago's Hull House in 1912 (Council on Social Work Education, 2000). Influenced by the Children's Bureau research efforts, the "Widow's Pension" was a proposal recommending that children be supported in their natural homes rather than institutional settings.

Beyond the scope of the settlement house movement, social work stretched its wings and entered into a number of fields new to social services: medical social work, psychiatric social work, school social work, occupational social work, and family social work. Professional schools of social work, guided by the Association of Professional Schools of Social Work (APSSW), emerged. In the 1930s, the APSSW adopted increasingly stringent curriculum guidelines and accreditation requirements. Social work has clearly identified itself as a unique entity and field with dual approaches, commonly referred to as micro (clinical) and macro (administrative) foci. Today, the field embraces service provision focused on encouraging individual change in concert with bringing about social reform and systemic intervention.

Compassionate and genuinely concerned for the welfare of others, early social service workers paved the way for human services by constructively exercising compassion for their fellow human beings, creating practical services to meet client needs, developing organized programs, and instigating and lobbying for social policy reform.

Psychology and Mental Health Roots

As professions, psychology and mental health have contributed greatly to the human service profession by providing workers with a host of theories to better understand the human condition and practice skills to intervene when challenges arise. A cursory review of these two fields is provided.

Clifford Beers first entered the mental health field as a patient. He used his unique experience as a patient and later as a professional helper to shape the human service profession. Beers's most enduring legacy may be his advocacy of the principle that people are to be treated humanely, regardless of their condition or circumstances. After suffering a mental breakdown, he was con-

fined to an asylum for three years where he received harsh treatment. After his recovery, Beers published his autobiography, based on his experience in American psychiatric institutions, in 1908. His account aroused public concern about the care of people with mental illness. Beers continued his campaign by founding the Connecticut Society for Mental Hygiene, the National Committee for Mental Hygiene (later becoming the National Association for Mental Health and known today as the Mental Health Association), and, years later, the International Foundation for Mental Health Hygiene. Human service educators strive to instill Beers's message that people with mental illness are to be treated with respect and dignity, regardless of their circumstances.

The fields of psychiatry and psychology emerged at about the same time. There are so many prominent early figures that it is not possible to describe them all within this context. Two familiar key figures include Sigmund Freud (1856–1939) and Wilhelm Wundt (1832–1920). Of the two, Freud enjoyed the widest acceptance for his psychoanalytic theory focused on the dynamics of the inner person and the resulting human behavior. His influence is still felt today within human services, psychological treatment, and counseling. Wundt is best known for his establishment during the late 1870s of the first experimental psychological laboratory in Germany (Capuzzi and Gross, 1997). Wundt focused on researching how the mind is structured and did so by asking clients to self-reflect aloud. William James (1842–1910) adapted Wundt's approach and focused on the functions of the mind. His work in the United States attracted a great deal of attention, and he and his followers were labeled as "functionalists." G. Stanley Hall (1844–1924) is considered the "father of American psychology" by many and is credited with organizing the American Psychological Association (APA). Hall believed that the means of resolving social problems could best be discovered via empirical research. He collected information on children and their mental characteristics. Hall established the first psychological laboratory in the United States at Johns Hopkins University in 1883.

Significant contributions to the development of mental health counseling were also made by founding behaviorists such as Edward Thorndike (1874–1949), John Watson (1878–1958), and B. F. Skinner (1904–1990). Thorndike studied educational psychology and the psychology of animal learning. Thorndike is remembered for his stimulus response "laws" of effect, readiness, and exercise. Watson established an animal research laboratory where he became known for his behaviorist approach. He later applied his work on animals to human behavior and is well remembered for his classical conditioning of Albert by associating a loud noise with the presence of a white rat. Watson helped us to understand how conditioning may affect fears, phobias, and prejudice. He also coined the term "behaviorism." B. F. Skinner is perhaps the most influential learning theorist. Using basic principles of reinforcement, Skinner's operant conditioning theory is found in a wide array of successful human service interventions (token economies, programmed instruction, behavior modification, etc.) and is used with a variety of human service clientele (adolescent offenders, chronically mentally ill, mentally retarded, etc.).

Human service professionals use principles of educational psychology and learning theory to help clients change maladaptive behaviors, identify compensatory strategies, cope with the daily stresses of life, and function in our cyber-paced world. Behavioral theory is highly regarded in the human service arena today because of its emphasis on measurable outcomes and interactional strategies. Many interventions used in modern-day human service programs can trace their ancestry to behaviorally based theory and practice.

Historical events also influenced the development of the fields of psychology and mental health. War played a large part in advancing both of these fields. The U.S. armed forces used standardized assessment to place servicemen and women in military and industrial positions before and during World War II. Uncle Sam used psychologists and counselors to select and train military personnel for special assignments (Capuzzi and Gross, 1997). Mental health services were also needed to deal with the mental anguish soldiers were experiencing from battle and to help those who returned to their homes in need of vocational guidance. Picchioni and Bonk (1983) credited the government for inviting the counseling profession into the community by noting that a government official indicated that counseling is counseling, whether it is conducted in homes, schools, business or industrial settings, or churches. Human service professionals who provide services across these environments and more are still celebrating this induction today.

Following World War II, the National Institute for Mental Health was established in 1946, authorizing monies for research and demonstration focused on assisting persons with mental illness in the areas of prevention, diagnosis, and treatment. A series of political steps involving psychology and mental health followed, influencing the human service profession. The Mental Health Study Act (1955) initiated the existence of the Joint Commission on Mental Illness and Health. Also, a 1963 landmark decision led to passage of the Community Mental Health Centers Act (CMHCA). This legislation had a considerable impact on the expansion of the human service profession by mandating that outreach, counseling, and service coordination be offered in the community through more than 2,000 newly created mental health centers (Capuzzi and Gross, 1997). Human service professionals are contemporary front-line workers who are still implementing the services inspired 37 years ago through the CMHCA.

The list of key people and critical events from the psychological and mental health arena that influenced human services is too lengthy to cover within the confines of this chapter. These disciplines have advanced our understanding of human behavior and developed health services within communities. Human services, based on the work conducted in the mental health centers, have capitalized on the fruits of their labor by using theoretical approaches and adopting strategies for helping people. Suffice it to say that human service professionals attempt to help the client reflect inward to self and outward toward the environment to identify areas needing adjustment or change. Theoretical constructs provided by psychology and mental health leaders have provided an eclectic foundation from which human service professionals are able to draw in their work with a variety of people. This foundation has provided an integral understanding of client behavior in a multitude of settings.

Vocational and School Counseling Roots

Human service professionals can be found assisting school-aged clients and those transitioning from school to school, school to work, or job to job. School and work are two primary aspects of client life and often provide the opportunity to change current living conditions and address the associated challenges. Therefore, human service workers rely on the learning and practices that resulted from the fields of vocational and school guidance. Whether it be assessing client aptitude and vocational skills through rehabilitation case management, building client skills in vocational readiness workshops, job coaching in competitive employment settings, or assisting students of all ages to seek out appropriate educational experiences, human service professionals have benefited from vocational and school policy and research.

In 1881, Lysander S. Richards published *Vocophy,* a slim text that described a system whereby individuals could identify a vocational calling best suited to their abilities (Capuzzi and Gross, 1997). The profession of guidance was on the map. Frank Parsons, considered the "father of guidance," shared similar views. Parsons was active in social reform and focused his efforts

toward assisting people to make good occupational choices.

Later, Jesse Davis was credited with bringing vocational guidance into schools. After being extensively questioned by one of his Cornell University professors regarding his career plans, Davis realized that others were in need of this same guidance. Over his career, he introduced his developing guidance plans to schools in Detroit and Grand Rapids, Michigan. Using Social Darwinism as a foundation, two other individuals influenced the guidance movement from opposite coasts. In New York, Eli Weaver realized that the students with whom he worked were in need of vocational guidance. Even without additional monies, Weaver began recruiting teachers to spend time with students and help them identify their own skills and abilities and match them to the needs of the current job market. In Seattle, Anna Reed took a more commercial route toward guidance, urging that the world of business be used as a model and goal for upcoming students. She believed that students ought to focus their energies on making money. Reed also felt schools should direct young people to enter vocations whereby they could earn money.

Due to the increasing interest in vocational guidance, in 1906 the National Society for the Promotion of Industrial Education (NSPIE) was established. At the third national convention in 1913, the National Vocational Guidance Association (NVGA) was founded. Two more recent events that greatly influenced vocational services include the creation of the *Dictionary of Occupational Titles,* first published in 1946, and the Vocational Rehabilitation Act (1954), which recognized persons with disabilities as having unique needs for specialized services.

Sputnik is a familiar term to those who have studied vocational and school guidance history. In the 1950s, the Russians successfully launched Sputnik, the first artificial Earth satellite, into orbit. Fearing that the United States would be left behind in the race to space, the U.S. government mobilized. The goal was to identify promising young people who could be guided into studying mathematics and the sciences in preparation for careers that would develop the space program. The National Defense Education Act (NDEA) is considered a landmark in terms of establishing vocational and school guidance programs. Capuzzi and Gross (1997) recount that NDEA appropriated monies to pay for primary- and secondary-level school counselors and developed training programs to produce qualified public school counselors. Over the years, guidance has established itself as a profession and offers training programs within most universities. The field has adopted ethical guidelines, written professional competencies, and published a number of journals dedicated to the profession. Although professional organizations at the national level have split and changed names numerous times and school guidance programs have been under fire on occasion, the effects of NDEA are still evident today.

Human service professionals work alongside school guidance counselors in full-service schools, as tutors and counselors within Upward Bound programs, in residential settings with on-campus schools, and as colleagues when representing community agencies working with troubled youth. On the vocational track, human service professionals are employed as vocational rehabilitation case managers (with master of arts or master of science degrees), employment specialists, and in work-related capacities. Understanding school and work environments, negotiating steps to successfully transition within and across these domains, and being familiar with the tools of the trade (e.g., *Occupational Outlook Handbook, Dictionary of Occupational Titles,* and computer-based interest and aptitude assessment programs) are within the human service professional's capacity. Human service professionals offer kudos to early vocational theorists and school practitioners for clearing the vocational and school guidance forest to create the path evident today.

The combined fields of social services, psychology, mental health, and school and vocational

guidance have contributed greatly to the development of human services. Compassion for the human condition, theoretical constructs, practical interventions, and assessment practices are some of the benefits human services have received from these sister vocations. After reviewing the roots of human services, it is important to look at contemporary perspectives.

CONTEMPORARY PERSPECTIVES ON HUMAN SERVICE HISTORY

The human service movement began when the Mental Health Study Act was passed and a shortage of qualified human service workers emerged in the 1960s. This shortage prompted an increase in training programs for generalist human service workers at two- and four-year colleges (Burger and Youkeles, 2000). An increased emphasis on mental health care, proliferation of social service agencies, an ongoing shift to community-based services, and greater demand for more highly trained professionals, coupled with the social strife evident in the 1960s, all had a part in the emergence of the human service field. During this period, Harold McPheeters received a National Institute of Mental Health (NIMH) grant to support his proposal to develop a human service curriculum at the community college level, culminating in an associate's degree. Neukrug (2000) recounts that because of McPheeters's initiating efforts, he is often regarded as the "founder" of the contemporary human service field. Added to McPheeters's efforts is the timing and direction taken by the sister fields of psychology, counseling, and social work. While these already-established disciplines began to focus their attention on graduate-level training, the need for qualified entry-level human service professionals continued to grow. And, while these sister disciplines became more specialized and arguably more exclusive, human services remained broad-based and inclusive.

As we look into the programs that are in this organization (NOHSE), we will see an extremely wide variety of different orientations, professions. Not just social work, psychology or sociology, but also nursing; education; corrections; drug, alcohol, and substance abuse programs; gerontology; health sciences; allied health professional sciences; etc. (Maloney, personal interview, October 28, 1999).

Human services filled a niche that had been created by a variety of circumstances and has continued to the present day.

Two legislative acts spurred the development of the new field of human services. The 1964 Economic Opportunity Act and the 1966 Schneuer Sub-professional Career Act provided federal funds to recruit and train entry-level human service workers. These changes were necessary due to the predicted shortfall of qualified human service workers resulting from the deinstitutionalization and decentralization movements that began in the 1950s. Neukrug (2000) recounts that McPheeters, supported by an NIMH grant, began developing human service training programs at the associate level. Around this same time, four-year baccalaureate degree programs began emerging. During formal training, students learned the skills necessary to work with a variety of clients and other health professionals. Many of the routine and time-intensive duties that kept more highly trained practitioners from diagnosing and treating clients were perfectly matched to the skills of the newly trained human service workers. The involvement of human service workers helped to broaden the treatment focus from the individual client to include systems or forces surrounding the client. Systems included the client's family, environmental factors such as living conditions and work, larger systems such as community supports, and ultimately, societal constraints or supports. Human service workers observed and interviewed clients, making initial assessments. Gathering individual and family histories, directly observing clients, connecting individuals and families to community resources, working with other professional helpers and community groups, and developing resources when they did

not already exist were some of the tasks undertaken by the first human service workers. Maloney (Maloney, personal interview, October 28, 1999) asserted, "They [human service programs] can specialize and attract students to given areas within the field, namely drug and alcohol, for instance, and working with [persons] with mental retardation or the mentally ill." However, initially, human service workers are most aptly considered generalists who may go on to specialize in a specific genre of human service work once they enter the field.

After McPheeters's grant from the NIMH identified the need to train mental health workers, institutes of higher education responded. Purdue University created the first associate's degree program in 1965. By 1975, 174 associate and baccalaureate programs had been started, and by 1991, the Council for Standards in Human Service Education (2000) directory included 614 human service programs.

As more human service graduates joined community efforts, more highly trained professionals from sister fields began to question the competency of the less-trained human service workers. Likewise, competent human service workers confirmed their own ability to effectively accomplish tasks traditionally completed by their more highly educated counterparts. Tension and controversy ensued and continues to exist today, with education requirements, competency criteria, job titles, and delineation of professional tasks and responsibilities still unsettled.

The legitimacy of human services as a profession has been debated. This discussion has provided some of the impetus behind important aspects of the contemporary history of human services: professional identity, organization, and representation.

PROFESSIONAL IDENTITY

Human services' historical professional amalgam provides wonderful strength to the profession, yet this *interfusion* has also made it difficult to delineate a clear professional identity. Revisiting client needs by analyzing the responses to strategic research questions in the late 1960s, the Southern Regional Education Board (SREB) identified thirteen roles for the human service professional:

1. Administrator
2. Advocate
3. Assistant to specialist
4. Behavior changer
5. Broker
6. Caregiver
7. Community planner
8. Consultant
9. Data manager
10. Evaluator
11. Mobilizer
12. Outreach worker
13. Teacher/educator

Within these generalist roles, human service professionals must adhere to an acceptable standard of practice guided by a set of essential skills defined by competencies.

In addition to competencies, in the early 1980s, the two leading organizations in human service education determined that a set of ethical standards unique to human services needed to be developed for guidance and accountability purposes. On the basis of research followed by a committee process, ethical standards for the human service professions were written, revised, and adopted and are known today as the Ethical Standards of Human Service Professionals.

With professional roles defined and a standard of conduct tailored to the human service profession, a measure of competence remained undetermined. Taylor, Bradley, and Warren (1996) provided competencies extracted through job analysis research efforts. They found that human service professionals must be able to perform skills in the following twelve broadly defined competency areas, listed alphabetically:

1. advocacy
2. assessment
3. communication

4. community and service networking
5. community living skills and supports
6. crisis intervention
7. documentation
8. education, training, and self-development
9. facilitation of services
10. organizational participation
11. participant empowerment
12. vocational educational and career support

Through much effort, human services has emerged as a respected and unique profession. Human service professionals have positioned themselves as generalists performing numerous skills in frequently changing roles while serving a variety of population groups with different problems and in diverse settings. This generalist title encompasses many similarities and some differences of opinion.

Three leaders in the human service field—two past presidents and the then-current president of NOHSE—were interviewed in October 1999 during the NOHSE and CSHSE conference held in Baltimore, Maryland: David Maloney, Franklyn Rother, and Lynn McKinney, respectively. Maloney differentiated the field of human services from one of its sister professions by stating, "It is separate and different from social work in. . . .that our (human service) students are generalists and can face the demands and challenges of a much wider variety of human service work." Rother pointed out that human services has maintained a strong integrity to the concept of empowerment as one of its main components. McKinney added that human service professionals are practitioners and that human service education programs have a heavier emphasis on field internships than many of their counterparts, especially at the associate's and bachelor's degree levels (Diambra, 2000).

To further establish the professional identity of human service workers, a collaborative national effort between two- and four-year educational programs is needed to provide a smooth continuum of educating and training students and practitioners desiring to further develop their skills (Diambra, 2000). Building a strong aggregate of human service professionals through existing national organizations ensures that the issue of professional identity will be successfully resolved.

PROFESSIONAL ORGANIZATIONS

As credentialing standards and accountability become paramount in newly established programs and professions, a national body that would identify these standards soon became necessary. In the mid-1970s, the National Organization for Human Service Education (NOHSE) was formed shortly after degree programs were offered. Soon afterward, the Council for Standards in Human Service Education (CSHSE) was established. While the mission of NOHSE was to provide students and human service workers with a national organization for continued education through the unity of regional groups, CSHSE acted primarily as a standard-setting, program-credentialing, and competency-establishing body (Clubok, 1990). However, it is important to note that regional human service organizations were being established separate from one another around the same time that the national organization effort was initiated.

Since their early formation and initial growing pains, CSHSE and NOHSE have blossomed into full-fledged sister organizations working side-by-side, providing continued education, standards for practice, program-development guidelines, workshops and annual conferences across the country, together with a code of ethics to which all human service workers and educators can refer (Neukrug, 2000).

NOHSE

The National Organization for Human Service Education was founded at the Fifth Annual Faculty Development Conference of the Southern Regional Education Board in St. Louis, Missouri, in August 1975. Its mission was to draw together all interested parties and establish an ongoing dialogue to promote best practices for preparing human service workers.

NOHSE has identified for itself four main purposes:

1. Ensure a medium is available for collaboration and cooperation among students, practitioners and their agencies, and faculty.
2. Improve the education of human service students and professionals by cultivating exemplary teaching and research practices and by curriculum development.
3. Abet and provide assistance to other human service organizations at local, state, and national levels.
4. Champion creative means to improve human service education and delivery through conferences, institutes, publications, and symposia (National Organization for Human Service Education, 2000).

NOHSE is made up of six regional organizations: New England (founded just prior to NOHSE in the spring of 1975), Mid-Atlantic, Southern, Midwest, Northwest, and West. Each regional organization defines its own mission and agenda. The interdisciplinary makeup of NOHSE and regional membership reflects the multidimensional needs found within the human condition. Members are direct-care professionals, students, educators, administrators, agencies and institutions, and supervisors.

CSHSE

The Council for Standards in Human Service Education was established in 1979 via impetus from the National Institute for Mental Health grant. Three years earlier, the Southern Regional Education Board did a national survey of 300-plus training programs in human services. The purpose was to identify baseline data on program content and characteristics from which informed decisions and planning would occur in order to determine program standards (Council for Standards in Human Service Education, 2000). It was discovered that training programs had a number of overlapping variables: training aimed at generic skills for working in human services, faculty from a variety of disciplines within one program, common program policies, and student field (i.e., internship or practicum) experience requirements. A task force used these commonalities to create format and content area recommendations for accrediting human service education programs. Human service faculty, graduates, and providers were surveyed to ensure acceptability and appropriateness of each standard.

CSHSE lists five functions:

1. Applying national standards for training programs at the associate's and baccalaureate degree levels.
2. Reviewing and recognizing programs that meet established standards.
3. Sponsoring faculty development workshops in curriculum design, program policymaking, resource development, program evaluation, and other areas.
4. Offering vital technical and informational assistance to programs seeking to improve the quality and relevance of their training.

5. Publishing a quarterly bulletin to keep programs informed of Council activities, training information and resources, and issues and trends in human service education (Council for Standards in Human Service Education, 2000).

CONCLUSION

Today, the profession of human services continues its historical tradition of integrating knowledge, skills, and values from varied sources. This integration provides human services with a rich and diverse legacy upon which to build. The profession's development has been influenced by contributions from many disciplines, enactment of federal legislation, and the growth and activity of current professional organizations. As stated at the beginning of the chapter, today's human services contribute to tomorrow's profession. The sections that follow discuss present-day human services and indicate what we can anticipate for the future.

REFERENCES

Burger, W. R., and M. Youkeles (2000). *Human Services in Contemporary America,* 5th ed. Pacific Grove, CA: Brooks/Cole.

Capuzzi, D., and D. R. Gross (1997). *Introduction to the Counseling Profession,* 2nd ed. Boston, MA: Allyn and Bacon.

Clubok, M. (1990). "Development of Professional Organization for Human Service Educators and Workers." In S. Fullerton and D. Osher, eds., *History of the Human Services Movement* (pp. 71–83). Council for Standards in Human Service Education, Monograph Series, No. 7.

Council for Standards in Human Service Education. (2000). *Council for Standards for Human Service Educators.* [On-line]. Available: http://www.cshse.com/

Council on Social Work Education. (2000). *The Social Work History Station.* [On-line]. Available: http://www.boisestate.edu/socwork/dhuff/xx.htm

Diambra, J. F. (2000). "Human Services: A Bona Fide Profession in the Twenty-First Century." *Human Service Education, 20,* 3–8.

Harris, H. S., and D. C. Maloney (1996). *Human Services: Contemporary Issues and Trends.* Boston, MA: Allyn and Bacon.

National Organization for Human Service Education. (2000). *Purposes of the National Organization for Human Service Education.* [On-line]. Available: http://www.nohse.com/ index.html

Neukrug, E. (2000). *Theory, Practice, and Trends in Human Services: An Introduction to an Emerging Profession,* 2nd ed. Pacific Grove, CA: Brooks/Cole.

Picchioni, A. P., and E. C. Bonk (1983). *A Comprehensive History of Guidance in the United States.* Austin: Texas Personnel and Guidance Association.

Taylor, M., V. Bradley, and R. Warren (1996). *The Community Support Skill Standards.* Washington, DC: Human Service Research Institute.

Woodside, M., and T. McClam (1998). *An Introduction to Human Services,* 3rd ed. Pacific Grove, CA: Brooks/Cole.

HUMAN SERVICES AND WELFARE REFORM
A. THE NEW AMERICAN CONTRACT WITH THE POOR

FRANCES FOX PIVEN

At the height of the election campaign of 1996, President Clinton signed the bill that ended sixty years of federal responsibility for some economic assistance to poor women and children. Clinton claimed this would allow the states flexibility to experiment with approaches that would improve a failed welfare program. But early experience shows that, freed from federal constraints, many states are simply tightening eligibility requirements, slashing benefits, and diverting funds to other purposes.

Moreover, the federal lump sum grants to the states that replaced the AFDC program require the states to impose strict time limits on the receipt of aid, regardless of whether women follow the rules and are willing to work. These arrangements are likely to drive several million women and children deeper into poverty, which proponents think will goad poor women into finding jobs in a low-wage labor market that is glutted even while overall unemployment falls. Meanwhile, and less noticed, the legislation also rolled back food stamp aid for the working or unemployed poor and made legal immigrants ineligible for most federal programs.

The draconian new welfare law was the culmination of a contest between Democratic and Republican politicians to claim ownership of the welfare issue. The 1992 presidential campaign had brought welfare to center stage. George Bush bashed welfare in his January 1992 State of the Union message, and then Clinton tried to claim the issue by promising to "end welfare as we know it" with reforms that would mean "two years and off to work."

The race was on. At first the Clinton Administration talked of training and job creation, health care, and day care, all presumably to make it possible for mothers to work. However, as the dollar estimates of such programs mounted, the services and job promotion side of the Clinton plan shrank. Then the Republicans won control of Congress in 1994, regained the initiative in the welfare-bashing contest, and fashioned the main proposals that became law in 1996.

It was inevitable that the Republicans would try to go Clinton one better. They escalated the rhetoric of welfare bashing, then began to strip away the modest services the Democrats had proposed and to limit cash assistance even more. This bizarre competition moved AFDC—a relatively small program, reaching at its peak some five million women and nine million children and costing only about 1 percent of the federal

This is a revision of an article that first appeared in and is reprinted by permission of *The Progressive*, 409 East Main Street, Madison, WI 53703.

budget—to the center of American politics. By election night, Phil Gramm was proudly telling Michael Kinsley on CNN that all means-tested programs should simply be eliminated.

The core argument in this assault, by Democrats and Republicans alike, is that welfare is a system of perverse incentives, the source of a moral rot that is spreading in American society. Welfare encourages women to quit school or work and have out-of-wedlock babies. And, once on the dole, these women are trapped, becoming passive and dependent so that they can't summon the spirit and initiative to get off welfare and cannot even socialize their children properly. Welfare children, the argument goes, turn into school dropouts and delinquents and then into welfare users themselves. The solution: Eliminate the perverse incentives. This "tough love" approach will force poor mothers to take jobs and discourage them from having babies in the first place. And, once they are self-reliant, those that are raising children will become better mothers as well.

These arguments are by now so familiar that they have worn ruts in our minds. Still, I suppose they need to be answered, again and again. Welfare is said to be the cause of a tide of "illegitimacy," and the polemics can get very excited, as when Charles Murray announced in the *Wall Street Journal* in 1993 that illegitimacy was "the most important social problem of our time," driving poverty, crime, drugs, illiteracy, homelessness, and so on. But while out-of-wedlock births have increased, they have increased in all strata of society, not only among welfare recipients or potential recipients. Indeed, they have increased in all western countries. This is almost certainly the result of epochal changes in sexual and family mores, not the result of the AFDC program.

Moreover, the all-too-familiar view that welfare is the cause of out-of-wedlock births among black women does not stand up. The nonmarital birth rates of African American women have in fact not changed in two decades. What has changed is the marital birth rates, which have declined because fewer men in black communi-

ties have the income or the stability to be reasonable husbands. In any case, the percentage of single mothers collecting welfare has actually declined over time, which would not be true if women were having babies to get welfare. And birth rates, which are about the same for welfare families as other families, are actually higher in low-benefit states and lower in high-benefit states. So much for the facts, though the talk of wanton women is so inflamed that one has to wonder whether the facts matter.

The work argument doesn't make much sense either, or at least the surface claims don't. Presumably, jobs are out there that are adequate to support a family and that are going begging because women prefer the average cash welfare grant of $370 a month. But even during this economic upturn, the low-wage labor market remains saturated in the inner cities, where welfare recipients are concentrated, and there are also some 25 million part-time and temporary workers, many of whom would prefer regular full-time work if they could get it. No wonder real wages are not rising for the unskilled and the young, whose wages have plummeted since the early 1970s. Some five million heads of families earn at or near the minimum wage, which now falls short of the poverty line for a family of three. Fewer and fewer of these jobs pay health or pension benefits, and the work is hard and is getting harder, whether in the new manufacturing sites like chicken processing factories or garbage recycling plants or in speeded-up service-sector jobs where computers monitor keystrokes and absences. If anything, increasingly it is the low-wage job with no mobility that is the trap and welfare that sometimes provides for some women an opportunity to go back to school or enter a good training program, for example, that would be totally impossible without some assured income. Slashing welfare is a way to seal the low-wage trap.

Nor does it seem to be the case that women on welfare are passive or dependent, although we might well expect that pauper-level benefits, coupled with harassment by welfare agency staff and denunciations by politicians, are not good for morale. Nevertheless, more than half of welfare spells last less than a year, and some 70 percent last less than two years, although irregular work, a sick kid, or an abusive male partner may lead many women to turn to welfare more than once. This pattern might more reasonably be viewed as evidence of the initiative of poor women who take work when they can get it and when it pays enough to feed their kids and turn to welfare as a lifeline when they have to. Moreover, many women work while they are on welfare, packaging the inadequate income from wages and benefit checks.

If labor market conditions raise large questions about the good sense of sending the mothers of young children "off to work," the documented results of actual efforts to do just that argue their absurdity. We have in fact been "solving" the welfare problem for twenty-five years with a series of much-heralded welfare-to-work programs, all premised on the idea that what welfare mothers need is a little training and a big shove to make it in the job market. And for twenty-five years we have been evaluating the results of these reforms, called WIP or WIN or GAIN or JOBS or whatever. The results are trivial or non-existent. The programs increase the job success of women by tiny percentages, when they increase job placement at all, and they have a similarly negligible effect on earnings. Even tiny percentages produce a few smiling and successful women for the TV talk shows. But no TV host invites the women who couldn't make it in the jobs they got and had to return to welfare. And no one invites the mothers who suffer the harassment of being hustled from one work-preparedness scheme to another and who are then perhaps sanctioned with slashed benefits if they do not cooperate. Nor, needless to say, is much research directed to measure the material and psychic toll of this harassment.

If the usual claims for why we need to end welfare as we know it make no sense, then we have to look beyond these claims. What is going on is not policy making in the sense of rational and informed interventions by government to solve a named problem but rather a species of symbolic politics. Democrats and Republicans alike have hit on welfare bashing as a way to appease an anxious and increasingly angry electorate by telling a story about the sources of America's troubles that points the finger of blame at welfare mothers.

There are, of course, good reasons that the American public is dissatisfied and anxious. Our world is changing, in many ways for the worse. For one thing, the American class structure has been transformed in the past two decades as the rich have gotten much richer, the poor much poorer, and large swaths of the voting public poorer as well. In just two decades, as profits rose and overall wealth increased, most wages fell, and wages at the bottom fell steeply. Sixty percent of male wage earners lost on average over 20 percent. To stay in place, more people are working, and they are working longer and often harder as well. Perhaps worst of all, the future is wrenchingly uncertain: Automobile workers can no longer expect a bigger paycheck as time goes on. It may well be smaller, maybe much smaller, and the uncertainties they see for themselves are underlined for their sons and daughters. Meanwhile, the palpable evidence of the economic casualties has also increased in the form of visible poverty and pathology and of beggars and spreading homeless encampments in all the major cities.

Cultural changes are also contributing to widespread unease. Not least, sexual and family mores are changing, eroding a world in which men are men, women are women, and the rules for mating and family life are clear. Changes of this sort can generate a distinctive terror, perhaps because the meanings they challenge are so deeply imprinted in early childhood. At any rate, these cultural insecurities have become focal in American politics, helping to fuel the rise of Christian fundamentalism and its entry into Republican politics.

It matters greatly how leaders talk to an anxious and confused public. President Roosevelt and, to a lesser extent, Kennedy and Johnson helped focus the nation's attention on broad economic conditions that were transforming American life, and because they did they were able to build public support for government programs that would moderate the impact of those changes.

But neither Clinton nor the Democrats have had much to say to ease economic anxieties. Of course, government interventions to reverse declining wages and widening inequalities are inherently difficult in a more international economy. But the way out of the Great Depression was uncharted, too. Roosevelt tried one strategy after another, and he used the bully pulpit of the presidency to make clear the class stakes in New Deal interventions. The problem now is that, pinioned as they are by their concern for business investment, for bond market stability, and for fat cat campaign contributions, the Democrats never gave their own credo "It's the economy, stupid" much of a try. Instead, Clinton opted to pander to the worst strains in American politics. Confronting militantly well-organized Republican opposition, he borrowed their strategy of invoking cultural anxieties with speeches about family values and individual responsibility. And he used his presidential soapbox to tell a story about America's travails that pointed to women on welfare as the source of our social problems. The story works as well as it does because it meshes with our racism and our chauvinism, with our obsessive sexual preoccupations, and with our American dislike of the poor. It is also a story we are prepared to endorse by a history of American welfare practices that denigrate the people on welfare by keeping them so poor that they are outside the mainstream of American life, by stripping them of any procedural rights and endlessly investigating and disciplining them, and even going so far as to criminalize impoverished women with procedures like fingerprinting, all reminiscent of ancient practices for dealing with paupers with the brand, the lash, and the workhouse.

The irony is that the symbolic politics of welfare bashing is likely to aggravate the economic causes of American frustrations even while it provides them scapegoats on which to vent their anger. Welfare cutbacks will force millions of poor women into the low-wage labor market, where they will compete with other low-wage earners for whatever jobs they can find, with the result that already low wage levels will drop and working conditions worsen. This also is part of the story of welfare reform.

Still, it is not likely to be the end of the story. Earlier episodes of aggressive and reckless business politics helped precipitate the popular mobilizations that, together with electoral convulsions, made possible the political reforms of the early and mid-twentieth century. It is not likely that we will reverse the losses suffered at the end of the century without comparable social and political upheavals.

CHAPTER 3

HUMAN SERVICES
AND WELFARE REFORM

B. WELFARE REFORM'S IMPACT ON PEOPLE— CASE EXAMPLES: IMPLICATIONS FOR HUMAN SERVICE WORK AND HUMAN SERVICE WORKERS

MICHAEL SELIGER

Changes in federal welfare policy (and law) and the ways in which each state has chosen to implement federal law at the state level have immense implications for the way that individuals and families who previously were covered under broad protections and economic supports are now served or treated. These changes shape the way that front-line human service workers will interact with clients because the goals of those interactions may change and the circumstances of the human service worker's clients certainly have changed.

The case examples presented here are based on actual experiences of individuals who have been affected by these changes. These are composite examples, not "true stories of particular individuals." In many cases, the actual cases of individuals are even more dramatic than the composites described here. For example, a single mother who chose to study at the Bronx Educational Opportunity Center to obtain a good job in an allied health technical field was ordered to report to a menial Workfare job. She sought the advice of her case manager and staff at the EOC's Child Care Center and was referred to the Welfare Rights: Policy Law Center, where she became the lead plaintiff in a case that ultimately determined that the City could not require individuals to enter Workfare unless an assessment had been conducted that determined that was the most appropriate option for moving

toward independence. This individual, with support from the EOC and child care center, was able to complete her program and ultimately obtain a good job in the field she had been trained for while her child benefited from quality child care services. But most individuals would not have been able to successfully navigate the maze of regulations developed primarily to make the city and state eligible for the maximum amount of dollars available under federal law; caseworkers who made decisions based on their personal interpretation of recent training in a field of daily changes in rules and procedures; and a system whose procedures had been designed to push all but the most tenacious into a "jobs first" strategy regardless of their potential to benefit from training.

Most of these composite cases are based on experiences in New York City, but the essential elements are applicable to understanding the impact of "welfare reform" in any part of the country.

1. Diana Taveras. Diana had moved to New York City from the Dominican Republic four years ago. The mother of two children under the age of five, she had been on public assistance, staying home caring for her children until the rules governing her situation changed. She was "invited" by letter from the Human Resources

Administration (HRA, New York City's welfare agency) to come to her local center to meet with a caseworker about her being assigned to a Work Experience Program. When she came to the meeting with the caseworker, it was determined that she could not be assigned to a Work Experience assignment for several reasons. First, she did not have child care for her two children. The caseworker gave her information on possible options, including having a neighbor or relative care for the children, at a rate of pay less than $2 per hour per child, which HRA would pay. Diana was told that she was required to explore these options and return to the caseworker within two weeks, once the "problem" was solved. Failure to make an effort to obtain child care would result in sanctions that would reduce her welfare cash grant.

Second, Diana's limited English language ability was identified as a condition that would require remedying before she could be able to obtain employment. It was determined that she should be enrolled in a six-month ESL (English as a second language) program in which she would receive twenty hours of language classes every two weeks while being assigned to a work activity—in her case, as a kitchen assistant in a city public school. Other typical assignments included filing in city offices, painting public facilities, photocopying, park maintenance (primarily picking up garbage in the park), and other activities that might improve city facilities but provide little in the way of job skills that could be transferred to unsubsidized employment options.

Diana arranged for her two- and four-year-old to be cared for by a neighbor who also receives public assistance. The neighbor received a waiver exempting her from participating in the WEP program because she was caring for children in her home. (While the neighbor had a clean home and good intentions, she was not trained as a child care provider. This unlicensed home care option is encouraged by welfare officials because it is the least expensive option for them. It does not, however, ensure quality care for the next generation.)

After Diana had been in the ESL program for four months, maintaining satisfactory progress and good attendance (there are sanctions for anything less than 100% attendance), one of the children of the neighbor who cared for Diana's children became seriously ill. As a result, she could no longer care for Diana's children. When Diana stayed home to care for her children, she was threatened with sanctions and ultimately had to withdraw from the program because of a lack of child care. (The other mother could be required to enter WEP herself, once the child recovers from her illness, because she is no longer caring for children in her home!)

Even if Diana had been able to complete the ESL program, in twenty-six weeks she would have had only 260 hours of ESL instruction, which is not likely to be sufficient to enable her to compete for jobs requiring English language skills. The most likely scenario would have been her being assigned to continue in the same activity as she had been in for an additional twenty-six weeks, or a combination of "job search" and WEP-type activity.

In Diana's case, we see a number of issues and problems requiring the attention of human services organizations, including the following:

▬ There is a need for quality child care services, including both trained and supervised family day care providers and center-based care options. In most of New York City, both the quantity and the quality of child care options are unsatisfactory. Funding and training more workers are critical concerns.

▬ The options for people like Diana must make it possible to break out of the cycle of poverty. This would require realistic remedial and training services that could enable them to become competitive in the employment market. The experiences provided through any kind of Work Experience activity should enhance skills with a marketable value and need to be viewed as preparatory, rather than punitive, activity. The time allotted for these training activities must be realistic.

▬ The experiences that Diana goes through must be processed by a sensitive case manager who can assist her in making realistic long-term choices and growing from her experiences. (At many agencies that deliver ESL and related work activities, case management services are built into the design.)

— There is a need for a safety net to ensure that failure of child care arrangements (especially for informal child care) will not jeopardize any progress and gains that someone like Diana might have made.

— Assessment, at the beginning of Diana's being called in to participate in WEP, must be comprehensive and identify the barriers that preclude Diana's successful participation in programs and that preclude her from being able to benefit from those programs to the point that she would eventually achieve meaningful unsubsidized employment. Meaningful assessment and advisement, with clear goals, are needed to enable Diana and others like her to succeed.

There are too many Dianas and not enough jobs in the current economy. Major efforts are needed to improve the economic climate and options in most cities. While we try to upgrade Diana's skills, we also must try to increase her opportunities to become employed, possibly through local economic development initiatives that bring employment through new industrial or retail service activity in the area.

2. Harriet Lewis.   Harriet had been attending college when the changes in welfare regulations took effect. She needed thirty-six credits to graduate from a vocational technical program at Manhattan Community College. The mother of a four-year-old who was being cared for in the College Child Care Center, she was called in to her welfare center for a reassessment of her eligibility for Training Related Expenses (TREs). She was informed that her rate of progress toward the degree must be maintained at twelve or more credits per term for her to continue to be eligible for TREs and that she could receive only two more terms of TRE allowances. She also had to maintain an overall grade average of C or better. Unfortunately, because of an unexpected domestic crisis in which she was beaten by her (now former) boyfriend, she was unable to complete her coursework within the required time. She was directed to accept a Work Experience Program

assignment or to drop off welfare. (Because of a recent change in state and local policy, college campuses can serve as sites for WEP assignments. Previously, WEP forced more people to drop out of college, but now some people are enabled to balance college and WEP, with work assignments and class schedules complementing each other.)

With a WEP assignment in the college library that was not in conflict with her class schedule, she was able to complete her coursework in three terms. With counseling assistance, she was able to deal with her domestic situation and the emotional impact it had on herself and her child. She moved and obtained a protective order denying her ex-boyfriend access to her home or vicinity. Eventually, she obtained employment with good benefits and appears to be well on her way to an independent life.

For Harriet to succeed, a number of elements needed to work together, including the following:

— Cooperation between HRA and the college on the scheduling of WEP assignments for college students

— Counselor assistance to deal with Harriet's home crisis, which threatened to halt her school progress

— Availability of a child care option that met her needs as a student and as a WEP enrollee

— College staff committed to addressing the unique needs of public assistance recipients on campus, especially in today's climate

3. Joan Gumbs.   Joan might be viewed as an example of WEP success. When called in to be assessed for WEP, she was so afraid of the treatment that she would get on a WEP job that she went out and got a low-paying factory job processing fish in a frozen-food plant. The hours were long, and she had little time to take care of her children, who now stay most of the time with their grandmother. Joan makes enough money to pay a small amount to her mother for their care and was able to get her health benefits continued for one year under the city's Transitional Benefits program. She is pointed to as an example of what this program is supposed to accomplish. The welfare rolls have been reduced.

However, Joan remains at risk of falling back into the situation that she tried to leave. Consider the following:

— What happens if her mother is no longer able to care for her children because of health or economic problems?

— If there are more and more people trying to leave the welfare system, how can Joan ever get ahead at her new workplace if there is a constant stream of potential workers willing to work for a starting wage? Will the plant let her go rather than pay for benefits after her transitional benefits year is over?

— Working long hours leaves little time for her to improve herself through education or even to take care of herself physically and emotionally.

— With no time devoted to self-improvement educationally or through training, she will not be in a position to better her situation and is at risk of having nowhere to go if the opportunity that she has grabbed ever fails. (Even if she wanted to get into an evening training program, there are few places that also address child care needs in the evening. This is becoming a major concern as some people leave public assistance and then seek to better their situation.)

EMPOWERMENT: THEORY AND PRACTICE
A. EMPOWERMENT: TOWARD A NEW DEFINITION OF SELF-HELP

AUDREY COHEN

The purpose of human service work is to empower people.

What are human services®?[1] Stated most simply, they are the complex interactions that address and respond to human concerns. When successful, they make positive and lasting differences in peoples' lives, and they help improve the world. Now, in the beginning years of the twenty-first century, a major portion of our work force is engaged in these very activities, and the phenomenon extends even to those areas not normally considered human services. In manufacturing companies, for example, there are key human service components (i.e., customer service and human resource management) that may spell the difference between these companies' success and their failure.

The importance of human service work cannot be overstated. While we can agree on the overall nature of human services, the question is whether there is an overarching purpose that gives continuity to this broad and varied field. I believe there is. Empowerment is the purpose of human service work. Not only must human service professionals themselves be empowered but, in addition, their goal is to help others to become empowered, to increase their ability to manage their lives more effectively and realize their potential as creative, responsible, and productive members of society.

This is not a small charge, but it is essential and is achievable. Empowerment is both the result of effective human services and the force that makes such results possible. It should be an integral part of human development and education and the basis on which professional effectiveness is assessed.

Unfortunately, educational institutions rarely address empowerment as their central concern. In addition, the rapidly changing nature of our economy has transformed the types of knowledge and skills that people require in order to be empowered and to empower others. Most educational institutions are still based on a paradigm of learning developed for industrial societies, whereas today we live in a technologically sophisticated and service-centered postindustrial age.

In 1964, I founded an educational institution whose specific purpose was to develop a method of teaching and learning that was based on principles of empowerment and that prepared people for professional work in the new economy. During the more than thirty years of the institution's existence, it has expanded into both graduate and undergraduate education. Audrey Cohen College's unique educational approach—its

---

[1] Audrey Cohen College holds a trademark (1967) on the word combination "human services." That term was registered as part of its original name, "The College for Human Services." However, the approved and official registration certificate from the U.S. Patent Office specifically exempts the words "The College" from trademark protection, leaving "human services" as the protected entity. This is an interesting note when one considers how generic the term "human services" has become.

Purpose-Centered System of Education®[2]—also is being applied in public elementary and secondary schools throughout the country and has become a model for educational approaches for the twenty-first century. For three decades, the College has tested its ability to promote and achieve empowerment in the world outside the classroom. My hope is that in reaching out to you, the future generation of professionals preparing for human service careers, I will help you achieve your own empowerment and that of the citizens you serve.[3]

Empowerment is reciprocal. You become empowered as you assist in the empowerment of others. To achieve this reciprocity, education and implementation must occur simultaneously. Theory and practice must prevail throughout the preparation for professional practice.

A FOCUS ON PURPOSE

How does one achieve this necessary synthesis of theory and practice? At our institution, we addressed this question by first defining what constituted an effective human service professional. Our goal was to use this definition to determine the outcomes on which to base professional education. It took four years of extensive research to identify the principal characteristics of effective service. That research focused on exemplary professionals throughout the country and determined, through the use of the "critical incident" and other social science methodology, the tasks and results, the knowledge and actions, that made them outstanding. We discovered that there were eight critical, complex areas of effective performance that creative professionals mastered. These professionals, whether they were corporation presidents, managers, social workers, educators, lawyers, or physicians, continually and effectively addressed the identified areas of performance. These were also the key areas of empowering human service work that qualitatively and quantitatively made a positive difference in people's lives.[4]

---

[2] Audrey Cohen College currently has a patent pending on its Purpose-Centered System of Education. In addition, the college has trademarks on a number of key concepts describing its system of education, including the following terms and descriptive phrases that appear in this text: Purpose-Centered System of Education, Constructive Action, Dimension, and Purpose.

[3] From 1964 to 1970, the College was the vanguard of what became the national paraprofessional movement. In our initial efforts to address what constituted effective human service, I worked with people throughout New York City to design new, above-entry-level positions that could meet the need for improved human services and also address the lack of job opportunities, particularly for the poor. Based on my research and our work with community organizations, we defined about a dozen new job categories, including Educational Assistant, Legal Services Assistant, Case Manager, Social Work Assistant, and Counseling Assistant. The College then designed the first rudimentary model of the empowering human service curriculum. It then educated and trained low-income-community members to fill these new positions, integrated the positions into the New York City and State personnel structure, and generated widespread support for the new roles. The need for these positions was demonstrated, and we helped disseminate them for hundreds of thousands of people throughout the country. In 1970, the College moved on to its total redesign of professional education.

[4] The plan for development of a professional education required the involvement of those who were identified as excellent examples of the kind of professional the program was intended to prepare. For the purpose of gathering and analyzing this material, the College hired a research firm to interview sixty outstanding professionals in the area of human service. When the data produced a number of areas of performance that seemed generic to the work of outstanding professionals, a team of planners from the College, working with a group of consultants (which included researchers, content specialists, curriculum experts, faculty, and agency officials) began to take the elements that emerged from the research—the skills, knowledge, and values of the outstanding professionals—and tried to separate and make sense of them. The new ideas that emerged would not have provided the basis for a "new" paradigm for educating a "new" human service professional if we had relied exclusively upon the traditional model of higher education.

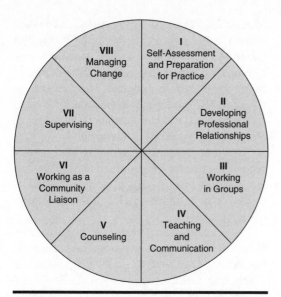

FIGURE 4.1 The Eight Performance Areas

At the College, we called these areas of performance Purposes®. Our first major educational breakthrough came when I decided to develop a curriculum focused around the Purposes, so that each semester, students training to become human service professionals develop competency in one of the eight generic areas of performance. The eight Purposes that empowering and creative service professionals master are self-assessment and preparation for practice, developing professional relationships, working in groups, teaching and communication, counseling, working as a community liaison, supervising, and managing change. Figure 4.1 illustrates these Purposes.

The College's curriculum moves human service professionals toward full self-empowerment by training them to address each of the eight Purposes we have identified. Equally important, students learn that their goal as human service professionals[5] includes consciously working to teach citizens to deal effectively with these Purposes themselves—to become less and less dependent. In other words, citizens would become empowered. As part of the human service process, our profession helps empower others. Our profession helps them recognize obstacles and call on resources, both internal and external, to overcome these barriers. Human service performance, under the College's paradigm, is successful on both societal and personal levels.

Dimensions of Knowledge and Action

Although defining the Purposes of human service education was the first step in implementing the concept of empowerment in the new curriculum, we also learned that our exemplary professionals worked holistically. This "holism" was clearly another critical factor in their success. Each time they addressed one of the Purposes in question, they considered a number of parameters, or Dimensions®, of their performance that they knew contributed to their success. Five essential Dimensions, key aspects of effective performance, were embedded in their empowering human service work. These Dimensions were concerned with selecting and achieving appropriate goals, acting ethically and resolving value conflicts, understanding oneself and others, understanding the systems within which people function, and developing the specific skills needed to achieve goals. These Dimensions, which remain constant whatever the situation, are shown in Figure 4.2.

This led to the second breakthrough in our human service paradigm: the decision to use these Dimensions as the organizers of the knowledge for each of the Purposes. They became the names of the classes students attended throughout their eight undergraduate semesters of study.

---

[5] In June 1974, the Conference to Found a New Profession, sponsored by Audrey Cohen College (formerly The College for Human Services) in New York City, marked the establishment of the Human Service Profession and the definition of a new professional role. A broad spectrum of national decision makers voiced their support for the profession and its practitioner: the human service professional.

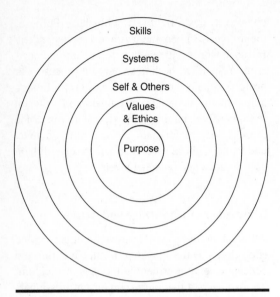

FIGURE 4.2   The Essential Dimensions® of Empowering Human Service

The first Dimension pertains to establishing appropriate goals and developing strategies for achieving them. Each term, students are required to set a service goal in relation to the semester's Purpose, work to achieve it, and apply both learning and practice in the context of this planned effort. They also are expected to teach those with whom they work the same purposive and self-directing skills. The second Dimension calls on the student to demonstrate a clear and consistent understanding of his or her values and those of others. It presupposes a belief in the unique value of each person and the capacity of each person for growth, increasing self-direction and creative and responsible participation in the world around them. The third Dimension involves a commitment to understanding oneself and others through both study and experience and is based on the understanding that everything we do is affected by our perception of ourselves and others. The fourth Dimension relates to understanding the role of systems in our daily life. As human service professionals, we are often incapacitated by lack of knowledge not only of the organizational systems that are closest to us (e.g., the particular office for which we work) but also how this system relates to

other offices, the total organization, and outside systems. A vital ingredient in becoming an effective human service professional is the acquisition of a thorough understanding of relevant systems and the ability to use them as resources. The final Dimension of performance relates to the acquisition of the written technical and interpersonal skills that are an essential part of professional behavior.

These Dimensions of effective performance become the lenses through which our students see the world of learning. They provide the framework by which we can teach and assess empowering practice.

At Audrey Cohen College, our students extrapolate from the theory drawn from the humanities, the social sciences, the sciences, and professional studies, and this theory is covered in the Dimension classes. Students learn how to work with people and organizations directly in order to identify their special needs. They master skills that include not only those involved in analysis and communications but also less tangible ones, such as effective interviewing and effective listening. They learn how to help others articulate their feelings, their strengths, their needs, and their goals. They learn how to encourage them to make realistic plans. Our students evaluate citizens' needs in relation to the resources that are available and the help the service provider can properly give in the situation. They learn that citizens are likely to have multiple needs that must be balanced and that may require quite different kinds of special help. Our professionals-in-training learn to look for other sources to provide the help that they cannot provide themselves. They learn to do all this with the goal of empowering those they are helping, empowering these citizens to meet the needs they themselves have defined and make their own choices as to the best methods of achieving their goals.

A Purpose-Centered System of Education®

The intersection of the eight performance areas and the five Dimensions, as illustrated in Figure 4.3, provide a general framework for human service practice. Wherever you are working (i.e.,

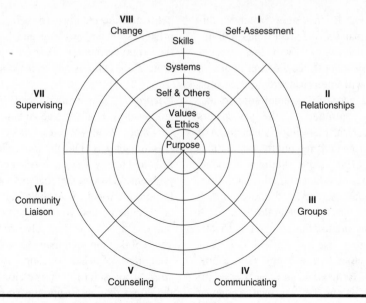

FIGURE 4.3   The Intersection of Dimensions® and Purposes

hospital, day care center, school, mental retardation facility) this framework facilitates integrated, rather than fragmented, service. It underscores, once again, a basic tenet of empowering human service practice: Human service professionals must perceive their work as a totality, not only meeting the needs of the citizen but also fostering a learning process that helps the same citizen to become empowered.

Constructive Action®

Assessment at Audrey Cohen College concentrates on students' abilities to effectively empower others. It cannot be concerned with minutiae. Our methodology for assessing the achievement of each semester's Purpose and, ultimately, assessing empowerment, requires that a student take Constructive Action®. A Constructive Action is a major service, designed and carried out in an organization during the semester and related to that semester's Purpose. The Constructive Action demonstrates how a student uses knowledge (what he or she is learning inside the classroom) as a basis for effective human services

outside the classroom. It documents the knowledge used and the process followed during the period of the Constructive Action. A successful Constructive Action improves the lives of citizens. It is conceived with the help of the citizens it serves. It can be carried out almost anywhere— in nursing homes, hospitals, schools, halfway houses, public and private agencies, and organizations that define the for-profit sector as well. Above all, it is a complex process of empowerment. It is a living case study.

Over the years, thousands of Constructive Actions have been carried out by students at our institution. They have ranged from reclaiming abandoned land and transforming it into a small neighborhood park in an area where no such resource had been available, to subtly incorporating necessary literacy training into parent education components in a Head Start program (many of those parents have earned general equivalency diplomas and are now pursuing higher education), to designing a training program for substance abuse counselors that was subsequently mandated for statewide use, to building bridges for young people at risk as they move from elementary to junior high school. In the latter instance, this meant that the human service practitioner in training, our student (who worked with these youngsters in elementary school), reached out to design support services with the prospective junior high school. Thus, the necessary special support and counseling was continued as the youngsters moved to the larger, far more impersonal arena of junior high school. In carrying out these and thousands of other Constructive Actions, students must address issues of values and ethics, relationships, and skills and systems, and above all they must demonstrate they can integrate them from all the Dimensions and use that integration to pursue their Purpose.

The Constructive Action begins with a proposal that addresses the goals and needs of a citizen or group of citizens. On approval, a plan of action is developed. This is done by our student (the human service professional in training), together with the citizen or citizens in question, a faculty member, and the student's supervisor in the organization in which the Constructive Action is to be performed.

The Constructive Action identifies academic success with professional accountability. This reflects the principle that classroom learning should be applicable to one's life, and it can be considered successful only if it helps both the student and the citizen to become empowered.

Empowerment from the Citizen's Viewpoint

In the process of carrying out the Constructive Action, both the human service professional-in-training and the citizen whose needs are being addressed learn to ask the right questions. If the citizen is not directly involved in the Constructive Action process, then the Purpose of the human service activity is illusory at best. Its achievement is difficult to assess.

Although one chapter does not present sufficient space to outline all the appropriate questions that a citizen should be able to answer, a sampling

helps provide insight into their depth and appropriateness. Like learning and assessment under the empowerment model, questions are framed around the Dimensions of learning and action.

Purpose®.   To evaluate the Purpose of the empowering Constructive Action, a citizen might be asked: Were you clear about your reason for seeking service? Did the professional listen carefully and help you to have a clearer idea about your problems? Do you feel that the questions asked by the professional were helpful, and could you answer them? Did you take part in planning what you ought to do to help solve your problem? Did you feel that the plan that was developed included *your* ideas of what you hoped would happen to *you?* As a result of the professional's services, did the things that were supposed to happen to you in the plan actually happen? In answering these and other questions, considerable detail is expected from the citizen.

Values and Ethics.   In assessing whether the professional was effective in the area of Values, some questions include: Did the professional draw conclusions about you and your problems that you felt were not true? Did the professional respect your feelings and opinions? Did the professional see your problem differently from how you see your problem? Did *you* question the professional's judgment of what is most important, or did you just accept it? Here, as in all areas of questioning, yes or no answers are not acceptable. The citizen is expected to provide a rationale for his or her actions.

Self and Others.   In determining whether the citizen has made progress in self-understanding as well as in understanding others, appropriate questions might include: Did the professional try to cooperate with you? Did you learn anything from the professional about yourself that would help you to solve your problems? Did the professional really help you to solve your problem?

System.   In looking at whether the citizen has expanded his or her ability to identify and work with the systems that provide service delivery, appropriate questions might include: Did the professional provide you with information about organizations that could help you? Were you able to meet your goals through accessing these organizations? Do you have a better understanding of the different organizations that can support you in your goals, and do you see how they are related to each other?

Skills.   The citizen is expected to have learned additional skills from empowering human service practice. That citizen might well be asked: Can you now be specific about how you can handle your own problems better? Did you acquire the skill to investigate resources for yourself or to plan and carry out ways of dealing with this and similar problems? Can you write a record of what is happening to you each day and indicate how any of the events you describe might be part of your problem?

Assessment: The Empowerment Chart.   In 1978, we developed the first Empowerment Chart, an additional tool to guide the student practitioner and the Purpose instructor through both the empowerment process and its assessment.[6] Two basic principles underlie the Chart's content: (1) providers of service can and should demonstrate the effectiveness of their services, and (2) recipients of services are empowered to the extent that they are involved in planning and assessing the services they receive.

The Empowerment Chart is designed for use by the citizen and practitioner as an integral part of the helping relationship. It is an instrument for planning and assessing service. Within the context of the citizen's needs, it helps the student see to what extent these needs are addressed. He or she is being effective in meeting three sets of goals simultaneously: the student's goals with regard to the citizen; the organizational/supervisor goals with regard to the same citizen; and, equally important, and too often overlooked, the citizen's goals with regard to the need he or she has defined.

Because these goals can be quite different, the Chart becomes a most effective educational tool. It will show the student to what extent he or she has been effective in meeting these three sets of goals. It will show whether the student has been able to bring the three points of view closer together. It will show whether there is true accomplishment.

It is not possible, within the confines of one chapter, to detail all the elements of the Empowerment Chart. However, let me begin the process with you by illustrating Step 1 of the Empowerment Chart: setting the long-term Purpose (Goal).

Our citizen is an abusing parent. Abusing parents represent a category of citizen far from empowerment. They are beset by such frustrations and difficulties that continued direct care and help are essential. Our citizen hurts his wife and his children. He hurts them physically and psychologically. He says he wants to change. If this is to occur, a broad range of services and skills are necessary. To actively involve this parent in the decision-making processes, to encourage him to take responsibilities in trying to change his life, and to teach him how to do this while respecting him as an individual are challenging enough. However, our student must also simultaneously deal with the professional at the organization providing service, who

---

[6] Productivity in the human services was described in detail in a monograph I wrote in 1978. *The Citizen as the Integrating Agent: Productivity in the Human Services* was published by Project Share, a national clearinghouse for improving the management of human services under the U.S. Department of Health, Education and Welfare, and was distributed through the U.S. Government Printing Office. The Empowerment Chart was shown in that monograph, and a step-by-step description of the process was included.

1. LONG-TERM PURPOSE (GOAL)

as stated by:

CITIZEN(S): *Stop hurting children and live better with others*

AGENCY/SUPERVISOR: *Develop self-esteem and improve relations with children*

PRACTITIONER: *Develop self-esteem and improve relations with children*

After you have completed your needs analysis, write down the problem or issue you feel you should address in your Constructive Action. Then write down the problem or issue as your Purpose® Instructor sees it. You may or may not agree.

FIGURE 4.4   The Empowerment Chart, Section 1

may have a very specific service approach that is not necessarily harmonious with empowering human service practice. Finally, our student has to confront his or her own perceptions about the citizen. Because of this totality, the Empowerment Chart helps define, on an individual-by-individual, step-by-step basis, a new way to deliver human services. Figure 4.4 illustrates the start of this process.

Our student is immediately aware of the three points of view he or she must strive to bring closer together. Other portions of the chart are derived from the long-term Purpose or goal. Throughout the empowering service process, the primary issue is what the citizen wants to accomplish. The citizen's goals may change during the service period, and such a change is often a positive one. At its best, it will indicate a growing capacity to deal with reality. Because the Citizen Empowerment Chart is intended to evaluate progress and service effectiveness over a period of time, it focuses on outcomes rather than processes.[7]

---

[7] A full example illustrating the usefulness of the Empowerment Chart is found in the monograph previously referred to: *The Citizen as the Integrating Agent: Productivity in the Human Services,* U.S. Government Printing Office, 1978.

EMPOWERMENT: THEORY AND PRACTICE
B. HOW ALUMNI PERCEIVE AND USE THE CONSTRUCTIVE ACTION

SHIRLEY CONYARD

ABSTRACT

This study was conducted among alumni (n = 309) of Audrey Cohen College to explore their perceptions of the Constructive Action process (the teaching and practice methodology developed by the College) and to determine whether they had continued to use the process in their professional and personal lives. The study also explored how alumni use the process and what parts of it they have found to be most helpful. Two hypotheses were tested, asserting that differences in participant characteristics on enrollment at Audrey Cohen College (age, GPA, transfer student, foreign-born, first-generation, and training site) and differences in participant characteristics at the time of the investigation (level of education, income, and position in employing organization) would be related to differences in how participants perceived and used the Constructive Action process. Two measures were used to test the hypotheses: *t*-test and chi-square. The findings support the research hypotheses: more than 70 percent of respondents continued to use the Constructive Action process in their professional lives, in graduate school (where applicable), and in their personal lives. More than 80 percent of respondents reported that the process had positively affected their professional lives. A similar percentage identified the parts of the Constructive Action process that were most helpful and described how they used the process. The results were statistically significant for differences in age, GPA, and transfer status at enrollment and for differences in level of education and position held in one's organization at the time of the study. In conclusion, the Constructive Action process was found to be an effective instrument for teaching students in the human services, and one with lasting impact on the personal and professional lives of alumni.

INTRODUCTION

The human service function is a process of directed change taking place as the result of interaction between human service workers, clients, and organizations (Cimmino, 1999). Training human service students is a comprehensive task, because training programs must carefully balance the time allotted to the human service delivery system (environment), education (classroom experience) and the role of the human service worker within the organization (field experience) (Cimmino, 1999). There is probably no aspect of human service education that has received more attention in recent years than how to connect the classroom experience with the field experience.

According to Simon (1999) this issue has generated much discussion and debate over the last forty years at institutions that provide education for human services.

To meet the challenge of providing a human service education that effectively and efficiently connects the classroom and the field experience, Audrey Cohen College developed a unique educational approach: the Purpose-Centered System of Education. This model stems from and reflects economic developments, including the growing predominance of the service sector and rapid globalization of the economy, which have required us to reexamine the every aspect of education (Cohen, 1978). The Purpose-Centered System of Education was designed to teach students to promote and achieve empowerment in the world outside the classroom (Cohen, 1999) and simultaneously to empower the students themselves. In other words, the College believes that empowerment should be reciprocal. In its 1975 proposal to establish bachelor's and master's degree programs in Human Services, the College asserted that the purpose of every human service was to help people become empowered to manage their own lives to the greatest extent possible and fulfill their potential as responsible and creative members of society (Cohen, 1976, 1977). The College, in a later publication, identified empowerment as the ultimate service goal, defining it as the people's ability to manage their lives, to recognize and meet their needs, and to fulfill their potential as creative, responsible, and productive members of society (Cohen, 1978). Others have sometimes articulated a similar goal for human services, though not necessarily calling for the empowerment of the student-practitioner. Describing human service intervention as the bridge between people and various subsystems in society, Eriksen (1977) said that the paramount goal of human services was to enable people to live more satisfying, autonomous, and productive lives.

The College's educational model focuses on eight Purposes or performance areas: Self-Assessment, Establishing Professional Relationships, Working in Groups, Teaching and Communication, Counseling, Community Liaison, Supervising, and Change. Each of these areas is examined from the perspective of five interdisciplinary Dimensions: Purpose, Values and Ethics, Self and Others, Systems, and Skills. The eight Purposes (performance areas), and the five Dimensions (comprising interdisciplinary knowledge and action) provide the framework for human services study and practice at Audrey Cohen College. A third major component of the College's model is the Constructive Action process. Students are required to engage in a field placement fourteen hours a week for fifteen weeks. For each consecutive Purpose, each student must carry out at the placement site a Constructive Action—that is, a significant action that is constructive for the agency and its clients.

Audrey Cohen College describes the Constructive Action as an "assessment tool, a method for pulling theory and practice together, and for joining the education site to the work site." It is considered a major piece of service delivery that is designed to improve the life of the citizen/client (Cohen, 1989). The College believes that all learning must be assessed in the context of an effort to solve a real problem; that is why students are required to demonstrate their learning in Constructive Action (Cohen, 1988). The Constructive Action process has six discrete components: (1) identification of purpose; (2) agency analysis; (3) needs assessment; (4) development of a plan of action (goals, objectives, strategies, and evaluation plan); (5) implementation of plan; and (6) assessment of outcomes.

RESEARCH DESIGN

Purpose

The purpose of the study was to investigate the validity of certain assumptions made by the College about the Constructive Action methodology. The assumptions studied were drawn from the writings of the founder of the College, Audrey

Cohen. The assumptions identified as the basis for the research were as follows: (1) the Constructive Action methodology, used as the basis for both learning and assessment, sets up a process that will serve the practitioner well throughout his or her working life; (2) the methodology helps to produce a practitioner who is always a learner, continually searching for useful theory and striving to improve his or her own performance; (3) the methodology helps to produce a practitioner who is better able to deal with the problems of life than he or she was at the outset of the education. If one learns to think and operate in this comprehensive way, one can turn all one's work into Constructive Actions (Cohen, 1989).

Research Questions

Based on the above assumptions, the following research questions were identified: (1) Have graduates of Audrey Cohen College continued to use components of the Constructive Action process in their professional lives or places of employment, in graduate school, and in their personal lives? (2) How has the Constructive Action format been used in their professional lives, graduate school, and personal lives? (3) Which components of the Constructive Action process have been most helpful?

Variables

Salient variables about the alumni were identified that would further help the College to understand alumni's perceptions of the Constructive Action process and how they are applying it. The variables pertain to alumni characteristics at enrollment in Audrey Cohen College and after graduation, at the time of the study. The variables at enrollment include age-traditional students (under the age of 23) vs. non-traditional students (23 and over); student status (transfer vs. non-transfer); grade point average (3.5 to 4.0 vs. 2.0 to 3.4); academic site (main campus vs. other campus), generation (first-generation college vs. non-

first-generation), birthplace (foreign-born vs. U.S.-born). The variables related to current status were defined as level of education (bachelor's degree vs. master's degree), income ($49,000 and under vs. $50,000 and over), and position held in the employing organization (administrative vs. non-administrative).

Hypotheses

The hypotheses that emerged from the above variables were as follows:

> *Hypothesis 1:* There will be differences in how alumni perceive and use the Constructive Action process that are related to their characteristics on enrollment in Audrey Cohen College.
>
> *Hypothesis 2:* There will be differences in how alumni perceive and use the Constructive Action process that are related to their characteristics at the time they fill out the survey.

To test the above hypotheses, six questions were formulated regarding graduates' continued use of the Constructive Action methodology, their perceptions of it, and how they used it. The six questions will be referred to as items 19, 20, 21, 22, 24, and 26. The questionnaire included thirty-five items. Item 23 was analyzed but not used for hypothesis testing because it dealt with graduate school, which was not part of either hypothesis.

METHOD

Population and Sample

The population consisted of a total of 1,682 alumni of the undergraduate Human Service program at Audrey Cohen College who had graduated prior to June 2000. To generate a sample, surveys were mailed to all potential respondents. After initial returns, a follow-up post card was mailed out and researchers attempted to make telephone contact. In addition, a snowball sampling method was employed which involved sample respondents providing addresses and telephone numbers of alumni who were not listed and/or inaccurately listed in the database. This process resulted in a final sample size of 309, indicating a response rate of roughly 20 percent. A preliminary review of data suggested that the demographic profile of the study population and the sample were similar in terms of gender (female 73.9 percent and male 26.15 percent), mean age prior to enrollment (35.0), and race/ethnicity (Blacks 74.8 percent, Hispanics/Latinos 15.8 percent, Whites 6.7 percent, Asians 2.6 percent). The sample had a slightly higher cumulative grade point average than the study population, with a mean of 3.4 and a median of 3.6.

Instrument/Data Collection

The instrument developed for this study was a four-page questionnaire that was mailed out to 1,682 alumni who had graduated from the School for Human Services undergraduate program between 1980 and 2000. Responses returned were 309. According to the Power Analysis Table, 309 is an appropriate sample size for a population between 1,600 and 1,700 (J. Cohen, 1977). The questionnaire had 35 questions: 14 open- and 21 closed-ended. Respondents were asked to select their answers to questions 22, 23, 24, and 26 on a seven-point Likert scale, with 1 representing the high end of the scale (positive perception) and 7 representing the low end of the scale (negative perception). Respondents were asked to rate their answers to questions 19, 20, and 21 on a four-point Likert scale that ranged from "strongly agree" to "strongly disagree." Questions 19–24 and 26 are reproduced below.

19. In my experience, the Constructive Action process is an excellent instrument for learning how to: integrate theory and practice or theory into practice; collect data; set goals and objectives; carry out research; focus on issues and needs; assess needs; and assess outcomes.
20. The Constructive Action process met my expectations as a learning tool.

21. I would highly recommend the Constructive Action process as an excellent learning tool.
22. Do you currently use the Constructive Action process in your professional life or place of employment? If yes, how do you use the Constructive Action: as a tool for planning; a tool for interviewing; assessing client needs; assessing program needs; case management; evaluating client outcomes; goal setting; evaluating program outcomes; implementing desired plan; in-service training; proposal writing; research/literature review; teaching tool; analyzing data; other.
23. Do you or did you use the Constructive Action process in graduate school? If yes, how do or did you use the Constructive Action process: analyzing data; evaluating outcomes; goal setting; needs assessment; project planning; plan implementation; research/literature review; writing up counseling cases; writing papers; and writing up law cases.
24. Do you currently use the Constructive Action process in your personal or private life? If yes, how do you use the Constructive Action: to analyze data; evaluate outcomes; set goals; assess needs, plan projects; implement plan; and carry out research/literature review.
26. Did the Constructive Action process have a positive impact on your professional career? If yes, indicate what impact: getting a job of my choosing; a promotion; a merit raise; an increase in pay; employee recognition; became a more organized planner; become a better counselor; increased my self-confidence; motivated me to continue my education.

The questionnaire included a comprehensive section on demographics, including level of education and employment; perceptions of the Constructive Action process and its current use as well as its effects on work, graduate school, and personal life; support systems; and obstacles to graduation. Last, respondents were asked for their perceptions about faculty teaching styles and the college's overall model of education.

Statistical Measurement

A number of items were combined to form a scale that focused on alumni perceptions of the Constructive Action process. An internal consistency test conducted on scale items showed a moderate to high degree of reliability (Alpha .91, reliability coefficients). The Conyard Constructive Action Tool for Learning Scale has seven items related to use of the Constructive Action methodology: to integrate theory and practice, collect data, set goals and objectives, carry out research, focus on issues and needs, assess needs, and assess outcomes (items 19a–g).

A two-tailed t-test and a chi-square test were used to test each hypothesis at a statistically significant level of $p < .05$. Descriptive analysis was use to classify alumni responses to the research questions.

FINDINGS

Research Questions

Do graduates from Audrey Cohen College continue to use components of the Constructive Action process in their professional lives or places of employment, in graduate school, and in their personal or private lives?

When asked if they continue to use the Constructive Action methodology in their professional lives or places of employment, 74.8 percent of respondents said "yes." The Constructive Action methodology is used as a tool for learning by 83.0 percent; as a tool for interviewing by 72.7 percent; for assessing client/citizen needs by 85.6 percent; for assessing program needs by 82.6 percent; for case management by 78.1 percent; for evaluating client/citizen outcomes by 80.4 percent; for goal setting by 86.2 percent; for evaluating program outcomes by 78.6 percent; for implementing desired plans by 81.3 percent; for in-service training by 64.0 percent; for proposal writing by 71.2 percent; for research/literature review by 81.4 percent; as a teaching tool by 78.8 percent; and for analyzing data by 77.9 percent.

The question, "Do you or did you use the Constructive Action process in graduate school?" was answered by 146 alumni, of whom 77.2 per-

cent said "yes." Among those who said yes, the Constructive Action process was used for analyzing data by 84.5 percent; for evaluating outcomes by 86.2 percent; for goal setting by 89.0 percent; for needs assessment by 89.2 percent; for project planning by 88.5 percent; for plan implementation by 76.6 percent; for research/literature review by 88.8 percent; for writing up counseling cases by 83.3 percent; for writing papers by 83.4 percent; and for writing up law cases by 68.7 percent.

When asked whether they had continued to use the Constructive Action methodology in their personal lives, 70.8 percent of respondents said "yes." Of this group, 83.4 percent use the Constructive Action process for analyzing data; 79.8 percent for evaluating outcomes; 93.4 percent for goal setting; 93.3 percent for needs assessment; 87.3 percent for project planning; 84.6 percent for plan implementation; and 82.6 percent for research/literature review.

Significant numbers of respondents found the Constructive Action process to be an excellent instrument for learning in the specific areas listed in the survey: integrating theory and practice, 91.7 percent; collecting data, 89.9 percent; setting goals and objectives, 91.4 percent; carrying out research, 88.8 percent; focusing on issues and needs, 92.2 percent; assessing needs, 90.6 percent; and assessing outcomes, 89.1 percent. In addition, 90.4 percent indicated that the Constructive Action methodology met their expectations as a learning tool, and 84.1 percent would highly recommend the Constructive Action methodology as an excellent learning tool.

To the question "Did the Constructive Action process have an impact on your professional career?" 88.6 percent of respondents said "yes." Among specific areas of impact, getting a job of their choosing was selected by 86.1 percent; getting a promotion by 84.5 percent; getting a merit raise by 71.4 percent; getting an increase in pay by 80.7 percent; getting recognition by 83.4 percent; becoming a more organized planner by 88.6 percent; becoming a better counselor by 83.6 percent; increasing self-confidence by 89.4 percent;

and being motivated to continue their education by 88.2 percent.

TESTING OF HYPOTHESES

Hypothesis 1: There will be differences in how alumni perceive and use the Constructive Action process that are related to their characteristics on enrollment in Audrey Cohen College.

Transfer or Non-Transfer Student. A chi-square test of the association between transfer and non-transfer students indicated a statistically significant association for item 22, "Do you currently use the Constructive Action methodology in your professional life or place of employment?" ($\chi^2 = 7.98$, $df = 1$, $p < .008$), and similar results for item 26, "Has the Constructive Action methodology had a significant impact on your professional life?" ($\chi^2 = 3.73$, $df = 1$, $p < .053$). With respect to items 19a–g, 20, 21, and 24, there was no statistically significant difference ($p > .05$).

Grade Point Average. The *t*-test indicated a statistical significant difference between grade point average (2.0–3.49 vs. 3.5–4.0) on items 19a–g, "In my experience, the Constructive Action process is an excellent tool for learning . . ." (means of 16.46 and 17.62, $t = p < .028$), and gave similar results on item 20, "The Constructive Action process met my expectations as a learning tool" (means of 2.31 and 2.50, $t = p < .028$), and item 21, "I would highly recommend the Constructive Action process as an excellent learning tool" (means of 2.20 and 2.39, $t = p < .049$). No differences were found with respect to grade point average on items 22, 24, and 26, $p > .05$.

Traditional or Non-Traditional Student: A chi-square test examining the association between traditional and non-traditional students indicated a statistically significant association for item 22, "Do you currently use the Constructive Action methodology in your professional life or place of employment?" ($\chi^2 = 13.81$, $df = 1$, $p < .001$), and item 26, "Did the Constructive Action methodology have a positive impact on your professional career?" ($\chi^2 = 9.94$, $df = 1$, $p < .005$). There were no differences between traditional and non-traditional students for items 19a–g, 20, 21, and 24 ($p > .05$).

Neither the *t*-test nor the chi-square test produced a statistically significant result for the following variables: first-generation vs. non-first-generation, foreign-born vs. U.S.-born, and main campus vs. other sites. The statistically significant level for the above variables was $p > .05$.

Hypothesis 2: There will be differences in how alumni perceive and use the Constructive Action process that are related to their characteristics at the time they fill out the survey.

Level of Education: A *t*-test indicated a statistically significant difference between bachelor's and master's degree holders for items 19a–g, "In my experience, carrying out the Constructive Action process is an excellent tool for learning . . ." (means of 16.59 and 17.88, $t = p < .009$), item 20, "The Constructive Action process met my expectations as a learning tool" (means of 2.31 and 2.57, $t = p < .001$), and item 21, "I would highly recommend the Constructive Action process as an excellent learning tool" (means 2.17 and 2.50, $t = p < .001$). A chi-square test examining the association between educational attainment and responses produced similar results for item 22, "Do you currently use the Constructive Action methodology in your professional life or place of employment?" ($\chi^2 = 4.09$, $df = 1$, $p < .049$), and item 24, "Do you currently use the Constructive Action methodology in your personal or private life?" ($\chi^2 = 8.51$, $df = 1$, $p < .004$.) The only item that did not show a difference for educational attainment was item 26 ($p > .05$).

Administrative or Non-Administrative Position. The *t*-test indicated a statistically significant difference between the responses of alumni in administrative and non-administrative positions for item 20, "The Constructive Action process met my expectations as a learning tool" (means of 2.60 and 2.37, $t = p < .006$) and item 21, "I would highly recommend the Constructive Action process as an excellent learning tool" (means of 2.46 and 2.27, $t = p < .034$). A chi-square test of the association between administrative and non-administrative positions produced similar results for item 22, "Do you currently use the Constructive Action methodology in your professional life or place of employment?" ($\chi^2 = 4.388$, $df = 1$, $p < .039$), and item 26, "Did the Constructive Action methodology have a positive impact on your professional career?"($\chi^2 = 10.55$, $df = 1$, $p < .001$). In looking at items 19a–g and 24, no significant results were found ($p > .05$). No differences related to income level were found for any items ($p > .05$).

DISCUSSION

The purpose of the study was to investigate whether alumni had continued to use the Constructive Action process in their professional lives or places of employment, in graduate school (where applicable), and in their personal lives and what its impact had been. The study also focused on alumni perceptions of the Constructive Action methodology, what parts of the Constructive Action methodology alumni had found to be most useful, and how they were using the Constructive Action methodology. The study examined status on enrollment and current status after graduation as variables that might affect alumni responses.

The findings support the assumptions made by Audrey Cohen College about the Constructive Action process as a methodology for teaching and practice.

More than 70 percent of respondents reported that they had continued to use the Constructive Action methodology in their professional lives or places of employment, in graduate

school (where applicable), and in their personal lives. The applications that had been most helpful to more than 80 percent of respondents were setting goals and objectives; assessing program needs (agency analysis); assessing client/citizen needs; implementing plans; evaluating outcomes; and research/literature review. More than 70 percent of respondents indicated that they used the Constructive Action methodology for interviewing clients/citizens; writing proposals, in-service training; teaching (in secondary education); analyzing data; writing research papers, and writing up counseling and law cases.

More than 90 percent of respondents reported that the Constructive Action process met their expectations as a learning tool, and more than 80 percent of the respondents saw the Constructive Action process as an excellent instrument for learning specific skills: how to integrate theory and practice; collect data; set goals and objectives; carry out research; focus on issues; carry out a needs assessment; and assess outcomes. More than 80 percent of respondents would highly recommend the Constructive Action process as an excellent learning tool.

More than 80 percent of respondents reported that the Constructive Action process had positively affected their professional careers. As a result of their experience with the Constructive Action process, more than 80 percent reported having become more organized planners, better counselors, and more self-confident; had been motivated to continue their education; and had gained recognition at their places of employment. More than 80 percent indicated that the Constructive Action process had helped them to get a job of their choosing, a promotion, and an increase in pay. *These results can be interpreted as evidence of the empowerment of students from continuing use of the Constructive Action process.*

Those who had completed their entire undergraduate education at Audrey Cohen College were more likely than students who had transferred to the College to make use of the Constructive

Action process in their professional lives or places of employment and more likely to report that the Constructive Action process had positively affected their professional careers. These results may reflect the longer exposure of non-transfer students to the Constructive Action process or the greater number of Constructive Actions completed. Most transfer students had completed only four Constructive Actions. The results also could reflect a lesser degree of commitment to the College's model of education among transfer students.

Respondents with a higher grade point average were more likely to report that the Constructive Action process is an excellent instrument for learning how to integrate theory and practice and to perform such tasks as setting goals and objectives, carrying out research, focusing on issues and needs, and assessing outcomes. They were also more likely to say that the Constructive Action process had met their expectations as a learning tool and that they would highly recommend it as an excellent learning tool. There were no differences related to grade point average on the other items. These results may reflect the level of respondents' understanding of the Constructive Action process. The results may also be based on the respondents' possession of skills needed to perform well in this type of accelerated, structured educational model. The Audrey Cohen College Human Service program is full-time only: students must carry five courses and a fourteen-hour-a-week internship from semester two through semester eight.

Non-traditional students (those over age 23 at enrollment) were more likely than traditional college-age students to make current use of the Constructive Action process in their professional lives or places of employment, and they were more likely to report that their experience of it had positively affected their professional careers. These findings may reflect several factors; for example, traditional students are older and more focused, they are more likely to be employed in human service organizations, and they are more

likely to have entered the College with years of experience in human services. All of these factors suggest that they are more likely than traditional students to have had the opportunity and the motivation to apply the Constructive Action process on a daily basis at their places of employment and to have developed a greater appreciation for its problem-solving properties.

Respondents who had subsequently earned a master's degree were more likely than those who had not progressed beyond the bachelor's degree to report that the Constructive Action process is an excellent instrument for learning how to integrate theory and practice and to perform such tasks as setting goals and objectives, carrying out research, focusing on issues and needs, and assessing outcomes, and they were also more likely to report making current use of the Constructive Action process both in their professional lives and their personal lives. It is noteworthy that respondents with a higher level of education were more likely to appreciate the Constructive Action process and to use it in their work and their personal lives. Possibly they had experienced how helpful the Constructive Action process had been in carrying out graduate work. It is also likely that they were better equipped with academic skills that enabled them to apply the Constructive Action process effectively and that they possessed a better understanding of how it could be used in many situations as a problem-solving instrument. Most important, these findings suggest that the Constructive Action process has lasting advantages of which graduates become more aware as they are exposed to further education and the more advanced practice that is likely to follow. They suggest that students who pursued graduate school successfully assimilated their later studies to the learning and practice methodology they had acquired at Audrey Cohen College.

Respondents in administrative positions were more likely than those in non-administrative positions to appreciate the Constructive Action process as an instrument for learning, to make current use of it in their professional lives, and to credit it with positive impacts on their professional careers. These findings reinforce the conclusions described in the previous paragraph. They suggest that respondents understand the empowering process of the Constructive Action methodology and its use as an instrument for bringing about positive change.

Income level was not a factor in responses to any of the questions. Throughout its history, Audrey Cohen College has taken pains to admit a diverse student body. Not much can be inferred from this finding, but it may suggest that the College has been successful in working with a diverse student body.

CONCLUSION AND IMPLICATIONS

The survey respondents included alumni who had graduated from the Human Service program up to twenty years previously. Results showed that more than 70 percent had continued to use the Constructive Action process in their places of employment, in their private lives, and where applicable, in graduate school. More than 80 percent of the respondents stated that the Constructive Action process had been helpful as a learning tool, and the same number reported that the Constructive Action process had positively affected their professional careers. The research findings clearly affirm the importance of the Constructive Action process in educating human service professionals at Audrey Cohen College. They also testify to the success of the College's overall educational model.

Grade point average and level of education significantly influenced the statistical results. Research shows that students who do well in school tend to have a higher level of satisfaction with their educational experience. Ward (2000) found that students with a higher level of education were likely to exhibit a higher level of knowledge and comprehension than students with a lower level of education. The implication here may be that if the College wants students to gain the greatest amount of learning and satisfaction from its programs, it should reconsider levels of student skills on admission, content of student academic services, content of mentoring programs, and counseling services. Further studies should be conducted to determine which services are needed by non-traditional and traditional students, how transfer students are best integrated into the College's program, and what extra services may be needed to increase the level of student skills. Continued study of these questions is recommended because the level of education (performance) may reflect not only students' skills but a lack of essential support services. The question is, what are essential services? The College may also want to carry out a similar study with its other programs, all of which use the same Constructive Action methodology, and compare the results.

It is not possible to generalize the results of this study to other student populations, because Audrey Cohen College's system of Purpose-Centered Education is unique. However, the results do suggest that Purpose-Centered Education provides a worthwhile model for other programs to study.

REFERENCES

Cimmino, P. F. (1999). "Basic Concepts and Definitions of Human Services." In H. Harris and D. Maloney, eds., *Human Services: Contemporary Issues and Trends.* Boston: Allyn and Bacon.

Cohen, A. (1976). Prisms. New York, NY.: College for Human Services and a grant from Improvement of Postsecondary Education, HEW.

Cohen, A. (1977). *Final Albany Document to Establish a Baccalaureate and Master's Program in Human Services.* New York: Audrey Cohen College. Nonpublished material.

Cohen, A. C. (1978). *The citizen as the Integrating Agent: Productivity in the Human Services* (Human Services Monograph Series). New York:

National Clearinghouse for Improving the Management of Human Services.

Cohen, A. C. (1982). *College for Human Services: Applied Transdisciplinary Curriculum.* New York: Audrey Cohen College and Ford Foundation.

Cohen, A. C. (1988). *The Third Alternative.* New York: Audrey Cohen College and Banbury Fund.

Cohen, A. C. (1989). *The Service Society and a Theory of Learning Linking Education, Work, and Life.* New York: Audrey Cohen College and Banbury Fund.

Cohen, A. C. (1999). "Empowerment: Toward a New Definition of Self-Help." In H. Harris and D. Maloney, eds., *Human Services: Contemporary Issues and Trends.* Boston: Allyn and Bacon.

Cohen, J. (1977). *Statistics: Power Analysis for Behavioral Sciences.* New York: Academic Press.

Eriksen, K. (1977). *Human Services Today.* Reston, VA: Reston Publishing Company.

Simon, E. (1999). "Field Practicum: Standards, Criteria, Supervision, and Education." In H. Harris and D. Maloney, eds., *Human Services: Contemporary Issues and Trends.* Boston: Allyn and Bacon.

Ward, S. (2000). "The Effects of Education Level on Illusion of Knowing and Comprehension Monitoring Activity." *Research for Educational Reform.* Grambling, LA: Directors of the Educational Research Quarterly.

KEY TERMS FOR PART ONE

After studying Chapters 1, 2, 3a, 3b, 4a, and 4b, you should have a command of the following key terms, major concepts, and principal topical references:

human services
multidisciplinary profession
intervention
professionalism
education
human service worker
facilitate
optimum human potential
human service ideology
Elizabethan Poor Laws
Mental Health Study Act
Manpower Development Act
Social Security
    Amendments—1962
Scheuer Sub-professional
    Career Act
Community Mental Health Act
human service delivery
    principles
goal of human services
medical model
public health model
human service model
generalist

roles of human service
    workers
constitutional protections
empowerment
conservative values
self-sufficiency
proactive
needs hierarchy
crisis intervention
service delivery system
client system
microsocial systems
macrosocial systems
social treatment
Southern Regional Education
    Board (SREB)
National Organization for
    Human Service Education
    (NOHSE)
Council for Standards in
    Human Service Education
    (CSHSE)
advocacy
cost-effective interventions

settlement house movement
Hull House
mental hygiene
psychoanalytic theory
American Psychological
    Association (APA)
behaviorism
Social Darwinism
*Occupational Outlook
    Handbook*
National Institute of Mental
    Health (NIMH)
welfare reform
Aid to Families with
    Dependent Children
    (AFDC)
American class structure
WEP
case study
Purpose-Centered education
holism
Constructive Action
research design

PIVOTAL ISSUES FOR DISCUSSION OF PART ONE

1. What are the differences between the human service profession and social work?
2. What are the most important human needs that must be met in our society? How are these needs being met today? What might be the priorities in the future?
3. What role(s) have the church and religion played in the historical development of human services?
4. What is the settlement house movement? How was it different from other charities at that time? How does it influence modern day human service practice?
5. What effect has welfare reform had in your state or locality? What are the current problems faced by clients in these programs?

6. List five federal laws that have had the greatest impact on the human service movement. How have these legislative acts been related to the needs of the American people?

7. Choose a pro or con position on welfare reform and list the reasons why your position is justified.

8. Call your state or regional welfare office and ask for a copy of the eligibility requirements and restrictions. Review and critique these materials and give a class presentation.

9. What is "empowerment" as a principle in human service practice? How does it operate in the context of your training and education as a human service professional?

10. Provide three examples of empowered human service clients. How can each of these people contribute to society in a relevant and meaningful way?

SUGGESTED READINGS FOR PART ONE _____

1. CSHSE Monograph (1990). *History of the Human Services Movement.*

2. Bloom, B. L. (1984). *Community Mental Health: A General Introduction,* 2nd ed. Pacific Grove, CA: Brooks/Cole.

3. Trattner, W. I. (1986). *From Poor Law to Welfare State: History of Social Welfare in America,* 3rd ed. New York: The Free Press.

4. Kamerman, S. B., and A. J. Kahn (1977). *Social Services: An Interventional Perspective.* Washington, DC: U.S. Government Printing Office.

5. Greenberg, J. (1965). *The Monday Voices.* New York: Holt, Rinehart and Winston.

6. Piven, F. F., and R. A. Cloward (1982). *The New Class War.* New York: Pantheon.

7. Woody, R. H., and associates (1984). *The Law and the Practice of Human Services.* San Francisco: Jossey-Bass.

8. Barton, W. E., and C. J. Sanborn, eds. (1978). *Law and the Mental Health Professions: Friction at the Interface.* New York: International University Press.

PART TWO

HUMAN SERVICE PROFESSIONALS: SKILLS, VALUES, AND STANDARDS

In Part Two, we will look at the skills, competencies, and values that are necessary for effectiveness in human services work.

In Chapter 5, Lorence Long and Maureen Doyle outline the values and the various roles and responsibilities that characterize a human service worker. To help you focus on the core qualities of the professional human service generalist, they provide a "generic" job description. Some of these qualities, such as being reliable, well-organized, focused, and attentive, are essential for success in working with many different kinds of agencies, programs, and clients.

In addition to these generic attributes, the human service worker must possess an array of special skills geared to the interpersonal helping process with individuals and with groups. Chapter 6 outlines the skills used in communicating with individual clients. John Hancock describes the principal techniques students must apply when interviewing and counseling clients. These skills and competencies represent a pivotal set of techniques and methods employed by all professionals in the helping fields. Barbara Somerville, in Chapter 7, invites you to examine how working with different kinds of groups, with different groups of clients, and in different situations will require you to become familiar with group dynamics and group functioning. After reading this chapter, you will know how groups are formed and organized and how human service professionals work with groups. You will also learn about the characteristics of groups, their stages of development, and leadership roles. Five vignettes related to different phases of group work vividly portray the tasks assigned to the human service worker in this area of professional responsibility.

Janet Hagen, in her Special Focus Feature, offers another example of how specific intervention themes such as conflict resolution are applied to work involving groups. Hagen shows the value of being aware of existing avenues and mechanics for resolving conflicts. Making use of existing resources is essential in many different situations in human service work.

Part Two concludes with Chapter 8, which addresses the implications of the National Community Support Skill Standards (CSSS) Project. As principal participants in the project and as national leaders in both NOHSE and CSHSE (discussed in Part One), Mary DiGiovanni, Franklyn M. Rother, and David C. Maloney present, interpret, and show

how these CSSS competencies relate to, or "crosswalk," the curriculum standards promoted by CSHSE. In this chapter the importance of standards is placed within a historical context of the continually evolving human service education and training movement. An examination of the CSSS competencies has strengthened and clarified the CSHSE standards, which are used as a basis for "program approval" of two-year and four-year undergraduate programs in human services across the United States. Eventually, these skill standards may well serve as a foundation for credentialing future human service graduates and workers.

Chapters 5 through 8 provide a broad overview of the knowledge, skills, and values associated with human service professionals. You will also know what standards or levels of competency the professional helper must demonstrate in individual and group work. In Part Three you will see how these responsibilities are especially relevant when working with children and families as human service clients.

LEARNING OBJECTIVES FOR PART TWO: HUMAN SERVICE PROFESSIONALS: SKILLS, VALUES, AND STANDARDS

After reading and studying Chapters 5, 6, 7, and 8,

— You will understand what is involved in undergraduate human service education.
— You will be familiar with generic human services training.
— You will be aware of the skills, knowledge, and values necessary for successful job performance in human services.
— You will know how standards of excellence can be utilized in the process of credentialing human service workers.
— You will see how specific interviewing techniques and methods are developed and applied in working with individual service clients.
— You will be familiar with how human service group work is developed and employed with clients in different circumstances.
— You will be familiar with conflict resolution and understand how it is used in human service group work.

WELCOME TO HUMAN SERVICES
A JOURNEY IN HELPING OTHERS

MARGARET J. FRENCH

Welcome to the career of human services—a journey in helping others! If you want to make a difference in your community; in the lives of others experiencing transition, change, and challenges; and in your own life, then this is the career for you. Human services is "that profession charged with responsibility to close the gap between traditional service systems and the needs and rights of the whole person, and to make society more whole in the process. Human Services has a cohesive underlying philosophy and ethic; a range of clearly defined tasks and goals; a specific body of knowledge; and a unique set of skills and a career ladder for its professionals" (Eriksen, 1977, p. 11).

Twenty-seven years ago (1970), I started on this journey as the Department Chair of the Mental Health Associate Program at Pitt Community College in Greenville, North Carolina. The program was one of several original programs in the South funded by a grant from the National Institute of Mental Health (NIMH). I worked closely with the Southern Regional Education Board (SREB) and the NIMH to ensure that the curriculum provided education for a generalist mental health worker. The Pitt Community College program also participated in various projects sponsored by SREB in the 1970s to determine activities engaged in by human service workers in entry-level jobs. But the profession started before 1970. The human service programs, as they are known nationally today, started with the vision of an extraordinary man, Dr. Harold McPheeters.

I first met Dr. McPheeters in 1971 at a conference hosted by SREB for program directors to train us about entry-level workers. I was absolutely amazed that Dr. McPheeters, a board psychiatrist, believed that generalist workers were needed to provide a variety of services to populations not being served and that these workers did not need a master's or doctoral degree. I remember him saying that we were not training "little psychologists" or "little social workers" or "little nurses." We were training generalists, which he and Jim King defined in 1971 as a person who "works with a limited number of clients and families in consultation with other professionals to provide 'across the board' human services as needed; is able to work in a variety of agencies and organizations that provide mental health services; is able to work cooperatively with all the existing professions in the field rather than affiliating directly with any one; is familiar with a number of therapeutic services and techniques rather than specializing in one or two areas; and is a 'beginning professional' who is expected to continue to grow and learn" (Neukrug, 1994, p. 42).

Human service programs provide an atmosphere of cooperative learning. We, as human service training staff, wanted a product called a "Human Service Worker." The process to produce this worker involved the training staff moving from the traditional teacher-directed learning to a more student-directed learning. The process elements involved creating a cooperative learning atmosphere for both faculty and students and using various methodologies and faculty to model attitudinal components. Because we were training generalists, we needed to be generalists. That involved faculty giving up some traditional thoughts and methodologies and gaining some new perspectives about themselves, their roles, their disciplines, and their students. And how exciting that was! Students and faculty became a being in the process of becoming. The faculty member was challenged to grow professionally and personally with colleagues and students in a cooperative effort and environment.

One of the program goals of human service programs was to produce individuals capable of establishing and maintaining a helping relationship; and, if the faculty wanted to facilitate persons to examine and attain personal qualities of empathy, trust, genuineness, acceptance, resourcefulness, and responsibility, faculty members needed to model these qualities—not just model, but *be* these qualities. Faculty could use this cooperative environment for their own personal and professional development and for that of their students. They created an environment where there was participative decision making, mutual assessment of needs, and mutual negotiations for setting goals. Most of all, the faculty was modeling for students the attitude of searching, expanding, and growing. The challenges were enormous and the rewards joyous!

Now there are approximately 500 programs nationwide, most of them leading to associate's and baccalaureate degrees and a few with some graduate programs. Basically, the programs have a similar profile with a different focus, depending on the degree level. For example, baccalaureate degrees place more emphasis on administrative/supervision skills, whereas associate's degrees focus on the skills, knowledge, and attitudinal characteristics needed by the entry-level, direct-service worker.

Generally, students entering the human services field come with different ages, socioeconomic backgrounds, value systems, intellectual levels, reading and comprehension levels, and academic capabilities. The programs take into account this vast range of needs and provide a training program that meets most of these needs without relaxing requirements, standards, or purposes.

This variety of students creates a family atmosphere, a cooperative environment. Different personalities, reactions, and abilities interact as in a family, but as time progresses each participant/student finds roles that he or she is comfortable with, sets personal or professional goals, is able to put some direction in her or his life, and forms a community where he or she belongs and experiences stability. Variety is also present among the instructors, methods of teaching, and requirements for courses. The variety allows students a choice and gives them a chance to be a part of determining their futures. In addition to specific expectations, a degree of flexibility allows for individual differences. Incorporating a multidisciplinary approach, most of the programs focus on the cognitive, medical, social, psychological, and spiritual components of human service work and the human service worker. Course components and a faculty from a variety of disciplines demonstrate the multidisciplinary approach, which reflects the diversity of the student populations.

Most human services curricula are designed to train and prepare graduates to fulfill a wide range of consumer needs in a variety of human service settings, to enable people to live more satisfying, more autonomous, and more productive lives. The programs combine liberal arts education, human services and mental health care courses, field placement courses, and specialty courses. A major emphasis is placed on experiential learning. Information is presented in the classroom situation, laboratory exercises, and application through field placements under supervision. Personal growth, attitudes, knowledge, and skills are distinct components of most human service programs.

To be specific, programs usually have three main phases of education and training that are intertwined over the training and education time frame. In the academic classroom phase, students gain general knowledge and skills in case management, interviewing, group dynamics, intervention and treatment, models of human development, characteristics of special populations, and planning and evaluation. Although students learn theory concepts, application of theory through various learning strategies and settings serves as the main focus.

The second phase is self-development, which is accomplished mainly in the group process courses. These small classes give students an opportunity to become aware of their own values and attitudes and how they affect relationships with clients as well as their own personal growth. The students are given the opportunity to focus on increased self-awareness by looking at their own biases, prejudices, and attitudes. The programs do not dictate change, although the student can see how these values affect him or her and as a result may choose to change.

Providing human services requires knowing oneself and applying that self-awareness to the development of helping relationships. It is necessary and essential to know oneself before one can know another or be helpful to him or her. Knowing oneself takes time and is never complete. We are, after all, complicated human beings, ever-changing and ever-growing. The following questions can serve as a guide as the student continues the process of personal growth:

1. How do I think and feel about myself?
2. How do I deal with my own fundamental needs?
3. What is my value system, and how does it define my behavior and my relationships with other people?
4. How do I relate to the society in which I live and work?
5. What is my life-style?
6. What is my basic philosophy? (Brill, 1990, p. 4)

The third phase is field experience, where students are placed in an agency to apply the knowledge and skill training received in the classroom. The opportunity to work in a human service agency is an invaluable experience, providing the means to put into action the knowledge, skills, and attitudes acquired in curriculum courses while exploring future job opportunities. The student is placed in a human service agency for approximately 250 hours in associate's degree programs and 350 clock hours in baccalaureate programs. Clock hours are under the direction of an agency supervisor and qualified faculty member. Field experience is arranged in a variety of human service agencies, such as mental health centers, group homes, developmental day-care centers, public schools, homeless shelters, nursing homes, substance abuse treatment centers, family violence programs, hospitals, and correctional facilities.

The programs train students to be direct caregivers. The curricula are skill oriented and allow the students to achieve personal and professional growth. The principles of "taking responsibility for your behavior," "asking for what you want," and "choosing to change" are integrated through every aspect of the program, including the field experiences.

To summarize, most human services programs seek to accomplish the following:

— To prepare graduates for a career in human services;
— To prepare graduates to effectively match consumer needs with available community resources;
— To increase the helper's capacity for self-awareness and personal growth;
— To promote a thoughtful, genuine, and empathetic attitude toward human beings;
— To expand and implement knowledge, skills, and attitudes necessary to help people help themselves;
— To facilitate articulation with upper-level degree programs.

The next stage of this career journey is the opportunity to work. As stated by my colleague,

Robert L. DeSoto, "students often reach new levels of insight during their field experience, beginning to decide about future employability options; the plus and negative features about agency structures, especially particular populations they may have the opportunity to work with." Frequently students are employed in the same setting where they completed their fieldwork or in similar settings.

Human service graduates work with people who are elderly, mentally ill, children with special needs, developmentally disabled, substance abusers, homeless, at-risk adolescents, or persons with HIV/AIDS. For example, Donna, Amanda, and Rosa became job coaches at a sheltered workshop after completing placements. Don became a substance abuse worker after completing a placement with an adolescent substance abuse treatment program. Carlos became a mediation youth director after completing his placement, and Charlene was employed by a correctional youth center after similar fieldwork experience with a county youth detention facility.

Other possible job positions available to graduates are residential services coordinator, activity director, women's shelter manager, youth services counselor, health care technician, psychiatric technician, hospice worker, and rehabilitation therapy assistant. These job titles may vary greatly across the nation, and this extraordinary variation demonstrates the fascinating job opportunities available to human service program graduates.

Another avenue on this journey is continuing formal education. Many students continue their education, transferring to universities to complete a four-year degree in a number of fields, such as rehabilitation counseling, social work, special education, or human services. And many have pursued the master and doctoral levels. For example, students who went on to receive a four-year degree were Edyth and Amanda. They received their AAS degrees in Human Services at Pitt Community College, transferred to East Carolina University, received a BS in Rehabilitation Services, and were employed in Greenville with special populations. Another student, Candy, after receiving her AAS degree from Pitt Community College, transferred to UNC-Charlotte, received her BSW, and returned to Greenville, North Carolina, where she was employed as an HIV/AIDS case manager with the Mental Health Center. Interestingly, she did her fieldwork as an AAS student in Project Outreach, an AIDS prevention program in Greenville.

So the journey began in the mid-1960s, and the human service career will continue to grow, change, and make a difference in the future. On this journey, the people, the programs, the competencies, the agencies, the professional organizations, and the consumers have enhanced the way the human service field has evolved. Most important have been the students, the ones willing to look at themselves and willing to achieve academically, develop professional skills, achieve success, and ultimately make a difference in the quality of life for the consumer. Welcome to the exciting, fulfilling, satisfying field of human services, where everyone experiences success.

REFERENCES

Brill, N. (1990). *Working with People: The Helping Process,* 4th ed. New York: Longman.

Eriksen, K. (1977). *Human Services Today.* Reston, VA: Reston Publishing.

"Everything You Wanted to Know about Human Services Technology," Pitt Community College, revised 1997.

French, M. "Human Services Advocacy: Strengthening Constituent Relationships and Program Visibility," paper presented at the NOHSE National Conference, St. Louis, MO, October 13, 1983.

Neukrug, E. (1994). *Theory, Practice and Trends in Human Services—An Overview of an Emerging Profession.* Pacific Grove, CA: Brooks/Cole.

CHAPTER 5

HUMAN SERVICES:
NECESSARY SKILLS AND VALUES

LORENCE A. LONG
MAUREEN DOYLE

To be effective, human service workers need to possess a certain combination of personal qualities, knowledge, skills, and values.

Workers must be able to deal with people who are upset, angry, depressed, or confused, without being swept away by any of these feelings themselves. It is essential that workers be good listeners yet be able to interject their own questions, statements, and judgments at an appropriate time.

Workers need to be well organized in a way that allows them to deal with a complex workload while being flexible enough to respond to interruptions. Workers must have a broad knowledge of human nature and social systems yet understand that each client is an individual, moving at his or her own pace toward self-discovery and the solution to his or her problem. It is desirable that workers display a deep interest in and commitment to their work, without neglecting their own development and their relationships with family and friends.

QUALITIES HUMAN SERVICE WORKERS SHARE WITH OTHER WORKERS

Many qualities needed by human service workers are the same as those generic characteristics required by architects, nurses, Wall Street brokers, carpenters, or any other workers. These include the following:

Being Responsible and Reliable. This cluster of characteristics involves being honest and taking responsibility for one's share of the work as well as for the mistakes that one commits. It means carefully doing the work that has been assigned. It includes coming to work on time and staying until the designated work time is over.

Addressing the Work in an Organized Way. Listening carefully to instructions, identifying sequences of tasks, allowing enough time for each part of the work, requesting assistance if time or resources are not adequate to get the job done, and asking for help if it is needed are all part of being organized. Workers are also expected to take the initiative when they know what to do and to try to anticipate problems and work cooperatively to solve them. Sometimes the organized worker must drop everything to meet an emergency and then reorganize to finish what had been begun earlier. Workers must be able to manage being interrupted without losing track of what they were working on before. The tasks that need to be done often exceed the time available to do them, so workers must prioritize, identifying what is most important to do first.

Listening Carefully, Paying Attention, and Focusing Energy on the Task at Hand. Workplaces are full of and surrounded by distractions: competition between individuals and groups, personal concerns, conflicts, diversions and amusements, friendships, and other attention-getters. It requires discipline to focus on one's work when these alternatives are close at hand.

Having a Constructive and Supportive Attitude.
The worker needs to be interested in learning and
should not be defensive about being criticized.
Such a worker tends to assume that problems have
solutions, even when the solutions are not obvious. She or he pitches in to do whatever is necessary. This worker treats other people—whether
chief, clerk, or client—with respect and understands that a key to success is to help clients, co-
workers, and supervisors be successful.

*Forming Positive Working Relationships with
Others.* Workers are attentive to the human
relations aspects of the job, willing to listen to
colleagues' work-related problems, reaching out
to co-workers and others to form links around
common interests, and being attuned to others'
cultures and backgrounds.

The qualities we have listed would make any
worker highly valued in virtually any setting,
including human service organizations. Some
readers may be surprised that we begin our discussion with these general qualities. Doesn't everyone
know that these are required for success? In our
experience, students and beginning workers are
more likely to undermine their own success in the
areas we have just outlined than in those matters
that are specific to human services.

SPECIAL SKILLS NEEDED BY HUMAN
SERVICE WORKERS

Human service workers need the following skills:

*Ability to Use Oneself to Help Others Move in a
Positive Direction.* Sometimes a human service
worker must interact powerfully with other people by setting limits, confronting the other person,
or engaging the person in an exciting activity. At
other times, the worker may choose to be silent,
let a client work out a problem on his or her own,
or invite the client to join in a quiet activity. One
must know not only how to do these things but

also when to do each one to maximize the effectiveness of the intervention.

*Ability to Communicate with Clients, Col-
leagues, and Others.* Workers are required to
create a climate in which clients feel free to disclose whatever concerns them. Workers need to
be able to hear what the client is saying without
letting their own judgments get in the way. They
must know how to use their imaginations in an
empathetic way to understand how the situation
looks from the client's point of view. It is important that they then find a way to let the clients
know that they have been heard, using paraphrasing or some other technique for this purpose.
"Being heard" includes recognizing and interpreting nonverbal, as well as verbal, forms of
expression.

Listening to the Words, and Then Some

SARAH'S CRY FOR HELP
*Sarah came into the office holding her little girl
firmly by the hand. "Can I talk to you?" she asked.*
   Fran said, "Sure. What's it about?"
   "I don't know how to start," Sarah said.
   "It's hard to talk about?" Fran asked gently.
   *Sarah was quiet for a moment. Then a tear ran
down her cheek. Fran offered her ever-ready box
of tissues. Sarah took one and blew her nose. Her
eyes filled.*
   "Sad . . . ," Fran said tentatively.
   *Sarah's daughter uttered a sound, but was
immediately shushed by her mother, who gripped
her hand even more tightly.*
   *"She can sit over here in this chair," Fran said.
The little girl, released, sat down, rubbing her
hand.*
   *Sarah said, "It's too much. I get to the point
that when she makes a noise, I want to hurt her. I
just can't control her."*
   *"You want her to be quiet, and do what you
want," Fran said.*
   *"My mother had the same trouble with me,"
Sarah said. "I was a very bad girl when I was little."*
   *"So you kind of see yourself in her, doing the
same types of things," Fran said.*
   "Yes," Sarah said, and sighed. She sat back.

"It was really important to you to say that, I think," Fran said.

"Yes, it was. I don't want her to turn out like me. And she will, unless I can change her," Sarah said.

"You seem determined, but not sure how to make her life different from yours, and your life different from your mother's?" Fran made this last phrase a question, because she thought this is what Sarah meant, but she wasn't sure.

"Yes. I couldn't bear it if I ended up like my mother, angry and drunk every night with nobody to love me."

"You sound hopeless, lost, when you say that," Fran said.

"I feel hopeless," Sarah said. "I guess I can't put it all on Susana, here."

"She reminds you of the trouble you want to stay away from, but she isn't really the cause of the trouble."

After a pause, Sarah said, "Right. I see that now. You saved me from doing something terrible."

"I just listened to what you were saying, yourself," Fran said.

Workers must also communicate the rules and expectations of the agency or other providers clearly so that clients understand what is required of them. Workers' own body language should correspond to their spoken language to avoid confusing the client.

Workers are required to tell the agency clearly in both written (case record or log) and oral (case conference) form what the client needs and how the worker has responded. Case records follow a specific format so that other workers can quickly find out the status of a client's situation and conform to the requirements of auditors from funding sources or regulatory bodies who are evaluating the agency's work.

Workers need to know how to use the telephone properly—communicating and receiving needed information accurately, completely, and clearly without breaking confidentiality and privacy rules regarding clients. Even acknowledging that someone is a client is a violation of the person's privacy, especially if such acknowledg-

ment would tend to suggest that the person is HIV-positive or has some other stigmatized condition. As technology becomes more complex, new challenges arise. For example, computer monitor screens containing client data may be seen by unauthorized persons who visit a worker's office.

Ability to Operate within the Agency's Framework to Solve Problems.
Workers are required to observe situations and individuals as objectively as possible, being able to separate inference from observation.

Separating Inference from Observation

EMILY'S SILENCE
The family therapy team met to debrief after the session.

"Did you notice that Emily did not say one word during the whole session?" Lloyd commented. "She is so uninvolved in this family!"

"I don't agree," Steve protested. "I think that Lucy intimidates her. She talked last week, when Lucy was away."

"I think she is getting ready to blast her father," Jeanine offered. "Did you notice how she looked at him as though she could kill him? Next session there's going to be an explosion."

"What are you all basing this on?" asked Jack. "She was silent, and that's that. Since none of you asked her why she didn't say anything, you can make up any meaning you want. You just don't know."

Everybody was silent for a moment after that.

Observations and assessments must be done with an agency's priorities in mind. When doing assessments, workers must distinguish between the more and the less important elements of a situation. This might involve differentiating between a presenting symptom and its related underlying problem or placing a style of behavior in the context of developmental levels or other critical issues.

Focusing on the Important Issues

WALTER
Desirée, a new worker at the day care center, called to a noisy three-year-old, "Walter, come here."

Walter responded gruffly, "Who you calling by my name?"

Desirée was about to reprimand him for his bad manners when her teacher said, "Isn't that good?! He's finally starting to speak in sentences!"

Desirée was shaken. She had assumed that her main goal was to make the children be well-behaved and polite. What the teacher said made her aware that she had been focused on an issue the teacher was not so concerned with.

Whatever activities are part of the agency's work—whether they be filling out forms, leading a group discussion, or advocating for a client—workers need to possess the skills involved. Workers also need to know emergency procedures, including how and when to contact emergency services personnel.

Workers need to be able to conceptualize a problem in terms of its relationship to the individual client's goals and to the goals of the program. Then they must break the problem down into objectives (what the worker, along with the client, will try to accomplish) and tasks (what needs to be done—and by whom—to achieve the objectives). Various parts of the problem may be selected for early action either because they are the most emergent or because they may be accomplished more easily. Skilled workers will be able to determine which parts should come first.

Workers also need to be able to make plans with clients (or sometimes for them, if the client is incapable) in a way that fits the client's abilities. Generally speaking, clients should participate in making plans for themselves to the extent of their capability because this strengthens the clients' decision-making and problem-solving skills as well as their self-esteem. Deciding things for clients should be a last resort. There is an old saying that applies here: "Whatever you do for me, I cannot do for myself."

Workers should be able to recognize the signs of progress that are appropriate and realistic for the client population they are working with.

Setting Realistic Goals for One's Work

FRANK'S PROGRESS

Mary had been working with Frank, a developmentally disabled child, in an effort to reduce his self-injuring behavior. She was using positive reinforcement to increase the frequency of a replacement behavior. When she met with Cliff for supervision, Mary confessed to being discouraged.

"He is still doing it, no matter how hard I try," Mary sighed.

"How many times a day?" Cliff asked.

"He banged his head seventy-five times while I was on the unit," Mary said.

"And a week ago?" Cliff wondered.

"Let me look at my notebook. He averaged 125 times. Okay, so it's better. But he's still doing it."

Cliff said, "I believe that a 40 percent improvement in a week is very good. You have to remember who you are dealing with. Frank has been institutionalized for nine years, and self-injuring behavior is one of his primary ways of stimulating himself. He's not going to stop it overnight. You are really doing very well."

"Oh," Mary said. "Well, I wish he would improve faster."

"Yes, I can understand that," said Cliff. "But you should expect that his improvement will slow down and maybe reverse at times. You're doing better than you should have expected to, given his history."

DIFFERENCES BETWEEN INFORMAL AND PROFESSIONAL HELPING

Some people believe that all that is needed to be a professional helper is to have the desire to help. They base this assumption on their own personal experiences of helping a friend or family member or babysitting for a neighbor's child.

Wanting to help is important. However, it can even get in the way of helping if it is not disciplined by skill, knowledge, and values of respect and understanding. A standard exercise in our beginning human service courses at LaGuardia Community College is to ask students to list ways of helping that are not helpful. Every class comes up with a long list, often based on personal experiences. All of us have been offered unwelcome advice, been given incorrect information, had limits set for us that were unfair, been lectured to by someone who didn't understand, or been offered assistance when perfectly capable of doing something for ourselves.

One aspect of the professional helping relationship is the unequal status of the helper and the person in need. Usually the helper has more experience and skill, better knowledge of resources, and some emotional distance from the problem. Often the worker's emotional distance enables the person in need to see the problem more clearly and to develop his or her own solution to the problem. It should be noted that different models of helping either emphasize or play down this difference in status (Corsini and Wedding, 1989).

Family members and friends may have trouble maintaining that emotional distance because they want to see a certain outcome. A professional helper—who is not vested in a particular outcome—should give the client information about various options and explore with the client the benefits and difficulties associated with each one. The client must ultimately make an informed decision. If a helper persuades a client to choose a certain option, the client may blame the worker for a poor result. This may lead to a lack of trust between worker and client and ultimately impede the helping process.

Another aspect of the professional helping relationship is that it usually lasts for a specific period of time. It is understood that the relationship will come to an end when the goals that have been set are accomplished, when the client's independence is more important than the remaining small gains that could be achieved by continuing, or when other factors intervene.

The professional helping relationship is clearly defined. Roles are specific and responsibilities clearly laid out. Often the helper's agency defines the ground rules for the helping activities and interactions, such as not giving clients money. Friendships and family relationships, on the other hand, are much more open-ended, shifting, and ambiguous, as they should be.

SPECIAL KNOWLEDGE NEEDED BY HUMAN SERVICE WORKERS

Agency-Related Knowledge.   In addition to the many personal qualities outlined, effective human service workers need certain kinds of knowledge. Part of this knowledge must be about the agency that employs them. What are the agency's goals? When workers are clear about goals, it is possible for them to make choices about competing claims on their time and judgments about whether an activity that is being considered fits within the scope of the agency's focus.

It is helpful to know the agency's history. Which workers joined the agency first? What functions are the core functions, and which ones were added later? What crises or scandals have "burned" the agency and led to defensive practices? All of these factors may explain otherwise puzzling attitudes and decisions.

Knowing the agency's philosophy about techniques and approaches is also helpful. Some approaches used elsewhere may be forbidden in a particular agency because of philosophical beliefs held by staff or board members. For example, some agencies are opposed to using behavior modification in working with clients, whereas others ground their approaches in behavior modification theories and practices. The agency's attitudes toward clients, government contracts, fundraising, interagency cooperation, and many other subjects will influence how workers are expected to proceed.

The worker must also be knowledgeable about the agency's accepted approaches and methods. If psychoanalysis, reality therapy, or the Montessori method is used, the worker needs to read the literature being published about that particular approach.

Knowledge of the agency's organizational structure, roles, departments, and services is also essential for the worker to be effective. Knowing whom to talk with about a particular problem, which department handles a certain matter, who supervises whom, and whether the agency performs certain functions or refers them elsewhere are important to a worker's success.

Familiarity with the agency's procedures is also expected of the worker. Whether procedures involve the agency's way of filling out a form, leading a group, writing up a psychosocial assessment, or taking a baseline on a child's behavior, the worker should thoroughly understand the reasons and regulations related to the procedure.

Knowledge about Clients and about the Field.
Workers are expected to be well informed about general characteristics of the types of clients with whom they deal on a regular basis. If the clients have a particular developmental pattern or certain cultural characteristics, the worker would read about and discuss these matters with knowledgeable people. Workers would be expected to attend conferences and meetings about such subjects and should regularly consult journals and other publications that present current information about their clients.

Should He Respond to a Cultural Style?

CHUCK'S DILEMMA

Chuck was visiting Ron, who ran a cultural arts program in the downtown area. Chuck said, "Ron, I want to ask about how you relate to your Hispanic clients. I have been getting larger numbers of them uptown, and I am not sure what kinds of changes I should make in my style and the program's style."

"Well," Ron said, "one thing that I have had to get accustomed to is saying hello to people personally. They expect to pay their respects to 'el Don' when they come into the agency. I don't always feel comfortable about spending the time when I have some deadline, but I know they will feel hurt unless I ask them to sit down and talk about family for a little while, before they go on to their activity."

"I can see how that would be a problem for me," Chuck said. "I am not very available to

clients. I expect staff members to do the face-to-face work. I don't mean that being distant is good, I just want to be as businesslike as possible."

"I think some of your Hispanic clients will feel that there is something missing in your program if they don't get to greet you," Ron said. "Most of them seem to want to be recognized by the head person."

"Okay, thanks," Chuck responded. "I can see I'm going to have to give this some thought."

In addition, the worker would attempt to keep abreast of new developments in the field. Human service concepts and approaches are always changing; what had been accepted as indisputable fact at one time can later be discounted. For example, until about thirty years ago, it was widely thought that the short lives of developmentally disabled people were not affected by putting them in large institutions that, in many cases, provided very poor care. What we now know is that developmentally disabled people live just as long as other people; their short lives were the *result* of poor care. A worker needs to keep up with these trends and must know where to find information about them.

Workers also need to know about the resources outside the agency that their clients must depend on. If new regulations are adopted by a referral agency, if public assistance grants are cut back, or if a new program opens in the community, the worker should be aware of the situation and involved in helping clients deal with the new development. Workers make referrals to outside agencies. They need to know how these agencies function so that they can prepare clients for a successful referral. It is imperative that they identify and develop relationships with contact people at these organizations.

Knowledge of the Dynamics of Working with Individuals and Groups.   Basic to nearly every human service activity is knowledge of the dynamics of relating to individuals: knowing about how relationships are formed, how they are worked through, and how they are ended. Relationships are the primary tool of the human service worker. Human service workers also need to understand how groups function so that they may make sense of what is happening in groups of people, including groups of colleagues as well as clients. A grasp of the concepts underlying these relationships is the basis for employing individual relationships and group dynamics to help clients move toward better lives.

VALUES FOR HUMAN SERVICE WORKERS

We have listed many professional and personal values in the preceding sections. Here are some that we believe deserve special emphasis:

Putting Clients' Needs First.   Given that clients are the reason that human service agencies and roles exist at all, it is surprising how easily other elements (e.g., agency success, professional recognition, and workload management) displace clients' needs as workers' first priority. This is especially distressing because clients are, once they enter the agency system, quite dependent on that system to meet their needs. Often the system is a mystery to the client; workers are the guides to what to expect as well as how to negotiate the system. Workers may find it necessary to rearrange their schedules, stay after regular working hours, go into neighborhoods they would rather not enter, and fill out multiple forms to meet the needs of clients. Workers are also empowered, within reason, to advocate within their own agencies on behalf of clients whose needs are not being met because of the system's inefficiencies. It should be obvious that clients are not to be exploited in any way—sexually, emotionally, or financially. Workers sometimes make serious mistakes in this area because they come into human services expecting that someone will be grateful for their efforts. While this may sometimes actually occur, resentment at having to be dependent often keeps clients from expressing gratitude. Workers must find their personal grati-

fications in the work, in their comradeship with colleagues, or in some other area. They cannot be allowed to steal it from clients.

Client Exploitation

THE TEMPTATION OF MARTHA
Gerda finally died, after long suffering. Her family was very grateful to Martha, who had managed the home care very efficiently and sensitively over seven years. Martha came to the house to pay her respects to the family. The subject turned to disposing of Gerda's possessions.

Gerda's older daughter was saying to Martha, "We are so grateful. You have always been there for us. Just let us know if there is anything we can do to show our appreciation."

As Martha thanked her perfunctorily, she turned and saw that a chair, which had been covered with a throw every time she had visited, was now revealed as the mate to her prized antique couch. She knew that it was worth several thousand dollars, and she suspected that the family did not know its value.

It should be understood that Martha, though a supervisor, was not well paid. Unlike many human service workers, she was used to helping people who had more money than she did. Gerda's children were working people, comfortable but not wealthy.

"That's a very handsome chair," Martha said.

Treating People Fairly.   Social agencies usually serve people who are discriminated against, for example, older people, disabled people, poor people, people from stigmatized races or ethnic groups, or people with a mental illness. Often while serving one stigmatized group, agencies follow their community's other patterns of exclusion. For example, a senior citizens program operates on a clublike basis, excluding disabled people or representatives of a minority group. Because of the damaging effects of discrimination, human service workers must commit themselves to going beyond this minimal level of accommodation.

Bias is not just about groups—it also has to do with individuals. Workers may find one client appealing and another disgusting. Each deserves to be treated fairly, however the worker feels about them.

Handling Clients' Information with Care.

Human service workers often know the intimate details of their clients' lives. Clients trust that this information will be confidential, or they would never confide in workers at all. So workers must keep this information from others—family members, debt collectors, and police officers— except when outsiders are authorized to have it. Yet workers must share the information within the agency so that the agency can respond appropriately when the primary worker is not available. Workers also offer the information to their supervisors to learn how to be more helpful to clients and to ensure that the work is being done properly. After all, the agency must monitor what the worker does. Another responsibility to share information occurs when clients pose a threat to themselves or to others. This double responsibility—proper disclosure without unduly violating clients' privacy—is a cornerstone of a worker's integrity.

Being Truthful.

Many people who enter human services as a profession are people who want to be liked. When someone at work asks them to give an opinion, they tend to sugarcoat it so the person will not be angry at them. This practice tends to obscure accurate understandings of what is going on in the work situation and robs colleagues and supervisors of accurate feedback.

This does not mean that one should go around saying exactly what one thinks, no matter what. It does mean that workers need to look for the right time and place to say what they think. Critical opinions may be expressed in the form of a question rather than a statement. It is desirable for workers to express themselves assertively, allowing for other people to have a differing point of view (Schulman, 1978, pp. 108–115). A goal for workers is to avoid assenting to an untruth, even if they do not feel they can tell the whole truth at the time.

SELF-AWARENESS AND SELF-MANAGEMENT

Responding to Criticism Non-Defensively.

Workers view criticism from colleagues and supervisors as an important aid in learning and are expected to offer frank and open accounts of their work—including mistakes—to their supervisors and, when appropriate, to their peers. It is always tempting to try to explain, excuse, or apologize for errors. The useful response is to acknowledge mistakes and to try to learn from them in a way that keeps the worker from repeating them very often.

Understanding One's Unique Ways of Acting, Responding, and Learning.

Each worker has different ways of thinking about and getting involved in experiences with clients and other staff members. One worker will be sensitive to family dynamics, another one will be especially capable in confronting aggressive clients, and another will know all the regulations about public assistance by heart. Some workers will do best when they work in private; others will thrive when collaborating in a team. An effective organization will use the different perspectives and responses of its workers in ways that allow each one to develop strengths and contribute them to the organization's life. Workers who want to grow will capitalize on their strengths and try to improve in their weak areas.

Managing One's Own Workload.

Working always involves meeting deadlines. Often the deadlines are not coordinated; a new one falls at the same time as another. The presentation to the community group must be prepared and delivered at the same time that the monthly client statistics must be handed in. Workers must have a way to decide what is most important and organize their time effectively. It is helpful if they know how to ask their colleagues for help in ways that do not lead to dependence but rather inspire, stimulate thinking, and spark renewed effort.

Knowing One's Limits.   The agency connection is what gives a worker legitimacy. As a worker for an agency, the worker is empowered to intervene in a deeply personal situation, access money and other resources, speak for and testify about clients in official proceedings, write records and reports that may determine the fate of individual clients or groups of clients, recommend that a child be removed from a family, plan programs that may involve large amounts of money and large numbers of people, and other powerful activities. Being rooted in the role that has been assigned to them is the worker's source of strength, authority, and authenticity.

Workers sometimes try to escape the limits of the calendar and the clock. There are so many interesting and worthwhile activities to become involved in that they overcommit their time and energy. Such overcommitment and its resulting stress leads to poor health, poor judgment, and erratic worker performance.

Workers are sometimes impatient to save the world because the needs of people are so great and the obstacles to meeting them so formidable. They sometimes set unreasonably high goals for their clients, setting them up for failure because the workers want so much to succeed. Some inexperienced or emotionally needy workers think of themselves as "Lone Rangers" or knights on horseback single-handedly rescuing clients from other insensitive workers. The truth is that one cannot carry out important and effective human service work alone. The cooperation of many others must be enlisted to meet any significant goal.

PRESCRIPTIONS FOR SELF-IMPROVEMENT

The preceding catalog of skills, knowledge, values, and personal qualities may intimidate some readers. It is a formidable list. If you know human service workers, you may know that not all of them have all these characteristics, at least not all of the time.

How does one go about developing these characteristics? The need for them is not just a matter of helping a worker improve; clients need dedicated, expert, skillful, and sensitive assistance from workers. That may be the *first* prescription for positive personal development: not forgetting that it is all done for the benefit of clients. Some other rewarding aspects of human service work may include professional recognition, community leadership, close association with interesting and dynamic people, the opportunity to challenge the power structure, intellectual stimulation, an opening for new arrangements in society, personal power, and many other values that draw people into lives of service. But if these become more important than serving clients, the helping effort will probably lose its focus and may even unwittingly harm clients.

The *second* prescription for positive personal development is to select our experiences carefully. None of us enter our roles fully formed. We grow into them, experience by experience. Often we learn more from our mistakes than from our successes. We all grow and change every moment. For that reason, it is important to select experiences that will help us grow positively. Work experiences early in the career of a human service worker will have an important formative impact, so it is critical that early experiences be carefully chosen. But even the most experienced workers are challenged to continually learn as the world changes around them.

The *third* prescription, then, is for the worker to form relationships with people who will challenge, stimulate, guide, and struggle in a positive way with the worker. The worker does not have to adopt the style or values of these people, although some may serve as role models. The joint process of learning with them is what is important. The beginning worker may, in turn, have an important influence on the others by asking seldom-heard questions, seeking explanations for customary ways of dealing with problems, or coming up with new ways of thinking about a topic. The process of dialogue and struggle, properly done, requires all participants to stretch and grow.

It is helpful if the worker can find these colleagues in the workplace; if not, they may be sought out in professional associations, civic groups, advocacy groups, or elsewhere. When a worker travels, it can be interesting to seek out human service workers who deal with similar problems in other locations to see how they think differently about these problems.

A *fourth* prescription is to read the professional literature. There are many different ideas about how to serve the needs of clients. Reading professional journals and other works that deal with human need and ways to meet it can give workers new tools and new perspectives to address their daily tasks.

A human service worker is always in the process of becoming someone new. Thoughtful application of the prescriptions above will make the "new" someone a more effective, informed, and thoughtful worker.

REFERENCES

Corsini, R. J., and D. Wedding (1989). *Current Psychotherapies.* Itasca, IL: F. E. Peacock.

Schulman, E. (1978). *Interventions in Human Services.* St. Louis, MO: C. V. Mosby.

SUGGESTED FURTHER READING

Brammer, L. M. (1988). *The Helping Relationship: Process and Skills,* 4th ed. Englewood Cliffs, NJ: Prentice-Hall.

Brill, N. (1990). *Working with People: The Helping Process,* 4th ed. New York: Longman.

Corey, M. S., and G. Corey (1992). *Becoming a Helper,* 2nd ed. Pacific Grove, CA: Brooks/Cole.

Egan, G. (1990). *The Skilled Helper: A Systematic Approach to Effective Helping,* 4th ed. Pacific Grove, CA: Brooks/Cole.

Kottler, J. (1991). *The Compleat Therapist.* San Francisco, CA: Jossey-Bass.

LaFramboise, T. D., and S. L. Foster (1989). *Counseling Across Cultures,* 3rd ed. Honolulu, HI: University of Hawaii Press.

Napier, R. W., and M. K. Gershenfeld (1993). *Groups: Theory and Experience.* Boston, MA: Houghton Mifflin Company.

Satir, V. (1989). *The New Peoplemaking.* Palo Alto, CA: Science and Behavior Books.

CHAPTER 6

TECHNIQUES AND SKILLS IN INTERVIEWING:

THE ROLE OF COMPETENCE-BASED LEARNING IN HUMAN SERVICE EDUCATION

JOHN M. HANCOCK

In the preceding article, Long and Doyle point out the various qualities, knowledge, skills, and values required of effective human service professionals. Ideally, individuals who are drawn to the human service field already possess some of the values, knowledge, and rudimentary communication skills they will need (Egan, 1994). Along these lines, the Council for Standards in Human Service Education (CSHSE) has established twenty-three standards that inform both associate and baccalaureate-degree human service programs and human service educators of the expected curriculum and competency that students need to acquire (DiGiovanni, Rother, and Maloney, 1999).

Fieldwork is considered to be an essential component of all human service programs and many undergraduate psychology programs (Boltuck, Peterson, and Murphy, 1980; Simon, 1999). Competence-based learning methods are frequently used to prepare students for success in fieldwork (LoCicero and Hancock, 2000), and human service agencies expect fieldwork students to have learned basic interviewing and counseling skills (Randolph, Graun, and Frates, 1997). Instruction in interviewing skills as a stand-alone course or as part of a broader counseling course is usually students' first exposure to competence-based learning. In an article I wrote with one of my colleagues, we described students' first exposure to competence-based learning (a stand-alone Interviewing Techniques course) as a pivotal course in human service education. We saw the development of human service skills, especially interviewing skills, as facilitating the establishment of students' identity as competent professional helpers (Hancock and LoCicero, 1995a).

CHALLENGES OF COMPETENCE-BASED LEARNING

Interviewing, which is typically the first competence-based course that students encounter, can be a challenge for both students and instructors. Unlike previous courses that mainly required students to be passive learners, competence-based courses require them to be active learners. A course in interviewing skills usually requires students to demonstrate competence by conducting a simulated interview while being observed by their classmates and the instructor or being videotaped for later viewing by the instructor. Requiring students to demonstrate competence has been found to cause anxiety for many (Sommers-Flanagan and Means, 1987). A survey of the literature revealed no information about instructors' reactions to teaching a competence-based course.

Based on my own experience and anecdotal information from other instructors, however, it would appear that instructors also become anxious about teaching a competence-based course—especially for the first time. In addition to playing the usual role of teacher, the instructor of a competence-based course must also (a) model communication skills, support, empathy, self-reflection, and a non-defensive stance; (b) provide a structure in which students help one another with skill development; and (c) observe and evaluate students' skills.

As a student, if you are required to take an interviewing course or conduct a simulated interview as part of another course, don't be surprised if you find yourself becoming anxious. This reaction is typical and normal. It does not mean that there is something wrong with you or that you are not cut out for human services. If you talk with some of your classmates, I am sure that they will tell you that they also feel anxious. If you have the opportunity to talk to a student who has already taken the interviewing course, I think that they will share that they were nervous at the beginning of the course but became more comfortable with interviewing as the course progressed. I also tell my interviewing students that their concerns and feelings in response to having to conduct their first simulated interview may be similar to clients' concerns about meeting with a human service worker for the first time. As an instructor, if this is your first time teaching a competence-based course or having students conduct simulated interviews as part of another course, don't be surprised to find that students are anxious and that you also feel apprehensive. If you can find a supportive colleague who teaches competence-based courses, I am sure they will welcome the opportunity to discuss the challenges of teaching such a course. As a teacher, your response to students' concerns and discomfort with being asked to demonstrate competence is critical. I would advise teachers to respond directly to students' performance anxiety by acknowledging and

affirming the normality of this reaction. The initial similar response of apprehension by students and instructor (but probably more intense for students) provides an opportunity for the instructor to model empathy and appropriate self-disclosure, thereby encouraging students' empathy for human service consumers.

INITIAL ROLE OF INSTRUCTOR

If the instructor structures competence-based courses to acknowledge and incorporate students' concerns and anxiety, students will be more likely to achieve the desired competence. One of the paradoxical consequences of over-focusing on skill development is that students often become anxious regarding their performance of the skills, especially when they are being observed. As pointed out by Whyte (1993):

> We ask students to learn a body of knowledge, values, and skills of the helping process, and then expect them to really listen to the people they are interviewing. Students find themselves attempting to remember all they learned while they are endeavoring to listen. (p. 49)

Therefore, it is essential that early in the course the instructor not only acknowledge but help students reduce and manage their level of performance anxiety. Instructors should respond with sensitivity to students' concerns and anxiety about having to conduct a simulated interview, affirming the normality of their reactions. The instructor should facilitate cohesiveness, helping students to become a supportive group for one another. This stance is supported by research suggesting that empathy is modeled most effectively when the model (in this case, the instructor) is perceived as warm and supportive (Eisenberg, 1994).

As an instructor, to defuse students' anxiety and my own apprehension, I have found that it is important to utilize audio and video equipment as early as possible in the course—ideally at the first class session so that students can get used to being observed and receiving feedback. For example, on the first day of class in my Interviewing Techniques course, I ask several pairs of students to talk with each other about whatever they wish while being videotaped and observed. I then conduct a formal interview with a student, with whom I have had no prior contact, during which I demonstrate basic interviewing skills. Following my interview, I ask students to compare and contrast the "social conversations" between students with my "formal interview." For the next couple of classes, prior to practicing interviewing skills, all students conduct a baseline simulated interview which is videotaped. Later in the course, students compare their baseline interview with their mid-term and final interviews and note skill improvement.

INITIAL ROLE OF STUDENTS

As a student in a competence-based course, you will be expected to (a) be open to learning by observing skills demonstrated by others, including both the instructor and fellow students; (b) tolerate a certain degree of discomfort in practicing new skills, especially while being observed and/or videotaped; (c) be open to receiving constructive feedback from your instructor and peers, and giving constructive feedback to peers; and (d) be willing to reflect upon and evaluate your own level of skill competence. I tell my students that the skills and professional role attitudes that I expect of them in the interviewing course will not only promote their success in this course but will help them succeed in other competence-based courses that prepare them for fieldwork experience and, over the long term, help them to become effective human service professionals.

RESOURCES AND INSTRUCTIONAL METHODS

Although text and didactic information is not the primary teaching method in competence-based

learning, having a text is still necessary. Selection of an appropriate text or texts is of critical importance for any course, including a competence-based course. Although there are numerous texts available that address interviewing skills and the helping/counseling process, most texts are either too generic or more appropriate for graduate-level counseling students than for undergraduate human service students. In addition, most texts are too comprehensive and cover more skills, including advanced skills, than can reasonably be taught in a one-semester course. I have not found any one text that I think is adequate in covering both micro-skill training and providing an exposure to a macro model of helping. In my opinion, the best micro-skill training text is Evans, Hearn, Uhlemann, and Ivey's *Essential Interviewing* (1998), which is a programmed learning text; whereas the best macro model helping text is Egan's *The Skilled Helper* (1994). Recently, in response to student feedback regarding the cost of having to buy two texts, I have been using one text that does a reasonable job in covering both micro-skills and the macro model of helping. The text is Ivey and Ivey's *Intentional Interviewing and Counseling* (2003). In addition, I have prepared a number of handouts (e.g., how to cope with silence during an interview) that students have found helpful.

Over my years in teaching competence-based courses such as Interviewing Techniques, Group Work, and Crisis Intervention, I have increased the frequency of videotaping with observer feedback (from the teacher and fellow students) and have integrated practicing skills in conjunction with text or didactic instruction. In addition to didactic information, I often show selected segments of Ivey, Gluckstern, and Ivey's (1992a) *Basic Attending Skills and Basic Listening Sequence* videos, or Murphy and Dillon's (1998) *Interviewing in Action: Process and Practice* video prior to having students practice the interviewing skills being covered. Students seem to benefit most from watching a video of an expert or the instructor demonstrating the skill prior to their practicing the micro-skill or a combination of micro-skills. It has also been my experience that text material is integrated better by students when issues arise in their simulated interviews that become topics of discussion following their or other students' simulated interviews.

Simulated Interviews

Although out-of-class assignments can reinforce classroom practice, they cannot replace in-class practice and simulated interviewing. According to Ivey and Ivey, researchers have found that "practicing the skills to mastery . . . appears to be important if the skills are to be maintained after training" (2003, p. 26). Instructors need to monitor skill development and provide ongoing feedback to students, and these tasks can best be accomplished by using class time to conduct and discuss practice-specific micro-skills via simulated interviews. If you are as fortunate as I am, your school will have an interactive lab equipped with a two-way mirror and audio/video equipment so that two students can be videotaped while conducting a simulated interview in one room while the instructor and students are observing through the two-way mirror or viewing TV monitors. Prior to our school having such a facility, I had to bring a portable video-recorder to a traditional classroom to record students' simulated interviews conducted at the front of the class in two regular chairs with students observing from their desks.

The use of simulated interviews is widely accepted as an effective training strategy (Bogels, 1994; Low, 1996). Several instructors have noted that they have classmates serve as interviewees (Fernald, 1995; Weiss, 1986), while Lane (1988) recommends using drama students to role-play the interviewees. Although I agree with Lane's rationale for recommending drama students, given the structure of my course in which practicing skill occurs during almost every class session, it is more convenient to have students in the course serve as interviewees. The best arrangement might be to have students practice skills with each other and utilize drama students for those simulated interviews used for evaluative purposes (e.g., mid-term and/or final grades).

Modeling Constructive Feedback and Encouraging Empathy

Discussion following practice sessions and simulated interviews provides an opportunity for modeling empathic, honest, and supportive feedback. In our survey of fieldwork students who had previously taken the interviewing course, we found that students rated feedback from the instructor, followed by feedback from students regarding their interviews, as the two most helpful components of the interviewing course in preparing them for fieldwork (LoCicero and Hancock, 2000). It has been my experience that students are often unprepared and reluctant to provide constructive feedback. Without instruction and modeling by instructors, students tend to hesitate to provide constructive feedback, and generally will provide only a global positive response such as "Good job!" Instructors need to encourage and, if necessary, model more specific feedback such as "Your use of key words helped the interviewee continue to share her story." My colleague and I have found that the student-interviewers show one or more of the following responses following their simulated interviews: "drawing a blank, severe self-criticism, or defensiveness" (Hancock and LoCicero, 1995b, p. 2). In my opinion, how the instructor structures the discussion following the simulated interview is of critical importance. The structure that I have developed is to have students spend a few minutes following the completion of a simulated interview filling out one of three forms depending on whether they were the interviewer, interviewee, or an observer. The observers, who are given their forms prior to the simulated interview, usually complete their forms before the interviewer or interviewee have done so. Following the interview, I instruct the observers that after they have completed their observation forms they are to share their observations with the rest of the group. I then go into the interview room and quickly debrief the interviewer and interviewee by asking the interviewer what they thought they did well in their interview. Typically, they will provide a rather limited response before sharing things they didn't like about their interview. I then ask the interviewee to share something that they liked about the interview. I have never encountered a situation in which the interviewee did not have more positive reactions than the interviewer. After a minute or two, I will leave them to check in with the observers. Typically, the observers will have a number of positive comments and one or two questions or criticisms regarding the interview. Usually the observers' questions or criticism are similar to the interviewer's self-criticism. I then have the interviewer and interviewee rejoin the class. I instruct students to share positive comments first and to offer questions about the interview by phrasing them as "I wonder" and to share constructive feedback by making "I statements" regarding what they would have done differently if they had been the interviewer. The sequential order of sharing is as follows: the student who conducted the interview, the student who was interviewed, the students who observed, and the instructor. It has been my experience that when the observers realize that the interviewer was aware of many of the weaknesses that they observed, they are more willing to share their observations regarding skill deficiency. It also helps if the interviewer solicits constructive suggestions (e.g., "tell me what I could have done better!") from their fellow students. To facilitate the development of students into a cohesive, supportive peer group, I have found that it is necessary to allot more time for processing the first couple of simulated interviews.

INTERVIEWING TECHNIQUES AND MICRO-SKILLS

Early in the semester, students practice micro-skills of attending and listening. They view videotapes showing both positive and negative examples of good attending and listening (Ivey, Gluckstern, and Ivey, 1992a). They are provided with an overview of a macro-model of helping and are informed that the purpose of the beginning stage of the interview is to help the client tell their story (Egan, 1994). Emphasis is placed on cultural influences that the skilled interviewer needs to be aware of in order to use an interviewing style that will be effective with a particular client (Ivey and Ivey, 2003).

In response to the often-observed phenomenon of novice student interviewers tending to give advice and reassurance, it is important for instructors not only to discourage this practice but to provide a rationale that students can understand. Students' expectations regarding their role as a helper should be explored. Many students have told me that prior to taking the interviewing course, they thought that as a helper they were supposed to ask questions and give advice. Comparing and contrasting the purpose of a social conversation with that of a helping interview can assist students to understand the rationale for refraining from offering reassurance or talking about themselves (i.e., self-disclosing personal information) while conducting a helping interview.

In my Interviewing Techniques course, I cover the following topics and micro-skills prior to the mid-term simulated interviews.

Preparing for the Interview

As recommended by Dillard and Reilly (1988, p. 101), I have students prepare for the interview by arranging the furniture in the interviewing room, including the location of the two chairs used by the interviewer and interviewee, and learning about the interviewee's presenting situation prior to the simulated interview. I also instruct students in all my competence courses that on the day they are scheduled to conduct a simulated interview for evaluative purposes, they will be expected to dress as if they were a staff member at a human service agency (e.g., no baseball caps). This makes the simulated interview a more realistic role-play and helps prepare students for fieldwork and being a professional human service worker. In preparing for the simulated interview, students are reminded of the critical importance of maintaining a nonjudgmental attitude and establishing rapport with the interviewee (Ragg, 2001; Samantrai, 1996).

Greeting the Client and Beginning the Interview

Students practice various greeting responses, such as "Hello, (Ms./Mr. interviewee's last name), my name is Ms./Mr. _____." I have found that having student interviewers use Ms./Mr. in their greetings helps socialize them into the role of a professional helper. Students are given the option of providing the interviewee with a directed opening regarding the purpose of the interview (e.g., "The director asked me to talk to you about your recent behavior on the unit.") or a non-directed opening such as "What would you like to talk about today?" (Murphy and Dillon, 1998).

Micro-Skills that Enhance Communication

Attending Skills.   Students practice sitting in a manner that is perceived by observers and interviewees as suggesting attentive body language and to avoid distracting mannerisms (Ivey, Gluckstern, and Ivey, 1992b). Having students view their videotapes is an excellent way for them to identify mannerisms they would like to eliminate (e.g., playing with their hair); however, in order to avoid causing embarrassment or making the interviewer feel defensive, this should not be done in class. Interviewers are encouraged to look, but not stare, at the interviewee, and to be aware of their tone of voice and rate of speech (e.g., not talking too fast). If you don't have access to videotaping equipment, audiotaping will suffice in providing interviewers with feedback regarding how they sound to others.

Observing Skills.   Students practice observing interviewees' body language, facial expressions, tones of voice, and rates of speech to identify clues regarding how they are feeling and responding to the interview. As suggested by Ivey and Ivey (2003), I encourage students to look for the "degree of harmony" between themselves and the interviewee, and to practice "mirroring" the interviewee (pp. 103–104). I also emphasize that interviewers should note (without providing immediate feedback) any discrepancies/incongruencies between the content and how interviewees express themselves both verbally and nonverbally. To practice using observation skills, I have students select a neutral event (e.g., going to the movies) and then select a card that tells them how to act (e.g., bored, pleased, scared, etc.) while being interviewed. Neither the interviewer nor the observers know what was on the interviewee's card until after the simulated interview. Before having the interviewee inform them of the emotion they attempted to convey, I have the interviewer and observers share their observations regarding the interviewee's nonverbal and verbal behaviors. In most cases, the interviewers and observers are aware of discrepancies between content and the interviewee's behavior. Students greatly enjoy this activity. With slight modifications, this exercise can also be used to practice reflection of feelings.

Questioning Skills.   According to Goldberg (1998), "Asking the right question helps the clients think more clearly, take greater responsibility for themselves, and accomplish their goals more easily." The most commonly used categories of questions are closed-ended versus open-ended questions. Closed-ended questions are "questions that could . . . be answered with a yes or no response" (Hutchins and Cole, 1997, p. 69).

By definition, open-ended questions (e.g., "What brings you in to see me today?") require more than a single-word response. In general, open-ended questions are preferable to closed-ended questions, especially at the beginning of the interview, because open-ended questions allow the interviewee to tell their story in their own words (Evans et al., 1998; Gordon, 1992; Ivey and Ivey, 2003). Closed-ended questions can be used to solicit specific information (e.g., "Do you have health insurance?") and to limit "verbal output . . . when interviewing a client who is excessively talkative and who overelaborates in response to interviewer queries" (Sommers-Flanagan and Sommers-Flanagan, 1999, p. 98). However, I have found that students who are beginning to learn interviewing skills need help in rewording their closed-ended questions into open-ended questions and asking fewer questions. As pointed out by Benjamin (1969), interviewers (and in my opinion, especially novice interviewers):

> . . . *ask too many questions, often meaningless ones. We ask questions that confuse the interviewee, that interrupt him. We ask questions the interviewee cannot possibly answer. We even ask questions we don't want the answers to, and consequently, we do not hear the answers when forthcoming (p. 65).*

To help students become less dependent on questioning during an interview, I have them practice asking no more than two questions in a row. Instead of questioning, students are asked to use other interviewing skills such as prompting with key words or reflecting content as an alternative intervention. I also encourage them to avoid asking multiple questions and leading questions. In my experience, students have difficulty with the wording of questions and often don't realize it until they review the audiotapes or videotapes of their interviews.

Encouraging Skills. Interviewees can be encouraged to continue talking if the interviewer uses a subtle nonverbal or verbal prompt, or a key word. Interviewers nodding their heads is a nonverbal prompt, while verbalizing "m-hm" is an example of a subtle verbal prompt (Westra, 1996). Prompting with key words, which some authors classify under reflection of content or paraphrasing, occurs when the interviewer repeats or echoes those words used frequently by the interviewee (DeJong and Berg, 1998). For example, if an interviewee states, "My parents just don't understand me; no one understands me!" the interviewer can simply repeat "Understand!" Typically the interviewee will elaborate and provide more specific detail regarding the significance of the key word (Ivey and Ivey, 2003). My interviewing students are surprised at how effective key words can be when used as an alternative to asking another question.

Listening Skills. According to Nichols, "the simple art of listening isn't always so simple" (1995, p. 3), a fact that students soon come to realize. Listening in the helping interview is not the same as being quiet while a friend talks. Instead, listening in the helping interview is an active process. According to Ivey and Ivey (2003), "Active listening demands that you participate fully by helping the client enlarge and enrich the story" (p. 125). Blocks to effective listening are those things that prevent the interviewer from being able to focus on the client's story. For example, rehearsing what to say before the interviewee has finished is a block to effective listening by the interviewer (Whyte, 1993).

Reflection of content or paraphrasing is similar to the use of key words, except that it involves repeating the essence of the client's message in a sentence or two. If we use the same example (i.e., "My parents just don't understand me; no one understands me!") that we used to illustrate the encouraging skill of prompting with key words (e.g., "Understand!") there are several possible reflections of content. An interviewer would be making a reflection of content if she or he responded to the interviewee by saying, "No one, including your parents, seems to understand you!" or "Not only your parents, but no one else, understands you!" In most cases a reflection of content involves responding to more than a single sentence of sharing by the interviewee. Although this is an essential listening skill, it is one that does not always come easily to novice interviewers:

> *Interviewers often feel awkward when making their first paraphrases; they feel as if they're restating the obvious. They often simply parrot back to clients what has just been said in a way that is rigid, stilted, and at times offensive.*
>
> Sommers-Flanagan and Sommers-Flanagan (1999, p. 79).

In addition to individual practicing, I have found it helpful to conduct a group exercise in which students take turns providing alternative paraphrases to an interviewee's statement. This exercise helps them realize that there is more than one correct reflection of content, and that the purpose of paraphrasing is to let the interviewee know that they have been heard (Ivey and Ivey, 2003).

Reflection of feelings is similar to paraphrasing, except that rather than reflecting on the content you are acknowledging and "providing feedback to the speaker about what they appear to be feeling" (Westra, 1996, p. 99). As pointed out by Sommers-Flanagan and Sommers-Flanagan (1999) "any attempt at reflecting clients' feelings should be considered a move towards interpersonal closeness or intimacy" (p. 82). It has been my experience that those students who are comfortable in the interviewer's role and able to establish rapport can easily master this skill; however, for most novice interviewers this is not the case. Key words that the interviewee uses that are emotionally explicit (e.g. "pissed") are easier for students to recognize than emotionally implied statements. For example, in the following statement, "My parents just don't understand me!" it is not clear what the interviewee is feeling. I advise students to be tentative ("It sounds like you are feeling _____ with your parents

because they don't seem to understand you?") and to check this out with the interviewee (e.g., "Is that correct?"). When I show the video of Carl Rogers's interview with Gloria (Rogers, 1961), I point out how Rogers checks with Gloria after he ventures a tentative reflection of feeling.

Summarization and Ending the Interview

Summarization consists of the interviewer providing an "overview of the story from the client's point of view before bringing in the interviewer's point of view" (Ivey and Ivey, 2003, p. 185). It includes both reflection of content and reflection of feelings, and central themes and issues discussed. It is a good way to end a session and to begin the next session.

Additional Topics/Skills Covered Following Mid-term

Topics covered prior to the mid-term interviews include basic attending skills and basic listening skills that are the foundation for helping. Following the mid-term, instructors and students benefit from reviewing previously covered skills and working on those skills that they identify as needing improvement. By this point in the semester, there is usually only limited time available to address new topics and skills. The material that I cover before the mid-term has been very consistent over time, whereas this has not been the case following the mid-term. Some of the topics and skills that I have covered between the mid-term and final simulated interviews include how to respond to silence, how to give feedback, confrontation, self-disclosure, information sharing, positive asset search, viewing a story from multiple perspectives, and integration of skills.

EVALUATING SKILL DEVELOPMENT

At the midpoint and the end of the semester, each student interviews a classmate while the instructor and other students observe and fill out feedback forms (see Appendix A). Each student reviews all observer forms and the interviewee feedback form. At the time that my colleague and I conducted our survey, in addition to reviewing various forms, students were asked to review the videotape of their simulated interview and write a reflective paper regarding their strengths and weaknesses as an interviewer (LoCicero and Hancock, 2000). My colleague and I were puzzled by students' relatively low rating of items regarding self-reflection. Three possible explanations occurred to us regarding students' responses to self-reflection. First, perhaps we overestimated the usefulness of self-reflection to students. Second, grading of students' self-reflection papers may have created anxiety and interfered with their effective use of self-reflection. Third, students may need more support and practice in self-reflection. Following a suggestion by my colleague Bob Wellman, students are now provided with more detailed and specific instructions and are required to select a five-minute segment of their simulated interview to transcribe and code (see Appendix B). They are instructed to provide an alternative response or revised wording for any of their transcribed verbalizations. The mid-term reflection paper has students compare their baseline interview with their mid-term interview and identify those skills that they need to work on before their final simulated interview. The final reflective paper has students compare their final simulated interview to their mid-term and identify those interview skills that they need to improve to be a more effective professional helper. Although students complain that this is a time-consuming project, they also report that having to transcribe helped them to identify areas of skill strength and skill deficiency, and to realize what they needed to do in order to become a more competent helping interviewer.

REFERENCES

Benjamin, A. (1969). *The Helping Interview*. Atlanta: Houghton Mifflin.

Bogels, S. M. (1994). "A Structured-Training Approach to Teaching Diagnostic Interviewing." *Teaching of Psychology, 17,* 144–150.

Boltuck, M. A., T. L. Peterson, and R. J. Murphy (1980). "Preparing Undergraduate Psychology Majors for Employment in the Human Service Delivery System." *Teaching of Psychology, 7,* 75–78.

DeJong, P., and I. K. Berg (1998). *Interviewing for Solutions*. Pacific Grove, CA: Brooks/Cole.

DiGiovanni, M., F. R. Rother, and D. C. Maloney (1999). "National Community Support Skill Standards Project: Implications for Human Services Education." In H. S. Harris and D. C. Maloney, eds., *Human Services: Contemporary Issues and Trends.* Boston: Allyn and Bacon.

Dillard, J. M., and R. R. Reilly (1988). *Systematic Interviewing: Communication Skills for Professional Effectiveness*. Columbus: Merrill.

Egan, G. (1994). *The Skilled Helper: A Problem-Management Approach to Helping*. Pacific Grove, CA: Brooks/Cole.

Eisenberg, N. (1994, August). *Empathy and Prosocial Behavior.* Paper presented at the Invited Address at the 102nd Annual Conference of the American Psychological Association, Los Angeles.

Evans, D. R., M. T. Hearn, M. R. Uhlemann, and A. E. Ivey (1998). *Essential Interviewing: A Programmed Approach to Effective Communication,* 5th ed. Pacific Grove, CA: Brooks/Cole.

Fernald, P. S. (1995). "Teaching Students to Listen Empathically." *Teaching of Psychology, 22,* 183–186.

Goldberg, M. C. (1998). *The Art of the Question*. New York: John Wiley and Sons.

Gordon, R. (1992). *Basic Interviewing Skills*. Itasca, IL: F. E. Peacock.

Hancock, J., and A. LoCicero. (1995a). "Interviewing Skills: A Pivotal Course." *The Link, 16*(3), 1–2.

Hancock, J., and A. LoCicero. (1995b). "Interviewing Skills: Facilitating Empathy." *The Link, 17*(1), 1–2.

Hutchins, D. E., and C. G. Cole (1997). *Helping Relationships and Strategies,* 3rd ed. Monterey, CA: Brooks/Cole.

Ivey, A. E., and M. B. Ivey (2003). *Intentional Interviewing and Counseling: Facilitating Client Development in a Multicultural Society.* Pacific Grove, CA: Brooks/Cole.

Ivey, A. E., N. B. Gluckstern, and M. B. Ivey (1992a). *Basic Attending Skills and Basic Listening Sequence (Videos):* Microtraining.

Ivey, A. E., N. B. Gluckstern, and M. B. Ivey (1992b). *Basic Attending Skills,* 3rd ed. Pacific Grove, CA: Microtraining Associates.

Lane, K. G. (1988). "Using Actors as 'Clients' for an Interviewing Simulation in an Undergraduate Clinical Psychology Course." *Teaching of Psychology, 15,* 162–164.

LoCicero, A., and J. Hancock (2000). "Preparing Students for Success in Fieldwork." *Teaching of Psychology, 27*(2), 117–120.

Low, K. G. (1996). "Teaching an Undergraduate Seminar in Psychotherapy." *Teaching of Psychology, 23,* 110–112.

Murphy, B. C., and S. Dillon (1998). *Interviewing in Action: Process and Practice.* Pacific Grove, CA: Brooks/Cole.

Nichols, M. P. (1995). *The Lost Art of Listening.* New York: Guilford Press.

Ragg, D. M. (2001). *Building Effective Helping Skills: The Foundation of Generalist Practice.* Boston: Allyn and Bacon.

Randolph, D. L., K. Graun, and B. Frates (1997). "Graduate and Undergraduate Internships in Human Services: A National Directory." *Counseling Education and Supervision, 26,* 279–285.

Rogers, C. R. (1961). "Client-Centered Therapy, Part I." In E. Shostrom, ed., *Three Approaches to Psychotherapy.* (Film). Santa Ana, CA: Psychology Films.

Samantrai, K. (1996). *Interviewing in Health and Human Services.* Chicago: Nelson-Hall.

Simon, E. (1999). "Field Practicum: Standards, Criteria, Supervision, and Evaluation." In H. S. Harris & D. C. Maloney, eds., *Human Services: Contemporary Issues and Trends.* Boston: Allyn and Bacon.

Sommers-Flanagan, J. M., and J. R. Means (1987). "Thou Shall Not Question: An Approach to Teaching Interviewing Skills." *Teaching of Psychology, 14,* 164–166.

Sommers-Flanagan, R., and J. S. Sommers-Flanagan (1999). *Clinical Interviewing,* 2nd ed. New York: John Wiley and Sons.

Weiss, A. R. (1986). "Teaching Counseling and Psychotherapy Skills Without Access to a Clinical Population: The Short Interview Method." *Teaching of Psychology, 13,* 145–147.

Westra, M. (1996). *Active Communication.* Pacific Grove, CA: Brooks/Cole.

Whyte, D. A. (1993). "Learning to Listen." *Human Service Education, 13*(1), 49–53.

USING SHORT-TERM PSYCHOTHERAPY TO TREAT POST-TRAUMATIC STRESS DISORDER (PTSD)

LYNNE SCHMELTER-DAVIS

It surprises many people to learn that the modal number of psychotherapy sessions per client is one. The average number of sessions for those who stay longer is three to six (Talmon, 1990). People stop coming *not* because they "drop out" but because they get better. Even a single session can reduce psychological symptoms, solve problems, and allow clients to continue making progress on their own (Talmon, 1990).

In these times of managed health care there are calls for quicker treatment with tangible therapy results. Most health insurance policies will reimburse the client for ten to twenty outpatient sessions per year for mental health reasons. Who benefits most from short-term therapy? Sifneos (1979) identifies the following important criteria:

- Evidence of a "meaningful relationship" with another person during early childhood;
- Capacity to relate flexibly to the evaluation during the interview and to experience and express feelings freely;
- At least average intelligence and psychological sophistication.

Talmon (1990) adds:

- The "worried well" who come for a mental health check-up essentially to ask whether they or their significant others are "normal."
- Patients who have a particularly "stuck" feeling (anger, grief, guilt, and so on) toward past events and are fed up with it.

USING SHORT-TERM THERAPY TO TREAT PTSD

The client, Elizabeth Brown, was a 30-year-old woman who had been referred to me by her physician. She had visited the doctor because of problems sleeping, feeling "tired all the time," trouble concentrating, and "feeling irritable most of the time." She told me upfront, on the telephone, that her health insurance would pay for ten sessions and she could not afford to pay on her own. Elizabeth made an appointment for the following week.

I began the first session by attempting to form a therapeutic alliance. While taking Elizabeth's history, I emphasized change and a positive expectation that a helpful solution could be found. At this point I learned that Elizabeth had been running a bit late to work at the World Trade Center on the morning of September 11th (it was now just before Christmas) and had arrived at "her" tower just as the first plane hit. Her office was on the 102nd floor. Most of her colleagues had died, and that day she saw many bodies as they fell to earth, and body parts as well. She thought she would be "fine" after a few days at home, but she now could see that instead of getting better she was getting worse. Her symptoms met the criteria for a diagnosis of Post-Traumatic Stress Disorder, and she was a good candidate for short-term psychotherapy to help restore her to her former psychological well-being. I felt it important to both give her factual information about PTSD and to create a therapeutic focus to help her not to feel overwhelmed. These results can be achieved by asking what is most painful for the patient *now* and discussing solutions for that specific problem. It is essential to encourage the patient's sense of autonomy and self-determination. In Elizabeth's case, she began with her insomnia because she said "the not sleeping is affecting everything else." I asked her what had helped her previously in times of stress and she said "warm baths, reading novels, and listening to music." She had not done any of that this time because she said she was too "upset." I suggested that she try all of those sleep aids that had worked for her in the past, *plus* I taught her a few relaxation exercises and gave her a progressive muscle relaxation tape to use at home. Also, I advised her to exercise outdoors (walking would be fine) each day to get physically tired enough to stay asleep.

By the time Elizabeth returned for a second session, her sleep had improved a bit and she felt encouraged because she had mobilized her own resources to heal herself. She also used the time between sessions to continue her therapy by joining a yoga class and taking walks in a beautiful natural environment.

Sessions two through six were used to focus on helping her examine personal values and explore how her behavior and experiences during the traumatic event had affected them. Her husband accompanied her to sessions seven and eight because of the potential impact of his behavior on Elizabeth, and vice-versa. He was appreciative of the opportunity to be helpful to his wife. After these sessions, Elizabeth joined a peer counseling group of September 11th "survivors" who met regularly to share their experiences and reactions to them. She was helped by the realization that many people had done the same things and felt the same emotions that she had.

Elizabeth was feeling much better by the last two sessions and was getting ready to return to her job, at an office that had relocated to New Jersey. If her symptoms had continued to be severe, I would have referred her to a physician for medication to help control them. Antidepressant medications may be particularly helpful in treating the core symptoms of PTSD (especially intrusive symptoms).

At the end of the ten agreed-upon sessions, I told Elizabeth that the door would always be open for her to return if needed.

As can be seen by this example, the use of short-term therapy can be an effective and efficient use of professional time and a great help to the client. Such therapy often utilizes behavioral, psychodynamic, family, and group therapies with the same client, so it is a good idea for the therapist to become comfortable using different techniques. Short-term therapy need not short-change the client simply because the number of sessions is limited.

REFERENCES

Sifneos, P. E. (1979). *Short-Term Dynamic Psychotherapy,* New York: Plenum.

Talmon, M. (1990). *Single-Session Therapy.* San Francisco: Jossey-Bass.

CHAPTER 7

HELPING SERVICES FOR GROUPS

BARBARA SOMERVILLE

Stephen is a human service worker in a large residential facility for seriously ill children and adolescents. The agency provides medical care, education, recreation, and counseling for its clients who, on average, remain there for several years. Stephen became aware that the teenagers really had no place to discuss typical topics of interest like dating, feelings about themselves, and their goals for the future. With his supervisor's permission, Stephen decided to organize what he called a "Rap Group" for eight teenage boys between the ages of fourteen and seventeen. He believed that by only having boys in the group and keeping the age range narrow, the members would more easily be able to speak to and understand one another.

Stephen thought a lot about the goals of the group. What did he want the members to get from participating? He decided that two of the most important goals would be to help the boys achieve a sense of belonging and to help them develop friendships that would extend beyond the time of the actual group meeting. Other goals included learning to relate socially (listening, taking turns, being polite) and having the opportunity to discuss issues of concern to them. Stephen knew that many different goals could be achieved within the same group. He chose one of the smaller recreation rooms as the location and decided to offer refreshments. The group would meet in the evening for an hour once a week for twelve weeks. Stephen approached several of the boys individually, explaining his ideas about the group. Some were not interested, but seven enthusiastically agreed to come. Stephen decided to run the

group with seven and not add any members later because he felt it would destroy the cohesion that he hoped the group would develop.

On the following Wednesday evening at 8:00, the seven new group members arrived at the recreation room feeling a little nervous and unsure. Stephen was there to greet them. During the first meeting the members introduced themselves, had cake and soda, and talked about what would happen in future meetings. Some of the boys asked if they could meet at 7:30 instead of 8:00, and the group voted on this. They also voted on whether to have refreshments every week. Stephen thought it was important that the members make decisions together rather than the leader deciding everything. After the boys left that first evening, Stephen was pleased with how the meeting had gone. They had all shown up, and all but one participated actively. (He would have to remember to try to involve that one boy in the next meeting.) They were talking and laughing on the way out, so they must have felt comfortable with one another. It was a good beginning.

Stephen continued to meet with his group every week. Gradually, feelings of closeness developed among the boys as they shared their questions and concerns. They were able to resolve the few conflicts that occurred during the third meeting, and at that point they decided to extend the time together from an hour to an hour and a half. Stephen worked hard with the group; his role changed as their needs changed. They talked about everything from girls to school to music. Some of the boys talked about the illnesses that had brought them to live there. Sometimes the conversation was light, and sometimes it was very personal. Stephen was proud of them as he watched them listen to one another and offer suggestions and support. He was glad to see real friendships begin to develop among some of the boys. He knew they were making progress and that soon it would be time to end the group.

Stephen began the tenth meeting with the reminder that they had all agreed to meet for twelve weeks and that, in two weeks, the group would be over. The boys seemed amazed that the time had passed so quickly. They also seemed a bit quiet that evening, and Stephen assumed they were reacting to the ending of the group. The following week they talked about how much they had enjoyed coming to meetings and that they would miss them. They decided to plan a party for their last time together. Stephen knew that it was important to encourage them to share their feelings about ending and to evaluate the progress they made. The last meeting of the group went well. They had their party and talked about the group being over. Someone suggested that they continue for another twelve weeks. Stephen had already considered this but decided against it. The boys achieved a sense of friendship and belonging (two of the initial goals) that enabled them to discuss issues outside the group. They didn't need the group as much as they had needed it in the beginning. Also, Stephen thought it was time to start a new twelve-week group with other teens so that they too could benefit from the process.

UNDERSTANDING GROUPS

From our birth until the time we die, most of us live our lives participating in groups. Our families, peer groups, church groups, and classes help us learn the norms of the society, enable us to acquire our values and beliefs, and help us develop our identities. Groups afford us the opportunity to try out new roles; they are the place where we can get feedback so we can know how we appear to others. They give us a sense of security that comes from belonging. Members of a group provide encouragement, support, and sometimes concrete help for one another. They offer new perspectives. Considering the influence group participation has on the individual, it is not surprising that the human service workers would find merit in helping clients within the context of the small group.

Before we examine the place of groups in human services, it would be helpful to understand exactly what we mean by a "group." If you are in an elevator with six other people, are you part of a group? Is your family a group? What about your human service class? Let's begin by looking at some definitions of "group."

> *Two or more people who, for longer than a few moments, interact with and influence one another and perceive one another as "us" (Myers, 1990).*
>
> *Two or more people who share a feeling of unity and who are bound together in relatively stable patterns of social interaction (Vander Zanden, 1990).*

In looking at these definitions, we can begin to see that groups have a certain set of characteristics that define them. If we examine these characteristics, we will begin to understand the nature of groups.

Two or More People.   Although a group must have at least two people, there is less agreement about the maximum number of people that can be considered a group. Generally, we believe that a group must be large enough for it to achieve its goals (more about goals later) and small enough for the members to interact comfortably with one another.

Interaction.   Members of a group must interact with one another in some meaningful way. Several people standing together in a moving elevator usually don't interact significantly, so we don't view this as a group. Obviously, speaking and listening form the basis of interaction. Examples of interacting within a group might include cooperating in completing a project, working together to learn something new, solving problems, and resolving conflicts. When a group of adolescents meets regularly after school to play basketball, they are interacting, as is a group of emotionally disturbed children who come together once a week to cook and bake.

Continuity. Members must interact over a period of time for them to truly be a group. If six students work together to rescue a cat from a tree on campus, would we consider them a group? Probably not, since their interaction took place for only a brief period of time. But those same students could be a group if they worked together during the semester on a term project, thereby interacting in an ongoing way over time. How long is enough time? Long enough for members to interact meaningfully, to influence one another, and to develop a feeling of "groupness" (explained shortly). In some cases, as in therapeutic encounter groups, this can happen in the space of a single, intensive weekend. In other cases, like a group of resistant predelinquent adolescents who attend only occasionally and are poorly motivated, it could take months. It is not really the length of time that is important but rather what occurs during the time they are together.

Influence. Members of a group generally influence one another. This is especially true when members have been together for a long time or they share a strong sense of group identification. This influence can be seen in many areas: The group may affect the ways members feel; their attitudes, values, and goals; what they believe; and how they act and look. We have only to consider the adolescent peer group for many examples of group influence on the individual. Sometimes the influence may be subtle, and it may affect some members more than others, but it is still usually present.

Common Purpose. Group members usually have similar purposes or goals in coming together. Note that goals need not be identical; they must just be similar enough so that the goals

of each member can be met within the context of the group. Consider the lunch group at the senior citizens' center. Although it is obvious that the members are all there to have lunch, one might be coming because the meal is free, another might attend for the chance to interact with others, and still another might come just to have something to do during the afternoon. Their goals are not the same, but they are certainly compatible.

Feeling of "Groupness." Members generally share a feeling of "belonging" to the group. This feeling is difficult to define but can generally be described as a sense of unity, group spirit, or being inside rather than outside the group's boundaries. It usually develops gradually over time as members continue to interact with and influence one another on a regular basis. They come to identify with one another, to see themselves as having characteristics, experiences, or goals in common. This sense of identification promotes the feeling of "us." Often a group culture may develop that enhances the members' sense of being part of the group. Examples may include dress (like the jackets worn by a certain gang), rituals (like ending each group meeting with a song), norms (celebrating members' birthdays in a special way), and even language (such as nicknames members may have for one another). These elements are certainly not always present, but when they do occur they tend to strengthen members' feelings of "groupness."

So in trying to decide whether your human service class is really a group, ask yourself these questions: Is the class small enough so that everyone can comfortably interact with everyone else? Do the students and professor actually interact with each other? Does the class meet over a significant period of time? Do the students and professor influence each other in any meaningful way? Do they have compatible goals that are being met in class? And finally, is there a feeling of unity or "us" in the class? If you can answer these questions in the affirmative, you may consider your class a true group.

THE USE OF GROUPS IN HUMAN SERVICES

There is a great deal of variety in the way groups are used in human services. Most human service agencies run groups; some will conduct several different kinds, according to the needs of their clients. Zastrow (1993), Heffernan et al. (1992), and others have described several different types of groups that may be found in human service settings. They vary in their purpose, activity, benefits to members, and skills required to lead them.

Recreation groups provide members with the opportunity for enjoyment and entertainment through sports, games, or crafts. They are found at YMCAs and YWCAs, community centers, hospitals, nursing homes, and other settings. Sometimes they arise spontaneously and may, in fact, be leaderless. In other cases they have leaders employed by the agency. One of their main goals is to provide members with the opportunity for social interaction. A number of people playing bingo in a nursing home is an example of this type of group.

Skill-building recreation groups are often found in the same settings as simple recreation groups and have the same goals of providing diversion and the opportunity for interaction. However, they have an additional purpose: to teach or improve member skill in some activity, such as sports, crafts, or cooking. Usually, the leader has some expertise in the activity being conducted. As members become proficient, self-esteem is often increased. An example is an after-school basketball group at the local community center.

Educational groups provide members with the opportunity to acquire knowledge or more complex skills. They are different from classes in that they encourage more interaction among members and, in fact, this is one of their goals. They may be led by human service workers who have both the skill required to conduct groups and sufficient expertise in the area being taught. Examples are assertiveness training groups, natural childbirth classes, and in-service training seminars.

Problem-solving groups may also be called task-oriented or decision-making groups. The goal of the group could be to solve a particular problem (like the lack of after-school care in a community) or make a decision that will affect many people (whether kindergarten in the public school should be extended to a full day). Although members may personally benefit in some way by participating in the group, their purpose in coming together and their roles within the group are related to the group's particular goals. Leadership in problem-solving groups may emerge from among the members or may be provided externally by the agency sponsoring the group. Examples include consumer groups, community action groups, and task forces.

Socialization groups may be led by human service workers and are found in a variety of settings, such as schools, prisons, psychiatric hospitals, and community centers. Their goals include helping clients to develop social skills, acceptable behavior, enhanced self-confidence, increased motivation, and more positive attitudes. They may be based on discussion or, especially with adolescents, may revolve first around an activity and then discussion. Socialization groups are very effective in working with delinquent and predelinquent youth.

Self-help groups are composed of people with similar problems or needs who come together to help themselves and one another. Leadership is usually selected from among the members, although sometimes human service workers may act as advisors. Depending on the group, the orientation might be recreational (like Parents Without Partners), therapeutic (like Alcoholics Anonymous), or problem-solving (like a group of parents of developmentally disabled children). Self-help groups are often found in churches, community centers, and hospitals.

Psychotherapy groups are usually led by trained professionals, often having advanced degrees. Either alone or together with individual therapy, the goal of psychotherapy groups is to help clients explore and resolve emotional problems. Family therapy and couples groups are special types of group therapy. Therapy groups are usually run in hospitals, mental health clinics, and other social agencies and by therapists in private practice.

STAGES OF GROUP DEVELOPMENT

Groups, like the people that make them up, are not static entities. They are constantly evolving and changing as they move toward the achievement of their goals. If you were to look in on the first meeting of a couples group, for example, you might see eight or ten people appearing a bit awkward and uncomfortable. Perhaps a few would be sitting silently; others might be laughing nervously, not sure of what to say or do. Suppose that, several weeks later, you had the opportunity to observe the group again. Chances are you would find members very busy discussing issues of importance to them, asking each other questions, giving feedback, and making suggestions. The uneasiness that you initially noticed would be gone, and in its place you would find friendship and concern. Finally, some time later, you might find yourself looking in on the group again, this time at one of its last meetings, and you may see that it has continued to change. Now members may be expressing regret, anxiety, or perhaps even resentment that the group is about to end. Perhaps they are planning a party for the last session or exchanging phone numbers to ensure continued contact. Could these be the same people you observed months before who seemed to have nothing to say to one another? Can groups really change that much? Indeed they can, and they do. We refer to these changes as the process of "group development." Several small-group theorists have proposed models of group development in which they describe the stages that groups pass through from the time they are formed until they end. One of the most valuable models was proposed by Margaret Hartford (1971), who outlined ten stages, or phases, in the development of a group.

Pregroup Phases.   This is the first stage in the development of a group, and as such it is one of the most important. There are three pregroup phases:

> *Pregroup private phase:* In this phase, a worker realizes that there is the need for a group, and he or she decides to start one. The worker may

or may not discuss these intentions with others. He or she thinks about the group and makes all the necessary decisions involved in the beginning (e.g., goals, number of members, length of meetings, and location). At this point, the group exists primarily in the mind of the worker.

Pregroup public phase: It is here that the worker's decision to form a group becomes known. Depending on the type of group, he or she may speak with each potential member individually to discuss joining (as in a psychotherapy group) or may send or post notices (as in a tenants' meeting). Potential members may be asked about their preferences regarding time, length of meeting, or meeting place.

Pregroup convening phase: This is the point at which the members come together for the first time. They engage in introductions and small talk, try to find mutual interests, and attempt to present themselves favorably. Members may be anxious and not sure that they want to belong. The worker's main task at this stage is to help them develop trust and a beginning commitment to the group. This can be done in many ways, such as restating the goals of the group, asking members to discuss their expectations, and pointing out areas of commonality. Sometimes structured group exercises are helpful. At this stage, the worker would also make known such things as number of weeks the group will meet, length of meetings, and whether refreshments will be served.

Case 1

Josie is a human service fieldwork intern placed in a program for the elderly in a community center in New York City. About eighty clients come to the center daily and participate in a range of recreation and crafts activities. Shortly after beginning her internship, Josie became aware that some of the clients were experiencing serious health problems that were beginning to impact on their sense of well-being and caused them anxiety about their ability to function independently in the future. She noticed that, although many of the clients spoke to her and her supervisor individually about their concerns, they rarely spoke about them with one another. She believed that the clients would benefit greatly from participating in a group situation where these issues and concerns could be discussed openly.

Josie, in the pregroup private phase of the development of the group, thought about her ideas for the group and then discussed them with her supervisor. The goals of the group, she decided, would be to provide an opportunity for mutual support and the sharing of concrete suggestions by clients who were experiencing similar health concerns. She decided that the group would be an open-ended one, would have six to eight members (both men and women), and would meet on Wednesdays after lunch for one hour. Finding a quiet, private place for the group to meet was not an easy task, but her supervisor offered the use of her office, which, if membership were limited to six, would be adequate.

In the pregroup public phase, Josie identified several clients who met the criteria for acceptance into the group. She spoke with each individually, explaining the purpose of the group and the potential benefits of belonging. She also mentioned the day, time, and place and gave an outline of what topics might be discussed. Two of the clients were not interested in joining, and two others did not attend program activities regularly enough to participate in the group. Josie was still able to identify five clients who were eager to be included, and she notified each that the first group meeting would be on the following Wednesday.

On that day, the group met for the first time (the pregroup convening phase). Josie was a little anxious as she had never led a group before and she quickly noticed that the members themselves seemed nervous as well. She knew that was to be expected. Most of them knew one another by sight but had never really spoken, and there was a lot of talk about the weather and the food offered at the center. There was also some nervous laughter among the members. Josie had prepared a group exercise that she developed to help them begin to get to know one another; they participated, reluctantly at first, but soon were enjoying themselves and seemed much less anxious. After the exercise, Josie explained the purpose of the group and her ideas about the kinds of things she thought they might like to discuss. She was fairly active in her

role as the leader because she realized that this would provide appropriate structure and make the members more comfortable, but she frequently asked for their comments and suggestions. She also tried to point out areas of commonality among members, noting, for example, that Hilda and Ann were both expert knitters and that Sam and Carmen were both born in California. The members spoke a bit about their health concerns, but the main focus of that first meeting was getting to know, and feel comfortable with, one another. By the time the hour was up, they seemed at ease, and some stated that they were looking forward to the next time they met.

Group Formation Phase.   During this phase, group norms and group identity begin to develop. Members start to find their roles within the group; they become committed and begin to influence one another. They begin to see that they have common goals, and they start working to attain them. They begin to see the group as an entity apart from other groups. This stage is very important, because without it, the collection of people will never become a true group. The worker should help members clarify their goals and expectations, reinforce appropriate roles, encourage them to share and identify, and stress the positive aspects of belonging.

Case 2

Liz is a recreation leader at a residential treatment center for girls. Her group, a cooking group of preteens, met for the first time two weeks ago. Liz had decided that planning and cooking a meal every week would allow the girls the opportunity to learn and practice such behaviors as sharing, taking turns, resolving conflicts, following directions, and working cooperatively. There were six girls in the group between the ages of ten and twelve. The group met weekly for about three hours, during which time they planned, shopped for, and prepared a simple meal and then enjoyed eating it with a few invited guests.

Liz knew that these first few meetings in the life of a group were very important in setting the stage for what would follow. For this reason, she dis-

*cussed the rules that the girls would have to fol-
low, such as being on time, using appropriate language, and helping to clean up. Liz was careful to
recognize and reinforce positive norms. For example, Ellen always arrived on time, and Liz remembered to mention this in the group in an approving
way. Sandra, who wanted very much to make the
dessert last week, was willing to compromise and
work on the soup, for which Liz thanked her. Liz
also saw different roles begin to emerge in the
group and did what she could to strengthen appropriate ones. Stephanie, for example, was the one
who seemed to try to help the other girls resolve
their disagreements, and Liz always remembered
to praise her for this.*

*Liz also tried to foster cohesiveness within the
group. One way she did this was by talking about
the group in a positive way and mentioning that
there were other girls who wanted to join but there
was no room for them. This made the members
feel that their group was special and important.
She also helped build cohesiveness by pointing
out areas of commonality among the girls, such as
the fact that Ellen and Stephanie both loved inline
skating. Liz was aware that she was a role model
for group members and tried to act accordingly in
her language and behavior and in the attitudes
and values she expressed. Although the group
members did have conflicts, especially in the next
stage, these conflicts were much easier to resolve
because of the way in which Liz handled the group
formation phase.*

Integration, Disintegration, or Reintegration.
This phase occurs in many but not all groups. This
is a period when members are no longer on their
best behavior. They may become disenchanted
with one another and with the group and may show
resistance, anger, hostility, or withdrawal. Power
struggles may develop, and decisions already made
may suddenly be reversed. The group may spend a
great deal of time focusing on interpersonal issues
in trying to resolve its conflicts. The worker's role
during this phase would include encouraging discussion and resolution of conflicts and helping
members see that this stage is a natural one in the

development of groups. Sometimes it may be necessary to change group purposes, roles, or tasks.
For example, a worker has put together a group of
concerned family members of patients in a
chronic-disease hospital. The group decides to
organize a trip for some of the patients with the
hospital's permission. Each member has a task to
perform (e.g., obtaining funds, arranging for the
bus, or getting the food). At first, everyone is very
enthusiastic, but as the group begins to move
toward this stage, some members think the trip is
too difficult to arrange. There is arguing about
whether members are accomplishing their
assigned tasks. One woman, who had often acted
as a leader, becomes very bossy, and the other
members object. The worker must intervene here
to help the group members solve their problems
and regain their enthusiasm. In general, if the
worker and members successfully resolve the
issues that arise at this stage, the group will move
forward into the next. However, if attempts at resolution fail, the group may not be able to continue.

Case 3

*Chris was employed as an assistant community
outreach worker at a local HIV/AIDS clinic in the
Bronx. He and his supervisor had been working
with local residents to plan a block party and fair
to increase community awareness of HIV/AIDS
prevention and related issues. Chris had identified
a group of eleven adults and teenagers who had
met weekly for nearly a month to plan the event. As
the group members were, for the most part, highly
motivated, Chris took on the role of advisor to the
group rather than the role of the leader. The actual
"leader" was Alba, an energetic and enthusiastic
young woman whom the others respected. It was
unanimously decided at the first meeting that she
would organize the group and run the meetings.
Also at that session, members identified tasks to be
accomplished, and each volunteered to take
responsibility for one of them. Sam, for example,
would contact the local police precinct to find out
about closing the street on the day of the fair.
Tamika agreed to visit the local merchants in a*

fund-raising effort to buy balloons and other decorations. Alan had friends in a band and agreed to ask them to play for free. Denise said she would call other community agencies to enlist their support and participation.

The second and third meetings of the group went smoothly. A date for the fair was set, decisions were made regarding important details, and some members reported their progress in their areas of responsibility. At the fourth meeting, Chris noticed that some members were absent and others very late. He mentioned this but otherwise allowed Alba to lead the meeting as usual. Suddenly, Denise said that she was finding it difficult to attend the meetings because she felt she was ignoring her children. Tamika agreed and added that she felt that her "job" (contacting local merchants) was more difficult and time-consuming than the others and she really hadn't had a chance to visit many of the stores. Sam, who came in late, expressed his annoyance at Tamika. He said that by not doing what she agreed to do she was letting the group down. Alba pointed out that by coming in so late Sam was also letting the group down, at which point Liz asked Alba who had put her in charge and suggested that the group reconsider whom they wanted as leader.

Chris watched and listened to what was happening and knew that these conflicts were common in the group's current stage of development. He knew also that he would have to help the group address these issues and resolve the conflicts or they might intensify and interfere with the group's ability to accomplish its tasks. He asked the members if he could have the floor for a few minutes, and they readily agreed. He explained that the problems they were experiencing often occurred after a group had met several times; this seemed to reassure them, and there was some relieved laughter. Chris then proceeded to help the group examine and resolve the issues that were presented: the leadership of the group (they all agreed that Alba was doing a fine job and should remain as leader), the uneven distribution of work (it was decided that Alan would help Tamika contact the local store owners), and attendance and punctuality (members restated their agreement to attend and be on time for all meetings). Members also agreed to try to handle future conflicts in a more constructive manner. To strengthen the members' commitment to the work of the group, Chris restated its purpose enthusiastically, pointing out the value of what they were doing to their own community.

Group Functioning and Maintenance Phase.

This phase of group development is very appropriately titled, whether it involves adolescents discussing personal problems, community residents planning a new day care program, or nurses organizing a holiday party on a pediatric ward. This is the stage in which most of the work of the group takes place. As the group becomes focused on achieving its goals, members become increasingly committed to the process and to one another. Defenses are lowered, and genuine affection and trust are felt. Group identity is strong. Generally by this stage a group culture has formed, and there are observable norms of behavior. For example, members may sit in the same place week after week; they may have group jokes that outsiders would not find funny; they may always start or end the meetings in the same way. This is usually a period of strong cohesion within the group. If a new member entered now, he or she would certainly feel like an outsider. During this phase, the worker should praise the work of the group and encourage members' efforts. Depending on the style of leadership (discussed later), the worker may or may not actually participate, but should be ready to intervene if conflicts develop.

Case 4

Hector is a social work assistant in a nonprofit nursing home in upstate New York. There are 250 residents in the home, and most have lived there for more than three years. Nearly all have family members living in the area, although many of the relatives don't visit. About six months ago, Hector organized a Family Council at the home made up of any relatives and close friends of the residents who chose to attend. The purpose of the group was to raise money for some "extras" for the residents and to address any issues and concerns that impacted on their quality of life. The group meets monthly and has twelve regular members, including an elected president and secretary; there are an additional six or eight members who have attended often but not every month.

The Family Council, like most groups, passed through a conflict phase, but with Hector's help the major issues were resolved. Now they were in the group functioning and maintenance phase, and he has been able to act more in the role of advisor, allowing them to set priorities, develop plans, and take action with minimal direction from him. Mr. Brown was elected council president and ran the meetings. They had just completed a successful clothing drive for the benefit of those residents who had need of clothing that they could not afford to buy. Mrs. Rivera, the council secretary, helped the group develop a questionnaire to assess the current needs of the residents. She was very well organized and often the one who kept the group focused on the task at hand. Hector was aware that group norms (such as members respecting one another's right to have the floor and people bringing coffee with them to the meetings) were being established and that members' roles were being more clearly defined. Attendance and punctuality were both good, and members were making good use of group time. In general, people were getting along well, and the group was becoming increasingly cohesive. The evidence for this was apparent: Members were willing to do their share toward making their projects a success, there was usually a positive feeling in the room (and sometimes very funny jokes were cracked), members often commented on the fact that they felt that what they were doing was worthwhile, members often encouraged others to join the council because of their positive experience, and conflicts were resolved without much difficulty when they occurred. Hector often pointed out his observations about how well the members were doing to reinforce their progress. When new members joined the council, there was a brief period of adjustment, but then the work continued as before.

Termination Phases.   This is an important point in a member's participation in a group; we will examine it again when we discuss worker skills

later on. It is important to realize that at some point the group will either end or, if it continues, members will eventually leave the group. Endings generally are emotional times for people, and throughout the process of termination the worker must be alert to the reactions of members and be prepared to help them deal with their feelings. Like the beginning of the group, the ending has three phases.

> *Pretermination phase:* This refers to the period immediately before the ending of the group or before a member leaves. In a short-term group, the members have known from the beginning that the group will end but should be reminded in advance. Workers should help the members enumerate and evaluate the group's accomplishments and failures. They should encourage members to discuss their feelings and, if necessary, help them work through the difficulties they have in breaking ties. It should be remembered that the worker, too, may have feelings about terminating.

> *Termination:* This refers to the last session of the group or the last session for a particular member. It may be a regular meeting, or it may be a party or special activity that was planned in the pretermination phase. These might help to formalize the ending and make separation easier. At the last meeting some members may make plans to stay in touch in the future, especially if the group was a close one.

> *Posttermination phase:* This stage in group development occurs only in some groups. Members may reconvene after the summer in a group that ended in June; some groups meet at regular or occasional intervals (like once or twice a year), much like a reunion, to keep in touch. Some groups that accomplish the task they were created to perform go on to become informal friendship groups. However, most groups in fact usually do end, although some members may stay in touch.

Case 5

Diana is employed as a social worker in a community mental health center in a large suburban town. Nearly two months ago she began a ten-week group of seven women who were recently separated or divorced. The group met weekly for two hours, and the members had developed a great deal of cohesiveness over the past several weeks. They were about to begin their eighth meeting, which Diana believed was the appropriate time to begin to discuss the realities of termination. When the members arrived and settled into their chairs, Diana began the group by reminding them that, after tonight, they would be meeting only twice more. Although the members knew that the group had contracted for ten sessions, many were surprised that there were only two remaining as time had seemed to move so quickly.

As Diana had led several similar groups, she was aware of her responsibilities during the pretermination phase of the group's development. During that session and the one that followed, she helped each member recognize the gains she had made during the past two months. Susan, for example, had found a job, something she had been very anxious about doing at the beginning of the group. Audrey was finally able to accept the fact that her husband was seeking a divorce and no longer tried to convince him to move back into the home. The acceptance would enable her to get on with her life in the months ahead. Each of the seven members had made progress toward achieving the goals she had expressed at the first group meeting, and Diana knew how important it was to recognize and reinforce this progress.

Diana also realized that each of the members had feelings about the fact that the group was ending, and she knew that it was crucial to allow each an opportunity to express those feelings. She asked the members to share their reactions to the ending of the group. Luisa said that she was grateful for the opportunity to participate and that she was looking forward to beginning a cooking class on Tuesday evenings after the group was over. Ann expressed sadness that she wouldn't be seeing other members every week anymore, as the group had grown to become an important part of her life. Sarah began to cry and said she was very worried because she had no one else in her life to offer her the kind of support she had gotten from the other members. As she was listening, Diana made a

mental note to speak with Sarah after the meeting to give her the name and number of a social worker at the clinic whom Sarah could see if she was feeling the need to do so after the group terminated.

At the ninth meeting, Diana asked the group if they would like to plan a party or activity for the following week. She knew that this was an important way to help members achieve closure around the group experience. They decided not to have a special activity but rather to bring in some refreshments and otherwise have the last group meeting be similar to all the others.

The actual termination phase of the group occurred at the tenth and last meeting. While having coffee and cookies, the women discussed some of their concerns and plans for the future. Sarah tried to convince Diana to allow the group to meet a few more times, which she briefly considered. She realized, though, that the women had gained a great deal from the group and that it was best to end at the tenth week as planned. She explained this, and they understood. Diana reminded the members that they could always contact the clinic if they ever felt the need to do so in the future. The cohesion that the group had achieved was very much in evidence, and there was some sadness at the final good-byes.

Diana's group never met again and thus did not experience a posttermination phase in the true sense. A few of the women got together for dinner but eventually lost touch with one another. Although Diana herself felt as though something was "missing" the following Tuesday evening, she knew that the group had been a success and that the members' lives had been changed in a very positive way as a result of participating in the group experience.

In considering the development of any group, it is important to remember that although all groups may pass through stages as they grow and change, there is a great deal of variation in the timing and sometimes in the order in which the stages occur. At times a group might regress to a former stage, as when, for example, an unexpected change in leadership causes a group to move from the group functioning and maintenance phase back to the conflict that typifies the disintegration phase. Some groups may skip certain stages completely.

The leader has a great deal of responsibility in helping the group grow and develop. The definition of the leader's role and the tasks performed will change as the group moves from stage to stage. It is important, then, for the leader to be aware of which stage the group is in at any given time and the ways in which to help the group successfully negotiate that stage.

FACTORS TO CONSIDER IN FORMING A NEW GROUP

Suppose that you are a beginning human service worker employed in a nursing home. Although the facility is clean and the residents are well cared for, you've noticed that many of them seem bored and lonely. You've also seen that, except for meal times, few residents actually interact with each other. Your supervisor confirms your perceptions and asks how you might change the situation. You decide, then, to form a group. You realize that there are some important choices to be made in setting up your group and that these decisions will affect the experiences of both the members and the leader for the duration of the group's life. Let's examine these variables.

Group Goals.   Before you begin to put together a group, you must understand your goals. Why do you want to run a group? What do you hope the group will accomplish? How might the individual members benefit from participating? In a nursing home, some examples of goals include providing social interaction, learning a skill, increasing self-image, strengthening memory, and promoting independence of functioning. It is especially important to understand your goals because, as we will see, many of the decisions you will make in setting up your group will depend on how you define your goals.

Group Type.   Once you are clear about the goals, you must decide on the type of group that would best help you and the clients achieve those goals. A bingo group, for example, would certainly help to relieve boredom and stimulate mental activity, but perhaps a discussion group might be a better choice. A discussion group would provide more interaction among members and might promote friendships that would continue to exist beyond the group. The point here is that there are many different types of groups that could be run in any particular setting; it is up to you to consider each type and choose the one that would best help meet the goals.

Group Size.   How many clients should you include in your group? There are many factors to consider in making this decision. Among the most important are your goals and the type of group you've decided to run. A bingo or exercise group could obviously be larger than a discussion group. Another factor to consider in determining group size is the setting in which your group will take place; if you are limited to a small space, you must have a small group. It is also worthwhile to examine member characteristics here. Those with short attention spans or behavioral problems, for example, might do better in a smaller group, where they would benefit from more attention from the leader and other members. In general, you must be sure that your group is large enough for members to have a true group experience yet not so large that some don't have an opportunity to participate.

Member Characteristics.   Factors such as age and gender may or may not be important to take into account in establishing a group. Once again, you must first look at your goals and then at the type of group you are creating. Age and gender are probably not important in most nursing home groups, but they could certainly be significant factors in a group for adolescents in a community center. What about other member characteristics? Depending on the type of group and the nature of the client population, you may want to consider a potential member's level of motivation, attention span, personality, ways of dealing with frustration and anger, strengths and weaknesses, and life situation. In selecting members for your group, it's important to think not only about whether a particular client might benefit from the group experience but also about the effect that person might have on other members and on the group process. A confused and aggressive nursing home resident might benefit from the social contact provided by a discussion group, but how would the other members' experiences in the group be affected by including this person? These factors must be carefully considered.

Group Setting.   To some extent, the location of the group will be determined by the type of group you're running. A cooking group tends to work best in a kitchen; a sport group may require a gym or other open space. In groups that focus on discussion as their main activity, the comfort and privacy of members should be the most important consideration in choosing a location. Factors such as size of room, seating, and lighting could promote or hinder interaction. Consider, for example, the difference between holding a therapy group in a classroom-type setting (large space, hard chairs, fluorescent lights, cold floor) versus the same group meeting in a room more like a living room with comfortable sofas, table lamps, and carpeting. While we acknowledge the impact of setting on group process, in reality many human service workers have little choice about where to run their groups. Agency space is often quite limited, and sometimes we gratefully take whatever room we can get.

Closed- or Open-Ended Group.   A closed-ended group is a group in which membership remains stable for the life of the group; that is, certain members join the group when it is formed,

they generally remain in the group throughout its duration, and no new members are added. An example of a closed-ended group is a college seminar that usually begins and ends with the same students. In an open-ended group, new members are added as other members leave. Although the number may remain constant, the actual membership changes over time. Alcoholics Anonymous groups are open ended. There are advantages to both types. Open-ended groups are sometimes more dynamic, constantly changing as members come and go. They also eventually allow participation by a greater number of people. Closed-ended groups may become more cohesive as members come to feel comfortable with one another. Whether a closed- or open-ended group will work best depends on the goals of the group, the needs of the client population, and in some cases the policy of the agency.

Number and Length of Sessions.   A long-term group is one that continues for months or even years. Long-term groups are often open ended. A short-term group is one that will meet only for a specified length of time or number of sessions. A college seminar is short term, usually meeting for one semester. Some group workers believe in the advantages of running short-term groups. Members often work harder on changing behavior or accomplishing tasks if they know they have only a limited amount of time to achieve what they've set out to do. In some cases, though, it would make more sense to organize a long-term group. Returning to our nursing home example, an activity or discussion group would best be long term with continued social contact and mental stimulation to meet the ongoing needs of the residents. The length of each session must also be determined and the nature of the group and the needs of its members considered. A therapeutic group of young addicts in recovery could last for hours, whereas a reality orientation group of confused clients might last only thirty minutes. The session must be long enough so that all members can participate and the group is able to make progress toward its goals. In some cases, sufficient time must be allotted for a specific task to be accomplished or project completed. However, if a group session is too long, members may become bored and restless.

Selection of a Program.   Within the context of group goals and type, the leader must make some decisions about programming in the group. Programming refers to what the group will actually do when it meets; it is through programming that the goals of the group are reached. If a crafts group is being planned, thought must be given to the kinds of crafts projects that will be undertaken. If it's a cooking group, what kinds of food will be prepared, and how will tasks be organized? What topics would be appropriate for a discussion group? A program, if appropriately chosen and carried out, will facilitate reaching group goals. It is very important to the success of the group that it be carefully planned in advance.

It is clear from our discussion thus far that there are many options, possibilities, and variables that must be considered during the group formation process. It is important that a group leader consider each of these to facilitate maximum effectiveness of the group.

GROUP LEADERSHIP

According to Zastrow (1993), leadership exists within a group whenever one person exerts influence over another and thereby helps the group achieve its goals. Most members, at times, engage in leadership behavior; however, in most groups the human service worker is generally the acknowledged leader. The ways in which the worker defines his or her role and performance in carrying out leadership tasks are crucial to the success of the group.

More than fifty years ago, Kurt Lewin and his colleagues (R. Lippitt and R. K. White), pioneers in the field of social psychology, identified three distinct styles of group leadership and described the ways in which they affect group performance. These are presented by Vander Zanden (1990) and are still considered current and valid today.

In the authoritarian style, the leader determines the policies of the group. He or she assigns tasks, gives detailed directions, and frequently praises or criticizes members according to their performance. Although he or she is active within the leadership role, the leader rarely participates in the ongoing activities of the group. This type of leadership often produces a great deal of frustration among group members and feelings of hostility toward the leader. The group may be very productive as long as the leader is there, but members don't work nearly as hard when he or she is absent.

In the laissez-faire style of leadership, the leader remains passive and uninvolved; he or she may even be perceived by group members as withdrawn. The leader is willing to provide materials, help, and suggestions but generally does so only when these are requested. He or she tends not to evaluate member performance. In groups led according to this style, there may be high levels of aggression among members, and group morale and productivity are normally low.

Finally, there is the democratic style, in which the leader encourages the members to determine the group's goals and the means of achieving them. Alternatives are suggested, but it is the members who make the decision. This type of leader usually participates in the activities of the group and evaluates member performance fairly and objectively. In this type of group, cohesion is high. Members are happier, friendlier toward one another, and more group oriented. They are motivated to work hard, even in the leader's absence.

The research by Lewis and others who study the dynamics of small groups clearly illustrates the impact of leadership behavior on group performance, goal attainment, and member satisfaction.

Leadership style will vary, depending on the nature of the group, its stage of development, and the needs of the members. The personality of the leader will also affect the ways in which he or she carries out this role, much the same way that your professor's personality will affect the way classes are conducted. Be that as it may, what exactly does a group leader do? What skills are required to lead a group? How is the process of working with groups different from working with individuals? In a sense, there is a great deal of similarity between helping clients individually and in groups. In the first place, the values are the same. Human service workers believe in honesty, in the inherent worth of the person, in being nonjudgmental, in promoting self-determination, and in protecting confidentiality, regardless of whether the clients are being seen in a group or one at a time. The basic helping skills are also the same. Among them are observing, listening, questioning, assessing, clarifying, confronting, and giving feedback. (These skills are discussed in different contexts throughout this book.) These skills, and others, are necessary for the human service worker to have and use with individual clients and with groups.

Schmolling, Youkeles, and Burger (1993) have further identified seven skills that are involved more specifically in working with groups: selecting group members, establishing goals, establishing group norms, intervening, promoting interaction, appraising and evaluating, and terminating.

Let's examine the way these skills are used in practice.

Selecting Group Members.   In putting together a new group or replacing a member who has left an existing group, it is important for the worker to consider several factors, including personality, motivation, interests, and perhaps age and gender. The needs of the individual members, as well as the balance within the group, must be taken into account. The worker should approach potential members individually and explain the goals of the group and when and where it will meet. Partici-

pation is generally more successful if members know as much as possible about the group before it actually begins.

Establishing Goals.   As we've discussed, the group worker must be active in establishing goals for the group, sometimes with input from the members. A tenants' group, for example, may have as its goal to get the landlord to provide a night security guard. A community group of working parents might have as a goal the development of an after-school program for members' children. The worker must be careful to establish only goals that are feasible for the members to attain within the amount of time available.

Members have their own goals in joining a group. Some examples are to resolve a personal conflict, to interact with others, or to do something useful. The single father who participates in the parents' group to build a playground may, in addition to wanting the playground, see the group as a way of meeting new people and having an evening out.

Establishing Group Norms.   The worker must be active in setting clear rules of behavior at the beginning of the group. This is important so that the group can work together to achieve its goals. Different norms would be significant in different groups. In a treatment group for substance abusers, maintaining confidentiality would be central to the functioning of the group. The worker would explain to the members why it would be vital not to discuss the group with any nonmembers. In a group of community residents who come together to fund and build a playground, one important norm would be for members to carry out their tasks thoroughly and on time. If the members didn't do this, the playground would never get built.

Intervening.   A worker running a group must listen carefully and be ready to step in at any time. Sometimes, leaders may point out something they are observing (e.g., that one member consistently arrives late or that one member often stands up for another). Sometimes, leaders may make a suggestion, offer a different perspective, provide feedback, or help settle a conflict. How much or how little the worker intervenes should depend primarily on the needs of the group and its members. But human service workers have their own styles of relating to others, which would affect the way they participate in the group process.

Promoting Interaction.   Positive interaction among members is generally necessary for the group to do the work it was intended to do. It also furthers the opportunity for mutual support and helps to develop group cohesiveness. Whether the group is baking a cake, planning a rent strike, or discussing the problems of childhood, it is important that members speak to one another and listen as well. How does the worker promote positive interaction among members? He or she may help members express themselves clearly; relate the concerns of one member to the concerns of another; encourage politeness; be an active listener; and take turns. Also, helping members explore and resolve conflicts, if they exist, goes a long way toward promoting positive interaction.

Appraising and Evaluating.   Workers must continually examine what is occurring in the group. For example, they must evaluate how well members relate to one another, the level of member satisfaction, the extent to which the group is moving toward attaining its goals, the presence of any conflicts or obstacles, and their own performance as group leaders. Sometimes leaders may choose to involve the members in this evaluation. Depending on the outcome of the evaluation, leaders may decide to intervene in a specific way. If, for example, leaders determine that the group is not as organized as it should be, they may choose to help members assign tasks and responsibilities. Or, if

leaders notice that the members are uneasy with one another, they may design a group exercise to increase familiarity. Evaluation, then, often implies action.

Termination.   A group may end for different reasons. If it is a short-term group meeting for a limited number of sessions, it will end at the last session. If the group was created to solve a particular problem, it will generally end when the problem is solved. Sometimes, as in the case of long-term groups, the actual group doesn't end but individual members may leave. This is, in a sense, a personal ending. As we discussed in the section on the stages of group development, workers have some very specific tasks to achieve in the process of termination. First, they must give the group notice, in advance, that the group will be ending. Even in a group that is scheduled to end, the members may not realize when the termination will occur. Second, because different people react to endings in different ways, leaders must allow members the opportunity to explore and express their feelings around the end of the group. Some may feel sad, anxious, or even angry. Third, workers may encourage the group to plan some sort of party or other celebration to make its ending. This is especially important in groups that have become particularly close. Finally, workers may want to discuss with the members some plan for addressing issues or problems that may occur after the group is over. Termination is the last stage in the evolution of a group, and as such it is important to handle it in a professional manner.

Skill in establishing and leading groups, like generic human service skills, is developed gradually over time. Knowledge gained in class, experience and supervision in the field, and on-the-job learning after graduation all contribute to the acquisition of these skills. One of the students' most important resources, though, is the ability to examine and critically evaluate their own feelings and behavior when working with groups.

REFERENCES

Hartford, M. E. (1971). *Groups in Social Work.* New York: Columbia University Press.

Heffernan, J., G. Shuttlesworth, and R. Ambrosino (1992). *Social Work and Social Welfare, An Introduction,* 2nd ed. St. Paul: West.

Myers, D. C. (1990). *Social Psychology,* 3rd ed. New York: McGraw-Hill.

Schmolling, P. Jr., M. Youkeles, and W. R. Burger (1993). *Human Services in Contemporary America,* 3rd ed. Pacific Grove, CA: Brooks/Cole.

Vander Zanden, J. W. (1990). *Sociology: The Core,* 2nd ed. New York: McGraw-Hill.

Zastrow, C. (1993). *Social Work with Groups,* 3rd ed. Chicago: Nelson-Hall.

SUGGESTED FURTHER READING

Mehr, J. (1992). *Human Services,* 5th ed. Boston: Allyn and Bacon.

Skidmore, R. A., M. G. Thackeray, and O. W. Farley (1991). *Introduction to Social Work,* 5th ed. Englewood Cliffs, NJ: Prentice-Hall.

CONFLICT RESOLUTION:
AN EXAMPLE OF USING SKILLS IN WORKING WITH GROUPS

JANET HAGEN

Conflict is a hallmark of being human. It is a factor in every facet of human relationships: within and between individuals, social groups, institutions, and nations. Conflict, of itself, is a positive force that, if harnessed, can move people and situations forward. Getting rid of conflict in any situation is therefore a questionable goal in that it is probably not achievable and very likely dysfunctional from a growth perspective. Intuitively, the student of conflict understands this basic functionality of conflict. Where there is only one voice, there is only one course. Where there are many voices, there are many choices. Indeed, effective groups often consciously bring conflict into an otherwise smooth problem-solving scenario by "playing the devil's advocate" and thereby introducing alternative points of view. The intra- and interpersonal and the intra- and interinstitutional dynamics at play in conflict are powerful engines that can lead to major contributions.

Conflict at its worst is destructive and is associated with human suffering and violence. It is no wonder, then, that some people and some groups tend to avoid conflict at all costs. The possible negative consequences of conflict handled badly far outweigh, in this view, the potential benefits of conflict handled well. Again, one does not need to look far to find many examples of conflict that has been subverted or, alternatively, conflict that has exploded.

The ubiquitous nature of conflict results in an interdisciplinary approach to its study. Law, soci-ology, anthropology, psychology, political science, education, business, human services, and others fields contribute to the understanding of conflict, both the problems and the promise. The nature of conflict studied varies by discipline, and different disciplines focus on different aspects. Law scholars, for example, focus primarily on conflicts handled through the legal system. Scholars in anthropology may focus on variations of conflict resolution through culture. All areas have contributions to be made in and from other areas. In this way the field of conflict and conflict resolution is truly interdisciplinary.

INFORMAL DISPUTE RESOLUTION

People deal with conflict without outside intervention every day. According to Deutsch (1973), the attitude that is most useful to effectively solving interpersonal conflict is one of concern for others with concurrent concern for self and an ability to understand and respond to another's needs as well as one's own. Different theorists postulate different conflict resolution styles. Blake and Mouton (1964) reported five: confronting, forcing, accommodating, compromising, and withdrawing. Putman and Wilson (1982), who developed a scale to measure communication styles in organizational conflicts, reported three styles: control, nonconfrontation, and solution orientation. Thomas and Kilmann (1974) report five styles: competing, collaborating, compromising, avoiding, and accommodating. Although there is a tendency to believe that one style is superior to all others, human behavior in conflict resolution, as in all other situations, must be taken in context. Thus, at certain times avoiding may be preferable to competing, which may be preferable at certain times to accommodating. The literature on coping and adapting is consistent in that the greater the number of behavioral strategies an individual can use, the better that person's ability to adjust. Most of us have one or two preferred styles for conflict resolution. Identifying those preferred styles with an eye toward developing other strategies for resolution can help ensure constructive outcomes.

Capozzoli (1995) listed four outcomes of conflict handled constructively and four outcomes of conflict mishandled. These outcomes can be used to evaluate the state of conflict resolution skills in interpersonal relationships, whatever the context. In constructive conflict the results are positive: People change and grow, a solution is generated, everyone affected is involved, and cohesiveness is developed. In destructive conflict the results are negative: No decision is reached and the problem still exists, energy is diverted from important tasks, morale is affected, and groups of people are polarized.

Some of the common themes that can lead to conflict, according to Capozzoli (1995), are differences in values, attitudes, needs, expectations, perception, resources, and personalities. In the conflict resolution process, a first step is often an exploration of the problem. The themes listed above can provide an initial framework by which to understand the conflict. Active listening and problem solving, two basic human service strategies, are paramount in effective conflict resolution.

FORMAL DISPUTE RESOLUTION

The Legal System

Until recently, the primary formal method of resolving conflict was through the court system—through a civil case or criminal case. In a civil case, the plaintiff, whose person or property has been injured, files a complaint against the defendant, who may be held liable for the particular injury. Civil law, also called torts, is considered to involve private wrongs between citizens. Criminal law is also about private wrongs between citizens (in fact, many crimes are also torts). However, in the case of criminal law, the wrongs are so serious as to be considered a crime against society. In criminal law, the governing unit brings charges against the person who may be found guilty. In civil law, the person who was wronged files the case. In criminal law, the state files the case. Because crimes are thought of as being against society, the particular victim is often displaced in the judicial process. As a response to the efforts of victims' advocate groups, the 1982 Omnibus Victim and Protection Act was enacted. This act provided, among other things, that victim impact statements be a part of sentencing, that victims be protected from intimidation, and that victims have a right to restitution.

ALTERNATIVE DISPUTE RESOLUTION

Alternative dispute resolution (ADR) refers to any of a group of procedures that formally resolve disputes through mechanisms other than the court system. Generally, ADR refers to arbitration or mediation in their varied forms. The goals of ADR are (1) to relieve court congestion, cost, and delay; (2) to enhance community involvement; (3) to facilitate access to justice; and (4) to provide more effective resolution (Carper, Mietus, Shoemaker, and West, 1995).

Arbitration. Arbitration is a formal process, similar to the legal process, whereby parties in conflict select a neutral third party to hear and decide the outcome of their conflict. The arbitrator acts as judge and jury in that the arbitrator is both the finder of fact and the finder of law.

Often, arbitration is binding. Every state and the federal government has statutes that provide for the judicial enforcement of a private arbitrator if the parties agreed to binding arbitration. Arbitration agreements are often part of an existing contract whereby the parties to the contract agree to use binding arbitration instead of the judicial system should a conflict arise, although it is possible that parties to a dispute will agree on arbitration without a prior contract. Arbitrators often have a high level of expertise in the topical area of the dispute. Organizations such as the American Arbitration Association provide procedural rules and administrative expertise.

Mediation.   Mediation involves the use of a neutral third party to assist voluntary parties to resolve their dispute. A solution is not imposed by the mediator; rather, the mediator facilitates the process by which the parties are empowered to develop a satisfactory solution of their own. The basic principles of mediation involve (1) a voluntary process; (2) the mediator serves as a neutral third party; (3) the role of the mediator is to facilitate the process whereby the needs of both parties are met; (4) the process is fair in that both parties perceive that the agreement was fair, regardless of how the mediator perceives the agreement; and (5) the basic process to mediation is (a) establishing ground rules, (b) telling and hearing each side of the story, (c) coming up with options for solving the conflict, (d) choosing and acting on the most viable alternatives, and (e) following up to ensure compliance.

The credentials required for mediation vary from state to state. Some states have licensing requirements, and others don't. Credentialed or not, mediators must have the following capabilities: (1) the ability to remain neutral—to allow parties to own the problem and solution; (2) active listening; (3) the ability to facilitate the empowerment of both parties; (4) the ability to stay on task in the mediation process; and (5) credibility, integrity, and respect for confidentiality. From this list, it is plain to see that the skills of a mediator include many of the skills of a successful human service practitioner. Some of the professional organizations to which mediators belong are the Academy of Family Mediators, Victim–Offender Mediation, and the American Bar Association. Five types of mediation programs are reviewed here: civil, child custody, family, victim-offender, and school programs.

Civil mediation programs in many communities are staffed by volunteer mediators with a coordinator often paid by the local court system. In this case, the first step for all civil cases filed, including small-claims court, is the opportunity to bypass litigation through mediation. In my county, the mediation coordinator sets aside one morning per week, at which time all disputants in new cases must appear. The goals and process of mediation are reviewed, as are the advantages. Those parties who are willing to proceed with mediation are provided with a volunteer mediator on the spot, and the mediation process begins. There are variations in the process, but parties to a formally filed complaint are offered the opportunity to try mediation first. If an agreement is reached, the civil charges are dropped.

Child-custody mediation in most jurisdictions is mandated, but reaching an agreement is not. Divorces usually occur after many years of unresolved conflict, yet it is critical for the minor children that some consensus be reached for mutually providing for their care. The skills of the mediator in this type of mediation are critical because the patterns of dysfunctional communication are likely to be firmly entrenched. A current controversy in the arena of divorce mediation concerns domestic abuse. On one side of the controversy are those who believe that, in cases of abuse, the power differential is so great that mediation cannot empower the person who was abused. Mediation, in this case, revictimizes the person by becoming an extension of the abuse. On the other side of the controversy is the thinking that the process of mediation can, in and of itself, empower people who were abused to take charge of their own needs and the needs of their children. At a very minimum, it is necessary for mediators to possess very highly developed skills, an awareness of the dynamics of abuse, and a clear understanding of their own personal issues that may come into play.

Family (or parent–teen) mediation helps parents and teens renegotiate conflicts in daily living and make realistic agreements. Often the initial conflicts that are mediated and agreements made are just the surface problems. Easily mediated are agreements for household chores, curfews, and allowance. Once negotiated and followed through, these successes can lead to new levels of trust. The higher trust allows for further mediation of more serious issues. Often the family mediation will require that participants address related issues, such as substance abuse, in a therapeutic setting. In these cases, referral must be made because mediation is not a substitute for counseling or other therapeutic programs. Once the underlying issues have been addressed, mediation can continue and is more likely to be successful since those issues will no longer serve to thwart the agreements.

Victim–offender mediation is the mediation of conflict between crime victims and their offenders. In this process, the mediator facilitates the ability of the parties to address informational and emotional needs, victim losses, and a restitution plan. Research has shown that victim–offender mediation is rated very highly by victims and results in a higher proportion of full restitution payment. Mark Umbreit has played a major role in the development of victim–offender mediation, as have the Mennonite Church and the concept of restorative justice (Zehr, 1990). The basic process of victim–offender mediation consists of four stages (Umbreit, 1994): intake, preparation, mediation, and follow-up. In the *intake phase,* the court refers the offender, the intake worker contacts the victim, and a mediator is assigned. In the

preparation phase, the mediator meets separately with the victim and the offender to explain the program, listen to the story of each person, and help the parties identify the potential benefits of the process. In the *mediation phase,* if both parties agree to participate, the mediator has a joint meeting with both parties. At this meeting the role of the mediator is reviewed, the ground rules are established, and each person is allowed to tell his or her story to the other person. Victims get a chance to meet the person who victimized them and ask questions like, How did you decide on my house? Will you come back? Why did you pick me? In the mediation, victims are able to see offenders as people, who often turn out not to be as frightening as they had imagined. The offender is put in the position of having to face squarely the person they have wronged. This process allows both parties to deal with each other as people rather than stereotypes. Meetings usually last one to two hours with a mutually acceptable restitution agreement developed. Mediators retain their neutral third-party status throughout to facilitate the process, and they do not influence the actual agreement. After the referral agency, often the court, approves the restitution agreement, the *follow-up phase* commences. In this stage, the restitution agreement is monitored until it is completed and final paperwork completed to close the case.

In some jurisdictions, mediation is mandated for the offender, although the victim always has a choice whether to mediate. The process of recovering from the trauma of being the target of crime varies for each person, and to prevent revictimization the victim must retain autonomy. Most victim–offender mediation programs start with juveniles involved in property crime and often develop quickly, and mediation for crimes such as burglary are now quite common. In the last ten years, increasingly more serious crimes have been mediated. A soon-to-be-released documentary, *Glimmer of Hope,* by the National Film Board of Canada, follows the mediation of a family trying to come to terms with the rape and murder of their nineteen-year-old-daughter. In this often painful video, it becomes clear that victim-offender mediation has the potential to facilitate healing, reconciliation, and closure.

School mediation programs provide children with an opportunity to resolve their own disputes. Effective programs generally provide three components: (1) conflict management curriculum in the classroom, (2) modeling of conflict resolution by adults, and (3) trained student mediators who provide services to other students. According to Schrumpf, Crawford, and Usadel (1991), peer mediation in a school setting helps students solve problems peacefully and develop skills to solve their own problems. It helps schools reduce disciplinary measures and increase time spent on matters other than discipline. Several different approaches have been used to implement peer mediation, the most promising of which, according to Wheeler (1995), is one whereby the school psychologist or counseling staff trains educators in conflict resolution principles, situations, and solutions. This training provides educators with the knowledge and materials to integrate conflict resolution into the classroom and to train specific students as mediators. The school psychologist or counselor then serves as an outside consultant. Peer mediators often work in pairs or with an adult supervisor to allow monitoring of the skill levels of the mediators. Some of the criteria for the selection of students as mediators include a good role model, representation from a cross section of student body, able to understand and learn mediation strategies, and good leadership abilities. As a human service professional, I recommend that thought be given to training *all* students as mediators. Too often I have seen selection criteria serve dysfunctionally in that "the rich get richer." This is a concept elaborated upon by Johnson and Johnson (1991), in reference to cooperative teams, that involves the ten-dency to select people who already have good skills to do more of what they are already good at and, simultaneously, to deny those with less-developed ability the chance to develop their skills. If we select peer mediators on the basis of previously demonstrated leadership skills, we are not supporting skill development of those in most need of the skills. Training and using *all* students as mediators would allow the development of leadership and problem-solving skills in more students. A downside to this philosophy is that although there is considerable evidence that many student mediators have greatly benefited from the experience (Deutsch, 1993), the major area of discontent is the lack of opportunity to mediate (Kaufman, 1991).

Although the school setting is different, the essentials of mediation principles are the same as in the aforementioned process and have been elaborated on already. Students must retain their neutrality, and parties to the dispute must enter mediation voluntarily. The voluntariness of mediation allows participants to "buy in" to the outcome. Alternative systems for resolution must be in place because students may choose not to mediate. Often the alternative is a solution imposed by school authorities. Within the ground rules are those problem areas that are outside mediation, usually those that break laws regarding weapons, drugs, or abuse.

School mediation programs generally report a high success rate in terms of whether the parties reach an agreement about how to solve their dispute. This success rate is usually 80 to 95 percent (Crary, 1992; Kaufman, 1991), which is comparable to other, nonschool mediation programs. Carruthers, Sweeney, Kamitta, and Harris (1996) compared the types of conflicts dealt with in various studies and determined that, in general, they can be categorized into gossip, property disputes, teasing/bullying, arguments, and fighting. The frequency of the type of conflict is situational and based on such things as the age and gender of the students and the setting of the school. Younger children tend to have disputes involving sharing and hurt feelings, whereas older children tend to have differences based on rumors/gossip or personal property. Urban settings are more likely to have disputes that become physical confrontations. No differences in types of conflicts by race have been established.

SUMMARY

Conflict, when managed positively, can provide constructive and mutually satisfying outcomes for those involved in the process. Effective communication skills are a critical element in most con-

flict resolution strategies, whether formal or informal. Generally, increasing interpersonal skills increases conflict resolution skills. Human service professionals are in a unique position wherein many of the skills that are imperative in conflict resolution are the same skills that serve as the foundation for human service strategies.

A variety of formal conflict resolution mechanisms exist: the legal system, arbitration, and mediation. Of the three, mediation is a process that most closely matches the core values of human service work: collaboration, respect, and the value of diversity. Open discussion of differences can establish an atmosphere in which conflict can become a positive agent for change.

REFERENCES

Blake, R. R., and I. S. Mouton (1964). *The Managerial Grid.* Houston: Gulf Publishing.

Capozzoli, T. (1995). "Conflict Resolution—A Key Ingredient in Successful Teams." *Supervision, 56*(12), 3–6.

Carper, D. L., N. J. Mietus, T. E. Shoemaker, and B. W. West (1995). *Understanding the Law.* St. Paul: West.

Carruthers, W., B. Sweeney, D. Kamitta, and G. Harris (1996). "Conflict Resolution: An Examination of the Research Literature and a Model for Program Evaluation." *School Counselor, 44,* 5–19.

Crary, D. R. (1992). "Community Benefits from Mediation: A Test of the 'Peace Virus' Hypothesis." *Mediation Quarterly, 9,* 241–252.

Deutsch, M. (1973). *The Resolution of Conflict: Constructive and Destructive Processes.* New Haven, CT: Yale University Press.

Deutsch, M. (1993). "Educating for a Peaceful World" *American Psychologist, 48,* 510–517.

Johnson, D. W., and R. T. Johnson (1991). *Learning Together and Alone: Cooperative, Competitive, and Individualistic Learning,* 3rd ed. Englewood Cliffs, NJ: Prentice-Hall.

Kaufman, S. (1991). *Assessment of the Implementation of Conflict Management Programs in 17 Ohio Schools: First-Year Report School Demonstration Project, 1990–93.* Columbus, OH: Ohio Commission on Dispute Resolution and Conflict Management.

Putman, L. L., and C. E. Wilson (1982). "Communications Strategies in Organizational Conflicts: Reliability and Validity of a Measurement Scale." *Communications Yearbook, 6,* 629–652.

Schrumpf, F., D. Crawford, and H. Usadel (1991). *Peer Mediation: Conflict Resolution in Schools.* Champaign, IL: Research Press.

Thomas, K. W., and R. H. Kilmann (1974). *Thomas-Kilmann Conflict Mode Instrument.* Tuxedo, NY: Xicom.

Umbreit, M. (1994). *Victim Meets Offender: The Impact of Restorative Justice and Mediation.* Monsey, NY: Willow Tree Press.

Wheeler, W. (1995). "Conflict Resolution through Peer Mediation." *Thrust for Educational Leadership, 25*(3), 32–35.

Zehr, H. (1990). *Changing Lenses: A New Focus for Crime and Justice.* Scottsdale, PA: Herald Press.

CHAPTER 8

NATIONAL COMMUNITY SUPPORT SKILL STANDARDS PROJECT:

IMPLICATIONS FOR HUMAN SERVICE EDUCATION

MARY DIGIOVANNI
FRANKLYN M. ROTHER
DAVID C. MALONEY

INTRODUCTION

This chapter reflects a necessary and timely effort to define, evaluate, and implement program standards for human service education with the most recent outcomes of the federally funded Community Support Skill Standards (CSSS) project. In the following pages, the reader will be given a detailed comparison and synthesis, where appropriate, of both the CSHSE standards and the CSSS competencies.

Historical Overview of the Need for, and Development of, National Skill Standards for CSHSPs

Changes in the societal expectations of human service delivery prompted by self-advocacy, scarce resources, and ideological shifts in the 1970s and 1980s led to a concentration on outcomes and quality-of-life issues. The purpose of human service interventions that promote changes in individual behavior, perspective, and social status and that provide life-sustaining supports became more focused on individualized support, institutional decentralization, and citizen participant involvement.

Human service agency providers became less hierarchical, encouraging recipient participation in their placement and treatment. This decentralization and flattening of organizational structures placed strong emphasis on collaboration among professionals working with recipients of services. At the same time, new community-based residential facilities and day activities programs promoted greater recipient participation and responsibility in improving their own life circumstances.

Direct care workers in these human service facilities were faced with new work demands and less supervision. An emphasis on tolerance of ambiguity, flexibility, and creativity in these new environments required greater future planning skills and a strong sense of personal professional behavior. This evolution of direct service worker skills required for professional performance in community support agency settings has converged with an inadequate labor pool, persistent low wages in the field, and the need for educational and training programs to teach the necessary values, vision, and competencies required for community support human service practice.

In 1993, the Human Services Research Institute in Cambridge, Massachusetts, received funding from the federal Departments of Education and Labor to participate in the original cohort of twenty-two industry pilot projects to identify national skill standards for entry-level and midlevel workers in community support human services settings. The vision of the National Skill Standards Board to establish skill standards for direct service workers by the year 2000 brought together members of consumer, employer, and educational organizations to research and determine the set of competencies required for direct service practitioners working in community support agencies.

A technical committee, headed by the HSRI project director, informed, guided, and participated in the three-year project, which led in 1996 to the publication of the Community Support Skill Standards (CSSS) (HSRI, 1996).

The implications for the pedagogy and structure of educational and training programs to effectively prepare students to meet the CSSS is the current focus of the Council for Standards in Human Service Education (CSHSE), the National Organization for Human Service Education (NOHSE), and the National Alliance for Direct Support Professionals (NADSP).

Higher Education Program Approval by CSHSE

Technical-, associate-, and baccalaureate-degree human service programs are encouraged to seek approval from the Council for Standards in Human Service Education. An approval process for master's degree programs in human services is currently in the initial stages of development. The twenty-three standards are comprehensive and uniform to all human service programs. They are organized into general program characteristics and curriculum (CSHSE, 1989).

The crosswalk match between the community support skill standards and the CSHSE program approval requirements, as well as the potential adjustments that can be made in CSHSE skills requirements to include all CSSS, will strengthen the utilization of the CSSS as a basis for worker

training and education in higher education human service programs.

CROSSWALK: THE RELATIONSHIP BETWEEN CSSS AND THE NATIONAL STANDARDS FOR HUMAN SERVICE WORKER EDUCATION AND TRAINING PROGRAMS (CSHSE)

The main objective of the crosswalk was to determine how closely the national skill standards (CSSS) corresponded to the council standards (CSHSE). The crosswalk revealed that there was a direct correlation between the council standards and the national community support skill standards. The council standards were then strengthened to incorporate the concepts of the national community support standards into the program characteristics and curriculum. The council has endorsed the community support skill standards and strengthened the council standards to incorporate the CSSS. (The crosswalk is shown in Table 8.1).

Dissemination of the CSSS through regional and national conference presentations and publications of NOHSE and CSHSE will inform human service educators about the necessary skills, knowledge, and attitudes required of the CSHSP. These national skill standards will:

- provide a framework for curriculum development for human service programs;
- set performance appraisal standards for field internships;
- delineate specific competency performance standards for students' educational completion; and
- provide human service agencies with guidelines for hiring and retaining workers.

THE CSSS: SKILL STANDARDS FOR DIRECT SERVICE WORKERS IN THE HUMAN SERVICES

The twelve competency categories defined by the CSSS project are described as follows. Included in the descriptions are the specific skill standards delineated by each competency area.

Categorical Interpretations

Competency Area 1: Participant Empowerment. The competent community-based support human service practitioner (CSHSP) enhances the ability of the participant to lead a self-determining life by providing the support and information necessary to build self-esteem and assertiveness and to make decisions.

Skill Standard A.   The competent CSHSP assists and supports the participant to develop strategies, make informed choices, follow through on responsibilities, and take risks.

Skill Standard B.   The competent CSHSP promotes participant partnership in the design of support services, consulting the person and involving him or her in the support process.

Skill Standard C.   The competent CSHSP provides opportunities for the participant to be a self-advocate by increasing awareness of self-advocacy methods and techniques, encouraging and assisting the participant to speak on his or her own behalf, and providing information on peer support and self-advocacy groups.

Skill Standard D.   The competent CSHSP provides information about human, legal, civil rights, and other resources and facilitates access to such information and assists the participant to use information for self-advocacy and decision making about living, work, and social relationships.

Sequence of Training.   At the secondary educational level, it is felt that basic concepts of participant support and encouragement should be developed in the CSHSP. Awareness of individual needs and respect for helping to motivate participants toward independent functioning are the priority goals in this competency area at this level of training. At the secondary level, it is felt that standards

1B and C can be achieved with both interactive classroom and role-playing exercises. Associate- and baccalaureate-degree levels of education will share the full set of standards as a foundation for practice in the human service field.

Competency Area 2: Communication.   The community-based support human service practitioner should be knowledgeable about the range of effective communication strategies and skills necessary to establish a collaborative relationship with the participant.

Skill Standard A.   The competent CSHSP uses effective, sensitive communication skills to build rapport and channels of communication by recognizing and adapting to the range of participant communication steps.

Skill Standard B.   The competent CSHSP has knowledge of and uses modes of communication that are appropriate to the communication needs of participants.

Sequence of Training.   At the secondary level, trainees should be directed toward gathering and organizing competencies in the communication area. At this level, these workers would be basic assistants in the client intake process and would focus on welcoming skills and helping clients complete initial registration materials. These activities would still require close supervision. Associate and baccalaureate degree professionals would be trained to assume independent responsibilities in the intake process and would be more closely supervised in the direct care and helping activities associated with entry-level positions of responsibility. Response and adaptive skills in interpersonal communication (both verbal and nonverbal) would focus the training and practicum experiences of the CSHSP.

Competency Area 3: Assessment.   The community-based support human service practitioner should be knowledgeable about formal and informal assessment practices to respond to the needs, desires, and interests of the participants.

Skill Standard A.   The competent CSHSP initiates or assists in the initiation of an assessment process by gathering information (e.g., participant's self-assessment and history, prior records, test results, evaluation results, and additional evaluation) and informing the participant about what to expect throughout the assessment process.

Skill Standard B.   The competent CSHSP conducts or arranges for assessment to determine the needs, preferences, and capabilities of the participants using appropriate assessment tools and strategies, reviewing the process for inconsistencies, and making corrections as necessary.

Skill Standard C.   The competent CSHSP discusses findings and recommendations with the participant in a clear and understandable manner, following up on results and reevaluating the findings as necessary.

Sequence of Training.   It is felt that the initial analysis and diagnosis of client needs should be primarily exclusive to the baccalaureate degree level of training (and perhaps beyond.) Because most third-party sources of reimbursement of client services require some form of initial diagnostic assessment, and this normally is assumed in the intake process, it should be principally limited to upper levels of training and experience. Consequently, it is not recommended for the secondary level and should be limited to basic gathering, organizing, and informational services at the associate degree level.

Competency Area 4: Community and Service Networking.   The community-based support human service practitioner should be knowledgeable about the formal and informal supports available in his or her community and skilled in assisting the participant to identify and gain access to such supports.

Skill Standard A.   The competent CSHSP helps to identify the needs of the participant for community supports, working with the participant's informal support system, and assisting with or initiating identified community connections.

Skill Standard B.   The competent CSHSP researches, develops, and maintains information on community and other resources relevant to the needs of participants.

Skill Standard C.   The competent CSHSP ensures participant access to needed community resources coordinating supports across agencies.

Skill Standard D.   The competent CSHSP participates in outreach to potential participants.

Sequence of Training.   All levels of training the CSHSP should include both the awareness of and the basic referral to community resources. The CSHSP would be trained on foundational matching of participant needs and available resources to meeting those needs in the community.

Actual research skills applied to community resources (surveying and collating agency and service information in the community) should be limited to more formal levels of training and education and are routinely incorporated into the introductory and survey courses at the associate and baccalaureate levels.

Competency Area 5: Facilitation of Services

Skill Standard A.   The competent CSHSP maintains collaborative professional relationships with the participant and all support team members (including family and friends), follows ethical standards of practice (e.g., confidentiality and informed consent), and recognizes his or her own personal limitations.

Skill Standard B.   The competent CSHSP assists and/or facilitates the development of an individualized plan on the basis of participant preferences, needs, and interests.

Skill Standard C. The competent CSHSP assists and/or facilitates the implementation of an individualized plan to achieve specific outcomes derived from participants' preferences, needs, and interests.

Skill Standard D. The competent CSHSP assists and/or facilitates the review of the achievement of individual participant outcomes.

Sequence of Training. All levels of training of the CSHSP should include a basic level of understanding and application of ethics in the profession (e.g., client confidentiality). Likewise, there should be functional awareness of what is involved in developing and implementing an individual service, treatment, or educational plan for the participant. At the associate and baccalaureate levels, it is expected that trainees would acquire greater self-awareness and outcome evaluation of individual participant plans.

Competency Area 6: Community Living Skills and Supports. The community-based support human service practitioner has the ability to match specific supports and interventions to the unique needs of individual participants and recognizes the importance of friends, family, and community relationships.

Skill Standard A. The competent CSHSP assists the participant to meet his or her physical (e.g., health, grooming, toileting, and eating) and personal management needs (e.g., human development and sexuality) by teaching skills, providing supports, and building on individual strengths and capabilities.

Skill Standard B. The competent CSHSP assists the participant with household management (e.g., meal prep, laundry, cleaning, and decorating) and with transportation needs to maximize his or her skills, abilities, and independence.

Skill Standard C. The competent CSHSP assists with identifying, securing, and using needed equipment (e.g., adaptive equipment), and therapies (e.g., physical, occupational, and communication).

Skill Standard D. The competent CSHSP supports the participant in the development of friendships and other relationships.

Skill Standard E. The competent CSHSP assists the participant in recruiting and training service providers as needed.

Sequence of Training. Secondary training of the CSHSP would include the more basic development of participant skills in life management and everyday achievement of basic household and social functioning. Associate and baccalaureate programs should incorporate all five standards in this area and would differ only in the amount of ongoing experience and for the level of challenge the participant population presents.

Competency Area 7: Education, Training, and Self-Development. The community-based support human service practitioner should be able to identify areas for self improvement, pursue necessary educational/training resources, and share knowledge with others.

Skill Standard A. The competent CSHSP completes required training education/certification, continues professional development, and keeps abreast of relevant resources and information.

Skill Standard B. The competent CSHSP educates participants, co-workers, and community members about issues by providing information and support and facilitating training.

Sequence of Training. The secondary level would be primarily excluded from more formal levels of credentials, licensing, and/or certification but would be routinely exposed to upper-level role models in their work environment. (*Note:* Students who graduate from substance abuse education programs for substance abuse certification and those who graduate from human service education programs at the two-year level may be eligible for a license or certification as an entry-level social service assistant.)

Associate and baccalaureate programs could more relevantly train the CSHSP for qualifying for the credentialing process. The amount of supervised experience criteria (e.g., levels of examination) would differentiate these levels of training in the credentialing process and would vary from state to state.

Competency Area 8: Advocacy. The community-based support human service practitioner should be knowledgeable about the diverse challenges facing participants (e.g., human rights, legal, administrative, and financial) and should be able to identify and use effective advocacy strategies to overcome such challenges.

Skill Standard A. The competent CSHSP and the participant identify advocacy issues by gathering information and reviewing and analyzing all aspects of the problem.

Skill Standard B. The competent CSHSP has current knowledge of laws, services, and community resources to assist and educate participants to secure needed supports.

Skill Standard C. The competent CSHSP facilitates, assists, and/or represents the participant when there are barriers to his or her service needs and lobbies decision makers when appropriate to overcome barriers to service.

Skill Standard D. The competent CSHSP interacts with and educates community members and organizations (e.g., employers, landlords, and civic organizations) when relevant to participants' needs or services.

Sequence of Training. Advocacy skills are social action competencies that evolve from more advanced training and exposure of the CSHSP to all levels of sociopolitical activism, lobbying, and grassroots community organizing. It is believed these are best reserved for associate and baccalaureate programs with opportunities for community- and state-level practicum experiences.

Competency Area 9: Vocational, Educational, and Career Supports. The community-based support worker should be knowledgeable about the career- and education-related concerns of the participant and should be able to mobilize the resources and support necessary to assist the participant in reaching his or her goals.

Skill Standard A. The competent CSHSP explores with the participant his or her vocational interests and aptitudes, assists in preparing for job or school entry, and reviews opportunities for continued career growth.

Skill Standard B. The competent CSHSP assists the participant in identifying job or training opportunities and marketing his or her capabilities and services.

Skill Standard C. The competent CSHSP collaborates with employers and school personnel to support the participant, adapt the environment, and provide job retention supports.

Sequence of Training. In this area of competency standards, it is felt that the thrust (vocational guidance and counseling of participants) would be best served at the two- and four-year levels of training where the CSHSP would be exposed to understanding basic vocational development theory (e.g., Roe and Super), various career training resources (state and federal), and the availability and eligibility of vocational and employment training.

Competency Area 10: Crisis Intervention. The community-based support human service practitioner should be knowledgeable about crisis prevention, intervention, and resolution techniques and should match such techniques to particular circumstances and individuals.

Skill Standard A. The competent CSHSP identifies the crisis, defuses the situation, evaluates and determines an intervention strategy, and contacts necessary supports.

Skill Standard B. The competent CSHSP continues to monitor crisis situations, discussing the incident with authorized staff and participant(s), adjusting supports and the environment, and complying with regulations for reporting.

Sequence of Training. Secondary programs do not engage their students in clinical intervention procedures and are not recommended for inclusion in these standards. In both associate and baccalaureate programs, there is a basic need to train and educate the CSHSP on foundations of crisis intervention. Prevention and postvention skills would be more readily appropriate to four-year programs.

Competency Area 11: Organizational Participation. The community-based support human service practitioner is familiar with the mission and practices of the support organization and participates in the life of the organization.

Skill Standard A. The competent CSHSP contributes to program evaluations and helps set organizational priorities to ensure quality.

Skill Standard B. The competent CSHSP incorporates sensitivity to cultural, religious, racial, disability, and gender issues into daily practices and interactions.

Skill Standard C. The competent CSHSP provides and accepts co-worker support, participating in supportive supervision and performance evaluation and contributing to the screening of potential employees.

Skill Standard D. The competent CSHSP provides input into budget priorities, identifying ways to provide services in a more cost-beneficial manner.

Sequence of Training. In this area of entry-level competencies, the CSHSP would be familiar with administrative, management, and budgetary processes and as such would be best served at

advanced levels of training and education (associate and baccalaureate programs.) This same consideration would apply to Skill Standard B, which relates to multicultural awareness and diversity.

Competency Area 12: Documentation. The community-based support worker is aware of the requirements for documentation in his or her organization and is able to manage these requirements efficiently.

Skill Standard A. The competent CSHSP maintains accurate records; collects, compiles, and evaluates data; and submits records to appropriate sources in a timely fashion.

Skill Standard B. The competent CSHSP maintains standards of confidentiality and ethical practice.

Skill Standard C. The competent CSHSP learns and remains current with appropriate documentation systems, setting priorities and developing a system to manage documentation.

Sequence of Training. All levels of training again should address training of the CSHSP in legal and ethical issues of the human service profession. Skill Standard 12B is also addressed in the previous discussion of skill standards.

In the ongoing responsibilities for record keeping, reporting, data management, and so on, it is felt that those competencies would be incorporated more exclusively at the associate and baccalaureate levels of training, inasmuch as both levels of the CSHSP would routinely require the same.

In Table 8.1 you will see an analysis of the "goodness-of-fit" between the twelve areas of competency from the CSSS and where these may be located within the CSHSE standards.

Table 8.2 is designed to exhibit the relevant placement at which entry-level skills standards would be most appropriately incorporated in relationship to level of educational programs (i.e., technical, associate, and baccalaureate levels). In

TABLE 8.1   Crosswalk: The Relationship between the Community Support Skill Standards and the National Standards for Human Service Education and Training Programs

CSSS STANDARD	CSHSE STANDARD NO.	COUNCIL DESCRIPTION
1. Participant empowerment	Standard 1	1. Primary program objective
	Standard 2	2. Philosophical base
	Standard 5	5. Procedures for admitting, retaining, and dismissing students
	Standard 19	19. Client-related values and attitudes
2. Communication	Standard 17	17. Interpersonal skills
3. Assessment	Standard 14	14. Generic planning and evaluation skills
4. Community and service networking	Standard 3	3. Community needs assessment
	Standard 12	12. Context and dimension of human service work
	Standard 21	21. Minimum field requirements
	Standard 22	22. Academic credit field experience
	Standard 23	23. Supervision
5. Facilitation of services	Standard 14	14. Generic planning and evaluation skills
	Standard 19	19. Client-related values and attitudes
6. Community/living skills and supports	Standard 13	13. Human service populations
7. Education training and self-development	Standard 10	10. Articulation
	Standard 20	20. Self-development
8. Advocacy	Standard 1	1. Primary program objectives
	Standard 11	11. History of human services
	Standard 19	19. Client-related values and attitudes
9. Vocational/educational and career supports	Standard 14	14. Generic planning and career supports
10. Crisis intervention	Standard 16	16. Intervention skills
11. Organizational participation	Standard 19	19. Client-related values and attitudes
12. Documentation	Standard 15	15. Information management skills
	Standard 19	19. Client-related values and attitudes

No change in council standards 4, 6, 7, 8, 9, and 18, which do not apply to CSSS.

the previous section, the CSHSE curriculum standard that most directly relates to each entry-level skill standard category has been cross-referenced. In sum, each of the twelve categories of the CSSS community support skill standards in the first column on the left of the chart is crosswalked to which level of educational program it is best suited for. Obviously, some categories of skill standards will be relevant to all levels of educational programs, whereas others will relate only to certain levels of program training. Regarding entry-level competency, the focus has been, and remains

TABLE 8.2   Educational Levels for Addressing Community Support Skill Standards: A Model for Sequencing the Content of the Community Support Skill Standards through Secondary and Postsecondary Programs

CSSS	SECONDARY	TWO-YEAR PROGRAMS	FOUR-YEAR PROGRAMS
1. Participant empowerment	BC	ABCD	ABCD
2. Communication	A	AB	AB
3. Assessment		A	ABC
4. Community and service networking	AB	ABCD	ABCD
5. Facilitation of services	AC	ABCD	ABCD
6. Community living skills and supports	BD	ABCDE	ABCDE
7. Education, training, and self-development		AB	AB
8. Advocacy		ABCD	ABCD
9. Vocational, education, and career support		ABC	ABC
10. Crisis intervention		AB	AB
11. Organizational participation		ABD	ABCD
12. Documentation	B	AB	ABC

today, exclusive to associate and baccalaureate educational programs. For purposes of relating competency standards of the National Skill Standards Project in the broadest possible way, the present report and crosswalk exercises have been extended downward to secondary education whenever it was appropriate to do so.

FUTURE DIRECTIONS AND CONSIDERATIONS

Faculty Requirements

Faculty at all levels—secondary, technical, associate, and baccalaureate institutions—need to possess experience and competency in those skill standards areas in which they teach. Because of the necessary skills development required of the learner to become a community support human service practitioner, it is important that faculty in these human service programs demonstrate competency in the teaching of the required worker skills areas and bring to the classroom professional experience that supports the hands-on knowledge and skills that learners must acquire in becoming effective CSHSPs.

The future of human service education will require educators and administrators at educational institutions to be drawn from the growing pool of human service professionals who are obtaining graduate degrees in human services and demonstrate excellence in the application of their learning to their practice.

Competency-Based Curriculum Goals and Objectives

Curriculum goals and objectives need to be based on competency. Assessment strategies to determine that learners have absorbed and integrated the necessary knowledge and skills required of a CSHSP must be clearly reflected in the overall program curriculum and specifically stated in course or training module assessment standards for completion of degree or training certification requirements. A partial list of activities may include the following:

- testing for knowledge retention;
- skill building through structured and supervised internships;
- in-class demonstrations and proactive experiences; and
- required field site visits and learner reflective feedback through process recordings, logging, or journal methods.

New technologies and techniques influencing educational delivery systems include distance learning through

- virtual classrooms;
- interactive computer software;
- programmed instruction;
- guided study;
- portfolio assessment; and
- CD-ROM vignettes and expanded performance assessments through
  - peer assessment evaluations;
  - participant assessment; and
  - consumer satisfaction surveys.

Curriculum Review, Evaluation, and Redevelopment Matching Curriculum Content to Competency Outcomes

Educational and training programs must reorient curriculum content to competency outcomes that lead to curriculum review, evaluation, and redevelopment. At all educational levels, curriculum content taught must match competency outcomes learned. It is not enough for training and educational program curricula to reflect the necessary content for student-practitioners becoming CSHSPs. Learners must demonstrate competency and mastery of the activity performance indicators that will reflect achievement of each skill standard.

To accomplish this goal, human service program coordinators and faculty must stay in contact with the national, state, and local employment trends and the ongoing knowledge and skill changes and then reflect all this in the competency requirements for learner educational program completion. Ways of staying current about human service competency requirements include

- maintaining a representative community provider advisory board;
- joining national, regional, and local human service organizations;
- participating in a broad range of human service information workshops and conferences; and
- reading materials from journals and governmental publications.

Regularly scheduled curriculum review and program evaluation will support redevelopment of curriculum content to match competency outcomes. Most higher education institutions have a five-year cycle in conjunction with preparations to regional accreditation organizations. The CSHSE has a five-year reapproval cycle.

Supervision of Student CSHSPs

Identification and recruitment of qualified professionals to supervise students in required internships and field practice is a crucial component of an effective training and educational program. Although a wide variety of degree levels and certifications/licensures are appropriate professional credentials for supervision, the supervisor must also be oriented to and supportive of the learner's demonstration of competency in his or her performance of activities related to each skill standard. Adequate and appropriate field site supervision has emerged as a major concern of human service training and education programs. Qualified and committed professionals to supervise students to become CSHSPs becomes essential to effective worker training and education.

Development and support of this critical component of student learning in field internships requires such strategies as

- advisory board participation in agency supervisory selection;

— development of field sites by a staff field developer;
— training of supervisors in the supervisory expectations of students in field internships;
— student feedback to instructors through class seminars and written feedback mechanisms;
— maintenance and updates to student learning contracts as internship experiences change; and
— recognition by the educational institutions of the contributions made by field supervisors with students in field internships.

Monitoring of Field Experiences and Internships

The maintenance of sufficient monitoring of field experiences and internships by faculty and staff of high schools, colleges, and training providers will be necessary for the quality control of field site supervision and the verification of competency outcomes by student interns. Use of learning contracts between the learner, the field site supervisor, and the faculty member to elaborate the specific activity performance indicator to meet a skill standard will assist in reviewing the efficacy of the field site as an appropriate and adequate placement for students studying to become CSHSPs.

Other monitoring tools may be useful in relation to the training or educational institution and level of skill standards achievement. These may include

— periodic redevelopment of a utilized field internship site;
— annual supervisory skills conference;
— updates of supervisory field manual based on changing expectations of the field; and
— student feedback in classroom seminars and written documentation of field experiences.

Professional Development for Faculty

Faculty should be supported in the maintenance of active involvement in professional organizations. This can include

— formal memberships in national, regional, statewide, or local organizations and associations;

— attendance at seminars, workshops, and conferences that keep them abreast of changes in the human service field and their impact on the program curriculum and learning objectives;
— sabbatical leaves focused on human service professional renewal activities; and
— institutional resources that support technological assistance to human service educators through library resources, computer equipment and software resources, Internet access, and interactive teleconferencing.

Faculty members' professional growth has been a critical area of concern in recent years because travel, research, and support resources for professional development have been reduced in institutional budgets during this period of fiscal exigency.

Technical Assistance to Training and Educational Institutions

Technical assistance in the development of curriculum content and competency outcomes assessment is important to quality program development and quality control in the implementation of the CSSS as a basis for education and training CSHSPs. The CSHSE currently provides technical assistance when human service education programs seek program approval. The implementation of the crosswalk recommendations will facilitate the integration of the CSSS into the approval and reapproval process. Other organizations should be identified to assist in technical assistance activities.

Utilization of the crosswalk document as a guide for articulation agreements between secondary and technical schools and associate's degree programs, associate's and baccalaureate degree programs, and baccalaureate to graduate program admissions, targeting members of CSHSE and NOHSE would expand the mission of integrating the Community Support Skill Standards into existing and developing human service education program curriculums. Human service educators knowledgeable and supportive of the Community Support Skill Standards could provide technical assistance training and education on curriculum infusion and competency performance assessment.

Support and Resources that Promote CSSS

Educational and training institutions need to identify and direct appropriate levels of support and resources that promote CSSS development for students studying to become CSHSPs. It must be recognized by training providers and educational institutions that implementation of the CSSS into human service programs will be labor-intensive and technologically demanding, because it will require low faculty-student ratios and adequate methodological and computer technological sup-

port. The effectiveness and efficiency of CSHSPs in their careers necessitate

- adequate faculty and staff personnel;
- properly equipped training and education settings;
- appropriate field site supervision; and
- sufficient technological support.

Seeking resource support will require

- assistance from local and county human service agencies;
- lobbying local, county, state, and federal governmental agencies and elected officials;
- participating in research and grant activities that promote the skill standards; and
- approaching business and industry for contributions to specific efforts to support the implementation of CSSS and recognize excellence of achievement by community-based human service agencies and CSHSPs.

REFERENCES

CSHSE. (1989). *National Standards for Human Service Worker Education and Training Programs.*

HSRI. (1996). *Community Support Skills Standards (CSSS).*

SUGGESTED FURTHER READING

Taylor, M., V. Bradley, and R. Warren, Jr. (1996). *The Community Support Skill Standards: Tools for Managing Change and Achieving Outcomes: Skill Standards for Direct Service Workers in the Human Services.* Human Services Research Insti- tute (HSRI) 2336 Cambridge St., Cambridge, MA 02140. Mailing address for the Council for Standards is Attn: Mary DiGiovanni, Northern Essex Community College, Elliott Way, Haverhill, MA 01830.

THE HUMAN SERVICE WORKER:
A GENERIC JOB DESCRIPTION

A JOINT PUBLICATION OF NOHSE AND CSHSE

HUMAN SERVICES

Making a Difference in People's Lives

The field of human services is a broadly defined one, uniquely approaching the objective of meeting human needs through an interdisciplinary knowledge base, focusing on prevention as well as remediation of problems, and maintaining a commitment to improving the overall quality of life of service populations. The human service profession is one that promotes improved service delivery systems by not only addressing the quality of direct services but also seeking to improve accessibility, accountability, and coordination among professionals and agencies in service delivery.

Human Service Workers

"Human service worker" is a generic term for people who hold professional and paraprofessional jobs in such diverse settings as group homes and halfway houses; correctional, mental retardation, and community mental health centers; family, child, and youth service agencies; and programs concerned with alcoholism, drug abuse, family violence, and aging. Depending on the employment setting and the kinds of clients served there, job titles and duties vary a great deal.

The primary purpose of the human service worker is to assist individuals and communities to function as effectively as possible in the major domains of living.

A strong desire to help others is an important consideration for a job as a human service worker. Individuals who show patience, understanding, and caring in their dealings with others are highly valued by employers. Other important personal traits include communication skills, a strong sense of responsibility, and the ability to manage time effectively.

Generic Human Service Worker Competencies

The following six statements describe the major generic knowledge, skills, and attitudes that appear to be required in all human service work. The training and preparation of the individual worker within this framework will change as a function of the work setting, the specific client population served, and the level of organizational work.

1. *Understanding the nature of human systems: individual, group, organization, community, and society and their major interactions.* All workers will have preparation that helps them to understand human development, group dynamics, organizational structure, how communities are organized, how national policy is set, and how social systems interact in producing human problems.

2. *Understanding the conditions that promote or limit optimal functioning and classes of deviations from desired functioning in the major human systems.* Workers will have understanding of the major models of causation that are concerned with both the promotion of healthy functioning and with treatment and rehabilitation. This includes medically oriented, socially oriented, psychologically behavioral oriented, and educationally oriented models.

3. *Skill in identifying and selecting interventions that promote growth and goal attainment.* The worker will be able to conduct a competent problem analysis and to select those strategies, services, or interventions that are appropriate to helping clients attain a desired outcome. Interventions may include assistance, referral, advocacy, or direct counseling.

4. *Skill in planning, implementing, and evaluating interventions.* The worker will be able to design a plan of action for an identified problem and implement the plan in a systematic way. This requires an understanding of problem analysis, decision analysis, and design of work plans. This generic skill can be used with all social systems and adapted for use with individual clients or organizations. Skill in evaluating the interventions is essential.

5. *Consistent behavior in selecting interventions that are congruent with the values of oneself, clients, the employing organization, and the human service profession.* This cluster requires awareness of one's own value orientation, an understanding of organizational values as expressed in the mandate or goal statement of the organization, human service ethics, and an appreciation of the client's values, lifestyle, and goals.

6. *Process skills that are required to plan and implement services.* This cluster is based on the assumption that the worker uses himself as the main tool for responding to service needs. The worker must be skillful in verbal and oral communication, interpersonal relationships, and other related personal skills, such as self-discipline and time management. It requires that the worker be interested in and motivated to conduct the role that he has agreed to fulfill and to apply himself to all aspects of the work that the role requires.

Where Human Service Workers Work

Working conditions vary. Human service workers in social service agencies generally spend part of the time in the office and the rest of the time in the field. Most work a forty-hour week. Some evening and weekend work may be necessary, but compensatory time off is usually granted.

Human service workers in community-based settings move around a great deal in the course of a work week. They may be inside one day and outdoors on a field visit the next. They, too, work a standard forty-hour week.

Human services workers in residential settings generally work in shifts. Because residents of group homes need supervision in the evening and at night seven days a week, evening and weekend hours are required.

Despite differences in what they are called and what they do, human service workers generally perform under the direction of professional staff. Those employed in mental health settings, for example, may be assigned to assist a treatment team made up of social workers, psychologists, and other human service professionals. The amount of responsibility these workers assume and the degree of supervision they receive vary a great deal. Some workers are on their own most of the time and have little direct supervision; others work under close direction.

Human service workers in community, residential care, or institutional settings provide direct services such as leading a group, organizing an activity, or offering individual counseling. They may handle some administrative support tasks, too. Specific job duties reflect organizational policy and staffing patterns as well as the worker's educational preparation and experience.

Because so many human service jobs involve direct contact with people who are impaired and therefore vulnerable to exploitation, employers try to be selective in hiring. Applicants are screened for appropriate personal qualifications. Relevant academic preparation is generally required and volunteer or work experience preferred.

Job Outlook

Employment of human service workers is expected to grow much faster than the average for all occupations through the year 2005. Opportunities for qualified applicants are expected to be excellent not only because of projected rapid growth in the occupation but also because of substantial replacement needs. Turnover among counselors in group homes is reported to be especially high.

Employment prospects should be favorable in facilities and programs that serve the elderly, mentally impaired, or developmentally disabled. Adult day care, a relatively new concept, is expected to expand significantly because of very rapid growth in the number of people of advanced age, together with the growing awareness of the value of day programs for adults in need of care and supervision.

Although projected growth in the elderly population is the dominant factor in the anticipated expansion of adult day care, public response to the needs of people who are handicapped or mentally ill underlies anticipated employment growth in group homes and residential care facilities. As more and more mentally retarded or developmentally disabled individuals reach the age of twenty-one and thereby lose their eligibility for programs and services offered by the public schools, the need for community-based alternatives can be expected to grow. Pressures to respond to the needs of the chronically mentally ill can also be expected to persist. For many years, as deinstitutionalization has proceeded, chronic mental patients have been left to their own devices. If the movement to help the homeless and chronically mentally ill gains momentum, more community-based programs and group residences will be established, and demand for human service workers will increase accordingly. State and local governments will remain a major employer of human service workers, and replacement needs alone will generate many job openings in the public sector.

Salary Range

According to limited data available, starting salaries for human service workers ranged from $25,000 to $30,000 a year in 2000. Experienced workers earned up to about $43,000 annually, depending on the amount of experience and the employer.

Employment

Human service workers held about 375,000 jobs in 1998. About one-fourth were employed by state and local governments, primarily in hospitals and outpatient mental health centers, facilities for the mentally retarded and developmentally disabled, and public welfare agencies. Another fourth worked in agencies offering adult day care, group meals, crisis intervention, counseling, and other social services. Some supervised residents of group homes and halfway houses. Human service workers also held jobs in clinics, community mental health centers, and private psychiatric hospitals.

Examples of Occupational Titles of Human Service Workers

Case Worker	Family Support Worker
Youth Worker	
Residential Counselor	Social Service Liaison
	Behavioral Management Aide
Case Management Aide	
	Eligibility Counselor
Alcohol Counselor	Adult Day Care Worker
Drug Abuse Counselor	
	Life Skills Instructor
Client Advocate	Neighborhood Worker
Social Service Aide	Group Activities Aide
	Therapeutic Assistant
Social Service Technician	Case Monitor
	Child Advocate
Probation Officer	Juvenile Court Liaison
Parole Officer	Group Home Worker
Gerontology Aide	Crisis Intervention Counselor
Home Health Aide	
Child Abuse Worker	Community Organizer
	Community Outreach Worker
Mental Health Aide	
	Community Action Worker
Intake Interviewer	

Social Work Assistant	Residential Manager
Psychological Aide	Halfway House Counselor
Assistant Case Manager	Rehabilitation Case Worker

NOHSE: A History of Commitment

The National Organization for Human Service Education (NOHSE) was founded in 1975 at the Fifth Annual Faculty Development Conference of the Southern Regional Education Board. NOHSE grew out of the perceived need by professional care providers and legislators for improved methods of service delivery. NOHSE, with the early support of the National Institute of Mental Health and SREB, has striven to promote excellence in human service delivery in an increasingly complex world.

Through the professional efforts of NOHSE members, many programs of care have been developed to address unique social, behavioral, and educational issues. NOHSE's focus includes supporting and promoting improvements in direct service, public education, program development, planning and evaluation, administration, and public policy.

Members of NOHSE are drawn from diverse educational and professional backgrounds. Professional backgrounds and experience in corrections, mental health, child care, social services, human resource management, gerontology, developmental disabilities, addictions, recreation, and education reflect this diversity.

The applied philosophy of NOHSE addresses the diverse needs of society by supporting educators and professionals in developing innovative models of service and education.

Purposes of NOHSE

1. To provide a medium for cooperation and communication among human service organizations and individual practitioners, faculty, and students.

2. To foster excellence in teaching, research, and curriculum development for improving the education of human service delivery personnel.
3. To encourage, support, and assist the development of local, state, and national organizations of human services.
4. To sponsor forums via conferences, institutes, and symposia that foster creative approaches to meeting human service needs.

Council for Standards in Human Service Education

Founded in 1979 to improve the quality, consistency, and relevance of human service training programs, the Council for Standards in Human Service Education (CSHSE) is the only national organization providing standards and assistance to accomplish these goals. The council achieves its purpose by the following efforts:

1. Applying national standards for training programs at the associate and baccalaureate degree levels;
2. Reviewing and recognizing programs that meet established standards;
3. Sponsoring faculty development workshops in curriculum design, program policy making, resource development, program evaluation, and other areas;
4. Offering vital technical and informational assistance to programs seeking to improve the quality and relevance of their training;
5. Publishing a quarterly bulletin to keep programs informed of council activities, training information and resources, issues, and trends in human service education.

Through a membership of educational programs, the council provides an organization and an opportunity for all constituencies of the undergraduate human service field to work together in developing and promoting sound programs of human service training as the essential foundation for effective and relevant service delivery.

KEY TERMS FOR PART TWO_____

After studying Chapters 5, 6, 7, and 8, you should have a command of the following key terms, major concepts, and principal topical references:

active listening	summarization	group leadership
closed-ended questions	PTSD	initial disclosure
nonverbal encouragers	brief therapy	conflict resolution
open-ended questions	crosswalk	skill standards
reflecting feelings	group cohesiveness	empathy
attending behaviors	unconditional positive regard	constructive confrontation
key words	Community Support Skill	generic skills
observing skills	Standards (CSSS)	credentialing
reflecting content		

PIVOTAL ISSUES FOR DISCUSSION OF PART TWO_____

1. Make a list of short-range human service interventions, long-term interventions, direct service interventions, and indirect interventions. How do these approaches differ when working with individual clients as opposed to working with groups?

2. Interview a social worker, clinical psychologist, and a psychiatrist and ask what each must possess as skills in performing their respective work. How are they different? Similar?

3. What is the managed health care movement in human services and mental health? What are the major issues in this recent movement? How do they affect the human service client, worker, and intervention services?

4. Give examples of how group approaches are used in human services. What are the advantages and disadvantages of groups?

5. Why is credentialing (i.e., licensure, certification, registration, etc.) a critical issue for future human service workers?

6. Make a list of the ten most important skills human service workers need to have, the ten most important bodies of knowledge, and the ten most important values. Can these be measured or tested for in human service students? How? When? Where? By whom?

7. Why should interviewers avoid giving advice to their interviewees?

8. Discuss the challenges of competency-based learning from both the students' perspective and that of the instructor.

9. Compare and contrast social conversation and formal interviewing.

SUGGESTED READINGS FOR PART TWO _____

1. Benjamin, A. (1969). *The Helping Interview.* Atlanta, GA: Houghton Mifflin.

2. CSHSE. (1989, September). *Field Work in Human Services Education.* Monograph Issue #6.

3. Ivey, A. E., M. B. Ivey, and L. Imek-Downing (1987). *Counseling and Psychotherapy: Integrating Skills, Theory, and Practice* (2nd ed.) Englewood Cliffs, NJ: Prentice-Hall.

4. Evans, D. R., M. T. Hearn, M. R. Uhlemann, & A. E. Ivey (1998). *Essential Interviewing: A Programmed Approach to Effective Communication,* 5th ed. Pacific Grove, CA: Brooks/Cole.

5. Schram, B., and B. R. Mandell (1983). *Human Services: Strategies of Intervention.* New York: John Wiley and Sons.

6. Nichols, M. P. (1995). *The Lost Art of Listening.* New York: Guilford Press.

PART THREE

HUMAN SERVICE WORK WITH FAMILIES AND CHILDREN

Part 3 contains four chapters focusing on topics related to families and children: domestic violence, the child welfare system, child abuse, and youth services. Services to families and children play important roles in the context of preventing spousal abuse, filling the gaps left by welfare reform, supporting working parents, and promoting the healthy development of children.

In Chapter 9, Maria Munoz-Kantha discusses domestic violence in terms of the causes and dimensions of the problem as well as the human service response. After reading this chapter, you will be able to identify the characteristics of a battered woman and understand the pattern of violence and the impact on the family.

In Chapter 10, David Liederman, Madelyn DeWoody, and Megan Sylvester describe the work of the child welfare delivery system in the United States. David Liederman is the executive director of the Child Welfare League of America, a private umbrella organization devoted to serving the needs and solving the problems of children. In addition to providing a wide variety of child welfare services, the League has another function, which is to advocate for children. It is important to note that the League maintains an extensive research effort so that, when campaigning for an issue, they can present the strongest case based on facts. The authors also discuss emerging issues such as addressing the special needs of children with incarcerated parents and striving for cultural competence.

In Chapter 11, James Edell Lopez discusses child abuse and neglect in terms of its extent, characteristics, and strategies for helping. You will understand the different ways children are maltreated and how to identify them. You will also learn about intervention approaches to treatment. Child maltreatment and domestic violence both reflect families in crisis and disorder. Frequently horrifying examples are exposed in the national media.

Chapter 12, by Walter de Oliveira and Christopher R. Edginton, is a comprehensive discussion of youth and human services. You will see adolescence as a developmental stage and understand its place within the context of society. A historical overview of the various organizations that target youth will give you a perspective on the ways that help is delivered. Different paradigms for serving youth are presented to allow you to compare different models and assumptions. In addition, the authors cover approaches to intervention and ways of categorizing youth development programs. The discussion concludes with a look toward the future.

In the Special Focus Feature, Rafael Mendez describes a teen pregnancy prevention program called Pregnant Productions. This program of improvisational scenarios takes place in a community setting.

LEARNING OBJECTIVES FOR PART THREE: HUMAN SERVICE WORK WITH FAMILIES AND CHILDREN

After reading and studying Chapters 9, 10, 11, and 12,

— You will be familiar with human service issues associated with domestic and family violence.
— You will understand the current dynamics and causes of child sexual abuse and know what responses and resources are typically available within human services.
— You will be aware of the origins, functions, and services provided by the Child Welfare League of America.
— You will become familiar with the core child welfare service in the United States.
— You will be aware of an innovative approach to prevent teenage pregnancies.

CHAPTER 9

DOMESTIC VIOLENCE, BATTERED WOMEN, AND DIMENSIONS OF THE PROBLEM

MARIA MUNOZ-KANTHA

Throughout history, society has disregarded family violence and its implications on the family system, regardless of the fact that earlier theorists made attempts to bring it to the attention of the public. Benjamin Wadsworth, an influential seventeenth-century New England writer on marital ethics, wrote:

> *If therefore the Husband is bitter against his wife, beating her or striking her (as some vile wretches do), with unkind carriage, ill language, hard words, morose peevish, surely behavior; nay if he is not kind, loving, tender in his words and carriage to her; he then shames his profession of Christianity, he breaks the Divine Law, dishonors God and himself too, the same is true of the Wife too. If she strikes her Husband (as some shameless, impudent wretches will) if she's unkind in her carriage, give ill language, is sullen, pouty, so cross that she'll scarce eat or speak sometimes; nay if she neglects to manifest real love kindness, in her words or carriage either; she's then a shame to her profession of Christianity . . . the indisputable Authority, the plain Command of the Great God, required Husbands and Wives, to have and manifest very great affection, love and kindness to one another (quoted in Morgan, 1966).*

This social issue presents a serious problem for society because violence against women and children has increased in the last twenty years. The physical abuse of women is increasingly recognized as a serious, widespread community problem that must be addressed by the medical, legal, law enforcement, academic, corporate, political, religious, and human service fields. Every year in the United States, three to four million women are beaten in their homes by their husbands, ex-husbands, boyfriends, lovers, or family members. These women often suffer severe emotional suffering and physical injuries that can be serious enough to result in death.

The last three decades since the 1960s witnessed a new national awareness of violence faced by women and children. Prior to the 1970s the focus was on rape by strangers or acquaintances. Violence in the family system was viewed as an intrapsychic issue rather than a societal widespread problem. In the past fifteen years, much data on violence against women has been gathered with regard to prevalence and outcome in the area of advocacy, medical care, mental health, criminal justice, and academic communities (Browne, 1986; Schechter, 1982). Major feminist movements, research, and policy initiatives now address aggression within the family system. Rape laws have been amended to protect victims of assault by marital partners. Nearly every state has passed legislation addressing domestic violence.

In 1972, the first refuge for battered women opened in Britain. Others soon opened throughout Britain (Sutton, 1978) and other parts of Europe, the United States, Canada, and Australia (Warrior, 1976), as activists traveled throughout countries sharing ideas and providing support for opening and expanding new refuges.

The battered women's movement has now extended throughout much of the world, providing shelter and support and working for social change. Although several books have been published on the topic of wife assault and family violence, few researchers considered the impact of this behavior on the children who were exposed to this violence. Most of the early literature focused on the incidence of violence against women and society's inadequate response represented by community agencies, justice, health, and social service systems (e.g., Gelles and Straus, 1988). The impact of the violence on the child was not considered unless the child was physically abused as well.

Early studies on shelters for battered women began to identify the needs of children admitted to the shelters with their mothers. At least 70 percent of all battered women seeking shelter have children who accompany them, and 17 percent of the women bring along three or more children (MacLeod, 1989). Shelter staff pointed out that the women were most vulnerable and that the children presented themselves with a number of emotional, cognitive, and behavioral problems that required immediate intervention. However, at the times when the children had the greatest need for nurturance, the mothers were unavailable as a result of their own overwhelming needs related to their victimization.

Given the complex nature of this problematic public issue, how do human service workers deal with battered women and their children? Both societal and intrapsychic determinants of reactions to "battered women" may determine how human service workers respond and intervene in providing services.

Utilization of human service workers has expanded rapidly over the past three decades. Today the single largest category of personnel providing direct services to children and families are paraprofessionals. The most recent trend has been the development of bachelor's degree programs in human services. Despite the degrees, we are finding gaps and problems with curriculum development. Students are confronted with their own reactions to societal problems and are requesting more training in identifying issues, dynamics, and interventions.

Extent of Domestic Violence

1. According to FBI statistics, wife beating results in more injuries that require medical treatment than rape, automobile accidents, and muggings combined in this country. Statistics for 1984 indicated that 2,116 spouses were killed by their mates. Another study conducted in 1988 by Stark and Flitcraft revealed that spouse abuse occurs in 20 to 30 percent of all families.

2. Family violence calls constitute about 25 percent of all calls to most police departments.

3. Eighty-six percent of injuries received by police officers are reported to be caused by calls involving domestic violence (confrontations with the batterers).

4. Violence against women and children is pervasive and does not discriminate; it cuts across lines of income, color, class, and culture. There are many variations, ranging from the most subtle and indirect to the most blatant, including psychological, emotional, and verbal abuse. These variations include sexual harassment, rape, incest, prostitution, economic deprivation, genital mutilation, murder, and oppression. Testimonies from an international hearing on violence against women held on February 13, 1993, at the Church Center in New York emphasized the need for society to recognize violence against women as a human rights violation rather than a private family matter. They estimated that 1,000 women per year are killed by their husbands or partners. Women from all over the world testified and revealed their inner pain within a cultural context. Women within many different cultures are seen as property of the husbands. In fact, wife beating is expected when a woman "steps out of line," in spite of religious and cultural taboos against violence.

Sources of the Problem

1. Alcohol—Alcohol is involved in at least 60 percent of domestic violence cases. However, alcohol is not the cause; it is only the excuse or defense level of rationalization for violence (Fitch and Papantonio, 1983).

2. Sex Role Stereotypes: Power Issues—Men are taught and conditioned that to be masculine is to be powerful, and to exert control is normal. It is common in many homes to stress values and beliefs that designate the man as the authority figure and the woman as subservient. Of course, not all women in these relationships experience abuse, but a traditional marriage does tend to reinforce certain gender roles. Many women are also taught early in their development that to be feminine is to be helpless, dependent, and vulnerable.

3. Cultural Values and Norms—Our cultural values, social norms, family expectations, and psychological processes work together to encourage men to be abusers and women to be abused. Historically, women have been oppressed and beaten with the acknowledgment of their families, friends, and community. Within my own clinical practice, I have treated battered women from various socioeconomic levels, cultures, religions, and races involved in cases in which family members interrupted acts of violence but facilitated its continuation by keeping it a secret for the sake of not shaming the family.

4. Cycle of Intergenerational Abuse—A wife- or woman-batterer has often learned from his father (identification with the aggressor) that a real man expresses his anger by using his fists, not by crying or verbalizing his frustrations. In this process, the male also learns to disrespect women and the woman learns to inherit her mother's passivity by watching her get exposed to years of abusive behaviors. For some couples, there seems to be a pattern of violence that is repeated from generation to generation. Some families perceive violence as normal; it is internalized to the point that defenses like denial, aggression, suppression, anxiety, and identification with the aggressor play an important role. In some families the abuse takes place among siblings as well as between parents and children, therefore creating blurred boundaries within the contextual family system.

5. Low Self-Esteem—A wife-beater usually feels inferior and powerless in other areas of his life. It does not matter whether he has an excellent job or is unemployed—he feels unsuccessful, angry with himself, and worthless. The batterer displaces and projects his own anger onto his wife or partner. A woman who endures this kind of abuse internalizes inferiority, hopelessness, worthlessness, and a temporary form of helplessness.

6. Economics—Many battered women are housewives with no money of their own, no work skills, and dependent children. However, it is important to note that there is a high number of professional women who stop working to take care of their children, later finding themselves trapped in an abusive situation. Women in these situations usually tend to get depressed and lost in the shadow of the "super woman" (the woman who performs all of the roles of the traditional stay-at-home mother, while working full time). Often, this depression is correlated to the experience of living with extreme emotional and physical stress and deprivation for an extended period of time.

7. Specific Causes of Violence—In a domestic violence situation, anything can precipitate abuse: a bad day at work, a delayed dinner, unpaid bills, an affair, or accusations of infidelity. Often, there is little awareness or insight into the level of abuse to come at the time that the abuser starts to abuse. His vision is microscopic, not macroscopic.

8. Societal Denial—The last three decades have been marked by a growing public awareness of wife assault or wife beating. The belief that all family life is safe and secure is shattered by the alarming frequency of reported violence. Yet, this topic that was once considered a family secret or acceptable behavior seems to be interwoven with the very fabric of society's attitudes and values. Extensive data in this area remain shocking to society while our statistics on violence continue to rise. Denial continues to be a major problem. An example would be the famous and controversial case involving the great football player O. J. Simpson, America's all-American football hero, a mentor to many and a model for all. Prior to the 1994 murders and subsequent trial, in spite of his long problems with domestic violence toward his ex-wife, O. J. continued to be idealized, protected, supported, and rallied around; there seemed to be more public sympathy for him than for his victimized ex-wife.

CHARACTERISTICS OF ABUSE

Abuse has several dimensions. It can be emotional, physical, or sexual. It can occur every day or once in a while. It can happen in public places or in the privacy of someone's home. Abuse can leave a woman with bruises and bumps on her body or inner emotional pain that no one else can see. Here are some common characteristics of abuse.

Physical Abuse

Does her partner:

- Hit, slap, shove, bite, cut, choke, kick, burn, or spit on her?
- Throw objects at her?
- Hold her hostage?
- Hurt or threaten her with a weapon such as a gun, knife, chain, hammer, belt, scissors, brick, or other heavy objects?
- Abandon her or lock her out of her house or car?

— Neglect her when she's ill or pregnant?
— Endanger her and children by driving in a wild, reckless way?
— Refuse to give her money for food and clothing?

Emotional Abuse

Does her partner say or do things that embarrass, humiliate, ridicule, or insult her? Does he say:

— You are stupid, dirty, crazy.
— You are a fat, lazy, ugly whore.
— You can't do anything right.
— You are not a good mother.
— Nobody would ever want you.
— You don't deserve anything.
— Your mother is a whore.

Does he:

— Refuse to give her attention as a way of punishing her?
— Threaten to hurt her or the children?
— Refuse to let her work, have friends, or go out?
— Feel threatened by her assertive and competent friends?
— Force her to sign over property or give him her personal belongings?
— Take away gifts that he gave her when he becomes angry?
— Brag about his love affairs?
— Berate women?
— Accuse her of having extramarital affairs?
— Manipulate her with lies, contradictions, promises, or false hopes?
— Hide money from her and the children?

Sexual Abuse

Does her partner:

— Force her to have sex when she does not want to?
— Force her to perform sexual acts?
— Criticize her sexual performance?
— Refuse to have sex with her?
— Force her to have sex when she is ill or when it puts her health in danger?
— Force her to have sex with other people or force her to watch others having sex?

— Tell her about his sexual relations with other people?
— Have sex that she considers sadistic, or sex that is painful?

Destructive Acts

Does her partner:

— Break furniture, flood rooms, ransack, or dump garbage in her home?
— Throw food and pots out of the window?
— Slash tires, break windows, steal, or tamper with parts of the car to break it down?
— Kill pets to punish or scare her?
— Destroy her clothes, jewelry, family pictures, or other personal possessions that he knows are important to her?

WHAT IS DOMESTIC VIOLENCE?

According to Evelyn White (1985), the terms *abuse* and *battering* are used interchangeably to describe a relationship with a partner who hurts a woman physically and/or emotionally. However, there are some differences in their meaning. This awareness can be helpful to the human service worker when providing assistance to a victim of domestic violence. White defines *battering* as a means of punching, hitting, striking, or the actual physical act of one person beating another. *Abuse* may include physical assault, but it also covers a wide range of hurtful behavior. Threats, insulting talk, sexual coercion, and property destruction are all considered forms of abuse.

Domestic violence is a general term used to describe the battering or abusive acts within an intimate relationship. For example, a shelter worker, counselor, social worker, psychologist, or legal advocate who helps battered women and their children might say that she or he works in the field of domestic violence.

Physical abuse, emotional abuse, sexual abuse, and destructive acts are all dimensions of domestic violence. Some forms of abuse are considered serious offenses that can be prosecuted; others are simply behaviors that no one should tolerate. A woman's partner has no more right to hit, threaten, or hurt her than to assault a stranger in the community or streets. A woman has a right over her body, mind, and soul; it is to be respected and should not be violated or demeaned.

Battered Woman

The term "battered woman" was first described by a women's movement in Britain. It was a powerful phrase. The everyday word "battered" had been successfully used to describe persistently abused children; much later the phrase was utilized by the movement to convey the traumatic experience of persistent and severe violence against women. Many believed that the problems associated with violence are primarily perceived as contextual, associated with violent repression of women by men. Therefore, allowing women to escape this predicament and release themselves from violence and its consequences is vital (Dobash and Dobash, 1992).

How Does Battering Begin and Continue?

Battering can begin at any time during a relationship and continue throughout it. It can happen in a companion relationship, on a first date, on a wedding night, and after good and bad times. Statistics show that many men are under the influence of alcohol or drugs when they become violent or abusive. However, it is important to note that substances do not cause the abuse. In some families it is repeated from generation to generation and can start at any interval.

The Cycle of Battering

Dr. Lenore Walker describes the cyclical pattern of battering as a process that can only be ended when the batterer takes responsibility for his abusive behavior. Only he can change or learn how to control his behavior. Within the cycle of violence the *first stage* refers to the process by which a man is irritable, uncommunicative, and quick-tempered. He may claim to be upset about his job and have a short attention span. He breaks dishes, throws objects, has shouting fits, but then quickly apologizes. It is during this period that the abused woman may report feeling as though she is walking on eggshells. She repeatedly tries to pacify him in order to prevent him from having another explosive episode. When there are children involved, quite often they, too, learn quickly to pacify their father's violent behavior. An adolescent child in my private practice described her feelings:

> I had to help my mother because she was afraid, I felt I needed to protect her, it was so frightening, while I was in school it was difficult to concentrate because I always feared coming home to a dead body. I remember life at home as extremely violent, my father cut my older brother's arm with a machete while my brother protected my mother. Following this, he threw my older sister down the stairs and knocked out my other brother's tooth. It was a nightmare. Now I am a victim of abuse; I let my boyfriend beat me, at times I feel I deserve it.

The *second stage* is what Dr. Walker describes as an increase in the tension leading up to physical or verbal explosion. It can be precipitated by a disagreement, traffic ticket, late meal, or misplaced keys. The event can trigger the batterer into a violent rage that can result in his attacking the person he is closest to. During this stage an abused woman may be beaten for seemingly minor or nonexistent reasons. Another woman in my practice reported that her husband beat her following a dinner party they held for some business associates. He accused her of being provocative and too outspoken. He criticized her clothing and also accused her of wanting him to lose the business deal.

Dr. Walker refers to the *third* stage as the "honeymoon phase." The batterer becomes extremely loving, gentle, kind, and apologetic for his abusive behavior. The client described above stated two days later in her session: "He loves me, he is genuinely sorry. I think it was the alcohol and cocaine that did it, after all, he just bought me that beautiful house in Rye, NY. . . . He promised me that he would never hit me again. . . . After all now he feels successful and just like his father. . . . You know his father is just like him. . . . My mother-in-law puts up with it. I'm sure we'll be fine." The battered woman believes these promises because she doesn't want to be beaten again, nor does she want to lose what appears to be a caring and nurturing provider. In this stage her partner romances her, brings flowers, buys gifts, takes her out to dinner, and spends extra time with the children. She believes that her household has been magically transformed into the classic happy family. She enters a period of denial and repression, overlooking the previous dynamics. Another client reported, "he lost his job because of his temper; upon his return home, he beat me so badly that my children begged him to stop while they cleaned up the blood off my body. One more time we were forced to go on welfare. He became enraged at any little thing like the children making a little noise. I was forced to work nights in a cleaning company. One evening I returned home to find my eight-year-old boy tied up to the bed post, beaten and scared. I found my husband crying in the living room, begging for mercy. I felt sad for him, he apologized and said he would never do it again. I believed him; his sadness and tears manipulated me. For the next few weeks he was wonderful to me and the children. Another incident occurred when I came home early and found him in bed with my ten-year-old daughter. I was devastated it was my fault, you know things would be better if he found a job. We eventually dropped welfare and had two incomes. I believed him." In reality the honeymoon phase wanes. It presents the battered woman and her children with a dilemma; they fall gradually from power, prosperity, or influence.

CHANGING ATTITUDES

The recognition of domestic violence as a deeply rooted problem in our society has come from several sources, most notably the women's movement and antirape organizers. Grassroots activists and human service professionals have borrowed counseling and organizing principles from the rape crisis movement to illustrate and address the similar plight of the battered woman. As public consciousness about sexism and its violent impact on all women's lives began to grow, shelters for battered women and their children opened, and social and legal reforms began to take place. Abused women took flight and organized supporters across the country.

Although it continues to face many cultural and economic challenges, the battered women's movement is here to stay. Abused women should be made aware that there is no need to feel shame about domestic violence. They should be educated about the physical, emotional, and sexual abuse counseling programs that are working to change the attitudes of battered women, their children, and batterers.

Given the complex nature of this problem, theorists have developed interventions and techniques that have been helpful to the counseling professionals working with battered women and children. The optimal goal in dealing with domestic violence is to keep the abuse from ever happening again, to prevent the explosive elements in a potentially abusive family system.

STRATEGIES AND INTERVENTIONS

Battered women who leave their homes frequently stay at the house of a relative, friend, or neighbor for a few days or months. There they hope to get support, comfort, safety, and distance from the batterer. Others choose to contact a battered women's hotline, where they get help with immediate intervention and referrals. A woman usually makes the first contact with the shelter by calling a twenty-four-hour hotline. She may have read about the shelter or gotten the number from a friend, doctor, church, social service agency, library, school, police officer, or a public service announcement or newspaper. During the hotline call the staff member evaluates the needs of the woman and the ability of the shelter to provide services. Usually women who have significant chemical dependencies or severe mental health problems are referred to more appropriate services where there are professionals to help via an interdisciplinary approach. Those who have been abused and are in need of shelter discuss their current situations with staff members and review the services available for shelter placement. If admission is indicated, a staff member will review the circumstances and make a decision whether to admit. If there is no room, a referral is made to another shelter. Once a decision to admit has been made, the living arrangements, fees, and guidelines are reviewed. However, no woman is rejected because of income or status. The woman is then asked to participate and cooperate in shelter life. Once an agreement has been made, travel arrangements are made either by giving the victim specific public transportation directions to the shelter or by arranging pickup by the shelter staff. When the woman and her children arrive at the shelter, they are greeted and oriented by a member of the staff who assures them safety, makes an assessment, and reviews shelter rules and routines. The family then meets the other families. Within twenty-four hours, the client is assigned a counselor who will continue to obtain information for intake and necessary services. These goals may include a methodology to include legal services, finances, school arrangements, Medicaid, emergency funds, and support counseling for all members. Some shelters refer to a case manager as the primary counselor and advocate for the family.

Services Available

■ **Counseling**—Short-term therapy, crisis intervention, assessment of the psychological needs of women and children is provided.

■ **Support Groups**—Group discussions revolve around each member's perceptions, peer support, and role modeling, especially in the area of problem solv-

ing and conflict resolution. Activity groups are provided for relaxation as well as the enhancement of everyday living skills.

■ **Family Sessions**—Family sessions are provided to help the client and children have a better understanding of family violence, current crisis, relocation, and conflict resolution.

■ **Legal Services**—A legal advocate will be available to provide information on a woman's legal rights and options. Clients will also be informed about family court laws and acts.

■ **Outreach Services**—Outreach services are also provided to the community whereby an assessment can be done in the area of need, advocacy, counseling, and referrals to appropriate facilities.

■ **Empowerment**—Each woman will be oriented to the cycle of battering and intergenerational patterns of abuse and their impact on the family system. They will become empowered to work through their issues in a therapeutic environment with the appropriate support staff, volunteers, and advocates.

■ **Children's Program**—This program provides a fun, safe place for children to play and explore their feelings through the course of play and artwork. The counseling component provides the children with individual sessions to work through their feelings of aggression, anger, sadness, and trauma.

■ **Community Education**—Domestic violence programs conduct presentations and seminars to community groups, professional associations, civic clubs, schools, training institutes, parent groups, and other institutions about family violence and related issues. They promote awareness of the scope of the problem, provide concrete information about available services, and offer information on recruiting volunteers and advocates for legislation and lobbying.

Leaving the Shelter

The average stay in a shelter for battered women is ninety days. When the family prepares to leave the shelter, an exit interview is conducted and follow-up contacts are made. Referrals to transitional housing, appropriate agencies, or to nonresidential service programs are made to provide support for the woman and children as they readjust to life outside the protected environment. If the woman returns home to the abuser, she is advised to seek nonresidential counseling with her abuser. The goal of the shelter staff is to assist the woman in whatever choice she makes without judging that choice, regardless of personal opinion.

Counselor Intervention and Self-Awareness

Treatment of a battered woman and her children is extremely difficult for the family, counselor, and community. The thought of someone being abused presents conflict for all involved. It is important for counselors to be aware of their feelings while working with battered families. Dr. Kim Oates (1986) refers to the battered professional as one who identifies with the client in a nonproductive way. Sometimes they are not aware that their feelings of anger lead them to overidentify with the battered client. In situations like these, Oates advises that counselors seek their own counseling to work through these feelings prior to making an attempt to work with battered families.

Last, human service workers must be ready to make an assessment and work with the battered family in a productive fashion to promote a healthier and a more positive environment.

CONCLUSION

It is quite difficult to realize that although public awareness and understanding of domestic violence in our society has greatly advanced over the last two decades, statistics on battered women and children continue to rise. In spite of the challenge, we recognize that it is our responsibility to raise and develop healthier families. We hope to guide our children and their families to safety, success, and challenging endeavors, without having to expose them to personal and familial violence. The pain caused by domestic violence is multilayered and can, in a sense, create a fragmented self, family, and society, which are not easily repaired.

The achievements of the battered women's movement are massive and inspiring. The goal of social change is macroscopic, with serious implications for the improvement of the institution of family, gender issues, and the psychological development of children. The achievement of such goals relies on the commitment of staff, community, public policy, legislation, advocates, educators, human services, volunteers, criminal justice system, and community-based programs. At the very least, their collaborative efforts have shown support for women throughout the world and have brought the issue to the public arena.

REFERENCES

Browne, A. (1986). "Assault and Homicide at Home: When Battered Women Kill." In M. J. Sakes and L. Saxe, eds., *Advances in Applied Social Psychology, Vol. 3*. Hillside, NJ: Lawrence Erlbaum.

Dobash, E. R., and P. R. Dobash (1992). *Women and Violence and Social Change*. London: Routledge, Chapman and Hall.

Fagan, J., and A. Browne (1982). "Violence between Spouses and Intimates." In J. A. Reiss and J. A. Roth, eds. *Understanding and Controlling Violence*. Washington DC: National Academy Press.

Fitch, F. J., and A. Papantonio (1983). "Men Who Batter: Some Pertinent Characteristics." *Journal of Nervous and Mental Disorders, 171*(3), 190–192.

Gelles, R. J., and M. A. Strauss (1988). *Intimate Violence*. New York: Simon and Schuster.

MacLeod, L. (1989). *Wife Battering and the Web of Hope: Progress, Dilemmas, and Vision of Prevention*. Ottawa: Health and Welfare Canada.

Morgan, E. S. (1966). *The Puritan Family*. Westport, CT: Greenwood Press.

Oates, K. (1986). *Child Abuse: A Community Concern*. New York: Brunner/Mazel, Inc.

Schechter, S. (1982). *Woman and Male Violence*. Boston, MA: South End Press.

Sutton, J. (1978). "The Growth of the British Movement for Battered Women," *Victimology, (3–4)2*, 576–584.

White, E. (1985). *Chain, Chain, Change*. Seal Press. Library of Congress.

Warrior, B. (1976). *Working on Wife Abuse*, 1st ed., subsequent editions published annually, Cambridge, MA.

SUGGESTED FURTHER READING _____

Jaffe, P., D. Wolfe, and S. Wilson (1990). *Children of Battered Women*. Beverly Hills, CA: Sage Publications.

Jaffe, P., S. Wilson, and L. Zak (1986). "Emotional and Physical Health Problems of Battered Women." *Canadian Journal of Psychiatry, 31,* 625–629.

Krugman, S. (1987). "Trauma in the Family: Perspectives on the Intergenerational Transmission of Violence." In B. A. Van der Kolk, ed., *Psychological Trauma* (pp. 127–151). Washington, DC: American Psychiatric Press.

Stark, E., and A. Flitcraft (1988). "Violence among Intimates: An Epidemiological Review." In V. Van Hasselt, ed. *Handbook of Family Violence*. New York: Plenum.

Steinmetz, S. K., and M. A. Straus (1974). *Violence in the Family*. New York: Harper and Row.

Walker, L. E. A. (1984). *The Battered Woman Syndrome*. New York: Springer.

CHAPTER 10

THE CHILD WELFARE DELIVERY SYSTEM IN THE UNITED STATES

DAVID S. LIEDERMAN
MADELYN DEWOODY
MEGAN C. SYLVESTER

Child welfare is a field of human services that focuses on the general well-being of children. It incorporates services and efforts designed to promote children's physical, psychological, and social development. Child welfare and social service agencies offer a range of services to children and their families to ensure the health and well-being of children.

The general principle is that child welfare is the responsibility, first and foremost, of the child's family, with human services supporting and complementing the role of the family. There are situations, however, when families encounter difficulties meeting the needs and fostering the development of their children. These difficulties may be so severe as to put the children at risk of physical, emotional, or developmental harm. The federal government has organized a system of child welfare services specifically designed to assist children and their families, supporting the strengths of families whenever possible, and intervening when necessary to ensure the safety and well-being of children. Child welfare services may be provided by public and private nonprofit agencies and usually are provided by social workers. They may take many forms, depending on the child's and family's situation and needs.

THE CORE CHILD WELFARE SERVICES

In general, child welfare services fall into four core categories:

1. Services to support and strengthen families
2. Protective services
3. Out-of-home care services
4. Adoption services

Services to Support and Strengthen Families

For many children and their families, child welfare services involve supportive services that are provided to assist the family in remaining together. These services are designed to support, reinforce, and strengthen the ability of parents to meet the needs of their children. When a child welfare agency provides services to support and strengthen families, it does not assume the responsibilities of the parent. Instead, the agency supports parents in protecting and promoting the well-being of their children and strengthens parents' ability to solve problems that may result in the abuse or neglect of their children.

There are three major types of supportive services: family resource, support, and educational services; family-centered services; and intensive family crisis services.

Family Resource, Support, and Educational Services. These services, which are broad and often overlap, assist adults in their roles as parents. Resource services are varied and include, as examples, providing referrals for services needed by the family and helping with transportation. Support services are likewise diverse and include,

141

as one example, parent support groups, often facilitated by the group members themselves. Educational services seek to develop parenting skills and often involve parenting classes where parents learn, among other things, children's stages of development.

Family-Centered Services.   These services help families with problems that threaten the well-being of children and the family as a whole. They are designed to remedy problems as early as possible. These services can include the following:

— Family counseling;
— Parent education programs designed to enhance parents' knowledge and skills;
— The identification and use of social support networks that include individuals, groups, and organizations;
— Advocacy to obtain services for families when services do not currently exist;
— Case management services to facilitate access to needed services and coordinate multiple resources.

Intensive Family-Centered Crisis Services. These services are designed to assist a family when a crisis is so serious that it may result in the removal of the child from the home. Intensive family-centered crisis services attempt to ensure the safety and well-being of the child and strengthen and preserve the family in order to avoid the unnecessary placement of children outside the home. Services may include crisis intervention counseling, alcohol and drug treatment, and parenting education.

Three specific services that can support and strengthen families are child day care, housing, and adolescent pregnancy prevention and parenting services. *Child day care* responds to the needs of children, families, and communities. Child day care can be provided in family day care homes, group child day care homes, and child day care centers and may be offered for part of the day, full days, or, in the case of respite care, twenty-four hours a day. *Adolescent pregnancy prevention*

and parenting services have become an important component of child welfare services as the rate of teenagers giving birth to children has increased dramatically over the last decade. Child welfare services include education and referral services related to preventing pregnancy and services for parenting teenagers, such as parenting education and assistance in locating child care and completing their education. *Housing services* have become increasingly important as the number of homeless children and families in America and the number of children who live in substandard conditions have risen. Child welfare agencies help meet the housing needs of children and their families by linking them to public housing resources and social services and by advocating for more and better affordable housing.

Protective Services.   Protective services are designed to protect children from abuse or neglect (sometimes referred to as maltreatment) by their parents or caregivers and to improve the functioning of the family so that children are no longer at risk. The specific types of maltreatment to which child welfare services respond include the following (Katz-Sanford, Howe, and McGrath, 1975):

— Physical abuse: physical injury to a child;
— Sexual abuse: sexual maltreatment of a child;
— Emotional abuse and neglect: emotional injury to a child or failure to meet the child's emotional or affectional needs;
— Deprivation of necessities: failure to provide adequate food, shelter, or clothing;
— Inadequate supervision: leaving children for long periods of time without access to an adult who can meet their needs and protect them from harm;
— Medical neglect: failure to seek essential medical care for the child;
— Educational neglect: failure to enroll a child in school or indifference to the child's failure to attend school;
— Exploitation or overwork: forcing a child to work for unreasonably long periods of time or to perform unreasonable work;

— Exposure of a child to unhealthy circumstances: subjecting a child to adult behavior that is considered "morally injurious," such as criminal activity, prostitution, alcoholism, or drug addiction.

Protective services are provided by the public agency—often referred to as child protective services (CPS)—mandated by law to respond to reports of child abuse and neglect and to intervene to protect children.

Protective services are offered to accomplish several purposes: to strengthen families who are experiencing problems that can lead or have led to abuse or neglect; to enable children to remain safely with their parents; to temporarily separate a child at imminent risk of harm from his or her parent; to reunify children with their parents whenever possible; and to ensure a child permanency with another family when the child cannot return to his or her parent without serious risk of harm (Association of Public Child Welfare Administrators, 1988).

Protective services include the following:

Case Finding and Intake.   The agency receives reports of child abuse and neglect. Reports received by protective services agencies generally fall into two categories: problems in the parent-child relationship, such as physical abuse, neglect, abandonment, the absence of the parent, or conflict between a parent and an adolescent; and problems that a child is experiencing, such as emotional difficulties, runaway behavior, failure to attend school, or physical problems.

When a report of abuse or neglect is made, the child protective service agency is responsible for investigating the situation. Contact is made with the family, others with knowledge of the situation, and the child. The agency will determine whether abuse or neglect has occurred (often referred to as "substantiation" of the report) and whether there is a substantial and immediate risk to the child that would warrant taking steps to remove the child from the home to a setting of safety.

Case Planning.   The agency assists families after abuse or neglect is reported and substantiated. At the heart of protective services is work with the family to prevent further abuse or neglect and to correct the problems that led to maltreatment of the child. The needs of the parents and the child are addressed through a range of services, such as extended day care centers and crisis nurseries to prevent further maltreatment; homemaker services; counseling services; and emergency caregiving services.

Court Involvement in Protective Services. Decisions are made by the courts regarding where a child will live and the changes that a family must make. Protective service agencies seek court action when parents are not able or willing to make the changes needed for their child's well-being or the situation presents a danger to the child so that the child can be protected only by placing him or her outside the family. In these situations, the court will order the child to be removed from custody of his or her parents and placed in out-of-home care. Only about 20 percent of the cases reported to protective services agencies require court action.

Out-of-Home Care Services for Children

Out-of-home care services are utilized when the situation presents such a risk to the child that the child must be separated from his or her parents and placed with another family or in another setting. In these situations, the public agency responsible for protecting children will seek court action to authorize placement of the child outside the home. There are three major types of out-of-home care services: family foster care, kinship care, and residential group care. These services, provided as twenty-four-hour-a-day care, are designed as temporary services for the child while the agency works with the family to correct the problems that led to placement of the child.

Out-of-home care in all settings also includes services to meet the social, emotional, educational, and developmental needs of the child:

— *Family foster care.* Family foster care is provided by adults who are not related to the child and who are licensed or approved as foster parents by a child welfare agency.

— *Kinship care.* Kinship care is the placement of children with relatives. Many agencies consider relatives as the first choice for out-of-home care because remaining with family members is often less disruptive for the child.

— *Group residential care.* Group residential care is composed of a variety of services. One type is group care, that is, living facilities located within residential communities that care for a small group of unrelated children, usually four to eight in number. Residential care, another type of care, is usually provided to a larger number of children or adolescents and involves highly structured, intensive, and planned therapeutic interventions for children and adolescents who have significant emotional or behavioral disorders.

Adoption Services

Adoption is a child welfare service that provides a new permanent family for children whose birth parents are unable or unwilling to provide them with the love, support, and nurturing they need. Adoption services meet the needs of three groups of children who need adoptive families: (1) healthy infants; (2) children with "special needs," such as children with disabilities, older children seeking permanent families, and sibling groups of children to be placed together with an adoptive family; and (3) children from other countries.

Agencies that provide adoption services identify prospective adoptive parents for children awaiting adoption; assess the ability of prospective parents to meet the needs of children waiting to be adopted; prepare the child and birth parent(s) for adoption; place the child with the adoptive family; assist the adoptive family in finalizing the adoption; and provide postadoption support services, such as casework services, linkages to community resources, and parenting groups.

EMERGING CHILD WELFARE ISSUES

Pediatric AIDS and HIV Infection

Child welfare professionals are confronting a new reality in the form of acquired immunodeficiency syndrome (AIDS) and the human immunodeficiency virus (HIV) that causes AIDS. Growing numbers of children are acquiring HIV from mothers who are themselves infected with HIV and, as a result, their lives are medically, psychologically, and socially threatened. Some of these children are "boarder babies," in hospitals awaiting homes because they are ready for discharge, but their parents are unable to take responsibility for them or bring them home. Other children who have been infected with HIV live with their parents, who cannot provide for them. In many instances, their parents are also involved with drugs, which compounds the problem. In addition to children with HIV infection, there are children who are not infected with HIV whose parents are dying, leaving them orphaned by AIDS. Child welfare agencies must be prepared to help through such services as placing the children with extended families or by finding adoptive families to care for them.

Child welfare agencies provide a range of services to meet the needs of children and families who are affected by HIV/AIDS. Some programs are community based and provide services to ensure that children who are infected with HIV receive the therapeutic, developmental, and educational services they need; help parents understand and manage the child's illness; and support the efforts of the child and the family to deal with the grief and bereavement issues that accompany the disease. Specific services may include information and referral for needed financial, medical, mental health, and social services; crisis intervention services when the immediate needs of the child place stress on the family; family therapy; and case management and coordination of medical and psychological treatment. For children whose families are not available or able to care for them, child welfare agencies provide specialized foster care—twenty-four-hour-a-day care by foster parents who are specially trained to meet the special needs of these children. Children who are healthy or who have been infected with HIV and have lost their parents to AIDS likewise need child welfare services. Child welfare agencies work with the extended family to prepare them to care for children who are attempting to cope with the loss of their parents from AIDS and provide ongoing supportive services to both the child and the family after placing the child. For other children, child welfare agencies recruit and train adoptive parents, offering a broad range of education and supportive services to ensure that adoptive families understand and can meet the significant psychosocial needs of these children.

Children with Incarcerated Parents

As our country's rate of incarceration escalates, child welfare professionals are encountering growing numbers of children who have parents in prison. We currently estimate that 1.5 million U.S. children have an incarcerated parent, and many thousands of others have experienced the incarceration of a parent at some point in their lives. As a result of parental incarceration and the criminal behaviors that precede it, many of these children experience disrupted and multiple placements, decreased quality of care, and an ongoing lack of contact with their parents. They are at increased risk for poor academic performance, truancy, early pregnancy, substance abuse, delinquency, and adult incarceration.

The growing number of children with parents in prison has serious implications for the child welfare system. Approximately 42,000 children with parents in prison currently live in out-of-home care, and we suspect that many more of these children have intermittent contact with child welfare services. The children of incarcerated mothers are particularly vulnerable because these mothers are often the sole caregivers and sole support of their families. Although most children of incarcerated mothers live with grandparents or other relative caregivers, they are at risk of place-

ment in the child welfare system if fragile family caregiving relationships deteriorate.

Until recently, few statistics on children of offenders and very little research have been available. As their numbers increase, though, child welfare professionals are recognizing that this is a particularly vulnerable group of children. Consequently, there has been a recent movement to develop policies and practices that address their special needs. In particular, child welfare agencies are beginning to consider ways of identifying and gathering information about the children in their caseloads who have parents in prison, strengthening reunification and permanency planning services to those families, and providing specialized training to improve caseworkers' and foster parents' capacity to help children and families separated by incarceration.

Cultural Competence

Cultural competence is a personal and organizational commitment to learn about one another and how individual cultural differences affect how we act, feel, and present ourselves. The purpose of cultural competence is the sharing of knowledge about all aspects of culture (gender, religion, age, sexuality, education, and socioeconomic level), not just the racial/ethnic culture of people of color. Cultural competence is an enrichment process that allows everyone to share and learn. Cultural competence is part of best practice. To efficiently and effectively carry out all the processes that are encompassed by best practice, the cultural implications should be identified and integrated into organizational operations. These processes include the planning, organization, and administration of social work services; the establishment of state and local regulations; content training and teaching in schools of social work; in-service training and staff development; board orientation and development; fiscal planning; and community relations.

The child welfare field is currently undergoing rapid and dramatic change as it struggles to provide quality services to children and their families. One of the most critical challenges the field faces is the need to understand and respond effectively to striking changes in the multicultural nature of American society—changes brought about by the mixture of racial, ethnic, social, cultural, and religious traditions of the children and families who make up our diverse society. These changes, coupled with the demands of a more outcome-driven environment, a more punitive outlook by society on the families served in child welfare, an anti-immigration sentiment, and the impact of managed care, challenge today's leaders. Child welfare executives face the dilemma of whether to include striving toward cultural competence as an organizational goal, given the range of pressures that impact their agencies.

Currently, children of color are disproportionately represented in the child welfare system, particularly in out-of-home care and the juvenile justice system. Unfortunately, children of color remain in these systems for longer periods of time and are less likely to be reunited with their families than children of European descent. Children of color in the child welfare system are ethnically diverse and include mainly those of Latino, African American, Asian American, and Native American cultures.

A common characteristic among children and families served in child welfare is poverty. One in five children in America is poor. The ramifications of poverty—unemployment, inadequate education, inferior or nonexistent health care, substandard housing, and welfare dependence—all increase the likelihood that children in poor families will at some point need the services of the child welfare system.

A crucial issue raised by the increase in the number of people of diverse cultures in the child welfare system is the degree to which current policies, programs, and services are relevant to the cultural values, traditions, needs, and expectations of the populations served. The child welfare system faces a challenge to extend itself in support of the premise that provision of effective child welfare services is directly related to the knowledge and understanding of, as well as sensitivity and responsiveness to, the culture of the client population. This, as well as the formidable task of recruiting and retaining a qualified, diverse staff, presents not only challenges but also opportunities for more effective leadership, management, and service delivery.

Child welfare agencies respond to issues of cultural diversity in many different ways. Many child welfare agency management teams are aggressively shaping an organizational agenda that encompasses a broadened vision, expanded goals and objectives, and modified policies, procedures, and programs to better meet clients' needs. The management teams of these enlightened organizations are also attempting to raise their individual comfort levels by gaining an understanding of their own cultural backgrounds and biases, the cultures of others, and multicultural organizational behavior. These management teams are learning how to positively manage the impact of diversity in their organizations—indeed, how to celebrate and enjoy the benefits of cultural diversity.

Conversely, many child welfare agencies and management team members are reluctant to develop a personal and professional agenda regarding the diverse populations of children and families served by the systems they administer. Many see no need to address the subject of cultural diversity, often because of a belief that acknowledging cultural difference could appear to condone discrimination. This "one size fits all" approach denies the existence of the current pluralistic society in the United States, the changing face of child welfare, and the resulting cultural diversity that is an inevitable part of the day-to-day experience.

As child welfare professionals, it is our responsibility not only to understand but also to build a consensus around the best way to develop programs, policies, and practices that recognize and support cultural differences. Through the development and implementation of appropriate and responsive programs, policies, and practices, we can effect systemic change. The number of people of color living in this country will drastically increase in the next few decades. The problems we currently face in the child welfare system will only be exacerbated if we do not take the necessary steps to stem the tide of children of color into the system.

Substance Abuse

As the abuse of alcohol and other drugs has continued to escalate and growing numbers of women have begun to use illegal drugs, child welfare agencies have observed a significant relationship between alcohol and other drug abuse and the well-being of children. Dramatic increases in the number of child abuse reports and in the number of children entering foster care have been specifically tied to parental alcohol and drug abuse. Child welfare agencies are responding to record numbers of child protective service referrals concerning drug-exposed infants, many of whom may also have been infected with the AIDS virus and who may be medically fragile, and older children who have experienced abuse or neglect because of their parents' substance abuse. In all age groups, growing numbers of children who have been affected by their parents' alcohol and drug problems are entering foster care.

Child welfare agencies are called on to respond to the needs of families who require immediate and intensive help in resolving their alcohol or drug dependency. Agencies must also help families correct the problems that alcohol and drugs create for their children. Child welfare agencies provide services to prevent and intervene early in situations involving child abuse and substance abuse, such as outreach to newborns and mothers; referrals for needed financial, housing, and social services; child day care; and coordination with community alcohol and drug treatment services. Special services may be needed by pregnant women who are abusing alcohol or other drugs. Early detection, proper prenatal care, and medical and substance abuse treatment services can be mobilized to reduce the damage that alcohol and drugs can cause for both the mother and the fetus.

Child welfare agencies also meet the needs of infants and toddlers who were prenatally exposed to alcohol and other drugs and older children whose parents, because of substance abuse, have not provided the psychological, social, and developmental environment that children need for healthy growth. Child welfare agencies, through child protective services, assess the risk to children posed by parental substance abuse; determine whether the child may remain safely at home with the parent or should be placed away from the parent to ensure the child's safety; and provide or coordinate the range of health, educational, and developmental services that children need. Substance abuse, which is often a complex and long-standing problem, presents the child welfare system with special challenges to protect children, provide effective services to parents and to children who may have significant health and developmental needs, and plan for permanent families for children whose parents are unable to care for them because of substance abuse.

INSTITUTIONAL SYSTEMS

Child welfare services are provided by agencies in both the public and the private sectors. Services to support and strengthen families, out-of-home care services, and adoption services are provided by public child welfare agencies and private nonprofit agencies in the voluntary sector. Public child welfare agencies often combine the way in which they provide these services, directly providing some services and contracting with private nonprofit agencies to provide other services. Private nonprofit agencies may provide a range of child welfare services or may specialize in certain services such as adoption or residential care for children with serious emotional disturbances.

Protective services traditionally have been undertaken only by government agencies charged by law with the protection of children—child protective services (CPS) agencies located within public welfare departments; law enforcement agencies; and the courts. Although CPS agencies and law enforcement agencies both investigate reports of child abuse and neglect, CPS and law enforcement investigations differ. The CPS agencies are concerned only with child protection; their efforts focus on determining whether a child has been mistreated and whether the child can remain safely with his or her parents. Law enforcement agencies focus on whether criminal charges should be filed in response to child maltreatment. Family and juvenile courts consider cases arising from CPS and law enforcement investigations. The courts will, when appropriate, declare a child in need of protection; remove custody of the child from the parent(s) and place the child in the custody of the CPS agency, and approve the child's placement in out-of-home care. When the court has made such decisions, the court will periodically review the progress that is being made toward resolving the problems that led to the child's placement and the progress that is being made toward finding a permanent family for the child. When criminal charges are filed, the court with jurisdiction over criminal matters may also become involved in the case.

CHILD WELFARE LAW

Child welfare services are shaped largely by federal and state law.

Federal Law

The Child Abuse Prevention and Treatment Act (CAPTA) of 1974. This federal legislation, enacted in response to growing public concern about child abuse, provides financial assistance to states and communities to prevent, identify, and treat child abuse and neglect. To receive funds, states must designate an agency with responsibility for investigating abuse and neglect; establish a reporting system for all known or suspected instances of child abuse and neglect; enact laws that protect all children under the age of eighteen from

mental injury, physical injury, and sexual abuse; and develop a system that provides a *guardian ad litem* who represents the interests of abused and neglected children when their cases go to court.

CAPTA was amended in 1996 (P. L. 104–235). Highlights include provisions for the establishment of citizen review panels to evaluate state child protection policies and procedures, provisions for termination of parental rights in cases of abandoned infants, and provisions for public disclosure of information in fatalities caused by child abuse and neglect.

The Indian Child Welfare Act of 1978. This legislation was designed to expand the services available to support and strengthen Native American families and to put safeguards in place regarding the custody and placement of Native American children. The law directs agencies to work closely with Native American children, families, and tribes when there has been a report of child abuse or neglect and requires the placement of Native American children who have been abused or neglected with Native American families whenever possible. Importantly, the law also recognizes the authority of tribal courts to handle Native American child welfare matters.

The Adoption Assistance and Child Welfare Act of 1980 (PL 96–272). This legislation, also known as Public Law 96–272, is considered the most important child welfare legislation enacted over the past several decades. Public Law 96–272 provides federal support for children in foster care, requires that states have in place a planning process designed to ensure that children who are placed out of their homes will have a permanent home in a reasonable period of time, and provides a subsidy program to meet the special needs of children who are adopted. The law sets forth certain standards for child welfare services that states must meet to receive federal funds. These standards, which have significantly affected the way that child welfare services are provided, include the following:

▬ "Reasonable efforts" must be made to keep children with their families whenever possible. States are expected to have in place prevention, intervention, and crisis services such as day care, crisis counseling, and access to emergency financial assistance.

▬ Permanency planning services are to be provided to children and their families when children have been removed from their parents' custody because of abuse and neglect. These services include "reasonable efforts" to reunite children and their families whenever possible. When reunification is not possible, alternative permanent plans are required, such as placement with extended family or adoption.

▬ Out-of-home placements are to be made in the "least restrictive setting." When children are placed in out-of-home care, the type of care selected for the child must be in the most "family-like" setting appropriate to the child's needs and in close proximity to parents. Generally, a child will be placed with extended family or in family foster care. If the child has special medical, mental health, or developmental needs, a group or residential care setting may be most appropriate.

▬ Detailed case plans and regular case reviews must be prepared to help ensure that the child has a permanent home as soon as possible after being placed in out-of-home care.

The Independent Living Initiative Title IV-E of the Social Security Act. This legislation funds services for adolescents in out-of-home care who will not be reunited with their families and who will leave care at age eighteen to live on their own. Services must be designed to teach basic living skills, provide educational and job training opportunities, and assist youth in locating housing.

The Omnibus Budget Reconciliation Act of 1993 (PL 103–66). The 1993 OBRA established a new subpart of Title IV-B of the Social Security Act titled Family Preservation and Support Services. This program provides funding for (1) community-based family support programs that work with families before a crisis occurs to enhance child development and increase family stability; (2) family preservation programs that serve families in crisis or at risk of having their children placed in out-of-home care and provide follow-up services,

including family reunification; and (3) evaluation, research, training, and technical assistance in the area of family support and family preservation. The law targeted nearly $1 billion for the five years (1994–98) for which the Family Preservation and Family Support Program was authorized.

Personal Responsibility and Work Opportunity Reconciliation Act of 1996 (PL 104–193). This act eliminated the federal guarantee of a basic floor of economic security for every family. The law abolished Aid to Families with Dependent Children (AFDC), the primary federal cash aid program for families, and created a block grant program, Temporary Assistance to Needy Families (TANF), for low-income families with children deemed eligible by the states. Under the TANF program, states receive a fixed level of resources for income support and work programs without regard to subsequent changes in the level of need in a state. The law established a sixty-month lifetime limit on TANF assistance for each family, although states may set a shorter state time limit. The law also tightened eligibility for the Supplemental Security Income (SSI) program, thereby denying cash assistance to thousands of disabled children.

As a result of the welfare overhaul, vulnerable families may be at increased risk for entering the child welfare system. A loss of income or support—caused by such factors as a TANF time limit, an insufficient supply of decent jobs, or state eligibility restrictions on cash assistance—may prevent families from providing basic food and shelter for their children and may result in hunger, homelessness, child neglect, or other family crises. Severe economic problems also heighten stress in families and in some cases may lead to child abuse or other forms of family violence. In addition, families that lose SSI benefits for children with disabilities may be forced to seek assistance from the child welfare system.

Multiethnic Placement Act of 1994 (PL 103–382). This act addressed the issue of transracial adoption by prohibiting discrimination in foster and adoptive placement on the basis of race, color, or national origin. It also required agencies to engage in diligent recruitment efforts to ensure that children needing placement are served in a timely and effective manner. The original MEPA statute contained specific language explicitly allowing agencies to consider a child's cultural, ethnic, or racial background and the ability of foster and adoptive parents to meet the child's needs.

MEPA was amended in 1996 (PL 104–188) to omit the original language that explicitly allowed agencies to consider a child's cultural, ethnic, or racial background. MEPA's recruitment provisions remain unchanged, however, and states must continue to seek out potential adoptive families who reflect the ethnic and racial diversity of children needing placement.

State Law

Each state addresses child welfare services in its statutes. In most states, the law does the following:

— Directs that services be available to help strengthen and support families;
— Defines the conduct that constitutes child abuse and neglect;
— Identifies the agency responsible for receiving, screening, and investigating reports of child abuse and neglect and protecting children;
— Identifies the court that has jurisdiction over child abuse and neglect cases and that has the authority to remove the custody of children from their parents;
— Specifies the duties of the agency in working with children and families toward preserving and reunifying families;
— Sets forth the conditions under which parental rights can be terminated and a child freed for adoption; and
— Describes the procedures for adoption.

PUBLIC POLICY

Child welfare services also include efforts to ensure that government decision-making is based on what children and their families need. It involves clearly defining child welfare issues and analyzing the merits of various approaches to enhancing the strengths of children and their families and meeting their needs. There are a number of child welfare policy issues that have been and will continue to be debated, including the proper role of the federal and state governments in protecting children, the balance between protecting children and preserving families, determinations about when in-home services are most appropriate and when out-of-home care should be used, and the extent to which resources should be allocated between prevention and treatment services.

THE CHILD WELFARE LEAGUE OF AMERICA, INC.

The Child Welfare League of America, Inc. (CWLA), the largest and oldest membership organization for child protection in North America, represents the public and voluntary child welfare sectors. The CWLA supports its more than 800 member organizations through policy, practice, and research initiatives within seven major program areas: adolescent pregnancy services, child protection, services to support and strengthen families, family foster care and kinship care, group care, adoption, and child day care. In addition, CWLA has eleven special initiatives: cultural competence, HIV infection and AIDS, chemical dependency, youth services, child and youth care credentialing, housing and homelessness, recruiting and retaining competent staff, state commissioners' roundtable, performance evaluation, child welfare and the law, and rural child welfare services.

CWLA is the world's largest publisher of child welfare materials. Its Publications Division reaches more than half a million professionals annually through its production and distribution of books, monographs, research reports, newsletters, a quarterly magazine, and a scholarly professional journal.

A major component of CWLA's work is its advocacy on Capitol Hill on behalf of children. Its Public Policy Division is committed to significantly improving the full array of federally funded services and supports needed to address the escalating crisis facing at-risk children and families and the child welfare system itself.

REFERENCES

Association of Public Child Welfare Administrators (1988). *Guidelines for a Model System of Protective Services for Abused and Neglected Children and Their Families.* Washington, DC: American Public Welfare Association.

Katz-Sanford, R., A. W. Howe, and M. McGrath, eds. (1975, Spring). "Child Neglect Laws in America" [Special issue]. *Family Law Quarterly, 9*(1).

SUGGESTED FURTHER READING

Costin, L. B., C. J. Bell, and S. W. Downs, eds. (1991). *Child Welfare: Policies and Practice,* 4th ed. New York: Longman.

Helfer, R. E., and R. S. Kempe (1987). *The Battered Child,* 4th ed. Chicago: The University of Chicago Press.

Kadushin, A., and J. A. Martin (1988). *Child Welfare Services,* 4th ed. New York: Macmillan.

Laird, J., and A. Hartman, eds. (1985). *A Handbook of Child Welfare: Context, Knowledge, and Practice.* New York: The Free Press.

Maidman, F., ed. (1984). *Child Welfare: A Sourcebook of Knowledge and Practice.* New York: Child Welfare League of America, Inc.

Pecora, P. J., J. K. Whittaker, and A. N. Maluccio, eds. (1992). *The Child Welfare Challenge: Policy, Practice, and Research.* New York: Aldine De Gruyter.

CHAPTER 11

CHILD MALTREATMENT AND ABUSE:
THE PROBLEM AND HUMAN SERVICES

JAMES EDELL LOPEZ

Child abuse occurs every day. The following example received national attention and became a contemporary symbol of child abuse.

> *Early Monday morning, November 2, 1987, six-year-old Lisa "Steinberg" (it was discovered later she was not legally adopted) was rushed to St. Vincent's Hospital. EMS workers picked her up unconscious from the bathroom floor in the apartment of Joel Steinberg, an attorney, and his companion, Hedda Nussbaum, a former writer and editor of children's books. The girl was covered with bruises, brutally beaten by Steinberg several times the day and evening before, the last time fatally for "staring" at him. One of the bruises on her head was delivered with such force that her brain shifted position inside her skull (a condition known as subdural hematoma). Subsequent investigation and court hearings found that Steinberg had also frequently brutally battered Nussbaum, his companion; she and Lisa had come to the attention of police as well as medical and Special Services for Children authorities several times in the past. After three days in the hospital in a coma, and with her brain permanently damaged, life support equipment was removed (Fontana, 1991).*

Renewed concern over child abuse as a major social problem emerged in the 1960s. The main agents were Dr. C. H. Kempe, a pediatrician, and his associates who practiced medicine in Denver, Colorado (Corby, 1987). Their work with children led them to conclude that severe physical maltreatment was a problem that occurred more often than previously thought. Kempe published his findings in 1962 in a now-classic article in the *Journal of the American Medical Association* in which the term "battered child syndrome" was first used (Kempe et al., 1962).

The article focused on children who were physically battered by their parents or caretakers and argued for psychological factors as the dominant cause of abuse. Unrealistic parental expectations for children, he argued, frequently led to frustration and physical abuse. The abuse, in Kempe's view, was likely to continue and worsen unless some form of intervention took place. Above all, Kempe's concern was to protect the child, and his model of intervention was either to remove children from the parents or place them in the hospital and then treat the parent (Kempe et al., 1962, pp. 17–24).

Kempe and his associates widely influenced how disciplines such as medicine, psychology, social work, and human and social services understand, treat, and prevent child abuse. The emerging public concern from his efforts with child maltreatment brought two major benefits. First, it resulted in more funding allocated to research on child abuse, and over time other theories and broader perspectives have developed (Fontana, 1991). Today, three decades of research and intervention have produced a basic knowledge—though it is still incomplete—concerning incidence, cause, treatment, and prevention. Second, the increased public attention to child abuse spurred widespread government involvement. By 1968, all fifty states had enacted some form of law that mandated reporting of suspected child abuse cases. In 1974, after ten years of debate and controversy, Congress signed the Child Abuse Prevention and Treatment Act (PL 93–247) into law. While individual states determine their own definitions of maltreatment, the federal legislation helped to create standards to identify and manage child abuse cases (McCurdy and Daro, 1993).

Twenty-five years after Kempe's article had focused national attention on child maltreatment, the case of Lisa Steinberg showed that the problem was still present. As Dr. Fontana, Chairman of the Mayor's Task Force on Child Abuse and Neglect and Medical Director of the New York Foundling Hospital has said, "We rediscover child abuse whenever an abused child's death makes headlines. This, our reawakening, is Lisa's legacy" (1991, p. 6).

THE PROBLEM OF CHILD MALTREATMENT

What Is Child Abuse?

What constitutes child abuse has been the subject of debate and disagreement since Kempe's article was published. An effective definition of child maltreatment, Mayhall and Norgard (1983) point out, should include (1) what is legally considered harmful to the child; (2) when and what must be reported; (3) when intervention occurs, how, and by whom; (4) what is "imminent danger" and when it occurs; and (5) when the court system is justified in intervening in the family and overriding the authority of the parents (possibly terminating their parental rights) to protect children. The debate turns on one central issue: The definition given to child abuse determines the establishment and enforcement of child abuse laws [for a description of how child protective services (CPS) use the law to determine whether child maltreatment has occurred, see the section "Social Service Response"]. It is not surprising, then, that the original Child Abuse Prevention and Treatment Act signed into law in 1974 has undergone two major revisions, reflecting the complex-

ity of the maltreatment problem. The current definition follows:

> *Child abuse and neglect means the physical or mental injury, sexual abuse or exploitation, neglectful treatment, or maltreatment of a child under the age of eighteen, or the age specified by the child protection law of the State in question, by a person (including any employee of a residential facility or any staff person providing out-of-home care) who is responsible for the child's welfare under circumstances which indicate that the child's health or welfare is harmed or threatened thereby, as determined in accordance with regulations prescribed by the Secretary (Child Abuse Amendments of 1984, Section 102).*

What Is the Extent of the Child Abuse Problem?

The extent of the child abuse problem is subject to wide debate. The debate centers on two issues. First, while the federal government helped to establish a set of standards to identify and manage child abuse cases through the Child Abuse Prevention and Treatment Act, it is still the individual states that establish definitions of maltreatment, procedures for investigation, services that are offered, and systems of data collection (McCurdy and Daro, 1993). Thus, part of the problem in estimating the number of child abuse cases nationwide is the lack of uniform procedures across the states for collecting data. For example, forty-two states have a central reporting registry. But half of those states maintain statistics on the calendar year and the other half on the fiscal year. Methods of counting child abuse cases present more of a problem. While some states count two or more reports of the same episode of maltreatment as one report, other states consider these as separate reports (McCurdy and Daro, 1993).

Despite these difficulties, the National Committee for the Prevention of Child Abuse (NCPCA) each year since 1986 has conducted a survey of federally appointed liaisons for child abuse and neglect in each of the fifty states. This survey obtains data on (1) the number of child abuse reports and the characteristics of those reports; (2) the number of child abuse fatalities; and (3) changes in funding and how that affects services offered to children (McCurdy and Daro, 1993).

The NCPCA estimates that in 1992, 2,936,000 children were reported to state CPS agencies as alleged victims of abuse. That makes 45 children per 1000 reported for maltreatment in the United States (McCurdy and Daro, 1993); 45 percent of these were due to neglect, 27 percent to physical abuse, 17 percent to sexual abuse, 7 percent to emotional maltreatment, and 8 percent to other reasons.

The forty states that were able to provide data for 1992 (forty-nine states responded to the NCPCA query, and nine of these could not provide data) recorded an average 7.8 percent increase in reports of child abuse between 1991 and 1992. Child abuse reports have grown at an average of 6 percent per year during the period from 1985 to 1992 (Daro and Mitchell, 1987). While it is difficult to sort out the relative contributions of increased public awareness, changes in reporting systems, and actual cases to the increased number of reports, most state liaisons contacted by NCPCA stated they believed the increase to be due to a real increase in maltreatment, resulting from increased economic stress and substance abuse.

The second and more serious problem in estimating the extent of the child abuse problem stems from reliance on "formal reports," that is, the number of reports of maltreatment made to CPSs discussed above. Such formal reports, critics charge, may seriously underestimate the incidence of maltreatment. Evidence for this position comes from studies and interviews with random samples of individuals that reveal higher rates of maltreatment than do formal reports (Straus et al., 1980).

One study done in 1980 estimated that between 3.1 and 4 million children are kicked or punched by their parents at some point during their childhood. These shocking findings were not substantiated in a follow-up study done ten years later. That study showed a decrease in the most serious forms of physical violence but did substantiate previously reported levels of pushing and slapping. Moreover, interviews with random samples of individuals corroborate the findings in these surveys. The gap between cases "formally reported" and the actual incidence suggested by the foregoing reports was highlighted by the National Incidence Study, which showed that only 33 percent of the cases identified by professionals throughout the country were ever formally reported (Westat, 1981).

Neither the formal reports nor the interviews with random samples give a definitive statement about numbers. They do, however, provide a base to discuss the extent of the problem and the frequency of the types of maltreatment. As Daro points out, the figures "make a powerful case for public intervention" (1988, p. 15).

What Are the Consequences of Maltreatment?

Any consideration of the consequences of child maltreatment must focus on concern for human suffering and its individual, social, and moral effects. First, child abuse causes physical trauma. In addition to bruises, serious injuries such as fractures, subdural hematomas (bleeding inside the skull), and so on, children who are abused may suffer from serious and recurrent medical problems, such as damage to the central nervous system, leaving the child with seizures, mental retardation, and sensory deficits. Not directly related to the episode of abuse are medical problems such as lack of immunizations, inadequate hygiene, poor nutrition, and anemia, among others (Martin, 1980).

Abused children are also at risk of various psychological problems, such as mental retardation, learning disorders, and language delays. Evidence for this risk comes from clinicians and from research that has documented maltreated children to have more developmental problems compared to control groups. Maltreated children are also at greater risk for depression, fearfulness, mistrust toward adults, lack of age-appropriate relationships with peers, as well as poor self-image (Elmer, 1977).

Second, there is the issue of what happens to maltreated children as they grow into adulthood. The most obvious long-term effect of abuse is its influence on how abused children later parent their own children. The concept of generational transmission of abuse was posited first by Steele and Pollock (1971). While an abused child who later became an abusive parent is commonly referred to in the literature as a cause of maltreatment, research on it is not conclusive (see the section "Who Are the Perpetrators of Maltreatment?" for a discussion of this issue). Other long-term consequences of abuse include delinquency, criminal behavior, school dropouts, teenage parenthood, and increased risk of repeated violent assaults on others (Martin, 1980).

Third, given these consequences, it is not surprising that there are increased social costs associated with medical care, hospitalization and rehabilitative services, emergency placements and foster care, special education, counseling, and so on. More difficult to assess, but no less real, are costs associated with adult criminals, criminal justice system and incarceration, and loss of earnings (Daro, 1988, pp. 149–155).

Finally, there are quality-of-life issues. Abused children may be unhappy children and adults, face bouts of clinical depression, and experience difficulties in relationships, especially those of love or attachment (Martin, 1980).

FOUR TYPES OF MALTREATMENT

Kempe's original article focused on physical abuse. Further research has expanded Kempe's focus on this one dimension of maltreatment to elaborate a typology of four kinds of abuse: physical abuse, neglect, emotional maltreatment, and sexual abuse. Such research has organized maltreatment into groups that share more or less similar kinds of characteristics and therefore similar underlying causes and types of intervention.

Legal definitions of child abuse and maltreatment vary from state to state. In the following section, New York definitions will be used as a guide.

Physical Abuse

Kempe's concept of the "battered child syndrome" informed both the research and the public campaign against child abuse. Hence, the popular image of the maltreated child is one who has been physically battered, and this form of maltreatment has wide public recognition as abuse.

A physically abused child is a person younger than eighteen years of age whose parents or legal caretakers inflict (or allow to be inflicted) a physical injury (other than an accident) that creates risk of death, disfigurement, or impairment of health or function of any body organ (New York State Family Court Act, Section 1012[e]).

Recent research has challenged lumping all physical abuse cases into one category, suggesting that physical abuse is too broad a term, one that encompasses variation not only in abusive behavior but also types of families that commit the abuse. Gil (1981) suggested dividing up physical abuse into levels of severity, since abuse that results in broken bones or permanent brain damage—as in the case of Lisa Steinberg—merit more concern and a different level of intervention as compared to incidents resulting in minor bruises. Other studies have focused on grouping cases of physical abuse into clusters on the basis of the characteristics of families. Different studies identify and use different characteristics to categorize families. Boisvert (1972, pp. 475–476), for example, collected data on characteristics of perpetrators, age of the child, and the nature of the injury. Kent et al. (1983), by contrast, developed subgroups on the basis of the type of intervention most likely to be successful with certain families. For example, Kent's category "spare the rod" referred to families that need to learn modes of discipline other than corporal punishment.

About 27 percent of cases reported to child protective services in 1992 involved physical abuse. Severely abused children tend to be younger than those experiencing "minor" forms of abuse. More children who are physically abused are hospitalized compared to those who are subjected to other forms of maltreatment. Physical abuse—more than any other form of maltreatment—causes death among children. In 1990, there were 1,060 confirmed fatalities resulting from child abuse and neglect in the United States; in 1991, there were 1,176; in 1992, with incomplete data, there were 869 confirmed fatalities, although the projected figure was 1,261 (McCurdy and Daro, 1993, p. 15). Between 1990 and 1992, 59 percent of these fatalities were due to physical abuse (McCurdy and Daro, 1993, p. 16).

How Is Physical Abuse Identified?   Physical abuse leaves marks on the body that are observable; consequently, it tends to be easier to identify than other forms of maltreatment. Reports of physical abuse generally come from observations of children made by physicians, health care providers, teachers, day care center personnel, friends, or neighbors.

What Are the Warning Signs?   The typical warning signs of physical abuse include bruises, burns, welts, scars, repeated accidental injuries, and broken bones. Besides medical evaluation, a key piece of information used to separate abuse from accidents is the parents' ability to explain the injury (see Table 11.1) (Weston, 1980, pp. 241–50).

Physical Neglect

If physical abuse is the most prevalent image of the abused child, cases of neglect are perhaps the form of maltreatment most removed from public awareness. Yet neglect is the most widespread form of child maltreatment. In 1992, 45 percent of the total number of maltreatment cases reported

TABLE 11.1   Indicators of Physical Abuse

Physical Indicators
- Bruises and welts
- Burns
- Fractures
- Lacerations or abrasions
- Human bite marks
- Frequent injuries that are "accidental" or "unexplained"

Behavioral Indicators
- Wary of adult contact
- Apprehensive when other children cry
- Behavioral extremes: aggressiveness, withdrawal
- Frightened of parents
- Afraid to go home
- Seeks affection from any adult

Parent's Behavioral Indicators
- Seems unconcerned about child
- Misuses alcohol or drugs
- Disciplines child too harshly
- Has a history of abuse

Adapted from: Weston, J. T. (1980). "The Pathology of Child Abuse and Neglect." In *The Battered Child,* C. H. Kempe and R. E. Helfer, eds. Chicago: University of Chicago Press, pp. 241–272.

were for neglect. Between 1990 and 1992, 37 percent of confirmed child abuse and neglect fatalities were due to neglect (McCurdy and Daro, 1993, p. 4).

A case of neglect refers to a child younger than eighteen years of age whose physical, mental, or emotional condition has been impaired (or is in danger of becoming impaired) because of a lack of a minimum degree of care. This breaks down into (1) failure to supply the child with adequate food, clothing, shelter, education, or medical care, even though the parents are financially able to do so, or are offered the means to do so, and (2) failure to provide the child with proper supervision (e.g., because of inattentiveness while under the influence of drugs or alcohol). Neglect also refers to children abandoned by their parents (New York State Family Court Act, Section

1012[f]). The NCPCA estimates that during 1991 and 1992, at least 4,696 children were reported abandoned by eighteen states (only twenty-three states collect data on abandonment; eighteen provided information for the survey). There are problems in estimating abandonment: The small number of states that collect data give an incomplete picture, and the system of data collection in many states does not maintain a separate category for abandonment, so these cases are lumped under neglect (McCurdy and Daro, 1993, p. 12).

Research portrays neglect as a homogeneous grouping. Certain characteristics of families tend to be associated with neglect in the majority of cases. These characteristics include lack of adequate financial and material resources, thus limiting the family's ability to care for children. For example, 51 percent of children reported for neglect lived in single-parent families; 43 percent of these caretakers were unemployed (AAPC, 1984). Other characteristics include poor housing and living conditions and large, multiproblem families (BPA, 1977). Above all, one factor consistently associated with neglect is lack of social support. Children who are neglected come from families that often are completely isolated from an informal network of social supports among family and friends. Research portrays one type of family consistently involved in neglect: a poor and socially isolated family in which the needs of the child are lost in the struggle for daily existence (Cantwell, 1980). It is not surprising that neglect, more than other forms of maltreatment, is likely to occur by itself and not in combination with other forms of maltreatment. Consequently, studies differentiate among neglect cases on the basis of behavior—educational neglect, medical neglect, abandonment, and so on (Miller, 1982). Neglect as a category of maltreatment contrasts with physical abuse, where researchers have separated out different types of families.

How Is Neglect Identified?   Like physical abuse but to a lesser degree, neglect results in observable signs that are noted by people who are in daily or frequent contact with the child, such as teachers, welfare caseworkers, day care personnel, physicians, and health care workers.

What Are the Warning Signs?   Suspicion of neglect does not turn on observation of a single episode of behavior; rather, it is a consistent lack of clean clothing or regular hygiene that results in skin or other medical conditions as well as consistent tardiness or absenteeism from school that are considered signs of potential neglect (see Table 11.2) (Miller, 1982).

The impact of neglect on children is severe. One study showed that neglected children received the lowest ratings in self-esteem and confidence. Families that neglect children appear to be among the most resistant to intervention (Elmer, 1977).

Emotional Maltreatment

Emotional maltreatment is defined as "impairment of emotional health" and "impairment of

TABLE 11.2   Indicators of Neglect

Physical Indicators
- Consistent hunger, poor hygiene
- Inappropriate dress
- Consistent lack of supervision
- Abandonment

Behavioral Indicators
- Begging or stealing food
- Poor school attendance
- Constant fatigue

Parent's Behavioral Indicators
- Misuses drugs or alcohol
- Disorganized home life
- Isolation from friends
- Chronic illness
- Exposes child to unsafe living conditions

Adapted from: Weston, J. T. (1980). "The Pathology of Child Abuse and Neglect." In *The Battered Child,* C. H. Kempe and R. E. Helfer, eds. Chicago: University of Chicago Press, pp. 241–272.

mental or emotional condition." These refer to a condition of substantially reduced psychological or intellectual functioning and include behavior related to failure to thrive, lack of control of aggressive impulses, acting out, and misbehavior (New York State Family Court Act, Section 1012[h]).

Emotional maltreatment is pervasive. It tends to occur with other forms of maltreatment, unlike physical abuse or neglect, which tend to exist alone. The National Clinical Evaluation Study found that sixty percent of all abuse cases in 1983 were accompanied by emotional maltreatment. Yet, the practical problems in measuring emotional maltreatment, assessing its impact on children, and developing effective treatment make it the most ambiguous form of maltreatment. First, it is not as visible as physical abuse or even neglect—constant criticism and shouting don't leave visible marks on children—and its consequences are more difficult to pinpoint. Second, not all states have statutes that mandate reports of maltreatment. These difficulties account for why, until recently, emotional maltreatment was omitted from policy and research. In fact, emotional maltreatment has been considered a "residual category," covering behaviors not in physical abuse, neglect, and sexual abuse categories (Daro, 1988, p. 35). These difficulties are reflected in the low reporting of emotional maltreatment: In 1992, only 7 percent of all child maltreatment reports were for emotional maltreatment (McCurdy and Daro, 1993).

In an effort to clarify these ambiguities, research has attempted to subdivide the emotional maltreatment category into small groups that make identification and treatment easier. Dean (1979) identified three types: (a) emotional neglect, (b) emotional assault (verbal attacks), and (c) emotional abuse (acts that prevent development of a positive self-image). Another study focused on differentiating the category in terms of behavior: rejection, coldness, inappropriate control, and extreme inconsistency (Garbarino, 1977). In addition to these efforts at categoriza-

tion, the medical profession has identified Munchausen syndrome as a form of emotional maltreatment. This refers to a situation where parents believe the child is ill or exhibit "paranoid" thinking about the child's health—and may even make frequent visits to different doctors—despite all medical evidence to the contrary (Woollcott et al., 1982).

Given these difficulties, it comes as no surprise that researchers so far have been unable to develop a profile of parents who emotionally maltreat children, as they have in neglect cases. Characteristics of families that emotionally maltreat children are also found among those who physically abuse children, such as lack of parenting skills and social isolation, making identification and treatment of cases much more difficult.

How Is Emotional Maltreatment Identified?
Identification is made by someone who has specialized daily or frequent contact with the child or family, such as a school counselor or a therapist.

What Are the Warning Signs?   Common warning signs include speech disorders, lags in physical development, and failure to thrive. Parents who emotionally maltreat children blame or belittle the child, withhold love, or don't seem to care much about the child's problems (see Table 11.3) (Carroll, 1980).

Sexual Abuse

The concern over sexual abuse as a major problem is reflected in the growing numbers of reports of this form of maltreatment. In 1992, 17 percent of all maltreatment reports involved sexual abuse (McCurdy and Daro, 1993, p. 4). If neglect cases tend to be associated with poverty, sexual abuse cuts across socioeconomic boundaries and is found in all communities and at all income and educational levels.

A sexually abused child is one less than eighteen years of age whose parents or legal caretakers commit (or allow to be committed) a sex offense

TABLE 11.3   Indicators of Emotional Maltreatment

Physical Indicators
- Speech disorders
- Lags in physical development
- Failure to thrive

Behavioral Indicators
- Habits, e.g., sucking, rocking
- Conduct disorders, e.g., antisocial, destructive
- Behavioral extremes

Parent's Behavioral Indicators
- Treats children in family unequally
- Blames or belittles child
- Cold or rejecting, withholding love

Adapted from: Weston, J. T. (1980). "The Pathology of Child Abuse and Neglect." In *The Battered Child,* C. H. Kempe and R. E. Helfer, eds. Chicago: University of Chicago Press, pp. 241–272.

against the child or allow the child to engage in, or promote using a child in sexual performance (New York State Family Court Act, Section 1012[e]).

Children reported as sexually abused are generally female (75 percent of cases) and older compared to other forms of maltreated children. Interviews with random groups of adults suggest that sexual abuse may also occur when children are younger, and many victims may be boys. In 50 percent of the cases, a parent or stepparent is responsible for the abuse; the remaining cases involve other adults who are usually known to the family (Kempe, 1980).

How Is Sexual Abuse Identified?   Identification of sexual abuse is difficult since verbal reports and physical symptoms are not available in most cases. Identification, therefore, depends on observation of the behavior of victims of sex abuse, their family members, or even a self-report at a later age. Social workers and others must be trained to identify the physical and behavioral signs of abuse.

What Are the Warning Signs?   Children who are sexually abused often have difficulty walking or sitting, have pain in the genital area, or suffer from sexually transmitted disease. Moreover, such children often have poor peer relationships, withdraw from social contact, or demonstrate infantile behavior. Parents who abuse children often misuse alcohol or other drugs or lack social and emotional contacts (see Table 11.4) (Kempe, 1980).

Public awareness of sexual abuse has led to instruction in schools to prevent abuse. Such instruction has included lessons on both inappropriate touching and the child's disclosure of such acts to someone they trust. The effectiveness of prevention efforts that rely on children is unknown and poses an important research question.

Who Are the Perpetrators of Maltreatment?

Studies have identified various characteristics of families that contribute to a higher likelihood of maltreatment. These range from psychological disorders and limited income and material resources to stress caused by unemployment, among other situations. But who are the people

TABLE 11.4   Indicators of Sexual Abuse

Physical Indicators
- Pain or itching in the genital area
- Venereal disease
- Bruises in genital area

Behavioral Indicators
- Unusual sexual behavior or knowledge
- Reports sexual abuse
- Withdrawal, fantasy, or infantile behavior

Parent's Behavioral Indicators
- Protective or jealous of child
- Encourages child to engage in prostitution
- Lacks social and emotional contacts

Adapted from: Weston, J. T. (1980). "The Pathology of Child Abuse and Neglect." In *The Battered Child,* C. H. Kempe and R. E. Helfer, eds. Chicago: University of Chicago Press, pp. 241–272.

who abuse children? Fontana has written that they "are not usually monsters or seriously deranged individuals, but rather parents deserving of help" (1991, p. 13). Research findings support this statement. Severely disturbed and psychotic individuals constitute no more than 10 percent of all cases of maltreatment (Kempe and Kempe, 1978). Rather, most parents who maltreat children suffer from various personality disorders or internal conflict. For example, Sever and Janzen (1982) studied sexually abusive families and noted that 71 percent abused alcohol. Moreover, Olson (1976), focusing on development of psychological profiles of parents who sexually maltreat children, found a high percentage have rigid or authoritarian personalities, emotional immaturity, or drug or alcohol dependence. Divorce and remarriage also pose a risk factor for maltreatment. Research noted that children in step-parent families showed a higher incidence of sexual abuse and other forms of maltreatment (Russell, 1984).

Finally, as noted earlier, childhood abuse of the parent is one of the most widely cited causal factors of maltreatment. Hunter and Kilstrom (1979) studied 255 mothers who gave birth to premature babies. Nine out of ten of the mothers who abused their babies had a history of abuse, lending support to the concept of generational transmission of abuse. However, 17 percent of the control group who did not abuse their babies also reported a history of past abuse. The data clearly show that while not all abused children grow up to become abusers themselves, an increased risk exists. Why some abused children become abusive parents and others do not is unknown.

Why Does Maltreatment Happen?

Three basic categories of theories are used in research to explain child maltreatment: (1) psychodynamic, (2) learning, and (3) environmental. These theories try to elucidate the relationship between either a specific individual (perpetrator of maltreatment) or a set of environmental conditions with the incidence of maltreatment.

Psychodynamic Theories.   Psychodynamic theories emphasize the psychological problems of parents and consequently their levels of personal and social functioning in explaining why abuse occurs. These theories argues that individuals with personal problems or severe or moderate psychological disorders are less able to care for their children. It is not a deficit of skills; rather, such parents do not have the personal capacity to care consistently for children. For example, parental depression can contribute to abuse. The intervention model associated with a psychodynamic perspective is therapeutic services provided to individuals, families, or groups. The nature and duration of therapy would vary according to the type and severity of maltreatment (Steele, 1980).

Learning Theories.   In contrast to psychodynamic theories, which focus on psychological problems of parents, learning theories emphasize lack of skills and knowledge. According to this theory, abuse occurs because parents don't know how to care for their children. The theory argues that parents can be taught how to care for children through learning new information or skills. Such information is imparted in parenting education classes and support groups (Steele, 1980).

Environmental Theories.   The theories covered so far have focused on the individual. The final theory moves from an individual focus to broader environmental conditions. Rather than psychological problems or lack of skill, this perspective looks at macrolevel factors such as poverty, racism, and sexism as causes of maltreatment. For example, poverty and a lack of material resources are associated with child neglect. Other researchers identify a correlation (if not causal relationship) between pornography and sexual violence/abuse toward women and children. Moreover, critics charge, poverty and the social conditions it produces—unemployment, underemployment, poor housing, lack of access to education, and health care—underlie the psychological problems and lack of knowledge that psycho-dynamic and learning theories attempt to address.

The intervention model suggested by this approach seeks policy changes to reduce poverty; to improve housing, health insurance and access to health care; and to increase vocational training and employment opportunities (Martin, 1980).

Ecological Model. None of these perspectives is incorrect, but each one alone is insufficient to explain maltreatment. The causes of maltreatment probably lie in individuals and society. The use of ecological theories in social work, developed by Germain and Gitterman (1980), focuses not just on the individual or on society but rather the interaction between these two domains and the impact of those interactions on children. The challenge for research is to specify these interactions and refine existing typologies of maltreatment so that cases with similar patterns of causation can be grouped together to enhance prevention and treatment efforts.

SOCIAL SERVICE RESPONSE: MANDATED REPORTING AND CHILD PROTECTIVE SERVICES

In 1973, the New York State Legislature signed into law the Child Protective Services Act of 1973 (CPSA). Other states have similar laws; as with the definitions of abuse, New York will be used as a model to explain the general process. The CPSA mandates certain persons and officials to report cases of suspected child abuse and maltreatment. It specifies what must be reported and how a report is to be made as well as the penalties for not reporting and the legal protection afforded to those who report.

Whenever child abuse or maltreatment is suspected, New York social service law mandates that a report be made immediately by telephone. Oral reports are made to the State Central Register of Child Abuse and Maltreatment (SCR). Social service law also mandates that a written report be filed with the local CPS within forty-eight hours of the oral report. Generally, information given during the oral report includes the names and addresses of the child and parents or caretakers; the child's age, sex, and race; and the nature and extent of the injuries or maltreatment. Reports can be made even if information is missing. Written reports are admissible as evidence in judicial proceedings related to child abuse. Moreover, any person or official or institution that acts in "good faith" in making the report has immunity from liability, both civil and criminal, that might result from the report. Conversely, a person who willfully fails to make a report is subject to penalty (a Class-A misdemeanor).

What Happens When a Report Is Made?

Once a report is made to the Central State Register, social service law mandates that local CPS workers investigate the report and provide or arrange and monitor services for children and families.

Investigation. The goal of the investigation is to determine whether "credible evidence" of abuse exists. Credible evidence is evidence that is worthy of belief. The investigation involves fact finding through interviews and observation. The CPS caseworker will contact people able to give information relevant to the case. These include the reporter, children, parents or caretakers, school personnel, physicians and health professionals, service providers, relatives, and neighbors.

Determination and Assessment. The final step is determining whether the report is "indicated" or "unfounded." This determination must be made within ninety days of the oral report. After the facts are gathered, they are compared to statutory definitions of abuse and maltreatment, and a decision is made as to whether there is credible evidence of abuse. During this process, the stresses in the family are evaluated. This process normally includes an assessment of the child's behavior and level of developmental functioning, the parents' capacity to care for the child, past and current family functioning, potential harm to the child; environmental factors; and supports to the family. Specific problems are also assessed, such as health problems, marital conflict, housing conditions, and substance abuse.

If the investigation determines that credible evidence does not exist, the report is considered "unfounded." If the investigation determines that credible evidence exists, the report is "indicated," and the family is offered appropriate services. When the report is indicated, a service plan is developed for the child/family that aims to ensure the child's well-being and preserve and stabilize the family. Service plans usually contain a description of the problem, an assessment of individual problems and needs, and goals to be achieved. The services needed to attain the goals are specified, along with their expected duration.

Service Provision and Monitoring. Services can be provided by the New York State Department of Social Services or from community-based agencies. The caseworker is responsible for arranging/coordinating and monitoring the services delivered.

In cases where the child's injuries are severe, there is a past history of abuse, and the parents refuse to cooperate, CPS turns to family court. The role of the court is to impose treatment or protective services on the parents. In some cases, a police officer, caseworker, or physician (in the capacity of a representative of a hospital) can take the child into protective custody. Removal of a child from the home under protective custody occurs under specific conditions, that is, when the child is in "imminent danger" and there is not enough time to apply for an order of temporary removal from family court. It carries responsibility to take specific actions such as bringing the child to an area designated by rules of the family court and making reasonable efforts to inform the parents of the child's placement.

Child protective service workers often use emergency foster care placements during investigation or following confirmation of a report to ensure the safety of the child. Foster care is defined as "full-time, substitute care of children outside their own homes . . . [that] occurs in family homes, group homes and institutions" (Encyclopedia of Social Work, 1987). After abuse is substantiated, Green and Haggerty (1968) estimate that when children are returned to their homes, there is a 50 percent chance that abuse would continue and a 10 percent chance that death might occur. While it is preferable to maintain the family unit, workers weigh the social/emotional damage created by removal of children from the parents and their placement in foster care against the potential harm if children remain with parents. In general, workers try to minimize the number of children placed in foster care and the length of their stay. As of May 1993, New York City foster care caseload was 48,560.

A large number of community-based agencies provide therapeutic and other services to families that maltreat children. Such services follow a psychosocial model built on the premise that effective intervention rests on combining provision of therapeutic services to individual clients with community or social interventions. The psychosocial model dominates service planning at community-based agencies and take place in multidisciplinary teams (formed of medical, legal, mental health, and social service specialists) that review reports and assess treatment needs.

Services are offered from a family perspective, that is, treating the family unit as opposed to individuals, usually over six to nine months. Direct services to parents may include parenting education, hospital-based perinatal services, group therapy, home visitor services, and various support groups.

Services to maltreated children include therapeutic day care, outpatient psychiatric treatment, and various special services for adolescents. Also, crisis intervention services exist that respond immediately to families in distress, such as twenty-four-hour hotlines or crisis nurseries. Finally, caseworkers provide concrete services to families, including resolving problems related to income, housing, medical care, public assistance, day care, vocational training, and employment opportunities.

WHAT STUDENTS OF HUMAN AND SOCIAL SERVICES SHOULD KNOW ABOUT CHILD ABUSE AND MALTREATMENT

Students should be aware not only of the legal definitions of abuse and maltreatment but also of the physical and behavioral indicators of abuse.

Under New York social service law (Section 413), certain persons and officials are required to report suspected cases of child maltreatment. These reports are made when (1) there is reasonable cause to suspect that a child is abused or maltreated, or (2) if the parent or legal caretaker states, from personal knowledge, facts, or conditions that would constitute abuse. See Table 11.5 for a list of mandated reporters.

Observation of indicators of abuse is often the only way caseworkers can identify suspected cases of abuse (see Tables 11.1–11.4 for the indicators of abuse). The presence of one of these signs, however, does not automatically signify abuse; there may be legitimate explanations. If physical or behavioral signs of abuse occur frequently, however, in sufficient number or as part of a pattern, there is cause to suspect child abuse or maltreatment and make a report. The mandated reporter does not have to be certain that abuse exists before reporting; cases are reported when they are suspected and on the basis of the existence of signs and the reporter's experience and training.

TABLE 11.5 List of Mandated Reporters

Physicians	School Officials
Surgeons	Residents
Medical Examiners	Interns
Coroners	Registered Nurses
Police Officers	Hospital Personnel
Dentists	Christian Science
Osteopaths	Practitioners
Chiropractors	Day Care Center
Podiatrists	Workers
Social Service	Foster Care Workers
Workers	Mental Health
Law Enforcement	Professionals
Officials	Psychologists
Peace Officers	

Source: New York State Social Services Law, Section 413.

CONCLUSION

More than forty years after Kempe's original paper was published, studies of child abuse continue to elaborate on a set of theoretical frameworks, models, and empirical findings that contribute to understanding the basic parameter of the problem—its causes, incidence, treatment, and prevention. Though far from complete, such knowledge consistently points out one central fact: Knowledge alone is insufficient; it needs to be put into action individually, socially, and politically to be effective.

REFERENCES

American Association for Protecting Children (1984). *Highlights of Official Child Neglect and Abuse Reporting.* Denver: American Humane Society.

Berkeley Planning Associates (1977). *Child Abuse and Neglect Treatment Programs: Final Report and Summary of Findings from the Evaluation of the Joint OCT/SRS National Demonstration Program in Child Abuse and Neglect.* Prepared for the National Center for Health Services Research under Contracts No. 106–74–120 and No. 230–75–0076.

Boisvert, M. (1972). "The Battered Child Syndrome." *Social Casework, 53* (October), pp. 475–480.

Cantwell, H. B. (1980). "Child Neglect." In C. H. Kempe and R. E. Helfer, eds., *The Battered Child.* pp. 183–197. Chicago: University of Chicago Press.

Carroll, C. A. (1980). "The Function of Protective Services in Child Abuse and Neglect," In C. H. Kempe and R. E. Helfer, eds., *The Battered Child.* pp. 275–287. Chicago: University of Chicago Press.

Corby, B. (1987). *Working with Child Abuse.* England: Open University Press.

Daro, D. (1988). *Confronting Child Abuse: Research for Effective Program Design.* New York: The Free Press.

Daro, D., and L. Mitchell (1987). *Deaths Due to Maltreatment Soar: The Results of the Eighth Semi-Annual Fifty-State Survey.* Chicago: National Committee for Prevention of Child Abuse.

Dean, D. (1979). "Emotional Abuse of Children." *Children Today, 8* (July-August), 18–27.

Elmer, E. (1977). "A Follow-Up of Traumatized Children." *Pediatrics, 59* (February), 273–279.

Fontana, V. J. (1991). *Save the Family, Save the Child.* New York: Dutton.

Garbarino, J. (1977). "The Human Ecology of Child Maltreatment: A Conceptual Model for Research." *Journal of Marriage and the Family, 39* (November), 721–735.

Germain, C. D., and A. Gitterman (1980). *The Life Model of Social Work Practice.* New York: Columbia University Press.

Gil, D. (1981). "The United States versus Child Abuse." In L. Pelton, ed., *Social Context of Child Abuse and Neglect.* New York: Human Services Press.

Green, M., and R. Haggerty (1968). *Ambulatory Pediatrics.* Philadelphia, PA: Saunders.

Hunter, R. S., and N. Kilstrom (1979). "Breaking the Cycle in Abusive Families." *American Journal of Psychiatry, 136,* 1320–1322.

Kempe, C. H. (1980). "Incest and Other Forms of Sexual Abuse." In C. H. Kempe and R. E. Helfer, eds., *The Battered Child.* pp. 198–214. Chicago: University of Chicago Press.

Kempe, C. H., F. N. Silverman, B. F. Steele, W. Droegemueller, and H. K. Silver (1962). "The Battered Child Syndrome." *Journal of the American Medical Association, 181*(17), 17–24.

Kempe, R. S., and C. H. Kempe (1978). *Child Abuse.* Cambridge, MA: Harvard University Press.

Kent, J., H. Weisberg, B. Lamar, and T. Marx (1983). "Understanding the Etiology of Child Abuse: A Preliminary Typology of Cases." *Children and Youth Services Review, 5*(1), 7–29.

McCurdy, M. A., and D. Daro (1993). *Current Trends in Child Abuse Reporting and Fatalities: The Results of the 1992 Annual Fifty-State Survey.* National Committee for Prevention of Child Abuse.

Martin, H. P. (1980). "The Consequences of Being Abused and Neglected: How the Child Fares." In C. H. Kempe and R. E. Helfer, eds., *The Battered Child,* pp. 347–366. Chicago: University of Chicago Press.

Mayhall, P. D., and K. E. Norgard (1983). *Child Abuse and Neglect.* New York: John Wiley and Sons.

Miller, K. (1982). "Child Abuse and Neglect." *Journal of Family Practice, 14*(3) (March), 571–595.

New York State Family Court Act, Sections 1012 (e, f, h).

Olson, R. (1976). "Index of Suspicion: Screening of Child Abusers." *American Journal of Nursing, 76* (January), 108–110.

Russell, D. (1984). *Sexual Exploitation: Rape, Child Sexual Abuse, and Sexual Harassment.* Beverly Hills, CA: Sage.

Sever, J., and C. Janzen (1982). "Contradictions to Reconstitution of Sexually Abusive Families. *Child Welfare, 61*(5) (May), 279–288.

Steele, B. (1980). "Psychodynamic Factors in Child Abuse." In C. H. Kempe and R. E. Helfer, eds., *The Battered Child.* pp. 49–85. Chicago: University of Chicago Press.

Steele, B., and C. Pollock (1971). "The Battered Child's Parents." In A. S. Skolnick and J. H. Skolnick, eds., *Family in Transition.* Boston: Little, Brown.

Straus, M. A. (1980). "Stress and Child Abuse." In C. H. Kempe and R. E. Helfer, eds., *The Battered Child.* pp. 86–103. Chicago: University of Chicago Press.

Straus, M., R. Gelles, and S. Steinmetz (1980). *Behind Closed Doors: Violence in the American Family.* Garden City, NY: Anchor Press.

Westat and Development Associates (1981). *National Study of the Incidence and Severity of Child Abuse and Neglect.* Prepared for the National Center on Child Abuse and Neglect under Contract No. 105–76–1137.

Weston, J. T. (1980). "The Pathology of Child Abuse and Neglect." In C. H. Kempe and R. E. Helfer, eds., *The Battered Child.* pp. 241–272. Chicago: University of Chicago Press.

Woollcott, P., Jr., T. Aceto, Jr., C. Rutt, M. Bloom, and R. Glick (1982). "Doctor Shopping with the Child as Proxy Patient: A Variant of Child Abuse." *The Journal of Pediatrics, 101*(2) (August), 297–301.

SUGGESTED FURTHER READING

Kempe, R. S., C. Cutler, and J. Dean (1980). "The Infant with Failure-to-Thrive." In C. H. Kempe and R. E. Helfer, eds., *The Battered Child.* pp. 163–182. Chicago: University of Chicago Press.

Wolock, I., and B. Horowitz (1979). "Child Maltreatment and Material Deprivation among AFDC-Recipient Families." *Social Service Review, 53* (June), 175–194.

CHAPTER 12

YOUTH AND HUMAN SERVICES

WALTER DE OLIVEIRA
CHRISTOPHER R. EDGINTON

The challenges, issues, and problems faced by young persons in contemporary society have shaped a professional field dedicated to providing programs and services to these youth. As in other human service areas, youth service workers aim to empower individuals, promote healthy development, and assist individual youth to optimize their well-being. Those working in this area often serve as role models, helping the youth to solve problems, clarify values, and acquire useful life skills.

Because youth constitutes a stage of development, working with youth demands a comprehensive understanding of this life stage. Those working with youth must comprehend the construction of youth cultures as well as the biopsychological transformations of this developmental stage. The work requires a deep understanding of the social, cultural, political, economic, and other factors that shape society and therefore human existence.

Youth today are faced with a world that presents many challenges and carries many risks. Although the world has always presented such challenges and risks, the complexities of modern life have created completely new dimensions that call for new ways of thinking and of pursuing meaningful solutions. Not all adults are prepared to offer these solutions. The human service profession has a responsibility to participate in the search for significant, relevant, and meaningful ways of promoting healthy development in young people. To this effort, the human service profession brings a holistic perspective, one that can serve as an organizing framework to ensure that the well-being of youth is effectively addressed.

In this chapter, we examine some relevant issues related to the development of youth, and then we explore the ways in which human service professionals work with young people. A brief historical overview of services dedicated to youth in the United States is presented next. The foundations of professional practice are examined in the context of current orientations to intervention with youth. The definition of the field, which has always presented a problem for practitioners and scholars, is then explored. Three paradigms identified by the authors are provided to illuminate the complexities faced by professionals in the field. It is not our intention in this chapter to deal with all or even most issues facing youth in contemporary society. At best, we intend to provide a few concepts, ideas, and constructs pertaining to the field and suggest some bases and strategies to guide professional intervention.

YOUTH IN CONTEMPORARY SOCIETY

Youth, or adolescence, is a relatively undefined period of time between childhood and adult life. The term *youth* has been largely used to indicate the period that starts with the biological transformations of prepubescence up to the time when most persons are expected to be ready to carry the responsibilities of adulthood, including sustaining themselves economically. Generally, in modern societies youth starts anywhere between nine and twelve years of age and can be extended up to twenty to twenty-five years of age.

167

To a large extent, adolescence is a transitional life period in which youth experience great excitement, learning opportunities, growth, and exploration of themselves and the world. It is also the phase of life in which individuals are required to grow into responsible, ethical, reflective, capable, and competent adults. At the same time, adolescents are often treated by society (and sometimes viewed by themselves) as helpless children. The Carnegie Corporation of New York (1997) writes

Adolescence is one of the most fascinating transitions in the lifespan: a time of accelerated growth and change, second only to infancy; a time of expanding horizons, self-discovery, and emerging independence; a time of metamorphosis from childhood to adulthood. Its beginning is associated with profound biological, physical, behavioral and social transformation. . . . The advance of this crucially formative phase can shape an individual's life course and thus the future of our society.

Erik Eriksen (1968) refers to this period as a "moratorium." In Erikson's view, this is a period of permissiveness, a protected phase of existence, in which the individual is provided opportunities to freely and openly explore life, often in a playful manner. Also, it is a period of transition in which values are formed and tested, vocation is discovered and rediscovered, and life skills are learned, enhanced, and put into practice. As Peiss (1996) has written, "in the twentieth century, youth is regarded as a distinctive stage of life, a time of self-expression and experimentation before the experience of marriage, children, and work" (p. 26). However, the open and free exploration of life, the search for self and for meaning, and the desire for participation in life events expose youth to many risks.

While youth experience much joy and growth, adolescence is also a period that produces stress, anxiety, confusion, role ambiguity, and dissonance with societal customs and norms. These disruptions can be attributed to the influence of biological transformations and the pressures of the environment. Adolescents face such problems as a need to adjust to a rapidly changing body and the urge to search for meaning in life and a personal and social identity. The seductions offered by society may provide additional stress and anxiety, especially given the fact that adolescents may not yet be ready to make mature decisions, as noted by Mitchell (1996). On the other hand, adult society has not been totally successful in offering solid values and meaning to the youth. Further, there is a lack of universally accessible preventive services in contrast to a nearly constant exposure, and sometimes pressure, to use and abuse alcohol and drugs and to engage in unprotected sex. Youth are also exposed to many other health-related risks, including poor nutrition and dietary habits, depression and other mental health problems, early pregnancy, alienation from family and from school (sometimes to the point of dropping out), and the lure of gangs, just to name a few.

The works of Coleman and Hendry (1980), Thompson (1991), and Edginton and Oliveira (1995b) suggest that adolescence, as a developmental phase, can be viewed from a number of different perspectives. These include (1) a stage of human growth, (2) a transitional phase in life, (3) a social pattern, and (4) a philosophical stance. Viewing youth development as a stage of human growth brings into focus physiological and psychological changes that the person experiences during preadolescence and adolescence. Inherent in this perspective is the tendency to perceive traits as biologically determined and therefore out of reach for mechanisms of social influence and social engineering (Coleman and Hendry, 1980). For example, the typical stereotyped view of adolescents as rebels may be explained biologically and therefore viewed as a natural part of human development. These traits are virtually out of reach of intervention.

A counterpoint to viewing youth as a biological stage is to understand youth as a transitional process. As Coleman and Hendry (1980) have written, "Too much individual variation exists for young people of the same chronological age to be classified together." The transitional perspective implies that the process of maturation depends to a great extent on internal as well as external forces. Internal forces are determined by physical and psychological development. External forces influencing this process of transition "originate from peers, parents, teachers, and the society at large" (Coleman and Hendry, 1980, p. 2). These combined influences direct the development of individuals as they move toward occupying adult roles in society. Some pressures will work for speeding individuals toward assuming adult roles, whereas others may impede this process.

The view of youth development as a social pattern looks into the social roles youth are expected to play. Preparation for career and job market, citizenship, marriage, family life and other duties, and rights of a citizen are the prominent guiding principles for the development of youth. Organizations must comply with the principles of ethical citizenship and therefore become an integral part of promoting social values as defined by established social and cultural norms. These norms are transmitted through rituals, education, and other social mechanisms. Youth service organizations define their mission and adopt the norms they think are best according to their own sets of values and beliefs. Organizations exert their power to transmit social values perceived as best to foster youth development.

From a philosophical point of view, youth can be seen, for example, as a phase of existence in which ethical behavior is to be acquired. Participation in social life relates to instilling in the youth responsibility and respect for others. By late adolescence, youth must decide how they are going to live their adult lives (e.g., in family units, etc.), make social choices, and other choices for lifestyles. From the point of view of society, the task is to promote autonomy and provide opportunities for development within the context of societal norms, values and expectations. The focus is on offering youth opportunities to make healthy choices of their own.

YOUTH AND THE HUMAN SERVICE PROFESSION

What is the mission of the human service profession pertaining to youth? What unique or special roles do human service organizations play in society in relation to youth? In what sectors of our society do we find youth-serving human service organizations operating? Cimmino (1993) defines human services as a helping profession that assists people in meeting important needs in their lives. While those trained in human services cannot claim to be the only ones delivering human services, as noted by Cimmino, human service organizations target population groups at risk for a number of problems that favor an unhealthy life. As mentioned above, youth are particularly at risk, and the human service profession therefore has a great stake in helping them.

A leading professional body dedicated to preparing and certifying future youth-serving professionals to work with America's youth and family members, American Humanics, Inc., suggests that human service organizations dedicated to youth should be committed to "service to people," but they also point out that these organizations "must play a leadership role in helping solve society's problems" (American Humanics, 1996, p. 14). Another perspective is offered by the Drucker Foundation for Nonprofit Management, suggesting that the mission of human service organizations with a strong commitment to social concerns is one of changing lives (The Drucker Foundation, 1996, p. 48):

> *This mission is accomplished . . . by addressing the needs of the spirit, the mind, and the body—of individuals, the community, and society. This sector and its organizations also create for the individuals within society and the community a meaningful sphere of effective and responsible citizenship.*

The human service profession focuses on enhancing the quality of life of individual clients and of the communities to which these clients belong. Human service organizations focused on youth identify problems and assist clients to solve these problems. Because of the intricacies and complexities of adolescence as a phase of life and as biological as well as social phenomena, however, youth-serving professionals are concerned with a variety of issues that cannot be dealt with from only a problem-solving perspective. Moreover, the youth-serving professional has to understand youth for what they are and understand the issues involved in assisting people who are moving through biological and social transitions to take their places as full members of society. Further, they have to gain knowledge and an appreciation of the social issues that lead to the problems and risks youth face today. In other words, it is not enough to define a problem, such as involvement in gangs, and then try to find out how can one "save" the youth from such engagement. The professional is called to perform a much more difficult task, one of analyzing the factors that promote youth gang membership, including issues related to family participation and peer pressure; concerns related to loneliness, solitude, and belonging; the search for an individual as well as a social identity; and other issues, such as the glamorization of violence and drugs in contemporary society. Amidst all these situations the central and most compelling question that must be addressed is, How do you reach the youth client in a manner that is meaningful and relevant and that builds trust and promotes positive change?

To answer the major questions posed to youth-serving professionals in their mission of promoting the healthy development of the youth, we will explore how a variety of organizations provide programs and services with various degrees of success. We will begin by briefly reviewing the historical evolution of youth-serving organizations in United States.

A BRIEF HISTORY OF YOUTH SERVICE ORGANIZATIONS IN THE UNITED STATES

Young people's movements organized by churches in America have been in place since at least 1675. The youth service movement in the United States can be traced to the early 1800s. During that period, several religiously affiliated youth programs were established, including the Sunday School Movement for Children (1820), the Young Men's Bible Society (1823), and the Young Men's Missionary Society (1826). These organizations served as a springboard for the first program specifically designed for youth, established in Philadelphia as the Juvenile Missionary Society of the First Reformed Presbyterian Church in 1831.

In a global sense, the appearance of programs targeting youth in the early to mid-1800s can be tied to the tidal wave of social changes as society moved from an agrarian into an industrial culture. Social, political, and economic conditions brought about by the Industrial Revolution called for immediate reforms. Everyday life in America became heavily impacted by overcrowding of newly created industrialized cities, massive immigration, and economic turmoil. Fast urbanization was accompanied by lack of infrastructure, poverty, poor sanitation, harsh child labor conditions, lack of minimally habitable housing, lack of open space and play areas, racial violence, and an overall problem of transition to a new cultural urban/industrial identity. Analyzing the consequences of continuous industrialization, James (1993) notes, "the social conditions of the 1890s were so harsh that they set the tone for reform in the early twentieth century, firmly establishing the undercurrent of dread that made reform appear indisputably necessary" (p. 177).

Industrialization created a perceived need for social change and led to a political atmosphere of progressive liberalism. As a result, there was a greater awareness of the conditions of children and youth, who then came to be perceived as objects of exploitation, deprivation, and prey to the new ills of urban life. New paradigms emerged, both in the realms of community and social institutions and on how children and youth came to be perceived. The emergence of professional areas such as social work, recreation, psychoanalysis, and public health helped shape new institutions, influenced social policy, and often framed new and unique perspectives on issues related to youth. In education, disciplines other than psychology started to affect curriculum and instruction. One of these disciplines was sociology, which changed the emphasis traditionally put by psychologists on the individual to the social structure and the contributions of education to the preservation and progress of society (Wilds, 1956, pp. 547–548).

The works of Jane Addams (e.g., 1907), Luther H. Gulick (e.g., 1938), John Dewey (e.g., 1916), G. Stanley Hall (e.g., 1904), Joseph Lee (e.g., 1915), Jacob Riis (e.g., 1892), and others highlight the development of a general social focus on children and youth. These American leaders were in tune with the schools of thought fostered by scholars such as Sigmund Freud, Friedrich Frobel, Johan Heinrich Pestalozzi, and Jean Jacques Rousseau, whose ideas were gradually absorbed in newly created youth programs and services. Several themes were prevalent in the emergence of youth services, including a focus on "child-saving" activities, a concern for the "moral welfare" of youth, and the idea of play as a central life activity. All these constructs provided a broad spectrum of interpretations of youth and their roles in society and resulted in the creation of several kinds of youth organizations. Some of these organizations were essentially proactive, promoting character building as a prevention against social ills. Others were reactive to the turmoil of the urban condition.

The emergence of youth movements in the late 1800s was characterized by a decrease in church control of youth programs, a concern for volunteer assemblage (the traditional basis of youth organizations), and a growing infusion of paramilitary values and beliefs. These factors led to a rise in adult-sponsored youth organizations, a growth in secular influence, and a lessening of ecclesiastic control of youth activities, rituals, and language (Kett, 1977, pp. 189–198). The foundation of the YMCA of the USA (1851) and YWCA of the USA (1855) represent a transition between evangelical and secular influences on the estab-

lishment of youth organizations. The emergence of such organizations as the Loyal Temperance Legion of the Women's Christian Temperance Union (1877), the Boys and Girls Clubs of America (1860–1906), National Grange Junior (1888), Woodcraft Indians (1902), Junior American Citizens Committee (1906), Boy Scouts of America (1910), Camp Fire Boys and Girls (1910), Girl Scouts of the USA (1912), and Order of DeMolay (1919), among others, testify to new influences and to an atmosphere of secular moral commitment and character building in the United States.

The efforts of the individuals and organizations contributing to the development of the youth service movement established the groundwork for the introduction of new paradigms in the community's perception of youth. Over the past several decades these basic themes have remained constant with attempts at greater definition and focus. The latter part of the twentieth century and the beginning of the twenty-first have witnessed the rise of new concerns for the welfare of youth, resulting in new orientations, services, and ideas. Yet, much of the core foundations established in the early 1900s remain.

YOUTH STUDIES, YOUTH WORK, YOUTH DEVELOPMENT, YOUTH SERVICES, YOUTH LEADERSHIP . . . WHAT DOES IT ALL MEAN?

Parallel to the appearance and development of youth organizations and youth services, ideas evolved and disciplinary fields blossomed. Much was accomplished in the study of youth and in reflecting on the practice of those working with youth. Definitions and terminology emerged. Today, the student may find many terms to describe what sometimes is viewed as different disciplines and sometimes nothing else but nomenclature to define ongoing professional dialogues.

People working with youth use various terms to refer to their professional fields. Sometimes these terms are used interchangeably, and sometimes professionals can be very particular about the terminology. It is useful for the human service professional to be acquainted with this terminology while acknowledging that these terms have not been cast in stone and for all purposes are not even clearly defined.

Generally speaking, the phrase *youth studies* refers to the domain of sociologists who study youth from the point of view of their inclusion in social phenomena. The study of youth as a culture or a subculture of society is part of the youth studies domain usually found in anthropological and sociological departments and publications.

Youth work has been mainly used in two ways. First, it has been used to define those professionals who work directly with youth, especially in the context of outreach work. Usually, outreach youth work is directed toward disenfranchised youth. Youth workers are found working with youth in the streets, shelters, and other unusual places where youth congregate. Because of their geographical and sometimes philosophical and ideological distance from central bureaucracies and supervision, the term *detached youth work* has emerged to describe professional, philosophical, and ideological stances.

Second, the term *youth work* has been applied to those working with youth inside character-building organizations, usually in the context of offering recreation and leisure programs. In that sense, youth workers are found in organizations such as Boy Scouts, Girl Scouts, 4H, Camp Fire, YWCAs and YMCAs, and other similar organizations. Still, some have suggested that the term *youth work* should be applied to all who work with youth, indiscriminately.

The use of the term *youth development* is somewhat complicated by the fact that it can relate (1) to the evolution of life stages and (2) to the overall field of working with youth. Many important authors and organizations subscribe to using the term to define the entirety of the youth-serving profession and the field of study (e.g., Pittman and Wright, 1991). On the other hand, youth development has been traditionally used as a basic concept by character-building organizations.

The earlier conceptualization of youth development by character-building organizations was elaborated in the midst of much social change brought about by the Industrial Revolution. In that view, youth were described as potential prey to environmental ills. To provide for *healthy youth development*, these organizations took on the task of protecting the youth against these physical, moral, and spiritual ills. Youth development, in these terms, has moral and religious connotations, and in fact the character-building concept was usually referred to as *moral education*. Newly emerging approaches in the postindustrial world have led to a host of new definitions of what constitutes positive youth development. As Edginton and Oliveira (1995a) have pointed out, youth development has become a multidimensional construct.

Youth leaders is a phrase that is often used interchangeably with *youth workers*. However, the leadership component is commonly associated with working inside the realm of character building, leisure or recreation and less with the term *youth work* as used to define those who work with the disenfranchised. The Institute for Youth Leaders at the University of Northern Iowa uses the phrase *youth leadership* in reference to working with youth in general, usually in partnership with community organizations.

Another term frequently used in the domain of working with youth is *youth services*. This refers to all services targeting youth. Usually such services are also committed to work with families and community, as it has been recognized that working with youth is incomplete if not involving those more close to the clientele. Youth services can be delivered by institutions such as schools, health centers, community centers, churches, and/or other agencies, institutions, and organizations. Such services may directly or indirectly involve clients' peers, educators, family, spiritual leaders, health care providers, and other community leaders.

PARADIGMS IN THE PRACTICE OF YOUTH SERVICES

When we refer to a youth service paradigm, we mean the conjunction of values, beliefs, concepts, and consequent principles, definitions, approaches, and methods that establish guidelines for professional practice. In this section we present three paradigms that define youth services' professional practice: the remedial, the prosocial, and the integrative.

The Remedial Paradigm

A major philosophical stance on youth that remains pervasive today emerged at the turn of the twentieth century. This approach, which we refer to as the remedial paradigm, essentially equates youth with problems. The basis for this view comes from social constructs born from the discipline of psychology that captured youth and adolescence as phases of life characterized by stress and turmoil. This concept was diffused by works of, among others, G. Stanley Hall (e.g., 1904), who is usually credited as creating the term *adolescence*. This early conceptualization of adolescence and an emphasis on the emerging problems of a newly born industrialized urban society, including delinquency, led to an association of the terms *youth* and *adolescence* with turmoil, stress, and, ultimately, problems. In this view, the context of relationships between youth and adult society is permeated by adversarial, troubled interactions. One of the consequences of this view is the idea of youth as almost inherently in need to be treated or fixed. This approach implies a need for intervention, and interventions based on the medical model and mechanisms of social control have typically been responses to these articulated needs. A contemporary result of this development is the general idea of "youth at risk," which has become a stigmatizing statement guiding much of the social mechanisms in place to work with youth in Western societies.

The remedial paradigm draws from discipline models that analyze youth and propose intervention within a framework of causes and consequences. In that way of thinking, inappropriate behavior is always a consequence of previous lived experiences and influences. The focus is on the individual, even though there may be identified causes behind the individual's behavior. In the remedial paradigm, knowledge about youth and about intervening with youth is drawn from theoretical approaches that look for causes and consequences of behavior. The main tenet is that kids are, in principle, trouble, in trouble, and at risk. To help youth who are in trouble, youth organizations operating under the remedial paradigm establish services and programs that focus on social control. The idea is that the youth need to be helped in such a way as to be resocialized into the society as it exists. Society is fine—the youth are to blame for not fitting in.

Because youth behavior is often described as deviance and labeled antisocial, programs based on the remedial paradigm focus on problems, not on persons. Individual youth, then, become nothing more than the problem they represent. The focus is drug use and abuse, teenage pregnancy, truancy, juvenile delinquency, runaways, and dropouts. The youth are to be treated, and the behavior is the focus of the treatment. The basis for intervention is the medical model, and the forms of intervening are mainly counseling, therapy, or corrections. Part of the intervention focuses on isolating the youth on the basis of the principle of infection and quarantine: The bad can contaminate the good and so must be isolated and treated, not left unsupervised.

The Prosocial Paradigm

Traditionally, the prosocial paradigm is based on the concept of youth development as defined in earlier works of character-building organizations. As noted above, traditional youth service organizations view themselves as protecting youth from the ills brought by modern life, as they conceptualize youth as potential prey to environmental ills. In this conceptualization, youth service organizations must intervene to prevent youth from falling into the cracks of immorality, delinquency, and other problems brought by industrialization and urbanization. The basic purpose of intervention is the promotion of morals and "good character." The main strategy is to form good habits by focusing on age-appropriate and morally founded "positive," wholesome activities. In this way the organizations' mission is fulfilled by providing positive alternatives for youth, in contrast to the "bad" activities present in the environment. One major objective in this strategy is filling up youths' free time with the positive activities provided by professionals.

However, the prosocial view has evolved, and a new philosophical approach proposes youth as competent individuals who, given proper assistance, will naturally become responsible adults ready to assume their roles in a complex society. Authors such as White (e.g., 1963) and Smith (1974) and more recently the works of Baizerman (1987), Howard (1997) and Oliveira, Baizerman, and Pellet (1993), among others, suggest that human development must build on the potential competence of youth. The role of adults becomes one of motivating youth toward building competence that results in effective interaction with the environment.

The Integrative Paradigm

This approach to youth services views children and youth as integral parts of community and social development. Authors who hold this construct, including Baizerman (1987), Banks (1997), Heath and McLaughlin (1993), Oliveira (1994), Oliveira and Montecinos (1997), Smith (1988), and others, acknowledge that youth sometimes achieve social integration in positive, healthy, constructive ways and sometimes respond negatively to a variety of social phenomena. Negative responses may occur because of the youth's developmental predisposition and vulnerability (Mitchell, 1996). These authors suggest mostly that participation of all members of society is required to provide for an overall positive social and community development. Exclusion is a generator of social problems and reflects on individuals' dysfunction. The main anxieties of today's world can be explained, to a great extent, by the alienation common to those who feel excluded

from the benefits of social and material wealth. Inclusion, participation, and integration become the essence of the search for solutions.

In the integrative paradigm, children and youth are perceived as potential collaborators and contributors to society rather than problems to be fixed. Their involvement and participation in decision making is encouraged. The community has a moral responsibility in nurturing youth by creating, with them, an environment conducive to healthy development. Youth-serving organizations not only help the client directly but also assist in the process of creating a healthy environment while seeking authentic definitions for individual, community, and social development. Tolerance, resilience, reflective thinking, social justice, solidarity, caring, courage, honesty, integrity, and collaboration—as well as self-awareness, self-reliance, liberation, and independence—are among the core values driving this paradigm.

Youth are, in themselves, a transformational force in society. In the integrative paradigm, youth activities and idiosyncrasies are therefore not to be feared but mostly welcomed. Like all human beings, youth are in the process of becoming. We are all unfinished, uncompleted beings inhabiting a likewise unfinished reality. We must be conscious of being unfinished, and aware of our incompleteness. Risk taking and other forms of youth expression must be seen as a natural part of healthy development and therefore not to be "treated" but discussed within a framework of collective social support.

Accepting the above principles makes the mission of youth service organizations truly transformational. The role of youth service workers in these organizations becomes one of learning about and supporting and enabling this transformational force. Youth service professionals are, then, committed to understanding the youth's place in the social, cultural, and political world and helping youth understand themselves as active participants in this world. Further, the youth service professional must be an advocate for what the youth represent as a force of change while nevertheless being ready to discuss with the youth their own shortfalls within the possibilities created by their stages of development.

ORIENTATIONS TO INTERVENTIONS WITH YOUTH

Having discussed the paradigms commonly used to understand and intervene with youth, we next provide some examples of how these paradigms are integrated into professional practice and how they play out in the everyday working lives of professionals. Of course, the gigantic dimensions of the youth-serving human service field does not allow for an analysis of all orientations to working with youth. Instead, we intend to provide a few, limited examples of how these paradigms are translated into programs and services.

The authors have argued in a previous publication (Edginton and Oliveira, 1995a) that there is a need to establish definitions, theories, and models to explain, control, and ultimately predict the consequences of our professional interventions. In the realm of intervention with youth, different kinds of organizations, including higher education and public and nonprofit agencies and foundations, have become major players in organizing the professional field. These organizations, working in isolation or collaboratively, have developed several orientations and models for intervention. As a result, the youth-serving field has been influenced by many different theoretical and practical developments, and organizations have become role models in the search for understanding youth, understanding issues related to youth, and promoting forms of intervention with youth within the context of youth-serving human services. We will provide a brief, incomplete, and mostly impressionistic view of some of these orientations and models for working with youth.

As indicated in Table 12.1, Edginton and Oliveira (1995a) distilled a number of orientations to services provided by youth-serving professionals. They analyzed the characteristics of

orientations to youth services utilizing the following variables: (1) goals, (2) assumptions/perceptions of youth, (3) basic values and concepts of development, (4) typical settings, (5) program formats, and (6) professional roles. The orientations distilled in Table 12.1 fall under eight categories: leisure, sports/fitness, social services, character building, religious, vocational/career, advocacy/social policy, and social pedagogy.

Also, Table 12.1 shows the main professional approaches to working within the realm of youth services. The work of Edginton and Oliveira provides a way for the human service professional to better understand the realm of youth-serving agencies while exposing the worker to some fundamental ideas on how to conduct intervention in the field and within the context of youth-serving organizations.

The orientations to working with youth presented in Table 12.1 reflect not only the philosophies and paradigms adopted by youth workers but also the sectorial distribution and categorization of youth-serving organizations in society and how these organizations structure and deliver their programs and services. Human service organizations that focus on youth are pervasive in all economic sectors of American society, including the private, voluntary, not-for-profit or quasi-public, and public sectors. These organizations can be defined or referred to in many different ways, including character building, membership driven, youth clubs, religious oriented, mental health services, rehabilitation services, social work, crisis intervention, counseling services, community service, and community organizations.

Human service organizations that focus on youth provide a large array of programs and services. Such programs and services could be classified in a number of ways to include direct service programs; referral and counseling services, information services, facilities and areas, outreach services, and programs that facilitate or enable behaviors. Erickson (1994) notes that youth-serving organizations provide a "nonformal system of education through which members may

TABLE 12.1   Orientations to Youth Work and Youth Development

	LEISURE ORIENTATION	SPORTS/FITNESS ORIENTATION	SOCIAL SERVICE ORIENTATION	CHARACTER-BUILDING ORIENTATION
1. Goals	Constructive use of free time; enhancement/ development of lifetime leisure skills; promotion of quality of life	Motor skill development; competition; fair play; social interaction	Promote youth welfare through provision of social services	Moral/character building; "positive" socialization; friendship development; civic education; strengthening family values
2. Assumptions/ Perceptions of Youth	Participants; customers	Participants; team members	Clients	Participants; customers; members
3. Basic values and concepts of development	Leisure as a social instrument; pursued as an end in itself; enabling/ expanding human potential	Sport teaches competition and cooperation; skill development; promotes fun, fitness and friend making	Welfare as community's right; welfare as community's benefit; helping; caring	Promotion of civic spirit; promotion of democratic values through moral education
4. Typical settings (examples)	Local park and recreation departments; nonprofit sports associations; commercial leisure organizations; schools; camps	Local park and recreation departments; AAU; AYSO; Hershey Track and Field; Police Athletic League; Pony Baseball; Pop Warner Football; YABA	Rehabilitation centers; juvenile justice system; government social welfare agencies; treatment centers	Boy Scouts of America; Girl Scouts of the USA; Boys & Girls Clubs of America; Camp Fire Boys and Girls; Girls, Inc.; YMCA of the USA; YWCA of the USA
5. Program Formats	Classes/instruc- tion; drop-in; special events; contests; clubs; leagues	Leagues; clinics; tournaments; clubs; special events	Counseling; training; rehabilitation programs; mentoring	Clubs; classes/ instructional; social recreation; special events; outdoor/adventure activities
6. Professional Roles	Instructor, event manager; camp counselor; program leader	Coach; official volunteer; manager; fund-raising coordinator	Social worker; therapist, counselor; trainer/instructor; psychologist; mentor	Counselor; instructor; fund-raiser; volunteer coordinator; program leader

Source: Edginton, C., and W. Oliveira (1995). A model of youth work orientations. *Humanics: The Journal of Leadership for Youth and Human Services, 4*(2): 3–7. Used by permission.

RELIGIOUS ORIENTATION	VOCATIONAL/CAREER ORIENTATION	ADVOCACY/SOCIAL POLICY ORIENTATION	SOCIAL PEDAGOGY ORIENTATION
Spiritual fulfillment through practicing charity; moral education; character building	Career exploration; work habits/attitude; career skills; opportunities for cooperative work	Fostering debate on youth concerns and problems; defending youth's rights before public and private institutions	Bringing youth and adults together to build stronger sense of community; providing youth services based on social pedagogy philosophies and principles.
Receivers/deliverers of charity services; disciples; learners	Clients; partners	Constituents; clients	Partners; learners
Search of spiritual elevation and fulfillment; helping the disadvantaged, the destitute and the oppressed	Fitting youth into the job market; revealing youth's personal inclinations; facilitating youth's realization as worker and/or human being	State responsibility for protection of youth; equality; rights of citizenship	Phenomenological understanding of youth; emphasis on the impact of encounters and relationships
Young Life; Salvation Army; Athletes in Action; Youth for Christ; Church Youth Groups	4-H; WAVE, Inc.; Job Corps; governmental agencies	Child Welfare League of America; National Coalition of Hispanic Health and Human Service Organizations; National Network of Runaway and Youth Services	Youth agencies, street corners; governmental agencies
Charity, spiritual education; social recreation; special events; service projects; encounters	Vocational programs; job training; job-seeking support; skill building	Lobbying; community organizations; public education; fostering political power structures	Encounters; social education
Spiritual leader; program leader	Instructor; trainer; counselor; placement advisor; mentor	Lobbyist; community organizer; fact finder; public relations coordinator; canvasser	Outreach worker; detached youth worker; social educator

learn a broad spectrum of skills, attitudes and values" (p. 3).

Finally, a framework for categorizing youth development programs has been presented by Edginton and Oliveira (1995b). They suggest that most programs may fall under the following areas: academic enrichment, leisure activities, sports and fitness, health promotion, social services, peer mentoring, life skill building, vocational/career, advocacy, leadership development, service learning (community/civic), outreach services, and clubs/special interest groups.

YOUTH AND YOUTH WORKERS AS METAPHORS FOR THE FUTURE

There are many problems facing youth today. Since the advent of the Industrial Revolution and through the new information era, youth-serving workers have tried to keep pace with the challenges facing youth. The workers have to struggle to understand the rapid social changes influencing youth behavior while trying to educate society about the necessity of providing services that attend to youth needs. Youth-serving workers have become as varied in specializations as the problems they face. Be they working in corrections departments or character-building organizations or as detached youth workers, recreation leaders, child abuse investigators, or in other capacities, youth-serving workers find themselves many times in the same position as the youth: as persons caught in the middle of historical changes, in situations that call for fast adjustment while stirring excitement and risk. The task of both youth workers and youth is to create and preserve an identity that has to be at the same time solid enough to resist the constant bombardment of sometimes meaningless and negative stimuli and flexible enough to adjust to the fast changes and concrete necessities presented in social life and by the job market.

The ability of youth and youth workers to adapt and adjust to rapidly changing conditions is of utmost importance for the future of society. Our youth represent our future, and our youth workers are the leaders who play a fundamental role in helping shape this future. Youth are vulnerable because of their biological developmental characteristics and because of the environments in which they live. The youth leader must recognize this vulnerability and help the youth through the formation of their identities, and their initiation into the future.

Youth workers are essentially educators. Whether they relate to youth in the context of street life, in playgrounds, inside of correctional facilities, or in a summer camp, their task is essentially to educate the youth, the society, and themselves. Paulo Freire, one of the greatest educators of the twentieth century, contends that education must occur within the context of collaboration between the educator and the student. In this context, the educator joins the youth as co-investigators of the world in search for the truth. Education, therefore, must make youth feel that they are not isolated, alienated, and unattached to the world. The task of youth workers is to help youth in their quest for meaning as well as in their efforts to acquire a sense of belonging. This makes the role of the youth worker key in delivering formal and informal education and in helping society understand and embrace youth for what they are.

The youth worker who recognizes this profound task, of helping shape the future of society, is engaged in a pedagogy that is essentially libertarian. Such a pedagogy works toward humanization, liberating, empowering, and educating individuals and groups who otherwise may feel oppressed and excluded. Youth service work embracing such a task incorporates the following principles:

1. Youth workers are engaged in a movement of inquiry, directed toward humanization, to transform situations. Such a movement of inquiry implies fellowship and solidarity versus individualism and isolation.

2. *Helping* is based on knowledge as well as on sincerity and ethical behavior. Authentic, sincere dedication and thinking to create knowledge is concerned with reality and takes place not in isolation but only through communication. Transfer of knowledge about society and knowledge that is useful to help individuals within a given social environment can occur only in the context of collaboration within the realm of the society.

3. The youth leader and the youth are not in oppositional but in cooperative positions. The leader must present him- or herself as open to authentic dialogue and collaboration with the youth. The leader and the youth must find common grounds for their quests, intentions, and practice. Youth leaders and youth are to become inquiring partners.

4. Youth leaders and youth must overcome authoritarianism and an alienating elitism. A libertarian approach to youth services embodies authentic communication. Both professionals and youth teach and learn with each other through dialogue. They are both responsible for a process in which all grow. Youth are critical co-investigators in dialogue with the professionals. Authority must be on the side of freedom, not against it.

5. Youth work, as education, is constantly remade in the praxis. Praxis means reflection on practice and practice based on reflection. One without the other is grossly incomplete.

6. Youth and youth-serving workers will greatly profit from engaging in critical thinking. This means to consider reality critically and not to accept it blindly as it is presented. Reality is a process that undergoes constant transformation. Reality can be shaped by interests.

7. Youth can develop their power to perceive critically the way they exist in the world. They can come to see the world not as a static reality but as a reality in process, in transformation. The youth must be aware of their responsibility in transforming the world, and the youth worker is responsible for transmitting that awareness.

8. Critical intervention is one main objective of youth-serving workers.

9. In order to *be,* youth and youth workers must work on *becoming.* We are incomplete human beings, incomplete persons, and professionals-in-the-making. Lifelong learning is a gift, a talent, and an effort to pursue with devotion.

10. The youth worker is engaged, and must help the youth to engage, in a struggle for liberation and humanization.

Although these principles are not conclusive, they present a general framework for those working with youth in different capacities. The future of our world is in the hands of those who are today at a young age. They will be instrumental in bringing about the needed transformations that can lead to a better world. We envision this future as a world in which all human beings can engage in meaningful occupations and have their basic needs met and their well-being and happiness promoted—in deed as well as in words. In such a world, people have bountiful opportunities to optimize their development within the context of a sustainable society.

REFERENCES

Addams, J. [1907](1964). *Democracy and Social Ethics.* Edited by Ann Firor Scott. Reprint, Cambridge, MA: Belknap Press of the Harvard University Press.

American Humanics (1996). *American Humanics 1996 Progress Report—The Momentum of Many Makes A World of Difference.* Kansas City, MO: American Humanics, Inc.

Baizerman, M. (1987). *Why a Community Needs Its Adolescents.* Paper presented at the Regional Conference on Adolescent Health Issues. Sponsored by the United States Public Health Service, Region IV. Dallas, TX, November.

Banks, S. (1997). "Community Youthwork: A British Perspective." *Humanics: The Journal of Leadership in Youth and Human Services, 6*(2), 7–10.

Carnegie Corporation of New York (1997). *Great Transitions: Preparing Adolescents for a New Century.* Available at http://www.carnegie.org.

Cimmino, P. (1993). *Exactly What Is Human Services? The Evolution of a Profession: Academic Discipline and Social Science.* Bronx, NY: Council for Standards in Human Services Education Monograph Series.

Coleman, J. C., and L. Hendry (1980). *The Nature of Adolescence.* London: Routledge.

Dewey, J. (1916). *Democracy and Education: An Introduction to the Philosophy of Education.* New York: Macmillan.

The Drucker Foundation (1996). "About the Drucker Foundation." *Leader to Leader, 1*(1), 48.

Edginton, C., and Oliveira, W. (1995a). A Model of Youth Work Orientations. *Humanics: The Journal of Leadership for Youth and Human Services, 4*(2), 3–7.

Edginton, C., and W. Oliveira (1995b). "Youth Development: A Program Framework." *PERS Review, 1*(2), 22–27.

Erickson, J. B. (1994). *Directory of American Youth Organizations.* Minneapolis: Free Spirit.

Eriksen, E. H. (1968). *Identity, Youth and Crisis.* New York: W.W. Norton.

Gulick, L. H. (1938). *Education for American Life. A New Program for the State of New York.* New York: McGraw-Hill.

Hall, G. S. (1904). *Adolescence, Its Psychology and Its Relations to Physiology, Anthropology, Sociology, Sex, Crime, Religion and Education.* New York: D. Appleton.

Heath, S. B., and M. W. McLaughlin (1993). *Identity and Inner-City Youth.* New York: Teaching College Press.

Howard, B. (1997). "Assets vs. Risks: The Selling of Rival Youth Development Strategies." *Youth Today, 6*(5): 1, 18–21.

James, T. (1993). "The Winnowing of Organizations." In S.B. Heath and M.W. McLaughlin, *Identity and Inner City Youth.* New York: Teaching College Press.

Kett, J. F. (1977). *Rites of Passage: Adolescence in America, 1790 to the Present.* New York: Basic Books.

Lee, J. (1915). *Play in Education.* New York: Macmillan.

Mitchell, J. J. (1996). *Adolescent Vulnerability.* Calgary, Alberta, Canada: Detselig Enterprises.

Oliveira, W. (1994). *We Are in the Streets Because They Are in the Streets: The Emergence and Praxis of Street Social Education in Brazil.* Doctoral dissertation, University of Minnesota.

Oliveira, W., M. Baizerman, and L. Pellet (1993). "Street Kids: Aspirations and the Future." In H. Campfens, ed., *Poverty and Interventions.* Thousand Oaks, CA: Sage Publications.

Oliveira, W., and Montecinos, C. (1997). "Education in the Open Environment." *Humanics: The Journal of Leadership in Youth and Human Services, 6*(2), 3–6.

Peiss, K. (1996). *Cheap Amusements: Working Women and Leisure in Turn-of-the-Century New York.* Philadelphia: Temple University Press.

Pittman, K. J., and Wright, M. (1991). *A Rationale for Enhancing the Role of the Non-School Voluntary Sector in Youth Development.* Washington, DC: Center for Youth Development and Research, Academy for Educational Development.

Riis, J. (1892). *The Children of the Poor.* New York: Scribner's Sons.

Smith, M. (1988). *Developing Youthwork.* Philadelphia: Open University Press.

Smith, M. B. (1974). Toward a Conception of the Competent Self. In H.V. Kraemer, ed., *Youth and Culture: A Human Development Approach.* Monterey, CA: Brooks/Cole.

Thompson, J. (1991). *The Price You Pay to Wear Tennis Shoes to Work.* Doctoral dissertation: Union Institute.

White, R. M. (1963). "Ego and reality in psychoanalytic theory: A proposal for independent ego energies." *Psychological Issues, 3*(3).

Wilds, E. H. (1956). *The Foundations of Modern Education.* New York: Rinehart.

PREGNANT PRODUCTIONS:
A VYGOTSKY-INSPIRED APPROACH
TO TEENS AND TEEN PREGNANCY

RAFAEL MENDEZ

CREATING ENVIRONMENTS OF POSSIBILITIES: A CULTURAL-PERFORMATORY PROGRAM TO PROMOTE HUMAN DEVELOPMENT

James and Jamal are fifteen-year-old African American teenagers who recently performed a duet of monologues before an adult audience.

Act I, Scene 1

"Hi! My name is James and I'm from Flatbush, I've been there you know. I'm from _Brooklyn,_ man. You know, playing the shorties—it's fun, man. I went to this party one night and all the shorties were passing me by. The shorties were good, man, all kinds of girls. I met this one girl, man, she was something, nice body, hair in braids; ooh she was cool! We were getting it on and all and then she asked me to walk her to the bus stop. Well, you know what happened, man; _we got it on_. It was cool and everything, and I said I'd call her. I didn't know if I would but the whole thing was PHAT!

Then, she calls me up a few weeks later, you know what I mean, and _tells me she's pregnant!_ No way, man. I mean, No Way! She is sweating me and no way. I mean, I want to be responsible and maybe I should be a one-woman man, but I'm a PLAYER. Yeah man, I'm a player. I like playing the shorties. I don't know what to do. I just don't know. There's a way I care and there's a way I don't care at all."

Scene 2

"Hey man, my name is Jamal and I'm from HARLEM, and James, he's my man! We went to this party a few days ago and it was cool. We met these shorties and James, well, he's a player and he _got it on;_ you know what I mean? So he walked this shorty to the bus stop and they were gone a long time. Now she says she's pregnant. Sometimes my man doesn't think about the consequences of what he's doin', about safe sex and all, you know, if you're gonna be a player. Man, I think he needs to take responsibility for what's gone down. He says he doesn't care. He needs to make a decision about what kind of man he wants to be. Whatever he decides, I'm behind him because _he's my man;_ you known what I mean? I think he needs to do the right thing. I'll stand by his side whatever he does. That's what I think; what do you think?"

James and Jamal are members of an innovative teen pregnancy prevention program called Pregnant Productions, currently in Harlem. It is structured and functions as a cultural production company where adolescents create and produce cultural events for the community based on issues of sexuality and teen pregnancy. The theoretical premise of Pregnant Productions was inspired by Lev Vygotsky's theories of human development. It is one of the few but increasing number of Vygotskian programs in the United States. James and Jamal's monologues are from a cultural event they participated in creating and producing.

James performed a character who wonders whether he is going to be a "player" and date many girls or whether he is going to be a "one-woman man." The youth of Pregnant Productions collectively developed this scenario by improvisationally directing James during rehearsals to perform as a character who is conflicted over whether he was going to care about anybody's life, including his own. His was a demanding performance; its development took weeks.

At the time of this performance, James was dating and having sex with a number of different young women. He is handsome and charismatic, and many of the girls in the programs were attracted to him. James did not like to admit that he enjoyed the attention. During the rehearsals, James was very reluctant to perform his character, saying, "I don't want to do this . . . I don't want to say I had sex with this girl . . . who is now telling me she is afraid that she is pregnant . . . and hell I don't even like her anyway . . . and now she is becoming a real pain and I don't really care about her . . . no, no, we ain't having this . . . I don't want to say those things because it will make me look bad."

WHAT ARE ZONES OF PROXIMAL DEVELOPMENT?

Pregnant Productions meets weekly. The two directors (the program coordinator and the social worker) organize twenty-five at-risk teenagers between the ages of twelve and eighteen to produce cultural events addressing the social, economic, and emotional issues of teen pregnancy. The purpose of the weekly rehearsals is to produce six public performances throughout the year. The activity of producing these events provides the structure wherein the youth collectively participate in creating what Lev Vygotsky (1978) calls zones of proximal development (ZPD) and what we call social environments. Vygotsky's discovery of ZPDs is the identification of psychological processes (e.g., thinking, speaking, remembering,

and problem solving) as produced through participation in and internalization of social-cultural-historical forms of activity (i.e., social behavior). The ZPD is the difference between what one can do with others and what one can do by oneself (Vygotsky, 1978, 1987). In the activity of creating social environments, youth can developmentally address the complexity of emotional/social issues that affect them.

One of the purposes of these public performances is to create a community dialogue *led by the youths* on the topic of teen pregnancy. The themes of teenage sexuality and pregnancy are not in any way important for their public performance to be an effective developmental activity; any theme would do. The themes of teen sexuality are helpful in the public performances. Through these public performances, the teens produce new social environments in which they lead a dialogue with adults about their views and emotions about sexuality in a social context where they won't be dismissed. The teens of Pregnant Productions create a new "zone of proximal development" with the community. This reorganizes their social location from perceived victims or problems to actual leaders in the community.

With the support of the directors, the cast did a lot of work with James, supporting and directing his performance. They let him know that through his performance he would be providing leadership to those who see his performance and are grappling with similar issues. If James feels as if he doesn't care, *he can perform not caring.* He is repeatedly reminded that this would be a giving activity. He would be performing for the community what actually goes on for many teens, and the cast and the community can build a new social environment with it.

WHO WAS LEV VYGOTSKY?

Building new social environments is fundamental to a Vygotskian approach to human development. The investigations of Lev Vygotsky, a renowned

Russian developmental psychologist, in the 1920s and 1930s, led to a methodological breakthrough in the *conceptualization of human development.* His theories provide insight into the process by which human beings have the capacity for continuous qualitative change-development. Vygotsky died young, in 1933, and his work was repressed by Stalin's government. In the past decade, his theories have been translated and have become internationally popular. Vygotsky recognized in early childhood play a distinguishing characteristic of human beings: that humans create and can transform the totality of their social environments, producing human development. He distinguished his conception of human development from the traditional Piagetian concept of fixed stages of development by focusing on social activity (Vygotsky, 1978, 1987, 1993). Vygotsky identified developmental activity (the activity that promotes development) as the activity of creating new social environments, which he described as having the dialectic character of being simultaneously the tool and the result. Participating in creating new social environments is a collective activity in which people can create the possibility of breaking out of predetermined social roles (Newman, 1994).

One of the directors tells James that although oftentimes a person cannot control how he or she feels, he or she can make a conscious decision on *what to do.* James was directed to perform his conflict: to perform not being sure whether he wanted to be a young African American man who cares about African American women or someone who just doesn't care. James was supported to *perform feeling many different ways* about how he would like to be during the course of a day. This support allowed James to stretch beyond himself without denying who he is (a youth with emotional conflicts about caring).

James requested that someone join him in his monologue who would support him. So a friend got up and improvised, saying, "Hi, I'm Jamal, and James is my man. Let me tell you about what

James said; I believe in safe sex; I am somebody who cares a lot about people, and sometimes James doesn't care, but that's okay, 'cause he is still my man, and I am there for my man, and I'm going to help him get through this." Using performance, Jamal creatively expressed his support and caring for both the collective performance and his friend James, without siding with James's feelings of not caring.

CREATING POSSIBILITIES BY BREAKING OUT OF PREDETERMINED ROLES

The rehearsals and production of this monologue supported James and the others in *the activity of creating new social environments.* The purpose of these new social environments is to support the youths in breaking out of their predetermined roles. Ordinarily, James would not have asked for help. That's not cool. Ordinarily, Jamal would have had to pick a side: support his friend, or support the others. We describe these environments as *activity* where they can perform on and about emotional issues of their lives. The themes the youths choose to perform *do not* necessarily need to be from their direct experience for the activity to be developmental. The themes they choose are what they're interested in performing, which is empowering and increases their collective participation while minimizing coercion.

Their *performance* is not an attempt to act out their biographies as some kind of psychodrama. There is no attempt to explore anyone's inner experience or to relive past experiences. *Performance* is the conscious activity of producing how we are in the world. We have no theoretical commitment to the concept of truth. We do not attempt to discover what actually happened to them when younger, for example. *In performance, we respond to the activity of the statement being said,* not its truth or falsity. Our commitment is to knowledge, which is socially arrived at and, in life, changes and renews itself with each moment of interaction (Hoffman,

1993). What is important is the activity of collectively building a supportive social environment, moment to moment, where people can exercise their capacity for continuous emotional development. We agree with Gergen and Kaye's (1993) urging for a therapeutic approach that is not based on truth. We believe that what is therapeutic is supporting human development. We believe that the activity of creating new social environments to perform best promotes human development.

DIALECTICS: THE UNITY OF LEARNING AND DEVELOPMENT

Pregnant Productions is the activity of participants creating the social environment necessary to perform experiences on and about their lifetimes in a genre they create. Here they care about what they are collectively doing together (producing their cultural event) and about each other. The production of the cultural event is a developmental activity to the degree that it is simultaneously both the tool and the result, the unity of learning and the development (Newman and Holzman, 1993).

In a society and culture where often it is not "cool" or common to care about others, the members of Pregnant Productions created a social environment where they could creatively care by *performing caring* (i.e., giving direction and support to James) and collectively building something meaningful together. They created new ways of *being* for themselves. In the activity of this Vygotsky-inspired methodology, the youths learn that they can create a social environment (a cultural performance) that allows them to learn and develop (a tool and a result).

DEVELOPING YOUTHS AS LEADERS

Pregnant Productions' organizing concept, a cultural production company, maximizes Vygotsky's concept of human development as the activity of creating ZPDs. Pregnant Productions' weekly rehearsals for productions include organizing the community. Building an audience is part of producing public performances. For example, Pregnant Productions is currently funded through a grant by the Urban League and hosted by the Minisink Community Center in Harlem, which provides a dance studio as space. Pregnant Productions produces after-school cultural events at the Minisink Community Center. The teens invite the members of the community center, advisory board members, local community agencies, parents, and classmates to attend. Inviting people to their event enhances their collective responsibility and caring for what they produce. It is a significant activity of building a new ZPD with the community. They also travel to other neighborhood centers to produce after-school events.

At the conclusion of their cultural performance, a dialogue takes place between the cast and the audience. This portion of their public performance creates a new social environment (ZPD) and an important dimension of Pregnant Productions: a community dialogue with the possibility for community development.

At one such discussion, the monologues between James and Jamal emerged as the focal point between the adults and the teenage performers. The adults were noticeably affected by the frankness and conflictedness of the monologues. They asked pointed and direct questions about sex: "Are you having sex?" "Do you use condoms?" "What do you do when you don't have a condom?" The youths confidently and openly responded. They received applause and praise. At times, their frankness was unsettling to some: "If I have the opportunity but I don't have a condom, I'm still going to get busy [have sex]."

The youths created through their performance and production a new social context—a new social location where they could provide leadership to the adult community on critical and complex topics. This is not to say that the youths have the answers, but they did create a new context where meaningful dialogue was possible. They were able to effectively tell the adults that many but not all of them were having sex, that condoms need to be readily available, and that more open discussions were needed. These youths transformed their social location through the activity of creating the context for and leading this community dialogue, dialectically transforming themselves.

WHY YOUTH MUST PROVIDE LEADERSHIP

Adults, particularly parents and teachers, too often assume that they know what goes on with teenagers merely because they were once teenagers themselves. This is an error that causes adolescents to reject parental advice. Contemporary society and culture are changing very rapidly. Today, children are more worldwise than their parents. Youngsters of nine and ten are likely to understand how fast things are changing better than adults who perceive the rate of change as if it were twenty-five years ago. This is not to put down caring adults but to point out that our rapidly changing world demands a new approach to learning and development. Adults get stuck in their roles as parents and teachers, restricting the kind of dialogue and intimacy they can have with adolescents. The topic of sex is one example.

Frequently, as the teens prepare for public performances, the issue of censorship arises. The older youths often want to perform scenes with street language and expressions common to their youth culture which some adults think is vulgar, or they'll want a dance routine that may be viewed as too sexually suggestive: "Let's be real," they say. Although sensitivity to representatives of funding sources is an important consideration (and the youths understand this), we think censorship is coercive. It is contradictory to tell youths they need to break out of their roles and then continue the authoritarian practice of determining their roles. This is antidevelopmental.

PERFORMANCE REINITIATES DEVELOPMENT

Pregnant Productions is a cultural-performatory approach to the complex issue of teen pregnancy. It is designed to reinitiate emotional development with teenagers. Development often is impeded by the internalization of and identification with predetermined social roles: "Oh no, I couldn't do that; that's not me." In contrast to traditional psychological approaches, Pregnant Productions provides an *activity-theoretic* framework for the critical question, "How do we promote human development in the context of social decay?" We use *performance* as an activity to break free of roles and identity. Traditional psychology has taught that development is a private matter that happens to individuated selves, that it is an internal process, that all people pass through fixed stages of development, that a strong sense of identity is key to mental health, and that our learning is a function of how developed we already are. This traditional stagist theory of human development is being challenged by activity theorists inspired by Vygotsky.

WHO CREATED PREGNANT PRODUCTIONS?

For nearly twenty years, the Eastside Institute and the International Center for Human Development have been dedicated to the practice and advancement of new methodological approaches to psychology and human development. The Eastside Institute has created an independent institution (a professional environment outside the constraints of traditionally funded institutions) where Vygotsky's investigations have informed our work. In turn, we developed and advanced Vygotsky's theories. We practice a Vygotsky-inspired approach, which we call social therapy, in a number of therapeutic-, cultural-, educational-, and community-based settings. Pregnant Productions is our contribution to the social issue of teen pregnancy.

Pregnant Productions is neither educational nor psychological in methodology. Rather, it is a cultural-performatory approach to human development. It teaches building new kinds of social environments that promote *learning and development.* To us, for civilization to advance, humans need to be able to create new social environments and new forms of life. We need to create human development.

THE STRUCTURE FOR PREGNANT PRODUCTIONS

The organizing task for the youths of Pregnant Productions is to figure out how and what they want to produce and give to the community. These decisions provide the structure for building a creative social environment that is at once beyond what they know how to do (in advance of their development) and a cultural orientation that they can easily relate to (as a goal within their reach). Do they want to produce a comedy, a variety show, a musical, or a drama? What content do they want to put in their show that will teach the community about who they are as young people (their interests, their conflicts, the issues they're grappling with)? These are decisions they must make in creating their cultural production.

Creating these cultural events is a giving activity that has the potential to simultaneously transform their relationship to their community and thus who they are. In the activity of producing these events, they experience the history of their decisions and decision making. A comment, a joke, or an experience can be developed and transformed into a scene for the final production. This activity promotes the youths as *decision makers*—as people who can, through their decisions, create something meaningful. Learning the social and emotional skills of performance creates the *possibility* that as decision makers they can break free from overly determined social roles and create their own lives.

ACTIVITY THEORY: DEVELOPMENTAL PSYCHOLOGY'S NEW TRADITION

This cultural performatory approach is on the cutting edge of contemporary culturally oriented cognitive, educational, and developmental psychology known as *activity theory.* Pregnant Productions was created in response to a request by funding agencies (the South Bronx Teen Pregnancy Network and A Better Bronx for Youth) that were frustrated with existing preventive programs that had limited impact on their youths and community.

Youth programs most often attempt to respond to issues of teen pregnancy with traditional educational and/or psychological programs. Traditional educational programs want adolescents to make what adults believe are "better" decisions (e.g., to not have sex or at least to use a condom and not get pregnant). Their underlying theoretical perspective suggests that if youths were better educated about the trials and tribulations of teen parenthood, abortions, and sexually transmitted diseases, they would make better decisions (e.g., not get pregnant). The complex social and institutional arrangements that produce high teenage unemployment, poor literacy rates, and an ever-increasing permanent underclass locate many educational programs (despite best intentions) as authoritarian and coercive.

Psychologically oriented programs usually incorporate pejorative value judgments. They view youths as "troubled," "at risk," or a "problem." Psychologically oriented programs tacitly impose behavioral expectations. They attempt to measure their success with indicators of particular behaviors they have deemed good or bad (i.e., adaptive or maladaptive). These behavioral expectations are undemocratic, coercive, and intrusive. They are part of the institutional arrangements that attempt to overdetermine societal roles. They are, in effect, antidevelopmental.

Pregnant Productions' innovative developmental approach is activity-theoretic. It advances Vygotsky's concept of ZPDs. We understand Vygotsky's use of the term *zone* to mean certain kinds of *human activity* (not a particular area) that create new social environments. We identify the activity of *performance* as the activity that best promotes human development. *Performing* requires the simultaneous activity of creating the social environment where one can perform (the tool and the result).

Pregnant Productions recognizes the unlimited human potential to create social environments where human development is possible. Vygotsky noted how traditional theories of learning do not explain how children's imitations of the language they hear differ from the imitations of a parrot. How is it that the child eventually becomes a speaker, whereas the parrot never does? To Vygotsky, what distinguishes the child from the parrot is *activity* (Newman, 1996). To understand human development we need to see that human beings engage in conjoint (not privatized) socio-cultural activity.

Vygotsky viewed human development as a joint social activity (Newman and Holzman, 1993). For example, children learn to speak in a social context (the ZDP) of being related to as a speaker, not an imitator. Parents encourage children to do what they do not yet know how to do— to be *ahead of themselves*. In this way, Vygotsky turned upside down the prevailing wisdom holding that what and how much an individual can learn depends on their level of development. Children learn in a way that contributes to their emotional, intellectual, and social development as the social environment supports their active participation in creating their development.

WHAT DO WE MEAN BY PERFORMANCE?

Our cultural-performatory approach is a critical contribution to the question of human development at this moment in history when there is a crisis in human development. Contemporary society, characterized by social decay, random violence, and increased poverty, creates profound obstacles for human development. Pregnant Productions'

cultural-performatory approach is radically democratic in that it's all-inclusive and insists that participants assume collective responsibility for what they are doing together; it's noninterpretive. We describe it as a new kind of play—a continuous performance of life.

The program relates to the youths as being capable of unlimited continuous development. With appropriate support, youth can build social environments where they can be the creators of their own lives. Collectively, they can explore and learn about the multitude of life choices open to them. The underlying premise of the program is that youth can go through a developmental transformation of their emotionality in much the way children acquire language (the activity of acquiring language transforms who children are). By virtue of this transformation, they're in a new social location to face important life decisions. They can become *better decision makers;* they can make choices in a developmental way, as people who make decisions in the activity of creating their own lives.

At Pregnant Productions, *performance* is the centerpiece of our program. Our concept of performance is inspired by Vygotsky's observation of child's play as characteristic of the social activity that best promotes development. It is distinct from acting. In the activity of play we can see children attempting to perform things they do not know how to do. In child's play, one *performs ahead,* or *in advance of, one's development.* Performance is the developmental dialectic of being and becoming. The improvisational qualities of child's play are maximized through the activity of youths creating, developing, and performing their own cultural events.

PERFORMANCE (NOT IDENTITY) PROMOTES DEVELOPMENT

Performance promotes development by engaging and breaking from one's identity. Frequently, people will behave in a particular emotive manner and justify their behavior by saying that they cannot change: "This is who I am." William, a young man in the program, was much taller and bigger than his peers. He had an intimidating presence. Merely by sitting he conveyed a don't-mess-with-me attitude. When initially directed to participate, he snarled, "Why I gotta do that?" When asked whether he was aware of his menacing posture, he said, "No man, I'm just chillin'. This is just the way I am." People often identify with their social attitudes and believe they cannot change.

Through performance, people can creatively perform who they are not and reinitiate development. If you can *perform* the behavior of you being who you are (like William performing himself being intimidating by just sitting), it is reasonable to assume that the behavior is not somehow naturally and unalterably determined. It is a performance of you being you. William was directed in a variety of scenarios to perform being intimidating and then asked to perform being gentle and considerate and then nerdy and silly. It was then clear to William that being intimidating was a behavioral choice, not who he is. Performance, on and off stage, is a self-defining activity.

If you can perform you doing that particular behavior that you identify as "you being you," you can also perform you doing something else. Just because you are performing does not mean you're being insincere. There is no justification for William saying, "I was only pretending to be nice; It's not really me." Why would pretending to be nice be any less "really you"? An advantage of the cultural-performatory approach over traditional psychological modalities is that it supports people in being less defensive. Performance gives people more access for going beyond the limits of their identities (Newman, 1996).

For the youths, creating and producing cultural events supports the activity of performance by providing a meaningful structure, a time, and a date for the public performance. *The activity of performing who they are becoming creatively transforms who they are.* In creating a cultural event, the members get to perform activities on and about issues and concerns that affect their lives. This is different from, and more demanding than, merely acting in a role.

Performance denotes the creative developmental activity of going beyond yourself to who you are not. When we say the youths perform, we mean they perform *who they are not*—they perform beyond themselves. Performance is not coercively getting someone to be someone else. We are not referring to role-playing. For example, when James was conflicted about performing his character, he was not asked to *act as if he cared* in coercive conformity to the politically correct way to feel. Rather, he was directed to *perform not caring.* We think it's coercive to ask a youth to be someone else. Performance is getting you (who will always remain you) to create you, to go beyond yourself. We do not mean simply taking on another role—that is merely acting or pretending to be someone else. Acting or role-playing requires only memorizing a script; it's imitation by replication, or mimicry. Performance is creating you by going beyond your identity.

PERFORMANCE: CREATIVE IMITATION, NOT ACTING

Performance is creative imitation. It is the *creative activity* of "you not being you." It is taking you, and stretching you, as you go beyond your identity. It is not a logic of either-you-are-this-or-that. Rather, it is a process logic, dialectically speaking; it is helping you *be you and not you simultaneously* (Newman, 1996). Creative imitation is grounded in the activity of child's play. Children's imitation includes internalizing and making use of the examples of others, but it is not simply being exactly like them in a replicative form. Rather, it is using models in the social process of actually creating something new. And what is created new is you (Newman, 1996). Creative imitation makes use of others as models and examples, but it's not simply replicating others.

To creatively imitate and perform is to take what you have, including the examples of others, and to create something new out of it, which is you. People, especially children, see someone do something that impresses them, and they try to imitate their model, but they do it their way, through creative imitation, and not replication.

Performance is demanding because people, even young people, are resistant to the idea that they can change, that they can develop. People can develop at any point in life—that is our discovery about development inspired by Vygotsky's activity-theoretic framework (Newman, 1996). Adolescents, just like adults, have already internalized that they are who they are. Once one becomes identified, one does not abandon that identity easily. They say, "This is who I am." Traditional psychology considers the formation of identity positively and views adolescence as a critical time for identity formation. The Vygotskian concept of development does not require identity formation for healthy development. We believe that identity (those predetermined social roles and expectations) restricts development.

Vygotsky recognized the unlimited human potential for continuous development. While daily life situations do not ordinarily support performatory activity, people can learn to transform their social environments and perform. For example, if people can learn to stop a scene during a rehearsal and say, "Let's do it again, only differently," they can stop a routine life situation by saying, "Let's try that again, differently." People can use performance to create and direct their lives and relationships. This is the activity-theoretic practice of our Vygotsky-inspired methodology of building and sustaining environments conducive to growth. The task is to grow and develop in whatever social circumstance.

THE ADULT DIRECTORS' ROLE IN PREGNANT PRODUCTIONS

Rehearsing for their cultural events gives shape and structure to teenage play: Children and adolescents enjoy repeating activity so they can improve. The use of cultural tools, such as improvisation and dance, is a form of play. As Vygotsky observed, when children are at play, they also create the social conditions for their play (the tool and the result). The directors support this activity by presenting activities that can promote their skills, such as directions on how to posture or gesture and to project one's voice. They provide cultural skills such as poetry reading and writing and dance instruction, that are important elements in supporting the youths' continuing participation. The directors' role is to support and direct the teens in conceptualizing and producing the rehearsals and public events.

The methodological pursuit of the directors is to support the cast's activity of performance. Their advanced skills allow them to perform as positive role models on how to collectively work together. They focus on supporting the youth in their activity of assuming and maintaining collective responsibility and care for what is being produced. The directors are a key element in this Vygotskian concept of the *learner/mentor relationship* (Vygotsky, 1978). They actively participate in the building of the social environment. The directors assist in reviewing the rehearsals, from how they began with one idea and creatively developed it into a production. This helps the youths model and creatively imitate the activity of directing and providing leadership.

CREATING SOMETHING MEANINGFUL TOGETHER

Creating a new social environment is goal oriented, even if the goal is just for fun. Performance is not an activity in itself. Rather, performance is the totality of the creative activity—the tool and the result. During rehearsal, the youths, through the activity of creating something that they care about, begin to direct one another and begin to care. They develop collective responsibility for their activity. Ultimately, they do not want to put on a poor show.

PERFORMING TALKING ABOUT SEX AND SEXUALITY

Sex is a subject in which both adults and youth are socialized into bragging about certain kinds of experiences, imagined or not. Sex is highly privatized—most people do not say what they think and feel. They want to avoid being humiliated. Mistakenly, many people believe they are the only ones who have had a certain experience or who feel or think a certain way.

At one rehearsal, the cast performed a series of monologues about their parents telling them about sex. Through their performance, they playfully poked fun at their parents, exposing the difficulty that most parents experience in talking about sex with their teenagers. One youth performed his father, saying, "Son, I have three words for you: Don't do it!" Another performed his father, saying, "Son, don't forget, use protection." "Right Dad, I'll carry a gun."

In creating these scenes, the youths performed on and about issues that are relevant to them while having fun discussing and performing the issues of their lifetimes. Once, a young man raised the topic of sexual harassment of boys by older girls, of being "attacked" in the restroom. This is not something that the boys wanted to be part of any final production. They didn't want others to know that it happened. Most adults have no idea that this goes on. The boys had plenty to say on this issue that would never have come up if the adults were choosing the topics.

CREATING CHOICES AND NEW POSSIBILITIES FOR DEVELOPMENT

Common issues for young women are the following: How do you not give in to the pressures of a young man? How do you not cave in to the pressure to brag about what you are doing, even when you are not doing anything? How do you keep your self-respect? How do you avoid not setting up other girls? Young women can be very com-petitive. A good-looking guy comes around, and young women can be hurtful and abusive to one another as they try to get the guy's attention.

The directors help raise the question and the possibility: Can we do this is in a way that is not hurtful to one another by creating improvisational scenes? Members were directed to create a variety of responses to scenes they created. The performances support developing emotional skills and *the possibility* of creating new choices for themselves and others. At rehearsals the girls set up a scene where Vanessa and Tim are hugging in the park. Carol, Tim's girlfriend, sees and confronts them. In their original improvisation, the girls fight over Tim. The director then suggests that they repeat the scene with a different ending. In the second version, the girls identify Tim as a manipulator; they create an alliance, and both dump the two-timing Tim. This cultural-performatory approach supports the development of a variety of ways of dealing with a situation—*creating possibilities and choices for development.*

Performance affords young women the opportunity to explore what kind of woman they want to grow up to be. It exposes them to more than one choice. It helps demonstrate that the decision is theirs to make and is not based merely on feelings or on who others think they are but on what may be most developmental. It is the conscious, continuous activity of deciding how you want to *perform,* every minute of every hour of every day. The performance activity occurs not just during rehearsals. It is *the opportunity to perform* every moment of every day instead of behaving in societally determined and conditioned social roles. If they can stop and repeat a scene in a play, why not at school or at home or anywhere?

The directors support the continuous activity of creating developmental environments where new performances can occur. At one rehearsal, the cast was making masks for their costumes. In the corner were two young men who did not want to make their own masks but wanted to help Victoria make hers. They were obviously flirting and being sexy with each other. The director asked them to join everyone else, that they could flirt and be sexy while being with the entire cast. "You mean you don't want us to stop?" they asked with surprise. "No," the director said. "We don't want to tell you what to do; rather we'd like you to continue to perform being sexy with all of us. We want you to create a new way of being sexy that's social and inclusive, not private." The director facilitated the cast performing a new way of being sexy that was not private, exclusive, competitive, or naughty.

The adults direct and participate in the performance activity and function as models. During one rehearsal, the cast was performing an exercise, a collective story, where each member contributes to the development of a scene. Christopher made a joke about rape within the story line. Beverly said it was not funny. No one else responded. The director intervened by asking, "Did people hear what Beverly said?" When no one responded, the director asked Beverly to repeat her comment, which she did. Then the group continued. As the collective story continued, Christopher, within the context of his character in the collective story, said he wanted to apologize for what he had previously said.

Christopher's improvisation was both very creative and something most adults are not likely to do. There was no coercive attempt by the director for Christopher or others to respond to Beverly in any particular manner. Through the continuation of the performance, a ZPD was created where Christopher could creatively go beyond himself, not by pretending to be someone else but by creatively stretching himself to create a new Christopher; one who would apologize. It was a decent and supportive act toward Beverly and the other young women. The director thanked him for that performance and supported him in recognizing that what he said had an impact on people.

His creative performance was moving, and his response to the young woman, rather than ignoring her, helped transform the entire cast.

CREATING NEW ENVIRONMENTS, NEW MEANING, AND NEW FORMS OF LIFE

The cultural-performatory approach focuses on how to transform the social environment and provide the conditions for a meaningful discourse. Having meaningful dialogue requires organizing the social environment to promote meaningful dialogue. Conversation, as an activity, as a form of human social life, has the potential to be developmental. It is not the content or the rhetoric of a conversation but its form—that existential moment when human beings touch one another—that has the potential to create development. It is through the social activity of conversation that people can collectively and continuously create a variety of things, including their relationships, their decisions, and their lives. If people stay in their socially structured environmental arrangements, they will simply interpret whatever gets said so that it fits into the already existing arrangement and understanding. The assumption that if people say something different people will hear it differently never happens that way. It's in the totality of the activity of conversation—in the language we create— where we create meaning (Bruner, 1993). There has to be a carefully supported restructuring of the social environment to allow people to break out of their roles and develop.

Pregnant Productions focuses on promoting development by allowing youths the opportunity to build something—a cultural production or a ZPD. In collectively organizing the event (doing all the things to make it happen) and in working to accomplish the event (assuming collective responsibility), they perform ahead of themselves (from not having the slightest idea of how to produce an event to participating and experiencing its completion). Collectively, they participate in a process of planning, communicating, making decisions, and taking responsibility for what they build and how they build it. In performing these activities, they are able to break out of their socially overdetermined behavior. They learn that there are choices and how to make choices, including when and whether to have sex or get pregnant. They learn how to create social environments where they are supported to do what they don't know how to do.

Our performers learn that although individually they may get stuck in a certain way of behaving, they can use their friends, their family, and their classmates in a joint activity and collectively come up with many choices and possibilities. In this alienated and decaying society, they learn the activity of creating new social environments and creating new forms of life—their own lives, including their future.

REFERENCES

Bruner, J. (1993). "Explaining and Interpreting: Two Ways of Using Mind." In G. Harman, ed. *Conceptions of the Human Mind: Essays in Honor of George Miller.* Hillsdale, NJ: Lawrence Erlbaum.

Gergen, K. J., and J. Kaye (1993). "Beyond Narrative in the Negotiations of Therapeutic Meaning." In S. McNamee and K. J. Gergen, eds., *Therapy as Social Construction.* London: Sage.

Hoffman, L. (1993). "A Reflexive Stance for Family Therapy." In S. McNamee and K. Gergen, eds., *Therapy as Social Construction.* London: Sage.

Newman, F. (1994). *Let's Develop! A Guide to Continuous Personal Growth.* New York: Castillo International.

Newman, F. (1996). *Performance of a Lifetime: A Practical-Philosophical Guide to the Joyous Life.* New York: Castillo International.

Newman, F., and L. Holzman (1993). *Lev Vygotsky: Revolutionary Scientist.* London: Routledge.

Vygotsky, L. S. (1978). *Mind in Society.* Cambridge: Harvard University Press.

Vygotsky, L. S. (1987). *The Collected Works of L. S. Vygotsky. Vol. 1.* New York: Plenum.

Vygotsky, L. S. (1993). *The Collected Works of L. S. Vygotsky. Vol. 2.* New York: Plenum.

KEY TERMS FOR PART THREE

After studying Chapters 9, 10, 11, and 12, you should have a command of the following key terms, major concepts, and principal topical references:

domestic violence	out-of-home services	child protective services
battered woman	adoption services	youth definition
rape laws	children with incarcerated	contemporary society
shelter	parents	youth work
extent of domestic violence	cultural competence	youth movement and
sources of domestic violence	substance abuse	organizations
characteristics of abuse	child welfare law	youth leader/worker
cycle of battering	public policy	remedial paradigm
changing social attitudes	child abuse	prosocial paradigm
intervention strategies	extent of child abuse	integrative paradigm
services for domestic	maltreatment	youth work orientations
violence clients	physical abuse	Vygotsky-inspired approach
child welfare delivery system	physical neglect	cultural-performance
core child services	emotional maltreatment	approach
supportive services	sexual abuse	activity theory
protective services	mandated reporting	

PIVOTAL ISSUES FOR DISCUSSION OF PART THREE

1. Make a series of lists of special consumer (client) populations in human services. Organize the lists by major demographic variables (i.e., age, gender, ethnicity, race, level of intellectual functioning, mental status, employment, income, number in family, physical condition, amount of education, criminal background). How and where are these consumers served? By whom? What are their special issues in receiving and responding to help?

2. What are the major causes of child sexual abuse? What can be done to reduce and/or eliminate this social issue?

3. Inquire within your community as to what services/programs are available to teenagers who are pregnant. What needs do these teenagers have? How are these needs being met locally?

4. What are your state's laws governing the "mandated reporters" for child abuse? Secure a copy of these laws through your state representative or senator. Make copies for your class and prepare a brief presentation on key points.

5. Call your local office for child welfare and get a set of brochures they have on programs offered for children.

6. Visit the closest juvenile court for a day and observe the proceedings that are open to the public. Write a journal of what you observed.

7. What is the relationship between drug and alcohol abuse and domestic violence? How does spousal abuse, in some cases, continue to be perpetuated in second or third primary relationships involving the same woman? What can be done to help such a person?

SUGGESTED READINGS FOR PART THREE _____

1. Berger, K. S. (1997). *The Developing Person.* New York: Worth.

2. Holzman, L. (1995). "Creating Developmental Learning Environments: A Vygostkian Practice." *School Psychology International, 16,* 199–212.

3. McNamee, S. (1993). "Reconstructing Identity: The Communal Construction of Crisis." In S. McNamee and K. J. Gergen, eds., *Therapy as Social Construction.* London: Sage.

4. McNamee, S., and K. J. Gergen, eds. (1993). *Therapy as Social Construction.* London: Sage.

5. Ryan, W. (1976). *Blaming the Victim.* New York: Vintage.

PART FOUR

HUMAN SERVICE CLIENTS:
SPECIAL POPULATIONS

In Part Three you read about human service work with children and adolescents. Part Four deals with other client populations: people living with HIV and AIDS, the homeless, alcohol and drug abusers, older adults, and people controlled by the criminal justice system. You will find that human service worker skills transfer and are useful in a wide range of situations. You will also see the importance of understanding what is unique to specific client populations. Knowledge of client particularities, including individual differences, is critical for effective helping.

Currently a large proportion of human service clients emerge from the HIV/AIDS epidemic. In Chapter 13, Wm. Lynn McKinney presents a comprehensive and practical description of the problem of the HIV/AIDS infection and its far-reaching implications. The information in this chapter will solidify your understanding of how this disease develops, how it is transmitted and spreads, the major effects of the infection, and how to address the needs of these clients within the human service field. You will also appreciate the special nature of this tragic social problem and the unique challenges it presents to the human service professional.

In Chapter 14, Lorence Long discusses the wide array of reasons why individuals become homeless, the range of different types of homeless people, the special problems associated with being homeless, and the nature and scope of services typically available to address these problems. The size of this client population has increased tremendously in recent years, challenging the human service delivery system in all areas of the United States. The material in this chapter will acquaint you with the basic and essential knowledge related to homelessness, and you will become more aware of the extensiveness of the problem.

Marcel Duclos and Marianne Gfroerer in Chapter 15 detail the special needs and demands of clients who abuse alcohol and other substances. This chapter will acquaint you with the scope of the problem of alcohol and substance abuse and familiarize you with some basic issues in working with these human service clients. Education, prevention, and intervention programs are described, and the need for specialized training and credentialing is discussed and defended.

In Chapter 16, Kathleen Niccum explores the human service needs of the increasing population of older adults. You will learn to identify the physical, psychological, and social aspects of aging as well as understand the special needs and issues of older adults. Additionally, you will become familiar with the types of human services provided to older people and the various career opportunities available in this rapidly expanding area of human services.

To conclude Part Four, David Whelan in Chapter 17 discusses the role of human services in the criminal justice system. The magnitude of the human service needs and the costs involved in serving this population are staggering when we consider the huge number of people in prison, those on probation, and those awaiting trial or sentencing. Think about this population when you read about changing human service system(s) in Part Five.

LEARNING OBJECTIVES FOR PART FOUR: HUMAN SERVICE CLIENTS: SPECIAL POPULATIONS

After reading and studying Chapters 13, 14, 15, 16, and 17,

— You will understand the current scope of the HIV and AIDS epidemic and the major emerging support considerations in human services.

— You will appreciate and comprehend the origins of homelessness, populations affected, and what is being done in human services to help these individuals and families.

— You will be aware of the needs of the substance abuse and dependency client and the types of support provided by human service professionals.

— You will know about the range and variety of human service programs designed to assist older adults with challenges related to the aging process.

— You will learn about the various clients and components of the criminal justice system.

CHAPTER 13

WORKING WITH PEOPLE WHO LIVE WITH HIV AND AIDS:
THE PROBLEM AND HUMAN SERVICES

WM. LYNN MCKINNEY

As a human service worker, you are almost certain to have clients who are people living with human immunodeficiency virus (HIV) and persons living with AIDS (PWAs). This is true because AIDS affects people of all ages, sexual orientations, and ethnic and minority groups and because the needs of PWAs and people living with HIV are numerous and span virtually all human service programs. Because AIDS is an illness, there are medical needs. Since most PWAs eventually must stop working, they have income needs. The number of children who have HIV is growing, and these young people may have educational needs. For several reasons, there are likely to be psychological and social needs.

First of all, AIDS occurs primarily in people younger than fifty, which means that PWAs must deal with a fatal illness at an early age. Second, AIDS is found mainly in marginalized people such as homosexual men, injection drug users, and racial and ethnic minorities. Still another reason that PWAs may have psychological needs is that many of them will have many friends who are seriously ill or who have died. The effects of such losses are potentially enormous. Thus, the entire human service system is involved in working with people living with AIDS and HIV. So, as you enter the field, it is important that you know about HIV and AIDS and society's reactions to the disease.

Working with people with AIDS and HIV presents particular challenges. Many people with

this illness will not have close ties with their families who may have turned their backs on what is perceived to be a social embarrassment. Most will be poor, some because they were poor when they became sick and others because the disease is impoverishing. Death from AIDS-related causes can be horrible; the diseases and infections that affect a PWA can leave people thin and weak and seemingly defenseless for long periods of time. Unlike those with other illnesses, PWAs may be very sick and close to death for a while and then go through long periods of good health when they can lead happy, productive lives. As more cases of AIDS are diagnosed among drug users, more clients may be difficult to work with. Finally, with more women contracting the virus and dying, there are orphaned children who are not infected as well as children who were born with the virus. Many of these children are not or cannot be cared for by their mothers or other relatives.

However, working in the HIV field can be rewarding. As you must know, as you are planning to enter the human service field, all work with people is rewarding. If your interest is in research, you can become involved with learning more about the virus, thus increasing the probability of a cure, a vaccine, or better care for people who are HIV positive. If you work with individual clients, you will no doubt develop intense, deep relationships with many of them; some of these will be enormously enriching, revealing to you some of the best aspects of humanity. Work with HIV will probably stretch you professionally, broadening your knowledge and experience so that, should you decide to change jobs, you will present an attractive array of qualifications to prospective employers. Finally, you can gain satisfaction knowing that you are working with people, many of whom live on society's margins, and doing what you can in response to a pandemic—a worldwide outbreak of a disease affecting an extraordinarily large percentage of the population.

You probably knew some things about HIV by the time you entered college. But because it is a politically charged issue, the quantity and quality of HIV education varies greatly. Although we may review in this chapter some material that you already know, there will also be material that is new to you. The objectives of this chapter are (1) to solidify your basic medical understanding of HIV and AIDS, (2) to help you understand some of the social ramifications of HIV, and (3) to acquaint you with current issues. This chapter is only an introduction to the topic. Reading about HIV and AIDS in books, newspapers, and professional journals should be a part of your professional growth. We urge you to become involved in AIDS service organizations (ASOs) as well. Practical experience is an excellent means to expand your knowledge.

HIV AND AIDS AS MEDICAL ISSUES

In 1985 the specific virus that is believed to cause AIDS was identified. It is human immunodeficiency virus (HIV). Today there are two strains of HIV active in the United States. The most prevalent strain is HIV-1, which has been with us since the early 1980s. The virus is constantly mutating as new medications are developed. We still know much less about HIV and AIDS than we wish we did. Fortunately, research is revealing new information to us regularly.

Acquired immune deficiency syndrome (AIDS) was first noted in the United States very early in 1981, but it was not until three or four

years later that it was identified as a syndrome and given a name. Doctors in San Francisco and New York began to notice that they were treating a new group of patients, primarily gay and bisexual men in their twenties and thirties, for a series of diseases that were highly unusual among healthy young people. Initially what doctors were seeing was called gay-related immune deficiency (GRID) because it was noted exclusively in gay men. Eventually the medical profession developed the description Acquired Immune Deficiency Syndrome (AIDS). The words that make up the acronym AIDS provide specific meaning. (For an incisive account of the early years of the disease in the United States and for insight into the politics of this illness, read *And the Band Played On* by Randy Shilts.)

The A in AIDS, which stands for "Acquired," indicates how a person gets the disease. AIDS is a communicable disease; a person must get it from someone else. In this sense, it is like hepatitis, a cold, or measles. AIDS is not inherited like some diseases such as sickle cell anemia and Tay-Sachs disease. Unlike some other diseases, (e.g., cancer), it does not just begin inside an individual, in many cases for unknown reasons. People have to get AIDS from someone else, and it is not easy to get (we emphasize this fact and explain what it means later in this chapter).

The I and the D stand for "immune deficiency," which refers to the characteristics of this disease that make it unlike any other disease. Instead of making you sick directly, HIV attacks the helper T cells in the human body. These helper T cells are important for us to be able to fight off infections. When they become weakened, our bodies become vulnerable to other diseases, virtually all of which we ordinarily are resistant to. This literally causes a deficiency of the body's immune system, leaving the infected individual susceptible to a wide variety of infections that ordinarily would not affect noninfected individuals.

Finally, the S stands for "syndrome." A syndrome is a collection of symptoms and effects of other diseases. AIDS is considered to be a syndrome because a person with AIDS does not die of AIDS but rather of other diseases, most of which were rarely seen in the United States until the advent of AIDS. These diseases, commonly called "opportunistic infections," can occur because T cells are destroyed and can no longer ward off infections.

People with HIV may continue to be asymptomatic for many years, but eventually symptoms will appear and a diagnosis of AIDS can be made. For two reasons it is important to have a clear diagnosis. First, there is a psychological impact on the infected individual of having AIDS versus having HIV. Different sorts of supportive services may be necessary as an individual progresses from knowing that he or she is infected with HIV to knowing that he or she has AIDS.

Second, once someone is determined to have AIDS, he or she may become eligible for a variety of state and federal programs. Initially a person was diagnosed with AIDS if he or she had any one of two or three diseases or opportunistic infections; pneumocystis carinii pneumonia (PCP) and Kaposi's sarcoma, a rare form of skin cancer, were the most common. In early 1993, the Centers for Disease Control (CDC) in Atlanta changed the way in which it defined whether a person had AIDS. Now a person is classified as having AIDS if his or her helper T lymphocyte count falls below 200 (ordinarily the helper T count ranges from 800 to 1,200) and if he or she also has at least one of the specific diseases associated with AIDS.

The definition was changed because it had been much more useful in diagnosing AIDS in men than it was in women. Since women experience the disease differently and since more and more women now have AIDS, it was important to change the definition.

The two opportunistic infections that are the greatest killers of men are PCP and toxoplasmosis. Toxoplasmosis is a chronic, severe brain infection. Toxo is a common parasite that is found in most everyone. As is true of all other opportunistic infections, it is fought off by healthy immune systems. However, in individuals whose immune systems are compromised, toxo can become activated, resulting in blindness, paralysis, and dementia. Fortunately there are now prophylactic treatments for both of these diseases.

Women with HIV are more likely to develop other diseases, particularly yeast infections, invasive cervical cancer, recurrent bacterial pneumonias, and bloodstream infections. Recently an increase in the number of cases of pulmonary tuberculosis has been noted.

Unless it is your intention to enter the medical field, this is probably enough for you to know about the medical aspects of AIDS and HIV. As you become involved with PWAs, you may need to increase your medical knowledge, but, as we repeat often in this chapter, knowledge about AIDS is increasing rapidly, and you should learn more as part of your continuing professional development and as the need confronts you.

The Transmission of HIV

HIV is transmitted through bodily fluids, specifically blood, semen, and vaginal fluid. Although the virus is present in other bodily fluids such as tears and sweat, it is found in such slight concentrations that these fluids are not considered dangerous. HIV is difficult to transmit. There are very few ways in which HIV can be transmitted from one person to another. Unprotected sex and sharing needles are the two most common ways. A third way is across the placenta from an infected woman to her unborn child. Until 1985, HIV was occasionally transmitted by blood transfusions, but since that time the U.S. blood supply has been considered safe because of donor screening and because all blood to be used for transfusions is tested before it is given to someone.

HIV is not easy to catch because, for a person to be exposed to the virus, it must enter a person's bloodstream. This can occur when individuals share an unsterilized needle to inject steroids or other drugs. It can also occur during unprotected sex, either vaginal, anal, or oral. But again, for infection to occur, the skin must be broken. This often occurs during anal intercourse, can occur during vaginal intercourse, and can occur during oral sex if the person performing oral sex has skin breaks such as canker sores or unhealthy gums. Tears in the skin need only be microscopic in size for transmission to occur.

Sexual transmission of HIV from men to women is much more common than from women to men. This is true because the skin must be broken for the virus to cross from one individual to another and because the virus is present in dangerous concentrations in semen. It is more likely that the lining of the vagina or anus will experience a tear during sex than it is that the penis will suffer some sort of skin break. Infection from a man to a woman is more likely because sex commonly results in the ejaculation of semen. The most risky form of sex between men is unprotected (i.e., without a condom) anal intercourse.

Infection is less likely during oral sex but can occur if semen is ejaculated. It is possible for the person performing oral sex to infect his or her partner only if infected blood somehow enters the sexual partner's penis such as if he or she has strep throat or other infectious lesions in the throat. Sex between two women and oral sex by a man on a woman rarely result in transmission, but it is possible. Use of dental dams during such oral sex is urged.

One quarter of babies born to infected mothers are born with the virus, but we now know that pregnant HIV-positive women who take AZT during the last three months of pregnancy and receive an infusion of AZT during labor and delivery can reduce to 8 percent the probability that their babies will be born infected. Why the virus crosses the placenta in some cases and not in others is not known at this time. As part of your continuing professional growth, you should regularly read newspaper and journal articles about AIDS and HIV to stay informed. Research is making great strides, and you, as a human service student

and professional, are responsible for keeping your knowledge current.

Epidemiology

The epidemiology of a disease is the way in which it spreads. AIDS was first recognized among gay men in New York and San Francisco when doctors began treating patients who were suffering from pneumocystis carinii pneumonia (PCP) and from Kaposi's sarcoma, a skin and/or blood vessel cancer. Ordinarily most people are immune to both of these diseases unless they are pregnant or elderly, but because HIV destroys the immune system, infected people can develop these and other opportunistic infections. It is believed that HIV was introduced to the North American continent by an infected gay man who had sex with other men who then had sex with others. Because of this, for the first decade of its existence, AIDS most heavily affected the gay male population in the United States. This is not true of the epidemiology of the disease in other countries, where it is almost exclusively a heterosexual disease.

Because large numbers of gay men live in the largest American cities, nearly all early recognized AIDS cases were found in New York, San Francisco, Chicago, and Los Angeles. However, the epidemiology of the disease has changed in recent years. AIDS is still primarily an urban disease, but cases are now reported in virtually all cities and towns across the country and among all demographics.

In response to scientific discoveries about how HIV was spread, many gay males altered their sexual behaviors, thus somewhat slowing the transmission of HIV in the homosexual population. The Centers for Disease Control (CDC) reported in late 1997 that AIDS had dropped from first to second as the leading killer of adults between the ages of twenty-five and forty-four. There was a 26 percent drop in the rate of AIDS deaths from 1995 to 1996, the first decline since the epidemic began in 1981. However, there has been slow spread of the disease into the general heterosexual population, and minority populations are now particularly vulnerable. Currently, 20 percent of reported AIDS cases occur in women, and sex with infected men has replaced drug use as the primary means for women to contract the virus.

In part because of the spread of the illness and in part because people with HIV are living longer, there are now many more people who have the virus. It is estimated that nearly 250,000 people with AIDS were living in 1996. Although progress may seem maddeningly slow, researchers are regularly discovering new prophylactic and infection treatments. Many of these delay the onset of opportunistic infections and thus improve the quality of life of PWAs and people living with HIV. Other treatments appear to dramatically prolong the lives of PWAs.

Predictions for the Future

The CDC is the reporting body that tracks AIDS and other diseases. Its predictions about the spread of AIDS have been reasonably accurate for the past several years. The CDC has reported that AIDS replaced murder as the tenth most common cause of death in the United States in 1990 and the ninth most common cause in 1991 and would probably continue to climb the statistical ladder. Among young people in 1990, AIDS was the third most common cause of death; only cancer and accidents killed more young Americans. In 1993, AIDS became the most common cause of death among men aged twenty-five to forty-five and, as reported above, has now dropped to second.

The epidemiology of AIDS varies in different countries. In some African countries, AIDS is much more prevalent than in the United States and is exclusively a heterosexual disease. In Zimbabwe, for example, one of every seven persons is believed to be infected, or 1.5 million out of a population of only 10.5 million people. Roughly 80 percent of new infections are occurring in developing countries. It was expected that by the year 2000, 2 percent or more of the world's population would be infected with HIV. A vaccine is yet to be developed.

These grim statistics underscore the importance of clear, early AIDS education for all people. But this education may not be enough. Many young Americans do not believe that they are vulnerable to the virus because they are not members of the groups most heavily infected; and because of the length of time it takes for symptoms to appear (perhaps ten or more years), most believe that they don't know anyone with HIV. This sense of "invincibility" results in willingness to engage in high-risk sexual practices. There are many indicators suggesting that young gay men are resuming unsafe sex practices. In late 1997 the CDC reported that cases of gonorrhea in gay men in many U.S. clinics had doubled. This is in contrast to the overall decline in gonorrhea cases in the United States. As a human service worker, you must take responsibility for helping everyone with whom you work understand this disease and how it is spread.

HIV AND AIDS AS SOCIAL ISSUES

Throughout this chapter we use the terms HIV and AIDS in a variety of ways. It is important to remember that HIV is the virus and AIDS is the name for the resulting illness.

As is true of many new diseases, AIDS raised an array of sociopolitical issues. These issues resulted from the unusual epidemiology that was discussed above and from the fact that HIV was transmitted by practices that Americans would prefer not to talk about. We discuss three major social issues in this chapter: (1) who has AIDS, (2) AIDS education, and (3) infection as the result of personal behavior.

Who Is Most at Risk for HIV?

Quite likely no disease that has affected and will affect virtually all Americans has been so poorly understood as HIV. It is clearly the most highly politicized disease of our times, primarily because it was initially found only in gay and bisexual men and was thought of as a "gay disease." To have HIV/AIDS meant shame and embarrassment for many sufferers and their families, and people tried to hide it. Initially people tried to cover up the fact that both the actor Rock Hudson and pianist Liberace had contracted AIDS. More recently, after Rudolph Nureyev died, his relatives brought suit against his doctor in France for revealing that AIDS-related diseases had killed the legendary dancer. Obituaries in large and small cities and towns across the country routinely veil the real cause of death with such phrases as "after a lengthy illness." Surviving family members continue to deny that the deceased had AIDS and, in many cases, that he or she was gay, bisexual, or a needle drug user.

Most heterosexual Americans, unless they are touched through the illness of family members or friends or become particularly interested in the disease, assume that HIV is something that they would never have to worry about. We now know that everyone must be concerned about AIDS. It is almost certain that every one of us knows someone who has HIV or AIDS or who has died of the disease. If you do not know someone who has the virus, it may be because they have chosen not to reveal their status to you. From college classrooms to corporate boardrooms, HIV and AIDS are affecting all racial, religious, and socioeconomic groups.

HIV quickly moved beyond the gay male population, primarily into the population of injection drug users and then into racial and ethnic minorities. In 1996, 60 percent of all AIDS cases in the United States occurred among African Americans and Latinos. African Americans are only 12 percent of our population yet account for 41 percent of AIDS cases, and Latinos, who comprise 9 percent of the population, account for 19 percent of people living with AIDS. Although overall the incidence of AIDS is declining, there was a 19 percent increase in diagnoses among heterosexual black men and a 12 percent increase among heterosexual black women in 1996.

Because HIV is transmitted almost exclusively by unprotected sex and sharing needles, the American population has been squeamish about discussing it. Because children are considered to be asexual and because society legislates as if it disapproved of sex between unmarried people and between members of the same sex, we have been unable to develop a consistent policy concerning AIDS education.

HIV Prevention/Education Issues

The spread of HIV could be greatly reduced if everyone stopped having sex and using drugs. Equally true is the fact that tuberculosis would soon be a disease of the past if we all stopped breathing. All of these have about the same probability. The spread would also be slowed if everyone who is not in a long-term, monogamous relationship in which both partners know they are HIV negative would always use a condom when having sex and if everyone who used injection drugs would either never share their needles or would "clean their works," that is, use bleach to clean needles before passing them on to the next person. Since we know this, it would seem to be a simple matter to teach people to use condoms and to clean their works. However, education about these two forms of HIV prevention has encountered great resistance in our society.

Much of our society shuns gay people and drug users and is squeamish about discussing sex. In numerous communities, elementary and secondary schools are not allowed to discuss sex at all. Although the climate has improved in the last decade, the 1993 reigning Miss America was prohibited from using the words "condom" and "AIDS" in some high schools while on a speaking tour in Florida. In some schools in which sex education is allowed, gay sex may not be discussed. Many people make the erroneous assumption that young people are actually encouraged to try out behaviors they might learn about in sex education classes. Use of condoms conflicts with some religious teachings. And many people believe it is impossible that they, or anyone they know, could ever become infected or even know someone with HIV or AIDS. So, some

Americans are growing up not knowing they may be vulnerable to a fatal illness, and they are not being taught how to avoid contracting it.

Reluctance to be clear about HIV has resulted in surveys revealing that 25 percent of respondents believed that you could get HIV from a mosquito, 33 percent thought that you could contract HIV by donating blood, and 25 percent believed that an HIV vaccine exists. All of these are absolutely false.

There is continuing resistance in this country to advertising about condoms on radio and television, on billboards, and in the print media. Virtually everyone in our society over the age of twelve probably knows about condoms, but without advertising, the use of condoms has not increased as much as needed. Instead of promoting condom use, we have continued to pretend that young people are not having sex, and we have continued to tell them not to. A 1993 survey of teenagers revealed that 56 percent of teens aged sixteen and seventeen had had intercourse at least once. It may be best for young people not to have sex, but until we can ensure that they will abstain, it is important for us to convince them to protect themselves from a disease that currently is almost certainly fatal.

The resistance to helping people clean their needles with bleach had been even stronger. But now, needle exchange programs are operating throughout the country. In such programs, injection drug users are encouraged to turn in their used needles for clean needles each time they use them.

There are three very important HIV education messages that every American, particularly young people, ought to know. First, do not have sex outside marriage or a long-term monogamous relationship, or, if you do, learn the HIV status of your partner and always use a condom during sex. To be blunt, the message needs to be, "If it is up, it is covered." And, always use a dental dam if performing oral sex on a woman. Second, do not use drugs, or, if you do, either do not share needles or clean your needles carefully with a bleach solution after each injection. Finally, women

who are HIV positive should carefully consider the risks to themselves and their unborn children should pregnancy occur.

As the gay community learned early in the epidemic, sex without penetration is not only possible but quite erotic and, for many gay males, has become the method of choice. It certainly is preferable to contracting an almost certainly fatal illness.

NEEDS OF PERSONS LIVING WITH HIV AND AIDS

There are three major continuing needs of PWAs: (1) fighting discrimination and violence, (2) having access to affordable health care, and (3) receiving assistance with everyday life. As you can see, these needs span the whole human service field, involving politics, economics, psychology, and human development. If you decide to work in the AIDS field, your clients will have many problems that most of us may never have to confront. With recent dramatic medical advances, PWAs are living longer and there is a new set of problems, including reentering the job market, finding sources to pay for very expensive medications, and psychologically trying to adjust to the possibility of living for a much longer time than previously thought.

The first step that a PWA or you, if you are an advocate or case manager, should take is to contact your local AIDS service organization. Virtually every city now has one, and many smaller areas do, too. These organizations are usually nonprofit, but there is an increasing number of for-profit agencies that will provide an array of services. These may be affordable if your client has insurance coverage. In the southeastern New England area there are several nonprofit agencies. One is AIDS Project RI in Providence, Rhode Island. It was formally incorporated in 1985 by a small group of volunteers in response to the growing numbers of AIDS cases in the area. With an annual budget of roughly $900,000, the Project offers education, outreach to the gay and minority communities, case management, and a national newsletter in Spanish entitled *Quipu.* Another nonprofit organization is AIDS Care of RI, whose purpose is to provide housing assistance and case management for PWAs.

AIDS service organizations (ASOs) vary. Some focus more on education and less on direct services. They may provide a strong referral service. Others are direct service organizations that assist clients with a broad range of needs. And now more non-AIDS organizations are providing AIDS-related services such as support groups, counseling, and testing. An ASO may provide a caseworker to your client, in which case you may no longer need to be involved with HIV issues, but you may need to follow your client for other reasons not related to HIV. You should stay involved until you are certain that your client is being well served.

Medical and Dental Needs

There is no vaccine for HIV, and none is on the horizon. Nor is there a cure for HIV. The medical needs of persons with HIV and AIDS focus on prevention and treatment of the specific opportunistic infections to which an individual becomes vulnerable. Dental needs are greater than those of people who do not have the virus. HIV positive people should have their teeth cleaned four times yearly, as more symptoms appear in the oral cavity than elsewhere; PWAs need high-quality dental care. The problem that many confront is the small number of dentists who are willing to treat them.

Many people, once they learn they are HIV positive, begin to take one of a small number of medications that are believed both to prolong and to improve the quality of life of those living with HIV. The choice of which drug to take depends on a variety of factors, including the preferences of one's doctor, the drug currently thought to be most effective, and the insurance plan of the patient. Most common in 1997 was a so-called "cocktail" of three medications, often

AZT, a protease inhibitor, and one other. This combination of drugs shows great promise in dramatically prolonging the lives of PWAs.

From the perspective of the medical profession, PWAs present risks to medical personnel. Many medical and dental procedures result in blood loss, and that blood must be viewed as lethal. Astute and ethical physicians and dentists insist that all their staff take universal precautions, such as wearing rubber gloves when working with all their patients, not just PWAs. They and their patients may not know who is and who is not carrying the virus. Universal precautions reduce enormously the risk of transmission, although there have been a small number of accidents that resulted in infected blood entering the bloodstream of a medical worker. People with the virus should also insist that medical personnel use universal precautions, since they are at much greater risk for other diseases than are noninfected people. In fact, all of us should insist that universal precautions be taken by all medical and dental personnel who treat us and our clients. These measures serve to protect all of us.

As a human service worker, you may have to advocate for or be a case manager for a PWA. This responsibility will require your negotiating with the medical establishment. For some PWAs this presents no problems, but for others it is quite difficult. There are still only a few doctors, mostly in cities, who have chosen to specialize in treating PWAs and therefore know enough about the disease to be "patient friendly." In your role as advocate, you may need to be very tough in insisting that your clients get the treatment they need. There may be times when your client has no one else to help him or her and may be too ill to manage his or her health care effectively.

Income Assistance

Because of prophylaxis and newly developed treatments, PWAs may live for many years after learning of their HIV status. People with HIV and

AIDS may eventually have to quit work because their energy levels simply do not permit them to continue. Unemployment will likely result in a dramatic reduction in income. They may need assistance in getting access to the government programs to which they are entitled. Many PWAs have never had to rely on income assistance programs, and they may be completely ignorant of the process of applying for benefits.

By federal law, having AIDS means that a person is disabled. This entitles PWAs to Supplemental Security Disability Income (SSDI). The process of applying is not very complicated, but it can be nearly impossible for someone who is very ill. If the disease requires hospitalization or relocation, your client may need your dedicated and skilled assistance. Beyond that, it takes five months to begin to collect SSDI benefits. The federal government wants to make sure that they are supporting people only if they are truly sick, so they have imposed a waiting period. Once begun, the benefits are paid retroactively, but the delay can be financially devastating. Many must apply for General Public Assistance to support themselves while waiting for their SSDI benefits to begin.

We noted above that the change in the definition of who has AIDS has had an impact on the lives of PWAs. Because the disease is now defined by a combination of helper T cell count and one disease commonly associated with AIDS, many more people qualify for SSDI. Previously it was necessary to have either Kaposi's or PCP. Since many women PWAs never developed either of these diseases, they were prevented from qualifying for disability income. This change in federal law has helped ease some of the money problems of many PWAs, particularly women. For all people with AIDS, the changing medical picture also affects who becomes eligible for federal benefits.

Now, with the development of protease inhibitors and the more common practice of prescribing a combination of drugs, PWAs who routinely assumed that they would live no more than six more months are learning that they may live for fifteen or twenty years. These people must begin to consider retirement plans again, how to secure employment that lets them monitor their energy levels, and how to secure health insurance that will pay monthly medical costs that may be as high as $3,000.

Housing

Housing may be an issue for your clients living with HIV and AIDS. The Americans with Disabilities Act (ADA) of 1992 protects PWAs in the areas of housing, employment, and public accommodation. Still, not everyone is aware of the law or intends to obey it. This may mean that individuals who suddenly become sick, lose their jobs, and may have to "come out" to family and friends now also have no place to live. Subsidized housing is a possibility, but the waiting lists in virtually all cities are so long that this option is not always feasible. AIDS service organizations, such as AIDS Care of RI, help people with housing needs, so you should make yourself aware of what is available in your area.

Many PWAs own their own homes and are able to stay in them. Others move in with friends or family. Some, however, may have no place to go. Fortunately, a growing number of residential facilities are dedicated to PWAs who otherwise might be homeless. AIDS Care of RI owns two residences with individual rooms for PWAs who help keep the houses clean and cook communally. In addition, the organization rents apartments throughout the area and provides scattered-site housing and other support services for many more people.

A part of AIDS Care of RI is what was formerly called the Family AIDS Center for Treatment and Support (FACTS), a home for up to seven children born to HIV-positive mothers who may or may not have the virus and whose families cannot or will not care for them. These examples from Providence were chosen to illustrate the breadth of services available even in a small city (population slightly under 200,000).

Employment

People with HIV who are working may need flexible hours or a reduction to part-time work. As noted above, the disease is unpredictable. After a serious bout of one of the infections (e.g., PCP), a PWA may enter a long phase in which he or she feels well, has good energy, and lives a normal life. Some people then return to full-time employment at their previous jobs, and some volunteer their time with ASOs. Again, federal law protects these workers. They may not be discriminated against because they have AIDS. However, this law does not prevent some employers from firing their employees if they suspect they are ill. You may have to assist your clients in returning to or maintaining their jobs. If you plan to work in the field of HIV, you should begin to learn the process for filing discrimination complaints.

Social Services

Persons living with AIDS may need a range of social services such as transportation, counseling, assistance with meals, legal aid, and companionship. These services may be available through a variety of sources, but you may need to help your clients access them. Again, the best first step is to contact your local AIDS organization and ask for assistance. They may provide a caseworker, a buddy program, counseling, support groups, and so on. Or you may need to find those services from a variety of sources. The nature and extent of needed services will depend on how capable and/or how ill your client is.

An excellent example of a social service program is the Food and Friends program, which operates in Washington, DC. Those PWAs who are too ill to shop and cook for themselves, who cannot leave their apartments or houses, and who have no one to care for them can call Food and Friends, which will deliver nutritious, abundant meals directly to the PWA. Many PWAs, once they are functioning well once again, become volunteers in the program, helping to prepare and deliver meals. In this way, the cost of the program is kept to a minimum and people invest in caring for one another.

WORKING WITH PWAS

Working with persons with HIV and AIDS will be both challenging and rewarding. Some are very angry that they are ill and vent their anger on anyone who comes close. Others may focus on being as healthy as possible, including maintaining strong mental health. Others, following the stages of dying outlined years ago by Elisabeth Kubler-Ross, will react differently at different times.

Working with PWAs today is much different from what it was like a few years ago because the stigma of the disease is lower, there are many more organizations that provide help, we know more about the illness, people are living longer, and there are vastly more competent, knowledgeable people who can provide assistance.

AIDS Agencies

Starting with the Gay Men's Health Crisis in New York and the Shanti Project in San Francisco in the early 1980s, nonprofit ASOs were created as the need arose. They are funded in part by local, state, and federal government dollars, but most receive the majority of their income from private donations, fund-raisers, and grants. Most have major fund-raising events annually. A common one is a pledge walk of some sort, such as the Walk for Life in Providence. Usually held on the first Sunday of June, The Walk is the major annual fund-raiser for the AIDS Project of RI. Individuals who plan to walk ask their friends and relatives to sponsor them, usually by donating a specific amount for each of the ten kilometers of the walk. The proceeds, regularly around $200,000, are sometimes shared with other, smaller ASOs in the area. Such walks are festive occasions with balloons, politicians, food, entertainment, and good cheer. In recent years bikes rides have become popular, with rides now taking place between Boston and New York, between San Francisco and Los Angeles, and between other cities. Local media provide good coverage of these events.

Self-Help Groups

Self-help groups use peer-helper models to provide emotional support. These groups lower the cost of caring for people with HIV and AIDS because they are low- or no-cost organizations. Groups have been formed for people living with HIV and AIDS, partners of PWAs, and the "worried well"—groups of individuals who attempt to deal with the emotions of being HIV negative while so many of their friends are sick or dead. Larger cities have separate groups for men and women and for people who speak various languages.

Volunteers as Important Resources

All ASOs rely heavily on volunteers. The best examples are probably the buddy programs. Most were started in the early 1980s with the (accurate) belief that the human service needs resulting from the AIDS crisis would far exceed the capability of the system to respond. They are also evidence that, for a long time, the system refused to respond and did not provide necessary services. And they are continuing testimony to the American spirit of caring and volunteerism.

The Buddy Program at AIDS Project RI is a good example. Started in 1985 by a small group of volunteers, it now provides training and support for more than 150 buddies. Buddies undergo a forty-hour training program that teaches them about AIDS and how to work effectively with HIV-positive people. They then may be assigned a buddy, that is, a person living with AIDS who has requested a buddy. Each pair negotiates its own terms, but commonly the relationship provides emotional support and companionship plus whatever tangible assistance is needed. The buddy may, for example, provide transportation, pick up prescriptions from a pharmacy, arrange for hospitalization or visits to the doctor, see that the PWA is eating properly, or negotiate with landlords. Buddy programs have provided emotional support and help for thousands of people who, without them, would have died sooner and been much more isolated. Being a buddy can be emotionally wrenching, so buddy support groups are common. Groups of buddies meet biweekly or monthly to provide one another with necessary emotional support and periodically consult ASO staff for support and direction.

Special Needs and Skills of Workers

Human service workers who work with people living with HIV and AIDS must have the customary set of skills, knowledge, and attitudes that all human service workers should have. They should go beyond these, however. First, always keep in mind that these people are living, not dying. This fact is very important for you to remember. However, courses about death and dying and experience with people who are terminally ill are useful. Second, a solid understanding of the entire human service system and how to make it respond is essential, since PWAs nearly always need a broad array of services. If not dealing directly with all involved government and nonprofit agencies and organizations, you will at least be making referrals, so you must know the entire system. Third, advocacy skills are critical. You may have to act on behalf of your client, who, for whatever reasons, may be unable to do so for him- or herself. Fourth, and very important, you must be aware of cultural differences.

Your clients may belong to cultural groups other than your own. Issues in HIV education vary among different populations, as do reactions to HIV and AIDS. Part of the reason that the death rates from AIDS among minorities seem to be higher than that of whites is that members of minority groups have less access to appropriate medical care and, even if they have access, may choose not to fully avail themselves of the care.

CURRENT ISSUES

Some issues have been with us nearly since the beginning of the epidemic. For example, questions and concerns about testing for the virus arose as soon as a test was available. Other issues, such as insurance coverage, arose later. Pertinent issues will change over time, and you must read widely so that you will know what the issues are at any given time. Unlike the early days of the 1980s, when we were just beginning to notice AIDS, the media now cover the topic extensively and in a balanced way. It should not be difficult for you to stay informed of how the illness and treatments are changing.

Mandatory HIV Antibody Testing

Some Americans believe that one way to stop the spread of HIV is to test everyone, or, if not all people, at least selected groups such as gay men, drug users, and people applying for marriage licenses. Setting aside civil rights questions for the moment, the issues around testing everyone concern the costs and benefits, how to account for the three- to six-month latency period between exposure and the development of the antibody response, and the psychological preparation needed for people to receive test results. Is it more effective to spend scarce HIV dollars on HIV education and research than on testing? Which has the most probability of slowing the spread of the epidemic? At the present time, mandatory testing affects very few people; people entering and serving in the military are a good example of a population that is regularly tested. In addition, a 1997 New York law requires the testing of all newborns.

Mandatory Reporting of Sex Partners

It has been community health policy and practice for many years that individuals testing positive for gonorrhea or syphilis provide the names of their recent sex partners. This has not been true for people testing positive for HIV, partly because of intense pressure from AIDS activist groups who feared that individual civil rights would be violated and partly from concern of public policy officials that even fewer people would choose to be tested if they had to provide the names of partners or if their names were reported to a federal agency. All states maintain registries of diagnosed cases. In 1997, twenty-six states required doctors to report the names of HIV-positive people to confidential state registries, but the debate continues. In 1997, the prestigious *New England Journal of Medicine* came out in favor of mandatory reporting at the federal level, so policies will continue to change.

Deciding Whether or Not to Be Tested

People who have engaged in high-risk behaviors such as unprotected sex and sharing needles must decide whether they should be tested for the virus. This is not an easy decision to make. The strongest argument for being tested is that, if the test results are positive, a person's health can be monitored and, if changes occur, action can be taken. The argument against being tested is that the news of a positive result can seem to be a death sentence. Some individuals know that they could not cope with such information. The best source of counseling about the testing issue is probably an AIDS organization.

Health Insurance Coverage

As we are painfully aware, health insurance coverage in the United States varies. Many people are insured through their places of employment while others are not. Even people who are insured may find that their insurance is not adequate after a diagnosis of AIDS.

People who are not insured must rely on government programs, particularly Medicaid, the program that provides health care coverage for indigent people. Although Medicaid provides basic care, it does not cover many additional services that PWAs may want or need. Coverage varies from state to state.

Medications

Because AIDS is fatal, those who contract it are intensely concerned about which medications are available to them and, perhaps even more so, about the progress of AIDS research and the speed with which the Food and Drug Administration (FDA) approves new drugs. There are always rumors, and sometimes facts, about experimental treatments that are available in other countries but not in the United States. Because of protests in the early 1990s by AIDS activist groups such AIDS Coalition to Unleash Power (ACT UP), the speed with which drug trials are conducted and new drugs approved by the FDA has increased.

Strain on the U.S. Health Care System

Treatment of HIV is expensive because people who have it may need a variety of intensive interventions over many years, many of them requiring hospitalization. Recently, however, the total amount paid by insurance companies for inpatient care has been declining. The cost of the much less expensive outpatient care is increasing. The common medications are very expensive, with the average monthly cost of AZT and ddI plus one of the protease inhibitors running from $1,000 to $3,000.

People with HIV/AIDS can suddenly become very ill with life-threatening infections. After hospitalization and appropriate medication, they may return to their lives for months or years without further enormous expense, or they may suffer a series of costly hospitalizations, one right after another. The course of the disease is unpredictable. What is predictable is the fact that treatment will be quite expensive. Current estimates are that each case of AIDS costs roughly $100,000.

Questions about health care always must revolve around how much value we place on a human life. For some, no expense is too great. For others, particularly when the causal factor is AIDS, nearly any cost is too great. The issue of cost will only escalate in the future because people with HIV/AIDS are living longer.

Who Is Responsible for AIDS?

While the U.S. Constitution is thought to protect all Americans, those of us in human services know well that discrimination continues in our society. Examples include the Rodney King beating in Los Angeles in 1992, the passage of Amendment 2 by Colorado voters in November 1992, and the enormous public reaction to President Clinton's 1993 efforts to allow openly gay men and lesbians into the military.

In the example of AIDS, this discrimination manifests itself as a form of "blaming the victim." According to this way of thinking, people who contract HIV do so because they violate society's norms by either using needle drugs or engaging in illicit or socially unaccepted (gay, extramarital, or premarital) sex. Some groups in our society then find it easy to adopt the position that people bring HIV on themselves. Since individuals are responsible for their own behaviors, some of which result in contracting HIV, these individuals are ultimately responsible themselves for becoming ill. Thus, society should have no responsibility toward them. The rule then would seem to be this: Either obey society's rules, or we don't care if you sicken and die. Taken to its logical extreme, this should mean that we refuse to provide treatment for victims of skin cancer who had spent time trying to get a tan, for victims of lung cancer who had smoked, for victims of cirrhosis who were heavy drinkers, and so on. So, we essentially would have groups of disposable people.

When translated into policy, this could mean that people with HIV and AIDS should be openly discriminated against in housing or employment or public accommodation. It could mean reductions in access to health care benefits. It could mean the stripping of civil liberties such as the right to privacy. People with HIV and AIDS could find that their health status is public information. Because the disease initially affected gay men almost exclusively, public attitudes toward homosexuality are closely tied to antipathy toward PWAs.

Some segments of American society would immediately stop all HIV education, relying instead on exhortations that there be no sex except between legally married heterosexual couples. However noble or ideal that goal might seem to be, it ignores the data on sexual activity in America.

As long as the HIV epidemic continues, these issues will be debated. As a human service worker, you will find yourself in an important role. You could be asked to provide expert testimony in court. You may be interviewed by people from the media. At the very least, you are a voter who should be well informed about the issues.

CONCLUSION

We reiterate that you will almost certainly work with people living with HIV and AIDS if you become a human service worker. This work can be richly rewarding, as can any human service work. But, because it involves life-threatening illness and death, it can be debilitating as well. Only you can decide whether specializing in this area would be a good choice for you.

We urge you to consider a career working in one of the many kinds of AIDS organizations. To make such a decision, you must carefully examine your attitudes toward sexual orientation, toward members of racial and ethnic minority groups, and toward people who use needles. If you are disapproving or squeamish, either work through your issues or select another area in which to specialize. Do not enter this line of work as a means for improving your attitudes toward gay people, members of minority groups, or drug users, or for proselytizing or preaching. People with HIV bring unique problems. They need your help and support. It would be unethical for you to use them for your own purposes.

To help you decide whether HIV work would be a good choice for you, begin to volunteer in a setting that provides services to people living with HIV and AIDS. Answer the telephone, raise money through phone-a-thons or a Walk for Life or other means, stuff envelopes, staff the hotline, or become a buddy. Interview people who work in such agencies. Get to know other volunteers. You can gain valuable additional experience by doing a field placement or internship working with people living with HIV and AIDS. Even if working with people living with AIDS is not your preference, you will undoubtedly work with people who are HIV positive, so you must learn as much as you can about the disease and the needs of people who have it.

SUGGESTIONS FOR FURTHER LEARNING

Information on HIV/AIDS is changing rapidly. The best way to stay current with this topic is using the Internet as your resource. One site that would give you all the information you need is:

http://www.thebody.com/whatis.html

CHAPTER 14

HUMAN SERVICES
FOR HOMELESS PEOPLE

LORENCE A. LONG

Before 1980, homeless people in the United States included a relatively small number of substance abusers and some unhospitalized people with a mental illness. Since that date, a number of factors, including the booming cost of real estate, a prolonged economic recession, a shrinking job market with declining real wages, and expanding substance abuse, joined with other factors to multiply the numbers and types of homeless people. An industry has developed to meet their needs. This chapter introduces the programs, workers, and clients in this area of human services.

DESCRIPTION OF THE PROBLEM

A homeless person is one who has no right to a living space. Other people do have such rights, through ownership, payment of rent, or through an enforceable relationship with a person who has the right to be in a particular living space (see Jahiel, 1992, Chapter 1, for a discussion of official definitions).

Thus, a person who pays rent to live in a farm shed is homeless because the shed is not a living space. Residency in the shed could not be enforced, even though the person paid rent. Following the same train of thought, a person who lives in a car or in a subway tunnel is homeless because the space is not legally a dwelling.

For a different reason, a person who is staying in a friend's apartment is homeless or at the edge of homelessness because he or she may be ousted from the living space at the whim of the friend.

The most recent prior residence of homeless people has usually been someone else's living space where the homeless person was staying temporarily and was then asked to leave.

Homelessness is a problem that almost never appears by itself. People become homeless because of another problem: family conflict, substance abuse, unemployment, low income, mental illness, physical illness, and so forth. Thus, there is no single pattern or cause of homelessness and no standard approach or service that would be effective for all homeless people.

Once a person becomes homeless, she or he may have very different experiences from other homeless people. Some people live on the street, while others live in shelters or with friends. Each of these situations has its special challenges, and each influences the homeless person in certain ways.

If a person goes through many difficult experiences while being homeless, these may limit the person's ability to resume life in his or her own living space. Homeless people who must make the most profound adjustment to their status would be those persons who live outdoors or in a nonliving space, such as in a subway tunnel. To survive in these settings, a person must adjust to the following conditions:

- The fear of abuse or attack;
- The need to be constantly alert, with little sleep;
- The difficulty of surviving extremes of weather;
- The lack of a balanced diet;
- Strained relations with other people.

211

Making these adjustments over a period of time often has the paradoxical effect of making it unbearable for people to be indoors.

Living in shelters often has its own drawbacks. These may include bullying by other residents (or groups of residents), actual physical or sexual abuse, and the theft of belongings by residents or staff. Lack of privacy is very common in shelters, as is the regimentation—everyone must do everything at the same time and in the same way—that usually accompanies institutional living. Overcrowding may make all the above factors worse. There may be no organized activities or services and badly prepared food. The general lack of resources tends to create dependence on the staff for every small attention or service, sometimes accompanied by dictatorial or preferential treatment by staff members.

Staying with friends or relatives may also have its problems, especially if the living space is overcrowded. Tensions between those living together may reach a point where conflict breaks out and the homeless person must leave. This type of accommodation is frequently the first stop on a series of steps within homelessness. A common transition to homelessness begins with the person staying in one or more friends' apartments and then moving on to shelters or the street as these temporary arrangements break down.

The challenges of surviving while homeless may keep the person from having sufficient time, energy, or motivation to address the problem that led to homelessness in the first place.

SOME TYPES OF HOMELESS PERSONS

Here is a thumbnail sketch of a "typical" homeless person:

> Luke lives in a cardboard box behind a maintenance shed at the local cemetery. He avoids contact with other people, but keeps up a busy conversation with himself. He gets enough to eat by sifting through the dumpsters at several local restaurants. He has severe skin problems from poor personal sanitation, body vermin, and exposure.

Here is another "typical" homeless person:

> Francine is staying with her two children in the Salvation Army's family shelter. She fled her abusive husband in another city. She came here, hoping he wouldn't track her down. One of her children is very restless and active, unable to stay still for more than a moment. The other child has a severe case of asthma. Both have been out of school for a month and a half while Francine has been traveling from place to place (Molnar, 1988).

Consider a third "typical" homeless person:

> Dorothy is living in the big city for the first time. She is staying in an abandoned warehouse with four other teenagers, also runaways or throwaways. She left her home in the Midwest to avoid the screaming fights she had with her aunt who has raised her since she was six months old. The fights were mostly over Dorothy's boyfriends and what time Dorothy should come home on a school night. Dorothy is supporting herself by providing (mostly) oral sex to men who drive down the Boulevard looking for young women to do what Dorothy does.

Perhaps less obvious types of homeless people would be the following:

- Juan, who works full time but doesn't make enough money to afford a room or apartment.
- Steve and Rose, a husband and wife whose family of five is staying in his brother's apartment while he looks for another job.
- Joyce, a woman with three children who now lives in a shelter for single women because her children were taken away when her substance abuse got in the way of her parenting.
- Jack, a Vietnam war veteran who begs on one of the main streets for quarters to support his habit of smoking rock cocaine.
- Tasha, a pregnant young woman who was ordered to leave her mother's house when her condition was discovered.

The list of situations could go on and on. Each is different in some important way from the others.

SERVICES FOR HOMELESS PEOPLE

The types of services that homeless people need are as varied as the types of situations they experience. Their most important needs are those common to every person:

Food	Housing	Clothing
Medical care	Income	Employment
Bath or shower facilities	A dependable routine	Belonging to other persons and a place
Safety	Privacy	

Note that "shelter" is not listed as a general human need. Although shelter is useful as a temporary aid for persons who have no place at all, it is not adequate as a long-term arrangement. People need housing, which may be defined as a living space where a person or her or his family has a right to be. Such a place must be safe, secure, private, and adequate in terms of space, temperature, and accessibility.

Some homeless people may also need the following:

Education	Job training	Social services
Substance abuse treatment	Supervised housing	Psychiatric treatment
Rehabilitation services	Individual or family counseling	Case management services

To be effective, services must be delivered in a manner that the homeless person will accept. In providing services to Luke, for example, the service must take into account his extreme discomfort in relating to other people. He has made many adjustments to succeed at living outdoors. If he is to begin to live in a more customary way, he will have to adopt a whole new set of behaviors.

What will work with Luke? Should he be approached boldly with requests for immediate change, or gently over a period of time? Which of the many services he needs—mental health, personal sanitation, nutrition, housing, and soon—should come first? Can these services be delivered where he is, or will he have to come indoors in order to receive them?

Some Types of Services for Homeless People

The range of services for homeless or near-homeless people is very broad. If homelessness is viewed as a process rather than a state of being, some services are aimed at the early part of the process. These include the following:

Eviction Prevention Services. Many tenants become homeless because they do not know their rights. The landlord usually has a lawyer to facilitate the eviction process, but the tenant often does not have a legal representative. Private or public funds may be used to ensure that tenants' rights are safeguarded and that unwarranted evictions do not occur.

Diversion Services. Interventions by this type of program involve the anticipation or interruption of the homelessness process by reaching out to offer resources or counseling to those likely to become homeless or who are at the point of homelessness. The resources might include providing money to pay a high rent, money to pay back rent, family crisis counseling, or conflict resolution services. (Note that many common supports and services fulfill the diversion function. Helping a person who is unemployed get a job, providing family counseling, providing financial support through public assistance, and overcoming discrimination in housing and employment all lessen the likelihood that people will become homeless.)

Special challenges for planners and workers in providing these services include how to identify those individuals or families most at risk so that action can be taken before they cross over the line into homelessness. Another obstacle to overcome is the difficulty that community leaders and funders have in conceptualizing and devoting resources to preventive, rather than remedial—the more common tendency—services (National Housing Institute, 1993).

Once a person does become homeless, other types of services may be available. In some communities, these may be the only types of services that exist. Services vary enormously from community to community. Some localities do their best to deny any support to homeless people on the theory that homeless people will then go elsewhere.

Some of the types of services provided for people who are homeless are the following:

Shelters.   Shelters may be buildings devoted to temporarily housing homeless people, or they may be hotels, motels, or other lodging places that are used for the same purpose. Shelters may have one-day stay limits or may allow guests to remain indefinitely as long as they obey the rules. Since shelters are often crowded and usually provide little or no privacy to their guests, many people cannot tolerate the closeness, noise, confusion, and conflict that result.

Some shelters are structured as transitional shelters, introducing the guest to programming that prepares the guest to live in permanent housing. The program may include orientation to tenant-landlord relations, rent-paying, minor maintenance of an apartment or room, connection with services and other resources in the neighborhood where the client will live, and so forth. The success of transitional shelters is closely related to the availability of decent, affordable, permanent housing when the client has completed the program.

Workers in shelters need to find ways to help guests move toward permanent housing even though staying in the shelter may provide more benefits for the guest. This must be done not through making life in the shelter miserable for them but through helping them prepare to move on. Another type of challenge is to treat guests fairly—which does not always mean treating each one exactly the same. Some shelter staff members find themselves treating all guests punitively when one or two of them are guilty of breaking rules. This approach can create a residence where everyone is miserable. The alternative is to (1) get to know the guests as soon as they enter, (2) form relationships with them, (3) observe them systematically during their stay, and (4) involve guests in governance issues so that they can help the staff make decisions about rule breaking.

Food Programs.   Food programs may be involved in preparing and offering food directly to homeless people, or they may be networks of scavengers and suppliers who locate and distribute free or inexpensive food to the direct providers.

Food pantries are one type of direct service food program. They provide unprepared food to both homeless and housed poor people who prepare and consume the food off the premises of the food pantry. Soup kitchens, a second type, cook and serve meals to homeless people and others who appear at a specified time or day.

Food suppliers to homeless services may gather, store, and distribute government surplus foods, leftover prepared food from restaurants or caterers, and private donations of food from manufacturers and food producers. They supply soup kitchens, food pantries, and shelters. These programs address a problem of hunger that is wider than homelessness.

Some homeless people qualify for U.S. government food stamps. In some cases when people are living in shelters, they pool their purchases so that everyone living there may enjoy a better menu.

Challenges for those who work in this area include providing for the special dietary needs of people who may have been severely malnourished in the recent past. It is essential to offer the appropriate foods to some who may need special diets because of diabetes or other medical conditions. Another challenge is providing sound nutrition for pregnant women and for young children and infants.

Health Care.   Because of their exposure to severe weather conditions, poor nutrition, lack of personal sanitation, and risk of injury, many homeless people have serious medical problems. Their lack of access to regular medical care over a period of time may mean that conditions that would ordinarily have been easily treated have advanced to a critical state. In addition, standard health care services for poor people impose conditions—repeated visits, long waits, fragmented care, impersonal or condescending service—that present insuperable barriers to participation by homeless people.

All these conditions have led to the development of special medical services for homeless people. These services typically are provided in shelters, soup kitchens, and day programs where homeless people gather. They offer more personal attention and are attuned to the typical problems and attitudes of their patients. Health care professionals deliver direct medical care and screen for more serious problems that may require referral to a hospital or substance abuse program. In many cases, the medical service tries to establish Medicaid eligibility for a patient, partly to garner reimbursement for the services it provides and also to give the homeless person access to other medical facilities.

Among the challenges for human service workers in this area are the following:

— Making a successful referral to a standard medical service, given the bureaucratic barriers that keep many people from getting the medical help they need;
— Achieving a helpful balance between exasperation at the behavior that has led to the homeless person's overlapping emotional, medical and social problems, and a too-sympathetic provision of service without raising expectations for changes in self-destructive behavior;
— Avoiding being manipulated to provide medicines that may be sold on the street to get money for drink or drugs.

Substance Abuse Programs.   Abuse of alcohol or some illegal drug may lead people to become homeless as they become increasingly unable to focus on paying rent or working steadily. Substance abuse may also develop into a problem after a person has become homeless (Wright, 1989, p. 99). Homeless persons may try to deal with depression, low self-esteem, symptoms of mental illness, physical pain, or other problems through the use of drugs or alcohol. Substance abuse then makes it difficult for them to face the emotional challenge of getting their lives together. It is easier to continue with the lifestyle that is buffered by the substance abuse.

Many shelters and other homeless programs deal with substance abuse by simply barring all persons who have obviously taken too much of some mind- or mood-altering substance. The person may be required to stay out of the program for a stated period of time. This protects the shelter from the fighting, damage, and demoralization that often accompany on-premises substance abuse. In a few cases, it may bring the excluded person to realize that substance abuse must be stopped. More often, substance abuse continues until the person suffers an accident or health emergency. Then the person is taken to a hospital for treatment, and there is an opportunity to raise the question of substance abuse treatment when the patient has recovered from the injury or ailment that led to hospitalization.

It is impossible to provide substance abuse treatment while a person is "living rough," as the English call living outdoors. The street dweller must be housed either in a hospital (perhaps for detoxification) or in a low-expectation shelter while her or his nutrition, personal sanitation, and level of fear are brought near normal. These changes alone may produce positive personality and behavior changes. Once the person is stabilized, expectations can be raised. Group and individual counseling sessions, assessment of mental and physical health needs, detoxification, and other processes may begin. The person may be moved to another shelter or to a place within the same shelter where abstinence is expected. This is a high-status program that is clean and pleasant and may offer various perks in terms of flexible routines, small stipends, better food, and so forth. Alcoholics Anonymous–type groups will probably be an important aspect of the program. Referrals may be made to residential drug or alcohol treatment programs. As the person makes further progress, referrals to permanent housing may be made and work begun on helping the person define and realize other personal goals.

The most difficult challenge for workers in this area is the high relapse rate of their clients. Workers must learn not to take such failures personally and to hope that the next time the client abstains he or she will be able to maintain abstinence for a longer period of time.

Mental Health Services. Many commentators on the problem of homelessness have blamed psychiatric hospitals for contributing to the problem of homelessness by discharging long-time patients who should have been kept in the hospital (Torrey, 1988). It would be more accurate to say that psychiatric wards and hospitals contribute to the severity of homelessness by refusing to admit people with mental illnesses until they reach a critical state of danger to themselves and others. The person who is simply incapable of self-care is not eligible for hospitalization, in most cases. Most of the mentally ill people who are homeless have never been hospitalized or have been hospitalized only briefly. Psychiatric emergency room staff may respond to a mentally ill homeless person by sending the person back to the streets with a supply of medication but no support.

Mental health outreach and treatment teams have been organized to provide services to sheltered and unsheltered homeless persons. These teams gently and nonthreateningly build relationships of trust with mentally ill homeless people, often by providing food or some other simple service in a nondemanding manner. Their clients often are so distrustful of other people that building such relationships takes a very long time. Once a relationship has been established, the team would provide a further service that the homeless client recognizes as something needed. Step is built on step, until the person is willing to go to get services and eventually enter a day program or a residence.

The mental health team may go so far as to bring medication to the homeless person who is living outdoors, establishing a pattern of regular administration of the medication. Experience has shown that it is very difficult to maintain consistent medication patterns in unstructured living situations. The team would also be prepared to call in the appropriate authorities to commit the homeless person to a hospital if the person's condition were to become dangerous.

As with medical services, a challenge for workers in this area is to balance sympathy for the client's problems with a demand for cooperation and self-care in a way that helps the person move forward without being scared off.

Social Services. Social services help to bridge the gap between the homeless person and the network of services that exist to assist the person. Connecting the person with publicly funded benefits, with family members, with shelters, with counseling, meals, medical care, mental health care, and many other resources is the job of the social service team.

Social service workers have historically had the freedom to move from behind a desk or to go outside a service organization's building to overcome the limitations of bureaucratic boundaries and limited perspectives.

Social service workers are required to develop expertise in a number of roles. These include intake, in which the client's needs are identified and plans are made for the work the agency will do with the client. A second role is that of finding resources, such as housing, income, medical care, or other resources that are not available within the agency. The third role is referral, in which an attempt is made to make a positive connection between the client and the outside organization that can supply the client's needs. If an obstacle arises to meeting the person's needs, the worker may become an advocate, who speaks for the client or a whole class of clients to get the needed resource.

The social service worker may also function as a counselor, helping clients to focus when they are confused or helping them to sort out their preferred choices among various alternatives.

There is a special type of social service worker called a case manager. This worker coordinates the process of meeting all the needs that a particular client has. This may involve making comprehensive plans with and for the client, contacting a number of different organizations, and arranging contacts between the client and the organizations so that they don't make conflicting recommendations or requirements as the client's needs are addressed.

Special challenges for workers in social services are related to the multiple problems that homeless people have. These problems may have become quite severe over time. In addition, organizations that provide the services that are needed may place obstacles in the way of serving the client. In some communities, the needed services—especially affordable housing or housing with supportive services—do not exist.

Job-Related Services. Helping a person end his or her homelessness involves connecting the person with an income. For some people, the income will be derived from disability payments or public assistance. But even those who are disabled may be capable of supporting themselves through work. This service is one that comes toward the end of the process of assisting homeless persons, after medical, mental health, and at least temporary housing needs are met.

People who have been homeless for a period of time may need more than help in getting a job. They may need job readiness training, which provides joblike activities to help the homeless person accept the time structures that are so important to employers: regular attendance and on-time attendance. Job readiness may also address issues such as acceptable dress, grooming, résumé, speech patterns, and attitudes toward supervisors and co-workers. In addition, work skills may need to be taught or polished. Practical matters such as child care, money for transportation, an address for responses to applications, and other, similar factors may need to be arranged.

Self-confidence may need to be built up through worklike activities in nonwork settings. Many shelters and other homeless programs involve clients in helping activities to build their self-confidence.

For clients who are disabled, some special rehabilitative measures may be appropriate. One of these may be the provision of a job coach, whose duties are to accompany the trainee to a regular work site, to teach the required skills on the job, and to help the person reach competitive levels of

work. The job coach then gradually leaves the site to train another person elsewhere.

The most distressing special challenge for workers in this area is the fact that even good training cannot overcome the problems of a sluggish economy. This challenge is exacerbated by the fact that racial or ethnic discrimination may deny well-prepared candidates opportunities to learn or to demonstrate their skills. The stigma of homelessness may accompany the potential employee to the workplace and limit her or his chances to relate professionally to employer, colleagues, and customers.

Education Services for Homeless Children. Just as adults need jobs, children need an education. Homelessness, by requiring families to move from one area to another, breaks up the relationship between children and their schools. Homeless parents are often completely occupied with carrying out the survival tasks of the family or overwhelmed with a sense of failure so that the educational needs of their children are neglected.

Shelters where children will be temporarily housed sometimes develop one-room schools to provide tutoring and informal classes. Such efforts cannot replace the resources of a regular school. However, homeless children admitted to regular schools are often subjected to the scorn of other children. They often try to keep the others from learning of their homeless status.

Challenges for workers in this area stem primarily from interruptions in schooling that children have experienced, leaving them behind others in their grade levels in many instances. In addition, a worker may form a strong educational relationship with a child, only to have the child disappear from the school or the community when the family either chooses or is forced to move on.

Legal Services. In many communities, services for homeless people are difficult to access. Bureaucratic barriers may make it difficult for homeless persons to get benefits to which they may be entitled. Legal services provide information, instruction, and, when necessary, legal action to enable homeless individuals to qualify for these benefits. Often nonlawyers are trained in the procedures that are necessary to prepare individuals to present their claims.

In addition, homeless people as a class may be treated badly or refused services they need in a particular community. In many cases, it has been through the efforts of advocates who have brought suits to compel communities to provide what homeless people need that any support or accommodation was offered to them at all. In some cases, the suits merely sought protection for homeless people to be free from harassment by police forces and other municipal employees.

One challenge facing workers in this area is frustration that the original plaintiff may not enjoy justice, even if the case is won. Lawsuits often take years to resolve. The original plaintiffs may not be around to benefit from the decision, if it is favorable. Lawsuits may also create a situation in which officials claim that they can do nothing until the lawsuit is resolved.

Courts have been reluctant to compel states and cities to spend money to provide services. Results of court actions have often been minimal or made only after months and years of delay. (For a fuller discussion, see Hopper, 1990.)

Having said this, it must be recognized that it is often only through court action that any positive movement toward justice has occurred. Bringing a suit can sometimes create a climate in which officials take action to solve the problem, making the case moot.

Housing.   In the late 1970s and the 1980s, the price of housing in the United States reached a very high level. Inexpensive apartments in urban areas became attractive to middle-class city dwellers. Many of these were turned into cooperative dwelling units that required substantial sums of money for purchase as well as high maintenance costs. Many people with low incomes were priced out of the market and became homeless. People—young adults, first-time parents, persons

leaving a relationship—who in earlier decades would have had little trouble establishing a household were unable to do so.

Before this time, even persons with other severe problems—substance abuse, mental illness, family conflict, low income, and so forth—could count on finding some sort of affordable housing. But after 1980, steep cutbacks in federal support for low-income housing coincided with factors like neighborhood resistance to the siting of low-income housing to sharply curtail the availability of affordable housing. A substantial increase in the supply of affordable housing would bring much of homelessness to an end.

Housing services for homeless people provide support for the transition from living outdoors or in shelters into regular housing. Where the service itself owns or controls the housing space, the service becomes the landlord as well as the service provider. These roles may conflict, especially when concern for the welfare or peace of mind of other residents leads the organization to make the difficult decision to evict a resident who is causing problems. On the other hand, the service provider as landlord has more control over the situation than if other landlords are providing the housing.

Among the factors that housing providers must take into account are helping newly housed people to take responsibility for cleaning and maintaining the living space, taking medication (where appropriate), and participating in on- and off-premises activities that help clients meet their assigned goals.

When the landlord is another person or organization, the service provider must locate the housing unit, prepare the client to survive the screening interview and other requirements, assure the landlord of the availability of problem-solving support, and refer and connect the newly housed client to local services.

The major challenge confronting the worker in this area is the lack of housing. Even when units can be found, the landlord or screening committee may be very particular about who is allowed to occupy the scarce housing unit. The landlord may not feel bound to put the housing unit into livable condition, so the client may be plagued by vermin, lack of heat, or safety and security problems. And the landlord may feel comfortable with evicting a difficult tenant, since there is plenty of demand for the housing unit.

A second type of challenge is based on the difficulty many clients have in adjusting to being good tenants. They may not feel quite the same sense of urgency that the worker feels about keeping their housing. Or they may be unable or unwilling to focus on paying rent on time, being quiet at late hours, and cleaning up after themselves—all important elements of successful tenancy. In any event, they may need time and consistent feedback to become accustomed to these practices.

Clothing Services. Clothing services seldom stand alone. They are usually included as part of a day program or a shelter. The homeless person has great difficulty getting clothing washed, keeping it from being stolen, keeping it clean and undamaged (while having no secure or dry place to store it), and getting it mended when it is torn. The person's prospects of getting a job or even being treated decently on the street depend in part on wearing clean, well-pressed clothes.

Nearly all homeless programs either have secondhand clothing to distribute or know where such clothing can be found. In some cases, manufacturers contribute out-of-style, faded, off-color, or otherwise unsellable clothing to programs for homeless people.

Some programs attempt to launder or clean the clothing of homeless people. This requires care because of the possibility that the clothes may be infested by lice or other body parasites. Washing and cleaning methods must be used that will kill these parasites.

Personal Sanitation Facilities. One of the persistent problems faced by homeless people is the quest for opportunities for washing, bathing,

washing hair, and cleaning teeth. Although offensive body odor may be used as a defense against harassment, especially by women, being clean is a widely held value among residents of the United States, including homeless people. Public restrooms are often the only place that homeless people can use for this purpose. In an effort to keep them out, communities and businesses have locked or closed many of the public restrooms across the United States.

Personal sanitation facilities are usually included in other programs for homeless people, such as day programs and shelters. Where they are available to persons who live outdoors, they are very popular.

Personal Storage Facilities. Homeless people have great difficulty keeping personal belongings, including identification papers, from being lost, damaged, or stolen. The personal possessions, family photographs, documents, clothing, and odds and ends that all of us collect are at great risk when a person becomes homeless. Such things are important reminders of our personal history and identity. "Sweeps" of squatters' camps by sanitation personnel or police in which all belongings are destroyed are particularly cruel.

Programs for homeless people are often reluctant to provide places to keep personal belongings, partly because these are sometimes left behind when the homeless person moves on and partly because some homeless people collect large quantities of objects that appear to other people to be of little value. There is not enough spare space in many programs for all the things that guests would like to store. Nevertheless, some programs provide a small locker for each resident or client to facilitate personal storage.

Mail Drops and Addresses. Homeless people, like everyone else, need to be able to receive mail. Some programs provide mail drops where a person can pick up mail. Having an address for job applications, benefit applications, voter registration, and other important functions is essential.

This is another service that is usually included within a more diverse program.

Travel Support. In many communities, services for homeless people are conceived of as rest stops for homeless travelers who are traveling to one of the coasts or to a large city. Stays are limited to a few days or even one day. Meals, personal sanitation, and some petty cash for travel assistance are available. Homeless persons are not encouraged to stay longer to find work or housing in the community because the community does not wish to accommodate persons who are likely to become dependent on local taxpayers or charitable organizations. This type of service is usually located in small communities along major travel routes. Residents of these communities who become homeless usually move elsewhere to avoid having to face their former neighbors on the street or in the store.

Self-Help. Although much of the homeless service system is based on "doing for" homeless people, there are a number of types of projects that show that homeless people can often do things for themselves. These organizations range from standard agencies in which homeless people have been given a clear responsibility for a certain aspect of the work (e.g., managing a shelter or providing counseling services) to self-help organizations where nonhomeless people are considered unqualified to take on any responsible role. One of the principles of self-help is that only those who have been through a particular experience are qualified to help others go through it because they understand the experience better than an outsider could.

Other principles of self-help (Long, 1988, p. 18ff.) include the following:

— That the person who has been through the situation and is now successful can be a powerful role model for a person who is now struggling with the same situation;
— That a person with a problem who is placed in the role of helper becomes stronger and more self-disciplined through assuming the helping role;
— That a person who becomes a helper enjoys enhanced status that helps the person to overcome the stig-

matized condition that led to the need for help in the first place;
— That belonging to a self-help group provides support and a social network;
— That having an active, supporting role helps the person overcome the dependent, passive role that is so unacceptable in U.S. culture;
— That the best way to challenge the stigma associated with an undesirable condition (such as homelessness) is for those who are going through it to demonstrate their strengths by becoming advocates for themselves.

Given these factors, it may be very helpful to hire a person who has been homeless to assist professional staff people in homeless service programs. This person may be useful in teaching the staff what the experience of homelessness is really like as well as being effective in reaching out to homeless people.

One challenge related to working in this area is that homelessness, unlike other stigmatized conditions, is one that a person may recover from completely. Many people, once they have been housed, have no wish to identify with other people who are now homeless. Housed persons often do not regard themselves as being potentially homeless, requiring continuing support. Therefore, the potential leadership of a homeless self-help group may continually be lost to the mainstream. Although this is often wonderful for the individual, it weakens the group's ability to maintain and renew itself.

A second challenge for human service professionals is that they will probably be excluded from, or given a limited role in, any true self-help group. It is often difficult for professionals to accept the idea that experience is the sole qualification for effective human service work. But unless they accept this principle, they will find themselves undermining the essential self-help dynamic.

Special Problems of Services for Homeless People

Many programs to meet the needs of homeless people began as the result of enormous efforts by deeply dedicated persons who worked for very low pay, or no pay at all, to help those who were seen as most helpless.

"Doing For."   It is this "helpless" image that leads to one of the problems with homeless services: More than other types of assistance programs, homeless services have "done for" rather than "done with" their clients. The resurgence of homelessness occurred at the same time as, and in some cases was caused by, substantial cutbacks in various types of government-sponsored aid programs. Many established social agencies were slow to provide services that met the needs of homeless people. Volunteers with little social welfare experience stepped into the breach to assist those who had lost their housing. Their style reflected the assumptions of an earlier era characterized by noblesse oblige, when it was assumed that well-to-do people knew what was best for poorer folks. Several decades of lessons of the value of client participation and self-help, learned in the 1960s and 1970s, were largely ignored in the case of homelessness. The result was that homeless people were not encouraged to develop their own organizations and movements to address their problems. They ended up as dependent clients rather than as advocates for themselves.

Built-in Deterrents.   A second type of problem with homeless services is the fear that homeless people would become too comfortable as recipients of services and not be motivated to rehabilitate themselves. Therefore, many services have built-in limitations or irritating features that are intended to block indefinite dependency. This echoes the ambivalence that is reflected in the restrictive nature of many human services in the United States, whose culture does not encourage providing unconditional assistance to people in need (Piven and Cloward, 1971). Among the features that are intended to be deterrents are the following:

- Strict and burdensome eligibility procedures;
- Lack of comfort and privacy;
- Limits to services—such as length of stay in shelters—even when alternatives do not exist;

- Unpleasant, demeaning or patronizing attitudes by staff members toward clients.

Fragmented Services.   A third type of problem with homeless services is that they are seldom integrated into a set of services that address all the needs of a person. Often an organization may meet just one need, and do that in a limited way. There may be a number of different soup kitchens in the community, each of which serves food on a different day. Different shelters may have different rules about eligibility, length of stay, required behavior, and other features. In addition, services for families and those for single individuals are often provided by different service organizations.

While services are fragmented and specialized, homeless people nearly always have a cluster of problems. An early mental health worker commented:

> *You can't separate the problems. They go hand in hand. We have a lot of hybrid people in our program—such as the woman we were working with earlier this week who abuses drugs, who may have hepatitis, who also has symptomatology that at times looks schizophrenic, who has a seizure disorder and is having seizures regularly at the shelter, and who also is five months pregnant (Alcohol, Drug Abuse, and Mental Health Administration, 1983, p. 14).*

Lack of Focus on Permanent Housing.   A fourth type of problem with homeless services is that they often do not assist the homeless person to make a transition to permanent housing. This is most often due to a lack of affordable permanent housing in the community.

Another factor keeping homeless services from focusing on placing homeless people in permanent housing is that the funds that support homeless services are restricted to emergency aid and may not be used to provide permanent housing. The U.S. government throughout the 1980s and early 1990s sharply limited the amount of money available to support the provision of permanent housing while allowing the amounts used for emergency aid to balloon.

In addition, many homeless persons belong to racial or ethnic groups that are subjected to discrimination in housing. Thus the service would have to overcome not only prejudice against homeless people but also prejudice against historic victims of housing discrimination in the services' communities. Such an approach could seriously weaken the service program's base of support, and require members of the agency's staff to come to terms with their own discriminatory attitudes.

Staff Resentment.   Some workers in homeless programs are paid so little that they are only a step away from homelessness themselves. They may have strong feelings of jealousy toward their homeless clients, who may be eligible for valued services or housing opportunities that the staff members desperately need themselves.

Denial of Services.   Many communities have taken the position that providing services of any kind to homeless people will attract them from other parts of the area or nation. These communities have done their best to remove any amenity that could be seen as making existence within the community possible for homeless people. In some cases, police forces have been allowed to harass homeless people with the hope that those who were pressured would go elsewhere. In many of these communities, legal suits have been brought in behalf of the homeless people; these suits are usually successful because courts have held that homelessness is not a violation of the law per se. Therefore, courts reason, homeless people are entitled to equal protection under the law. Localities that have been forced to provide services through this means may do so in a hostile manner that is meant to subvert the decision of the court.

CONCLUSION

Because of inadequate amounts of affordable housing, full employment, and support services that would help people live more successfully in their communities, a visible incidence of homelessness has spread to every area of the United States. A new industry with many different services, large numbers of employees, high costs ($550 million in 1994 in New York City alone), and hundreds of thousands of clients has sprung up. Once thought to be temporary, the homelessness industry has become a well-established arm of the service-providing network.

Without actually saying so, the nation has apparently "decided" that homelessness, with its personal and public costs, is more desirable than its alternatives. And human services has, opportunistically, benefitted from this trend. It is important to remember that other choices could have been made, indeed, can still be made, to reverse this policy and return the nation to a condition that existed before 1980, when homelessness was rare and shocking, as well it should be.

REFERENCES

Alcohol, Drug Abuse, and Mental Health Administration (1983). *Alcohol, Drug Abuse, and Mental Health Problems of the Homeless: Proceedings of a Roundtable*. Rockville, MD: U.S. Department of Health and Human Services.

Hopper, K. (1990). "Advocacy for the Homeless in the 1980s." In C. L. M. Caton, ed. *Homeless in America.* New York: Oxford University Press.

Jahiel, R., ed. (1992). *Homelessness: A Prevention-Oriented Approach.* Baltimore: Johns Hopkins Press.

Long, L. A. (1988). *Consumer-Run Self-Help Programs Serving Homeless People with a Mental Illness. Vol. 3.* Rockville, MD: National Institute of Mental Health.

Molnar, J. (1988). *Home Is Where the Heart Is: The Crisis of Homeless Children and Families in New York City.* New York: Bank Street College of Education.

National Housing Institute (1993). *Preventing Homelessness: A Study of State and Local Homelessness*

Prevention Programs. Orange, NJ: National Housing Institute.

Piven, F., and R. Cloward (1971). *Regulating the Poor: The Functions of Public Welfare*. New York: Vintage Books.

Torrey, E. F. (1988). *Nowhere to Go: The Tragic Odyssey of the Homeless Mentally Ill*. New York: Harper & Row.

Wright, J. D. (1989). *Address Unknown: The Homeless in America*. Hawthorne, NY: Aldine de Gruyter.

SUGGESTED FURTHER READING

Bassuk, E. L., ed. (1990). *Community Care for Homeless Families: A Program Design Manual*. Newton Centre, MA: The Better Homes Foundation.

Bingham, R. D., R. E. Green, and S. B. White, eds. (1987). *The Homeless in Contemporary Society*. Newbury Park, CA: Sage Publications.

Caton, C. L. M., ed. (1990). *Homeless in America*. New York: Oxford University Press.

Cohen, N. L., ed. (1990). *Psychiatry Takes to the Streets: Outreach and Crisis Intervention for the Mentally Ill*. New York: The Guilford Press.

Haus, A., ed. (1988). *Working with Homeless People: A Guide for Staff and Volunteers*. New York: Columbia University Community Services.

CHAPTER 15

HELPING FOR ALCOHOL AND DRUG ABUSE

MARCEL A. DUCLOS
MARIANNE GFROERER

The statistics describing the use and abuse of alcohol and other mind-altering drugs ring familiar on the nightly news, find bold print in the newspapers, and flavor everyday conversations. General hospitals treat medical/surgical patients suffering from medical complications due to abuse and dependency. Emergency mental health and medical services are often faced with management of the intoxicated person. Community mental health centers daily confront the detrimental poly-drug use of scores of deinstitutionalized patients, including the dually diagnosed. School personnel, counselors, teachers, and administrators alike witness the ebb and flow of the season's most preferred or most accessible substance on the school grounds. They must additionally contend with the far-reaching effects of substance use on students, families, and neighborhoods. Along with community workers and social service agency staff, law enforcement officers also struggle to overcome a gnawing defeatism when children and youth sustain, as victims, the ravages of their own or others' use in a cycle of destruction and even death.

No age group, no socioeconomic status, no level of education, no geographic area—urban, suburban, or rural, mountain, plain, or coast—no occupation or profession, and no religious affiliation—whether church, temple, synagogue, or mosque—protects from the insidious and infectious spread of the problem. Our society's cultural heritage of ambivalence reveals itself by the earliest promotion of the use of alcohol in the colonies and the colonial militia, combined with a primitive "righteous" response to inebriation. No time period in U.S. history, not even the years of Prohibition, provided a drug abuse–free environment for the growth and development of citizens. Nor can such an environment be anticipated for the near future. It is a dream, an idealistic vision. Human service practitioners must face the disillusionment of the present reality and continue to attend hopefully in the expectation of manageable goals realistically attainable by troubled and afflicted clients.

At-risk behaviors due to disinhibition and impaired judgment caused by mind-altering substances obligate human service practitioners to consider strategies—educational, medical, economic, political, sociological, psychological, and spiritual—to address the problems on the contemporary scene. These problems include the ones the nation shuns the most: the growing AIDS epidemic, all forms of child abuse, and the persisting plague of violence in our society. The long multicultural history of the human services teaches that the "cure" of human ills, including substance abuse problems, cannot come from logic alone but requires authentic caring. For the human service practitioner, caring in its concrete, active form means consistent and care-filled attention to the details of a realistic treatment plan.

CHALLENGES FACED BY HUMAN SERVICE WORKERS

The human service worker stands, as a generalist, in the middle of a network of providers, ready to work cooperatively with the many specialists assessing, developing treatment/service plans, delivering care, evaluations, and outcomes. In the arena of alcohol and drug abuse, the key challenge to the worker remains the same: achieving the earliest detection for possible prevention. Yet in the reality of the service delivery systems, the challenge almost always involves the detection of intoxication, the history of abuse, the possibility of dependence, and/or risk as victim or victimizer. No accurate or appropriate care can be designed and provided in any context without knowledge of the effects of drugs on a client's life. Failure to identify the contributing and resulting connections between substance abuse and the client's presenting problems with health, the law, money, work, school, society, family, and self will spell a decisive failure in care, however well packaged the plan and well intentioned the delivery. The old psychiatric rule "diagnosis predicts prognosis and therefore directs treatment" applies here as well.

The first challenge, then, is one of accuracy. However, much client care may be a matter of heart; it must be guided by knowledge and experience. Accurate knowledge of the psychoactive substance use disorders and their associated intoxication and withdrawal syndromes arms the worker with necessary information to intervene at the earliest possible moment. The continuum of care reaches from direct immediate crisis intervention to consultation and referral as required.

The second challenge lies in the subjective domain, in the human service worker's own personal story. Few individuals can claim never to have been touched by the effects of substance-induced behaviors, though they might claim, for themselves, lifelong abstinence. Whether in personal, social, or professional experiences, the human service worker will have accumulated learned responses to this population. The challenge of empathic acceptance, of healthy emotional distance, or disidentification of a client-enhancing response to countertransference calls for clear, helpful supervision. Whether the service being delivered to the client entails modest assistance with some agency paperwork or involves the complex, long-term work of case management, the energy at the meeting of client and practitioner will generate the atmosphere of change. It therefore becomes an inner challenge for the worker to know her or his own story and to use that level of awareness to promote the client's good and to attempt to cause no harm.

The third challenge pertains to the temptation of the human service practitioner to view himself or herself as competent to function as a substance abuse counselor despite a lack of specialized academic training and clinical experience. The treatment of substance abuse and dependence is a multidisciplinary enterprise. The work of a substance abuse counselor is defined by observable and measurable competencies. For the human service worker who serves an addicted population, it is an ethical imperative to know one's limits of competence and role within the agency and to consult and refer as necessary.

The worker who is unfamiliar with the neurological impairments caused by particular substances abused would be in danger of placing the client, self, and others in physical and/or psychological jeopardy. Depressants, stimulants, narcotics, and hallucinogens present their own sets of impairments and their own relative levels of danger. Confusion about the client's antecedent or resultant developmental and personality disorders would make the adoption of an individualized helping style difficult. Early trauma in combination with many years, even decades, of substance abuse exacts heroic transformational work on the part of the recovering person. Overestimation of the addicted person's ability to stop using and become sober without sufficient time for emotional healing and behavior change would lead to errors in the selection of strategy, in the expectation of outcomes, and in the fundamental process of defining the real problems. The nature of the disorder and of rehabilitation leads to paradoxes for the recovering addict as well as for the human service practitioner.

Again, the history of drug use gives us a clue about the paradoxical nature of psychoactive substances, of the disease of substance addiction, and of the recovery process. The ancients and the alchemists taught that nature cured disease with either similars or opposites, depending on the illness. Substance abuse and dependence is such a disease. The substances themselves produce their opposites: depressants can rebound into anxiety; stimulants can plunge into depression; narcotics produce their own pain; hallucinogens can lead to loss of self. That which the user originally sought through partaking of the drug eventually eludes the abuser. The drug exacts due payment for all experiences—soothing, exciting, painless, or expansive. All that was beyond the ego's humble ability to integrate into the psyche and beyond the body's physiological capacity to metabolize into vital energy returns with a vengeance.

The enslaving addiction to the drug releases the abuser to an opposite dependence, binding her or him to a committed pursuit of inner freedom hard won by selfless courage. In the tradition of recovery, the paradox of the twelve-step program of Alcoholics Anonymous (and Narcotics Anonymous) describe that which will nurse the recovering person back to sanity with an elixir of opposites—a bitter medicine that many will reject. No recovery program anywhere can sidestep the necessary laws of nature that direct bodies, minds, and souls from illness to health.

The client's life calls for a complete turnaround—nothing less will do. The cleverness and cunning that characterized the addiction must become slowness and carefulness, accepting the wisdom of another, allowing the unshakable inner self to put aside the false grandiose ego projected by the substance. A new life begins only with the death of the old one. It is ultimately the paradox of life and death because substance dependency is a matter of life and death.

HUMAN SERVICE RESPONSES TO SUBSTANCE ABUSE

The human services respond to the problem of addiction in society in three ways: education, prevention, and treatment. The choice of response is determined by the level of addiction, which is the target of the approach. Limiting considerations to the individual, the human services distinguish between the person who has never used drugs for recreation, the one who only rarely uses chemicals for recreation, the person who uses frequently and whose abuse leads to some personal and professional problems, the individual who is dependent to the point of resulting medical complications, and the small percentage of individuals who, in their chemical dependency, are also socially isolated and face predictable death. Because chemical dependency is potentially life threatening, the human services respond according to the immediacy of the danger to self and others.

Education

Successful drug education programs have incorporated in their materials and services the knowledge, attitudes, and behavior necessary to optimize the choice of a drug abuse–free life. Some programs emphasize convincing the audience of the dangers of drugs, whereas other programs underline the objective facts about the substances, advocating neither abstinence nor reasonable use. Other programs utilize the power of identification with a noteworthy person in recovery to score a point with the listeners or viewers. Still other programs, especially those geared toward the school- and college-age population, are even more direct in their approach, providing training in assertively resisting encircling pressures.

Prevention

Prevention does not only refer to those persuasive efforts aimed at stopping abuse before it starts. It also involves those interventions aimed at signaling to a user in the early stages of abuse that continued use could result in damaging consequences. Early diagnosis with crisis monitoring, crisis intervention, and referral are such interventions. For those individuals who are in the later stages of abuse that lead to dependency, the prevention efforts address the goal of halting the slide to that conclusion. In this instance, intervention efforts could take the form of early treatment, monitored maintenance, or social/medical detoxification. The motto "the best defense is a good offense" applies in this domain.

Treatment

Because drug abuse and drug dependence are characterized as mental disorders in the *Diagnostic and Statistical Manual of Mental Disorders* (DSM-IV), medicine, nursing, and psychology are the disciplines that have traditionally taken responsibility for the treatment of these illnesses. Social work and mental health counseling have also sought to remedy the social and societal ills related to substance addiction. The profession of substance abuse counseling, newly emergent in the early 1970s, has now taken on a prominent role in the treatment of individuals suffering from substance- related disorders. Human service providers who are certified by the International Certification Reciprocity Consortium as alcohol and drug abuse counselors have given evidence of specialized competence in their assigned roles and functions as they work alongside some of the other traditional professions. These particular individuals have passed an objective exam and have been successful in an oral defense of a case presentation before a member state board. They also may choose to become a member of the National Association of Alcoholism and Drug Abuse Counselors (NAADAC).

All of these professionals, according to their own training and skills, cooperate to promote the client's achievement of physical and psychological health, social and financial stability, and behavioral and interpersonal satisfaction. In all of this there still remains a key role for the generalist in the human service field: that of case manager, as the coordinator of all those services that promote follow-through and attainment of the treatment goals.

Whether the goals are abstinence after detoxification, management of disruptive behavior, stability of employment or housing, or improved overall self-care and health, the variety of treatment settings and assortment of approaches employed is as diverse as the developmental needs and problems of the clients. Depending on the severity of the addiction, the setting might be an in-hospital treatment program, a residential center, or a day program or out-patient individual, family, or group contact. The human service worker plays a valuable role in all of these settings as a team member with other providers.

It is important to note that treatment facilities vary, depending on the population served and the substance treated. Though they have commonalities worth acknowledging, treatment facilities may, in order to focus on specific areas of need, specialize in work with the elderly, adolescents, women's issues, cocaine or heroin abuse, homeless individuals, or the dually diagnosed. In each case, the facility will function along standard guidelines of substance abuse treatment but with its own particular focus. With this in mind, an outline of the most commonly found treatment facilities follows.

In-Hospital Treatment Program

Used for:

- Detoxification from physical dependence
- Individuals unable to remain substance-free without supervision

Provides:

- Medical monitoring of withdrawal
- Group psychoeducational counseling and introduction to support groups such as AA/NA
- Possibly some social services/case management

Length of stay:

- Twelve to twenty-eight days (some may be as brief as three to seven days, depending on insurance coverage)
- May transition into outpatient program

Residential Treatment Center

Used for:

- Long-term maintenance of sobriety/drug abstinence after detoxification
- Individuals without financial resources in need of halfway house/therapeutic community for recovery

Provides:

— Necessities of daily living (shelter, nutrition, life-skills training, education)
— Role modeling, direct reality-based feedback in daily living situations, and promotion of self-discipline

Length of stay:

— Three months to two years (usually funded by public or private nonprofit agencies)
— Includes assistance for vocational, social, and emotional transition back into community/family living

Outpatient Services

Used for:

— Transitional treatment after detoxification or residential treatment
— Individuals with early stage or less severe problems, those not physically addicted, those able to maintain employment during treatment, or those living in a stable and supportive environment
— Individuals unable to afford or not eligible for in-hospital or residential treatment programs

Provides:

— Counseling, education, support system for individual, couple, family, or group
— Possibly some case management, transportation, and socialization
— Assessment and referral to more intensive types of treatment if needed

Length of stay:

— Participation varies according to need and facility; may be once a day, all day, each evening, twice weekly, or once every two weeks; some facilities provide open-ended "drop-in" groups for occasional support of program "graduates"
— No set limit on length of service use; may be fee-for-service based on ability to pay or supported by public or private funds

Skills and Training Needed by Human Service Workers

To function as a valuable and valued team member in such settings, the human service student must be attentive to the skills needed in the field. Employers expect trained human service practitioners to understand how the health and human services work. Students must, therefore, gain skills in coordinating the services a client receives while being able to help the same client access the services of other agencies as the need arises. Given the multiplicity of needs and problems that the substance abuser presents, the student is obligated to at least know how to access the multiple services required to meet treatment goals developed by the program.

Knowing the resources is one thing, but helping the client to choose and use a service is another. Perhaps the most fundamental skill that the student has to offer this troubled client is the skill of professional helping. To be more specific, this is the art of attending: the quiet, focused, other-centered attention that develops an investment in the process of change on the part of the client. Consistent, focused attending can raise a client's self-esteem; foster, perhaps even repair, trust; and increase feelings of effectiveness. These basic building blocks of a successful life are the inevitable results of the authentic, professional, helping relationship. This is really the central gift at the heart of all the human service practitioner's efforts. To attend in a way that invites the client into eventual self-direction stands out as the main contribution that can enliven the delivery of care.

Students in the field of human services who seek additional proficiency in the area of alcohol and drug abuse may seek specific training in the following skills:

1. Taking an alcohol and drug use history
2. Identifying abuse and dependency, including the withdrawal syndromes
3. Recognizing the complications of drug interactions
4. Using the pertinent resources in the community
5. Imparting accurate information about abusable substances
6. Adapting services to the needs of specific populations

A question remains to be addressed: What specific body of knowledge and array of skills would provide the proficiency required to work effectively in the service delivery field of alcohol and drug abuse as an independent professional? For the sake of brevity, this article will only identify and parenthetically discuss major categories of competency.

These categories have been grouped under the headings of the Twelve Core Functions of a Counselor, which define and describe a professional human service provider as a specialist in more than forty states. Furthermore, training for these core functions is available at the associate's, bachelor's, and master's levels of formal education. It is also available to individuals through approved professional workshops, staff development, and continuing education courses. Currently, the federally funded network of Addiction Training Centers (ATCs) and the Center for Substance Abuse Treatment have identified and published the Addiction Counselor Competencies report, which summarizes the knowledge- and skill-based instruction leading to eligibility for certification, registration, or licensing through the aforementioned consortium under the laws of member state boards. These same competencies ensure competent and ethical practice for the protection of the consumers of substance abuse services.

Under these guidelines, a specialist/counselor in this field must be able to screen potential clients to determine whether they are eligible and appropriate for admission into the available program. If the person in need meets the established criteria for admission, the counselor will conduct the intake process to ensure the clarity of the emerging treatment contract and development of trust and rapport between the client and the program. At this point, the counselor will orient the client in the ways and means, rules, and structure of the recovery program, providing an inner and outer safe milieu for the start of the work of recovery. With the information gathered so far by all the professionals involved, the counselor will pursue the formulation of an assessment of the individual's strengths, weaknesses, problems, and needs relevant to the mutual work of change. The focus of both client and counselor becomes the partnership necessary to decide on an individualized treatment plan. Problem identification, rank ordering of changeable problems, time lines of change, and methodologies all become part of the client-approved plan or strategy for change.

This plan must be multidimensional. It must include all the domains of human growth and development and all the health and human services as necessary. To this end, the specialist must be a fundamentally sound individual, group, and family counselor. Because of the problems and needs of clients beset by the ravages of chemical addiction, the specialist must be able to coordinate the many services prescribed in the treatment plan. In the course of treatment, there will almost always be at least one crisis. The certified counselor will be able to respond to crises in a way that maximizes safeguarding the client's rehabilitation and turns the threat to recovery into an opportunity for continuing growth.

Throughout the treatment efforts, imparting accurate and germane information about addictions and the road to recovery remains a major function of the trained counselor. When the needs of the client cannot be met by a particular provider or by a particular program, the obligation to refer guides the accessing of other sources of help. This obligation may be exercised from the moment of screening to the time of discharge, aftercare, and follow-up.

Finally, in carrying out all of the above functions, including intra- and interagency consultations, the human service specialist in this field of addictions as in all other branches of this profession must be able to accurately keep records and write reports. It is essential that all records and reports maintain overall privacy and confidentiality while being clear, understandable, and complete. Careful handling of information allows for the effective continuum of care for the client's benefit.

Alcohol and drugs are perhaps the most constant variable in the synergistic forces that trouble the lives of human service clients. The arguments in favor of continued specialized training flow from the case management records of service delivery agencies. Whether as a generalist, specialist/counselor, or student practitioner, the goals of the human service worker in helping for alcohol and drug abuse remain ultimately the same. The worker's purpose is to encourage, assist, and enhance the recovery process with specific skills, knowledge, humanity, and genuine caring. It is to promote a life that will empower the recovering person to be, as an anonymous poet wrote, "tender enough to cry, human enough to make mistakes, strong enough to absorb pain, and resilient enough to come back and try again."

SUGGESTED FURTHER READING

Abadinsky, H. (1993). *Drug Abuse: An Introduction*, 2nd ed. Chicago: Nelson-Hall.

Ackerman, R. J., ed. (1986). *Growing in the Shadow: Children of Alcoholics*. Pompano Beach, FL: Health Communications.

Addiction Counselor Competencies (1993). *Addiction Training Center Program*. Washington, DC: U.S. Department of Health and Human Services.

Alcoholics Anonymous. (1976). *The Story of How Many Thousands of Men and Women Have Recovered from Alcoholism*. New York Alcoholics Anonymous World Services.

Bauer, J. (1982). *Alcoholism and Women: The Background and the Psychology*. Toronto: Inner City Books.

Boaz, D. (1993). *Embrace Your Child-Self, Change Your Life—A Workbook*. Seattle: Lane's End Publishing.

Chandler, M. (1987). *Whiskey's Song: An Explicit Story of Surviving in an Alcoholic Home*. Pompano Beach, FL: Health Communications.

Chappelle, F., T. G. Durham, D. Lauderman, D. J. Powell, L. Siembad, and N. Simonds, eds. (1992). *Counselor Development: A Training Manual for Drug and Alcohol Abuse Counselors*.

Clancy, J. (1996). *Anger and Addiction: Breaking the Relapse Cycle*. Madison, CT: Psychological Press.

Clayton, L., and R. Van Nostrand (1993). *The Professional Alcohol and Drug Counselor Supervisor's Handbook*. Holmes Beach, FL: Learning Publications, Inc.

Clemmens, M. C. (1997). *Getting beyond Sobriety: Clinical Approaches to Long-Term Recovery*. San Francisco: Jossey-Bass.

Columbia Assessment Services, Inc. (1996). *Role Delineation Study for Alcohol and Other Drug Abuse Counselors*. Raleigh, NC: ICRC/AODA.

Cultural Competence for Evaluators: Guide for Alcohol and Other Drug Abuse Practitioners Working with Ethnic and Racial Communities (1992). DHHS-A&DA and MH Administration.

Doweiko, H. F., (1993). *Concepts of Chemical Dependence*, 2nd ed. Pacific Grove, CA: Brooks/Cole.

Dusek, D. E., and D. A. Girdano (1993). *Drug: A Factual Account*. New York: McGraw-Hill.

Estes, N. J., and M. Heinemann (1992). *Alcoholism: Development, Consequences and Interventions*. St. Louis: Mosby.

Evans, K., and J. M. Sullivan (1990). *Dual Diagnosis: Counseling the Mentally Ill Substance Abuser*. New York: Guilford.

Evans, K., and J. M. Sullivan (1995) *Treating Addicted Survivors of Trauma*. New York: Guilford.

Flores, P. J. (1988). *Group Psychotherapy with Addicted Populations*. New York: Haworth.

Freeman, E. M. (1992). *The Addiction Process: Effective Social Work Approaches*. New York: Longman.

Galanter, M. and H. D. Kleher (1994). *Textbook of Substance Abuse Treatment*. Washington, DC: American Psychiatric Press.

Goode, E. (1993). *Drugs in American Society*. New York: McGraw-Hill.

Goodwin, D. (1975). *Is Alcoholism Hereditary?* New York: Oxford University Press.

Hanson, G., and P. Venturelli (1995). *Drugs and Society*. Boston: Jones and Bartlett.

Herdman, J. W. (1994). *Global Criteria: The 12 Core Functions of the Substance Abuse Counselor*. Holmes Beach, FL: Learning Publications.

Inaba, D. S. and W. H. Cohen (1993). *Uppers, Downers, All Arounders: Physical and Mental Effects of Psychoactive Drugs*. Ashland, OR: CNS Productions, Inc.

Jacobs, M. R. (1981). *Problems Presented by Alcoholic Clients: A Handbook of Counseling Strategies*. Toronto: Addiction Research Foundation. Fourth Force in Counseling. Vol. 70.

Khantzian, E. J., K. S. Halliday, and W. E. McAuliffe (1990). *Addiction and the Vulnerable Self: Modified Dynamic Group Therapy for Substance Abusers.* New York: Guilford.

Kinney, J. K. (1992). *Clinical Manual of Substance Abuse.* St. Louis: Mosby.

Kinney, J. K., and G. Leaton (1995). *Loosening the Grip.* St. Louis: Mosby.

Kleinman, M. A. (1992). *Against Excess: Drug Policy for Results.* New York: Basic Books.

Kulewicz, S. F. (1990). *The Twelve Core Functions of a Counselor.* Marlborough: Counselor Publications.

Lawson, G., and A. Lawson (1989). *Alcoholism and Substance Abuse in Special Populations.* Rockville, MD: Aspen.

Leonard, L. S. (1989). *Witness to the Fire: Creativity and the Veil of Addiction.* Boston: Shambala.

McNeece, C. A., and D. M. DiNitto (1994). *Chemical Dependency: A Systems Approach.* Englewood Cliffs, NJ: Prentice-Hall.

Mark, L., J. Olesen, and J. Fallon (1993). *A Manual for Chemical Dependency and Psychiatric Treatment.* Santa Fe, NM: CL Productions.

Miller, Norman S. (1995). *Addiction Psychiatry: Current Diagnosis and Treatment.* New York: Wiley-Liss.

Roebuck, J. B., and R. G. Kessler (1972). *The Etiology of Alcoholism.* Springfield, IL: Charles C. Thomas.

Roy, O., and C. Ksir (1993). *Drugs, Society, and Human Behavior.* St. Louis: Mosby.

Royce, J. E. (1989). *Alcohol Problems and Alcoholism: A Comprehensive Survey.* New York: Free Press.

Steinglass, P. (1987). *The Alcoholic Family.* New York: Basic Books.

Thombs, D. L. (1994). *Introduction to Addictive Behaviors.* New York: Guilford.

Vaillant, G. E. (1983). *The Natural History of Alcoholism.* Cambridge, MA: Harvard University Press.

Ward, D. A.. (1983). *Alcoholism: Introduction to Theory and Treatment.* Dubuque, IA: Kendall/Hunt.

Washton, A. M., ed. (1995). *Psychotherapy and Substance Abuse.* New York: Guilford.

A SOCIAL NORMS APPROACH TO REDUCTION OF ALCOHOL AND DRUG ABUSE AMONG COLLEGE STUDENTS

FRANKLYN M. ROTHER

HISTORICAL OVERVIEW

During the late 1980s colleges and universities experienced a growing number of serious alcohol and drug problems among students both on and off campus (Haines, 1996). Binge-drinking rates varied greatly according to the individual campus culture, yet headlines in the national media highlighting deaths and injuries during campus parties, class breaks, and other social events propelled this problem into the national spotlight. College students were just beginning to be recognized as an "at-risk" group for alcohol and drug abuse.

Prevention and education program initiatives funded by FIPSE (Fund for the Improvement of Postsecondary Education) grants and New Jersey State Department of Health had produced "disappointing outcomes" in terms of reducing use and abuse of alcohol and drugs among college students (Haines, 1996). The experiences of higher education institutions conducting and publishing research in this area were replicated in the results of prevention and education awareness programs at colleges and universities throughout the state of New Jersey (Rowan, 2001).

In 1985, a Monmouth County addictions services coordinator and a State Department of Health addictions director approached the coordinator for the human service program at Brookdale Community College to propose the development of courses in addiction studies for students seeking careers in the addictions field. They also requested that a representative of the college participate in a statewide task force to discuss the college's potential involvement in professional training efforts, and to report on campus prevention and education efforts.

In 1987, a task force supported by the Division of Alcoholism of the New Jersey State Department of Health, consisting of representatives from sixteen colleges and universities, evolved into New Jersey Higher Education Consortium on Alcohol and Other Drug Abuse Prevention and Education (Rowan). The Brookdale Community College representative became the first elected president of the statewide consortium. In 1989, the Southern and Northern Regional Consortia were established through FIPSE grants, and in 1993, a FIPSE-sponsored regional consortium was formed in central New Jersey.

During this era, college administrative practices favoring disciplinary intervention actions, as well as general acceptance of alcohol abuse as a "rite of passage" for college students, impeded prevention program efforts. The members of the four New Jersey consortia recognized that public acceptance of the traditional view of college student drinking behavior could be countered only by a structured, specific, and persistent informational program. College students needed to be recognized as an "at-risk" population for drug and alcohol abuse (Rowan). Across the country, prevention interventions at colleges were meeting the same public resistance, with the same tragic effects.

A PARADIGM EMERGES

During the 1980s, Wesley Perkins and Alan Berkowitz of Hobart and William Smith Colleges (HWS) began to study the linkage between student perceptions of their peers' drinking behavior and students' self-reports of their own alcohol consumption. As these researchers collected data from other institutions across the country, evidence emerged indicating that misperceptions of drinking norms greatly influenced individual alcohol abuse. Perkins and Berkowitz theorized that discussing student misperceptions and presenting authentic data on college student drinking behavior could reduce actual high-risk drinking behavior (Berkowitz and Perkins, 1986).

The research conducted by Perkins and Berkowitz on misperceptions of drinking norms demonstrated a relationship between actual alcohol use reported by students and their misperceptions of the amount their peers used. They found this relationship between misperceptions and behavior on every campus studied, and they concluded that a "reign of error" led to increased negative drinking behavior. Thus, "imaginary peers" influenced students' drinking behavior because of the belief that "everyone was doing it!" (Berkowitz, 1998). This self-fulfilling prophesy led to an assumption that binge drinking was the peer norm among college students, thus promoting actual increases in this behavior.

High-risk drinking was found to have greater prevalence

- in the Northeast region of the United States;
- at smaller colleges without graduate programs;
- among single undergraduates, 17–24 years old;
- in residential student housing environments;

- among student bodies with low religious participation and affiliation;
- at colleges with predominantly students of European American descent;
- at colleges oriented toward sports and athletic events;
- at institutions with fraternities and sororities. (Perkins, 2002)

In addition to the physiological effects of misuse of alcohol among students, other alcohol-related problems surfaced in the studies conducted by Perkins and Berkowitz, including the following:

- accidents while intoxicated;
- DWI/DUI convictions;
- interference with other students' academic pursuits and sleep;
- attempts to make unwanted sexual contact;
- unprotected sexual activity;
- violent behavior;
- destruction of property.

The consortium decided to adopt a social norms approach in the form of a media campaign called "Know It!"

COMPONENTS OF A SOCIAL NORMS PROJECT

Brookdale Community College implemented a Social Norms Misperceptions Campaign in 1998–1999. The campaign has been expanded yearly as new activities were added. Currently, Brookdale's social norms project includes the following components, which will be explained individually:

- The "Hunt"
- Test/survey
- Campus banners
- Special events
- Campus newsletter and student publications
- Blues Net/Cable
- Curriculum infusion and overheads
- Faculty and staff training and involvement
- Peer educator training

- Non-alcoholic happy hours
- Website banners
- Campaign materials
- Peer norms survey
- Evaluation

The Hunt

In August 2001, the grant director met with a small committee to determine a strategy for the Social Norms Campaign. The college marketing director offered a singular proposal for the fall semester: a contest or "Hunt" for facts about student drinking behavior. A prize would be awarded to each student who completed The Hunt: a T-shirt imprinted with the words, "I Won the Know It Hunt."

Signs were posted around the campus with social norms statistics about Brookdale Students. One sign was placed in three high-traffic areas. During orientation week and the opening of the semester, approximately 6,000 flyers were distributed to students. Faculty members continued to distribute instructions for participating in The Hunt throughout the fall semester and into the spring 2002 semester.

Test/Survey

During the spring semester, The Hunt became a search for "factoids" about binge drinking. Faculty members were recruited to distribute more flyers, newsletters, and the T-shirts. Nearly thirty faculty members participated, but only about a half dozen consistently distributed every flyer and newsletter in their classes prior to implementing The Hunt for the "factoids" that would lead to winning a T-shirt.

Distribution of the same materials also continued through the efforts of two college work study students, a faculty member, and other students. At least 5,000 additional flyers and newsletters were distributed during the first half of the spring semester.

Campus Banners

Two "Know It!" banners, each 50 feet long and 3 feet high, were produced and raised over the library entrance and the college commons during the spring semester. The banners supplemented "The Hunt" begun in the fall. These large banners remained up until mid-April.

Special Events

A faculty member from the psychology department organized a group of students in the spring semester to carry a banner stating "Free Sex," with one student dressed in a beer can costume and several other students clustered around her. The group spent two hours walking around the campus distributing flyers and newsletters about misperceptions regarding binge drinking among Brookdale students. This event attracted much attention and controversy. Some faculty members reported that their afternoon classes on that day were buzzing about the event. Discussion focused on its "taste" or "lack thereof," as well as the use of a message about "free sex" to bring attention to a different message about binge drinking.

Campus Newsletter and Student Publications

Dr. Eugene DeRobertis of Brookdale's psychology department researched and published a newsletter on the Social Norms project, entitled *The Sobering News.* The newsletter was printed on a single sheet of brightly colored paper and published biweekly from October to April. The "factoids" for the second Hunt were included in several of the newsletter publications *(The Sobering News)* so that students could find the answers and win the T-shirt. Between 500 and 1,000 copies of each issue were published and distributed.

The Student Life weekly publication *Brookdale Happenings* regularly includes "Know It!" factoids. *The Stall,* the student newspaper, has published a story each year about the Social Norms project.

Blues Net/Cable

The Brookdale Blues Net/Cable Station broadcasted 15-second "factoids" concerning misperceptions about alcohol use among students. These announcements were broadcast continuously during the fall and spring. At approximately 50 TV sites throughout the campus, Blues Net broadcasts included one "factoid" every few minutes. The cable station broadcasts occur during breaks in the broadcast of course media instruction and other productions. The campus radio station also offered public service announcements.

Curriculum Infusion and Overheads

Over the years learning modules about Social Norms Theory have been developed in psychology, sociology, history and education. Overheads were produced for seventy-five faculty members teaching introductory psychology, sociology, human service, and criminal justice courses. The overheads summarized the "factoids" about binge drinking and provided information about the social science research method utilized, and explain "misperceptions theory" in relation to attribution theory. Most faculty members distributed the Social Norms facts flyers without much discussion. Some faculty members reported that students wanted to discuss the survey messages. Students often questioned the survey results, disputed the definition of binge drinking, and suggested that the "factoids" did not reflect their experiences.

Distribution of flyers by faculty members during class sessions appeared to bring about greater depth of discussion that was lacking when posting the messages around campus. Some faculty members were interested in their students' reactions, and several questioned the timing of the surveys in the early part of the spring semester and speculated on the impact that certain holidays and testing periods might have had on the survey results. Often faculty members reported critical class discussion that demonstrated relevant application of course content to the survey facts.

Faculty and Staff Training and Involvement

During the fall 2000 adjunct meeting, part-time faculty in the psychology department were introduced to curriculum infusion materials developed by full-time faculty. The Peer Norms modules are correlated with the Biology of the Brain, Attribution Theory, Social Science Statistics, and Perception and Sensation. Feedback from the faculty who used these materials indicated that students engaged in lively discussions about the meaning of the survey results and the "real" effects of binge drinking. Continuation of the "Know It!" campaign has led to ongoing dialogue between faculty and students regarding the meaning of the messages. One of the messages, concerning drinking at athletic events, was particularly controversial. There were concerns about the perception that students drink at these events. These "Know It!" posters were removed from areas in and around athletic facilities.

Peer Educator Training

Recruiting students and training them as peer educators can assist the effective implementation of a Social Norms campaign. This core student group participates in the on-campus distribution of campaign materials and related activities. Student interest has been high and consistent in some years and low and inconsistent in others.

Non-Alcoholic Happy Hours

Five Non-Alcoholic Happy Hours are held during the year. Between 200 and 400 students, faculty, and staff members attend each event. Flyers and newsletters are distributed, together with food and non-alcoholic beverages. These Non-Alcoholic Happy Hours garner the most consistent attendance of all campus activities. Literature distributed at each event includes information concerning drug/alcohol abuse prevention and the role of the Social Norms Project. This activity has also generated interest in student clubs regarding participation in abuse prevention activities. It also serves as a way of recruiting students into the Human Service club, where they can be trained as peer educators. Materials concerning the Non-Alcoholic Happy Hours are imprinted with the "Know It!" logo and, where possible, one of the misperception messages.

Website Banners

Production of website banners has been delayed because of a number of technological changes at the college and questions about the "ethics" issues that might have to be addressed in promoting these messages.

Campaign Materials

"Factoids" highlighting aspects of the campus peer norms survey of Brookdale students are printed on posters and flyers distributed in the classrooms of participating faculty and throughout the campus. Thousands of flyers are distributed in these classrooms. Some faculty members have presented students with pens, highlighters, stress balls, or keychains as rewards for class participation. The "Know It!" campaign, and other prevention messages appear on these materials.

Peer Norms Survey

Peer norms surveys are collected from the introductory general education courses during the spring semester of each year. Approximately 500 surveys are collected in a "convenience survey" of students during their freshman year. Faculty members have been very cooperative in supporting the project.

Evaluation

In the 2000–2001 Social Norms campaign evaluation, Dr. Wesley Perkins indicated that Brookdale Community College had basically flat-lined in the exposure to the message categories (going up by a few percentage points). The data remained the same from year to year in "actual use reported" and "perceptions of peers' use," with one notable increase in "perceptions of peer drinking in the last two weeks." Dr. Perkins pointed out that the two categories of "exposure to the message" revealed that 55 percent of the students were somewhat familiar with the Social Norms campaign, with only 30 percent reporting non-exposure. We can work toward increasing this exposure.

Looking at the data more closely, members of the Social Norms Project found that Brookdale students tended to cluster their own use below the "binge drinking" thresholds, with 80 percent reporting consumption of two drinks or fewer in a row in the last two weeks. This suggests that the low thresholds of "actual drinking" among our students (particularly binge drinking) makes it more difficult to achieve reductions. Cross-tabulation report data from 2000 and 2001 actually demonstrated an increase of students reporting consumption of fewer than three drinks, from 78.9 percent in 2000 to 80.5 percent in 2001. When you add in the percentages of "less than five drinks," with five drinks being the binge drinking threshold, there is a wider gap: 88.7 percent (2000) versus 91.6 percent in (2001). In 2000, 3 percent were invalid responses, the remaining 97 percent of responses were at or above the binge threshold and in 2001 2 percent were invalid responses with the remaining 98 percent of responses above the binge threshold.

This is good news! More than two-thirds of the students reported "actual use" at or below the binge threshold. Over 50 percent believed that their friends consumed five or fewer drinks in a row at a party.

CONSIDERATIONS AND CONCLUSIONS

Implementing an effective social norms project requires the following steps:

- Collecting baseline data.
- Developing a message that highlights non-binge norms.
- Ensuring credibility of the message source.
- Delivering the message to the target student population.
- Supporting message retention within the target student population.

To implement the above steps, human service educators involved in a social norms project must have a campus environment with the following elements:

1. Leadership support, from the college's president to the deans
2. Involvement of key campus administrative personnel:
   - Dean of Students
   - Director of Student Life
   - Health Administrator
   - Campus Police Chief
   - Director of Marketing
   - Public Relations Administrator

3. Commitment from faculty members to serve in the following capacities:
   - Advisors and/or task committee members
   - Participants in classroom activities
   - Presenters at conferences and workshops
   - Developers of materials
4. Involvement and participation of students in the following roles:
   - Peer educators
   - Advisors on what works
   - Participants in social norms activities
   - Messengers carrying the "Know It!" Facts

Social norms projects also require consistent, substantial, and sustained resources. Mini-grants to New Jersey Statewide Consortia member colleges through the New Jersey Department of Health and Rowan University were reduced by one-third in 2002–2003 due to state budgetary restraints in the current economic climate. The college contributes substantial financial support through the Marketing and Student Life departments, and is expected to continue that support. Large commuter colleges in high population markets with a diverse student population face especially difficult challenges in maintaining a focused and sustained labor-intensive media campaign.

REFERENCES

Annual Grant Reports of Brookdale Community College—Center for Addictions Studies—unpublished.

Berkowitz, A. D. (1998). "The Proactive Prevention Model: Helping Students Translate Healthy Beliefs into Health Actions." *About Campus,* September/Octover 1998.

Berkowitz, A. D. (2002). Responding to the Critics: Answers to Common Questions and Concerns About the Social Norms Approach. The Report on Social Norms: Working Paper #7. Little Falls, NJ: PaperClip Communications.

Berkowitz, A. D. & Perkins, H. W. (1986). Problem Drinking Among College Students: A Review of Recent Research. *Journal of American College Health.*

Haines, M. P. (1996). *A Social Norms Approach to Preventing Drinking at Colleges and Universities.*

Newton, MA: The Higher Education Center for Alcohol and Other Drug Prevention, Education Development Center, Inc.

Perkins, H.W. (2002). *Social Norms and the Prevention of Alcohol Misuse in Collegiate Contexts.* Journal of Studies on Alcohol, Supplement 14: 164–172.

Rother, F. (2001). Annual Grant Report-Brookdale Community College. Lincroft, NJ: Center for Addictions Studies, Brookdale Community College.

Rother, F. (2002). Annual Grant Report-Brookdale Community College. Lincroft, NJ: Center for Addictions Studies, Brookdale Community College.

http://www.edc.org/hec/socialnorms/theory/html
http://www.rowan.edu/open/depts/cas/tabacco_social
http://www.socialnorm.org

CHAPTER 16

HELPING SERVICES FOR OLDER ADULTS

KATHLEEN J. NICCUM

In the past three decades it has become increasingly common knowledge that, as a population, there is a "graying of America." Increased life expectancy, the aging of the "baby boomers," and population expansion have each contributed to our awareness of the reshaping of our previous "population pyramid." Within that general trend, 13 percent are over 65, with the fastest growth in the nonwhite population, especially Latinos and Asian Americans (Gelfand and Yee, 1991). By the year 2030, it is expected that one-fifth of the population in the United States will be over 65. The U.S. Department of Commerce (cited in Katz and Karuza, 1992) reports that the United States has the fourth largest population of adults 60 years of age and older in the world. The increasing number of older persons is creating a new market for service programs such as travel agencies, adult education, human services, and most aspects of health care.

Older adults are more different than alike. Physically and psychologically, people age at different rates, and what is true for one 70-year-old may not be true for another. Many people know older adults who are "old" at 60 and others who are "young" at 80. Health, outlook on life, and agility often affect how old or young one feels. This is because the aging process reflects a combination of genetic and environmental factors that include one's activity level, attitude, diet, stress, and lifestyle.

PHYSICAL ASPECTS OF AGING

The aging process begins at conception and continues throughout one's lifetime. Many of the changes associated with the normal aging process occur slowly and gradually. For instance, one's vision changes with age. Declining visual acuity begins in early adulthood but usually does not interfere with a person's functioning until much later in life. By the age of fifty or fifty-five years, most people wear glasses or use reading glasses to accommodate the changes in their vision. The effects of aging on visual changes include reduced visual acuity, reduced accommodation (decreased flexibility of the lens), reduced capacity to adjust to changes in illumination (dark adaptation), shift in color vision, and increased susceptibility to some types of visual illusions (Huyck and Hoyer, 1982).

Hearing loss may begin in one's early twenties and progress slowly throughout life. Approximately 30 percent of the older population in the United States is affected by a hearing loss, which can frequently be alleviated by the use of hearing aids. A major auditory loss that can occur later in life, called presbycusis, is caused primarily by deteriorative changes in the middle ear. It mainly affects the discrimination of pitch (especially higher tones) and the threshold for hearing high-frequency tones.

The other senses also show slight declines with age, although many people do not notice the changes. In addition, older adults tend to have less physical strength and stamina than younger people. In general, though, people adapt to the physical and perceptual changes of aging with little awareness of its process.

Although older adults are now healthier and live longer than they did at the turn of the twentieth century, they still account for more than

239

one-third of all health care costs. They continue to have more chronic conditions than do younger people, with arthritis, hypertension, and heart conditions being some of the most common ones (U.S. Senate, 1991). Even though 80 percent of older people have at least one chronic condition, only 20 percent of people 65 and older have some degree of disability associated with it (Katz and Karuza, 1992).

Alzheimer's disease, a progressive, degenerative disease that attacks the brain and results in impaired memory, thinking, and behavior, affects only 10 percent of the population over 65 years of age. However, more than 50 percent of nursing home residents have this disease or a related disorder. Early symptoms of the disease include forgetfulness, shortened attention span, trouble with simple math, difficulty expressing thoughts, unpredictable moods, and a decreasing desire to try new things or meet new people. As the disease progresses, the symptoms become more debilitating and include severe loss of memory (including dressing skills and names of family members and friends), mood and personality changes (including outbursts of anger and suspicion), total loss of judgment and concentration, inability to complete routine household tasks, and inability to handle personal hygiene.

A number of illnesses and conditions, such as drug reactions, thyroid problems, and malnutrition, may manifest symptoms similar to those of Alzheimer's disease. Thus, it is very important that people undergo thorough evaluations (physical, neurological, and psychological) to eliminate potential causes that might have a cure. Alzheimer's disease occurs when there are changes in the nerve endings and brain cells that interfere with normal brain functions. There are various theories about why these changes occur, but there is no conclusive proof of a cause of Alzheimer's disease.

PSYCHOLOGICAL ASPECTS OF AGING

Old age is a developmental stage of life. Exactly when it occurs depends upon which developmental theory is being used or what resource is being referenced. There is no one consistent age range corresponding to middle age or older adulthood among the definitions created by lifespan theorists, society, or the government. For instance, the Age Discrimination in Employment Act (ADEA) uses 40 as the time when age discrimination occurs, whereas the government frequently uses the age of 65 for full entitlement to its aging programs, such as Medicare and Social Security. Other organizations, such as the American Association of Retired Persons (AARP), accepts members as young as 50, whereas many senior discount programs start at age 60 or 65.

Often, it is presumed that older adults become more rigid, set in their ways, stubborn, grouchy, and crotchety as they age. These are stereotypes and are not supported by research related to the aging process. Grouchy 70-year-olds were probably grouchy 20-year-olds. However, there are a number of emotional events, such as the death of a loved one or a move to a nursing home, that may affect behavior. Thus, it is important when working with older adults to avoid relying on age stereotypes and instead to view people as individuals.

Aging also has an effect on various aspects of intelligence. For example, crystallized intelligence (knowledge acquired through experience) depends on sociocultural influences and encompasses the skills one learns in school and through acculturation, including verbal comprehension, numerical skills, and the ability to perceive relationships and carry out formal reasoning. Crystallized intelligence continues to improve with age (Peterson, 1983).

Fluid intelligence, on the other hand, refers to one's general mental ability independent of acquired knowledge, experience, or learning. It depends more on genetic endowment and consists of the ability to perceive complex relationships, use short-term memory, create concepts, and use abstract reasoning. Fluid intelligence begins to decline slightly during the middle years and slowly continues to decline throughout the remainder of life (Peterson, 1983).

Older adults often seem to have more difficulty learning and remembering information than younger people. Hayslip and Kennelly (1985) suggest that age differences in learning may be a product of the interaction between cognitive and noncognitive influences. Cognitive influences refer to basic learning processes, including memory function as it relates to learning, intelligence, and problem-solving skills. Noncognitive factors that affect learning include (1) health, (2) ability to see and hear, (3) ability to understand and build on past experiences, (4) energy level, (5) ability to overcome fear and inhibition that could limit involvement in the learning process, and (6) motivation to learn (Lowy and O'Connor, 1986; Peterson, 1983).

Depression and low morale may impair memory and decrease learning performance. Depression, which is prevalent in the older population, is frequently associated with fear and anxiety concerning real or anticipated losses. Many of these losses are indirectly related to aging, such as loss of income with retirement, loss of health with chronic conditions, and loss of family and friends through death. Biological changes within the central nervous system and the increased incidence of physical illnesses, as well as the side effects of medications, also may contribute to higher rates of depression. Symptoms of depression include changes in appetite (eating more or less); changes in sleep patterns (sleeping excessively or disruptive sleep); changes in activity level (decreased or agitated, purposeless); loss of interest in hobbies or usual activities; low self-esteem; guilt; decrease in the ability to think, understand, and concentrate; and thoughts of suicide. In addition, older adults have more psychosomatic complaints, more frustration with memory impairment, withdrawal behaviors, apathy, and increased alcoholism (Frengley, 1987).

Overall, healthy aging means making adjustments and adapting to change as needed. In the later years of life, some changes, especially those associated with illness, may occur with little or no warning. Gradual changes in physical ability are easier to adapt to than sudden changes. However, a positive attitude, flexibility, and philosophical beliefs help many people to accept changes, even sudden ones, and to continue to look forward to the future.

ECONOMIC ASPECTS OF AGING

Although there has been a steep decline in poverty for both men and women following the Social Security Act amendments in the 1960s, older women are much more likely than men to have incomes below the poverty level. In 1987, the poverty rate for older white women was 12.5 percent, for older white men it was 6.8 percent, for older African American women it was 40.2 percent, and for older African American men it was 24.6 percent. Thus, older men and women often have different financial and social resources available to them, some of which are influenced by gender and race (Hess, 1990).

The life expectancy for women is estimated to be seven years longer than for men. Although a portion of this difference in mortality can be explained by hormonal and genetic factors, much of it is due to acquired risks and health habits. However, as women increase their stress levels and acquire unhealthy habits, the difference in mortality rates is beginning to narrow (Hess, 1990).

According to the U.S. Bureau of the Census (cited in Hess, 1990), American men who are 65 or older are almost twice as likely to be married than women of the same age group, who are three and a half times more likely to be widowed. Thus, more older women live alone and thus are more likely to enter a nursing home if an illness makes it difficult to maintain their own home. In contrast, older men who become disabled are more apt to be cared for at home by their spouse. Thus, even though women usually live longer than men, they do not necessarily have a better quality of life.

CULTURAL ASPECTS OF AGING

Cultural diversity is a growing part of American life. Human service workers need to know about cultural and racial differences (between and within races and cultures) to best meet the needs of older minorities. For instance, within the Native American population, the elderly are respected, seen as a source of strength, and receive social support from their families. However, this may be less true for some families who do not live on a reservation (Yee, 1990).

The African American population has traditionally been viewed as taking care of its own family members. Many African American older adults live in intergenerational families or at least help younger family members with child care. Throughout the years, African American women have been a significant source of strength and support for their families. Thus, older women may be more respected than older men in the African American culture (Yee, 1990).

Overall, the Latino/Hispanic population has a strong extended-family orientation that can provide a sense of belonging and security to its members. For this population, family often includes biological family members as well as close friends and the godparents of children. Godparents traditionally have social support privileges in addition to family responsibilities in the Latino culture (Yee, 1990).

Although there is diversity within and among minority groups, these populations share more similar life experiences with each other than they do with the white population. Most, if not all, of the minority populations have had to contend with racist prejudices and stereotypes. They have been forced to develop inner strength to help them adapt in their life struggles. In turn, these strengths have helped them adjust to their own aging challenges (Yee, 1990).

NURSING HOMES

Approximately 5 percent of people over the age of 65 live in long-term-care institutions, primarily in nursing homes. Over 70 percent of nursing home residents are women (predominantly white women), and most are over 80 years of age. Although most older adults prefer to live in their own homes, they move to nursing homes when

they are no longer able to live alone, when family members are unable or unwilling to assist them, or when there are no community services available to help meet their needs.

Adjusting to life in a nursing home is difficult for many people and requires a number of dramatic adjustments. There are major losses to handle including a decrease in independence, a loss of privacy, a decreased personal sense of control, a loss of personal possessions, an inability to come and go at will, and a drain on financial resources. Frequently, the nursing home is viewed as the place to die, and in reality most of the residents never return to their homes or communities. Many nursing homes do not provide adequate mental stimulation or opportunities for independence, personal empowerment, socialization, community involvement, or independence.

AGE DISCRIMINATION

It was during the 1960s that Robert Butler (the former director of the National Institute on Aging) coined the term "ageism" to mean a process of systematically stereotyping and discriminating against people because they are old (Butler, 1975). Age discrimination, which is often more subtle than other forms of discrimination because of the false stereotypes that equate age with ability, has been prevalent for generations. Typical myths and stereotypes include (1) aging is a constant downhill decline, (2) older people are unproductive, (3) there is a marked decline in intelligence after middle age, (4) people get senile as they age, and (5) older people cannot learn new things.

Age discrimination has hampered the ability of many older people to obtain employment or to further their careers. To address ageism problems, the Age Discrimination in Employment Act (ADEA) was passed in 1967 to promote employment on the basis of ability rather than age. It has been amended since that time and currently prohibits discrimination on the basis of age in hiring; job retention; compensation, and other terms, conditions, and privileges of employment. It protects workers who are 40 years of age and older, and it has eliminated mandatory retirement for all but a few careers that are still being studied for safety factors. Even though research has been refuting age stereotypes since the 1920s, many ageist beliefs still remain today.

Older Workers

The labor force is getting older, and employers are beginning to recognize that older workers are an untapped resource. Presently, approximately 30 percent of workers leave their careers during their late fifties or early sixties. For those who are 65 or older, 46 percent were employed in 1950, compared to 16 percent in 1988 (Peterson and Coberly, 1988). Although people are retiring younger, many retired people start new careers or look for part-time work that offers flexibility in days and hours of work. Older adults are now healthier, better educated, better informed, and more active than in the past, which makes them better candidates for continued employment—barring age discrimination.

As the work force gets older and the labor pool of young people shrinks, employers are being challenged to address the issue of employing and training older workers. A number of studies indicate that many managers harbor some prejudices toward older workers. For example, a 1985 study by AARP concluded that, overall, human resource managers perceived older workers positively and valued their experience, knowledge, work habits, and attitudes. However, the managers also held some negative perceptions that included the view that older workers were resistant to change, had physical limitations, did not learn new tasks quickly, and were not comfortable with new technology (AARP, 1987). Another survey of corporate managers found that managers said they valued both older and younger workers. However, they did not attribute positive motives to older workers who desired retraining, favored the career development of younger workers, viewed older workers as less likely to be promoted, and believed older workers had more trouble adjusting to change (Peterson and Coberly, 1988).

Overall, the work performance of older workers does not support the above negative beliefs. In general, the attitudes and work behaviors of older employees are compatible with effective organizational functioning. Older workers have greater job satisfaction and greater loyalty to their organizations, resulting in a lower turnover rate than that of younger employees. Furthermore, the rate of absenteeism for healthy older adults is lower than it is for their younger counterparts. The older population also has fewer injuries on the job, but if there is an injury, the recovery time is longer (Doering, Rhodes, and Schuster, 1983).

Older Clients

It is important for human service workers to understand the aging process and to avoid the trappings of ageism with its myths and stereotypes. It also is helpful to know that negative attitudes, low self-esteem, and depression may be barriers to learning, seeking social services, or participating in counseling or activity programs.

Human service workers will benefit from assessing the individual needs of the older clients with whom they work. It will be helpful to gain information about the person's background, past experiences, culture, strengths, limitations, interests, needs, and motivation level. This information can then be incorporated into the planning of training/retraining programs, educational or activity programs, and intervention and social service programs.

Developing rapport, trust, and respect is vital in building a relationship with an older person. Often, the human service worker will be younger than the client, thus making it important to establish one's credibility. It is essential to never "talk down" to an older client, even if the person suffers from Alzheimer's disease or another form of dementia.

When working with people who have hearing problems, be sure that the person has heard the entire question or instruction to avoid inappropriate responses. If the person asks to have information repeated, it may help to lower voice pitch. This modification will benefit those who cannot hear higher-frequency pitch and who have difficulty distinguishing vowels and soft consonants such as s, p, f, th, sh, and ph. Also, it is helpful to face the hearing-impaired person when talking, to talk slower, and to have the person's attention before beginning to speak.

PROGRAMMING TECHNIQUES

Research in gerontology (the study of aging) has shown that healthy older people continue to learn as they age. However, they may benefit from the use of specific teaching techniques to enhance their learning. Many adults become more cautious with age, which makes it appear that they need more time to do tasks and to answer questions (less likely to guess). Thus, they will need more time and encouragement to respond in learning situations.

Older adults also may benefit from teaching techniques that help them organize information so that it is more easily remembered. Often, they are less likely to spontaneously organize new information as a way to aid remembering it. A helpful tool could be the use of advance organizers that involve organizing information into categories, sequences, or relationships. Examples of advance organizers that human service workers might use during an educational program include providing handouts on a given topic, providing a written outline of what will be covered during a training session, or verbally giving an overview of the program's agenda.

Older adults also need more time to recall information once it is learned. When planning programs for this population, it is helpful to use a slower pace, incorporate their previous knowledge and experience when possible, focus on one task at a time, avoid time limits, and give lots of

positive feedback. In addition, repeating and rephrasing information during a learning session will enhance its retention. The use of mediators, which involves associating a word to be learned with some other word, image, or story, is another example of how to increase learning performance. Also, short breaks may be beneficial if the learning activity lasts more than thirty minutes (Sterns and Doverspike, 1987; Peterson, 1983).

The use of concrete examples and maintaining a clear focus may be helpful in individual/group counseling, discussion groups, and educational programs with older adults. This type of approach may decrease anxiety, enhance the understanding of the client, and assist in staying on topic. Older adults may benefit from learning to set goals and timelines, to use brainstorming techniques, and to address specific problems. There may be a tendency for the client to ramble and talk about a number of problems, so the human service worker will need to help the client stay focused for the best results.

Older persons' past experiences may block, modify, or enhance their participation in various kinds of programs. For instance, they may be reluctant to participate in government entitlement programs or social service programs because of their pride and belief that seeking help is a sign of weakness. They may not seek counseling because of a previously learned belief that they should be able to deal with their own problems independently or that "normal" people do not receive help. They may not participate in educational programs because they have the misperception that they are too old to learn. In learning situations, if they have been taught to do a task a certain way, it may take a great deal of time to unlearn the task and then to relearn to do it another way; or they may resist learning something that is contrary to what they had learned previously, thus making it difficult to integrate the new information (Harvey and Jahns, 1988).

Past experiences, however, also can make learning more meaningful. For example, sometimes it is easier to apply information to a new task if there is a way to relate to it. Likewise, past experience can provide a bridge for combining the old with the new, especially if the new knowledge now makes the old information more meaningful and useful (Sterns and Doverspike, 1987).

A desire to participate and learn is important for learning to take place at any age. Older adults may have an interest in learning but fear failing at the task, be anxious about participating, or believe that they are not able to learn new information. In mixed age groups, they may fear failing in the eyes of their peers or doing less well than younger participants. Human service workers will need to be aware of the potential reluctance of older clients to enroll in educational programs. To encourage participation, the human service worker may need to change the format of a program or help the clients work through the reasons they are hesitant to get involved.

Research has shown that age decrements in learning ability are affected by health, as defined by the presence of chronic disease such as coronary artery disease, arteriosclerosis, and hypertension. In addition to poor health, chronically ill people may be depressed, have low morale, and become tired more quickly than their healthy peers, which can impair their learning. Although knowledge can be empowering and can aid decision-making skills for most people, it is imperative for chronically ill people. Providing patient education can help people understand the physical and psychological aspects of their illness and may help them maintain independence and a sense of control over their lives. Human service workers will need to account for chronic conditions whenever they program activities, educational tasks, or other services for chronically ill older adults.

The physical setting where older adults receive services, educational programs, or come to participate in activities is important to consider when programming for this population. For a community-based group, the place should be located on a bus line, have parking close to the building, and be wheelchair accessible. In any setting, the room should be free from noise dis-

tractions. The noise level could hinder the learning process, since some older adults may not hear well or their attention may be drawn toward the noise rather than attending to what is being said. In addition, increased lighting is needed to compensate for potential visual problems and glares. Also, because of poor circulation, many older adults prefer a warm room with temperatures in the upper seventies.

Some equipment and teaching materials may need to be considered differently for older age groups. As people get older, certain colors such as dark green, blue, and violet become harder to see as the lenses of the eyes become yellow. However, red, yellow, and orange stay more vivid and, thus, become the preferred colors to use on flipcharts and printed material. It also helps to use large print, write legibly, and have a contrast between the paper and ink. If using film projectors, be aware that it takes a longer time for older adults to adapt to light and darkness. Thus, it will help to wait a short time to start a film after the lights have been dimmed. After a film, lighting should be restored slowly, and there should be a short interval before people get up and move around.

When working with older adults who live in nursing homes, the human service worker should address the psychosocial needs of the residents and help them feel empowered in their restricted environment. Also, it is important to avoid both labeling residents as patients and focusing on their illnesses. Residents need to have mental, physical, and social stimulation regardless of their mental status. They need to have individualized care plans that reflect their individual needs (medical and emotional), and they need to be treated with respect. It is important, too, for residents to have a sense of personal control, to make choices, to have privacy, to have a support network, and to participate in their care as much as possible. Although some residents are not alert to time and place, they still should be treated as adults, with dignity and respect.

Overall, human service workers help older clients in a number of different ways. They may provide educational programs or training sessions geared toward the needs of older learners. They may assist with retirement issues, adjustment to widowhood, or other issues related to the aging process. In addition, they may help older clients learn new skills, develop new hobbies, expand their interests, and learn how to empower themselves and enrich their lives.

JOB OPPORTUNITIES FOR HUMAN SERVICE WORKERS

As the population ages, more social services will be needed to meet the needs of older adults. Human service agencies will need to target more efforts toward rural and minority elderly. These two populations may need more assistance than the general older population but may be more reluctant to ask for help. Human service workers may have to do more home visits and learn about the older client's culture to establish a supportive, therapeutic relationship. It also may be helpful to become fluent in a second language, such as Spanish, to decrease the language barrier when working with minority clients (such as Latinos) who may still be struggling to learn English. Many programs will be aimed at helping people maintain their independence, in turn helping maintain or increase their self-image or self-esteem.

There is an increasing need for case management skills to plan and organize services and resources needed by many older adults to remain independent. This may involve coordinating and integrating a variety of services from different programs. For instance, a person may need low-cost housing, Meals-on-Wheels (a program that delivers hot meals to older adults in their homes or at a designated site), assistance with medication costs, transportation, and involvement in a social, therapeutic program to decrease loneliness, isolation, and depression.

Working with older adults can provide an enriching experience and an opportunity to learn from the wisdom and life experiences of the client. Human service workers who want to work with older adults can find employment in a variety of settings. For instance, they may want to work in a corporation and assist in providing training/retraining programs, wellness programs, or elder-care services. In a long-term-care facility (retirement center or nursing home), a human service worker may be employed as an activity director, social services director, coordinator of volunteers, admission coordinator, or marketing coordinator. There also are employment opportunities in senior citizen centers, adult day care programs, community multiservice centers, area agencies on aging, home care programs, respite programs, and organizations that provide advocacy services. In addition, human service workers may be involved in programs that provide training and education, counseling and group work, and crisis intervention or that help older clients access community resources such as housing, transportation, and financial assistance.

Human service workers who have an interest in working with older adults may find employment opportunities after completing a two-year associate's degree or a four-year baccalaureate degree. Some colleges also offer a gerontology certificate, which requires a student to take a certain number of courses in gerontology and complete a practicum in a setting with older adults. It will be beneficial for human service workers who work with older adults to understand the aging process (physical, psychological, and sociological aspects) and to know how to use specific techniques that enhance learning in later life. In addition, knowledge about cultural diversity, advocacy, and caregiver issues will be important.

The large number of baby boomers (those born between 1946 and 1964) have had a major effect on the trends of society through each of their developmental stages. As they get older, they will influence how older adults are viewed and what services will be available. Older adults are now healthier and wealthier and are apt to stay in the mainstream of society. It is likely they will demand more community and leisure services, receive more retirement education, have second and third careers, and require more health services. It is an exciting and challenging time to be working with older adults, and there should be ample employment opportunities for human service workers in a variety of settings.

REFERENCES

About Alzheimer's Disease (1985). South Deerfield, MA: Channing L. Bete Co.

American Association of Retired Persons (1987). *Workers 45+: Today and Tomorrow*. Washington, DC: American Association of Retired Persons.

Butler, R. N. (1975). *Why Survive? Being Old in America*. New York: Harper and Row.

Doering, M., S. Rhodes, and M. Schuster (1983). *The Aging Worker: Research and Recommendations*. Oklahoma City, OK: Sage.

Frengley, J. D. (1987). "Depression." *Generations, 12* (1), 29–33.

Gelfand, D., and B. W. K. Yee (1991). "Trends and Forces: Influence of Immigration, Migration, and Acculturation on the Fabric of Aging in America." *Generations, 15*(4), 7–10.

Harvey, R. L., and I. R. Jahns (1988). "Using Advance Organizers to Facilitate Learning among Older Adults." *Educational Gerontology, 14*, 89–93.

Hayslip, B. Jr., and K. J. Kennelly (1985). "Cognitive and Noncognitive Factors Affecting Learning among Older Adults." In B. Lumsden, ed., *The Older Adult as Learner* (pp. 73–98). New York: Hemisphere.

Hess, B. B. (1990). "Gender and Aging: The Demographic Parameters." *Generations, 14*(3), 12–15.

Huyck, M. H., and J. J. Hoyer (1982). *Adult Development and Aging*. Madison, WI: Wm. C. Brown.

Katz, P. R., and J. Karuza (1992). "Service Delivery in an Aging Population: Implications for the Future." *Generations, 16*(4), 49–54.

Lowy, L., and D. O'Connor (1986). *Why Education in the Later Years?* New York: Macmillan.

Peterson, D.A. (1983). *Facilitating Education for Older Learners*. San Francisco: Jossey-Bass.

Peterson, D., and S. Coberly (1988). "The Older Worker: Myths and Realities." In R. Morris and S. A. Bass, eds., *Retirement Reconsidered: Economic and Social Roles for Older People*. (pp. 116–128). New York: Springer.

Redmond, R. X. (1986). "The Training Needs of Older Workers." *Vocational Education Journal, 61,* 38–40.

Sterns, H. L., and D. Doverspike (1987). "Training and Developing the Older Worker: Implications for Human Resource Management." In H. Dennis, ed., *Fourteen Steps in Managing an Aging Workforce*. pp. 97–109. New York: Lexington.

United States Senate Special Committee on Aging (1991). *Developments in Aging: 1990 Volume 1* (Rept. 102–28, Vol. 1), Washington, DC: U.S. Government Printing Office.

Yee, B. W. K. (1990). "Gender and Family Issues in Minority Groups." *Generations, 14*(3), 39–42.

CHAPTER 17

HUMAN SERVICES AND CRIMINAL JUSTICE:
PEOPLE AND THE SYSTEM

DAVID C. WHELAN

The criminal justice system continues to be a growing job market during the early years of the twenty-first century. Crime is big business for both the public and the private sector, since there are so many cooperative ventures, interchangeable programs, and a large number of potential clients. Police departments across the country are converting to community policing alternatives to replace traditional policing efforts. The courts are expanding in the areas of probation and intermediate sanction alternatives, and the correctional component remains pressured to rehabilitate and reintegrate its clientele. Where does the human service professional fit into this mix?

For decades, the criminal justice system has been recruiting, selecting, and training people with a traditional criminal justice education or any closely related social science major. The diverse needs of police, courts, and corrections have changed the focus of entry-level positions. It is no secret that the criminal justice system is affected by social, economic, psychological, and political forces. The human service professional is educated in a comprehensive area that is certainly suited for work in criminal justice.

This chapter outlines three components of the criminal justice system, the different client populations surrounding those components, and the potential for human service students to work with those people within the system.

POLICE

Policing has changed over the past three decades. The bulk of police research, done in the 1960s and 1970s, has allowed police departments to utilize new community policing concepts. Studies on the role of police officers in the community, limits of preventive patrol, police response time to crime scenes, and alternative patrol management strategies have changed the scope of modern policing. Police management has finally put into practice the theory they were aware of all along: that to be successful in fighting crime, the police need the community, and the community needs the police.

What this means for individual police officers is that they must interact with members of the public at different levels now as compared to past years. Several community policing initiatives have put police officers directly into the eye of different neighborhoods on bicycles, in strip-mall substations, in schools, and on foot patrol. Community policing is designed to ensure that police officers are not isolated from the communities they serve.

Another approach, often synonymous with community policing, is problem-solving policing. Typically coordinated with crime analysis data, this strategy asks police officers to converge on problems that cause particular types of criminal activity. Police are then asked to work with all the constituencies available to them to solve the problem at hand, including public and private social service agencies, business owners, and local citizens. It is hoped that the police and the various components of the community can work together to find solutions to the problem, and thereby reduce criminal activity. Police officers are asked to become active participants in the process of solving root problems. The traditional police officer who sees him- or herself solely as a crimefighter does not fit easily into a department of the twenty-first century.

Community- and problem-oriented policing is a natural choice for the human service professional who desires a career in police service. Since almost all police departments do not have extensive numbers of civilians working within the department, other than in communications and records, the only work available is in the rank and file. The community-at-large offers the police officer a wide variety of populations to deal with. In addition to violent and property criminals, police deal with gangs, drug users, prostitutes, the mentally ill and challenged, the alcohol abuser, homeless, and juvenile issues. Policing provides a full range of human service clients and problems with the additional responsibility of enforcing laws and maintaining social order.

There has been a long debate over whether police officers should have a college education. The President's Commission on Law Enforcement (1968) encouraged, "The ultimate aim of all police departments should be that all personnel with general enforcement powers have baccalaureate degrees" (p. 27). Advocates argue that a degree gives police officers the necessary experience and knowledge to work in a diverse, multicultural environment. Detractors cite the fact that a college requirement limits the potential pool of applicants and could potentially be discriminatory. Sherman (1978) stated that "there is no conclusive evidence that officers with college degrees perform more effectively than those without degrees." There has been no evidence to the contrary since Sherman's statement almost two decades ago. Although only a small proportion of police depart-

ments require college for employment, most agencies have educational support policies and provide incentives or benefits for recruits and officers with some college (Alpert and Dunham, 1997).

The most important aspect of this argument is the fact that a college education can only strengthen the potential performance level of the police officer. In a community- or problem-oriented police environment, education would logically reinforce training and background. Equally as important for the human service graduate, there is no conclusive evidence that *any particular type of bachelor's degree* is more valuable than any other when entering police work or performing in the field. The role of education is to ensure that police officers are informed decision makers who base their actions on a logical interpretation of facts and application of diverse knowledge (Radelet and Carter, 1994). Clearly, there remains a consensus that higher education of any type, including human services, augments the value of police work.

COURTS AND CORRECTIONS

These two components of the criminal justice system are closely related in terms of administration, employment, and volunteer opportunities for human service professionals. There are employment options at the local, state, and federal levels for court officers, investigators, probation officers, and parole officers. There are also a number of jobs that do not require enforcement or supervision responsibilities, performed by "civilians."

Courts

As a civilian, an individual can work in both paid and volunteer positions. There are divisions within the court that people can work in, depending on their area of interest or specialization. Most local or county courts are broken down into three basic divisions: criminal, civil, and family. Each court may have one or more programs in which civilians can become involved, that require both extensive interviews and training. In most cases, the training programs are run directly by the courts, but there may be a few programs where civilians are required to be trained by the state.

For example, in Camden County, New Jersey, there are a number of alternatives within the criminal court. The programs in this court vary, depending on the type of offense and the type of offender. There is a "drug court" program, a criminal case management program, and a "volunteers in probation" program, all housed within the criminal court. Drug courts have been established to selectively process felony drug cases, thereby reducing crowded felony dockets and case-processing time and providing a mechanism for more creative and effective dispositions.

Another example is the child placement review program, run by the family court, for children who have been abused or are in foster care. The children in this program may be there voluntarily or by court order. There are five child placement review "boards" per county, each with five to seven members. The panel meets approximately two times per month to review a certain number of cases and make recommendations to the court as to what should be done with the juveniles in question. Decisions are made solely on behalf of the court.

Court-appointed special advocates (CASA) are similar to child placement review board members in that both are under the auspices of the family court and represent children who are abused or in foster care. They are different in that all CASA interviews are done on-site—that is, in the family's home or residential housing. Reports are then submitted to the court on behalf of the child with CASA suggestions as to what should be done.

Defining what type of client one wants to deal with and getting the proper education, training, and background is of utmost importance in the courts. Giving time, whether in volunteer or paid position, remains a paramount consideration in this type of work, especially with juveniles. Most juveniles in the court system feel as if they have been let down

by someone in their lives, and they need to know that there is someone they can trust. If an individual is going to enter this field, he or she must know that time and trust mean everything. Juveniles, above all, need to know they have a safety net, and court personnel are that safety net.

Corrections

With the advent of community-based corrections, or intermediate sanctions, a variety of challenges have opened up for human service professionals at both the institutional and the vendor level. Although reintegration of the offender into the community remains the paramount theory driving community-based corrections, realistically these programs are also needed to resolve problems of excessive caseloads and overcrowded facilities.

Intermediate sanctions can be administered by the judiciary, probation departments, or correctional departments. Several examples of community-based corrections options follow:

Diversion Programs. The usual objectives of any diversion program are to try to change the offender while serving both the victim and the community and to remove offenders from the system (e.g., alcohol detoxification centers and family crisis intervention units for domestic violence).

Pretrial Release Programs. These are alternatives to the incarceration of accused offenders who are awaiting prosecution and who may not qualify for diversion (e.g., court intervention units and day reporting).

Probation. A sentencing alternative or sanction, probation is designed to keep offenders in the community under supervision. Treatment resources would be available under the many probation variations.

Fines, Fees, Restitution, and Community Service. These are primarily economic sanctions, used for diverse reasons in different types of cases.

Alternative Sanctions.   This form of intermediate sanction includes intensive supervision programs, boot camps, home confinement and electronic monitoring, and day reporting centers.

Halfway Houses.   Residential centers, or halfway houses, are designed to help former offenders make the transition from incarceration to productive membership in the community in supportive surroundings.

Parole.   Under this option, offenders are released from correctional institutions prior to the conclusion of their sentence. The parolee remains under supervision and must abide by conditions of release.

Related Services.   These services usually focus on fostering reintegration skills, including job readiness training, vocational training, and job development and placement.

There are separate programs for juveniles, including juvenile diversion, community alternatives to detention, probation, residential programs, and aftercare.

CONCLUSION

For community policing, court programs, and community-based corrections to be effective, the people who work within the system must be able to understand the particular problems, goals, and plans of each component. Unlike police work, most jobs in the courts and corrections, except the position of correctional officer, require a college degree. Human service students in the twenty-first century will find unlimited possibilities in the criminal justice system. Not only will there be significant turnovers through attrition, but strategies to reduce crime cannot, and will not, eliminate it completely.

REFERENCES

Alpert, G., and R. Dunham (1997). *Policing Urban America*. Prospect Heights, IL: Waveland Press.

President's Commission on Law Enforcement and Administration of Justice (1968). *The Challenge of Crime in a Free Society*. New York: Avon Books.

Radelet, L., and D. Carter (1994). *The Police and the Community*. New York: Macmillan.

Sherman, Lawrence W. (1978). *The Quality of Police Education*. San Francisco: Jossey-Bass.

SUGGESTED FURTHER READING

Champion, D. J. (1998). *Corrections in the United States: A Contemporary Perspective*. Upper Saddle River, NJ: Prentice-Hall.

McCarthy, B. R., and B. J. McCarthy, Jr. (1997). *Community-Based Corrections*. Belmont, CA: Wadsworth Publishing.

Silverman, I., and M. Vega (1996). *Corrections: A Comprehensive View*. St. Paul, MN: West.

ARCHITECTURE FOR JUSTICE:
DIRECT SUPERVISION MANAGEMENT

ANTHONY W. PELLICANE

In recent decades, a new development has taken place in the history of penology, one that is considered by some to be the first major prison innovation since the late eighteenth century.

Direct Supervision Management (DSM) is both a penal and architectural approach to the burgeoning population of the nation's jails. In practical use for fifteen years, Direct Supervision Management has been shown to increase effective control of inmates, increase staff efficiency, alleviate overcrowding, and reduce overall costs. The basic concept behind DSM is that through the design of the cell cluster (pod) and the management techniques of the corrections officers, inmates are dealt with in a pro-active manner, defusing potentially violent situations, as opposed to the traditional method of reacting to crises and disturbances after they occur.

The architectural design of a direct supervision facility differs from a traditional linear-oriented jail in several areas. The direct supervision facility incorporates a humane, barrier-free design into a podular structure that contains cells for 64 or more inmates as well as recreational and dining facilities. By having these services in each pod, movement of the inmates throughout the jail is drastically reduced, thereby eliminating one of the primary causes of disturbances. The tiered podular arrangement affords the corrections officer easy surveillance of the entire structure. This line-of-sight capability, not achieved in any other jail design, allows the officer to prevent problems,

effectively manage the inmates, and keep order. Due to the open design of the DSM pod, costly steel bars and doors, electronic locking systems, and stainless steel fixtures are eliminated, thus reducing construction costs. "Soft," commercial-grade furnishings enhance the comfort level of the pod and are less expensive than "hard," maximum-security products.

Essentially, there are three types of jails in the United States: linear indirect supervision, podular remote supervision, and podular direct supervision. Linear jails, those with long corridors of electronically locked cells, are the oldest; they afford corrections officers poor line-of-sight and require the extensive movement of inmates to and from their daily routines. Podular remote jails improve the line-of-sight of the officers; however, the officers are located in a remote operating station and do not interact with the inmates. Podular direct supervision jails locate a corrections officer inside the pod along with the inmates in order to supervise and manage the inmates.

The Direct Supervision Management approach is based on several key principles: effective control, effective supervision, competent staff, safety of staff and inmates, manageable and cost effective operations, and accurate classification. In a direct supervision environment, the corrections officer must understand human behavior and be able to control any situation that may arise. With well-trained staff people, potential difficulties within the pod can be prevented.

Initial classification of inmates is extremely important prior to placing them in a direct supervision atmosphere. Implicit in the understanding of effective control is the fundamental precept that some inmates (approximately 10 to 15 percent) will require maximum security. It is a fundamental precondition that inmates who exhibit violent tendencies, have serious behavioral difficulties, or have emotional or psychiatric problems be housed in maximum security areas. The objective is to house as few of the population as possible in these expensive units without compromising the principle that only compliant inmates are permitted to be housed in direct supervision housing units.

Throughout the country, overcrowding in jails has become endemic. Most notably, the jail population has exploded with drug-related and drunk-driver inmates who are either awaiting trial or sentenced and serving their time. With a great amount of backup in the county jails, a cost-efficient, staff-efficient solution is needed. With a 64-to-1 inmate to staff ratio and the option to double bunk if necessary, a direct supervision podular design can increase the capacity of existing institutions or can be used to create new, economically viable alternative institutions. This 64-to-1 ratio is currently used in the Federal Prison System and other direct supervision facilities.

The diminished need for vandal-proof and security-type furnishings, fixtures, and finishes throughout most of the facility lowers construction costs significantly. Over the past fifteen years, administrators have developed a knowledge base regarding the performance of commercial grade material in direct supervision facilities, and can select less costly alternatives to the security components without concern that future replacement costs will cancel out cost savings. The difference in cost is dramatic: building and furnishing a direct supervision facility may cost one-half as much as a traditional jail.

It is widely accepted that construction of a jail is 30 percent of the total cost of running the facility, while personnel garner the other 70 percent in expenditures. By its design, a direct supervision facility requires fewer personnel, due to the increased inmate-to-staff ratio and the reduction in inmate movement throughout the institution. By providing a self-contained housing block and well-trained staff in direct contact with the population, efficient use of personnel is maximized.

KEY TERMS FOR PART FOUR

After studying Chapters 13, 14, 15, 16, and 17, you should have a command of the following key terms, major concepts, and principal topical references:

cycle of abuse
societal denial
domestic violence
"graying of America"
Alzheimer's disease
Age Discrimination in
  Employment Act
gerontology
American Association of
  Retired Persons (AARP)

AIDS/PWAs
HIV-1, HIV-2
Centers for Disease
  Control
eviction prevention
  services
shelter
self-help
substance-related
  disorders

countertransference
A. A. & N. (narcotics) A.
DSM-IV
Project for Addictions
  Counselor Training
  (PACT)
International Certification
  Reciprocity Consortium
NAADAC

PIVOTAL ISSUES FOR DISCUSSION OF PART FOUR

1. Make a series of lists of special consumer (client) populations in human services. Organize the lists by major demographic variables (i.e., age, gender, ethnicity, race, level of intellectual functioning, mental status, employment, income, number in family, physical condition, amount of education, criminal background). How and where are these consumers served? By whom? What are their special issues in receiving and responding to help?

2. What is the relationship between drug and alcohol abuse and domestic violence? How does spousal abuse, in some cases, continue to be perpetuated in second or third primary relationships involving the same woman? What can be done to help such a person?

3. Visit an NA meeting. Visit an AA or ALANON meeting. What were your impressions, feelings, and reactions to what you observed? Are there similar resources on your campus? If not, what can you do to initiate the organization of a similar group for students on campus?

SUGGESTED READINGS FOR PART FOUR

1. Lamb, H. R. (1984). *The Homeless Mentally Ill*. Washington, DC: American Psychiatric Association.

2. Hope, M., and J. Young (1986). *The Faces of Homelessness*. Lexington, MA: Lexington Books.

3. Kozol, J. (1988). *Rachel and Her Children*: *Homeless Families in America*. New York: Crown.

4. Estes, C. L. (1979). *The Aging Enterprise*: *A Critical Examination of Social Policies and Services for the Aged*. San Francisco: Jossey-Bass.

5. Hilts, P. J. (1991). "AIDS Panel Backs Efforts to Exchange Drug Users' Needles." *The New York Times,* August 7, p. A1.

PART FIVE

CHANGING THE SYSTEM(S) IN HUMAN SERVICES

Part Five explores the ways in which the human service profession is affected by the political process, advocacy, prevention, community organizing, and the legal system.

As a human service professional, you will find yourself challenged with daily demands and seemingly insurmountable problems on the job. Despite these challenges, it is essential to save time and energy for a large overriding issue: the social context of human service problems and solutions. Frequently, securing public support through legislation and money for programs is the major first step needed to solve a problem. The chapters in Part Five deal with various aspects of obtaining public commitment to help with solving a problem or preventing its occurrence.

Harold McPheeters, in Chapter 18, discusses the roles of public policy and the political process in human services. Dr. McPheeters outlines ways to get your concern into the political spotlight. There are several avenues of involvement and influence. It may be necessary, for example, to lobby regulatory bodies or launch a media campaign. Additionally, many methods of political involvement are available, from voter registration drives to coalition building, that can influence who becomes the elected official and/or what that elected official represents.

Lee Stuart, in Chapter 19, discusses community organizing as a means of bringing about change and solving problems. He compares several different approaches that can be used to effect social change. A major focus of the chapter is the model of the Industrial Areas Foundation (IAF) based on the work of Saul Alinsky, which has implemented successful projects throughout the country and abroad for more than fifty years. The important principles used by the IAF network are explained, including the role of tension, power, leadership, and money. The author provides examples of four successful community organizing actions, explaining how each group used its power to achieve the desired results. Community organizing is one way that people can voluntarily participate in a process that can lead to change and thus improve their own lives.

In Chapter 20, Joseph Mehr deals with an important direction for human service programs: the shift in mental health service delivery from institutional care to community-based mental health programs. The author discusses how policy makers in the legislature and bureaucratic organizations influence the distribution of funding for delivery systems and how these processes affect training and education of human service workers. In this chapter, you will learn about a variety of new approaches to treatment programming and case management and gain a better appreciation of these dynamic systems of influence.

Christine Lewis Shane, in Chapter 21, discusses the impact of advocacy and legislation on people with disabilities. The author traces the history of social attitudes and legislation involving persons with disabilities, conveying the significance of the Americans with Disabilities Act and such terms as "reasonable accommodations." People with disabilities have been helped by political activism and advocacy. You will see how the issues of discrimination and civil rights, along with pressure from millions of disabled persons and their families, have been instrumental in bringing about legislative successes for the disabled.

Part Six provides you with basic reviews of legal foundations in the field of human services and some of the more important issues you will encounter as a professional human service worker as you are guided by ethical standards and lawful responsibilities. Practical advice is offered for career success and survival against "burnout" in the field. The final section, Part Seven, will introduce you to some of the more relevant trends emerging in human services including computer technology, cultural diversity, and service-learning. This section will also present the special role of research in human services and the more popular types of designs used specifically for the uniqueness of this field of study.

LEARNING OBJECTIVES FOR PART FIVE:
CHANGING THE SYSTEM(S) IN HUMAN SERVICES

After reading and studying Chapters 18, 19, 20, and 21,

— You will understand how social change can be brought about through the political and legislative systems.
— You will know how to use local, state, and federal contacts to gather information about social issues and to identify resources available for dealing with these issues.
— You will understand the concept of advocacy as it applies to the work of the human service professional.
— You will become familiar with the concept and practice of prevention in human services.
— You will learn about the trend toward service delivery in community-based settings.
— You will be able to describe the contemporary models of delivering services to those needing mental health care and the implications of recent changes in the focus of these programs.
— You will become familiar with the Americans with Disabilities Act of 1990 and its impact on human service clients.
— You will become aware of community organizing and understand its potential for empowerment and systemic change.

CHAPTER 18

POLICY, POLITICS, AND HUMAN SERVICES:
AN ADDRESS GIVEN TO MEMBERS OF THE NATIONAL ORGANIZATION FOR HUMAN SERVICE EDUCATION, ON OCTOBER 9, 1992

HAROLD L. McPHEETERS

I wish to begin with a few words of special appreciation for Dr. Ron Feinstein of your organization. Dr. Feinstein was one of the pioneers of the human service education movement. I have been privileged to have been with him in perhaps two dozen meetings as we forged some of the concepts and directions for the movement. I always found him to be knowledgeable, critical, analytic, and positively involved. It was a pleasure to have known him and worked with him, but I especially want to mention his leadership here because he was one of our most active human service educators in the area of public policy development and political action. A few months ago he died from a heart affliction while in the office of a Pennsylvania state senator on such a mission. We shall miss him.

In modern times the primary sanction and funding for both human service delivery programs and human service educational programs is government. The days when churches or private charitable organizations provided the major impetus for health and welfare services and funding have long receded despite some nostalgic urgings that somehow a "thousand points of light" might assume this responsibility. There are still many private and charitable groups involved in human service delivery, but most of them receive both their sanction and much of their funding from federal, state, or county governments. By *sanction,* I mean their charters and licenses for the programs and their staffs, required standards of operation, tax exemption, liability, and often public oversight. Funding may be provided through direct government grants or contracts or the fees from programs such as Medicaid and Medicare. Virtually all human service educational programs are located either in public institutions or in institutions that receive much of their funding from government sources.

Thus, for self-interest alone, human service educators must be involved in public policy and politics related to human services. In addition, human service educators, with their depth of understanding of human service needs and programs, should be involved in helping key government officials make better policy decisions for the human services. It is sometimes sad to see educators from the human service education programs turn away from involvement in policy development and politics or, worse yet, to constantly criticize and express contempt for public officials and politicians. Such an attitude helps no one, least of all one's own program and its graduates. Many of the most effective human service educators are active in public policy developments and find that their programs and graduates are more frequently requested and better regarded as a consequence.

The two areas of public policy and politics are closely related.

Public policy development is the process of helping national, state, and local governments and professional and voluntary associations decide what laws, regulations, programs, philosophies, and values are to be implemented and how. It also involves deciding how to obtain the funds and other necessary resources for the programs.

Politics is the process of nominating and electing officials to legislative and top executive positions in local, state, and federal governments (and sometimes judges) and drafting and enacting legislation to implement major policy directions.

PUBLIC POLICY

It is generally in the area of public policy development that human service professionals can have their greatest impact, but it is also the area in which they are least involved—at least as organized groups. This is probably because public policy development is not as well defined or as well publicized as politics. In fact, many times elected and appointed officials of government seem to have no particular interest in policy development—they have no vision of where they want their agency to be or how to get there. This is no different from private corporations or voluntary organizations that have no policy or planning mechanism for the future but simply keep on doing what they have always done despite changing times and needs.

There seem to be cycles in our society when we expect our institutions to behave in progressive and purposeful ways, while at other times in the cycle there is a trend to be preoccupied with the immediate bottom line. Such conservative thinking discourages policy development and planning; planning staff and research and development personnel are let go as "unnecessary middle-level managers." The disadvantages soon become evident, and then the cycle changes. As a nation we have been through a twelve-year cycle of conservatism, but now the tide appears to be turning. Unfortunately, the excesses of the recent past have left huge deficits and debts that will impede our nation and our institutions for some time to come.

But that is all the more reason for careful policy development, and it is likely that we shall see much more of it in the future. However, governments and all our agencies and institutions, primarily as a result of litigation and court orders, have recently begun to establish mechanisms for more sharply defining their policies and procedures, and those mechanisms provide the route for our inputs into the policy-making process. Among them are the following:

1. *Regulation writing.* Legislation is generally very broad in scope and leaves to the operating agencies the responsibility for developing the necessary policies, procedures, regulations, and so on. This is the process called "administrative law." Thirty years ago, this was likely to be a haphazard process that too frequently was never formally done or committed to writing. However, as a result of lawsuits from clients, families, staff, and so on, governments have instituted a whole set of legally mandated procedures for "administrative rule making." The procedures almost always provide for public hearings and comments and suggestions from interested individuals and organizations. This is where the inputs of human service educators should be made through the following steps:

   a. Learn the legal requirements and procedures of the administrative rule-making process for the relevant units of government and get on their mailing lists to receive notices of public hearings, dates, names of responsible official persons to receive comments, and so on for the writing of specific regulations.

b. Participate in public hearings. This may require making appointments to appear on the program and preparing written statements for the hearings. It is generally desirable to participate in hearings as an organization rather than as an individual, but either is generally acceptable. Presentations at hearings should be documented as much as possible and be cognizant of the realities of budgets, geographic realities, and so on facing the agency.

c. Send in written comments to preliminary drafts of regulations if one is unable to be present at the hearing. This is an entirely acceptable forum for letters from individuals. It is always best to make specific and well-documented suggestions rather than simple statements that the drafts are unacceptable or one-sided statements with no documentation or with biased documentation.

2. *Advisory Bodies to Public and Voluntary Agencies.* At still another level, public and voluntary agencies increasingly make use of citizen boards, advisory groups, and private consultants. Human service educators should be represented on such citizen bodies. Their organizations should take the initiative to suggest names of their members who will serve on those bodies, especially at the national and state levels, but there is nothing wrong with the educators suggesting their own names and their willingness to serve, especially to local agencies. Here, too, the persons who serve in such capacities should expect to represent the best interests of the total agency but also speak to the interests of the human service profession and its educational programs. This implies that the person becomes knowledgeable about the broadest issues affecting the agency and its operations.

3. *Special Task Groups and Studies.* Public and voluntary agencies and legislative research bodies frequently find themselves faced with the need for special studies of problems and the development of recommendations for addressing them. These special studies range from clinical issues such as how to best manage the problems of AIDS patients in the prisons or mental hospitals to organizational issues, such as how to best relate the state institutions organizationally and financially to local public and voluntary programs. Here again, human service educators should be represented on at least some of these citizen study bodies or as consultants to them.

4. *Networking with Other Organizations.* Many professional and advocacy organizations are also interested in public policy and will be using some of these same strategies to influence it. Human service educators should join with them. Most educators come from one of the traditional professions of social work, psychology, counseling, and so on. Join those professional organizations as well as advocacy organizations, such as mental health associations, associations for retarded citizens, and public welfare associations, and become active in their affairs so that you multiply your impact on the public policy process.

5. *Participation in Media Activities.* Another way of participating in the public policy debate, especially at the local level, is to take part in media activities, such as writing letters to editors, writing special articles for newspapers and magazines, and appearing on media panels and radio talk shows. These activities require some special talent at being brief and to-the-point with a special sensitivity to the perspective of the general public.

6. *Inviting Agency Officials and Policy Makers to Participate in Your Programs.* Many human service educators have found it useful to invite key persons from human service agencies and local policy makers to participate in their educational programs as speakers, panelists, or advisory committee members. In that way they come to know you and your program, so that they are likely to call on you when they face policy questions that they feel you may be able to answer. In any case, such persons should be invited to participate in such activities and kept on the mailing list to receive reports, newsletters, and so on from your program.

POLITICS

Participation in the political process is a more directed, promotional, and often adversarial process of working for the election of specific candidates or the enactment of specific pieces of legislation by the legislative body and then getting the responsible executive officer to sign the legislation. This process is better known, and it is the one that human service educators are more likely to use. However, because of the nature of the democratic process of our governments, it is also one in which there is a strong possibility of being on the losing side. This may be no problem unless it means that your candidate and all that he or she stands for is defeated and everyone in a responsible position is replaced.

The processes of working for the election of candidates and working for legislation are somewhat different although related. It should be clear to human service educators, as it is to members of Political Action Committees (PACs), that an elected official is much more likely to be responsive to someone who has worked actively in the election campaign than to a complete stranger.

How to Elect Candidates Supportive of Human Services

The general process of electing candidates to office is familiar to each of you, but there are a few specific pointers to keep in mind.

Register and Vote. This seems obvious, but it is astounding that so few eligible voters bother to get themselves registered or vote, and I am regularly surprised to discover that some of those nonvoters are persons who have very significant stakes in the election. In most jurisdictions it is better to register in a specific political party rather than as an independent. In many places "independents" are not allowed to vote in primary elections, where some of the most critical decisions are made.

Learn About the Candidates and Help Them Take Stands on Issues. Meet the candidates or learn about them and their positions on human service issues. At local and state levels it is not difficult to attend programs and events where the candidates are in attendance and discuss human service issues with them. At congressional and presidential levels this becomes more difficult

and is best done through established organizations. If it is not possible to reach the candidates themselves, talk with their campaign staff persons, but the most effective personal contacts will be made before the heat of campaigning consumes all the candidate's time. Send letters to candidates and ask for their response and commitments. Most candidates are eager to reply to such letters of concern.

Make Financial Contributions to Candidates and Parties. Political campaigns cost money, and many a campaign has been lost because money ran out too soon. This has been a special problem for women candidates. The political parties do not provide much financial support for candidates until the later stages of the campaign. At the early stages, especially at the level of the primaries, the candidates are on their own to finance their campaigns, and it is at this stage that individual contributions are especially welcomed. It is at this stage that candidates learn whether there is real *public* interest in their candidacies or whether it is just the special interests. Such early contributions are especially likely to be remembered.

EMILY's (Early Money Is Like Yeast) List is an organized effort to help with the early financing of the campaigns of Democratic women who support free choice, but the individual supporters from EMILY's List are sure to be remembered.

The two major sources of funds for political campaigns are (1) individual contributions and (2) contributions from PACS or private organizations with vested interests in the outcome of the election. Later contributions to political campaigns are important, be they from individuals or organizations, but they are likely to be more substantial and memorable when they come from groups that can pool their contributions as PACS do. Be careful not to violate the ethics rules for political contributions. Do not make large contributions in cash; use a check and note that it is a campaign contribution.

Join Political Parties and Work in Campaigns.
Join the political parties and work in the campaigns to reach the candidates with your suggestions and influence. It will help the candidate's campaign to have your organizational work and moral support. Organizational work is frequently crucial to a campaign, especially for a lesser-known candidate. When you work in their campaigns, the candidates get to know you as an individual and are likely to respect your opinions when and if they are elected. This can also be a useful way to get to know some of the other campaign workers who may later become the staff workers for the official if the campaign is successful.

How to Influence Legislation

Influencing legislation is tricky business. It has been said that the public is better off not to see how sausage is made or how bills become laws. There are many considerations.

Learn the Legislative Procedures. Learn the legislative procedures for how bills may be introduced and by which house, how they are referred to committees, which kinds of bills go to which committees, how they are likely to be amended, how they pass from house to house, and how they go to the executive officer for signature or veto. The procedures vary from place to place and even from time to time. To a considerable extent they depend on unwritten customs and temporary political alliances. Learn about these!

Keep Informed of All Bills of Interest. Keep on top of bills introduced in your legislative body and get copies of the ones relevant to your interests. There is almost always some kind of published daily record of the bills that have been introduced, to which committees they have been assigned, and their progress through the legislative session. Arrange to subscribe to this legislative journal or examine it regularly in a library that subscribes to it. It is not unusual to find bills that either conflict with ones that you are following or duplicate all or parts of them. Copies of bills are usually available the day following their introduction.

It is also important to keep aware of any amendments made in any of the bills that interest you. Opposition groups may have succeeded in totally reversing the intent of your bill or amending it with completely unacceptable changes. In the political process anything can happen! There is no widely published account of such amendments. It is vital to check with key committee members or staff persons (if there are staff persons).

Attend and Participate in Committee Hearings.
Committee hearings are usually short of time to consider all persons and groups who desire to be heard, so appointments may be required. Also, be brief and to the point with documentation whenever possible. Have your statement written and duplicated for handout. Be aware of the broad implications of your testimony (e.g., its cost implications, its impact on rural areas or minority groups) and be prepared for any kind of question or criticism. It is well to anticipate organized opposition and acknowledge it and any efforts that have been made to work out conflicts. Legislators take a dim view of proposals that draw opposition where there has been no indication of efforts of the opposing parties to negotiate their differences. Such bills very likely will be tabled until the next session when they will have to be reintroduced.

If you cannot arrange to participate in the hearings, try to get a written statement to the committee for its consideration. If the statement comes from an organized group that has documented support from relevant organizations (e.g., public agency administrators, health insurers), so much the better. It is better to get these statements to members of the specific committees that are considering the bills rather than to your personal representative or senator, but send your own representative an informational copy. And be timely with such statements! Be aware of the committee's schedule for when a vote is likely to be taken, and get statements to them ahead of that time.

Personal calls to committee members are also helpful, especially if they include the logic and reasoning for your position rather than just a message to vote for or against a specific bill. Formal petitions and messages that urge votes for one side or the other are tabulated but play little role in the committee's decision.

Contact Your Personal Legislators.   Your personal legislator should know what you want done, from either personal contacts or letters or telephone calls. The greater the number of legislators who are approached by different members of a group with a common interest, the better, especially when it comes to the vote, if and when the bill comes to the floor for a full vote. Your personal legislator may be willing and able to negotiate with members of the committee that is considering your bill while the bill is in committee. Be aware, however, that the issue should then probably have to be one with considerable political importance to justify your legislator's using his or her political capital.

Bills are introduced by individual legislators, but it is usually wise to carefully choose which legislator will make the introduction—usually one with some tenure and reputation for expertise in the area of the bill's concern. It is necessary to meet with that legislator and present your proposal and follow the legislator's advice. Keep in mind that bills introduced early in the session have a much better chance of passage than those introduced later.

Model bills will probably have to be rewritten to fit the state or local government's format. Most states have a bill-drafting unit to do that, but they require time to do this, so the initial contacts for a new bill should be made *well* ahead of the legislative session. It will definitely help to contact additional legislators who are willing to sign the bill as cosponsors. This shows wider interest.

Build Coalitions with Other Groups.   In the political process it is most important to build coalitions with other interest groups (e.g., other professional groups, public agencies, voluntary agencies), so that they support your bills while you support theirs. Remember, the political process is a democratic process that requires a majority vote. It is most difficult for an isolated group to generate that much clout. This also means that you must be willing and able to negotiate and compromise—sometimes on very short notice. But remain alert to the implications of your negotiations and compromises. Be especially careful of wording. A careless word or phrase can completely change the meaning of your bill!

Working with other groups in the political process will also give you a broader perspective on the community's or the state's problems and needs and the concerns of the legislators in addressing them. Legislators appreciate the advice of lobbying groups with broad perspectives because they see so many narrow interest groups who are oblivious to the broader concerns of the society. I recently heard a state legislator say that the most credible lobby group he sees is the medical society because it is prepared to discuss everything from public health and clinical treatment issues (e.g., AIDS, mental health commitment laws) to rehabilitation, licensure of various health professionals, organizational and financial issues such as Medicaid fees, health insurance for state employees, workers' compensation, and managed care organizations.

Be Prepared to Try Again Next Session.   Be prepared for your bill to die in committee, fail to pass both houses, or be vetoed. Most state legislatures have between 3,500 and 4,000 bills introduced each session, but only a few hundred, at most, pass and become signed into law. Many of those bills that succeed have been around for several previous sessions. Their sponsors have persisted and compromised and honed their political skills by developing coalitions, strengthening public support, and meeting with additional legislators. Representative democracy is a great concept, but it is frequently not a tidy or efficient process. However, it works in its own fashion, and it is important that you be there!

CHAPTER 19

COMMUNITY ORGANIZING AS HUMAN SERVICE

LEE STUART

Community organizing has a different emphasis from traditional human services, although it starts in the same place; namely, with a desire to create a just society where the dignity of people is upheld, where people may grow and develop to their full potential, and where people participate fully in the basic economic, social, and political structures of their society. Traditional human services usually (though not always) focus on a particular problem or set of problems presented by an individual or perhaps a family. In contrast, community organizing focuses first on building relationships among people and institutions in a community and then on particular issues of importance determined by these people and their institutions. The issue is not personal but collective and is not internal to the participants but external.

The purpose of traditional human services is to help people meet their needs, gain access to services, and develop autonomy. The purpose of community organizing is to build power for people and institutions who are usually "voiceless" in the dominant economic, social, and political structures. Through community organizing, power is created to allow participation in the public decisions that determine the community's fate. This participation is as an organized presence—people with real power—in contrast to participation as clients, victims, or individuals up against "the system."

The job of the human service professional is to be broker, advocate, or service provider for the client so that the client receives the services to which he or she is entitled; so that the client's suf-fering is limited; and, ideally, so that the client can one day achieve a way of life that no longer requires human service intervention. In contrast, the community organizer, together with local leaders, builds a mediating organization capable of dealing with multiple issues within a community. The purpose of the organization is not to provide a particular service or in fact any service at all. Its purpose is to build power for its members, to train them in the use of that power to deal with specific issues that affect their community, and to develop a culture of self-determination, collective leadership, and direct civic action.

Community organizing is unabashedly a political activity. Its premise is that a just society depends on people being political (i.e., involved in the public arena), determining their own needs, developing strategies to meet them, mobilizing themselves and others, negotiating, compromising, and claiming victories for themselves and their community. The leaders of the organization become their own brokers, advocates, and lobbyists. Because the members of such community organizations are usually from sectors outside "traditional power," their assumption of and organization for power can and does create tension.

The purpose of this chapter is to explain community organizing as a method of social change. The particular model of organizing discussed is that practiced by affiliates of the Industrial Areas Foundation. This model of organizing is commonly called "congregationally based organizing," emphasizing the core participation of religious congregations, or "broad-based organizing," emphasizing the diversity of membership. The starting assumptions are the following:

1. The world as it is, is not the world as it should be.
2. Human beings have the capacity to relate to one another and to act in concert with one another to bring the world as it is closer to the world as it should be.
3. Power is the currency of the world as it is. To advocate for social change and not work to build power is hypocritical. Therefore, organizations are built for power.
4. The core values of community organizing are rooted in the religious traditions of member congregations and the civic values inherent in the practice of plural democracy in an open society.

MOVEMENTS, AGENCIES, AND ORGANIZING: CONTRASTS IN APPROACH

In recent years, human beings, struggling for social change, have organized themselves in several ways. One way is to build a movement characterized by focus on a particular issue (e.g., Save the Whales, Pro-Life, the National Rifle Association, political campaigns). Movements are made up of people devoted to a particular cause. Participants have little relationship to one another (or to charismatic movement leaders) except through their status as true believers. Movements are essentially protest organizations. Movement methods include mass mobilization, demonstrations, leaflets, and high rhetoric. They rely heavily on outside funding and spend most of their money and time making sure that their issue is before the public eye through the media or before the public funders through special-interest lobbying.

Movements do not usually last after they win (or lose repeatedly), and they are particularly subject to dissolution or weakening when the charismatic leader is no longer present, whether through retirement, resignation, electoral loss, death, or assassination. The power of a particular movement is limited by its focus; by its very nature it excludes people who are not "true

believers" and inevitably creates a countermovement. It is not easy to turn a movement built on one issue toward another issue. This is not to say that movements are not effective in certain times; movements are not, however, a suitable vehicle for building sustained, multi-issue power.

A second form of organizing for social change has been the development of social service or civic agencies. These are usually developed as a reaction to a particular need, though in recent years the "multiservice agency" has become more common. Service agencies may be private voluntary efforts, such as, on a large scale, the Red Cross or March of Dimes or, on a smaller scale, soup kitchens, drop-in centers, or overnight emergency shelters. Service agencies may also be in the public domain, for example, public hospitals, city welfare agencies, shelters, or emergency services. The distinguishing mark of the social service agency is that it provides direct service to those in need.

Service agencies are usually staffed by professional administrators, experts in particular fields, or dedicated volunteers, and, when not directly part of government, they still receive their principal funding from government grants and contracts. Social service agencies thus often find themselves subject to changes in political support; with a change in administration, programs may lose funding. They also may find themselves changing and developing programs, not entirely on the basis of their original mission but on the basis of getting additional funding. Even the best social service delivery system creates a top-down, power-over relationship between provider and client. This inherently unequal power relationship can create or enhance dependence in the client.

As long as there is human need, programs and services will be necessary to meet those needs, particularly for people who cannot, for various reasons, meet their needs by themselves. Whereas some needs can be met through individual attention, other needs are not the result of a particular problem of an individual. For example, adequate housing, good schools, and the existence of living-wage jobs are social challenges that go well beyond an individual. Such conditions are structural, not personal, and intervention at the personal level, although it may be helpful to an individual, does little to address the underlying structure.

The community organizing approach would argue, therefore, that something beyond movements and social service agencies is required for a just society. The key distinction of community organizing as compared to movements or social service agencies is the form that participation takes. In movements and social service agencies, the participants or clients are proclaiming their lack of power. In community organizing, it is just the opposite: Participants have power and use it. In movements and service agencies, participation is essentially individualistic, whereas in community organizing, participation is collective and communal.

Community organizing is not, then, designed for a specific cause or to meet a particular need. The community organizer starts not from people's needs but from their strengths and vision for their community. The analysis of the "presenting problem" is not on an individual basis but a collective basis. The development of solutions is not left up to experts or outsiders but is the focus of intense deliberation among local leaders. The "iron rule" of organizing—"Never do anything for anyone that they can do for themselves"—is in stark opposition to so-called economic Darwinism (survival of the fittest, therefore, no need to do anything for anyone) or the social service model, which makes the client the object and the provider the agent in solving a particular problem (a program for every need).

KEY PRINCIPLES OF BROAD-BASED COMMUNITY ORGANIZING

The principles of broad-based community organizing discussed below are those practiced by affiliates of the Industrial Areas Foundation (IAF). The IAF, founded by Saul Alinsky in 1940, is the oldest and largest community organizing network in the United States. The IAF has nearly sixty affiliates in the United States as well as related organizing efforts in Great Britain, South Africa, and Germany (IAF, 1990; Greider, 1992; Penta, 1992; Rooney, 1995).

Purpose.   As stated previously, the purpose of the broad-based community organization is to acquire power. *Power* is the ability to get things done, a capacity to create change, and an ability to relate mutually with others so that a course of action in the common good can be recognized and followed. Power can be exercised in one of two ways: dominant power, which is the traditional power used over and against another, or relational power (Loomer, 1976), which is power used with another for a common good. The entire focus of community organizing is to build relational power, first within the organization and then between the organization and other power centers in the community. Broad-based community organizing recognizes two sources of power—organized people and organized money—and takes care to make sure that both are part of the organizing effort.

Focus.   Broad-based organizing is not, fundamentally, issue organizing. In fact, it often takes years of organizing before action is taken on an issue. Broad-based organizing assumes that there is no power without relationships and thus that building relationships takes priority over any and all issues. The relationships fostered in broad-based organizing are intentionally diverse. That is, an organization is intentionally created to cross racial, ethnic, linguistic, class, party affiliation, and geographic lines. If power is measured by the diversity and depth of relationships, then the broader the base, the greater the potential for power. Once the relationships are built, then action on any issue is available to the organization. In contrast to a movement, broad-based organizations can and do work on a multitude of issues.

Membership.   Membership in the broad-based organization is institutional, not individual. Movements recruit individuals, and clients are seen as individuals in social service delivery. The excessive individualism of society is thus reinforced by those models of social change that promote individual involvement. Given the dominant structure of government and market-based forces, it is precisely individual action that is most likely to fail or to be overwhelmed. Broad-based organizing recognizes that institutions are local centers of power and that an organization of institutions has significantly more capacity to effect change than a group of unrelated individuals. The institutions most commonly part of broad-based organizations are religious congregations, tenant and homeowner associations, block or neighborhood associations, and occasionally labor unions or worker associations. Often these are further affiliated with national networks that also can be called on to add their power (both as organized money and as organized people) to the local effort.

Institutional membership brings people who are already into relationship with one another into relationship with others who have similar relationships within their own institutions. Institutions have organized people and organized money, so they bring two of the important measures of power with them as they join together. Institutions also have their own histories, cultures, points of view, rituals, and affinities. Whereas a movement may be dominated by people of one point of view and a service agency may focus primarily on a particular need, broad-based organizations with diverse institutional membership are guaranteed to have members with sharply differing points of view.

Leadership.   Collective leadership, in contrast to leadership by a charismatic individual or staff

of experts, is emphasized in the building of a broad-based community organization. The primary qualities of good leaders of this type of organization are people who are angry at the way things are, who have a vision for how things might be, and who have the appetite to fight for their vision. These leaders must be willing to enter into public relationships with others of sharply differing backgrounds, outlooks, races, religions, and so on. They must be willing and able to mobilize their followers, to be accountable to one another, and to be part of a collective of leaders. Parochial or limited access to leadership is seen to diminish the power of the organization. Broad-based leaders understand that leaders are made, not born, and that they must not act alone. They understand that a diverse group of people in respectful relationship with one another can provide better, more representative, and wiser leadership than can any one person.

Two of the central values of broad-based organizations can be protected only with collective leadership. One of these is "An injury to one is an injury to all." The second, related to the first, is "Stand for the whole." Too much of modern politics is based on identity or membership in a suffering class (e.g., race or a particular form of disability). This type of division among people, most of whom have limited power compared to the dominant society, has the unfortunate consequence of pitting the "have nots" or "have a littles" against one another. This is ultimately self-defeating and does little to change the social structure that puts them in the "have not" or "have a little" category in the first place.

Money.   Organized money is one form of power, and broad-based organizations take special care to make sure that they have their own organized money. All member institutions pay dues, the amount of which is determined by the leaders themselves. The philosophy is simple: "Our money" is preferable to "other people's money" and allows a greater freedom of action.

In addition to dues, IAF affiliates receive support from the judicatories and national church bodies to which their members belong.

Mode of Action.   Leaders of broad-based community organizations learn to exercise their power by a discipline of direct civic action, reflection, and evaluation. The first step in developing a broad-based community organization is thousands of "individual relational meetings" consisting of one-on-one encounters among leaders of the institutions engaged in the organizing effort. These individual meetings begin to surface interests, energy, and vision and are the basis of all relationships within the organization. Hundreds of "house meetings" of ten to fifteen people are also conducted to gather a common understanding of issues and concerns. Gradually, as leaders work to distill what comes from the individual and house meetings, an agenda for action develops. This agenda is specific to the organization and leaders involved. In the South Bronx, for example, the first agenda for action included improvements in the local hospital, construction of new and rehabilitated housing, improving education, and raising the minimum wage. Other organizations have focused on public transportation, park maintenance, neighborhood clinics, job development, after-school programs, or street signs, again depending on the issues local leaders identify as their priorities.

Once the general agenda is adopted, leaders work to break down problems (e.g., drug dealing) to issues for action (e.g., a specific crackhouse or heroin distribution point). To be suitable for an effective action, the issue must be specific and in the interest of the organization. Leaders willing to work on the action must step forward. The issue must have a solution, and the action must target a specific person for accountability for producing the solution.

Regular participation in direct actions is the lifeblood of a broad-based community organization. Actions occur when leaders practice partici-

pation in public life. They learn to analyze problems, develop solutions, and negotiate settlements. They evaluate what they do and how they do it each step of the way. They learn to analyze their own power, that of their allies, and that of their opponents. They experience themselves as the instigators of change, and they take enormous pride, even years later, when they say, "These are the lights which were installed because of us." "I live in a home that my organization built—I helped fight for this land." "My children attend a high school that we made the Board of Education open." "My wages were restored to what I earned before my job with the city was privatized."

EXAMPLES OF ACTIONS

An "action" is a deliberate display of power, focused on a particular issue, and with a particular end in mind. A broad-based community organization is able to act on issues of widely differing complexity. Leaders within the organization are constantly exposed to and participate in different levels of action and thereby increase their capacity to evaluate social conditions, decide on necessary changes, and see the direct results of their work. An action early in the history of South Bronx Churches, an organization of thirty congregations in the South Bronx, concerned the removal of tires from a vacant lot. The vacant lot was next door to a member congregation, and the piles of tires served as breeding sites for mosquitos and rats. The leaders from the congregation met with the district supervisor of the sanitation department and demanded that the tires be removed. He informed them that the lot was privately owned and thus that the responsibility for clearing the lot was the owner's, not his. The leaders then researched the property records, found out who the owner was, and wrote a respectful letter to him, requesting that the tires be removed by a certain date because they were so offensive to the community. The owner, safe in a wealthy Westchester County enclave, answered, essentially saying that the tires were not his responsibility. At this point, the leaders wrote a second letter, telling the owner that on an upcoming Saturday they intended to rent a dump truck, load it with the tires, and bring them to his front yard, since it was apparent that he was not offended by stacks of tires in residential areas. Within days, the owner had rented his own truck and cleared and fenced the lot.

In another action, leaders from other congregations were angry over the state of their local supermarkets. It was not uncommon for them to find pools of blood leaking from the meat cabinets onto the floor. Much of the produce was well past its prime, and many of the canned goods and frozen foods were items removed from first-string supermarkets and dumped into secondary markets in the black and Hispanic neighborhoods of New York City such as the South Bronx. In addition, the prices of the inferior products were often higher than in wealthier neighborhoods, justified by the assumed cost of greater shoplifting in poorer areas.

The South Bronx Churches leaders educated themselves on agricultural and health department standards for markets. Armed with clipboards and inspection forms and wearing white lab coats and specially made buttons proclaiming themselves "SBC Market Inspectors," they entered their neighborhood store. The manager was shocked and tried to interfere. Some leaders then began "shopping," not for the rare high-quality merchandise, but for the brownest vegetables and the greenest, most spoiled meat. The market owner called the police. Responding to the call, the police looked at the evidence—in the leaders' shopping carts—and joined in the action against the owner. The leaders, now with police at their side, met with the owner and demanded that he clean up the store and bring in good products. They gave him two weeks and said they would be back. He agreed. When they returned in one week to check on his progress, little had changed. They began a picket line against the store, having purchased sample produce and meat as supporting props for the pickets. The owner got to work, and the store was put in decent shape. Needless to say, this owner remembers what happened when he tried to take advantage of the community; if local shoppers find the quality beginning to slide, they remind him of what happened before.

Another action concerned the lack of lights in a South Bronx subway station. Although the station was adjacent to a police precinct, even the police were reluctant to go down those dark stairs. Residents of public housing in the area, however, had to brave the darkness in the early morning and when returning from work in the evening or late at night. Muggings were common, and there had even been one murder. The South Bronx Churches leaders team went to work. They built a constituency of support by providing flashlight guides during the evening for people using the stairs. Thousands of people signed petitions demanding the installation of lights. The leaders went to a public hearing of the Transit Authority and presented their demands. They were told that what they were saying was ridiculous, that such a situation did not exist. They invited the head of transit to come see for himself; he agreed. The night he came, the leaders contacted one of the local TV news channels, and a cameraman and reporter were standing in the dark in the station. The Transit Authority official arrived and was guided down the stairs by flashlight, rapidly making promises to take care of the situation right away. At the bottom of the steps he met the camera and a few tough questions. Within two weeks, lights were installed.

Broad-based organizations can also take on very large projects. For example, in both East Brooklyn and the South Bronx, leaders of local organizations have been successful at building the most affordable homes in New York City in their Nehemiah Program. Building more than two thousand new homes in Brooklyn and more than five hundred in the South Bronx required sustained efforts over many years, first to acquire the land

and then to acquire the financing for construction. It took many hard struggles and negotiations, including massive demonstrations of more than five thousand people, before the city was willing to entertain the idea of locally controlled new housing development. Their more favored model was of housing development controlled by major banks and for-profit developers.

East Brooklyn Congregations and South Bronx Churches each raised millions of dollars in no-interest loans for construction capital, primarily from the judicatories and national church bodies of their member institutions. The City provided a $15,000 no-interest second mortgage to each buyer. The first three thousand homes were built under the supervision of a legendary New York builder, I. D. Robbins. The people who bought the Nehemiah homes in East Brooklyn and the South Bronx ended up in many cases paying less for their mortgage than they had paid in rent in public housing. In addition, block upon block of land that had been vacant and filled with rubble for more than twenty years had been transformed into thriving neighborhoods.

CONCLUSION

Broad-based organizations are often criticized for using confrontational tactics and creating tension. What the Industrial Areas Foundation and its affiliated organizations have learned over the past fifty years, however, is that without tension, there will be no change. This is particularly true when the people demanding the change are people who are outside of traditional power structures. It might seem ridiculous and unkind to put a supermarket manager on the spot for the blood spilling from his meat coolers or to embarrass a transit executive for the condition of his stations, but the fact is that in neighborhoods like the South Bronx, public officials and private interests have abandoned their responsibilities and do take advantage of the powerlessness of the local community. A shop owner on East 86th Street would never dream of offering the inferior produce and meat that is often the only available merchandise in the South Bronx.

In his *History of the Peloponnesian War* (1972 trans.), Thucydides pointed out that the "standard of justice depends on the equality of power to compel and that in fact the strong do what they have the power to do and the weak accept what they have to accept." This principle holds true today, and it is only by the use of power that the apparently weak can achieve a standard of justice. None of the achievements of South Bronx Churches, East Brooklyn Congregations, or the other affiliates of the Industrial Areas Foundation throughout the United States were accomplished simply because they were good ideas put forth by good people. The new schools, clinics, houses, apartments, street signs, bus stops, and so forth were brought into existence by the intentional, sustained use of power. This exercise of power by people who are assumed by dominant political and civic leaders to have none created tension. No matter how apparently reasonable the request (who could deny the necessity for lights on subway stairs?) all these results required a fight, sometimes over months or years, to get results.

Perhaps the most important human service available through community organizing is the claiming and exercising of power by people and institutions who have been marginalized by the dominant society. It is through the exercise of power that the marginalized can achieve justice. "Justice cannot be realized in a society in which some citizens are prevented from sharing in the decisions that shape the basic structures which determine their fate. Participation constitutes a right which is to be applied both in the economic and in the social and political field" (Haughey, 1977). Community organizing opens a new level of participation—not as client, not as victim, but as agent of power. In the fullness of human expression, this makes all the difference in the world.

REFERENCES

Greider, W. (1992). *Who Will Tell the People? The Betrayal of American Democracy.* New York: Simon and Schuster.

Haughey, J. C., ed. (1977). *The Faith That Does Justice: Examining the Christian Sources for Social Change.* New York: Paulist Press.

Industrial Areas Foundation (1990). *IAF: Fifty Years—Organizing for Change.* South San Francisco: Sapir Press.

Loomer, B. M. (1976). "Two Kinds of Power," The D. R. Sharpe Lecture on Social Ethics, October 29, 1975. *Criterion, 15*(1), 11–29.

Penta, L. J. (1992). "Organizing and Public Philosophy: The Industrial Areas Foundation." *Journal of Peace and Justice Studies,* 17–32.

Rooney, J. (1995). *Organizing the South Bronx.* Albany: State University of New York–Albany.

Thucydides. (1972). *History of the Peloponnesian War.* Translated by Rex Warner. London: Penguin Books.

CHAPTER 20

HUMAN SERVICES IN THE MENTAL HEALTH ARENA:
FROM INSTITUTION TO COMMUNITY

JOSEPH MEHR

As human services enters what is arguably its fifth decade, the field continues to be characterized by dramatic change. In the mental health arena, the past forty years have seen a move from the provision of public services in monolithic residential institutions (state hospitals) through an emphasis on institutional closure and the promotion of an ideal of community-based services. Some state hospitals have in fact closed, almost all are significantly smaller than they were, and those that remain are likely to become smaller yet. Unfortunately, although there has been growth in community mental health services during this period, that growth has not always paralleled the need for services for the chronically mentally ill in most parts of the country. The decades of the 1970s and 1980s were times of severe fiscal constraints for state and federal government. In many states the savings from closing institutions were not channeled into community services but were used to cover government budget deficits from other programs, most notably the soaring medical health care costs of Medicaid programs. It was an era with a lack of public and political will to pay the cost of needed human services in the mental health sector if such services would require the politician's nightmare—a tax increase.

Times continue to change. In 1993, the sequential Republican administrations of Presidents Ronald Reagan and George Bush were replaced by the Democratic administration of President Bill Clinton. President Clinton at first focused on a major attempt at health care reform, but that plan was soundly defeated by a Republican majority. The need to reduce the rate of growth of the federal deficit took precedence over any major new social service initiatives. During President Clinton's second term in office, the main emphasis was on deficit reduction, with some success. However, the emphasis on health care reform was not totally lost. Although no major federal initiative was taken, most state governments moved ahead into health care reform by instituting a managed care approach to health care for Medicaid and Medicare recipients. Although details vary from state to state, health care reform is in process across the nation.

However, even if changes at the state level are not successful or only partially successful, one can still anticipate continued change in the delivery of human services in the mental health arena. The changes that have occurred in mental health care over the past four decades have developed a momentum that will continue either more quickly or more slowly—but they will continue.

Understanding the immediate future (the next decade) of human services in public mental health systems is best achieved by viewing the impact over time of changes in mental health service delivery and the roles of human services that developed along with those changes. A detailed history of mental health service systems in the

United States is available from a variety of sources, including Fisher, Mehr, and Truckenbrod (1974); Grob (1994); and Mehr (1983, 1995). For our purposes here, a brief overview will suffice.

THE EARLY YEARS: A GRAND PLAN

After World War II, public policy regarding mental health services began to change drastically, and that change accelerated over the following decade. Through the mid-1950s the public mental hospital was the primary provider of mental health services, with inpatient census reaching a peak in 1955 of 558,922 (Mechanic and Rochefort, 1992). Public mental hospitals had become huge warehouses of the mentally ill, isolating patients from community life. In 1958, Harry C. Solomon, the new president of the American Psychiatric Association, described them as "antiquated, outmoded and rapidly becoming obsolete" (Grob, 1991).

Disenchantment with large public mental hospitals stemmed from a variety of sources. Intolerable conditions had been exposed through a variety of public media venues, including books, movies, and newspapers. Advances in treatment approaches, particularly the discovery of psychopharmacological medications that reduced the symptoms of major mental illness and the growing popularity of psychotherapy, suggested that the mentally ill could be treated in less restrictive settings.

From the late 1950s on, it became more and more accepted that the mentally ill could be treated in community clinics on an outpatient basis and that chronic hospitalization should be seen as a last resort. Community mental health centers had been opened all across the country, and as early as 1959 there were more than 1,400 such clinics in the United States.

Major legislative changes reflected the changing opinions of the times and added impetus to the growing community movement. In 1946 legislation was passed to establish the National Institute of Mental Health (NIMH). The Mental

Health Study Act was passed in 1955, providing funding for a Joint Commission on Mental Illness and Health that was to analyze and evaluate the needs of and resources for the mentally ill and make recommendations for a national mental health program. Of particular significance for human services were the manpower development recommendations of the commission (Albee, 1961). These recommendations suggested that, because of a lack of medical staff, nonmedical mental health workers (i.e., human service workers) would be a necessary part of providing mental health services if such services were increased. The recommendations of the commission regarding dramatically increasing community mental health services were sympathetically received by the Kennedy Administration and Congress and were codified in the Community Mental Health Centers Act of 1963, which proposed the development of 2,000, and funded the establishment of over 600, community mental health centers during the next decade.

From the mid-1960s to the mid-1970s, the principles of the community mental health movement were broadly accepted, and the locus of mental health services shifted dramatically from the public mental hospital to the community clinic. The community movement was, in a sense, a "grand plan" that had at its foundation a belief by many that the public mental hospital could be abandoned and replaced by a comprehensive community service system. That belief was, in fact, even shared by many who worked in public mental hospitals. The growing emphasis on community treatment, improvement in treatment technology, the passage of Medicare and Medicaid legislation in 1965, and the expansion of Supplemental Security Income, Social Security Disability Insurance, and housing subsidies to the mentally ill led to a dramatic reduction in the number of public mental hospital patients to 193,436 by 1975. It appeared that the community mental health movement was well on its way to changing the mental health delivery system, and the phenomenon of declining public mental hospital populations was given the name "deinstitutionalization."

At the dawn of the community mental health movement, the terms "human services" and "human service worker" had yet to be coined; there were, however, "human service workers" in fact if not in name. Most were nonprofessionals who worked in public mental hospitals under titles such as psychiatric aide, psychiatric technicians, or nurse's aide. Their role was initially quite limited. However, of all the staff in such settings, it was they who provided the lion's share of staff contact with patients. The growing recognition that traditional professionals would always be in short supply led to a number of organized efforts to expand the role of such workers and increase their competence. Some early efforts in this direction occurred at a few state mental hospitals, funded by NIMH Hospital Improvement Program (HIP) grants (Mehr, 1966, 1971). Later at NIMH, a special division was created, the Paraprofessional Manpower Development Branch, whose purpose was to provide technical assistance and grant funds to organizations (such as state departments of mental health and community mental health agencies) to develop training programs and career ladders for such individuals. On the academic side, in 1964 an associate-level degree program was started at Purdue University to train this type of mental health worker for jobs in both the community and the mental hospital. In 1966 the Southern Regional Education Board (SREB) sponsored a national conference of mental health and community college professionals to explore the training of mental health workers at two-year colleges. Subsequently, SREB received an NIMH grant to assist in the development of associate's degree or certificate programs in fourteen southern states.

The SREB'S Mental Health Division became a leader in the early human service/mental health manpower development arena. In 1969, SREB published a document that defined a series of roles and functions for mental health workers (SREB, 1969). In this groundbreaking monograph, SREB described thirteen proposed roles and four competence levels. The thirteen roles were as follows:

> Outreach Worker
> Broker
> Advocate
> Evaluator
> Teacher Educator
> Behavior Changer
> Mobilizer
> Consultant
> Community Planner
> Caregiver
> Data Manager
> Administrator
> Assistant to Specialist

Nine of the thirteen roles can be appropriate for an inpatient setting, but the focus of the roles and their definition was clearly on services in a community setting. The rapid expansion of community services during the era saw a concomitant expansion of the employment and use of nontraditional staff in both public mental hospitals and community mental health centers. The changes in the mental health system were viewed as so dramatic that they were often described as "revolutionary" (Rochefort, 1984), and great expectations were held for the success of the approach.

THE MIDDLE YEARS: DREAM VS. REALITY

Advocates of the community mental health movement had a dream—a vision of what the mental health system should look like. The nation would be fully covered by a network of 2,000 community mental health centers, each serving a population base of up to 250,000 people. The services offered would effectively replace the large public mental hospital. The chronically mentally ill would be served in less restrictive community programs; the public mental hospitals would either be entirely eliminated or be reduced in size and designed to serve only a very small segment of the mentally ill population. The services that would replace the public mental hospital were defined in a number of sources as follows: (1) to provide treatment by a basic mental health team for persons with acute mental illness, (2) to care for incompletely recovered mental patients either short of admission to a hospital or following discharge from the hospital, and (3) to provide a headquarters base for mental health consultants working with mental health counselors. In the early period, federally funded community mental health centers were required to have at least five essential services: inpatient, outpatient, emergency services, pre- and posthospital care, and education and mental health consultation.

For a number of years it appeared that the dream was becoming a reality. Public mental hospitals were getting smaller; some were closed. The community mental health center network was growing, and statistical data were being generated that documented the growth of community services. By 1985 the number of public mental hospital patients had declined to about 100,000 from over 550,000. In spite of that decline, patient care episodes for all types of mental health services had increased from 1.7 million in 1955 to 6.9 million in 1983 (Mechanic and Rochefort, 1992). Well over 50 percent of the patient care episodes in 1985 occurred in nonhospital settings. There had been a profound shift in the location of services as well as in the rate of episodes (Grob, 1991). A superficial view of the data supported the notion that the community mental health movement was moving toward success.

In actual practice, however, in many of the community mental health centers, the severely mentally ill person discharged from the public mental hospital did not receive adequate and comprehensive care. The increase in patient care episodes reflected a broadening of the clientele to encompass new groups that in previous years had no access to the mental health system—persons with problems of crisis, problems of satisfaction, and milder psychological problems rather than

severe mental illness (Grob, 1994). More typically, the chronically and severely mentally ill person discharged from the public mental hospital was placed in a nursing home or entered a cycle of short-term stays in the public mental hospital, discharge, and readmission. To be sure, there were many community mental health centers that did provide adequate service and could maintain a severely mentally ill person in his or her community, but the reality did not approach the dream.

A compounding problem for the vision of a reformed mental health system was the impact of declining fiscal support from government entities. In 1981, federal support for comprehensive community mental health centers was eliminated after only slightly more than 600 of the proposed 2,000 had been established (Kiesler, 1992). Medicaid did not keep pace with the growth of the number of poor, and Congress required states to tighten SSI and SSDI eligibility, which disproportionately affected the mentally ill. In general, the Reagan-Bush years saw significant cuts in funding for social programs even though the federal deficit continued to soar. In addition, a general antitax, antigovernment spending sentiment at the local level resulted in social service funding stagnation at the state level. By the mid to late 1980s, only a few state systems saw any increases in funding for mental health services.

The plight of the mentally ill in the community was further compromised by a general loss of housing availability. Federal housing programs suffered cutbacks, low-cost housing units were converted to middle-class housing through gentrification in most cities, and single-room-occupancy (SRO) hotels virtually disappeared. Homelessness has become a problem of much greater magnitude, highly visible on the nightly news, and present in every city in the country. The growth in numbers of homeless people is viewed by many to be a sign of the failure of the deinstitutionalization of public mental hospitals and the community mental health movement (Torrey, 1988).

In fact, the two groups, the homeless and the mentally ill, are quite different populations, even though they do overlap. Only about a quarter of the homeless have ever experienced prior psychiatric hospitalization (Rossi, 1990).

A number of factors came together in the 1980s to result in a two-tracked system consisting of continued use and need for public mental hospitals and a community mental health system substantially lacking in a full range of services for the most needy of the mentally ill. With a lack of new or expanded fiscal sources, the two tracks of the system competed for the same funds. In most states the downsizing of public mental hospitals continued. The fiscal savings from the downsizing in some states was put into funding new community programs. In other states, unfortunately, the mental health system lost the savings; they were used to cover state deficits in other areas. The two-tracked system was characterized by weak institutional linkages or mechanisms to ensure continuity and coordination of services. Severely mentally ill people were often released from public mental hospitals, after relatively brief periods of time, into communities without adequate support mechanisms (Grob, 1991).

During the 1980s the term "human services" became more and more commonly used in the mental health arena as the general field of human services developed. By 1987 there were almost 400 certificate and associate- and bachelor-level academic programs around the country and a growing number of master's degree programs (Cogan and Wood, 1987). The roles of human service workers in mental health have paralleled the changes in service from institutions to community. Although about as many human service workers continue to be employed in public mental hospitals, far more are working in community agencies. There has been a significant expansion in the number of human service workers who engage in the activity of case management because of the expansion of community mental health services, although the fiscal constraints of the 1980s

did, for a time, slow the growth of positions for human service workers.

RECENT TIMES: RETURN OF THE PENDULUM

The late 1980s and 1990s saw a reconsideration of the overly optimistic promises of the original community mental health movement. With few exceptions, most authorities no longer believe that public mental hospitals can be eliminated altogether. However, they will continue to be smaller, and the total available beds will be less than the 69,000 available in 1995 (Center for Mental Health Services, 1997). Although plagued by the negative stereotypes of decades past, which are reinforced by occasional scandals portrayed in the popular media, most public mental hospitals are consistently improving as they get smaller and become better staffed. The pendulum has swung to a somewhat more centrist position that has a goal of a system of mental health care that not only is balanced between public mental hospitals and a comprehensive community mental health system but also integrates public mental hospitals into the community mental health system.

The challenge for mental health policy makers and planners has recently been to find ways to fund the expansion of a community mental health system that is responsive to the public health needs of the indigent chronically and severely mentally ill. Some states have made dramatic efforts in this direction by systematically collecting funds saved by downsizing public mental hospitals and putting those funds into community programs specifically for the severely mentally ill. Notable examples include Massachusetts, Connecticut, Vermont, New Hampshire, Ohio, Kansas, and more recently New York, which reduced the number of resident patients by more than 50 percent between 1987 and 1995 (Mechanic and Rochefort, 1992; Center for Mental Health Services, 1997). The costs of aggressive comprehensive community care, although not cheap, are substantially less than care in a public mental hospital, and thus equivalent funds can purchase much more community care than hospital care. However, most states have discovered that additional revenues from the tax base will be needed if a fully comprehensive system is to be established to adequately address the mental health needs of the severely mentally ill.

A comprehensive system of mental health care must reflect the following principles:

— An organized, managed, coordinated system of care at the *local level* provides the best opportunity for individuals to access mental health services in, or close to, their home communities.
— Each community area should have sufficient core services to meet the needs of individuals who are most in need and most dependent on state-funded care. Core services will be immediately available and accessible to priority populations. Immediate priorities include assertive case management, residential/housing options, crisis/emergency response services (including prescreening to ensure appropriateness of admissions to restrictive levels of care and coordination of services to ensure continuity of care regardless of the location of the client).
— Individuals who are most in need and least able to afford care must be the priority for state-funded services.
— Individuals with special needs must be able to access services tailored to fit their needs.
— Services must be culturally relevant.
— Continuity of care between hospital and community services must be a consistent feature of the service system.
— An appropriate balance between inpatient, outpatient, and residential services must be achieved and maintained with the utilization of the most costly, restrictive levels of care being justified on the basis of clinical necessity.
— All service settings must provide high-quality care and treatment consistent with professional, nationally recognized standards of care.
— The system of care must be accountable to its users and the taxpayers for its outcomes, quality, efficiency, and effectiveness.
— The responsibility for ongoing planning and service system development at the local level must be shared between primary and secondary consumers, providers, advocates, and other interested stakeholders and parties.

HUMAN SERVICES IN MENTAL HEALTH: WHERE DO WE GO FROM HERE?

What direction will mental health service systems take in the next ten years? Prediction is a risky process. However, as pointed out earlier, whether or not community services for the severely and chronically mental ill are included in health care reform, the changes we have seen in the past several decades will continue. Public mental hospitals will be an integral part of the mental health service system, although they will be smaller, there will be fewer of them, and those that remain will provide a higher quality of care. They will be fully integrated into the networks of community care offered in their geographic areas. The community services offered by local agencies for the severely mentally ill will expand significantly as public mental hospitals continue to downsize and as priorities are set for the limited fiscal resources available for public mental health services.

As the community service system expands to provide adequate comprehensive services for the priority population of the severely and chronically mentally ill, existing programs will be expanded and new, more effective programs developed, opening opportunities for human service workers.

Three types of services in particular will be implemented that will require additional staffing of both traditionally credentialed professionals and human service professionals. These three services have been documented and recognized as highly effective in maintaining the severely and persistently mentally ill in the community, in improving their daily functioning, and in many cases in promoting recovery. One approach is usually called assertive community treatment (ACT), or intensive case management (ICM), and the second is called psychosocial rehabilitation. The third goes by a variety of labels but for convenience here is called family psychoeducational intervention.

Assertive Community Treatment has existed for more than twenty years but has not been uniformly implemented. It involves aggressive psychiatric care and medication supervision, intensive daily case management, assistance with housing and welfare entitlements, and the ability to respond to crises twenty-four hours a day. It is usually offered on a team basis, with caseloads of about ten clients per case manager. Sustained care over long periods of the client's lifetime is typically essential to maintain favorable results (Stein and Test, 1980, 1985; Olfson, 1990).

Experience in discharging clients to the community during the past several decades demonstrated that simply moving people to the community and providing traditional services was not the answer. Many clients who returned to the community were unable to remain there for long. Resources were not coordinated to assist clients in securing or maintaining needed services. The use of a service by individuals depends on their being knowledgeable not only about the nature of a problem but also about which of numerous agencies they should turn to for help. Persons who are chronically mentally ill have special needs and present special problems. The disruption to the client and family, and the interruption of productivity and cost to the taxpayer, is staggering when the client cannot be maintained in the community.

The role of the ACT case manager is to meet the needs of clients wherever and whenever required. The responsibilities of case managers are not restricted to predefined functions or limited in time and location. They must be available twenty-four hours a day, ready to go to the clients in their environment and perform assertively. What severely mentally ill clients need most is a person to help with their problems as they experience them, not as others might define them. They need a person on whom they can count for support. For case management to achieve its purpose, the case manager must have the authority required to ensure

client access to any of the programs or services provided by the agency. The case manager's effectiveness is defined in terms of client outcome. That means assisting clients with the appropriate services so that they have a life that is as productive, satisfying, and self-sufficient as possible.

The responsibilities of an ACT case manager are as follows:

1. *To identify members of the target population:* Includes being able to assess whether prospective clients meet eligibility criteria (i.e., that they are truly in the greatest need of attention); also entails maintaining good relationships with major referral sources—state hospitals, community mental health centers, shelters, single-room occupancy hotels, bus terminals and airports, and the families of people with mental illness or the individuals themselves—so that clients will be referred for service.

2. *To engage the new referrals in the program:* Initial engagement of a new client must be slow and careful so that the client will not be overwhelmed by offers of assistance; ideally, initial engagement should begin by assisting a client with a concrete task to demonstrate the advantages of participation in a case management program from the outset.

3. *To conduct assessments and, subsequently, to plan interventions on the basis of these assessments:* Consists of taking stock of a client's strengths, difficulties, existing resources, and remaining needs and then searching out novel ways to interrupt the chain of events that previously led to the person's distress in the community, subsequent rehospitalization, and/or homelessness; develop the intervention strategy in consultation with the client and his or her family if the client consents.

4. *To assume ultimate professional responsibility for clients:* Includes helping clients assemble individually tailored packages of community supports that are either provided directly by the ACT team or set up by the team in conjunction with other service providers; also means showing unusual tolerance for unresponsive or difficult behavior and refusing to "give up" on clients.

5. *To assist clients through outreach:* Consists of meeting with individuals on their own turf where their problems generally arise and where the solutions to their problems must be found; must have the flexibility to

meet with clients in very unconventional places, if necessary, such as low-rent hotels, welfare offices, public shelters, police lockups, street corners, and neighborhood coffee shops.

6. *To be able to attend to the concrete details of clients' everyday lives:* Entails paying close attention to matters of everyday living that might otherwise be taken for granted, such as food, clothing, shelter, medical care, entitlements, and money management; helping to make concrete matters seem less overwhelming so that living in the community becomes a viable and desirable alternative to institutional care.

7. *To provide clients with* in vivo *assistance and training:* Includes giving on-the-spot help and skills training to clients regarding a wide range of independent living tasks such as grocery shopping, laundry, leasing an apartment, managing a checking account, or cleaning a room; also involves encouraging clients to become involved in social, vocational, recreational, and self-help programs and even attending the first few meetings of these programs with clients to ease the transition.

8. *To arrange for psychiatric and other medical services for clients:* Entails helping clients obtain the highest quality services available while diffusing some of the confusing and stressful nature of making such arrangements; in some cases, in addition to assisting clients in arranging the visit, the ACT staff will have to physically accompany them to their doctor or psychiatrist appointments to help them negotiate the entire process.

9. *To provide interagency resource brokering and advocacy.*

10. *To develop new community resources:* Could entail searching for and making available to clients hidden resources or possibly developing currently nonexistent resources "from scratch"; includes creatively combining resources to come up with a new avenue for addressing a client's need when that need cannot be met by an existing resource.

11. *To facilitate inpatient psychiatric hospital admissions, when absolutely necessary, and to work with the inpatient staff while the client must be in the hospital:* Consists of being able to recognize signs that the client is truly in need of rehospitalization, initiating hospitalization if the client is unwilling to go voluntarily, and working with inpatient staff once the client is safely hospitalized to have a voice in the client's inpatient treatment and to take part in the subsequent discharge plans.

12. *To establish a partnership with families of clients in cases where client and family are still in contact and the relationship between client and family is one that has potential to be of some benefit to the client.*

The defined roles of an ACT case manager are similar to the roles previously identified by SREB and embody many of the philosophies and attitudes characteristic of human service workers (Mehr, 1995).

Psychosocial rehabilitation includes a variety of approaches designed to improve the daily social functioning of the chronically mentally ill by helping them develop or acquire social and instrumental skills and by developing environments that will support the maintenance of those skills. Although many mental health professionals have contributed to the development of the approach, two in particular stand out: William Anthony in Boston and Robert Paul Liberman in California (Anthony and Liberman, 1986).

In Liberman's approach, social skills training is delivered in group settings using structured modules for teaching social and independent living skills (Vaccaro et al., 1992). All patients receive competency-based instruction in four core skill areas: medication management, symptom management, basic conversation, and recreation and leisure. Classes are run four days per week, three hours per day, for a period of six months. Each of the classes is sixty to seventy-five minutes in length. The total length of instruction varies slightly from group to group because clients do not proceed to the next skill area until the material is learned. Ongoing progress is monitored through the use of "pop quizzes" administered during and after the social skills training classes. Patients are further assessed for knowledge and skills acquisition and maintenance at the end of the six-month intensive treatment phase and every six to twelve months thereafter. Therapists' competency and adherence to the model are regularly assessed as well, ensuring high degrees of fidelity to the model. Once patients complete the first six months of skills training, they enter into the generalization phase of the program. Case management efforts are directed toward helping patients generalize the skills learned in the classroom to other life areas. Case managers use behavioral learning interventions such as structured problem solving and role play in their practice. All patients periodically update their individualized written rehabilitation plans. These plans address goals in major life domains such as housing and household maintenance, symptomatic status, occupation, social and family life, and finances. Substantial evaluative research has accumulated to document the effectiveness of a psychosocial rehabilitative approach in relapse prevention and maintenance of clients in community settings and in the improvement of quality of life.

Family psychoeducational interventions have had remarkable results. Multiple outcome studies report a reduction in annual relapse rates for community-based severely mentally ill clients who are taking their medications by as much as 40 percent when they and their families are enrolled in family psychoeducational intervention.

This effect equals the reductions in relapse in medicated versus unmedicated consumers in most drug maintenance studies. The average relapse rates in these studies stand at just under 15 percent for family psychoeducation approaches and 40 percent for individual treatment, without family involvement. With twelve studies in the literature, from three countries, family psychoeducational intervention has accumulated the most consistent record of effectiveness of any psychosocial approach for a psychotic disorder. Three studies have recently been reported from China, including one with a sample of over 3,000 subjects. This record of efficacy is unequaled by all but medication itself and ACT (McFarlane et al., 1995)

The basic psychoeducational model consists of four treatment stages that roughly correspond to the phases of an episode of schizophrenia, from the acute phase through the slow recuperative and rehabilitation phases. These stages are joining, survival skills training/workshop, reentry, and social vocational rehabilitation. Approximately one year following an acute episode, most consumers begin

to evidence signs of a return to spontaneity and active engagement with those around them. This is usually the sign that the negative symptoms of psychosis are lifting and that the consumer can now be challenged more intensively. The focus of this phase deals more specifically with the rehabilitative needs of the consumer, addressing the two areas of functioning in which most deficits occur: social skills and the ability to get and maintain employment.

The more efficient multifamily version of the psychoeducational approach is designed to follow as closely as possible the treatment methodology used in the single-family condition but is conducted in a very different social format, namely, a group consisting of several patients, their families, and two clinicians. The engagement process is that clinicians meet with families for a minimum of three sessions until up to five persons and their families are assigned to a given group, whereupon there is an educational workshop for the group with the patients absent. This workshop deals with factual matters about etiology, prognosis, and treatment of schizophrenia to educate the family about their member's mental illness.

After the educational workshop, each multifamily group of up to five families meets biweekly, led by two cotherapists, and includes the patients. Throughout, the therapists facilitate problem solving to achieve clinical stability and functional adaptation. An individual patient's or family's problem is addressed by the entire multifamily group in a structured, clinician-guided, problem-solving process. These problems are almost always management issues created by schizophrenic symptoms and/or family members' uncertainties about the means for promoting recovery and rehabilitation. The clinicians facilitate the formation of "real" rather than transferential relationships between members of different families. After the second year, ongoing groups evolve into quasi-natural social networks, and the focus shifts from problem resolution to rehabilitation and enhancing the quality of life of the identified patient.

The implications for the future of human services in mental health that arise out of the broad expansion of ACT, psychosocial rehabilitation, and family psychoeducational intervention are significant. During the next ten years, there will be a need for thousands, perhaps tens of thousands, of new community staff nationwide who have, or can develop, the necessary attitudes, knowledge, and skills to be employed as ACT case managers, psychosocial rehabilitation technicians, and family intervention group leaders. Although some traditionally trained mental health professionals perform these roles, the human service professional who is a graduate of a two- or four-year human service program is more likely to enter the work force with an appropriate set of attitudes and skills already in place to be effective in these services. The potential skills market that will develop in the near future suggests that human service programs should evaluate their curricula to ensure that extensive training and education in these content areas are included to provide a supply of professionals who can meet the growing demand that will arise in these three areas.

REFERENCES

Albee, G. W. (1961). *Mental Health Manpower Trends.* New York: Basic Books.

Anthony, W. A., and R. P. Liberman (1986). "The Practice of Psychiatric Rehabilitation: Historical, Conceptual, and Research Base." *Schizophrenia Bulletin, 12*(4), 571–591.

Burt, M. R., and B. E. Cohen (1989). *America's Homeless: Numbers, Characteristics, and Programs That Serve Them.* Washington, DC: Urban Institute Press.

Center for Mental Health Services (1997). *Additions and Resident Patients at End of Year, State, and County Mental Hospitals, by Age and Diagnosis, by State, United States, 1995.* Rockville, MD: Author.

Cogan, D. B., and A. C. Wood (1987). "A Survey of the Introductory Course in Mental Health and Human Services." *Human Services Education, 8*(2), 22–27.

Fisher, W., J. Mehr, and P. Truckenbrod (1974). *Human Services: The Third Revolution in Mental Health.* Port Washington, NY: Alfred Publishing Co.

Grob, G. N. (1991). "The Severely and Chronically Mentally Ill in America: Retrospect and Prospect." *Transactions: Studies of the College of Physicians of Philadelphia, 13*(4), 337–362.

Grob, G. N. (1994). *The Mad among Us: A History of the Care of America's Mentally Ill.* New York: Free Press.

Kiesler, C. A. (1992). "U.S. Mental Health Policy: Doomed to Fail." *American Psychologist, 47*(9), 1077–1082.

McFarlane, W. R., B. Link, R. Dushay, J. Marchal, and J. Crilly (1995). "Psychoeducational Multiple Family Groups: Four Year Relapse Outcome in Schizophrenia." *Family Process, 34* (June), 127–144.

Mechanic, D., and D. A. Rochefort (1992, Spring). "A Policy of Inclusion for the Mentally Ill." *Health Affairs,* 128–150.

Mehr, J. (1966). "Hospital Staff Development Grant Proposal." Unpublished Manuscript, Elgin State Hospital, Elgin, IL.

Mehr, J. (1971). "Evaluating Non-Traditional Training for Psychiatric Aides." *Hospital and Community Psychiatry, 22*(1), 315–319.

Mehr, J. (1983). *Abnormal Psychology.* New York: Holt, Rinehart and Winston.

Mehr, J. (1995). *Human Services: Concepts and Intervention Strategies,* 6th ed. Boston: Allyn and Bacon.

NASMHPD (1993). Report #103–18, "Tipper Gore Mental Health Issues Group Considers the Role of Public Psych Hospitals in Health Care Reform." Alexandria, VA: National Association of State Mental Health Program Directors.

Olfson, M. (1990). "Assertive Community Treatment: An Evaluation of the Experimental Evidence." *Hospital and Community Psychiatry, 41*(6), 634–641.

Rochefort, D. A. (1984). "Origins of the Third Psychiatric Revolution: The Community Mental Health Centers Act of 1963." *Journal of Health Politics, Policy and Law, 9*(1), 17–25.

Rossi, P. H. (1990). "The Old Homeless and the New Homelessness in Historical Perspective." *American Psychologist, 24*(3), 232–239.

SREB (1969). *Roles and Functions for Different Levels of Mental Health Workers.* Atlanta: Southern Regional Education Board.

Stein, L. I., and M. A. Test (1980). "Alternative Mental Hospital Treatment: I. Conceptual Model Treatment Program and Clinical Evaluation." *Archives of General Psychiatry, 37*(2), 392–397.

Stein, L. I., and M. A. Test, eds. (1985). *The Training in Community Living Model: A Decade of Experience.* San Francisco: Jossey-Bass.

Torrey, E. F. (1988). *Nowhere to Go: The Tragic Odyssey of the Homeless Mentally Ill.* New York: Harper and Row.

Vaccaro, J. V., R. P. Liberman, C. J. Wallace, and G. Blackwell (1992). "Combining Social Skills Training and Assertive Case Management: The Social and Independent Living Skills Program of the Brentwood Veterans Affairs Medical Center." In R. P. Liberman, ed., "Effective Psychiatric Rehabilitation." *New Directions for Mental Health Services, 53*(Spring), 33–42.

CHAPTER 21

AMERICANS WITH DISABILITIES:
ADVOCACY, LAW, AND HUMAN SERVICES

CHRISTINE LEWIS SHANE

The types of programs and services provided to adults and children with disabilities are the result of historical and social debates about the nature of disability. That is, people's beliefs about disabilities shape how they behave toward the disabled. For example, in ancient Sparta (Greece), babies born with physical deformities were left on a hillside to perish; in Elizabethan England, the poor and infirm were consigned to almshouses or convicted of crimes of begging and vagrancy; and in the early twentieth century, persons who were mentally retarded were removed from their communities and sent to live in large state-run institutions. Today, attitudes about disabilities have changed. Persons with disabilities are no longer confined to the margins of society. Under law, Americans with disabilities are guaranteed the same social and economic rights enjoyed by all citizens of the United States.

There are 43 million disabled people in the United States. This figure does not include individuals with some forms of mental illness, learning disabilities, HIV (AIDS), or other chronic physical illnesses. If these people were included in the count, there would be approximately 49 million disabled people in the United States (Shapiro, 1994; West, 1993). The quality and types of programs and services provided for the growing numbers for people with disabilities largely depend on the attitudes and vision of those who are privileged to work with them.

HISTORICAL OVERVIEW OF SOCIETAL TREATMENT OF DISABILITY

Exclusion, Benevolence, and Independence

Throughout history, people with disabilities have been excluded from society, pitied, or placed in custodial care away from their families and friends. Even today, people with disabilities are not always encouraged to seek an independent lifestyle. Historically, a physical, emotional, or cognitive disability was seen as punishment for sin or a curse from the gods. Specific cultural themes are associated with disability and chronic illness. These themes or images are woven into the fabric of our societal perceptions about disability. These themes are revealed in the language, the visual images, and the human service models that society creates for children and adults with disabilities.

In not-so-subtle forms, the print and entertainment media contribute to the negative images associated with people who have disabilities. The antihero in the 1997 movie *Sling Blade* murders a man after he leaves the psychiatric hospital, and Lenny, the dimwitted but deadly character in *Of Mice and Men,* is portrayed as dangerous and threatening to society. Within the last ten years, however, television and movies began to convey positive images of people with disabilities. For example, Corky, a young man with mental retardation, was represented as a likable and competent teenager in the popular television series *Life Goes On.*

Many authors who study the historical treatment of persons with disabilities note that the quality of their treatment reflects the economic health of the society. When an economy is prosperous, society treats persons with disabilities in more humane ways, providing better services and more generous financial supports. When economic times are lean, societies tend to provide less to those individuals who are in need (Stone, 1984; Berkowitz, 1987). Wolfensberger (1972) argues that persons with disabilities are not valued by society and that our human service models tend to isolate them and underestimate their competency. He offers these historical images of people with disabilities:

Objects of Pity/Sickness. Disability is often associated with sickness and disease. During ancient times, the priest and temple staff cared for the sick and dying, sometimes curing them. A place within the temple grounds was set aside for the care of the infirm. The medulla and staff, the early symbols of the healing power of the priest, can be seen today on the insignia of the American Medical Association.

Objects of Fear/Dread. In the Middle Ages, European villagers collected alms for specific ships that sailed into their ports. The passengers on those ships were sick, mentally ill, and disabled people who were banished from their homes— forced to embark on voyages to unknown ports. When townsfolk saw the "ship of fools" approaching the harbor, they would collect enough supplies and money to send the ship off again. This is an example of society's tendency to banish and physically segregate people with disabilities. Early asylums and hospitals for the insane and infirm were built on top of hills, far away from cities and towns. It was believed that the "poisonous fumes" that emanated from the diseased would be carried away by the hilltop winds.

Objects of Charity. Perhaps the most persistent stereotype associated with people with disabilities is the charitable image. During the tenth and eleventh centuries, the common belief was that no beggar should be turned away because the beggar carried within him a holy spirit. To provide charity, therefore, was to gain blessings from God. Today, religious organizations continue to advocate and promote the welfare of persons who are in need of social supports.

The Eternal Child. Childlike images abound in the world of disability. The image of the "poster child" for charity campaigns suggest that persons with disabilities are eternally dependent and vulnerable. This childlike image of people with disabilities tends to limit expectations and diminish competence.

Wolfensberger's historical images of persons with disabilities are supported by events detailed by Joseph Shapiro in his book *No Pity* (1994). Shapiro demonstrates that a common societal response to disability is to provide help (however begrudgingly) and to segregate the disabled from the "able bodied." Social historians link increases in social commitment to the treatment of people with disabilities to increases in the government's care for wounded soldiers.

The notion that people with disabilities should be treated separately from the rest of the population changed over time. Historical events and laws illustrate how United States policy evolved from excluding people with disabilities to including and protecting the rights of people with disabilities. The following are some of the events offered by Shapiro and others:

1630   In colonial America, physical ability was valued in order to tame the wilderness and to defend the frontiers. The early settlers discouraged the immigration of individuals who could not care for themselves. People who were not self-sufficient could be returned to England by force.

1775	During the Revolutionary War, the Continental Congress assisted the colonies to support wounded soldiers.
1778	Marine hospitals were established for disabled sailors. This service evolved into the United States Public Health Service.
1854	Dorothea Dix advocated for the establishment of federally funded hospitals for the "deaf, dumb, feeble-minded and blind." Hospitals were established in New York, Massachusetts, and Maryland.
1865	The Civil War necessitated the establishment of the National Home for Disabled Union Soldiers and the rise of orthopedic medicine.
1886	The State of Mississippi spent 20 percent of its revenue on artificial arms and legs for former Confederate soldiers.
1917	During World War I, the federal government, which had denied adequate support to the disabled, revised its view and provided funds for soldiers and their families.
1918, 1920	Federal funds were allocated to rehabilitation and training for jobs. National attention was directed to the problems of workers who suffer accidents.
1921	The Veteran's Bureau was established to address the needs of military veterans.
1935	The Social Security Act established permanent assistance for the disabled.
1946	Federal programs were expanded for World War II veterans; the Veterans' Administration established the Paralyzed Veterans of America and the President's Committee on Employment and the Handicapped.
1950s	Parents' advocacy groups were established for the education of handicapped children.
1966	The Federal Bureau for the Handicapped provided funds for the education and training of special educators.
1973	Section 504 of the Rehabilitation Act of 1973 provided antidiscrimination protection for disabled individuals in federally funded programs and facilities.
1975	Education for All Handicapped Children Act prohibited the exclusion of children with handicaps from public education services.
1990	The Americans with Disabilities Act (ADA) prohibited discrimination against disabled persons in employment and public and private facilities.
1997	The Individuals wth Disabilities Education Act mandates that all children with disabilities receive a free and appropriate public education that emphasizes special education and services that prepare them for employment and independent living.

CHANGING ATTITUDES TOWARD DISABLED PEOPLE

A disability, of itself, is never as disabling as it first seems.

—Hockenberry rule

Despite the negative cultural stereotypes that persist throughout Western civilization, today persons with disabilities are protected by anti-discrimination laws. The purpose of the laws is to enable people with disabilities to participate in the mainstream of society. Like other minority groups, people with disabilities experience prejudice and are denied access to services. Changes in attitudes about disability came about because of advances in medicine, technology, and pressure from growing numbers of disabled people. People with disabilities demanded and received better education and employment. Today the disability rights movement is a viable political and social force in the United States. The disability rights movement, which began in the 1960s, is composed of like-minded groups who believe that the biggest problem with having a disability is dealing with society's negative attitudes.

MEDICINE, TECHNOLOGY, AND GROWTH IN NUMBERS

Less than 15 percent of people with disabilities are born with them. Most people acquire disability through illness, accident, or aging. Advances in medicine have increased the numbers of people living with disabilities in the United States. The development of antibiotics, insulin, and chemical therapies and the early detection of illness increased the life expectancy of diabetics, cancer patients, and others with chronic illness. Surgery, physical therapy, and rehabilitation increased the survival rates of trauma and accident victims. During World War I, only four hundred soldiers survived wounds that paralyzed them from the waist down. Ninety percent of those men died *before* they reached home. In World War II, two thousand soldiers survived the same wounds and came home. In the 1960s, 85 percent of those wounded soldiers were still alive (Scotch, 1984).

The increased life expectancy of the American population has increased the percentage of people who are "probably going to be disabled." That is, of the 32 million older Americans, one-third of the population is currently disabled. By the year 2020, there will be 57 million older Americans with an equal increase in the number of those with disabilities. The increase in the number of older Americans with disabilities will challenge the ability of the rest of the population to financially support the housing, medical, and social needs of the aging population.

Lifesaving interventions for low-birthweight infants or sick babies enable thousands of children to live. Some of these children will survive with lifelong disabilities. Although medical advances can increase survival rates, they do not necessarily provide a cure. For example, a baby born with spina bifida (a condition seen at birth in which the bottom of the spinal column is not fully developed) will live but may not walk. Amniocentesis may identify a fetus with a disability or illness, but medicine may not be able provide a cure.

The inability of medicine to cure disabilities necessitates the development of prosthetic devices and adaptive technologies. The development of artificial limbs and robotics enables people to live independent lifestyles. Motorized wheelchairs enable people who are paraplegic and quadriplegic to be mobile. Assistive technology allows people who cannot talk or hear to communicate through computerized speech and telecommunications systems. Equally important, the expansion of the home health industry and the availability of personal care assistants (PCAs) allows individuals with disabilities to live in their own homes.

ADVOCACY AND CIVIL RIGHTS

Anatomy is not destiny.

The 1960s and 1970s were watershed decades for the civil rights of millions of Americans. The civil rights movement for black Americans sought to eliminate cultural prejudices against people of color. The women's movement sought to eliminate gender bias in employment, marriage, interpersonal relationships, and medicine. Parents of children with mental retardation and adults with disabilities sought public education, antidiscrimination in employment, and access to public services and facilities (e.g., transportation, stores, movie theaters). The goals of these groups were supported by the increasingly liberal politics of the United States and public attention to the emotional and physical needs of returning Vietnam veterans.

During that time, eloquent and powerful speeches by the Reverend Martin Luther King about social injustices toward black Americans captured this nation's attention. The fact that a country based on the ideals of liberty, equality, and justice would bar individuals from economic opportunity and limit individual freedoms mobilized thousands of individuals to challenge discriminatory social patterns.

Protection from racial discrimination is guaranteed by the Civil Rights Act of 1964. This act prohibits discrimination in employment and public and private services on the basis of race, sex, religion, and national origin. Compliance with the Civil Rights Act is enforced by the federal Department of Justice (DOJ) and the Equal Employment Opportunity Commission (EEOC). Each state is required to have a Commission Against Discrimination to guard against discrimination on the local level.

As the civil rights movement gained greater acceptance, the women's movement emerged. In the 1960s, feminists Betty Friedan and Gloria Steinem helped bring the issues of gender equality and reproductive choice to the center of the nation's attention. In Massachusetts, the abortion issue was ignited by the arrest of Bill Baird for the distribution of contraceptives to unmarried women. The *Roe v. Wade* (410 U.S. 113 1973) Supreme Court decision legalized a woman's right to choose the termination of her pregnancy. The liberalization of sexual norms and gender roles supported the concept of making major life choices without regard to physiology and gender. The social view that "anatomy is not destiny" was shared by advocates in the disability community.

Civil Rights and Disability

Civil rights legislation for person with disabilities is rooted in social ideology and in fact. The relegation of thousands of people with mental retardation to state-run institutions initiated a national examination of living conditions for disabled people. In the 1960s and 1970s, state institutions for the mentally retarded were overcrowded and understaffed. Thousands of residents were housed in large, barren buildings and were often left unattended all day. People with severe disabilities were not clothed or taught to use bathrooms. In some institutions, groups of individuals were compelled to eat out of large pots, naked and without the proper use of utensils. The first federal lawsuits were filed on behalf of persons in institutions in the states of Alabama, Pennsylvania, and New York. The purpose of the litigation was to improve the dehumanizing conditions of the institutions and to provide treatment and training for those who lived there. Similar litigation was filed in Massachusetts and other states. On the basis of the courts' findings, thousands of people with disabilities were "deinstitutionalized" or released into publicly funded community programs (Boggs, 1993).

One of the first and most vocal advocacy groups for children with special needs consisted of parents and family members. Until 1974, school-age children with mental retardation, physical disabilities, or emotional illness were excluded from the local school system or taught in separate classrooms. The refusal of local school systems to "mainstream" or include children with special needs became a "civil rights" debate among parents, educators, and legislators. In 1974, the "right to a free and appropriate education regardless of the degree of handicap" became law with the passage of the Right to Education for All Handicapped Children Act of 1974.

The Rehabilitation Act of 1973

Ed Roberts, a college student with quadriplegia at the University of California, Berkeley, became active in student demonstrations for the civil rights of minorities and an early advocate for the disabled. As founder and, later, director of the Center for Independent Living, Roberts led the charge to make the university accessible to people with disabilities. Accessibility provisions included the installation of ramps and elevators, doorways, and living spaces to accommodate wheelchairs and allow students with disabilities to attend classes with nondisabled students. With the help of other advocates, Roberts was instrumental in attaining the passage of the Rehabilitation Act of 1973. This act expanded protections for person with disabilities in federally sponsored programs. The most important parts of the act are the definition of the term "individual with a handicap" and the antidiscrimination mandates attached to Section 504.

Legal definitions are important because terms categorize people and will dictate what goods, services, or protections people are entitled to. If an individual does not "qualify" under the terms of a law, he or she will be denied the law's protections. The Rehabilitation Act of 1973 defines "individual with a handicap" as any individual who

> *(i) has a physical or mental impairment which substantially limits one or more of such person's major life activities, (ii) has a record of such an impairment, or (iii) is regarded as having such an impairment. Handicap includes chronic physical illness such as tuberculosis.* (West, 1996)

The scope of this definition is broad enough to include current disability, history of disability, chronic illness, and perceptions. For the first time, an "individual with a handicap" was broadly defined to include persons who have, or are *perceived* to have, a mental or physical handicap that "substantially limits one or more of a person's major life activities." "Perceived to have a handicap" is an important concept because it challenges cultural assumptions about disabilities. Some persons are considered "disabled or unable" to perform a function because of their medical or emotional history (e.g., heart problems or mental illness) or because of the way they look due to accident or trauma. In other words, discrimination against individuals with disabilities, real or assumed, is prohibited. Major life activities include such areas as work, caring for oneself, and participation in recreation and leisure activities.

The Rehabilitation Act of 1973 protected people with disabilities only in federal government programs, in the Postal Service, and in contracts and entities (including state, county, and local governments) receiving federal funds over the amount of $2,500. The antidiscrimination clause of the act requires that "no otherwise qualified handicapped individual will be discriminated against or excluded from participation in any benefits of any program or activity receiving federal assistance." The inclusion of this statement had significant impact on how state programs operated. All federal and state government buildings and services were required to be accessible, federal jobs had to accommodate disabled employees, federal public transportation systems required renovations, and federally funded housing projects needed to comply with Section 504. Section 504 of the act, however, introduced legal concepts that extended broad protections to persons with disabilities. These concepts can be described as follows:

— *Reasonable accommodation:* This removes barriers or provides technical or environmental supports to enable otherwise qualified disabled individuals to perform the essential functions of a job. These accommodations may not impose an undue hardship on the employer or company.

— *Undue burden* (*undue hardship*): This occurs when an employer is not required to hire a disabled individual because of the expense or difficulty that would be incurred to accommodate the disabled individual.

— *Otherwise qualified individual:* This refers to a disabled person who has the qualifications, education, and ability to do the job with appropriate environmental adaptations.

— *Essential job functions:* These are those components or tasks of a job that are the primary elements that complete the job. If the essential function were eliminated from the job, the job would be significantly altered or eliminated. For example, if a janitor's job requires an employee to lift fifty pounds, then lifting heavy material is an essential job function. Secondary or additional job duties, such as "driver's license desirable," are not part of the essential job function.

The antidiscrimination prohibition and the legal concepts of reasonable accommodation and essential job function set the stage for even more assertive legislation for the rights of people with disabilities. The focus of the disability movement broadened toward a wider community context.

That is, instead of limiting demands to the federal government and government-subsidized programs, the disability community took its message to home and community.

The Americans with Disabilities Act of 1990

Although the regulation of the Americans with Disabilities Act can be extraordinarily detailed, the purpose of the law is quite simple. It is to prohibit discrimination against 43 million Americans who live with some type of disability by providing clear, comprehensible, strong, consistent and enforceable standards.

—Bishop and Jones, 1993

The Americans with Disabilities Act of 1990 (ADA) is considered landmark legislation for children and adults with disabilities. The purpose of the ADA is to ensure that disability does not prevent people from participating in the mainstream of American life (West, 1993, 1996). The reason the ADA is such an extraordinary piece of legislation is that unlike previous antidiscriminatory legislation for persons with disabilities, the provisions of the ADA apply to private as well as publicly financed business and services, covering areas such as employment, transportation, and communications.

An important feature of the ADA is that it addresses employment opportunities for people with disabilities by going beyond Section 504 of the Rehabilitation Act of 1973. The ADA applies to private employers who employ at least fifteen employees and clearly articulates definitions of disability. The ADA prohibits specific discriminatory employment practices. For example, employers cannot limit, classify, or segregate employees on the basis of disability. Employment decisions must be made on the basis of an individual's abilities, not on presupposed limitations. The ADA prohibits the use of screening devices, employment tests, or other selection criteria that discriminate against people with disabilities. It also protects individuals seeking employment who have a disabled spouse, child, or relative. This safeguard protects families from discrimination when an employer refuses to hire someone whose personal circumstances may increase the business's health insurance premiums.

In addition to employment, the ADA increases accessibility to social opportunities for people with disabilities. The law mandates that all public services and accommodations be accessible to disabled persons. As stated earlier, these services include movie theaters, restaurants, sports arenas, and all forms of transportation. A Harris survey (1986) found that nearly two-thirds of all disabled Americans had not gone to a movie theater in the previous year and that disabled people were one-third as likely to eat in a restaurant as people without disabilities. These findings suggest that people with disabilities remained segregated from the rest of society. Like the Rehabilitation Act of 1973, the ADA expanded the definition of disability. The ADA defines disability in three ways.

First, in functional terms, the ADA looks at how a disability affects a person in his or her home, community, or work environment. A disability need not be a recognized medical condition but can be a more subtle learning problem. A physical or mental impairment is defined as any "physiological disorder or condition, cosmetic disfigurement, or anatomical loss affecting one or more of the body's systems." Some of the systems identified include the cardiovascular, skin, and sensory organs. A mental impairment is defined as "any mental or physiological disorder, such as mental retardation, organic brain syndrome, emotional or mental illness, and specific learning disabilities." The ADA defines a contagious disease as a disability, including HIV (AIDS). Therefore, disability may limit an individual's ability to attain or to hold a job.

Second, a disabled individual must have a history or a record of disability or impairment. Finally, disability is legitimized when a person has a physical or mental impairment that is supported by *the attitudes of others toward the disability* or has none of the impairments defined but is *treated* as having such an impairment. This clause of the law addresses the issue of discrimination toward persons who are inappropriately labeled or treated as disabled. The ADA extends the definition to perception of disability, such as obesity, and to survivors of life-threatening illnesses who may still be perceived as sick, even if fully recovered.

Conditions that do not qualify under the ADA are those impairments that are not chronic, are of short duration, and do not leave a lasting impairment. These include the following:

- Broken limbs
- Sprained joints
- Appendicitis
- Transvestitism, pedophilia, exhibitionism, and gender and other sexual disorders; compulsive gambling; kleptomania; pyromania
- Psychotropic substance abuse involving illegal drugs
- Homosexuality and bisexuality

Costs. Eliminating discrimination against people with disabilities and guaranteeing access to public services and facilities costs money. The Rehabilitation Act of 1973 required a $1.55 billion federal aid package for programmatic compliance. The ADA demands the investment of private capital without federal reimbursement. For this reason, many still oppose the full implementation of the ADA. But disabled people want to work and participate fully in life.

Negative attitudes and limited access are major barriers to the full participation of people with disabilities. A 1994 Harris survey found that only 33 percent of disabled people held jobs, although 79 percent said they wanted to work. Advocates say that the cost of accommodating a disabled worker is less than maintaining the same person on welfare. Others point out that the average reasonable accommodation for a worker with disabilities costs less than $100. Accommodations include physical and temporal changes in the workplace. For example, a person who is blind can use a computer with special audio features and a braille printer. A person in a wheelchair may need a modified desk or a ramp into a building. A person with a stress-related disability may require a modified work schedule or frequent breaks during the workday.

Lack of Progress. Harris conducted another survey in 1998. This survey showed that opportunities for persons with disabilities had not changed significantly since the passage of the 1990 Act. There continued to be significant barriers to participation for persons with disabilities, especially in the area of employment. Recent U.S. Supreme Court decisions appeared to have narrowed the interpretation of the ADA and limited the legal protections provided to persons with disabilities.

Harris (1998) found that despite advocacy for persons with disabilities there continued to be a wide employment gap between nondisabled persons and disabled persons. Three in ten persons with disabilities were employed full- or part-time, compared to eight in ten adults without disabilities (1998 NOD, Harris, page 5). The low rate of employment for individuals with disabilities means a low income level as well. One in three persons with disabilities lived in households with incomes below $15,000 a year.

Limited employment opportunities for persons with disabilities have not been helped by recent Supreme Court decisions. The Court ruled, for example, that workers' labor union contracts can, in some instances, override the ADA. One ruling decided that a nondisabled senior union employee could take a disabled worker's job because of the union's seniority rules. In another instance, the court ruled that persons with physical disabilities that can be ameliorated by corrective measures, such as eyeglasses, are not eligible to be treated as individuals with disabilities under the ADA.

Despite the fact that progress has been somewhat slow, good things continue to happen for persons with disabilities. The 1999 Ticket to Work and Work Incentives Improvement Act (P.L. 160-1700) provides health and employment benefits to allow individuals with disabilities to return to work and keep federally funded health benefits. Families and individuals with disabilities continue to advocate for improved, individualized state and federal programs and services. Most important, persons with disabilities believe that the ADA has improved their lives (Harris, 1998).

CONSIDERATIONS FOR HUMAN SERVICE WORKERS

Attitudes and expectations are shaped by our personal experiences and histories. As human service workers, we need to be aware that our attitudes and beliefs about persons with disabilities will affect their lives. There are important ways in which human service workers can assist people with disabilities to attain their personal goals.

First, we must recognize the way in which society views people with disabilities. Understanding the historical treatment of persons with disabilities allows us to gain insights into the development and implementation of human service programs. Many of the cultural stereotypes previously described affect the design and imple-

mentation of human service programs today. For example, training and education programs for adults and children with disabilities provided in separate buildings and facilities limit opportunities for community integration. Likewise, unreliable special transportation services for disabled people limit their access to shopping centers, health care, recreational opportunities, and jobs. Lack of appropriate housing in the community forces adults to live in substandard housing or at home with their parents. By recognizing how negative stereotypes and attitudes can affect programs, human service workers can develop more positive service delivery models.

Second, we need to become familiar with the laws that protect the civil rights of people with disabilities. There are many opportunities for human service workers to ensure the participation of people with disabilities in the community. Physical barriers that deny access to buildings and prejudices that deny access to jobs are prohibited by law. The Vocational Rehabilitation Act of 1973 and the ADA extend antidiscrimination protection to people with disabilities. Human service workers need to inform and educate others about the provisions of the ADA and advocate for the rights of disabled people.

REFERENCES

Access New England (a publication of the ADA technical assistance center). Vol. 1, no. 3 (Summer 1977).

Berkowitz, E. (1987). *Disabled Policy: America's Programs for the Handicapped. A Twentieth Century Fund Report.* New York: Cambridge University Press.

Bishop, P., and A. Jones (1993). "Implementing the Americans with Disabilities Act of 1990: Assessing the Variables of Success." *Public Administration Review,* 53 (March /April), 122–128.

Boggs, E. (1993). "The Americans with Disabilities Act: Historical Legacy and Contemporary Challenges." Presented at symposium: Americans with Disabilities Act (held at the Starr Center for Mental Retardation, Florence Heller Graduate School

for advanced study in social welfare), Brandeis University, Waltham, MA.

Harris, L. (1986). *The ICD Survey of Disabled Americans: Bringing the Disabled Americans into the Mainstream.* New York: Louis Harris and Associates.

Harris, L. (1998). *N.O.D./Harris Survey of Americans with Disabilities.* New York: Louis Harris and Associates.

Scotch, R. (1984). *From Goodwill to Civil Rights: Transforming Federal Disability Policy.* Philadelphia: Temple University Press.

Shapiro, J. (1994). *No Pity: People with Disabilities Forging a New Civil Rights Movement.* New York: Times Books.

Silverstein, R. (2000). "The Emerging Disability Policy Framework: A Guide for Developing Public Policy for Persons with Disabilities." *Iowa Law Review, 85*(5).

Stone, D. (1984). *The Disabled State.* Philadelphia: Temple University Press.

Stone, D. (1988). *Policy Paradox and Political Reason.* London: Scott, Foresman.

West, J. (1993). *The Americans with Disabilities Act: From Policy to Practice.* New York: Milbank Memorial Fund.

West, J. (1996). *Implementing the Americans with Disabilities Act.* Oxford: Blackwell Press.

Wolfensberger, W. (1972). *Normalization: The Principle of Normalization in Human Services.* Toronto: National Association on Mental Retardation.

KEY TERMS FOR PART FIVE _____

After studying Chapters 18, 19, 20, and 21, you should have a command of the following key terms, major concepts, and principal topical references:

public policy	organized money	historical view of people with
regulation writing	modes of action	disabilities
advisory bodies	Supplemental Security Income	disability rights movement
special task groups and studies	Social Security Disability	civil rights
networking	Insurance	advocacy
media activities	community mental health	Rehabilitation Act
politics	movement	deinstitutionalization
elections	SRO	accessibility
influencing legislation	homelessness	physical impairment
lobbying	downsizing	mental impairment
coalitions	community mental health	anti-discrimination
opposition groups	services	reasonable accommodation
community organizing	Assertive Community	undue burden
organizing for social change	Treatment	otherwise qualified individual
social movements	Intensive Case Management	essential job functions
IAF	case management	cultural stereotypes of PWD
government	Americans with Disabilities	competency-based instruction
collective leadership	Act	

PIVOTAL ISSUES FOR DISCUSSION OF PART FIVE _____

1. Make one visit to each of the following public legislative activities and record your observations on each occasion.

    Public Legislative Hearing

    Subcommittee Hearing

    General Session—House

    General Session—Senate

    Make a list of all elected officials serving you as a constituent. Write to each official and request a list of pending bills having to do with human services that they, individually, support. Record their responses, collate the materials, and present your work in class.

2. What is the role of prevention/promotion in human services?

3. As a community leader, you are committed to maximizing prevention techniques in the delivery of community human services. Describe how you would develop prevention/promotion programs throughout your city or town. How would these programs be used in schools, agencies, hospitals and clinics, housing, police and public safety, and so on?

4. Request a copy of the Americans with Disabilities Act of 1990 from your U.S. congressperson and outline it.

5. Identify two current or recent community organizing projects in your region. Review and evaluate their relative success or failure and share your feelings with the class.

6. Visit a community-based group residence program. Interview the manager of the program and record the description of the program, the clients served, funding, and the problems and barriers encountered in administering the program. Be sure to include how to become a staff member and what is required in this work.

SUGGESTED READINGS FOR PART FIVE _____

1. Woods, R. H. (1984). *The Law and the Practice of Human Services.* San Francisco: Jossey-Bass.

2. Neugeboren, B. (1985). *Organization, Policy, and Practice in Human Services.* New York: Longman.

3. Fairweather, G., K. Sanders, and L. Tornatzky (1974). *Creating Change in Mental Health Organizations.* Elmsford, NY: Pergamon Press.

4. Hasenfeld, Y. (1983). *Human Services Organizations.* Englewood Cliffs, NJ: Prentice-Hall.

5. Shapiro, J. (1994). *No Pity: People with Disabilities Forging a New Civil Rights Movement.* New York: Times Books.

6. Mehr, J. *Human Services: Concepts and Interventional Stategies.* Boston: Allyn and Bacon.

7. World Health Organization (1975). *Organization of Mental Health Services in Developing Countries: Sixteenth Report of the Committee on Mental Health* (WGO Technical Report Series No. 564). Geneva: World Health Organization.

PART SIX

LAW, ETHICS, AND PROFESSIONAL ISSUES

Part Six directs the student's attention to two important areas of professional concern: (1) law and ethics, and (2) career issues. Nearly every undergraduate program in human service education includes both of these topics as part of its core curriculum.

In carrying out the work of a human service professional, you will be expected to know (and, in some cases, *required* to know) what laws apply to you as a professional and what laws apply to the clients you serve. In Chapter 22, David C. Maloney and Peter Clark outline and discuss the general role of law in our society, the nature of clients' rights and privileges, and the legal responsibilities of human service workers. These lawful foundations are essential to your preparation and will be a routine part of your day-to-day responsibilities in future work situations. Ethics are discussed in this chapter and again in Chapter 23, written by Naydean Blair. The thread running through both of these chapters is a recognition that the client should be treated as a person embodied and protected by legal rights. Although ethical guidelines will directly influence your work regardless of the location, many laws vary depending on the state in which you practice. In Chapter 22, laws are cited as they exist in Massachusetts. In Chapter 23, Texas laws are used as examples. To help you understand the challenges of learning how to do the right thing, at the right time, for the right reason, these chapters are followed by a Special Focus Feature presenting the official Code of Ethics for the human service professional.

Although you may be an "A" student, possess a high level of skills and knowledge, and be a moral and ethical person, it will still be a challenge to have a successful human service career. Chapter 24, by Miriam Clubok, is devoted to giving you insight and encouragement in feeling satisfied and productive as a human service worker. The chapter covers a variety of ways to enhance your professional growth and ensure your personal survival as you pursue your career in human services. The discussion emphasizes the concerns you should have for your client, self, and work setting. You will also find helpful the identification of eight tips, which, if followed, will enhance your personal and professional growth.

Part Six concludes with Chapter 25, which deals with understanding and avoiding stress-related burnout. Here, Frederick Sweitzer attempts to raise your awareness to both intrapersonal and interpersonal sources of stress and discusses ways to avoid these problems. Burnout may affect you directly in your career and indirectly when, for example, one of your co-workers becomes "burned-out" and you have to assume additional work responsibilities in the process.

As a professional human service worker, you will need to watch for emerging trends in the field in order to keep abreast of advances in technology and science that will reshape the nature of your work with others by offering the potential for better and more effective ways of understanding and assisting clients. This is the central focus of the book's final section, Part Seven.

LEARNING OBJECTIVES FOR PART SIX: LAW, ETHICS, AND PROFESSIONAL ISSUES

After reading and studying Chapters 22, 23, 24, and 25,

- You will become familiar with legal issues that apply to the human service profession.
- You will understand the range of ethical behaviors to which human service workers must adhere in their work with clients.
- You will know and appreciate what is involved in the development of a career in human services.
- You will understand the problem of job burnout, how it develops, and how to deal with it.

CHAPTER 22

LEGAL FOUNDATIONS IN HUMAN SERVICES:
CONSIDERATIONS FOR CLIENTS AND WORKERS

DAVID C. MALONEY AND PETER CLARK

It is our intent and purpose in this chapter to meet three basic goals for the reader. First, inasmuch as your work will be performed in the service of others, you will need to know what rights and privileges are given to clients by law and how these rights and privileges are typically dealt with by human service professionals. In this way, you may begin to appreciate the extent to which legal considerations will influence what you are required to do with and for the people you service, and you will understand what helping others involves with regard to their freedoms and their choices as recipients of your service.

Second, as a beginning student preparing to eventually enter the field of human services, you will need to understand how legal principles will influence the work you do. The readings to follow are designed to present relevant information regarding these principles.

Third, after reading this chapter, you will gain a greater appreciation of the law through your knowledge of the origins of those ethics that guide and direct the professional behaviors of human service workers by setting limits to help ensure that such workers always are doing the "right" thing, for the "right" reason, at the "right" time.

As "bookends" to the above goals, the authors will begin by providing a brief outline of the relationship between law and society and finish with some relevant applications of specific

laws in relation to human services and mental health.

LAW AND SOCIETY: BASIC PRINCIPLES

In modern civilizations, as well as in known past societies, humans united by a common bond of purpose have always had a shared reliance upon a set of rules that structure the conduct of behavior and the relationships between and among the group's members. Stability and continuity of society are the products of these laws and rules (Abel, 1995).

Laws are the rules of behavior that members of a given society are directed to follow. Whatever benefits are offered to members of a society (e.g., protection, support, income, status, freedom, etc.), those rewards are the product of adhering to the rules inherent to that society. In our society, our laws (rules) originate from two basic sources: either they have been *legislated* by federal and state elected bodies or they have *evolved* (case law) from the interpretations of our judiciary system (all branches, state and federal).

As a nation, our original basic principles of legislated law are set forth in our Constitution, its amendments, and the Bill of Rights. In the two hundred or so years since the required nine states ratified these sets of rules, all subsequent laws created and voted upon by federal and state legislatures have had to conform to the original constitutional laws. Thus, stability and continuity were preserved for every state in the Union and for the nation, a democratic republic, as a whole (Rembar, 1980).

Rights and Restrictions

The *products* of law are statements that describe the rules by which people, their activities, and their relationships are constantly governed. The *process* of law is the interpretation of those laws via the court system on a case-by-case basis. As original laws are upheld they are constantly being interpreted and reinterpreted through the judgments of the court(s). When new and different judgments are rendered and upheld via the appellate courts (state and federal) they become the prevailing (case) laws. Thus, law is not an arcane code, never to change or bend and intelligible only to lawyers and judges, but rather a substantive, living set of rules subject to review and reevaluation and available to criticism and modification and when in the best interests of all citizens, also subject to repeal. Law is not a monolith of rules, but always in flux as it adapts to social changes of the day.

Rights are insured for all citizens of this country by constitutional law. Human service workers should understand the rights guaranteed by the U.S. Constitution in its original form. There are few terms in the Constitution, or its twenty-six amendments, that the average human service student will need to consult a dictionary to comprehend. The conciseness and clarity of these writings are the cornerstones of their longevity and resilience. Collectively, they represent the heart of our civil court system and are exercised daily throughout the country.

Laws are also utilized to establish the limits of behavior; that is to say, they present the *restrictions* imposed both on individuals and on institutions (including the government itself). These limitations, properly administered, form the ground rules for our liberties and our freedoms as citizens. As a student of the Constitution, with all of its rights and restrictions, you will gradually grow to appreciate its depth, its power, its simplicity, and its utility for all citizens within our society, especially those in need.

Freedoms and "Humanitarian Ethos"

As citizens of a democratic republic, we enjoy a bounty of freedoms and liberties guaranteed by law. Countless numbers of disputes throughout our country's history have been ultimately resolved and remedied by the application of these laws. Another cornerstone of our society is the moral obligation we carry to help those who are in need and less fortunate than others, by nature or by circumstance. In the broadest historical review of these two centerpieces of modern civilization, there appears a gradual synthesis of legal philosophy (jurisprudence) and Judeo-Christian ethics, expressed as a marriage of earlier "common law" and later "civil law," especially as it applies to the poor, the disabled, the ill, the deprived, the disadvantaged, and others whom we deem "at risk." In each of these categories of subgroups in society we can identify the human service client, and thus we understand how our laws to protect and to help them are a reflection of our moral duty (humanitarian ethos) as a society.

Having explored the broad outlines of history, law, and social ethics, let us now see how these concepts are more specifically represented in the people we serve and the nature of the help we provide as professional human service workers.

RIGHTS OF HUMAN SERVICE CLIENTS

Only in the last three or four decades have the rights of human service clients been codified in laws. The initial impetus was provided by the debate concerning civil rights of racial and ethnic minorities in America and by the strength of the commitment of well-known activist leaders of that era, including Hubert Humphrey, Martin Luther King, Jr., and John and Robert Kennedy. Other groups in need were eventually also recognized (the physically disabled, the mentally ill, the mentally retarded, and so on). From these beginnings, programs on equal opportunity compensatory education, nondiscrimination in school and work, and other equal-rights concerns were legislated and made laws. Again, all of these efforts, being grounded on constitutional rights, guaranteed to all citizens a national spirit of moral obligation (humanitarian ethos) devoted to helping those in need.

Right of Privacy

Probably the most fundamental right of human service clients is their *right of privacy.* Inasmuch as such clients rely heavily on the trust of professionals, their intimate and personal revelations in therapy and treatment must be held, at all costs, confidential and private. For this reason, the Federal Privacy Act of 1974 was passed (referred to as PL 93-579).

The background of the law was a concern that consumers (clients) were not adequately informed of the records being maintained on them and were not able to have full access to these files. The original Privacy Act pertained to federally funded and administered programs as well as some non-federal programs receiving federal grant monies. All such programs had to abide by the regulations in the cases of consumers receiving services through such monies. The Social Security Administration, Department of Veterans Affairs, Supplemental Security Income (SSI) programs and other programs (Medicaid, Medicare, for example) that employ social workers, psychologists, psychiatrists, and other helping professionals were all affected.

The highlights and provisions of the law are summarized below. They represent guidelines that medical and health care professionals, human service agencies and institutions, and practicing providers must follow:

1. The individual on whom a record is maintained has the right to:

   a. find out what records are being maintained on him or her and how they are used and disseminated by the agency;

   b. prohibit those records that are to be used for a particular purpose in the agency from being used for any other purpose without his or her written consent;

   c. have access to records and be accompanied by a person of his or her choosing, whether as counsel or as support;

   d. have copies made of any or all of his or her records, although the agency may charge a fee for this service;

   e. correct or amend the record as he or she feels is necessary to render it complete and accurate.

2. The agency must secure the individual's written consent before it can release information from that person's record to another person or agency.

3. When an agency makes a disclosure of information, it must keep records of

   a. the date of the disclosure;

   b. the nature and purpose of the disclosure; and

   c. the name and address of the person or agency to whom disclosure was made.

   d. In addition, (a) through (c) must be retained by the agency for a minimum of five years or the life of the record, whichever is longer.

   e. (a) through (c) must be available to the individual whose record is involved.

   f. The agency keeps note of all amendments or corrections made by the individual to his or her record. If the information involved has been disclosed to someone prior to the addition of the corrections or amendments, the agency must inform all persons to whom the disclosure was made of the additions or corrections.

4. The individual has the right to correct or amend the record.

5. Agencies must follow certain guidelines in gathering material for their records:

   a. The agency must keep only information that is relevant and necessary for agency purposes.

   b. It must collect the information directly from the individual if it is information that may lead to negative decisions regarding federal benefits or rights.

   c. The agency must provide the following information to people whose records are maintained:

(1) by what authority the agency is allowed to gather the information;

(2) whether the information can be disclosed to the individual whose record is involved;

(3) the purposes for which the information is to be used;

(4) the effects on the informant, if any, of not providing all or part of the requested information.

6. The agency has a responsibility to set policies regarding the handling of records and the safeguarding of confidentiality.

7. A legally appointed guardian may act on behalf of an adult individual who has been declared incompetent, or if a minor is involved, the legal guardian and/or the parents of the child can act on behalf of the child.

8. There are situations in which an agency is allowed to maintain records on an individual that the agency does *not* have to disclose to the individual:

a. Material that would reveal the identity of a source who gave the information to the government under promise that identity of the source would be kept confidential does not have to be disclosed to the individual on whom the record is kept.

b. The agency does not have to disclose to the individual information that was gathered prior to the effective date of the Privacy Act if at the time an implied promise of confidentiality of the identity of the source was made.

c. An individual does not have to be given access to any information "compiled in reasonable anticipation of a civil action or proceeding."

d. Records maintained by the CIA do not have to be disclosed to the individual.

e. Records maintained by an agency concerned primarily with the enforcement of criminal laws do not have to be disclosed to the person.

9. An agency cannot require an individual on whom it keeps records to disclose to the agency his or her Social Security number.

10. A Privacy Protection Study Commission is established to

a. monitor application of the Federal Privacy Act;

b. study "data banks, automated data processing programs and information systems of governmental, regional, and private organizations to determine the standards in force for protection of personal information";

c. recommend additional legislative action as needed to protect privacy rights of the individual;

d. look for violations of the Federal Privacy Act;

e. study the information systems of governmental, regional, and private organizations to determine the procedures in force for the protection of personal information. Following this study, the Commission must recommend the extent, if any, to which the principles and/or requirements of the Privacy Act should be applied to those organizations not currently subject to them.

The Buckley Amendment.   Sponsored by Senator Robert Buckley of New York, this addition to the Acts of Privacy extended its mandated application to students (all ages, all levels) and to schools, training facilities, and educational institutions.

Recent Modifications to Privacy Laws.   The *Health Insurance Portability and Accountability Act* (HIPAA) was an outgrowth of earlier legislation sponsored by Senators Nancy Kassenbaum (R-KS) and Ted Kennedy (D-MA). The HIPAA law was designed to protect Americans who had been ill from losing their insurance when they changed jobs or residences. Another intent of the law was to streamline the health care system through the establishment of standards for transmitting information uniformly via electronic health claims. Last, these legal standards would have to be carried while still protecting the privacy of the client and preserving the security of the storage of this information.

The privacy rule focuses on the application of effective policies, procedures, and business service agreements to control the access and use of patient information.

The proposed security rule addresses the provider/organization's physical infrastructure such as access to offices, files, and computers to assure secure and private communication and maintenance of confidential patient information.

The essence of this recent modification is to safeguard the health care information of human service clients vis à vis the use of electronic-based storage and communication systems (primarily computers and their files). This information is now referred to as *Protected Health Information* (PHI). Such information and the standards for limiting the accessibility of this information applies, by law, to all human service work, from mammoth hospitals and medical insurance companies to individual, solo practices in psychology, social work, mental health counseling, and so on. It will be yet another area of legally based rules and information that human service workers will be required to know and operate within. Full implementation was scheduled for October 2003.

Accessibility and Release of Client Information.

Beginning with the client's first contact with the human service agency or worker, *all information,* including basic identification data such as name and address, is private and confidential. In other words, having *access* to it or *releasing* it to others is restricted by law.

The rules outlined earlier in the Privacy Acts identify who, by law, is allowed access to client information, and under what conditions the release of this information is allowed. Essentially, only the client, and those directly involved in working with that client, have access to client information. In releasing information on clients, the human service worker must secure signed consent by the client to release the information maintained by the agency or worker on that client.

We will now examine further details of clients' right to consent.

Right to Consent

Other than in very specifically defined circumstances which will be discussed later in this section, clients' legal right to grant consent or permission to do something on their behalf (e.g.,

consent to release information or consent to receive treatment) requires that an individual's permission be given knowingly, intelligently, and voluntarily. In the vast majority of situations this permission by the client is recorded in writing and confirmed by the signature of the client. In some cases, a witness's signature to the consent is also recorded.

Types of Consent.

There are basically two classes of consent, both of which can be legally binding if the consent is obtained according to proper procedure(s).

1. *Informed (Express) Consent*
   Written, signed, dated, and witnessed consents constitute informed or express consents. They may still, however, be invalid if the client can prove that consent was not given knowingly, intelligently, or voluntarily. Final questioning of the client, in the presence of another party (usually a professional colleague or a personal responsible party known to the client) may help to avoid any future consent issues. One such client question protocol would include:
   (1) "Do you understand what you are consenting to?"
   (2) "Do you understand why this consent is important?"
   (3) "Do you give your consent freely and voluntarily and not under threats or any other form of duress?"
2. *Implied Consent*
   There are times during which consent can be deduced from a client as a consequence of prior circumstances or previous consents. Examples might include consent to release information to insurance companies who require such information in order to process the billing claims for the services provided to the client. Some insurance companies require such consents from their subscribers at the time of application or enrollment. Another example would be drawing a blood sample from a patient who had been admitted to a hospital. In this case, consent would be implied based upon the consent on file that was taken during the admission process.

Extensions and Limitations to Rights of Privacy and Confidentiality

Confidentiality is a general standard of conduct that obliges a professional provider not to divulge information about a client to anyone. In this country, it directly includes all medical professionals (physicians, nurses, and so on), allied health professionals (occupational therapists, physical therapists, speech therapists, and so on), mental health professionals (psychologists, social workers, counselors, therapists, and so on), educators (principals, teachers, and so on), as well as fiduciary professionals (accountants, financial/estate planners, and so on).

Confidentiality and Privileged Communication. In contrast with confidentiality, *privileged communication* is a legal construct that refers to a rule in evidence law that "provides a litigant with the right to withhold evidence in a legal proceeding that was originally communicated in confidence" (Rule 504 of the Federal Rules of Evidence). In other words, standards on confidentiality have evolved to protect the client from having private information divulged within the courtroom. The underlying rationale for testimonial privilege is based upon the assumption that the benefit to justice in allowing the testimony is outweighed by the potential injury to the relationship between the professional and the client that is based squarely upon trust and confidence. In most situations, privileged communication is respected in the courts as it applies to doctors, lawyers, and "confessional" clergy, but in some states, like Massachusetts, it has also been extended to psychologists, social workers, and therapists. One important limitation to the construct of privileged communication is that the right to have information revealed in court is the client's choice and *not* that of the professional. As such, if the client consents to having information revealed in court, the professional has no legal recourse to refuse and may be punished for doing so (contempt finding); that is,

> . . . *clients, not therapists, are protected under privilege statutes. Once a client waives his/her*

> *privilege, a therapist is legally obligated to testify (unless the therapist is willing to assume the possible penalty for violations of the law by refusing on ethical grounds to break confidentiality).* (Jagim, R. D., et al., p.462, 1978).

"Need to Know." Restrictions on access to client information apply to other professionals who may be otherwise qualified but are not directly involved with the client as such. Professionals, despite working together at the same agency, hospital, or institution, do not have a professional right to access files of clients whom they are not directly servicing. In other words, they must have a "need to know" about such information. "Need to know" means that in order to carry out their work-related responsibilities, they must have access and exposure to the client file. If they fail to meet the "need to know" requirement, they have no right to access the client's file. Besides direct service providers, other professionals with a "need to know" would include clinical supervisors who meet regularly with workers to review and discuss cases they are working on, utilization review committees and internal audit teams who randomly evaluate client files for completeness and quality, and to a more limited extent, billing clerks, approved researchers, and external auditors doing site visitations.

Limits of Confidentiality. Under what conditions are the laws governing access and release of private and confidential client information intentionally breached or broken? The following list outlines those circumstances whereby confidentiality is limited by higher priorities or more important reasons.

1. If withholding information would threaten the client's safety or the safety of others.
   a. If the client is clearly dangerous to himself and refuses to accept further treatment, the therapist may take steps to seek involuntary hospitalization. The therapist may also contact members of the family or others if necessary to protect the safety of the client.

b. If the client threatens to kill or seriously hurt someone and the therapist believes he or she may carry out the threat, or if the client has a known history of physical violence and the therapist believes he or she will attempt to kill or inflict serious harm on someone, the therapist may:

   i. tell any reasonably identified victim;

   ii. notify the police;

   iii. arrange for the client to be hospitalized voluntarily; or

   iv. take steps toward involuntary hospitalization.

2. If it is necessary to place or keep the client in a hospital for psychiatric care.

3. If the therapist is a "mandated reporter" and is required to notify government agencies because he or she reasonably believes a child, a handicapped person, or an elderly person is suffering injury as a result of abuse or neglect.

4. If the client reveals information that pertains to an instance of physician misconduct. In such cases, the therapist is required to report the physician to the board of registration in medicine.

5. In the following types of legal proceedings:

   a. In a court proceeding wherein it is alleged that a child is without proper guardianship due to the death, unavailability, incapacity, or unfitness of the parent or guardian, or in a proceeding to dispense with the need for parental consent to adoption.

   b. In a child custody or adoption case if the judge thinks that the therapist has important evidence about a parent's ability to provide suitable care.

   c. In any other court proceeding in which the client might introduce his or her emotional condition as an element of a claim or defense. (For example, if the client is fired from a job and sues the employer for wrongful discharge and claims to have suffered emotional trauma, the client has "introduced their mental or emotional condition" and the therapist can be required to testify about issues and communications in therapy.)

   d. In the event of the client's death, the therapist may be required to testify in a proceeding where the mental or emotional condition is introduced as an issue.

e. If the client brings a legal action against the therapist and disclosure is necessary or relevant to a defense, the therapist may disclose confidential communications.

6. If it is necessary to provide information regarding the client's diagnosis, prognosis, and course of treatment to an insurance company that is paying for these services.

7. If the Agency must use a collection agency or other process to collect amounts the client owes for services. In this case, clinical information will not be released, other than the client's name and address.

Right to Treatment

Human service clients have a right to receive adequate and proper treatment. Application of this right is binding by law, regardless of the client's status (i.e., inpatient vs. outpatient, involuntary vs. voluntary, competent vs. incompetent). This right also applies to all clients regardless of their special classification (e.g., minors, criminal inmates, mental retardates, and so on). The adequacy and properness of treatment also extends to the number and competency of treatment providers. It further incorporates the accuracy and validity of diagnosis and assessment, which in most cases determines the type(s) of intervention best designed to deal with or treat the problem(s) identified diagnostically. The client's right to treatment also includes the right to the *least intrusive* treatment necessary to alleviate the particular problem. Factors such as permanency of change, non-beneficial side effects (including mental/physical debilitations), costs, time and follow-up services are just a few considerations. All of the foregoing issues related to the right to treatment help to define standards in the *quality of care* and its specific delivery. A final extension of the right to treatment is the client's *right to choose between treatments* and to be informed of the differences between treatment approaches or modalities. Unless otherwise directed, the responsibilities for ensuring clients' right to treatment lie with the human service providers.

Right to Refuse Treatment

While the right to refuse treatment has multiple reflections of legal support in the First, Eighth, and Fourteenth Amendments to the U.S. Constitution, it nevertheless creates endless debates on its utility and relevance, especially in the face of other legal issues that its argument automatically draws into fire (i.e., competence, safety, custody, etc.). As Kraft notes, it pits "patient against doctor, expert against layman, clinician against lawyer" (Kraft, 1985) In the wealth of related literature on the subject it appears that the problems or issues lie not with the refusal right itself, but rather, with the circumstances under which it is applied. Most actual cases of the right to refuse treatment involve (a) administration of medications as treatment, or (b) intrusive treatment modalities (psychosurgery, electroconvulsive treatment, insulin shock treatment, and so on), and (c) refusal is more likely to occur in underfunded public institutions than in well-staffed private hospitals (Ford, 1990; Michaels, 1981).

In contradiction to the commonly held position that such legal dilemmas are best clarified and settled in the appellate court system, it does not appear that the states or the supreme courts have thus far remedied the matter in any consistent manner, other than reiterating that such a right should, in fact, exist. If nothing else, the debate has underlined the need for the Right to Due Process.

Right to Due Process

This legal safeguard points to the protection of all of the rights of clients and ensures that prior to the loss of any of those rights, the client must be given "due process." Due process outlines the steps, mandated to be followed, in the case of any abridgement or loss of any right involving the client. Sufficient cause for the removal of any right must occur only by and through the following series of steps:

(a) *Right to Notice*—The right to a written form of petition, which spells out all essential elements of the case;
(b) *Right to Counsel*—Availability of an attorney to represent the client and his/her interests;
(c) *Right to a Hearing*—Fair and impartial review of all salient matters pertaining to the case;
(d) *Right to Appeal*—Any/all decisions rendered in the hearing may be appealed by the client to the local court(s), the State Court of Appeals (including the State Supreme Court), and the Federal Court of Appeals (including the Federal Supreme Court).

"Best Interests of the Child"

An individual is not generally considered legally competent until he or she reaches the statutory age—the age of majority—for taking responsibility for his or her decisions and behavior. Until such chronological age is met or exceeded, the individual remains defined as a "child"—that is, incompetent by reason of immaturity—or of the age of minority (a minor). Typically, until legally mature the minor falls under the custody or control of the child's parents, unless it can be proven that the parents, as custodians, are not acting in the child's "best interests."

On the basis of the "parens patriae" doctrine (i.e., the moral, legal duty of the state to protect its citizens), the state can assume legal custody of the child and make decisions in place of the parents. These situations most commonly arise from (a) the "dangerousness" of the child's behavior, (b) custody disputes emerging from divorce proceedings and/or physical custody issues arising after divorce, (c) child abuse and neglect (physical, sexual, emotional) by parents, and (d) involuntary commitments for treatment. Frequently the protection of the child's "best interests" is secured by the state appointing an intermediary guardian—a "guardian ad litem"—who will then act on the child's behalf. Such appointees are usually charged with investigating all of the salient issues surrounding the specific child's case and reporting back to the court (usually

Probate/Family Court or in some cases, Juvenile Court) with their recommendations.

Many legal dilemmas have been unearthed in cases dealing with the "parens patriae" doctrine, minors, and the Right of Due Process in those proceedings. In some highly publicized cases (in re *Gault* 1967), minor children were taken by police to detention centers without parental notice; hearings were held without principal parties present; no transcripts/recordings were made; and subsequently, commitments were effected without access to counsel. Needless to say, these convictions were reversed by the Supreme Court's decision. In more recent years, competency motions upheld by judges have frequently led to otherwise minor children being tried and adjudicated in adult court. It would appear these trends demonstrate a shift in the underlying juvenile justice rationale for the "best interests of the child" which was designed to offer the child "individualized justice and treatment rather than impartial justice and punishment" (Halleck, 1967, p. 245). Only time will tell.

Organizations dedicated to following these trends and advocating for minor children, such as the Child Welfare League of America, The American Professional Society on the Abuse of Children, and The National Association of Counsel for Children, monitor landmark cases, advocate and lobby for protective legislation, and evaluate/research strategies for improving the safety and welfare of all children.

Let us now turn our focus to those legal and ethical issues that directly apply to the profession of human services.

EFFECTS OF LAWS ON THE HUMAN SERVICE WORKER

Credentialing and Competence

Professional Licensing Law. Competence in one's profession is a prerequisite for any or all of those occupations associated with the field of human services. In most mental health professions, symbols of professional competency are expressed as licensing, certification, and/or registration. These credentials are generally administered by state or national boards that determine the required education, the amount and type of supervised training, passing scores for examinations, references, and so on.

For government-supported boards, the regulatory bases for these and other activities (i.e., complaint reviews, sanctions, suspensions, and so on) are laws passed in those states. These individual boards of licensing/registration routinely represent the separate professions of psychiatry, psychology, social work, mental health counseling, drug/alcohol counseling, rehabilitation counseling, and others. Allied health boards may represent other professional occupational groups (occupational and physical therapists, speech therapists, and other specialists).

Collectively, these regulatory state agencies attempt to assure the competencies of professional human service workers, to protect the interests of consumers, and to implement ethical and legal hearings when complaints against these professionals are filed.

So far, these comments have been directed to the separate professions that typically work with human service clients. Another movement with similar purpose and function may be found in the work of The *National Community Support Skill Standards Project,* which is designed to regulate the quality and competency of entry-level (two-year/four-year college degrees) human service workers. Please refer to Chapter 8 for additional specifics on this national credentialing program.

Professional Accountability and Peer Review. In the foregoing discussion, you have been introduced to how society formally recognizes a profession. In that recognition, leading to a credential, the profession also is made aware of its professional accountability to society. When, and if, society evaluates the professional or his/her practice as substandard, it attaches legal liability as a consequence. This liability is presented as a claim of malpractice and its review and judgment is made in one, or both, of two mechanisms: regulatory reviews conducted by the professional board representing the specific discipline involved, or formal legal complaints presented by means of the civil court system. In some legal cases, criminal charges may also be filed. Inasmuch as the latter two topics will be addressed later in this chapter, we will deal only with the former topic—regulatory reviews—at this point.

The most often utilized procedure for policing professionals in human services is by means of self-regulation via the professional credentialing boards in each state. It should be stated here that there is much state-by-state variance regarding the defined standards of care and how these standards are monitored in the practice of the specific discipline. One must be knowledgeable regarding the statutes governing one's chosen profession in the state in which one practices.

Notwithstanding the lack of uniform legal references to these credentialed professions, there are fairly common phases or steps involved in how they are processed in any state. In all cases, the professional is protected by the right to due process (notice, counsel, hearing, appeal, and so on).

If a complaint is received, the board will record the complaint with release consent and notify the practitioner, gathering verification of basic information. If the complaint is deemed viable, the board will then request pertinent file material, interviews with all principal parties, and statement of review findings. These activities are normally conducted by *colleagues,* or *peers,* appointed by the board for such occasions and representing the standard for self-regulation of its credentialed members. A final step incorporates the conclusion of the board for or against the individual in question. Positive findings typically result in dismissal of the complaint(s), whereas negative conclusions that substantiate the complaint(s) lead to a range of possible reprimands, from a formal warning issued by the board, to suspensions, or to

revocation of the professional credential. These *Peer Reviews* constitute the mainstream procedure for self-regulation of professionals. Boards may also refer the complaints to the proper legal authorities (District Attorney, Attorney General, U.S. Attorney) should their investigation uncover serious criminal behavior(s).

Malpractice in Service Delivery

The delivery of services to human service clients is universally a case process format. The case process for the vast majority of human service clients follows these general steps:

1. Intake—Initial data-gathering contacts with clients;
2. Assessment—Diagnosing/determining the problem(s);
3. Treatment Planning—Planning goals/objectives for helping;
4. Intervention—Implementing the help (therapy, medication, self-help, etc.);
5. Evaluation—Measuring outcomes of treatment;
6. Termination/Referral—Ending services or referring the client elsewhere.

The phases of case process that are most vulnerable to accusations of professional malpractice occur in Assessment/Diagnosis and/or Intervention/Treatment. During these phases, errors of commission or omission can occur. For example, the clinician may misdiagnose a client (commission) or may neglect to provide appropriate/proper treatment for a diagnosed condition (omission). In some cases, complaints may incorporate both types of errors in both phases of case process.

Diagnosis/Assessment. Clinical skills in the determination of the priority issues for clients vary from one profession to another. For instance, most readers would agree that the use of psychological tests in assessing client problems would be a good choice of tool(s) in such a task. The training and education, however, required to be competent in the administration, scoring, and interpretation of standardized tests lies almost exclusively with doctoral level psychologists. Thus, psychiatrists, social workers, and mental health counselors routinely utilize interviewing techniques to arrive at their diagnostic decisions. For psychiatrists, the mental status exam is the method of choice, while social workers rely on social histories and systems analysis (family, work, school, and so on) to assess the client's problem(s).

Problems for the professional arise when standards of care are ignored or violated. In the procedures for assessment and diagnosis, the professional must gather complete and relevant information on the client in order to accurately and reliably determine problems. Timeliness of data and information, validity of recorded observations, past assessments and issues, prior hospitalizations, medical issues, and the like must be gathered, reviewed, and interpreted before clinical judgments are rendered. In the use of tests, one's training and competency in testing must be considered. Latest editions of tests and their norms must be used. Referral questions to be answered by the tests must be clear and relevant. Moreover, in formulating the diagnosis, substantiation of symptomatic behaviors must be documented for each diagnostic label or code used. Thorough knowledge of the content and use of diagnostic reference tools such as the *Diagnostic and Statistical Manual of Mental Disorders, Fourth Edition* (DSM-IV), must be acquired. Faulty use of such tools, incomplete supportive information, misuse of tests, use of outdated editions of tests, and going beyond or outside one's level or area of clinical expertise, are examples of areas where diagnostic errors of commission and omission are typically made.

Therapy/Treatment Aside from misconduct violations within relationships with clients (a topic that will be addressed later in the chapter), human service workers are more often targets of malpractice suits related to therapy and treatment than to any other area of responsibility. Most often such suits are driven by claims of negligence in the delivery of such services. These actions can range from employing radical and inappropriate treatment methods to physical and/or mental harm arising from improper hospitalizations, medications, or other treatment. In all these circumstances, the plaintiff (the client) must demonstrate:

(a) A legal duty existed between practitioner and the injured party;
(b) The practitioner was derelict or negligent in that duty (by commission or omission);
(c) Harm or injury was experienced; and
(d) The harm or injury was caused by dereliction of duty (Hogan, 1979, p. 8).

Ultimately, the determination of whether a professional is guilty of dereliction/negligence of duty will rest upon whether the practitioner conformed to a required standard of care and followed a standard protocol (procedure) for treatment of what was originally diagnosed.

In essence, the student of human service practice must (a) know how to make accurate, valid diagnoses, and (b) since *diagnosis drives treatment*, understand which treatment protocols or approaches work most effectively with which diagnostic labels or conditions.

Relationship Issues

Civil and Regulatory Infractions.   Many of the complaints made by clients against mental health professionals arise from violations of the therapeutic relationship. Because of the intimacy and trust that form the bond of therapist and client, there cannot be any other relationships between the parties involved. "Dual relationships" are strictly taboo in professional codes of ethics inherent to the field, and penalties for violations can be severe.

Human service professionals cannot develop or encourage social relationships with their clients. Social activities, gift exchanges, regular telephone contacts, transportation arrangements, loans, favors, work, home visits, lunches and dinners, and so on are all outside the limits and boundaries of professionals working with needy clients to help them resolve life's issues and problems. Professional human service workers must be continuously vigilant as to their professional conduct and the limits of their involvement with clients. Along these lines, the most frequent malpractice complaint of clients against their therapist or counselor involves *sexual misconduct.*

Criminal Behavior. In some states such as Massachusetts, sexual misconduct is not only a violation of professional ethics (leading to possible civil litigation) but is also actionable as a criminal offense. Violators may not only lose their professional credential (license or certificate) but also may be subject to fines, civil monetary awards, and prison sentencing.

Consequently, human service workers must know and understand the legal responsibilities of their work, the specific ethical codes adopted by their professional association(s), and the penalties and consequences for ignoring or neglecting those professional responsibilities.

HUMAN SERVICE APPLICATIONS OF LAW

Up to this point in the chapter we have attempted to focus on lawful foundations involving the rights of human service clients and professional issues and responsibilities that human service workers must attend to and resolve. Now we will outline how the law is applied to the field of human services and offer selected noteworthy case references.

Competency and Civil Commitment

Historically during the 1950s and '60s, it was routinely acceptable to place seriously mentally ill patients into psychiatric facilities with legal support and by orders from the civil courts. These actions, known as civil commitments, were almost always involuntary and frequently lasted for long periods of time. The basis for these actions was

the legal tradition of *parens patriae,* referred to earlier as the prerogative of society to act on behalf of these impaired citizens who lack mental competency to make reasonable decisions on their own behalf and at the same time, to protect society from the potential danger they may present as disturbed individuals.

As a consequence of mental health reforms of the 1960s and '70s, laws were passed tightening the rules for involuntary civil commitments and establishing new public social policies regarding the deinstitutionalization of hospitalized mental patients and their re-entry to community-based outpatient treatment programs. At this time, before individuals who were petitioned for involuntary commitment to residential mental institutions could be admitted, four conditions had to be proven to exist:

1. The person is mentally ill;
2. The person poses an imminent risk of danger to self or to others as a result of the mental illness;
3. Treatment for the person's mental illness is available at the proposed treatment facility;
4. Hospitalization is the least restrictive alternative available for the person's treatment.

As a consequence of the release of large numbers of mental patients from hospitals and the more difficult standards required for involuntary commitments, more and more mentally ill patients had to rely upon community support systems for help. Unfortunately, over time we have witnessed the failures of these changes as more and more mentally ill persons have drifted into homelessness and faced the risks of surviving on the streets. Also noteworthy have been increases in the number and kinds of criminal behavior in which mentally ill individuals have been involved. In spite of the disadvantages of institutional care, it at least provided safety and minimum standards of treatment and care to these unfortunate and needy individuals.

Let us now examine other legal efforts of society to protect and assist those who are incapable of representing their own best interests.

The "Therapeutic State" and Pleas

The "Therapeutic State" is a jurisprudence view-point that sees an obligation of law and society to evaluate and interpret all mental health laws in terms of their value as therapy for the mentally ill.

The utility of the "Therapeutic State" is most apparent in trial court involving suspected mentally ill individuals who are being charged with criminal complaints. The first of these is the "competency to stand trial." Defendants are considered incompetent if, as a result of a mental disorder, they *cannot* (1) understand the nature of the trial proceedings, (2) participate meaningfully in their own defense, or (3) consult with their attorney. Competency here refers to the defendant's mental condition at the time of the trial. In other "therapeutic" pleas, insanity is reviewed in the defendant's mental state at the time of the alleged offense.

Defendants are commonly presumed to be mentally responsible for the crimes with which they are charged. If defendants plead *not guilty by reason of insanity,* they must present evidence to show they lacked the state of mind necessary to be held responsible for the crimes with which they have been charged. As a legally defined concept, insanity standards have evolved slowly over time and have varied, and do vary, from state to state. The origins of insanity standards began with the McNaughton Rule. Daniel McNaughton was an Englishman who in 1843 plotted to assassinate the British Prime Minister, Robert Peel. Outside 10 Downing Street in London, McNaughton shot and killed Peel's secretary, whom he mistook for Peel. Following arrest and at his arraignment on murder charges, McNaughton pleaded "not guilty by reason of insanity" (NGRI). After several psychiatric evaluations, he was declared legally insane and subsequently found innocent due to mental impairment. The judgment inspired heated debate within British society and eventually led to defining *two* requisite criteria: (a) the mental illness caused the subject to *not* know what they were doing; and (b) the mental illness caused the subject to *not* know that what they were doing was wrong. The major theme of criticism against the McNaughton Rule was that it was based on cognitive impairment and failed to consider motivation and control.

In 1954 an alternative to the McNaughton Rule emerged from a burglary case involving Monte Durham, a career criminal whose plea of not guilty by reason of insanity was rejected by the sitting judge and appealed by his attorneys on the basis that the McNaughton Rule was obsolete. Appellate Court Judge David Barelon in Washington DC ruled in favor of Durham and ordered a new trial with the standard for an insanity plea being "that an accused is not criminally responsible if his unlawful act was the *product* of a mental disease or mental defect." This eventually became the Durham Rule, or the *product test* for the insanity plea. As a result of its emphasis upon the testimony of psychiatrists and psychologists, the Durham Rule was eventually replaced in 1972 by the Brauner Rule, also known as the ALI Rule (American Law Institute). In the ALI Rule, a defendant is not responsible for criminal conduct if "at the time of such conduct as a result of mental disease or defect the defendant lacks substantial capacity either to *appreciate* the criminality (wrongdoing) of his conduct or to conform his conduct to the requirements of the law."

In the last thirty years, the use of insanity pleas has become far less frequent than the public may realize. Despite notorious cases involving such pleas, such as in the John Hinckley trial, less than one percent of defense pleas involve insanity. Moreover, the insanity defense has been successful in only a handful of all cases heard annually.

Guilty but Mentally Ill

A more recent, and to some, more reasonable legal position regarding the competency and sanity of defendants has been the plea or verdict option of finding a person so charged *guilty but mentally ill* (GBMI). In these rulings, the subject would be adjudicated appropriate treatment for the mental condition and when (and if) cured or relieved of the presenting disorder (the symptoms syndrome) would then begin the sentence applicable to the crime committed.

Mandated Reporting: MGL Chapter 51A

Another application of law to human services may be found in mandated reporting statutes governing the recording of suspected child abuse and neglect circumstances observed or suspected by human service workers who rout: ly work with children and families. The following excerpt taken from Massachusetts General Law (MGL) Chapter 51, Section A, typifies the spirit of such laws found in most states at this time.

> *Any physician, medical intern, medical examiner, dentist, nurse, public or private school teacher, educational administrator, guidance or family counselor, probation officer, social worker, foster parent or policeman, who in his professional capacity shall have reasonable cause to believe that a child under the age of eighteen years is suffering serious physical or emotional injury resulting from abuse inflicted upon him including sexual abuse, or from neglect, including malnutrition, or who is determined to be physically dependent upon an addictive drug at birth, shall immediately report such condition to the department by oral communication and making a written report within forty-eight hours after such oral communication; provided, however, that whenever such person so required to report is a member of the staff of a medical or other public or private institution, school or facility, he shall immediately either notify the department or notify the person in charge of such institution, school or facility, or that person's designated agent, whereupon such person in charge or his said agent shall then become responsible to make the report in the manner required by this section. Any such person so required to make such oral and written reports who fails to do so shall be punished by a fine of* not more than one thousand dollars. *(Massachusetts General Law, Chapter 51A)*

As noted, failure to report child abuse incidents will lead to adjudication of penalties including fines and imprisonment. As presented earlier, such reporting takes priority over the rights of confidentiality and, as such, protects the reporter from any such confidentiality infractions. The law also protects the reporter from any defamation, slander, or libel claims resulting from such reporting, whether the abuse claims are substantiated or not. In all cases, human service workers should recognize their mandated responsibilities in this law and should understand the purpose and protection it affords for both the client (child) and the worker.

CLOSING REMARKS AND FUTURE CHALLENGES

The law and human services are partners in serving and protecting those in need of help and assistance. While lawful foundations establish the structural underpinnings of our professional duties and responsibilities, they also serve to define the rights and privileges afforded to clients. In may different ways, the influences of law and of professional ethics permeate our daily work activities; thus, it is essential to know which laws apply to our work and our clients and how the directives are best utilized and integrated in day-to-day circumstances.

As you have read in this chapter, there is a "power" or "strength" one acquires in studying the law and professional ethics and in learning to exercise this knowledge on behalf of those we serve. As a human service professional, you will feel the power of the law and will know confidently and competently how you must follow and work with those future responsibilities regardless of job title or kind of agency, or individual client with whom you eventually work. Good luck, and never stop learning.

REFERENCES

Abel, R. L., ed. (1995). *The Law and Society Reader.* New York: New York University Press.

Ford, M. (1990). The Psychiatrist's Double-Bind: The Right to Refuse Treatment. *American Journal Of Psychiatry, 137,* 718–719.

Jagim, R. D., W. D. Wittman, and J. O. Noll (1978). "Mental Health Professionals' Attitudes toward Confidentiality, Privilege, and Third-Party Disclosures." *Professional Psychology,* 9(3).

Halleck, S. L. (1967). *Psychiatry and the Dilemmas of Crime.* New York: Harper & Row.

Hogan, D. B. (1979). *The Regulation of Psychotherapists. Volume III. A Review of Malpractice Suits in the United States.* Cambridge, MA: Ballenger Publishing.

Kraft, P. B. (1985). *The Right to Refuse Treatment: Professional Self-Esteem and Hopelessness.* In C. P. Ewing, ed., *Psychology, Psychiatry, and the Law: A Clinical and Forensic Handbook.* pp. 215–240. Sarasota, Florida: Professional Resource Exchange.

Michaels, R. (1981). *The Right to Refuse Psychiatric Treatment: Ethical Issues. Hospital and Community Psychiatry, 32,* 251–255.

Rembar, C. (1981). *The Law of the Land: The Evolution of our Legal System.* New York: Simon & Schuster.

Rinas, J., and S. Clyne-Jackson (1988). *Professional Conduct and Legal Concerns in Mental Health Practice.* Norwalk, CT: Appleton and Lange.

CHAPTER 23

LAW, ETHICS, AND THE HUMAN SERVICE WORKER

NAYDEAN BLAIR

The profession of human services has been struggling with its identity for many years. Although I've been working and teaching in the helping services, *I'm* confused. I cannot be sure that I truly understand all of the fundamental differences that set apart the various definitions. The students in my program in Houston are called mental health workers. A neighboring school with a similar curriculum calls its students human service workers, yet in another program nearby they are known as social work associates. To my knowledge these graduates compete for the same jobs and, when they get them, are expected to perform the same functions and have similar skills.

The confusion about what we call ourselves only adds to the dilemma when we consider law and ethics. Human service workers are employed in a variety of settings and work with a variety of clients, patients, and students. Every state has a set of students' rights, clients' rights, patients' rights, and laws governing inpatient and outpatient services. There are privacy laws telling us what information can or cannot be placed in records or released. The list of rules and regulations is endless. As soon as you feel you have a comfortable grasp of the rules concerning nursing home care, for example, you get offered a wonderful position in child protection services. Time to start over.

Ethics are a different concern altogether. Are ethics and values the same? Who tells us what ethical standards we will work by? Most professional organizations have established codes of conduct or ethical standards that provide guide-lines for acceptable behavior on the job. Who knows whether an ethical code is compromised? Who enforces these codes? I will attempt to address these and other issues concerning law and ethics in human services.

This chapter is based on personal experience and is not meant to provide you with a barrage of facts. It would be impossible to include all the laws and ethical standards that apply to the variety of students and colleagues who may be reading this book. Instead, I will share with you some of the ethical and legal concerns that are frequently discussed within the topics. Many are issues brought up by interns in their weekly seminars.

EARLY DEVELOPMENTS

To have a formal set of professional ethics by which to work, we must first decide who we are, what our mission is, and with whom we will affiliate. As a group, we became a separate entity when we gave ourselves a new name. By 1965 this country had reached a point at which the demand for the trained generalist mental health worker had reached crisis proportions. The early 1960s, with its War on Poverty, brought with it the need for soldiers to fight this war. The Southern Regional Education Board (SREB) planted the early seeds for what is known today as the Human Services Training Movement. The SREB obtained a grant from the Experimental and Special Training Branch of the National Institute of Mental Health (NIMH) to work with community colleges and to allow institutions to develop the first training programs. These early training programs were mainly called "mental health"; however, this terminology was changed to "human service worker" to give the field the broader perspective it needed.

Many states do not have a method by which to credential a human service worker who does not have a minimum of a bachelor's degree. Recently, agencies like the National Association of Social Workers (NASW) and the National Association of Alcoholism and Drug Abuse Counselors (NAADAC) have developed appropriate exams to be used by states if they choose to test at a lower level.

The Council for Standards in Human Service Education (CSHSE) has been laboring since its inception to establish minimum standards of competency. The CSHSE was created to develop a set of program training standards that would reflect the content of existing programs (McClam and Woodside, 1990). This was done on the assumption that the programs already in existence were based on community needs. Human service students who attend a program that is approved by CSHSE will receive training in values, attitudes, and professional ethics (standard 19, CSHSE Guidelines for Program Approval, 1989). We have now answered the questions of what a human service worker is and how it is distinguished from other helping professionals.

Texas is one state that requires all counselors to be licensed. The NASW and TCADA (the Texas equivalent to NAADAC) have a licensing procedure for paraprofessionals. They have their own code of ethics and committees to enforce it. In the first year that licensure was required for substance abuse counselors, many ethical complaints were filed. These complaints were investigated and action was taken.

WHAT ARE ETHICS?

Ethics, by definition, consist of "The study of the general nature of morals, and of the specific moral choices to be made by the individual in his relationship with others. The standard rules governing conduct of the members of a profession" (American Heritage Dictionary). The same book goes on to tell us that "a moral is concerned with judging the goodness or badness of human action and character." My understanding, then, is that ethics and morals are very subjective.

Any topic that is subjective can have many variables. For this reason, the codes of ethics for similar professions may be markedly different. For a good representative sample of the code of ethics for mental health professionals, I recommend that you read the appendix of *Issues and Ethics in the Helping Professions,* 4th ed., 1993, by Corey, Corey, and Callanan, published by Brooks/Cole.

Tony Ellis, in his article "The Nature of Morality" (Barker and Baldwin, 1991), contrasts morality with a set of norms that we refer to as customs. He goes on to tell us that sometimes there is really not a good answer to why we do the things we do; it's just because everyone around us thinks it's normal for the times. Ideally, in human services we have established customs that promote the well-being of our clients. Of course, there are those who feel that we cannot police our colleagues, and so laws are passed.

CURRENT TRENDS THAT CAUSE CONCERN

One of the ways we help our clients is to model healthy behavior. Ethical problems must be faced openly and honestly. To do this, we must take a close look at current trends that have caused much distress in our industry.

One obvious challenge related to many of the dilemmas we now face is agency survival. Social service providers are being held accountable now more than ever. Government funds are harder to acquire. Insurance companies want proof that a client will be healed. There is more competition for grants. Agencies that provide funding for training want to be assured that their clients will be able to find jobs when they complete a program. In essence, the people who pay the bills want results.

In 1991 Texas began a study of unethical practices of psychiatric hospitals in the state. Numerous complaints from consumers and concerned professionals prompted the action that led to the proposal of more than one hundred suggestions for reforms to be made in this field alone. The study uncovered what would be considered one of the largest scandals in Texas history.

Bounty Hunting

Bounty hunting is one of the oldest professions; however, one does not expect to find it in the mental health profession. Most states currently outlaw this in the medical fields, but the laws are vague or nonexistent in human services.

One of the most frequently used bounty-hunting techniques is to offer some kind of perk to professionals who refer to a particular hospital or clinic. These perks can be something as small as favors provided by the hospital, such as fruit baskets, free literature, or elaborate lunches. These special treats can also be quite substantial and may include vacations, free office space, or actual monetary kickbacks.

Many times bounty hunting can begin as a small unconscious act that seems to be an innocent give-and-take. One example can be tied to recent trends. An institution may offer to provide free training programs or workshops to a company or a business on topics such as drug testing, AIDS, or stress reduction. In return, this good relationship may prompt an employee assistance representative to refer employees to the facility. This institution may be offering the best available treatment; however, it may also simply have an excellent speaker's bureau. Who can be sure?

Advertising

Advertising and marketing is a multi billion-dollar business. None of us are immune to the seductiveness of a good commercial or a nicely done billboard. A few years ago while driving down the freeway, I looked up to see a huge sign showing a teenager, head in hands, looking very forlorn. The sign read, "Is your child restless, easily bored, acting out? Call us at . . . we provide a free evaluation and referral." Having two adolescents of my own and numerous friends of both teenagers hanging out at my house, I can safely describe most of them as restless and easily bored. What is "acting out"? I suppose it is something beyond what is normal. My fear is that it may be possible to exaggerate symptoms to come up with a diagnosis serious enough to have a child admitted to a residential facility for a twenty-eight-day stay at perhaps $1,000 per day, the average fee covered by insurance.

Making services available to the public is part of the job of a good mental health worker. Not all advertising, of course, is bad or unethical. We must, however, ask ourselves two questions: (1) Are we providing the least restrictive environment for care? (2) Who will benefit most from the service or treatment we recommend?

Accountability

Can we do what we say we can do? Can we provide a treatment that will improve the quality of living for our clients? Apparently not all of us can. One of the largest complaints is that many of our clients relapse into whatever it was that brought them to us to begin with. We simply do not keep honest or accurate statistics on our successes and failures. If we did and if we were honest, we might discover that often our recovery rate is not good. Good, however, is a relative term. We all know that we do not have cures and that the clients must ultimately help themselves. The ethical concern here is that our clients, all of them, are vulnerable, as are their families. They must rely on us, the professionals, to learn from our mistakes in treatment plan development, follow-through, and aftercare. We cannot wait for insurance companies or legislation to do this for us.

Many human service agencies rely heavily on public funding that requires a high degree of accountability. The records needed to substantiate progress, or rather, success, are difficult and time-consuming to keep, and easily lend themselves to error. As a profession, human services has not traditionally done a good job initiating changes in this area.

Bissell and Royce (1987) have this to say about accountability and how to learn from our mistakes: "If we are to retain credibility and share useful information with one another about what works for patients and what does not, we must insist on quality data and well-defined goals." We must hold ourselves and each other accountable for, at the very least, providing the best care with the resources and knowledge we have available.

Sexual Impropriety

Most studies done on professional liability in the helping professions show that nearly 25 percent of lawsuits involve some sort of sexual impropriety. Sexual contact is generally understood as physical touch of a clearly sexual nature (Markowitz, 1992). I am astonished at how many of my colleagues have involved themselves in this type of blatant misconduct. At least 50 percent of the offenders are repeats. Most of the therapists involved believe that the behavior is harmful or at the very least has no benefit for the client. Then for whose benefit is it?

Two facts are very clear. Every ethical code in the helping professions that I have read forbids sexual misconduct with clients. The other fact is that an accusation does not necessarily have to be substantiated for the therapist to appear guilty.

Example.   A few years ago, an intern that I was supervising was accused by a schizophrenic female client of touching her and propositioning her in inappropriate ways. The male intern emphatically denied the accusations and insisted that the client was angry because he had not responded to her sexual interest in him. The student felt that it was my job as his supervisor to defend his innocence with the agency. Instead, I

called the on-site supervisor and removed the student from the placement with the agreement that the matter would be dropped. Did I believe the student was guilty? In fact, I did not. I did feel, however, that it would be better for the student in the long run to choose not to fight this battle. The student felt a sense of disloyalty from me, and it took awhile before his respect could be regained. The point is that these battles are lost even if innocence can be proven, which is difficult to do.

According to the American Psychological Association Insurance Trust, which is the major insurer for psychologists, sexual relationships between the client and therapist cost them more money in suits than any other type of claim. For this reason a cap has been placed on how much can be recovered for such a suit.

Fraudulent Billing

Several years ago a family was referred to me whose son had just been released from a residential treatment center for substance abuse. The young man was in the facility for several months, and the parents' portion of the bill was in excess of $57,000. On close examination, the parents discovered that the statement contained charges for services that they were sure he did not receive. He was billed $100 each day for the services of the admitting physician, whom he saw about twice per week for ten minutes. He was billed for three hours of group therapy per day at $65 per hour. One therapy group had an average of twelve members; one was an education session with more than forty residents. He was charged $45 per day for therapeutic recreation, which he discovered was for the use of the swimming pool and athletic facilities since there was not a recreation specialist on site. The list of charges went on and on and averaged $1,127 per day.

Currently there are states that do not levy criminal penalties for health care providers who fraudulently bill patients or insurance companies for services that are not necessary or not provided.

The suspicions that have brought us to this situation are not without cause. There have been many, many abuses. Consumers will be the ones to cause a radical change to occur. They will insist on better care, and repeated lawsuits will force laws to be passed that will make us accountable.

Cases to Review

It would be unlikely that any human service worker could get through a whole month of working in the field without being able to provide some example of a behavior observed that they felt was unethical or perhaps that broke a basic law. Following are a few examples of actual circumstances where beginning human service workers have had to stop and think twice before they realized they were being caught up in a questionable behavior.

Case A.   Lila, a woman in her mid-forties, had returned to school after raising three children. She was completing her final mental health practicum working on the adolescent substance abuse ward of a private psychiatric hospital. The hospital staff was delighted with her skills and her ability to understand the turmoil many of these children had been through. After only a month at the hospital, Lila was cofacilitating a group of eight to ten adolescents. She was always well prepared and was offered a job at the hospital. A few weeks after she accepted a paid position, she was told there were going to be some staff cutbacks and that she would have to double up on group patients until further notice. The first afternoon was a nightmare. They had put the general psychiatric youth in with the substance abuse patients to bring the group number up to nineteen. Children were behaving inappropriately, and the group constantly needed several technicians available for control. After each session, it took Lila two to three hours to properly document all the charts about client progress. She was told not to sign her name to the charts belonging to the psychiatric patients because that was not an area in which she was licensed to work.

This case illustrates some ethical and legal concerns. Beginning workers are often cautious in expressing concerns about such things as the unmanageable size of the group or the fact that it could be very harmful to mix general psychiatric clients with substance abuse clients. Little can be accomplished if we spend a large part of our time containing acting-out behavior. The issue of being asked to provide care in an area for which we are not trained or licensed is an area in which we must take a stand.

Case B.   John, a newly licensed substance abuse counselor, was very excited when he got his first job with a halfway house that received state funds. After he had been on the job for only a few months, the facility was going to be examined for contract renewal. The staff was in a frenzy to ensure that all records were up to date and files in order. John was asked to work overtime to audit files of patients, some of whom had been discharged up to a year before his employment there. He was given an example and told how to properly document the records. He was told that this was usual and that often the patient load was too heavy for a busy counselor to get all the records done in a timely manner.

In essence, what John was being asked to do was falsify client records. Funding is an important issue; clients cannot receive care if funding is not continued. Facilities may lose their license if paperwork is not kept up properly. It is very true that keeping up with the piles of documents necessary is a cumbersome chore not enjoyed by many human service workers. Proper documentation requires a lot of time, and most of us feel our time is better spent elsewhere. Cleaning up paperwork problems left by our colleagues because of poor management cannot become our problem. This issue cannot be taken lightly, since we are often expected to do this unethical and illegal chore and we must know our position on the issue before entering an agency.

Case C.   Susan had always wanted to work with the elderly. Her first practicum was with a large, established nursing care facility that had a wonderful reputation for providing excellent care. She was assigned to work with the lead social worker and found her guidance invaluable. Halfway through the semester, an announcement was made that the facility would become a rehabilitation center. The residents who did not need rehab and were not covered under insurance would be assisted with relocation. The change was to be completed in thirty days. The process seemed to be going smoothly until Susan noticed that most of the residents were being strongly encouraged to move to one particular center that was not well known for its quality care and was more expensive than the average. This concerned her. She consulted her supervisor, who told her that she was doing what the management had told her to do and that it was not her place to question.

Making referrals is one duty that will consume a lot of our time. Our clients are always in a vulnerable position when they need a referral because they trust that we are giving them the best information we have available. They will most often go with whatever recommendation we make. It is our duty to make sure that we are informed about the most appropriate referral sources. If we knowingly refer for a motive other than wanting to provide the best care for a client, there will be no question that we are acting unethically.

Case D.   Art was working at a day treatment center for mentally retarded young adults. He really enjoyed the physical activities, and it gave him great satisfaction when the young people seemed to be enjoying themselves. One afternoon when they were playing basketball, another worker became frustrated with the low level of one of the clients and very forcefully threw the ball, hitting the client in the face and causing a very bad bruise.

Art, disturbed by the incident, went to his supervisor to discuss his concern. The supervisor was supportive. Art, however, did not see a change in his colleague's behavior and again approached his boss. This time the supervisor said that these people had accidents all the time and that it would be better if he just did his job and went about his business.

With inexperience often comes self-doubt. Art was not sure what could be considered excessive force in this situation and, quite frankly, did not understand his client's rights well enough to take a stand confidently on the issue. He did, however, have a real human feeling that this behavior was not right. This "feeling" that most of us have will most times be appropriate, and any action is better than none.

Lila, John, Susan, and Art all had similar but different ethical problems. All were new to the field, and all were questioning whether what they felt was wrong truly was wrong.

What do we teach human service students about working within a system? Woodside and McClam (1990) discuss being a good bureaucrat: learning to work within a system for the benefit of our clients. We take this a step further when we are being pragmatic. Let's face it, there is competition for most jobs out there. We cannot afford to challenge all the details we may find that offend our value system. On the other hand, it is important that new workers in the field understand, at the very least, where their limits are and how to approach a situation to achieve the best results.

WHAT ABOUT THE LAW?

Human service workers have typically been afraid of issues dealing with the law. I believe this is true for several reasons. First, we are intimidated by legal terms that tend to make us feel not so smart. Second, we think we will never need to know. Third, we often feel that we will always do a good job and that our clients will all think we're great. So why worry? Soon these excuses will no longer be sufficient to convince even ourselves.

Over the past few years, lawsuits have been rising at an incredible rate. One of the biggest reasons for this is that our clients are feeling a greater sense of empowerment. They are being heard and are no longer intimidated by physicians, therapists, or human service workers. We sometimes feel that as human service workers, we are not as liable as physicians. This is very untrue. Anyone can be sued.

Most laws are written in such a way that they are difficult to understand. The American Psychological Association publishes a series of books titled the Law and Mental Health Professionals Series. The books are each tailored by states and are divided into sections that are easy to read and understand. The books reference federal laws that may conflict and provide additional resources if questions arise.

At a minimum, mental health professionals need to understand the laws in their state affecting how they conduct business.

Client Rights

Do clients have rights? We would like to believe that they do. Unfortunately, sometimes we will discover that this is only a myth. We have many prepared forms for our clients to sign. Some of these forms will cause them to give up their privacy rights. Some forms will release the agency from the responsibility of providing good service. All states have some basic rights published for mental health patients. It is the responsibility of every human service worker to know, understand, and be able to explain to consumers their rights using words that they can understand. The wording may need to be changed depending on the agency setting, but below is an example of a basic set of clients' rights.

Sample of basic rights for all mental health patients in the state of Texas

1. You have all the rights of a citizen of the state of Texas and the United States of America, including the rights of habeas corpus (to ask a judge whether it is legal for you to be kept in a hospital), property rights, guardianship rights, religious freedom, the right to register and vote, the right to sue and be sued, the right to sign contracts, and all the rights relating to licenses, permits and privileges, and benefits under the law.

2. You have a right to be presumed mentally competent unless a court has ruled otherwise.

3. You have the right to a clean and humane environment in which you are protected from harm, have privacy with regard to personal needs, and are treated with respect and dignity.

4. You have the right to appropriate treatment in the most open place available that provides protection for you and the people around you.

5. You have the right to be free from mistreatment, abuse, neglect, and exploitation.

6. You have the right to be told in advance of any charges being made, the cost of services, sources of the program's reimbursement, and any limitations on length of services.

7. You have the right to fair compensation for labor performed for the hospital in accordance with the Fair Labor Standards Act.

8. Prior to admission, you have the right to be informed of all hospital rules and regulations concerning your conduct and course of treatment.

Communication

9. You have the right to talk and write to people outside the hospital. You have the right to have visitors in private, make private phone calls, and send and receive sealed and uncensored mail.

Confidentiality

10. You have the right to review the information contained in your medical record. If your doctor says you shouldn't see your record, you have the right to have, at your expense, another doctor of your choice review that decision. The right extends to your parent or conservator if you are a minor (unless you have admitted yourself to services) and to your legal guardian if you have been declared by a court to be legally incompetent.

11. You have the right to have your records kept private and to be told about the conditions under which information about you can be disclosed without your permission.

12. You have the right to be informed of the current and future use of products and of special observation and audiovisual techniques, such as one-way vision mirrors, tape recorders, television, movies, and photographs.

Consent

13. You have the right to refuse to take part in research without affecting your regular care.

14. You have the right to refuse any of the following:
- surgical procedures
- electroconvulsive therapy
- unusual medication
- hazardous assessment procedures
- audiovisual equipment
- and all other procedures for which your permission is required by law

15. You have the right to withdraw your permission at any time in matters to which you have previously consented.

Care and treatment

16. You have the right to a treatment plan for your stay in the hospital that is just for you. You have the right to take part in developing that plan as well as the treatment plan for your care after you leave the hospital.

17. You have the right to be told about the care, procedures, and treatment you will be given; the risks, side effects, and benefits of all medications and treatment you will receive, including those that are unusual or experimental; the other treatments that are available; and what may happen if you refuse the treatment.

18. You have the right not to be given medications you don't need or too much medication, including the right to refuse medication that is mood altering or mind altering, unless the right to refuse has been specifically taken away by court order.

19. You have the right not to be physically restrained unless your doctor orders it and writes it in your medical record. If you are restrained, you must be told the reason, how long you will be restrained, and what you have to do to be removed from restraint. The restraint has to be removed as soon as possible.

20. You have the right to meet with a staff responsible for your care and to be told of their professional discipline, job title, and responsibilities. In addition, you have the right to know about any proposed change in the appointment of staff, professional or otherwise, responsible for your care.

21. You have the right to request the opinion of another doctor at your own expense. You have the right to be granted a review of the treatment plan or specific procedure by another doctor who works for the hospital.

22. You have the right to be told why you are being transferred to any program within or outside the hospital.

At this point clients are told that if they have any questions or complaints concerning these rights, they can call the appropriate state office, and they are given the toll-free number.

Please note that there are special rights for persons apprehended for emergency detention and special rights if they are voluntary patients. These rights include such things as how long they can be detained without a hearing and the right to discharge themselves.

Many states use federal laws, such as the Federal Confidentiality Regulations, as a guide when developing standards for care. There may also be sets of rights established for special populations, such as the elderly and mentally or physically challenged clients. When you choose to work with a special-needs population, it is your duty to keep abreast of changing laws.

Confidentiality

To most of our clients, confidentiality means that we will keep what they tell us private. Many actually believe that we will tell no one. Little do most of them know that there are many people and many reasons information told in confidence may be shared. Our laws and code of ethics will dictate most of the guidelines. However, ultimately, our good judgment will provide us with the most prudent answer.

Human service professionals need to have a clear understanding of the privileged communication laws in their state. In Texas, for instance, the laws are different for civil and criminal cases. In criminal cases, the mental health worker–patient privilege is not recognized (Shuman, 1989). Every state has different definitions, exceptions, and waivers.

Under certain conditions there are common reasons for breaching the personal relationship we have with our clients. Most often, these are (1) the duty to warn and the duty to protect laws and (2) child abuse (in most states). The duty to warn and protect laws were passed in many states after the California Supreme Court ruled that a college psychologist did not take all the needed precautions when a student confided that he was going to kill a woman, who was easily identifiable, after she returned from a trip. The woman, Tatiana Tarasoff, was eventually killed and a lawsuit filed by her parents. Although the psychologist notified the campus police and wrote a formal letter of concern, he did not notify the woman or her family (Corey, Corey, and Callanan, 1993). If an intended victim's name is unknown, it's important to know how long a client can be restrained.

Protecting a client from him- or herself is another area that human service workers wrestle with frequently. There is no doubt that a confidence must be broken to save a life. Our often volatile clients have so few healthy coping skills that suicide seems, at times, to be the best answer. Although most of us are not in the position to be able to detain clients when we are concerned, we must have at our fingertips the resources and referrals necessary to protect human life.

Child abuse is against the law in every state. Reporting procedures may vary, but as a general rule all people involved in the helping services are obliged to report cases of child abuse, even if it breaks confidentiality.

When training our beginning mental health students, we always have them actually verbalize to their clients the exceptions to the confidentiality pact. We also encourage them, when they get to their practicum sites, to inform clients whether information will be disclosed in staff meetings and what the information will be used for.

Confidentiality is an even tougher issue when we discuss group work. We may have a good feeling for our genuine desire to keep confidence, but it's almost impossible to control the actions of twelve other people. The best rule of thumb is to discuss the issue openly with the group up front. It may often be necessary to screen more closely and perhaps have forms signed if you feel particularly insecure about a group. Corey, Corey, and Callanan (1993) discuss in some detail ways to encourage confiden-

tiality in groups and go on to relate exceptions to the confidentiality rules.

Domestic Issues

Every client population will have domestic issues to be resolved. Although it is best for us not to give legal advice, we must know some basic civil law to assist us in making wise referrals. For example, states vary in their opinion about who is a minor, who will pay child support, the statute of limitation for reporting child abuse, and the list goes on.

Basic Department of Education Laws

The laws pertaining to education and schools in your state are valuable tools to possess. Who is entitled to an education, and under what provisions are special needs provided for? What are the assessment tools available through the school system that may save your clients time and money? Who is considered a student? This information is especially important for those parents who have children in their twenties in college. When can students be considered independent and qualify for financial aid on their own?

Truancy, guardianship, and residency laws will also come in handy, as many of our clients will have difficulty in this area. Laws pertaining to minors are often different and unexpected.

Insurance

Insurance rules and regulations can and will change constantly. Insurance laws will dictate many things to a human service worker. Some examples are how long and what kind of treatment can be provided. The trend recently is to allow hospitalization for emergencies only. Both medical and mental health procedures must almost be a life-or-death situation to be covered. Outpatient services are encouraged, and new treatment methods are being developed to accommodate these regulations.

Insurance may also dictate the kind of documentation that will be kept on a client. In 1979 Congress passed the Privacy Act (P.L. 96–440) protecting third parties from the abuse of a search warrant. Many states have laws overriding this public law.

A relatively new term in our profession is "managed health care." What this really means is that someone other than a mental health professional may be telling us what is best for our clients. Employee assistance professionals have been learning the hard way that a marriage must occur between the insurance companies, the employers, and health care providers (Young, 1993). Managed health care will be very similar to what our clients understand as health maintenance organizations (HMOs). As part of our public understanding and educational skills, we may be called on to interpret what services are covered, which will most certainly affect our referrals.

ETHICS AND CULTURE

Lately, human service professionals have come to realize how necessary it has become to have a basic understanding of cultural differences if we are going to provide quality, ethical care. Many cities have become so diversified that it is impossible to work effectively, in any profession, without at least a few tools for being culturally appropriate. Daisy Kabagarama, in her book *Breaking the Ice: A Guide to Understanding People from Other Cultures* (1993), provides us with six keys to help prepare us to be culturally neutral.

1. *Genuine interest.* Genuine interest is cultivated by a realization that culture is a relative concept and that our interests need not have the hidden agenda of wanting to affirm beliefs in our own culture.
2. *A sense of curiosity and appreciation.* An openness to appreciate behaviors that are different from our own.
3. *Empathy.* The ability to place ourselves in another person's place. To be able to feel the same kinds of feelings.
4. *A nonjudgmental attitude.* Understanding before passing judgment.
5. *Flexibility.* Being open to changing our own behavior to fit the situation.
6. *Childlike learning mode.* Allow yourself to accept new meanings.

People are people, and the laws for working with all cultural groups are the same. The difference lies in remaining ethical, not imposing our own values, and protecting the rights of all without breaking the law.

Preparing to be Ethical

For most of us, our basic sense of right and wrong will guide us in the right direction. We'll remember what we've been taught by our parents, our teachers, our religion, and our community. We'll choose a few special people to use as models. We'll study the laws and codes of ethics of our professions. We'll make some mistakes, and we'll learn many lessons. There are a few suggestions I can add to assist you in becoming and remaining an ethical human service worker:

1. Write your own personal code of ethics. Use one of the professional codes, such as that of the APA or the NASW, as a guide and put it in your own language. Be flexible and willing to change as you mature.
2. Continually solicit feedback from colleagues. Get a second or third opinion if you feel in doubt about a behavior or belief.
3. Keep yourself healthy. You must be well to assist others in staying well. Understand your motivations, and you'll be able to maintain your boundaries.
4. Know your limitations and refer a client before you give incorrect, illegal, or unethical information.

SUMMARY

Human service work is a relatively new field of study and has yet to define itself clearly. Organizations such as the Council for Standards in Human Service Education and the National Organization for Human Service Education have brought the field a long way by publishing literature specific to the field. A basic brochure, *The Human Service Worker,* is available by writing to CSHSE, Mental Health Program, 5514 Clara Rd., Houston, Texas 77041.

REFERENCES

Barker, P. H., and S. Baldwin (1991). *Ethical Issues in Mental Health.* London: Chapman and Hall.

Bissell, L., and J. E. Royce (1987). *Ethics for Addiction Professionals.* Hazeldon Foundation.

Corey, G., M. S. Corey, and P. Callanan (1993). *Issues and Ethics in the Helping Profession.* Pacific Grove, CA: Brooks/Cole.

Kabagarama, D. (1993). *Breaking the Ice: A Guide to Understanding People from Other Cultures.* Boston: Allyn and Bacon.

Markowitz, L. (1992, December). "When Therapy Does Harm, Crossing the Line." *The Family Therapy Networker.*

McClam, T., and M. Woodside (1990). *An Introduction to Human Services.* Pacific Grove, CA: Brooks/Cole.

Shuman, D. W. (1989). *Law and Mental Health Professionals.* Washington, DC: American Psychological Association.

Young, V. (1993, January). "Managed Care." *The Advisor, 4*(6), 1–4.

SUGGESTED FURTHER READING

Corey, G. (1991). *Theory and Practice of Counseling and Psychotherapy.* Pacific Grove, CA: Brooks/Cole.

Fullerton, S., and D. Osher (1990). *History of the Human Services Movement.* Council for Standards in Human Service Education, Monograph Series.

Maeder, T. (1989, January). "Wounded Healers." *The Atlantic Monthly.*

Lum, D. (1992). *Social Work Practice and People of Color.* Pacific Grove, CA: Brooks/Cole.

Smith, M. (1992). "Psychiatric Reforms Are Proposed." *Houston Chronicle,* Sept 22.

ETHICAL STANDARDS OF HUMAN SERVICE PROFESSIONALS[1]

NATIONAL ORGANIZATION FOR HUMAN SERVICE EDUCATION

PREAMBLE

Human services is a profession developing in response to and in anticipation of the direction of human needs and human problems in the late twentieth century. Characterized particularly by an appreciation of human beings in all their diversity, human services offers assistance to its clients within the context of their community and environment. Human service professionals, regardless of whether they are students, faculty, or practitioners, promote and encourage the unique values and characteristics of human services. In so doing, human service professionals uphold the integrity and ethics of the profession, partake in constructive criticism of the profession, promote client and community well-being, and enhance their own professional growth.

The ethical guidelines presented are a set of standards of conduct that the human service professional considers in ethical and professional decision making. It is hoped that these guidelines will be of assistance when the human service professional is challenged by difficult ethical dilemmas. Although ethical codes are not legal documents, they may be used to assist in the adjudication of issues related to ethical human service behavior.

Human service professionals function in many ways and carry out many roles. They enter into professional-client relationships with individuals, families, groups, and communities, who are all referred to as "clients" in these standards. Among their roles are caregiver, case manager, broker, teacher/educator, behavior changer, consultant, outreach professional, mobilizer, advocate, community planner, community change organizer, evaluator, and administrator. The following standards are written with these multifaceted roles in mind.

THE HUMAN SERVICE PROFESSIONAL'S RESPONSIBILITY TO CLIENTS

STATEMENT 1 Human service professionals negotiate with clients the purpose, goals, and nature of the helping relationship prior to its onset, as well as inform clients of the limitations of the proposed relationship.

STATEMENT 2 Human service professionals respect the integrity and welfare of the client at all times. Each client is treated with respect, acceptance, and dignity.

STATEMENT 3 Human service professionals protect the client's right to privacy and confidentiality except when such confidentiality would cause harm to the client or others, when agency guidelines state otherwise, or under other stated conditions (e.g., local, state, or federal laws). Professionals inform clients of the limits of confidentiality prior to the onset of the helping relationship.

[1]Southern Regional Education Board, *Roles and Functions for Mental Health Workers: A Report of a Symposium.* Atlanta: Community Mental Health Worker Project, 1967. Used with permission.

STATEMENT 4 If it is suspected that danger or harm may occur to the client or to others as a result of a client's behavior, the human service professional acts in an appropriate and professional manner to protect the safety of those individuals. This may involve seeking consultation, supervision, and/or breaking the confidentiality of the relationship.

STATEMENT 5 Human service professionals protect the integrity, safety, and security of client records. All written client information that is shared with other professionals, except in the course of professional supervision, must have the client's prior written consent.

STATEMENT 6 Human service professionals are aware that in their relationships with clients, power and status are unequal. Therefore they recognize that dual or multiple relationships may increase the risk of harm to, or exploitation of, clients, and may impair their professional judgment. However, in some communities and situations, it may not be feasible to avoid social or other nonprofessional contact with clients. Human service professionals support the trust implicit in the helping relationship by avoiding dual relationships that may impair professional judgment, increase the risk of harm to clients, or lead to exploitation.

STATEMENT 7 Sexual relationships with current clients are not considered to be in the best interest of the client and are prohibited. Sexual relationships with previous clients are considered dual relationships and are addressed in Statement 6.

STATEMENT 8 The client's right to self-determination is protected by human service professionals. They recognize the client's right to receive or refuse services.

STATEMENT 9 Human service professionals recognize and build on client strengths.

THE HUMAN SERVICE PROFESSIONAL'S RESPONSIBILITY TO THE COMMUNITY AND SOCIETY

STATEMENT 10 Human service professionals are aware of local, state, and federal laws. They advocate for change in regulations and statutes when such legislation conflicts with ethical guidelines and/or client rights. Where laws are harmful to individuals, groups, or communities, human service professionals consider the conflict between the values of obeying the law and the values of serving people and may decide to initiate social action.

STATEMENT 11 Human service professionals keep informed about current social issues as they affect the client and the community. They share that information with clients, groups, and community as part of their work.

STATEMENT 12 Human service professionals understand the complex interaction between individuals, their families, the communities in which they live, and society.

STATEMENT 13 Human service professionals act as advocates in addressing unmet client and community needs. Human service professionals provide a mechanism for identifying unmet client needs, calling attention to these needs, and assisting in planning and mobilizing to advocate for those needs at the local community level.

STATEMENT 14 Human service professionals represent their qualifications to the public accurately.

STATEMENT 15 Human service professionals describe the effectiveness of programs, treatments, and/or techniques accurately.

STATEMENT 16 Human service professionals advocate for the rights of all members of society, particularly those who are members of minorities and groups at which discriminatory practices have historically been directed.

STATEMENT 17 Human service professionals provide services without discrimination or preference based on age, ethnicity, culture, race, disability, gender, religion, sexual orientation, or socioeconomic status.

STATEMENT 18 Human service professionals are knowledgeable about the cultures and communities within which they practice. They are aware of multiculturalism in society and its impact on the community as well as individuals within the community. They respect individuals and groups, their cultures and beliefs.

STATEMENT 19 Human service professionals are aware of their own cultural backgrounds, beliefs, and values, recognizing the potential for impact on their relationships with others.

STATEMENT 20   Human service professionals are aware of sociopolitical issues that differentially affect clients from diverse backgrounds.

STATEMENT 21   Human service professionals seek the training, experience, education and supervision necessary to ensure their effectiveness in working with culturally diverse client populations.

THE HUMAN SERVICE PROFESSIONAL'S RESPONSIBILITY TO COLLEAGUES

STATEMENT 22   Human service professionals avoid duplicating another professional's helping relationship with a client. They consult with other professionals who are assisting the client in a different type of relationship when it is in the best interest of the client to do so.

STATEMENT 23   When a human service professional has a conflict with a colleague, he or she first seeks out the colleague in an attempt to manage the problem. If necessary, the professional then seeks the assistance of supervisors, consultants or other professionals in efforts to manage the problem.

STATEMENT 24   Human service professionals respond appropriately to unethical behavior of colleagues. Usually this means initially talking directly with the colleague and, if no resolution is forthcoming, reporting the colleague's behavior to supervisory or administrative staff and/or to the professional organization(s) to which the colleague belongs.

STATEMENT 25   All consultations between human service professionals are kept confidential unless to do so would result in harm to clients or communities.

THE HUMAN SERVICE PROFESSIONAL'S RESPONSIBILITY TO THE PROFESSION

STATEMENT 26   Human service professionals know the limit and scope of their professional knowledge and offer services only within their knowledge and skill base.

STATEMENT 27   Human service professionals seek appropriate consultation and supervision to assist in decision-making when there are legal, ethical, or other dilemmas.

STATEMENT 28   Human service professionals act with integrity, honesty, genuineness, and objectivity.

STATEMENT 29   Human service professionals promote cooperation among related disciplines (e.g., psychology, counseling, social work, nursing, family and consumer sciences, medicine, education) to foster professional growth and interests within the various fields.

STATEMENT 30   Human service professionals promote the continuing development of their profession. They encourage membership in professional associations, support research endeavors, foster educational advancement, advocate for appropriate legislative actions, and participate in other related professional activities.

STATEMENT 31   Human service professionals continually seek out new and effective approaches to enhance their professional abilities.

THE HUMAN SERVICE PROFESSIONAL'S RESPONSIBILITY TO EMPLOYERS

STATEMENT 32   Human service professionals adhere to commitments made to their employer.

STATEMENT 33   Human service professionals participate in efforts to establish and maintain employment conditions that are conducive to high-quality client services. They assist in evaluating the effectiveness of the agency through reliable and valid assessment measures.

STATEMENT 34   When a conflict arises between fulfilling the responsibility to the employer and the responsibility to the client, human service professionals advise both of the conflict and work conjointly with all involved to manage the conflict.

THE HUMAN SERVICE PROFESSIONAL'S RESPONSIBILITY TO SELF

STATEMENT 35   Human service professionals strive to personify those characteristics typically associated with the profession (e.g., accountability, respect for others, genuineness, empathy, pragmatism).

STATEMENT 36 Human service professionals foster self-awareness and personal growth in themselves. They recognize that when professionals are aware of their own values, attitudes, cultural background, and personal needs, the process of helping others is less likely to be negatively impacted by those factors.

STATEMENT 37 Human service professionals recognize a commitment to lifelong learning and continually upgrade knowledge and skills to serve the populations better.

CHAPTER 24

HUMAN SERVICES AS A CAREER:
PERSONAL SURVIVAL
AND PROFESSIONAL GROWTH

MIRIAM CLUBOK

ACKNOWLEDGING MOTIVATION

"You're going to do what?" "You'll never get rich." "You'll be bogged down with paperwork and bureaucracy." "Why not accounting, computer science? Why human services?" Who hasn't heard these questions and more after revealing that they have chosen human services as a career? Usually these questions are answered in a superficial manner; the answers seem easy. But upon reflection, it soon becomes clear that people choose human services for more complex reasons. Success in human services requires that individuals identify their true motivation for this work, at least for themselves if not for friends and relatives.

Most persons, when asked, say they chose human services because they like people. They may cite times when others came to them for help and how they liked being a listener. Some may say that they have had problems they overcame, and they want to help others do the same. Some point to individuals who have helped them, inspiring them to become helpers in return. Although all of these statements are true, they may also be viewed as explanations for entering the profession that do not address the deeper-level motivations that people may have. When asked to reflect more deeply, human service workers will become aware of a different set of needs and motivations. They will admit such things as liking to feel needed, liking to feel in control and powerful, liking to feel important, enjoying being viewed as knowledgeable, and liking to be liked.

At first glance, admitting these feelings seems distasteful, even selfish. But human service workers are humans with human needs, wants, and desires. To deny these basic motivating forces would be dishonest and possibly dangerous. It is neither bad nor selfish to have these feelings, but if one refuses to acknowledge them, the danger lies in the likelihood of the worker unconsciously using the client to meet the worker's needs. When we are in touch with, for example, our need to be liked and depended on, we may be more likely to recognize that doing too much for the client is really meeting our need, not the client's. In their discussion of how personal needs influence the helping relationship, Danish, D'Augelli, and Hauer (1980) emphasize that all students should analyze their needs for becoming helpers to identify what is personally rewarding and to recognize how their needs will influence the helping process.

IDENTIFYING WORRIES

Just as being in touch with personal needs and motivations is essential to success in human services, so is being in touch with the worries and fears every student has as the protection of school is about to end and the entry to the real world of work approaches. Although a myriad of fears and concerns could be identified, generally they fall into three categories: fears about the clients, fears about oneself, and fears about the work environment. Facing these fears directly and examining them can help new workers to deal more realistically with their responsibilities and expectations.

Concerns for Client

One of the most frequently stated worries involves students' fears that they will not be able to help or may even harm the client. The fact is, however, that we cannot help every client, and survival in the field demands accepting this reality. Some clients resist change, often preferring a painful status quo to taking a risk. For some, all available options are poor ones, easing some aspect of the problem but creating new concerns. It is important to remember that making no choice because all options are flawed is also a choice. Ultimately, choices for change and responsibility for outcome are the client's, not the worker's. The worker, however, must assume primary responsibility for the helping *process*. That is, the worker must have or seek out relevant knowledge about the client's situation, utilize his or her skills to create and maintain a helping relationship, engage the client in problem solving and identification of all available choices, and operate in a professional manner, applying all the basic attitudes and values that are inherent in ethical practice (e.g., respect for individual dignity, client self-determination, and confidentiality).

Concerns for Self

Another common worry is that one may become too emotionally involved with a client. The truth is that workers cannot avoid becoming emotionally involved with clients to some extent. Most of those who enter the human service field are naturally empathetic and caring individuals. These qualities cannot always be turned off at 5:00 P.M., and to expect oneself to do so creates an unrealistic and unachievable goal. Instead, it is important to accept the fact that entering human services will place emotional demands on the worker, but

to avoid becoming overwhelmed some attitudinal and behavioral restructuring is needed. One of the most important attitudinal factors all workers need is a high degree of self-awareness. This is necessary in many aspects of human service work but is certainly critical to avoid the emotional exhaustion that can result from getting too involved with clients. All workers should learn early in their careers to constantly evaluate their behaviors and feelings. To do so does not make one selfish or egocentric, as some may fear. Instead, it helps sharpen the focus on clients or problem situations by forcing the worker to consciously identify what works, what doesn't, and what behaviors or actions may be originating from the worker's own unmet needs. When a worker learns to constantly think about his or her own behavior and attitudes toward clients, internal alarms will sound when signs of being too involved begin (e.g., too-frequent telephone calls, extended interviews, and a disproportionate amount of time spent worrying about the client). Honest self-reflection can help identify the reasons for the involvement, separate worker and client responsibility, and help the worker step back to evaluate what is happening in a more objective manner. After a worker's self-awareness has helped to identify danger signs, appropriate attitudinal and behavior changes must take place. Being realistic about one's own responsibility for the client, setting limits, utilizing supervisory and peer support, and involvement in satisfying personal relationships and activities outside the workplace are some of the major ways workers can distance themselves from overinvolvement.

Most new workers are concerned that they do not have enough knowledge or skill to be effective. While for some this concern may paralyze them into inaction, for most it is a useful concern that motivates workers to stay self-aware about what new knowledge or skills are needed, to seek out that information, and to constantly try to improve practice. Frankly, it is the new worker (or more experienced worker for that matter) who insists that he or she knows the "right" way to do everything and that his or her decisions are "best" who will pose much more risk than the worker who admits there is more to learn and a variety of choices that can be made. The fact is, human service workers operate in situations where complete knowledge of facts and outcomes is impossible to achieve, so as responsible professionals workers must learn to accept their limits while constantly striving to improve their practice. All human service workers must make a personal commitment to acquiring new knowledge and improving skills throughout their professional careers.

Work Environment Concerns

A third category of concerns deals with the work environment. New workers worry about whether they will get along with their colleagues and whether they can get along without the support and protection provided by the college environment. They worry about whether they can balance the demands of their personal and professional lives and whether they can have an impact on problems in their work environment. Although all of these concerns are valid, most new workers find that these concerns can be dealt with if they utilize for themselves the same skills they have learned for working with clients. The use of relationship-building skills works with colleagues as well as with clients. Application of problem-solving techniques helps in one's own life as well as with clients. Understanding the organization and bureaucracy in which one works is critical to professional survival and the possibility of effecting change (Lauffer, 1984). Learning to anticipate difficulties and identifying early signs of personal and professional problems is also essential.

THE ETs (EIGHT TIPS)

Although survival and professional growth in human service careers require that workers consider their own motivating forces and confront common worries, it is also helpful to have some specific guiding principles that can increase one's chances for a successful, satisfying career. What follows is what this writer calls her Eight Tips, or "ETs": a list of behaviors and qualities that, if internalized and used routinely, will likely maximize personal and professional rewards.

Be Professional in Attitude and Work Habits. Much has been written about whether the human services is a profession (Clubok, 1987, 1997; Fullerton, 1990), but the resolution of that issue is not a prerequisite for the necessity for human service workers to behave in a professional manner. What is meant by "being professional"? Clearly, a long list of qualities could be presented, but basically one must begin by demonstrating personal traits such as being collegial and polite in relationships with clients and colleagues. Using tact to achieve one's ends, learning to be appropriately assertive but still cooperative, managing time effectively, and accepting realistic limits to workplace changes all contribute to "professionalism." Critical but too-often-ignored qualities are dependability and punctuality. Many employers, when calling about references, identify these factors as their number-one concern. Agencies cannot function well (and indeed can suffer serious repercussions from such behaviors as missed deadlines or meetings), nor can workers meet their obligations to clients if they are in the habit of being late or missing appointments or deadlines. Finally, it is important for professionals to be clear about their roles but not to interpret them too narrowly. In other words, sometimes, when situations demand it, a "professional" worker will need to file, type letters, or do other tasks that may not be a specific part of one's job description. A professional attitude demands flexibility and a willingness to step in to meet needs when special circumstances arise.

Continue to Concentrate on Writing Skills. Proofread! Proofread! Proofread! No matter how much knowledge or skill one has, if written work contains misspellings and grammatical errors or is poorly organized, the worker risks being identified as less competent than he or she may really be, and the agency risks being viewed as careless and unprofessional. Furthermore, sloppy writing is often accompanied by sloppy documentation, and conceivably that could result in legal action against the worker and/or agency. It behooves all human service workers to take a close look at their writing skills and work to improve them. Career advancement is much less likely for individuals who, although able to relate well and think well, cannot translate their ideas to the printed page.

Do Not Compartmentalize Knowledge Areas. Those who think psychology is psychology, sociology is sociology, and interviewing skills are interviewing skills are making a serious mistake. All areas of knowledge relate to one another, and virtually all areas (theoretical and practical) have potential applications to practice situations. To breathe a sigh of relief once the good grade is achieved, thinking (for example), "Now I'll never have to worry about identifying those psychological defense mechanisms or demonstrating understanding of role theory concepts," can jeopardize optimal practice. Successful workers must learn to translate knowledge, value concepts, and skills to practice situations. Given any case situation, one should habitually ask oneself, "On what knowledge areas must I draw? What values must be operationalized here? What skills must I use? In what areas must I be particularly self-aware?" Every class or workshop offers potential for application in practice settings. To set aside or compartmentalize that information is irresponsible. The more able one is to identify practical applications from class material, the higher the level of success one will have in practice.

Be a Critical Thinker. Understanding problems, making decisions, and initiating change will create fewer new problems if one carefully analyzes facts, considers alternate reasons for behavior, and avoids making assumptions.

Because it is natural for human service workers to want to be "helpers," there is a tendency to make assumptions and to jump to solutions or interventions before all the relevant facts are known. In many cases, knowledge of even a few more details of a problem situation will lead to an entirely different definition of the problem and thus to a different direction for intervention. This point underscores the importance of good data collection, making and testing hypotheses, and the necessity to identify alternate meanings for client behaviors. Application of critical thinking skills in one's professional life is equally important and can help avoid many difficulties in career decisions.

Use Self-Talk. This tip refers to the necessity of having self-awareness and utilizing self-questioning skills to understand one's needs, feelings, and behaviors. Successful human service workers should acquire the habit of automatically questioning themselves and their decisions. Such questions may include the following: What is the *purpose* of this interaction? What do I wish to achieve? What knowledge do I need? Am I maximizing the client's right to self-determination and confidentiality? Am I really conveying a nonjudgmental attitude? Have I considered all explanations for behaviors and options for change? The list is endless, but acquiring this habit will unquestionably improve one's effectiveness in all professional situations.

Learn from Experience. In all situations, even negative ones, there is something to be learned. The habit of identifying what one can learn should begin in the classroom and should never end. Begin to question what is happening in every situation. Why is it boring, demoralizing, or unproductive (as the case may be)? What could be changed, and how? How can I use what I've learned from this in the future? It is no accident that professionals refer to their work as "practice." Human service workers "practice" their profession, and that word implies that all situations are not perfect but that we have the ability to identify what is working and what is not and to utilize that information to improve in the future.

Take Responsibility for Learning.   As a student, one needs to learn to speak up if material or instructions are incomplete or unclear. Students must learn to take initiative in utilizing all of the resources available to them (instructors, field supervisors, library) to seek out additional relevant knowledge and skills. This responsibility does not end when one's degree is conferred. When one is no longer faced with the learning demands of college, the responsibility for continued learning and professional growth falls squarely on the new worker. All human service workers should identify early in their careers with their primary professional organization, the National Organization for Human Service Education, and take advantage of the opportunities it offers, including its publications and national and regional conferences. Workers should regularly read several journals relevant to their area of work to keep informed of new knowledge and skills. Participation in a variety of workshops and professional meetings is critical for effective practice, professional growth, and career development.

Take Care of Yourself.   If one were to master all of the previous ETs, one would soon become stagnant and exhausted without attention to this final, critical one. It is not by chance that the human service field is replete with major publications about stress and burnout (Burnard, 1991; Edelwich and Brodsky, 1980; Pines and Aronson, 1980; Wessells et al., 1989). As new workers begin their careers, their high levels of energy and unrealistic expectations may develop into frustration and chronic disappointment unless conscious attention is paid to burnout prevention. Workers must learn to separate their professional and private lives and develop off-the-job satisfactions and relationships. Learning to accept responsibility for oneself, prioritizing responsibilities, iden-

tifying ways to vary one's work responsibilities, finding professional and personal supports, creating personal goals, and giving oneself tangible rewards are some of the ways human service workers can achieve the personal satisfaction needed to survive in a demanding career.

CAREER ENTRY AND MOBILITY

Preparation for entering the field of human services requires attention to several factors. Certainly, one must prepare a good résumé and should rehearse for a variety of interview questions and situations. Finding employment often requires looking broadly at the field and utilizing not only obvious sources (civil service opportunities, health and welfare directories, telephone books) but also less obvious sources such as private employers, personal contacts, and organizations that may offer opportunities for human service work but under less familiar job titles. It is also important that one be prepared to address the issue of what human services means and, particularly, how it is similar to and different from social work (Clubok, 1984, 1997). New professions are misunderstood professions. The ability to concisely explain the nature and goals of one's training and the specific skills acquired can "sell" a worker to an employer who may be unfamiliar with the human service degree.

Finding a position, however, is only the first challenge. Mobility within the field is another. To maximize one's opportunity to advance in the field, it is often necessary to further one's education by acquiring an advanced degree or specializing in specific knowledge and skill areas. In addition, the importance of "networking" in human services cannot be overemphasized. Many opportunities arise as a result of contacts and acquaintances made through professional workshops and conferences and community contacts. It is an unfortunate irony, however, that often advancement in the human service field places the worker in supervisory or management areas, removed from direct contact with the people and clients who inspired him or her to enter the field in the first place.

There is no question that there are many opportunities to enter and advance in the human service field. Success in doing so, however, is more likely if one acknowledges personal motivation for human service work, confronts fears, and learns and internalizes the ETs. Although the ETs may be easy to memorize and may even seem somewhat obvious, in reality, if workers are honest in self-appraisal, they will admit difficulty applying them conscientiously and in many instances will find themselves making excuses for *not* applying them.

Those who choose human services as a career must expect to be faced with many frustrations, including misunderstanding of the human service profession itself, turf issues with traditional professions, insufficient financial rewards, unappreciative clients, and decreasing funding and community resources accompanied by increasing caseloads and workplace demands. So why not choose accounting or computer science instead? The answer lies in the immeasurable rewards available in human services that compensate for the limitations. Few other fields, if any, offer the variety, challenges, opportunity for creativity, and personal satisfaction that comes from knowing that one has made a positive impact on individuals or the community. Change, when it occurs, even small change, can be exhilarating. Of course there are potential hazards and frustrations, but enthusiastic, thinking individuals, armed with knowledge, self-awareness, and problem-solving skills, can inoculate themselves against much of this. With discipline and determination, new workers can enter, survive, and grow in the field of human services, creating for themselves an exciting professional career and a satisfying personal life.

REFERENCES

Burnard, P. (1991). *Coping with Stress in the Health Professional: A Practical Guide.* New York: Chapman & Hall.

Clubok, M. (1984). "Four-Year Human Service Programs: How They Differ from Social Work." *Journal of the National Organization of Human Service Educators, 6,* 1–6.

Clubok, M. (1987). "Human Services: An 'Aspiring' Profession in Search of 'Professional' Identity." In R. Kronick, ed., *Curriculum Development in Human Service Education,* Council for Standards in Human Service Education Monograph Series, Issue No. 5, 1–7.

Clubok, M. (1997). "Baccalaureate-Level Human Services and Social Work: Similarities and Differences." *Human Service Education, 17.*

Danish, S., A. D'Augelli, and A. Hauer (1980). *Helping Skills: A Basic Training Program.* New York: Human Sciences Press.

Edelwich, J., and A. Brodsky (1980). *Burnout: Stages of Disillusionment in the Helping Professions.* New York: Human Sciences Press.

Fullerton, S. (1990). "A Historical Perspective of the Baccalaureate-Level Human Service Professional." *Human Service Education, 10,* 53–61.

Lauffer, A. (1984). *Understanding Your Social Agency,* 2nd ed. Beverly Hills, CA: Sage Publications.

Pines, A., and A. Aronson (1980). *Burnout: From Tedium to Personal Growth.* Riverside, NJ: Free Press.

Wessells, D. T., A. Kutschner, I. Feeland, F. Selder, D. Cherico, and E. Clark, eds. (1989). *Professional Burnout in Medicine and the Helping Professions.* New York: Haworth Press.

CHAPTER 25

BURNOUT:
AVOIDING THE TRAP

H. FREDERICK SWEITZER

Picture three human service workers, all of whom work at a mid-sized human service agency. The first is an efficient, happy professional. She arrives most days full of energy and enthusiasm, getting in a little early to check her mail and phone messages, read logs, do some paperwork, and compose herself before beginning to work with clients. She works quickly and efficiently yet seems to have time to talk to co-workers who need her opinion or to clients who need some extra attention. She is a tireless advocate for her clients in the community and at staff meetings, and it is a joy to watch her interact with them. She seems to have a feel for each one. Her paperwork is almost always in on time, and she has authored or coauthored several proposals for new programs and approaches at the agency. She works extra hours a few days each week and sometimes takes work home on weekends, but she doesn't seem to mind, and it doesn't appear to drain her energy.

The second worker often seems resentful and exhausted, but she is still trying hard to do a good job. She finds that she has to work weekends and evenings to stay caught up, and even this isn't working anymore. She sometimes forgets appointments or misses deadlines but snaps at people who remind her about these things. She has not been out with family or friends in months, although she occasionally goes out for beers on Friday with some other workers. Lately her supervisor has been leaning on her to work more efficiently.

The third worker never arrives before her shift begins and is often late. She takes a break each morning and afternoon, regardless of what is going on, and leaves precisely at the end of her shift, often arranging to leave a little early. She refuses to take work home or work on weekends under any circumstances. She interacts with clients as little as possible, is often short-tempered and impatient with them, and is heard to make cynical, disparaging comments about them in the halls and even in staff meetings. She is skeptical of any new ideas, rebuffs any attempts to involve her in change efforts, and makes fun of more enthusiastic workers. Her supervisor usually has to ask two or three times for reports or other paperwork, and when it does come in, it is not done well. She complains loudly about her pay, the clients, and "the system."

Of course the three portraits are stereotypes, but even if you've only been in the human service field for a little while, you have surely met people who are similar to these three. Perhaps you were on the receiving end of teachers, counselors, or other human service workers who fit these types. What may surprise you is that all three descriptions could be of the same person at different points in her career. The third worker, of course, is burned out, and her clients and co-workers are paying the price with her. Chances are, though, that most burned-out workers didn't start out that way, nor did they get that way quickly or abruptly. Most new workers swear they'll never be "like that." But burnout sets in slowly, usually without your knowledge. The second worker is showing signs of burnout but may not understand the phenomenon or want to admit it. One of the major misconceptions that new workers have is that burnout happens only to "bad" workers—something they are not and never will be. Certainly you want to see yourself as more similar to the first worker than the third. Don't be convinced, though, that it can't happen to you. It can, and once you are deep in burnout it is very difficult to turn it around. This chapter is about burnout prevention. It will help you examine ways that you can prevent burnout before it happens and recognize it when it begins.

WHAT IS BURNOUT?

Burnout is the result of persistent job-related stress. This phenomenon has been examined in a variety of professional contexts, and there are many different definitions of burnout. Christine Maslach, who has written extensively on burnout in the helping professions, emphasizes that burnout is a progressive process. It leads to physical and emotional exhaustion, rendering the worker depleted and drained; depersonalization of work and clients, so that the worker feels detached and even callous; and reduced personal accomplishment (Maslach, 1982). The exhaustion is not only physical but also emotional and even spiritual. The person feels irritable and displays negative attitudes toward the clients. Productivity declines, and the person often feels isolated and withdrawn. No two people are alike; we all manifest stress and the onset of burnout in slightly different ways. However, there are some common warning signs. Carey Cherniss, another author who has written on burnout in the helping professions, compiled this list (1980a):

Resistance to going to work	Guilt and blame
	Fatigue
Anger and resentment	Clock-watching
	Not returning client phone calls
Discouragement	
A sense of failure	Lack of concentration
Increasingly "going by the book"	Stereotyping clients
	Cynicism
Frequent colds or flu	Sleep disturbance
Postponing client contacts	Frequent gastrointestinal disturbances

Everyone probably experiences at least some of these symptoms some of the time. However, if you see a rise in frequency in any of them, pay attention. It does not necessarily mean you are burning out, but it could be a warning. Also, just because you aren't experiencing any of the symptoms on the list doesn't mean you aren't under stress; you may have some ways of showing stress other than the ones listed here. Additional reading on stress and burnout may help you recognize some of the ways that you show stress. You also need to determine how much stress you can take before you begin to be negatively affected. Don't hold yourself to someone else's standards. You may know a colleague who seems to be able to take more than you, but that does not make him or her a better worker or a better person. Furthermore, if either of you pushes beyond your limits, you will start to burn out, and you will become less effective very quickly.

Burnout in Human Services

Anyone can experience burnout, even those who are not employed in high-stress occupations. People in the helping professions, however, seem especially vulnerable. The kinds of people who select human services as a career are typically concerned with people and their problems, attuned to human suffering, and eager to make a difference. These very qualities make them vulnerable to working too many extra hours or to putting their clients' needs ahead of their own (Cherniss, 1980b; Corey and Corey, 1993; Mandell and Schram, 1983). There are also many aspects of human service work that can cause stress. Clients are often not appreciative of your efforts, change often comes slowly and sometimes is not seen for years, many agencies are understaffed and underfunded, and neither the pay nor the prestige are equivalent to other professions.

What Causes Burnout?

After reading the preceding paragraph, you may be wondering about who is to blame for burnout. Is it caused by the behavior and attitudes of individual workers, the characteristics of the agency, or the work they do? The answer is that all of these factors are involved. Certainly, some attitudes are necessary for human service work, such as patience, empathy, and tolerance for ambiguity (for an excellent discussion, see Mandell and Schram, 1983). If you don't have them or cannot develop them, you will burn out in a hurry. It is also important to have realistic expectations for your work. Both Russo (1993) and Bernstein and Halaszyn (1989) have written excellent books describing what new workers can expect. There are also signs of burnout that you should not ignore and many lists of "do's and don'ts" designed to prevent burnout; your agency may even have one. For example, some authors and agencies will tell you never to see clients outside your regular hours or shift, and some agencies offer recreation programs as stress reducers. The trouble with these prescriptions is that they may be true for human service workers in general but not for you.

On the other hand, some of the conditions described above are not the fault of individuals; they are characteristics of some human service organizations. It is possible to think about any organization as being "healthy" or "unhealthy," although that is a discussion outside the scope of this chapter (see Moracco, 1981). However, even within accepted definitions of health, caseloads, clarity of expectations, the amount of feedback and support offered, the nature of the clients, and the quality of communication all vary from setting to setting.

Burnout Prevention

Burnout is a result of the interaction between the worker and the work setting. This interaction is highly personal and individual. No two people are going to react the same way to a work setting, and you will find that you respond differently to the different agencies where you work. Therefore, I recommend you take a view of burnout that is similarly personal; instead of thinking about burnout in general terms, think of it in terms of yourself. The most important thing you can do to prevent burnout is get to know yourself better than you already do. As discussed earlier, you need to learn to recognize the ways in which you show stress. You also need to learn what stresses you. The answer to this question is both interpersonal and intrapersonal. Human service work involves many interpersonal relationships, and all of them have the potential for stress. As you think about the people you are going to work with, don't think in terms of good and bad clients, supervisors, coworkers, and work situations. Instead, pay careful attention to the things that stress *you*. These are interpersonal sources of stress. However, the reason people react differently to the same situation is that they have different personalities. Surely you can think of someone you know or work with who gets upset over things that don't bother you, and vice versa. Your personality will leave you vulnerable to stress and burnout in ways that the worker at the desk next to you is not. These are intrapersonal sources of stress. You need to try to understand what it is about you that makes you vulnerable to being upset by certain events. By understanding these two factors and the way they interact for you, you can take steps to prevent burnout from occurring or to stop it quickly when you see it starting to happen.

There is a lot to know about burnout, and this chapter is not going to cover it all. It is devoted to helping you develop self-awareness, specifically focusing on where and why you are vulnerable to burnout. If you understand more about why and how certain situations are stressful, the stress of those situations will lessen somewhat and you will have some clues about ways to combat burnout in your professional life.

INTRAPERSONAL STRESS

You enter the human service profession with a unique set of values, hopes, and motivations. Your life experience has given you certain strengths and also some areas that are sensitive or painful. Your strengths are an important asset in preventing burnout. Your sensitive and painful areas make you vulnerable to burnout in some unique ways. The more you know about your vulnerabilities, the better you can prevent burnout. Specifically, it is important for you to be aware of the needs you bring to your work, of any unresolved or partially resolved issues you may have, and of some of the fears about yourself that underlie some of your responses and response patterns.

The Needs You Bring

At some point in your education someone has probably asked you to think or write about the reasons you are considering human services as a career. Understanding and reminding yourself of these motivating factors can be a source of strength. Yet every one of them leaves you vulnerable to burnout in some way as well. Corey and Corey (1993) discuss several possible reasons for entering human services, or needs that workers bring with them, including the need to make an impact, the need to care for others, the need to help others avoid or overcome problems they themselves have struggled with, the need to provide answers, and the need to be needed. They also point out that each one of these motivations can cause problems.

There is an important distinction between wanting and needing. All the reasons listed above are good ones for entering human services, provided you substitute "desire" for "need." For example, wanting to care for others is fine, but as Corey and Corey point out, it is not fine if you always place caring for others above caring for yourself. Sometimes what you need conflicts with what the agency wants or needs. For example, you have worked a very full week and are very tired. Your supervisor explains that someone is out sick and asks if you would mind working over the weekend. If you choose to say yes to these requests from time to time, that is fine. However, if you find that you cannot say no, ever, then you may be someone who needs to put others' needs first in order to feel good about yourself. That can happen for a lot of reasons, but none of them offset the price you will pay if you don't learn to attend to your own needs as well as those of your clients. Eventually, you will be headed for burnout. Take some time to think about your own motivations for entering human services. If those desires turn into needs, in what specific ways will you be vulnerable to burning out?

Unresolved Issues

Each of us has struggled with different personal issues in our lives. You may have had a prolonged struggle with one of your parents during adolescence. You may have been a victim of abuse or assault. Perhaps you wrestled with substance abuse or an eating disorder. These struggles leave us all with issues that are unresolved or partially resolved. For example, you may have overcome your eating disorder, but the memory of those days may still be very painful for you. These issues could be thought of as your "unfinished business." This unfinished business does not have to come from some traumatic event or a particular struggle such as those described above. Family patterns are another source (Corey and Corey, 1993; Sweitzer and Jones, 1990). For example, if you were always the "mediator" in your family— the one who stepped in, calmed people down, and helped them resolve their differences—you may have some very strong feelings about conflicts. It may be hard for you to see someone in conflict and *not* step in to help, even though in some cases it is best to let people work it out for themselves.

Transactional analysis (or TA) is another useful perspective for uncovering your unfinished business. There are many books on TA, and an excellent one is *Born to Win,* by James and Jongeward (1971). According to TA, each of us has a number of ego states, which are cohesive systems of thoughts, feelings, and actions. All ego states are always present, but we act out of certain ones at certain times. They are often referred to as "tapes" because you can sometimes actually hear them in your thoughts. They are also called tapes because they are believed to be the result of messages you received and internalized (or "recorded") growing up. Many of those messages may be helpful to you. Those that are not helpful may represent your unfinished business.

A full discussion of ego states can be found in the sources listed below, but a brief one will be undertaken here. The ego states can be divided into three groups: parent, child, and adult. When you are acting in a parental way toward yourself or others, you are likely to be in your parent ego state. The Nurturing Parent is the part of you that is sympathetic, warm, and supportive of yourself and others. The Critical Parent, on the other hand, lets you (or others) know what should and should not be done. When you act, think, and feel as you did when you were a child, or in a child-like way, you are acting out of your child ego state. The Natural Child is the part of you that is spontaneous and uncensored. The Adaptive Child is the part that obeys the rules, compromises, and tries to get along. Finally, the Adult ego state is the one that is rational and deals with objective reality. It separates fact from opinion and calmly assesses the costs and benefits of certain courses of action.

Although some of the ego states may sound more attractive to you than others, they all have the potential to help you or hurt you. Too much or too little of any of them can be a problem. For example, too much criticism can make you unsure of yourself, but too little can also cause anxiety; you never know when you are doing something right or wrong. Cooperation and compromise are necessary to get along in the world, but people with too active an Adaptive Child can have trouble being appropriately assertive. Also, although ego states exist in all of us, they have different amounts of strength or energy, depending on the person. For example, I may find that my Critical Parent ego state is very active; I find myself thinking, feeling, and behaving out of that state often and vividly. You, on the other hand, may have a relatively quiet Critical Parent and a much more active and energetic Nurturing Parent. The situation you are in can also make a difference. You may find, for example, that your Adaptive Child is relatively quiet, except when you are around authority figures.

This is not the place for a full discussion of all the ego states, but you should be able to see their utility in uncovering your unfinished business. If you are overly critical with clients or quick to take yourself to task for the smallest failure, if you have trouble setting limits with clients or co-workers, or if you often find yourself fighting the urge to do something really rebellious, like skipping work or shouting at your boss, you may be dealing with an imbalance in the ego states. You are encouraged to explore TA further (see Corey and Corey, 1993; Corsini, 1989; Dusay, 1977; James and Jongeward, 1971).

Finally, your unfinished business can come from your membership in certain societal subgroups. Your vulnerable areas are not just the result of your personality or of your childhood and family experiences. They are also the result of your experience in society as a member of racial, ethnic, gender, and other subgroups. If you are a member of a group that has been discriminated against, you may have a hard time with clients who express prejudice, especially toward that group. If you are a member of a "majority" group, such as males, whites, or heterosexuals, and you have thought about issues of discrimination, you may feel guilty or hesitant around members of oppressed groups.

The point here is not that you must not have any unfinished business; all of us have some.

However, you need to be as aware as you can of what that business is and how those "sore spots" may be touched in your work. Often past struggles are the reason people choose human service work. They want to help others deal with or avoid problems that they experienced, and they feel their experience will be an asset. Corey and Corey (1993) point out that your experience certainly can be an asset and can help you establish empathic connections with clients. However, they also point out that some workers can unconsciously want clients to confront or resolve issues that they themselves have not yet resolved. This is called projection (Sweitzer and Jones, 1990). An example of this kind of projection occurs when a worker who struggles with expressing anger encourages his clients to express theirs at every opportunity.

Even if your unfinished business is not part of the reason you selected human services as a career, human service work will often stimulate those issues. Suppose you are working with a substance abuse population. As you work with a particular client, he begins to discuss his struggle with an overcritical father. Even though you have not had experience with being a substance abuser, you have had a similar struggle with your father or some other parent figure. You are likely to be touched by this client in some ways that seem mysterious at first. You may find yourself thinking about him when you are at home or when you wake up in the morning. This kind of preoccupation can be very draining. Also, some clients have an uncanny ability to sense your sore spots and will use them to manipulate you. If you have a strong need to be liked, for example, the client may withhold approval as a way to get you to relax a rule or go along with a rationalization.

Learning to recognize your unfinished business is an important part of burnout prevention. If you accept and face these issues, you are less likely to blame your clients or yourself or to need your clients to act in certain ways. You may also want to use a support group, a self-help book, a therapist, or some other approach to personal growth to have a place to deal with these issues and to absorb the emotional fallout of having them stimulated at work.

Fears about Yourself

One of the most frustrating, stressful situations for anyone is one in which they find themselves doing something they don't want to do or reacting in a way they don't want to react. Here are some examples:

— Your supervisor offers you some constructive criticism. As the conversation goes on, you find that you are getting angrier and angrier and are having a hard time listening. You keep coming up, mentally or verbally, with defenses for every criticism, and you imagine yourself telling the supervisor off.

— You are at a staff meeting in which an important policy is being discussed. You have something to say but can't seem to say it. Since others are very vocal, it is easy, although frustrating, for you to just sit there.

— You are struggling with your relationship with one of your clients. A co-worker who seems very skilled asks you how it's going with that client and, to your surprise, you hear yourself saying that things are fine.

— A client calls you at home and asks that you meet him right away. The matter does not seem like an emergency to you, but you leave your family at the dinner table and drive to meet your client.

These are not situations in which you find later, after much reflection, that you made a mistake. They are situations in which you know immediately afterward or even during the situation that you are not responding the way you want to. In fact, almost as soon as it is over, you can think of several ways to handle the situation that would have been better. Think about situations like this that have happened to you. Jot a few of them down.

Thinking about Difficult Situations

One very useful method for understanding yourself and learning from your experiences is to keep a journal and try to write in it every day. Record the events, thoughts, and feelings from each day that seem significant to you. If you get in the habit of writing, the journal can be useful in several ways, one of which is to learn more about the kinds of situations we have been discussing. Gerald Weinstein developed a method of reflecting on events that will be helpful to you here (Weinstein, 1980; Weinstein et al., 1975). Take a moment at the end of the day to recall any events that stand out in your mind. Pick out one or two (they can be positive or negative). Divide a piece of paper into three columns. In the left-hand column, record each action taken by you or others during the event. Record only those things that could be seen or heard, such as "she frowned," "he said thank you," or "they stomped out of the room." List them one at a time. Now read down the list and try to recall what you were thinking when the different actions occurred. When you recall something, enter it in the middle column, right across from the event. For example, you may have been thinking, "What did I do now?" when the people left the room. Finally, read the list again and try to recall what you were feeling at the time each action and thought occurred. Record what you recall in the extreme right-hand column. For example, you may have felt embarrassed, confused, or angry when they walked out. An example of this sort of analysis is included in Table 25.1. Take a look at it before proceeding.

You may find that these are isolated incidents or that they occur with just one person. You may also find, however, that these responses are part of a pattern for you. You may find that, in general, you are defensive about criticism, unable to speak in meetings, unable to say no to clients or to ask for help. Gerald Weinstein calls these tendencies dysfunctional patterns (Weinstein, 1981). Dysfunctional patterns are groups of thoughts, feelings, and actions that occur in response to a particular group or class of situations. See if you can identify any of these patterns in your work. Try using the format suggested by Weinstein (1981):

Whenever I'm in a situation where _____, I usually experience feelings of _____. The things I tell myself are _____, and what I

typically do is _____. Afterwards I feel _____. What I wish I could do instead is _____.

Here is an example to help you:

Whenever I am in a situation where I feel angry at a client, I usually experience feelings of anxiety and self-doubt. The things I tell myself are "Take it easy. It's not that bad. There's probably a good explanation, and besides, you don't want to upset him." What I typically do is smile, joke, or protest very weakly. Afterwards I feel like I let us both down. What I'd like to do is find a clear, respectful way to tell the client what is upsetting me.

Your journal is an excellent source for discovering these patterns. Look for common themes in your actions, thoughts, and feelings. Also, look for common themes in the events that caused those thoughts and feelings. Consider the situation analyzed in Table 25.1. It may be an isolated incident, but it may also be true that the person who wrote it has a pattern of hesitancy with difficult clients or of becoming confused about rules and procedures.

These patterns come from a variety of places. You may have had a difficult experience or set of experiences that "taught" you to react this way. They may come from your ego states or from the role you played growing up in your family (Corey and Corey, 1993). According to Weinstein, however, at the heart of these patterns is a "crusher" statement, which is a statement about ourselves that we do not want to hear. The pattern protects us from the crusher. In the example above, the crusher might be "I'm a mean, vindictive person. I have no compassion, and people should be afraid of me." The pattern protects you; you believe that if you *do* confront a client, it will confirm that you *are* that mean and vindictive person. In the example of the worker who is reluctant to speak up in meetings, the crusher might be, "I'm stupid. I don't belong here. If I answer wrong, everyone will see." As painful as the pattern is, it protects the worker from the crusher, which is even worse. If you are struggling with a dysfunctional pattern, discovering the crusher is the key to change. Just

TABLE 25.1 Situation Analysis Technique

ACTIONS	THOUGHTS	FEELINGS
I am sitting in the lounge with several residents. John walks in and sits down. There are several chairs available, but he sits right in front of me.	This guy is always looking for trouble. What is he doing?	Nervous, uncomfortable
I say hello. He nods. I continue my conversation with the residents.		
John squirms around in his chair several times. Finally, I notice the outline of a pack of cigarettes in his pants pocket (a clear violation of house rules).	What is his problem? Damn. He has cigarettes, and I'm supposed to take them away and take points. He has a terrible temper. He set this whole thing up.	Annoyed, angry, anxious
When I look up, he is looking right at me.	I have to do something now. He knows that I saw them.	Embarrassed, more anxious
I say, "What've you got in your pocket there, John?"		
John: "Where?"	Here we go.	
Me: "Right there."		
John: "Nothing! What are you talking about?"	He's not going to make this easy. I'm trying to be nice.	Nervous, angry
Me: "The cigarettes. You obviously wanted me to see them."		
John: "I did not! So what are you going to do about it anyway?"	If I punish him now, he's going to do something worse.	Confused, uncertain
Me: "What do you think I should do?"	I'm stalling, and he knows it.	Stupid
John: "I think you should leave me alone." His face is getting red.	I'm tired of this nonsense.	Angry, resentful
Me: "If you wanted that, you shouldn't have come in here. You could have just gone outside and smoked, you know."	I can't believe I just suggested he break a rule. I just wouldn't have had to deal with him if I hadn't seen him.	Upset at myself
John: "Go take a flying leap (expletives deleted)!" He jumps to his feet.	Uh oh! Are there any other staff around? I have to calm him down. The other kids are watching me.	Scared, self-conscious, alert

TABLE 25.1   *(continued)*

ACTIONS	THOUGHTS	FEELINGS
Me: "Look, if you just give me the cigarettes, I won't report this."	Maybe this will work.	Hopeful
John: "They're mine. No one takes my property!" He is clenching his fists.	He's not going to get physical over this, is he?	Frightened
Me: "You're not allowed to have them here, and you know it. I should take points away."		
John: "Do I get them back?"	I can't give them back.	Confused, desperate
Me: "I don't know. I'll think about it."		
John: "All right, but only because I like you."		
Me: "Thanks."	Thank God. I wonder if I did the right thing, though.	Relieved, embarrassed, angry

telling yourself "I'm not going to do it anymore" won't help; you've probably told yourself that many times already.

Irrational Beliefs

Albert Ellis offers another way to look at specific situations in which you are not responding the way you want to (Ellis and Grieger, 1977; Ellis and Harper, 1975). He believes that situations like the ones described are stressful because of what we believe they mean. Often we have irrational beliefs about how we are supposed to be. No one can live up to them and no one should, but we keep trying. When we fail, it is evidence that we are not the person we want to be. These beliefs often take the form of "shoulds" or "musts." Below are some beliefs to which human service workers are vulnerable, drawn from the work of Ellis; Corey and Corey (1993); and Bernstein and Halaszyn (1989):

> I must be successful with all my clients.
> I must be outstanding, clearly better than others I know or hear about.
> I must be respected and loved by my clients.
> Clients should listen to me and push themselves to change.
> I should always enjoy and grow from my work.

Try to see how these beliefs, especially the first three, may be operating in the four examples described earlier. We have already discussed the distinction between having goals for your clients (wanting) and needing them to behave in a certain way. Here, too, all these statements contain noble aspirations; it's fine to want them. But when you believe you must have them, you are setting yourself up for stress because none of them are achievable.

Your Fears and Burnout

These situations and patterns contribute to burnout in several ways. The situations are stressful, as is the knowledge that you didn't handle them the way you wanted to. If you are struggling with a pattern, not only are the situations stressful, but the knowledge that you keep falling into the pattern, sometimes despite vowing not to, adds to your stress. Finally, many of these situations and patterns will keep you from making the progress with clients or having the relationships with supervisors and co-workers that you want.

If either of these approaches to examining your fears about yourself intrigues you, you can explore it further. All the sources listed in this section discuss ways to overcome crushers or to replace irrational, stressful beliefs with more rational, encouraging ones. It takes focus and practice, but it will pay off for you in your work and your personal life.

INTERPERSONAL STRESS

There are three main groups of people you will interact with on the job: clients, supervisors, and co-workers. Each can be a source of great satisfaction and in some cases can give you lots of support. However, each can also be a cause of stress. Learning what behaviors in clients, co-workers, and supervisors are difficult for you is an important step in preventing burnout.

Clients

Although your experience with clients may be limited, if you have spent even a few hours volunteering at an agency, you already know something about how you react to clients, and you can learn more by reflecting on your experience. Before going on with this chapter, try this exercise. Think of a client you enjoy(ed) working with. Don't worry about why you enjoyed it; just get a picture of that person in your mind. Now describe the person in as much detail as you can, including both physical and behavioral characteristics. Here is a partial list of things to consider:

What does he or she look like? What is he or she wearing?

Recall the tone of voice, the body language, and the gestures this person uses.

What kinds of emotions have you seen that person display? Under what circumstances?

How does he or she react to you? To other clients?

Do this for as many clients as you can. Now try the same thing for clients you do not enjoy. Again, try to avoid analyzing yourself or them to discover why you don't enjoy them. You can also use your journal and the three-column processing described earlier.

If you look back over the descriptions of people and incidents you kept, you may see some patterns emerging. You may begin to see elements that are common to several different incidents, thereby getting clues to what kinds of clients, behaviors, or emotions are hard for you and which ones are easier. For example, you may notice that all the clients you do not enjoy are loud or aggressive in some way. As you review several incidents in your journal, you may notice that in many of the stressful situations a client challenged your authority in some way. See how many of these common elements you can find.

Perhaps you have some ideas already about what client behaviors you find most stressful or think you might find most stressful. The list below was compiled from the work of Cherniss (1980b), Corey and Corey (1993), and Russo (1993). Read it and see how you react to each client. If you are not sure, that's a good answer to give. In some cases you may be speculating; that is, you may never have actually experienced this behavior in clients, but you do have an idea how you would react. That's fine, too, but remember that you may respond differently when it actually occurs. Keeping a journal is a good way to check yourself.

Clients who "play the game"; they go along with agency rules, but they're not really making progress

Clients who lie to you

Clients who manipulate you to get something they want but cannot have

Clients who are never satisfied with what you have to give; they always seem to need more

Clients who are prone to angry outbursts at you

Clients who blame everyone but themselves for their problems

Clients who are always negative about everything

Clients who are sullen and give one-word answers or responses

Clients who ask again and again for suggestions and then reject every one

Clients who refuse to see their behavior as a problem

Clients who are very passive and won't do anything to help themselves

In their book, *Issues and Ethics in the Helping Professions,* Corey, Corey, and Callanan (1993) emphasize the importance of values awareness in relationships with clients. A value difference with a client over a matter that is important to the worker can be very stressful. The worker must decide whether to expose the difference by telling the client about it and, further, whether to try to influence the client to change his or her values (this is called "imposing" values). Of course the first step is to be aware of what your values are, especially in areas that may be challenged by your clients or your work. Some of the key areas discussed in their book include sexuality, race, the right to die, religion, and homosexuality. They also discuss value differences that can arise from cultural differences between workers and clients. The book contains a very useful chapter on values and many self-tests covering a wide range of value issues.

Some of your reactions to the hypothetical clients listed above may be triggered by value conflicts. For example, suppose that honesty and straightforwardness are strong values to you. For you, to be dishonest is wrong. Of course, you are dishonest occasionally, but you know it is wrong when you do it. You may be dealing with a client who has different values. In your client's experience, being honest, especially with human service workers and other authorities, means being taken advantage of by a service delivery system she perceives as unfair. For example, in some states a woman on welfare will have her benefits reduced if she is married, even if her husband is not employed. One way to lessen the stress of client interactions is to try to understand the values underlying their behavior. That way it will seem less like a willful transgression, although you may still object to (or in some settings even punish) the behavior.

A final issue involving client-related stress concerns the extent to which you may, consciously or unconsciously, be relying on clients to meet needs that should be met in other ways. For example, some workers need clients to make progress in order to feel successful. They will not say so directly and may even be unaware of it themselves, but the high level of stress they feel from client failures indicates this pattern. There is an important but subtle distinction here. Of course you *want* your clients to make progress; you want that progress for *them.* However, when you *need* your clients to succeed, you set yourself up for stress. Not all clients can or want to succeed, yet they all need your attention and respect, and you will need to be able to find satisfaction in working with them even when they don't make the progress you hope for. Another need most people have is to feel that their work is respected. Often human service workers find that their work is misunderstood and not valued by peers, family members, or people in the community. This gap can lead workers to depend on clients to provide them with a sense of respect. Also, many human service workers have to set limits with clients, and for many people that is difficult to do. A client in a residential program may challenge a rule. A client in a community agency may press you to give more assistance, services, or time than he or she is entitled to. A worker in those situations needs someone to confirm or validate the necessity of the limit setting. The client is not usually going to do that; in fact, they may often be angry about the limits being set. Workers who need that validation from clients spend unnecessary time and energy trying to get clients to *agree* with the limit when all they really have to do is be willing to abide by it.

Here is another exercise to try. List all the things you want from your work, such as intellectual stimulation, the knowledge that you are doing some good, continued professional growth, and so on. Now list the things that might happen on the job that will give you the things you listed as wants. How many of these involve clients? For each one that involves clients, make sure there are other people and situations that can serve to meet that need as well. Another useful exercise is to list all the things you hope your clients will accomplish. Make a long list, and don't worry about how achievable the goals are. Then go back over your list and eliminate unreasonable goals. You should then have a list of goals that are reasonable to hope for. Ask yourself, though, whether you need your clients to achieve any of them. If so, ask yourself why. Lots of goals are reasonable to hope and strive for, but none are reasonable to demand or need.

It has probably already occurred to you that there can be a connection between interpersonal and intrapersonal sources of stress. As you have thought about your reactions to the clients discussed in this section, you may see ways in which your unfinished business, your ego states, or your dysfunctional patterns all affect your client interactions. In turn, you may find that in answering the questions posed in this section of the chapter you will get clues to some intrapersonal issues that are operating for you.

You may also, at this point, be wondering what you are supposed to do with all this awareness. After all, your clients are not going to change, at least not right away. So now that you have some ideas about what clients are difficult for you and why, what can you do about it? One strategy is to learn more about the clients and about yourself. If you find out more about a particular client or client group—about the psychological and social factors that influence their behavior—their actions may not seem so mysterious and stressful. If you do not understand why you react in a certain way to a client or a prospective client, do some further self-exploration. You can take deliberate steps to modify your emotional reactions to certain clients, as discussed in the section on intrapersonal stress. You can also let supervisors and co-workers know that you will need some extra emotional support in dealing with a certain individual or group. How-

ever, while you can and should pursue all these avenues, it may well be that there are certain individuals or client populations that you should not work with, at least right now.

Supervisors

Your relationship with your supervisor is one of the most important ones in your professional life. It can be a wonderful source of learning and support. It can also be a major contributor to burnout. Notice that I did not say that your supervisor can provide support or cause burnout. As in any relationship, what happens with your supervisor is a result of the attitudes and behavior of both parties. You do not have to like your supervisor for the relationship to be productive, although it helps. You do, however, have to make sure that you are getting what you need. The better you know yourself, the better you will be able to communicate your needs to a supervisor. For example, it is important for you to consider how you react to criticism, praise, or the knowledge that you have made a mistake.

Although it is true that there are some supervisors who are not very good at their jobs, and you may have one of them someday, it is also possible to have a poor relationship with a perfectly competent supervisor. That is because no one approach to supervision works best for everyone. Here are two exercises to help you understand what is important to you in a supervisor. As you did with clients, take some time to recall supervisors you have had, in human services or other settings, with whom you had a good relationship. Describe each person in as much detail as you can. Don't worry yet about what it was that made the relationship a good one. Just write the most complete description possible. Do the same exercise for any supervisors with whom you had a difficult or unproductive relationship. Now go back and look at your descriptions and see whether there are some characteristics that all the successful—or unsuccessful—supervisors had in common.

Next, consider some specific aspects of supervision and several possible approaches to each one. You may have experienced many of these approaches in the supervisors you have worked with. Think about which ones seemed to work for you. If you have not had much experience, try to imagine how you would react to each of the approaches.

Data Collection. Supervisors have different ways of finding out how you are doing. In a direct supervision approach, your supervisor works alongside you or observes you directly. Self-report means that you meet with your supervisor and tell him or her what you have been doing. Using a peer review approach means that other workers in the agency observe your work and report to your supervisor about your progress.

Frequency of Contact. Some supervisors will set aside an hour or more each week to meet privately with you, whereas others may schedule private meetings less frequently or not at all. One approach is to wait for you to initiate a meeting or to wait until the supervisor senses a problem or has a concern. Some supervisors hold group meetings with several of their workers. Some don't schedule meetings at all but will pull you aside for a conversation if they see something particularly noteworthy. Finally, some supervisors are open to meeting with you outside of scheduled times, and some are not.

Format. Supervisors will set up supervision time differently. Some supervisors follow a structured format and some are more flexible. Some supervisors, although not following a structured format, are always the one to set the agenda for the meeting; they come with issues they want to discuss. Others will discuss only those concerns and issues that you bring to the meeting. Still others will reserve time for both.

In some cases, there is a mismatch between a worker and a supervisor. For example, you may be very sensitive to criticism and be working with a supervisor who is especially blunt. If you have a supervisor who does not work alongside you, having him or her show up to observe you may make you nervous. On the other hand, you may not like having your supervisor base his or her opinion of you on reports from other people. You may prefer an unstructured approach while your supervisor is very structured, or vice versa. Another important point to remember is that you may need different styles of supervision at different points in your career or in a specific job. You may, for example, need a high level of structure in your first job or in your first few months at a new job and then less as time goes on. A mismatch can occur when a supervisor does not change his or her style to match your changing needs. Therefore, you may recall a supervisor who was terrific in a job you had a few years ago, but that same supervisor would not be as effective for you today.

Of course, you will be better off if you can adjust to a variety of styles. However, if you have a mismatch, it can contribute to burnout in two ways. It can be a direct cause of burnout in that it is a stressful relationship, or it can be an indirect cause in that you are not getting the support and guidance you need to grow and to meet the emotional challenges of your work setting. If you are clear about what you need and why you are not getting it, you may be able to approach your supervisor and discuss the situation. If it is thought of and described as a mismatch and not as a failing on the part of you or your supervisor, you will increase the chances that both of you can make some changes and work out a successful relationship.

Co-Workers

Although your supervisor may be one of the most important professional relationships you have, your relationships with your co-workers are an important factor in burnout as well. There are many more of them than your supervisor, and you will probably spend more time with them. Often it is your co-workers who teach you the ropes of the agency, especially the unwritten rules that are such a powerful part of life in any organization. They can also be models and sources of support for you as you attempt to balance the many and sometimes conflicting demands placed on you by clients, supervisors, agency rules, and your own professional ideals and aspirations. When your relationships with co-workers are not good, it adds another source of stress to your work life and also denies you a potential source of support (Maslach, 1982).

Difficulties with co-workers are sometimes the result of a personality conflict; a certain amount of that is unavoidable. However, you may also find yourself frustrated with or resentful of the way some of your co-workers approach their jobs. I am not talking here about people who cut corners or avoid their responsibilities. You may see a co-worker who brings a lot of energy and commitment to the job but applies it in a way that puzzles or even troubles you. You may find yourself wondering what is wrong with that person. It may be that the person simply has an approach that differs from your way of doing things. It is possible to have value differences with co-workers just as with clients. Some of your co-workers may have a different theoretical perspective from you. Thinking of the differences as differences, as opposed to trying to decide who is "right," will help you live with and even learn from this diversity rather than be stressed by it.

Russo (1993) offers another productive way to look at these differences. He says that in adjusting to competing demands there are three general patterns of adjustment: identification with clients, with co-workers, and with the organization. He emphasizes that these are not personality types but choices that can be and are made by many different kinds of people. Workers who identify with clients believe their primary responsibility is to effect change on their clients' behalf. They are often impatient with policies and procedures,

with professional codes of conduct, and with "the system." Those who identify with co-workers see their primary allegiance to a professional code. These codes are issued by many different professional organizations and are very useful guides to professional conduct. However, those who identify with these organizations follow these rules and codes rigidly, with little regard for the nuances of individual clients and organizational settings. Finally, those who identify with the organization adhere to the rules and codes of the organization itself, rarely even considering deviating from them.

In reading these descriptions, you may find yourself drawn to one or the other, although not everyone falls strictly into one of these categories. Most likely, some seem strange, overly rigid, or even wrong to you. Russo, however, emphasizes that people often move from one category to another over the course of their careers and that there is a legitimate case to be made for each position. Understanding these categories may help you be more accepting of co-workers whose priorities are different from your own.

CONCLUSION

Many talented people leave the human service field because of burnout. Although nothing is wrong with changing careers, it is always sad to see someone who has the potential for a long and successful career leave the field early, often in a state of bitterness. You may find that human services is not for you; however, you should be able to avoid burning out. This chapter has tried to acquaint you with the role of self-awareness in burnout prevention. No two people have the same experiences in human services. That is because each person is unique, as is each agency and client group. If you understand the things about you and others that may lead you to burn out, you can take a more productive, proactive approach to stressful situations. You don't need to see yourself as weak or incompetent or view others as bad supervisors, co-workers, or clients. Instead, you can think of the situation as a mismatch and envision ways to make changes in yourself and/or in the situation.

There are a lot of other things about burnout that you may be interested in knowing. The books and articles referenced at the end of this chapter contain interesting and important information on dealing with burnout once it begins, the characteristics of clients and organizations that may lead to burnout, and comprehensive stress management plans that will help prevent burnout from occurring.

REFERENCES

Bernstein, G. S., and J. A. Halaszyn (1989). *Human Services? . . . That Must Be So Rewarding.* Baltimore: Paul H. Brookes Publishing Co.

Cherniss, C. (1980a). *Staff Burnout: Job Stress in the Human Services.* Beverly Hills, CA: Sage Publications.

Cherniss, C. (1980b). *Professional Burnout in Human Services Organizations.* New York: Praeger.

Corey, G., M. S. Corey, and P. Callanan (1993). *Issues and Ethics in the Helping Professions,* 4th ed. Pacific Grove, CA: Brooks/Cole.

Corey, M. S., and G. Corey (1993). *Becoming a Helper,* 2nd ed. Pacific Grove, CA: Brooks/Cole.

Corsini, R. J. (1989). *Current Psychotherapies,* 4th ed. Itasca, IL: Peacock.

Dusay, J. (1977). *Egograms: How I See You and You See Me.* New York: Harper and Row.

Ellis, A., and R. Grieger (1977). *Handbook of Rational Emotive Therapy.* New York: Springer.

Ellis, A., and R. A. Harper (1975). *A New Guide to Rational Living.* Englewood Cliffs, NJ: Prentice-Hall.

James, M., and D. Jongeward (1971). *Born to Win.* Reading, MA: Addison-Wesley.

Mandell, B. R., and B. Schram (1983). *Human Services: An Introduction.* New York: John Wiley and Sons.

Maslach, C. (1982). *Burnout: The Cost of Caring.* Englewood Cliffs, NJ: Prentice Hall.

Moracco, J. (1981). *Burnout in Counselors and Organizations.* ERIC/CAPS.

Russo, J. R. (1993). *Serving and Surviving as a Human Service Worker,* 2nd ed. Prospect Heights, IL: Waveland Press.

Sweitzer, H. F., and J. S. Jones (1990). "Self-Understanding in Human Service Education: Goals and Methods." *Human Service Education,* 10(1), 39–52.

Weinstein, G. (1980, Spring). "Asking the Right Questions." *Journal of Humanistic Education, 4,* 1–4.

Weinstein, G. (1981). "Self Science Education." In J. Fried, ed., *New Directions for Student Services: Education for Student Development.* San Francisco: Jossey Bass.

Weinstein, G., J. Hardin, and M. Weinstein (1975). *Education of the Self: A Trainer's Manual.* Amherst, MA: Mandella.

KEY TERMS FOR PART SIX

After studying Chapters 22, 23, 24, and 25, you should have a command of the following key terms, major concepts, and principal topical references:

National Association of Social
   Workers (NASW)
National Association of Drug
   Abuse Counselors
   (NAADAC)
"bounty hunting"
accountability
sexual misconduct
humanitarian ethos
access and release
billing fraud
confidentiality

informed consent
right of refusal
managed health care
Durham Rule
parens patriae
mandated reporting
"therapeutic state"
Health Maintenance
   Organization (HMO)
duty to warn
dual relationship

privileged communication
ETs
career mobility
Privacy Act (1974)
intrapersonal stress
interpersonal stress
McNaughton Rule
A.L.I. Rule
need to know
GBMI
due process

PIVOTAL ISSUES FOR DISCUSSION OF PART SIX

1. Read the Articles of the U.S. Constitution, the Amendments to the Constitution, and the Bill of Rights.

2. List three basic rights that human service clients have by law. Give an example for each as it may exist in any typical human service agency.

3. How can human service professionals protect themselves from professional liabilities?

4. Describe your career goals in human services. What requirements will you need to meet in order to reach your goals?

5. What are the signs of job burnout in human services? How do you plan to avoid or minimize this professional dilemma?

6. Identify three ways you can be a better human service worker.

7. What are your personal concerns and worries about working in human services? How do you plan to address them?

SUGGESTED READINGS FOR PART SIX

1. Woody, R. H., and Associates (1984). *The Law and the Practice of Human Services.* San Francisco, CA: Jossey-Bass.

2. Barton, W. E., and C. J. Sanborn, eds. (1978). *Law and Mental Health Professions: Friction at the Interface.* New York: International University Press.

3. Corey, M. S., and G. Corey (1993). *Becoming A Helper,* 2nd ed. Pacific Grove, CA: Brooks/Cole.

4. Corey, G., M. S. Corey, and P. Callanan (1993). *Issues and Ethics in the Helping Professions,* 4th ed. Pacific Grove, CA: Brooks/Cole.

PART SEVEN

EMERGING ISSUES
AND TRENDS

In Part Seven we will explore the changing demographic landscapes of American society, the impact of technological advances on human service work, and the research methodologies that provide challenges and opportunities for social experimentation and social change. A Special Focus Feature describes the transformative nature and impact of the Service-Learning movement.

In Chapter 26, R. Donna Petrie discusses differences "between and within" cultural groups and explores the challenges of working with clients who hold different beliefs and values. To be effective, human service workers may need to provide different kinds of caring for people in various groups. Awareness of one's own assumptions can make it easier to remain open to other points of view.

In Chapter 27, Stan Rosenzweig brings you up to date on technological advances that help you work more efficiently as a human service professional. The author provides historical support for his assertion that new technology is first viewed with suspicion and eventually becomes commonplace. He provides a virtual tour of the World Wide Web, explaining how the Internet can make the job of a human service professional easier and more rewarding. For technophobes, the author emphasizes the value of playful learning.

In Chapter 28, Eugene DeRobertis and Robert Saldarini describe the impact of computer technology, particularly the widespread use of telecommunications, on social interaction. The authors explore emerging trends in the use of technology that present challenges to a healthy social climate and optimal self-development. The authors describe the bridges and barriers that technology constructs for human contact.

In a Special Focus Feature, Linda Mass describes how the Service-Learning Program at Brookdale Community College helps human service students to clarify their chosen career paths and apply the knowledge they have acquired in the classroom, while simultaneously providing needed services to the community.

In Chapter 29, Rod Underwood and Michael Lee clarify how research is used in human services and why it is an important area of knowledge for contemporary human service workers. The authors provide clear descriptions of the many different types of research, describing their methodology, purpose, and use. From this discussion of research techniques you will grasp how different research approaches are used for specific purposes.

LEARNING OBJECTIVES FOR PART SEVEN: EMERGING ISSUES AND TRENDS

After reading and studying Chapters 26, 27, 28, and 29,

- You will appreciate the special concerns that cultural diversity presents for human service professionals.
- You will be aware of the ways in which subjectivity can hinder the effectiveness of human service workers.
- You will become aware of the growing importance of computer technology in the field of human services.
- You will learn how to use the Internet for various activities that are relevant to human services.
- You will know the basic components of research models used in human services.

CHAPTER 26

TRENDS AND CHALLENGES OF CULTURAL DIVERSITY

R. DONNA PETRIE

We are born in families, whether small or large, with one or more parenting figures. These families are embedded in a web of other families, all of which are part of a particular society or culture. In the United States families share a common culture because they all live in one country, but they also share a family culture that may or may not be like the culture of the nation. It is virtually impossible to overemphasize the influence an individual's family culture has on the day-to-day activities of any given person's life. In this country it is also nearly impossible to overestimate the points of difference within cultures and between cultures. Diversity itself has historically represented a core component of the democratic fabric of that which defines American life. This position and role is as viable today in 2003 as it was during the past two centuries.

The purpose of this chapter is to broadly introduce the challenges of multicultural human service work. These challenges are threefold. First, human service professionals need to have an understanding of specific value areas wherein misunderstanding between cultures is likely to occur; second, workers need to understand different cultural models of healing and caring; and finally, human service professionals, whether they think of themselves as bicultural or as "American," need to understand how they are seen as "agents" of mainstream American culture.

FUTURE POPULATION TRENDS

A decade ago the *New York Times* reported that the United States Census Bureau has had to recal-culate population growth (Pear, 1992). The population of the United States, it appears, will continue to grow through 2050 rather than decline after the year 2038. To summarize, for the years 1990 to 2025 there will be more babies born, particularly to new immigrants, and the proportion of men to women is likely to even out, as the life expectancy of men appears to be rising faster than that of women.

Despite this overall increase in the number of people in the United States, whites will account for a declining share in the population. The numbers of black Americans, Asian Americans, and Hispanic Americans will grow appreciably. Using the 1990 census, the Bureau predicts a 412.5 percent population growth for Asian and Pacific Islanders; a 237.5 percent growth in numbers for Hispanic Americans; a 109.1 percent increase in the number of Native American Indians, Eskimos, and Aleuts; and a 93.8 percent increase for black Americans. These figures contrast significantly with the 29.4 percent projected growth of white Americans from 1992 to 2050.

The Census Bureau makes the future trends somewhat more complex by noting that immigration by itself will account for the expected growth in the Asian American population and not the number of births. Birth rates are increasing among the black and Hispanic populations. The birth rate of whites, however, is not expected to increase. In the United States the youngest population group is Hispanic Americans. In fact, whereas the median age of all Americans is thirty-three, more than one-third of the Hispanic population in the United States is under the age of eighteen.

In addition to shifts in the growth of ethnic populations, other demographic variables are also changing. For example, in the age category of 55 years or older, 13 percent are over 65, with the quickest rate of change observed in the nonwhite population, especially Latinos and Asian Americans (Gelfand and Yee, 1991). With this sociocultural picture and the continuation of "urban sprawl," jobs traditionally available to typical city dwellers will be less available. Consequently, human service workers on the two coasts (namely New York, northern New Jersey, Long Island, Los Angeles, Anaheim, and Riverside, California) will likely experience more interpersonal racial and ethnic conflict because of the greater numbers of immigrants and the greater density mixes of black, white, yellow, and brown cultures. Other urban areas such as Miami and Fort Lauderdale, Florida; Houston, Galveston, and Brazoria, Texas; and San Francisco, Oakland, and San Jose, California, may also experience the effects of polarizing differences between Hispanics and Asians and between Asians and blacks (U.S. Department of Commerce, 1991). Color consciousness and ethnic intolerance, although long-standing and typically a white-black issue in this country, is no less a problem between and within other racial and ethnic groupings.

Social characteristics of various cultural groups in this country add to the complexity of the challenge of working with culturally diverse client populations. Whereas the percentage of persons twenty-five years of age and over who have not completed an elementary school education (zero to eight years) is lowest for Asian Americans (6.4 percent with five years or less completed) and highest for Hispanic Americans (34 percent), the percentage of whites is 11 percent and of blacks 17 percent. Level of education, unemployment, and poverty have a high degree of correspondence for all cultural groups in America, except for whites. The unemployment rate for whites is the lowest of all groups, as are

their numbers in families living below the poverty line, and this despite the fact that 11 percent of the white population has only an elementary school education (U.S. Department of Commerce, 1991).

These population trends can help us create an accurate picture of current and future clients seeking human services. People of color will continue to dominate the social welfare client rolls and will continue to have multiple problems. The clients will be very young or very old, their formal education will be limited, and they will have trouble finding work. If they are immigrants or children of immigrants, they will likely have problems navigating family and personal cultural issues as well.

Although individuals from this client population profile are well known to any entry-level human service professional, the human service model of helping does not automatically attribute deficiency or mental illness to these individuals (Schmolling, Youkeles, and Burger, 1992; Papajohn and Spiegel, 1975). On the contrary, many such clients, although wanting economic security, may not subscribe at all to the American values of materialism and of being "bigger and better" or more successful than one's forebears. Indeed, on many levels, not only their needs and wants may be different from mainstream cultural stereotypes presented in the media, but individual clients may be very different from the culture or family in which they were raised (Pedersen, 1976).

BASIC AREAS OF DIFFERENCE IN CULTURAL VALUES

We can safely assume that all people in the United States, regardless of cultural affiliation, want to have an *optimal life* (Speight, Myers, Cox, and Highlen, 1991). Given that definitions of an optimal life differ and that individuals living in an increasingly multicultural and multilingual society will often have to interact or negotiate with members of another culture, on what subjects are they likely to have interpersonal misunderstandings?

Apart from differences in individual communication style and language usage (Sarbaugh, 1988; Baruth and Manning, 1991), cultural anthropologists have categorized differences between ethnic groups in the following ways: (1) their understanding of authority, (2) their definitions of success, and (3) their beliefs about how people should conduct themselves and their relationships (Carter, 1991; Baruth and Manning, 1991). Understanding the values of each client group on the previously stated dimensions can help to clarify how an individual may be in conflict with his or her own culture or with the larger multiethnic culture. In the next several paragraphs we will look at a number of ethnic groups' general responses to these questions.

What motivates human beings? Are they basically good or well meaning, or are they born with evil intentions? The answer to this question is a basic building block of an individual's belief structure. Research has shown that blacks and Puerto Ricans often contrast sharply with Eurocentric Americans in their view of human nature (Carter, 1991). Although several studies of white, middle-class Americans provide mixed views of human nature, none offer evidence that Euro-Americans think human beings are born malevolent in character; blacks and Puerto Ricans are more fatalistic, believing some people do evil things because they are evil.

Similarly, Euro-Americans tend to differ from blacks, Chinese, Africans, Italians, Cubans, and Native American Indians in their belief that individuals exert control over life events and that each person should use willpower for one's own gain (Carter, 1991; Helms, 1992; Pinderhughes, 1989). While many blacks, Cubans, and Native Americans believe people live in nature and are partners with all of nature, other blacks, Italians, and Chinese believe that people have little control over natural forces or what happens to people and also what they can do about what has happened. Clearly, trying to help an individual who believes

that personal effort is futile because "that's the way things are" and that one must comply with fate is likely to "feel" frustrating and futile to Euro-American and Japanese American intake workers who have put themselves through college. Euro-American culture believes in action, in achievement, and in self-expression (Carter, 1991; Helms, 1992). Action is centered in the individual, who not only has the right but is expected to be autonomous from the group—to, in effect, place his or her goals ahead of those of the group (Carter, 1991). This "rugged individualism" is so widespread in the United States, it has become almost synonymous with American culture. But not all cultures in America hold individualistic values. Puerto Ricans, Italians, and Greeks, to name a few, do not (Carter, 1991), and, interestingly, some studies of Euro-American college students indicate a movement away from mastery over nature and action value orientations (Carter, 1991).

What is success, and what should be emphasized in social relations between people? Typically Euro-Americans believe success occurs somewhere in the future, that success is usually gained through individual effort, and that success will be observable in material gain or achievements (Carter, 1991; Helms, 1992). Few other cultures put as much emphasis on the value of delayed gratification or material well-being as white, middle-class Americans do. For other cultures, either traditional customs or the activities and events of the present are of central importance (Carter, 1991). So, again, human service college graduates who seek to help individuals from a different culture must be open to other definitions of success and achievement (Pinderhughes, 1989).

To summarize this section, human service workers who have graduated from college have learned how to function successfully within the mainstream value culture of this country. Specifically, they have been encultured by others who believe in rugged individualism, delayed gratification, material success, personal effort and responsibility, and the basic goodness of human nature. Because human service workers have negotiated the educational system, they can assist in educating clients about American culture and work habits so that clients may also become multicultural. The helper's self-knowledge can also prevent possible misunderstandings in interpersonal communication.

Still and all, there is no way to simplify cross-cultural diversity. Pinderhughes (1989) lists at least fourteen different sources of cultural differences between people. When within-group differences are added, as in immigrant second- and third-generation groups, gaining a comprehensive knowledge of any single culture becomes impossible. The best students can do to meet the challenges inherent in cross-cultural helping is to know their own culture, to stay open and accepting of other cultures, and to keep an eye on what "works" in the dominant or mainstream culture. C. Gilbert Wrenn (1987), a longtime researcher in cross-culture counseling and therapy, suggests that students (1) read positive long-range-thinking scholars who talk about the spiritual as well as the beautiful, (2) unlearn something every day to make way for change, (3) trust that there is a light at the end of the tunnel, and (4) risk acceptance and validation of another's experience. The latter point is important to the next section, which explores kinds of caring.

KINDS OF CARING

Textbooks in human services usually emphasize one-on-one talking or group talking as the most frequently used helping interventions. Sometimes the skills of brokering, advocacy, outreach, and community organizing are also added (Schmolling, Youkeles, and Burger, 1992; Okun, 1992; Shulman, 1982). There are other ways of intervening with clients. Madeleine M. Leininger (1987) persuasively argues for *transcultural caring* as an innovative and essential approach to helping people "live and survive in diverse and changing contexts" (p. 107). She believes that helpers must learn what "cultural-care" behaviors are likely to be accepted by helpees before "real care" or service can be given. Other researchers have highlighted culturally specific interventions, too. What follows are summary findings from Leininger (1987), McGowan (1988), Vontress (1991), Prince (1980), and Tseng and McDermott (1981) about kinds of caring in different cultures (see Table 26.1). The summaries are not meant to be exhaustive but rather to provide evidence of the diversity of helping methods.

Leininger (1987), from a study of thirty-five cultures, determined forty-two different ideas about caring for others. Those on the list that are usually taught in human service classes include trust, understanding, empathy, listening, and respect. But there were others current education does not suggest as appropriate to American culture: touching, loving, succoring, protecting, and sharing (Leininger, 1987). Whether there are universal elements basic to all cultures has not been determined because the process of helping is complex, and there is often a very hazy boundary between psychological and physical problems (Prince, 1980). Methods are made more complicated, too, by the fact that some cultures believe psychological suffering is a fact of living to be accepted rather than an idiosyncratic personality outlook that can be changed (Prince, 1980).

Aside from these qualities and purposes of helping, each culture has a characteristic stance on who can effectively do the helping. In many cultures only an expert can be a "healer." This point of view is true of mainstream American culture—our experts are those who have managed to successfully complete a number of years of postsecondary education. In Africa, as Vontress (1991) writes, the healing specialists include the herbalist, the fetish man, the medium (usually a woman who is able to transmit messages from the dead to the living), the sorcerer (usually one who can do evil), and the healers (perhaps an equiva-

TABLE 26.1   Value Emphases—Four Major Cultural Groups

	Value Authority	Value Extended Family Relationships	Value Personal Independence	Value Nature	Prefer Expert as Helper
Asian Americans (Includes individuals of island or mainland descent who understand Mandarin or Cantonese dialects)	H*	H	L	M	L
Black Americans (Includes individuals who identify with Caribbean or African origins)	H	H	H	M	H
Euro-Americans (Those individuals who would identify themselves as Caucasian, white, or of European descent)	L	L	H	M	H
Hispanic Americans (Those individuals who speak or understand Spanish or a variant dialect)	M	H	M	M	M

*Legend: H = high value or emphasis; M = moderate emphasis; L= low value or little emphasis

lent to our generalists). Although different from our experts, they are experts nonetheless.

In other cultures the community, using traditional rituals, acts in a collateral fashion with individuals to relieve their suffering. McGowan (1988) described the effectiveness of a community center providing preventive service programs for Puerto Ricans in a Brooklyn, New York, neighborhood. In effect, the program provided sociotherapy in that it maintained over a dozen programs for at-risk families—programs that included an after-school drop-in center, a thrift shop, a mothers' group, an advocacy clinic, an employment service, and a foster grandparent program. Clearly for Puerto Ricans, being with members of their community is important for healing. Another study (Leininger, 1987) found that family sharing (i.e. nonrelatives living with a "sponsor" family) was a particularly important ingredient in helping for the Vietnamese, Philippine Americans, and Mexican Americans. Ethnotherapy is another within-group treatment used by various cultural groups to explore and understand personal identity (Klein, 1976).

A final method of helping or caring, one form of which is currently sweeping the United States through twelve-step programs, is the use of self-healing methods. Aron (1992) describes *testimonio* (testimony) as a therapeutic tool in the treatment of people who have suffered psychological trauma. This method is not unlike the "qualification" at a twelve-step recovery meeting. There are other examples of self-healing techniques: prolonged sleep or social isolation found in Weir Mitchell's "rest cure," the Japanese Morita treatment (Prince, 1980; Tseng and McDermott, 1981), and autogenic training, a form of self-hypnosis practiced in Germany (Prince, 1980; Tseng and McDermott, 1981).

In summary, the challenges of cultural diversity in human services include not only differences in beliefs, attitudes, and customs between and within cultures but also varying opinions about who can help and how that help can be carried out. Clearly the combinations are so vast in number that any beginning professional might think working with clients outside one's own culture is impossible. It is not impossible, however, if the helping professional is accepting and open to others and has the knowledge described in the next section.

HUMAN SERVICE PROFESSIONALS IN THE UNITED STATES

Service professionals who are immigrants or first-generation Americans, especially if they are fluent in a language other than English, clearly have an "edge" in working within the culture in which they have their origins. The edge is linguistic. This is not to suggest that anyone who speaks Spanish is going to be a "better" helper to the Hispanic client population. Indeed, if the helper is Mexican American, she or he may have no point of reference, other than Spanish vocabulary, with an Argentinean or Cuban client.

The question remains: Can an American-trained human service entry-level professional, regardless of cultural background, work with diverse cultural groups? Clinicians answer "yes" if that helper understands he or she is an agent of

Euro-American culture and also a helper who by definition has power (Pinderhughes, 1989; Carter, 1991). Although it is important not to be "culturally encapsulated" (Pedersen, 1976), it is imperative to have specific knowledge of dominant American values (Carter, 1991). For Helms (1992), Carter (1991), and Pinderhughes (1989), that knowledge involves awareness that history affects how our institutions operate and that American history is a history of racial-cultural inequalities. Racism, sexism, ageism, and heterosexism operate unconsciously, so helpers must work to stay open, flexible, and empathic. Central to all "isms" is power and the underlying "better-than" or "less-than" dynamic between helper and helpee that is implicit or inherent to American values. Americans believe in power, in influence, and in the "better-than" ability of the expert. Although mainstream American culture does not value authority, we paradoxically give power to our "experts."

Thus, power exists with powerlessness, dominance with subservience, control with helplessness, and capability with incompetence—dangerous autonyms, but ones that those who seek help often carry within them. In effect, as Pinderhughes (1989) suggests, those who are without status or power in American culture often identify with the aggressor and feel doubly victimized. In other words, the "have-nots" not only don't have things but also hate themselves (thereby believing they deserve what they get) for not having things. Thus helpers, by recognizing that power is built into a helping experience, can speak the unspeakable (Ruebens and White, 1992) and clarify the needs and expectations of those interacting. That, by the way, includes the helper's needs and expectations of the client as well. In short, helpers must diminish their own defensiveness (Pedersen, 1988) and monitor and manage their feelings, perceptions, and attitudes (Pinderhughes, 1989). As helpers we must realize we have power and be willing to acknowledge what we know and can do and what we don't know and can't do.

As Pinderhughes (1989) further suggests, helpers must realize that all people need to feel positive about their cultural identity and that it is the responsibility of the helper to demonstrate mutuality, self-respect, and respect for clients in the helping relationship. Helpers need to allow clients the opportunity to exercise choice, and to collaborate in treatment goals and in treatment methods. Given that all people in America live in culturally diverse communities, it is important that the helper help all clients become multicultural. Learning to live harmoniously and with self-expression, both within a culture and with others of another culture, are the great rewards and challenges of living in a democratic society.

SUMMARY

Human service workers face the challenges of cross-cultural social service work. Cultural diversity demands an understanding of possible value differences in worldview, in who can be a helper, and how helping is experienced. The human service worker needs to be fully aware and culturally sensitive to self, others, and the helping relationship's interpersonal variables.

REFERENCES

Aron, A. (1991). "Testimonio: A Bridge between Psychotherapy and Sociotherapy." In E. Cole, E. D. Rothblum, and O. M. Espin, eds., *Refugee Women and Their Mental Health, Vol. 2, Women and Therapy,* 173–189. San Francisco: Jossey-Bass.

Baruth, L. G., and M. L. Manning (1991). *Multicultural Counseling and Psychotherapy: A Life Span Perspective.* New York: Macmillan.

Carter, R. T. (1991). "Cultural Values: A Review of Empirical Research and Implications for Counseling." *Journal of Counseling and Development, 70,* 164–173.

Gelfand, D., and B. W. K. Yee (1991). "Trends and Forces: Influence of Immigration, Migration, and Acculturation on the Fabric of Aging in America," *Generations, 15*(4), 7–10.

Helms, J. E. (1992). *A Race Is a Nice Thing to Have.* Topeka, KS: Content Communications.

Klein, J. (1976). "Ethnotherapy with Jews." *International Journal of Mental Health, 5*(2), 26–38.

Leininger, M. M. (1987). "Transcultural Caring: A Different Way to Help People." In P. Pedersen, ed., *Handbook of Cross-Cultural Counseling and Therapy.* pp. 107–115. New York: Praeger.

McGowan, B. G. (1988). "Helping Puerto Rican Families at Risk: Responsive Use of Time, Space, and Relationships," In C. Jacobs and D. D. Bowles, eds., *Ethnicity and Race: Critical Concepts in Social Work.* pp. 48–66. Silver Spring, MD: National Association of Social Workers.

Okun, B. F. (1992). *Effective Helping: Interviewing and Counseling Techniques,* 4th ed. Pacific Grove, CA: Brooks/Cole.

Papajohn, J., and J. Spiegel (1975). *Transactions in Families.* San Francisco: Jossey-Bass.

Pear, J. (1992). "Population Growth Outstrips Earlier U.S. Census Estimates." *The New York Times,* Dec. 4, 1992, pp. A1, D18.

Pedersen, P. (1976). "The Field of Intercultural Counseling." In P. Pedersen, W. J. Lonner, and J. G. Draguns, eds., *Counseling Across Cultures.* pp. 17–42. Honolulu: The University Press of Hawaii.

Pedersen, P. (1988). *A Handbook for Developing Multicultural Awareness.* Alexandria, VA: AACD.

Pinderhughes, E. (1989). *Understanding Race, Ethnicity, and Power.* New York: Macmillan.

Prince, R. (1980). "Variations in Psychotherapeutic Procedures." In H. Triandis and J. G. Durgens, eds., *Psychopathology, Vol. 6: Handbook of Cross-Cultural Psychology.* pp. 291–349. Boston: Allyn and Bacon.

Ruebens, P., and J. White (1992). "Speaking the Unspeakable: Race, Class, and Ethnicity: Differences within the Treatment Setting." Women's Therapy Centre Institute Workshop, October 24.

Sarbaugh, L. E. (1988). *Intercultural Communication.* New Brunswick, NJ: Transaction Books.

Schmolling, P. Jr., M. Youkeles, and W. R. Burger (1992). *Human Services in Contemporary America.* Monterey, CA: Brooks/Cole.

Shulman, E. D. (1982). *Intervention in the Human Services,* 3rd ed. St. Louis: C. V. Mosby.

Speight, S. L., L. J. Myers, C. I. Cox, and P. S. Highlen (1991). "A Redefinition of Multicultural Counseling." *Journal of Counseling and Development, 70,* 29–36.

Tseng, W., and J. F. McDermott, Jr. (1981). *Culture, Mind, and Therapy.* New York: Brunner/Mazel.

U.S. Department of Commerce (1991). *Statistical Abstract of United States, 1991.* Washington, DC: National Data Book.

Vontress, C. E. (1991). "Traditional Healing in Africa: Implications for Cross-Cultural Counseling." *Journal of Counseling and Development, 70,* 242–249.

Wrenn, C. G. (1987). "Afterword: The Culturally Encapsulated Counselor Revisited." In P. Pedersen, ed., *Handbook of Cross-Cultural Counseling and Therapy.* New York: Praeger, pp. 323–329.

CHAPTER 27

TECHNOLOGY AND HUMAN SERVICES

STAN ROSENZWEIG

KNOWLEDGE IS POWER

These days we benefit from technological advances in almost everything we do. Automobiles all run on computers (note that I didn't say *a* computer but *computers* [plural]). Your kitchen is computer-enhanced with high-tech components in your microwave oven, your refrigerator, and your dishwasher. Clothes washers and dryers, too, are computer processor controlled. Elevators and escalators all use integrated-circuit, high-tech components that are transparent to you.

The simple truth is that the "higher" the technology, the less you even notice it when you use it. Most of this new growth has come along with the virtual stealth of the B-1 bomber, so we don't even give it a second thought when we step on the gas, pop a bag of microwave popcorn, or set the clothes dryer to delicate.

Like the stealth B-1 bomber, however, although we don't always see high technology coming, it sure takes a lot of high maintenance to keep it going once we own it.

Technology is burgeoning not just at home but also in the workplace. Workplace growth, of course, is much more apparent, if not downright intimidating. Simple phones of the 1980s have been replaced by phone system terminals with complex keyboards, voice mail, and detailed instruction books. Computers have made their way to every desktop and to many briefcases—cell phones and pocket pagers are almost everywhere, and they are all being consolidated into a common voice-data integrated and unified messaging environment.

In the past few years, teletype and typewriters have disappeared altogether, while today everyone must know how to use fax machines and collating copiers that were unheard of only a few years ago.

Even in the fields of education and human services, usually the last to be funded for such improvements, change is evident. In school, our fourth-grader gets her homework assignment from her teacher by calling a voice mailbox at school, and her teacher gets her assignments from the school district the same way. Snow-day reports are listed in voice mail, are broadcast by fax to the media, and are posted on the Internet.

With each advance in technology, applications will become more transparent to you and easier to use. There will be many more changes, and they will occur at a much faster pace, bringing human service professionals both bad news and good news.

The bad news is that information technology is now so integrally important to your ability to do your job that you will have to be as technologically literate as possible. You will need to keep abreast of changes and be able to implement them in your everyday activities. In short, as the calendar advances, there will always be some sort of technology learning curve that we will need to be tuned in to.

The good news is that with this explosive growth, every day brings a new beginning for learning some new technology, and even those who are more technologically advanced will find that they have to start from square one each time there is a new paradigm shift. This means that, for you, it is never too late to jump in and become as valuable to your profession as the person next to you.

Marshall McLuhan said, "The medium is the message." *Process rules.* Recall the popular and populist slogan of the new paradigm: "You've got to be in it to win it."

So, take the plunge. Stop procrastinating and thinking like an adult. Instead, start thinking like a grade-schooler. The once popular "inner child" hasn't been heard from in some time now, but it's time we dusted off the little tike. Kids don't know what they don't know, and therefore can learn through play. Play, after all, is the perfect protocol for learning technology. The sooner you do this, the sooner you will accomplish the following:

1. Become more valuable to your clients, to your organization, and to yourself.
2. Find that your job is more interesting and more fun.
3. Feel the joy of empowerment that comes with unbridled access to the world's knowledge.

Are you keeping up? Can you use new techniques, for instance, to track your human service clients so they don't fall through the cracks? Can you single-handedly develop meaningful statistics to show what programs are working and what needs improvement? Can you keep in touch with your colleagues and your human service clients? Of course you can.

Here are some of the things you will accomplish with your newly acquired ability to harness modern computer technology:

First, you will manage finite resources better, and you will expend fewer of those resources developing and maintaining human service records. After all, record keeping is drudgery, but it still has to be done, especially if you are providing mandatory reports for grants or public funding. Computer-based accounting, clearly, is the most efficient means to this end.

In addition to simple accounting software, record keeping has been significantly improved through the use of commercial database management products. Many of these are high-cost, high-end products that you will come in contact with only if the organization you are connected with has specified them.

However, for training, practice, or to set up your own system for a small organization, there are several small office/home office (SOHO) products such as Microsoft Access, Borland's Paradox, and IBM's Lotus Approach that are highly recommended.

Computing is the obvious solution for those who have the need to track down information and share it with others. Principal uses of computers to communicate include the following:

1. Sharing information with co-workers through telecommunications transmission and work group collaboration. This is especially useful for collaborative projects among several individuals separated by significant distances. This chapter, for instance, had to be communicated to the book's editors. The most sensible means to do this was through the Internet from my computer to theirs.
2. Obtaining information from other databases. Any desktop computer with a modem can dial into any large information repository that is warehoused on a computer, *if* the warehoused information is made available to you (through password and communications access codes). This is a wonderful way to receive information from government agencies, to research facts and procedures, to receive updates of changes to laws and regulations, and so on.
3. For learning and individual staff development, computer communications brings the latest content, both in text and video, directly to your desktop.

BOOK? WHAT'S A BOOK?

Will books be replaced by computers? No, not completely, but many books have, indeed, been rendered obsolete by computers that bring readers the most timely updates to text. Moreover, desktop computer books are interactive, integrating audio, live action graphics, and full-motion video. So far, computers have not replaced books, which retain the following beneficial characteristics:

1. No batteries required
2. Totally portable and lightweight
3. Still easier to use (for a while, anyway)
4. Very low cost allows wider distribution
5. No hardware required to run them
6. Make excellent archives and summaries

Reading a traditional book, however, may fall short of the expectations of the MTV generation: (1) it's boring—no entertaining sound bites, (2) it requires an attention span exceeding current MTV standards and practices, and (3) it's not interactive: nothing to push or click.

What is the conclusion? I predict that books will evolve to fulfill two functions in today's professional world: (1) they will review and summarize computer-generated audio/visual training, and (2) they will provide a means for cost-effective distribution to people who have little or no computing infrastructure. The rise and fall of books notwithstanding, your new use of computing technology will prove most useful to you as a communications tool with clients, with staff, with other organizations, and for research and to simulate user groups and attend conferences and so on without being there.

SURFING WITHOUT THE OCEAN

Technology professionals are starting to hate the phrase "surfing the Web." Why? Because it gives people the impression that access to the Internet's World Wide Web is nothing more than a mindless, rock-and-roll, boob-tube type of activity that has little value other than to entertain.

Entertainment is nothing to sneer at, of course, and Internet technology certainly provides that. In fact, in addition to our previously voiced recommendation that you use play as a means to advance your own education in technol-

ogy, we second the recommendations of many major corporate human resource executives who believe that spending time with your computer for fun and amusement is the best way to improve technological skills. Just about every desktop computer in corporate America is now allowed to be installed with some number of computer games. Computer professionals do this so that you will advance from considering the desktop computer as new technology to be respected from afar to integrating it into your cognitive consciousness as you do with older, but no less useful, high-tech gear such as the telephone.

Yes, the common telephone, which we use every day without a conscious thought is, in fact, a technological advance without which all modern commerce would cease. But this wasn't always so. Back in 1877, William Orton, president of Western Union, the world's largest communications company, looked at the telephone as some of us look at computer technology today.

According to Sidney H. Aronson (1977), Orton turned down the chance to buy all rights to the telephone from Alexander G. Bell's new company. Orton's response to the merger offer was, "What use could this company make of an electrical toy?" Failure to appreciate the value of technology, for Western Union, didn't end there. Several years later, after commissioning Thomas Edison to invent the phonograph, Western Union didn't see the value of this technology either and gave the patent back to Edison.

The point here is that new technology often progresses from being odd, to novel, to entertaining, and then to highly productive. Those of us who are curious about it and are drawn to it will prosper, whereas those who eschew its potential will fail.

Because the Internet is so much in the news and on everyone's lips, let's see how to best use this newest of technologies for fun as well as for profit and improve our utilization skills enough to become complete users without deliberate thought, just as we use the phone. For example, here is a list of the everyday things I did using the Internet from my computer this week:

1. Sent forty-two quick messages to clients and suppliers without printing, stuffing envelopes, stamping, or mailing anything.
2. Researched the field of human services without leaving my office to gain a better understanding of who will be buying and reading a book like this (you).
3. Found out which was the lowest group airfare for our ski club's next vacation trip.
4. Updated my file on the latest treatments and diets for gout and Lyme disease, both of which are of interest to my family members.
5. Recovered and printed out a published sports analysis of the September 14, 1997, National Football League game between the New England Patriots and the New York Jets, which was the first meeting of these two teams since winning coach Bill Parcells left the former team to lead the latter.
6. Reviewed three new published works on entrepreneurial marketing.
7. Sent my monthly magazine column to the publisher.
8. Received and sent e-mail to family and friends around the world.

In addition, here are some things I could have done but didn't:

1. Make free phone calls to friends in Israel (or any other place where someone I know has a computer connected to the Internet).
2. Download (record on my computer from some distant computer) my favorite musical selection and play it at my convenience.
3. Download a movie and show it on my TV.
4. Research and learn about any subject of human knowledge from almost any library in the world.

That's not all. I am about to run out and buy a new computer to replace one of the seven we own. The current ones work fine for the things I have described, but they don't quite do enough of what your desktop computer can do if you buy one today, thanks to Gordon Moore.

LAW OF SUPPLY AND DEMAND

In 1968, Gordon Moore became the co-founder of Intel Corporation, and in 1971 he helped to develop the world's first microprocessor. Several years before that, however, in 1965, Moore made a startling observation that foresaw all that we do with technology today and has since come to be known as Moore's law.

Each new chip, said Moore, contained roughly twice as much capacity as its predecessor, and each chip was released within eighteen to twenty-four months of the previous chip.

To understand the magnitude of this observation, let's do some simple math. Say you borrow $10,000 from a friend or relative to invest in the ultimate sure thing: a safe bond that will double your money in eighteen months, after which time you will have $20,000, a tidy profit. In six years, though, you would compound that amount to $160,000. In six more years, you could cash out and retire on a satisfying $2.4 million. But if you let it ride, twenty-five years from now you would have $1,229,000,000.

True to Moore's law, in the twenty-five years following Moore's projection, the number of transistors on an ordinary desktop computer chip increased from 2,300 to over 10 million—and that was a few years ago.

So, my new computer will do all the things we expect from a PC, plus it will be able to listen to my dictation tapes, transcribe my speech to text, correct spelling and grammar, translate to a foreign language of my choice (if needed), and e-mail the finished article, column, or book chapter to my editor. Now that's fine for me, but what can all this pricey hardware do for you?

Your assignment, should you accept it, is to go out and get a computer with a communications connection, called a modem. Buy the largest and fastest one you can afford because these become old and tiny in eighteen months, thanks to Moore.

A PRIMER FOR PROFESSIONAL DEVELOPMENT

The U.S. Army divides training into two phases. First, they teach you how to be a soldier. Then they teach you how to use soldiering to do your job. It's a good formula, and it works. So, let's copy the

Army training formula and divide your technological education process into two phases: (1) basic training, or personal development; and (2) advanced training, or professional development.

For personal development, try this:

1. Sign up with an Internet service provider such as AOL, CompuServe, Netscape, Netcom, AT&T, Microsoft, and so on. This will work from home if your organization does not provide Internet access (or if it provides restricted access). If your organization provides unrestricted Internet access, especially to the Web, grab the information specialist and get yourself an account, an e-mail address, a password, and an instruction book.

2. Read the instructions and plow right in. Don't be afraid. It's not like driving a car, after all. Nothing will get wrecked, and no one will get hurt, so just do it. Remember, think like a child, not like an adult.

3. Stop watching TV with new versions of the same old storyline. Instead, log on and explore the richness of the Internet three or four times a week until you feel so comfortable with it that you don't even think about it. Learn how to learn all over again. Start by researching all the new ways to research (more details, later). Entertain yourself. See what others in your field are doing with technology. Enter a few chat groups.

4. Practice with software and seek out new things you can do with it. Do you already know how to use Microsoft Word? That one application has enough great communications and publishing features to keep you busy and productive for years.

5. Get comfortable with computer accounting by checking out local banks that let you use your computer to transfer funds, write and mail checks, view statements, and so on. It gives you good control of your economic life and is great practice with new technology.

6. Get a different perspective on the news. Check your favorite news provider on the Web each day. All the major broadcast companies have websites. In addition, new web-only companies are doing a bang-up job of presenting news and providing entertaining graphics.

For the advanced training we call professional development, do these two things:

1. Begin by seeking out advice and counsel of other human service professionals within your particular discipline or organization. I have found, through experience, that the learning curve is flattened significantly when you speak with those who have come from where you now stand.

2. Now that you are computer literate and Internet facile (relatively speaking), plan for professional development by blocking out a specific time slot each week to research the Internet for technical and general information that pertains to your specific discipline within human services.

Searching for information is easy and quite rewarding. The other day, I spent only an hour on-line searching through human service websites to test this procedure.

On my Microsoft Windows main computer screen, I clicked my Internet Web browser icon. The screen changed to the browser, and the computer dialed the number of my Internet service provider.

My default setting brings me to a kind of catalog/search site called Yahoo.com. Web addresses start with the hypertext transfer protocol (http), which makes Yahoo!'s address look like this: http://www.yahoo.com. On that first screen is a blank space where you can type in the words that you would like to search for. If you are new to the Internet: words and phrases that are in a different color from the regular text and/or are underlined can be clicked on for more information.

At the Yahoo! site, there is an underlined word "options" that can be clicked on for more information on how to make your search more successful.

At the Yahoo! site, I typed +*"Human Services"*+ *Computer.* The results gave me underlined words that would take me to sites maintained by the National Institute of Health (NIH), Computers Systems Laboratory (CSL), National Library of Medicine (NLM), Educational Technology Branch (ETB), and several private businesses selling to the human service market.

Yahoo! also includes underlined clickable choices to take me to competing search engines. The most famous ones, after Yahoo!, are Alta Vista, Webcrawler, HotBot, Lycos, Infoseek, Google, Ask Jeeves, and Image Surfer. In addition, there are links to interesting general purpose places like Yellow Pages, People Search, City

Maps, Get Local, Today's Web events, Weather, and so on.

Instead, I linked to a chat (Usenet) search engine called DejaNews. This is a place where you can eavesdrop, after the fact, on actual typed conversations that have transpired on every imaginable subject. Some are quite colorful, but in this case I was connected to sites addressing my original query.

In the case of our search topic, DejaNews had twenty-one groups of activity that included Usenet sites like k12.ed.health-pre, can.schoolnet.chat., gov.us.fed.congress, misc.jobs.resumes (a particularly interesting place, if you get my drift), ba.jobs.resumes (also interesting, for the same reason), and a Chicago seminar on adapting technology at the site alt.comp.blind-user.

Infoseek had 265 sites, or pages, that contained the phrase "human service"+ computer.

Excite had many locations to choose from, and I chose the following on the basis of their descriptions:

New Technology in the Human Services URL: http://www.fz.hse.nl/causa/swbib/sw_r61.htm Summary: For example, computers facilitate documentation, encourage the utilization of advanced research techniques, and free practitioners from paperwork, so that increased services can be offered. Keywords: computer technology, human services, documentation, research facilitation, evaluation, quality assurance, social work. These pages are part of the Web pages of the New Technology in the Human.

So, I drilled down a little deeper, and here is what I found by clicking at the above-referenced site:

Reference: Barker, N. C. (1986). The Implications of Computer Technology in the Delivery of Human Services. Journal of Sociology and Social Welfare, 13(1), 56–63.

Abstract: Social Service programs are nowadays required to operate efficiently and effectively. In order to ensure that this occurs, service delivery must be documented and evaluated like never before. Nonetheless, at the same time, clients are reporting in ever greater numbers to receive ser-

vices. Computer technology can assist practitioners to deal with this apparent conflict. For example, computers facilitate documentation, encourage the utilization of advanced research techniques, and free practitioners from paperwork, so that increased services can be offered. Accordingly, this technology can be used to improve the delivery of social services (Journal abstract.).

Keywords: computer technology, human services, documentation, research facilitation, evaluation, quality assurance, social work.

HOW DO YOU SPELL SUCCESS?

What do you really need to know about technology to succeed? Not that much, really. You don't have to, for instance, become a computer nerd or a technology guru (unless you want to, of course). Success, for you, can be defined as the ability to maximize your productivity for your clients, for your organization, for your family, and for yourself. You can best maximize your productivity, hence your success, if you learn to do the following:

- Identify what is truly needed from you professionally.
- Determine how best to meet those needs.
- Exploit technology, instead of people, to meet those needs.

CONCLUSION

As with any intellectual endeavor, experience is knowledge's greatest ally. In technology, play is the best means of gaining experience. The best way to learn how to use technology to become better at what you do, therefore, is simply to find a computer and have fun with it. Everything you do, when at play with computers, becomes productive technology training and makes you better at it. Eventually, you will become both proficient and productive. So sit back, fire up the old PC, and browse through the Internet for fun and profit.

REFERENCES

Aronson, S. H. (1977). *Bell's Electric Toy: The Social Impact of the Telephone.* ed. Ithiel de Sola Pool. (pp. 18–33). Cambridge, MA: MIT Press.

SUGGESTED FURTHER READING

Graham, G. (1995). *The 3-D Visual Dictionary of Computing.* Indianapolis: IDG Books.

Grimes, G. A. (1997). *Ten Minute Guide to Netscape for Windows.* Indianapolis: Que Publishing.

Maran, R. (1996). *Computers Simplified.* 3rd ed. Indianapolis: IDG Books.

Maran, R. (1995). *Internet & World Wide Web Simplified.* Indianapolis: IDG Books.

Simpson, A. (1995). *Your First Computer.* Alameda, CA: Sybex Publishing.

Underhill, B. (1997). *Windows 98: One Step at a Time.* Indianapolis: IDG Books.

Reference locations on the World Wide Web for further research and study:

http://yahoo.com
http://www.sau.edu
http://fdncenter.org

http://www.soton.ac.uk
http://infoseek.go.com

CHAPTER 28

TECHNOLOGY AND SOCIALITY IN THE NEW MILLENNIUM:
CURRENT CHALLENGES FOR THE HUMAN SERVICE GENERALIST

EUGENE M. DeROBERTIS AND ROBERT SALDARINI

Human services can be characterized as a broad social movement designed to counterbalance the emphasis on rugged individualism in American culture (Cimmino, 1999, p. 13). Thus, part and parcel of the human service orientation toward helping others is the notion that human service generalists place "a portion of responsibility on society for creating conditions that reduce opportunities for people to be successful by perpetuating social problems" (p. 14). Among the myriad challenges that human service generalists address in their work are problems involving the development of the self within the social context (p. 10). As is well known, Maslow's (1968) hierarchy of needs speaks to the importance of interpersonal relations in self-development with his articulation of needs for love and belongingness, esteem, and self-actualization. Hansell's motivation theory also addresses the need for a co-constitution of the self by noting that humans need intimacy, closeness, belonging, self-identity, and social roles (Schmolling and Burger, 1989). Accordingly, it is in the interest of competent service delivery for human service workers to be aware of burgeoning trends in the interpersonal dimension of our lives that pose new challenges to a healthy social climate and optimal self-development. Such trends can be found in the ever-increasing reliance on technology in American society.

TECHNOLOGY AND PARADOXICAL HUMAN CONNECTEDNESS

As the sun sets on the past century, so fades the concept of an individual "being out." With line and cell telephones, beepers, pagers, voice mail, and the Internet, technology has set up an almost ubiquitous communication network. People from all walks of American life are undergoing the process of becoming unceasingly connected. On the surface, it appears that this network would only enhance the quality of life. In fact, technology constantly allots new opportunities for individuals to manage their day-to-day affairs in a more convenient, even life-sustaining way. For example, technological means for managing work affairs, contacting baby-sitters, and going to school on-line offer great potential to help people with limited means meet their responsibilities and strive toward their aspirations.

Ironically, however, this unprecedented technological connectedness is also manifesting a relational paradox. Literature on the connection between the growing reliance on technology and increasing social alienation has been burgeoning since the mid-twentieth century. Recently, a study done at Carnegie Mellon University reported that individuals who spent just several hours a week on the Internet experienced higher levels of depression and loneliness (Kraut et al., 1998,

p. 1028). Thus, the new millennium beckons the exploration of how current technologies and technological trends set the stage for a pervasive sense of loneliness in today's culture.

TECHNOLOGY AS A CONTRIBUTOR TO ISOLATION AND LONELINESS

As was noted above, the notion that technology has the potential to exacerbate a sense of social alienation is far from contemporary. In 1958, Rollo May wrote:

> ... Human beings ... have lost their world, *lost their experience of community.* Riesman *presents a good deal of sociopsychological data in his study ... to demonstrate that the ... lonely, alienated character type is characteristic ... of people as a whole in our society and that the trends in that direction have been increasing over the past couple of decades. He makes the significant point that these people have only a* technical *communication with their world.... (May, Angel, and Ellenberger, 1958, pp. 56–57)*

Despite the enormous changes that have occurred in America since May wrote these words, societal behavior indicates that his observations continue to ring true in the twenty-first century. One can identify at least two interrelated ways in which the force of technology continues to contribute to a culture-wide feeling of loneliness. First, the deepening devotion to technology and its advancement has alienated individuals from sharing a sense of personal meaning and value in life. As Viktor E. Frankl (1978) once put it, "In the impersonal climate of industrial society ever more people obviously suffer from a sense of loneliness.... People cry for intimacy. And this cry is so urgent that intimacy is sought at any expense, on any level, ironically even on an impersonal level ... " (p. 82). Research in the area of television viewing, for example, attests to Frankl's observations. Studies show that lonely people not only watch more television (Canary and Spitzberg, 1993), but also attempt to use tele-

vision to alleviate their loneliness (Rook and Peplau, 1982; Rubinstein and Shaver, 1982).

Second, the increasing use of technological language has alienated people from their worlds by disposing them to interpret life in objectivistic, impersonal ways. For instance, in 1992 the Internet was most familiar to those who were trained in technology, yet "dot-com" is presently entrenched in conversational communication. *The New York Times Almanac* reports that 200 million people are members of the Internet community, and Information Technology (IT) "techno-babble" has become a mainstay of American language. As the millennium progresses, it will be worth noting the degree to which IT-based language contributes to the alienation and loneliness that May refers to in his continuing discussion of Riesman's famous book, *The Lonely Crowd* (Riesman, Glazer, and Denny, 1950): " ... People have only a *technical* communication with their world.... Their orientation [in Riesman's study], for example, was not 'I liked the play,' but 'The play was well done,' 'The article was well written,' and so forth" (May, 1958, p. 57). With this said, one can evaluate some of the dimensions of what may rightly be called "techno-loneliness" as they have come to manifest themselves.

For a more concrete understanding of the current, almost technophilic state of the American culture, one needs to examine the shift of technological empowerment from organization to individual. Corporations had possession of "the big machine" (i.e., technology) until well into the 1940s. This point has been widely illustrated in films such as Charlie Chaplin's 1936 *Modern Times.* However, as the transistor and microcircuits gave way to cost-effective digitization, technological tools such as computers no longer served solely as corporate number-crunching machines. With the advent of the Internet, the world received a true naked resource, a completely democratized source of information protected by the First Amendment. The new information technology was transformed into a powerful multimedia communication platform and directed toward an almost insatiable consumer market.

This new information infrastructure created communication vehicles that gave connected individuals the ability to "reach out and virtually touch" anyone in the world. Experiencing a heightened sense of empowerment, society at large began embracing these communication systems with exuberance in gadgets ranging from pagers to PCs. To be sure, people in the helping professions now had a more powerful vehicle to access all sorts of information from theoretical and empirical research within the social sciences to information regarding the various social subsystems needed to facilitate human service delivery. However, in tandem with the obvious benefits of efficient, effective information availability in everyday life, American culture has experienced a simultaneous expansion of social isolation.

This phenomenon of technology-induced alienation affects all age groups. In contemporary society, steady advances in communication technology have served to wire children to entertainment. Video entertainment, in a myriad of on-line and off-line forms, is replacing more socially oriented pursuits such as board games and playground activities. Further, video games are enabling parents to acquire personal time and establish a silent environment. Taking this to a broader perspective, one needs to focus on the fact that the video games children are playing often do not promote cooperative, pro-social values. Rather, the object of many of the favored games is to crush, kill, and destroy any and all competitors. Thus, the fact that video gaming is coming on strong as a kind of digitized babysitter raises a renewed concern over the impact of anti-social experiences on observational learning. Studies show that aggressiveness in young children increases with the correlative amount of violence that they view on television (Bandura, Ross, and Ross, 1963; Joy, Kimball, and Zabrack, 1977), and thus it seems reasonable that one

ought to be wary of the alienating potential of such entertainment. It is unsurprising that these concerns are supported by Daniel Goleman's (1995) assertions in the area of emotional intelligence that children's EQs are on a steady decline in America. As he notes, depressive symptomology affects approximately one-third of all teenagers (p. 232).

As the dawn of virtual reality (VR) gaming breaks, the isolation of this new dimension is already evident in its language. Specifically, the human participant is known as "the patron" and his or her virtual self becomes "the puppet." Disconnecting from the game grid is considered "falling into the meat." The virtual experience is a true detachment not only from others but also from one's own body. Should the market demand that VR gaming imitate current video trends, impressionable children will then have the opportunity to practice the worst forms of anti-social behavior in an ever-more-realistic environment sanctified under the word "fun."

Education has seen massive reform as a result of the exploding emergence of technology for instructional purposes. Pre-literate children are given lessons from training software to "touch the screen," whereby there is no need for a teacher. Reliance on the computer in lieu of human contact continues into higher education via distance learning. In the years to come, teachers will need to be aware of the pitfalls associated with replacing interpersonal exploration and discovery with repetitive text-image-driven affirmation of content. In tandem, school administrators cannot view distance education as a financially lucrative means of removing teachers from classrooms. The need for human contact is an important part of learning, and the isolated computer-student paradigm does not allow for the touch and feel of warm expression and full empathetic insight by another individual. In addition to the teacher-absent situation, removing the student from the traditional learning environment may alienate students from their peers as well. Unless the educational setting taps into interactive video classroom instruction, the student is visually isolated from classmates altogether.

Paralleling the world of education, the American workplace has seen revolutionary changes in its organization. Telecommuting is burgeoning as a popular alternative to the day-to-day physical commute to one's place of employment. In past decades business affairs were conducted in suits and dress shoes, but today a wide range of business proceedings can be held in "boxer shorts and bunny slippers." Without doubt, many who work only from their homes have begun a slow degradation away from cultural ritual whereby they no longer physically prepare to interact with others. For some, the isolation from colleagues and the limited social atmosphere of the home office has been manifested in correlative malaise (Katz, 1987).

On a broader scale, managers and clerical support staff throughout the country are spending significantly more time on their jobs, thus making the workday substantially longer than its perceived eight hours. In a recent study by Rosen and Weil (2000), the number of hours employees use technology after the "end of their work day" increased consistently throughout the 1990s. Included in their findings were the following observations:

> For the Managers/Executives, three-quarters are using their computer after work hours, half are using e-mail and the Internet, and other communication technologies. Clearly, technology has extended the workday long after standard work hours. In fact, when asked how much time they spend using technology after work hours, half said less than one hour per day, one-third said 1–2 hours per day, and one-sixth said they were hooked up for three or more hours a day.

Supporting this perspective, an article in *The New York Times* based on an Internet survey indicated that a quarter of all regular Internet users reported that the Internet had increased the time they spent at work (Markoff, 2000). As a result, people are spending less and less time with colleagues, friends, and loved ones.

With the Internet's vast communication capacity, technology continues its movement into social relations by intervening in the personal dimension. On-line and connected, the millennium years offer real-time chat. It would be difficult to dispute that when used to provide a cost-free channel for communication it serves its purpose well. At the same time, it must be acknowledged that it is the spirit in which this technology is appropriated that makes all the difference. Should chatting become a substitute for intimacy (e.g., cybersex), interpersonal encounters are avoided. When chatting acts as a habitual surrogate for human contact, the need to pursue a social life is forfeited. The proliferation and easy access to sex chat rooms and bulletin boards may provide a convenient way for some people to avoid investing time and energy into existing relationships. The demand for this type of service far exceeds any other, as pornographic Web sites are the leading E-businesses among those that are acknowledged as E-commerce.

THERAPEUTIC SERVICES AND TECHNO-LONELINESS

Rather than helping to reverse this trend of increasing alienation, psychology has often contributed to the technology-induced loneliness of American culture. As Knowles (1986) notes, psychologists have generally tended to overlook the fact that human beings exist as "real selves" in dialogue with others (p. 3). Simpatico with the individualistic current within American culture, mainstream psychology has more often chosen to identify human beings with their individual ego functions. People are reduced to organisms whose main task is to adapt to their environments via calculative thought processes and managerial tasks. Other people are thereby interpreted as potential need objects and never true subjectivities, or unique individuals. Thus, psychology has often been a symptom of technologized culture, unable to wrest us from our interpersonal alienation.

A look at the models that have dominated the American psychological milieu since the democratization of information technology will demonstrate the overtly technological current in psychology and psychotherapy. In the 1950s, behaviorism was the dominant force in American psychology. As is widely known, strict behaviorists saw people as biological machinery shaped by environmental contingencies. Consequently, attempts at psychotherapy from the behavioral perspective revolved around instituting processes that would cure individuals of their supposed dysfunctional training, so to speak. Counseling had little to do with anything like baring one's soul or engaging in interpersonal encounter. The job of the psychotherapist was to perform techniques designed to reorganize behavioral response patterns so as to allow one to once again obtain pleasure from one's environment. Human beings were viewed as objects of technical manipulation.

In the 1960s, with the advent of the so-called "cognitive revolution," cognitive psychology began picking up momentum in America and is currently the most prominent trend in mainstream psychology (Robins, Gosling, and Craik, 1999). Rather than employing a radically mechanistic view of human existence, cognitive psychologists began to see humans as complex biological computing systems (Ellis and Hunt, 1989). As Ellis and Hunt put it,

> The cognitive revolution was . . . the simultaneous development in six sciences of new knowledge bearing on mental processes. Computer science had by far the greatest impact on psychology. The information-processing (IP) or "computational" model of thinking has been the guiding metaphor of cognitive psychology ever since the 1960s (p. 515).

Utilizing the IP model as their theoretical foundation, cognitive psychotherapists have traditionally framed their work in terms of concepts such as logical decision-making, ego control, and self-regulation. The focus of psychotherapy is typically rational thinking and managerial functions (e.g., stress management, pain management). In the spirit of Gabriel Marcel's critique of modernity, traditional cognitive psychology views life as a set of problems to be solved by the individual ego, rather than a mystery to be shared with others. Rarely is there an emphasis on probing dialogue or a co-exploration of meaning, value, or purpose. Counsel itself is largely constructed from the language of the lonely.

The field of human services is grounded in a perspective that promotes "a sense of personal gratification in social life" (Cimmino, 1999, p. 13). Thus, the above analysis suggests that a genuine approach to the delivery of human services would be mindful of the potentially alienating characteristics of technology in the lives of clients. Accordingly, conscientious human service intervention can ideally provide an alternative to traditional intervention strategies and contribute to a therapeutic force that discloses technological entrenchment and guides clients away from the alienating potentials therein.

THE IMPACT OF TECHNOLOGICAL DISTANCING ON COMMUNICATIONS AND PROFESSIONAL ETHICS

Related specifically to the increasing use of communication technology in the human service field, an issue of growing concern is the need to use technologically mediated communications in a professional manner. Computer-facilitated communication is fast becoming an integral part of the work of human service agencies. Since human service workers must display competent communication skills in order to operate within various agency roles (Cimmino, 1999, p. 18), an understanding of the impact of current information technology on communications is essential.

E-mail is a form of communication that is primarily linear text processing. Since its inception, this means of communicating has quickly beckoned the creation of personalizing characteristics such as emoticons (i.e., faces created with keyboard characters for the purpose of communicating emotional intent). With comparable haste, the term "flaming" was coined to describe loaded and biased language, insults, and derogatory humor intended to offend the reader. Both the necessity of personalization techniques and the emergence of flaming bear witness to the fact that there is a certain shortcoming inherent in this new communication forum: many of the subtleties of human expression cannot be easily conveyed when talk is mediated by a text-driven processing platform. Perhaps more importantly, this distancing has the potential to generate an over-inflated sense of empowerment through anonymity. In effect, individuals are transformed into "sender" and "recipient."

The anonymity of computer-mediated interactions diminishes the sense of responsibility that is experienced when communication occurs in person. Without the identifying nature of a face-to-face dialogue, informal day-to-day discourse achieves a certain sterility that opens up the possibility for lapses in E-ethics. To quote Rollo May (May, Angel, and Ellenberger, 1958):

> The anonymous mode . . . is the mode of the individual living and acting in anonymous collectivity, such as the dancer in a masked ball or the soldier who kills and is killed by individuals whom he does not know. Certain individuals seek refuge in this mode as a means of escaping or fighting their fellow men; the latter is the case with the authors of anonymous letters . . . (p. 122)

The experience of technologically induced distancing can be taken up as license for a release of accountability. As this sense of pseudo-empowerment increases, individuals may seek to push the boundaries of social propriety. For example, there are documented instances of gross disrespect of authority as demonstrated by e-mailed insults, obscenity, and threats to teachers, employers, and government officials that would not have occurred prior to technologically induced anonymity. Given that the majority of computer-mediated communications are presented as detached from their authors, the human service generalist needs to be mindful of the temptation to stray from the ideals of professionalism in such communications under the cover of facelessness.

FINAL REMARKS

The new millennium is offering ever-expanding opportunities to enhance the quality of life as technology grows at a geometric rate. Current research is being done in areas of biotechnology and information storage that will render obsolete what is currently leading edge. Hewlett Packard and other research laboratories are working on molecular storage, in which information processing will be molecules wide and atoms deep. Already, pharmaceutical companies prepare to program medication. Yet, it should not be ignored that a vicarious byproduct of technology's greatness is its propensity to obstruct fulfillment of the human need for interpersonal contact and personal growth through social engagement.

The Amish community demonstrates a view of technology that contrasts strikingly with mainstream culture; i.e., containment of technology is viewed as necessary for community. Education of Amish children is completely devoid of scientific theory and the applications of contemporary technologies. Their lives center on human interaction, whereby any object that isolates a member from the community becomes irrelevant. Present-day Americans could benefit from acknowledging the wisdom of the Amish social philosophy. Technology in the new millennium creates both bridges and barriers to human contact. Competent human service delivery in the new millennium will require a fundamental grasp of the benefits and drawbacks of technology in the social world.

REFERENCES

Bandura, A., D. Ross, and S. A. Ross (1963). "Vicarious Reinforcement and Imitative Learning." *Journal of Abnormal and Social Psychology, 67,* 601–607.

Canary, D. J., and B. H. Spitzberg (1993). "Loneliness and Media Gratification." *Communication Research, 20,* 800–821.

Cimmino, P. F. (1999). "Basic Concepts and Definitions of Human Services." In H. S. Harris and D. C. Maloney, eds., *Human Services: Contemporary Issues and Trends* (pp. 9–21). Boston: Allyn and Bacon.

Ellis, H., & R. R. Hunt (1989). *Fundamentals of Human Memory and Cognition.* Dubuque, IA: Wm. C. Brown.

Frankl, V. E. (1978). *The Unheard Cry for Meaning.* New York: Washington Square Press.

Goleman, D. (1995). *Emotional Intelligence.* New York: Bantam.

Joy, L. A., M. Kimball, and M. L. Zabrack (1977). *Television Exposure and Children's Aggression Behavior.* Paper presented at the Annual Meeting of the Canadian Psychological Association, Vancouver, BC, Canada.

Katz, A. (1987). "The Management, Control, and Evaluation of a Telecommuting Project: A Case Study." *Information & Management, 13* (2), 179–190.

Knowles, R. T. (1986). *Human Development and Human Possibility.* New York: University Press of America.

Kraut, R., M. Patterson, V. Lundmark, S. Kiesler, T. Mukopadhyay, and W. Scherlis (1998). "Internet Paradox: A Social Technology that Reduces Social Involvement and Psychological Well-Being?" *American Psychologist, 53* (9), 1017–1031.

Markoff, J. (2000, Feb. 16). "Portrait of a Newer, Lonelier Crowd Is Captured in an Internet Survey." *The New York Times.* Retrieved March 23, 2000, from http://www.nytimes.com/library/tech/00/04/biztech/articles/12sur.html

Maslow, A. (1968). *Toward a Psychology of Being.* New York: Van Nostrand Reinhold Company.

May, R., E. Angel, and H. Ellenberger (1958). *Existence.* New York: Basic Books.

Riesman, D., N. Glazer, and R. Denny (1950). *The Lonely Crowd.* Massachusetts: Yale Press.

Robins, R. W., S. D. Gosling, and K. H. Craik (1999). "An Empirical Analysis of Trends in Psychology." *American Psychologist, 54* (2), 117–128.

Rook, K. S., and L. A. Peplau (1982). "Perspectives on Helping the Lonely." In L. A. Peplau and D. Perlman, eds., *Loneliness: A Sourcebook of Current Theory, Research and Therapy.* pp. 351–378. New York: John Wiley and Sons.

Rosen, L., and M. Weil (2000, April 13). "Results of Our 49-Month Study of Business Attitudes Show Clerical/Support Staff, Managers and Executives Using More Technology at Work and at Home and Becoming More Hesitant Toward New Technology". Retrieved May 10, 2000 from Technostress website: http://www.technostress.com/busstudy2000.htm

Rubinstein, D., and P. Shaver (1982). *In Search of Intimacy.* New York: Delacorte Press.

Schmolling, M. Y., and W. R. Burger (1989). *Human Services in Contemporary Society.* Pacific Grove, CA: Brooks/Cole.

HOW SERVICE-LEARNING EXPERIENCES TRANSFORM STUDENTS' LIVES

LINDA MASS

The philosophy of Brookdale Community College includes the following statement: "Effective education promotes awareness of the intricate relationships which exist among people, and between individuals and their environment. . . . Therefore, we urge students to accept their responsibility for improving society." This philosophical tenet is best exemplified in Brookdale's Service-Learning Program, which provides students with the opportunity to apply knowledge gained in the classroom in a community service project while satisfying course requirements. The Service-Learning Program at Brookdale Community College focuses on providing "both meaningful service to the community and meaningful experiences for the student-learner." These goals are reached by "incorporating student volunteerism within an academic framework, while providing many needed services to the community" (Service-Learning Faculty Guide, 1998).

Service-Learning refers to the integration of community service into an organized setting in which the server reflects upon the meaning of the service performed. Combining the service experience with a reflective educational structure generates powerful benefits that go beyond what either the service or the learning can offer separately. More specifically, by combining service and learning, students who perform community service will be able to see the connections between their work and the underlying values and issues behind the social problems being addressed. "Service-Learning programs emphasize the accomplishments of tasks which meet human needs in combination with conscious educational growth" (Kendall, 1990, p. 40).

Service-Learning falls along the same continuum as Experiential Learning, although there are some basic differences between Experiential Learning and Service-Learning. One of the primary differences is that Experiential Learning focuses primarily on the benefits to students. The focus in Service-Learning is twofold, acknowledging the reciprocal benefits to both the community and the student-participant, with the primary focus on the community.

Service-Learning is an appropriate pedagogy for experiences that have elements of performance skills and/or social awareness components that are best developed through participation. There are many different definitions and styles of Service-Learning, but there are common threads and core elements that all programs must have to be considered "good practice."

An effective Service-Learning program:

— Engages people in responsible and challenging actions for the common good;
— Provides structured opportunities for people to reflect critically;
— Articulates clear service and learning goals for everyone involved;
— Includes training, supervision, monitoring, recognition and support.

The Service-Learning Program at Brookdale Community College began its twelfth year of operation in Fall 2002. At its inception in 1991, the program had twenty-two student participants from two courses in two disciplines, Psychology (Human Services) and Sociology. Between 1991 and 2002 the Service-Learning Program at Brookdale Community College has engaged more than 5,000 students in providing more than 150,000 hours of volunteer community service activities with over 250 nonprofit community organizations (including public schools) located in and around Monmouth County, New Jersey. These students come from over 40 courses, across disciplines which include nursing, psychology, English, political science, criminal justice, communication, culinary arts, humanities, environmental studies, oceanography, sociology, business, and technology.

Human service students participate in greater numbers than students from other disciplines and programs. Students report that their service-learning experiences have provided them with a greater understanding of their community, the role of human service workers, and the dynamics of community agencies and social service agencies, as well as a realization that they can play an active role in addressing social issues. Students find that their experiences provide a clearer picture of their chosen career paths. Many students report that service-learning has confirmed their career choice, while others have changed their majors as a result of the life-changing effect of their service experience.

What kinds of work do Brookdale students do?

- They tutor "at-risk" youth.
- They assist activity directors at nursing homes.
- They coach youth involved in community recreation programs.
- They test the water in local lakes and streams for contamination, and they recruit people for and coordinate beach sweeps along our shores.
- They are counseling assistants to the Division for Youth and Family Services (DYFS), which operates group homes for girls. They are mentors to young men in detention centers.
- They are teacher's aides in our public schools and after-school programs.
- They prepare lunches in local soup kitchens, coordinate food collection for local pantries, and deliver meals to homebound individuals.
- They provide companionship to the frail elderly in adult day care facilities.
- They assist teachers in all of our Head Start Centers.

Service-Learning is not a "new" concept. During the late 1960s and early 1970s students were following the call to "get involved" in their communities. Many young people and adults worked in their communities to address social problems. But the movement didn't last. Jane C. Kendall identifies three primary lessons from the community service movement of the 1960s and 1970s that we can build on today:

- Programs must be integrated into the central mission and goals of the schools and agencies where they are based;
- Emphasis is to be placed on the relationship between the server and "those served" as a reciprocal exchange between equals;
- Service alone does not ensure that either significant learning or effective service will occur.

Today, hundreds of colleges and universities have incorporated Service-Learning programs into their college missions and institutional fabric. National associations that provide training and support to faculty and Service-Learning practitioners have grown. Federal funding from the National Corporation for Community and National Service continues to support the development and expansion of Service-Learning programs throughout the country. Brookdale Community College is proud of its commitment to its Service-Learning Program. Its growth and development testifies to this commitment. We continue to serve as a national and regional model program and a resource to colleges and universities in New Jersey and throughout the United States.

REFERENCES

Kendall, J. C., and Associates (1990). *Combining Service and Learning: A Resource Book for Community and Public Service.* Raleigh, NC: National Society for Internships and Experiential Education.

Additional Facts about Brookdale's Service-Learning Program

- The impact of Brookdale's Service-Learning Program has reached far beyond the Lincroft campus. The Middle States Evaluators cited it in 1989 as having "potential as a national model due to its creativity, success, and relatively low cost."

- In 1990 our program was selected as one of seven National Model Community Service Programs. Other institutions selected included Stanford, the University of Vermont, and the University of Michigan.

- Our program model has been demonstrated at local, state, national, and international conferences over the past ten years. In addition, we have provided numerous hours of technical assistance to colleges in New Jersey, including Monmouth University, Stockton College, and Raritan Valley Community College, and assisted in the establishment of Service-Learning programs at colleges across the United States.

- During the past three years we have been involved in the training of more than eighty K–12 teachers on "Service-Learning: Community As Classroom."

- We were one of the four founding colleges and universities of the New Jersey Higher Education Service-Learning Consortium. As a consortium, we received funding for capacity building from the National Commission for Community Service from 1993 to 1997. The Consortium currently has twelve member institutions.

CHAPTER 29

RESEARCH MODELS IN HUMAN SERVICES

ROD UNDERWOOD AND MICHAEL LEE

WHAT IS RESEARCH?

Research yields a particular form or type of information. Its value lies in the fact that the information is collected rigorously in a systematic way, and thus should be free from bias; when it is applied, its limitations are known. Another way of conceptualizing research is to think of it as a type of investigation or as a process leading to a greater understanding of the world. There are many different ways to gather information. The scientific method is one such procedure. Because it is so widespread, we commonly think that the scientific method is the only way to gain new knowledge. However, this is not the case. New knowledge can come from a variety of other processes, such as a religious or spiritual experience. Such an experience can give new insights and different understandings of human problems. However, an important limitation to knowledge acquired by religious means is that it is difficult to verify. Another related procedure is philosophical analysis, which examines important issues and dilemmas in our lives. Although such analysis might sometimes use information that comes from research, it does not necessarily set out to investigate using the scientific method.

If research is information gained using a particular method and as a consequence has distinctive characteristics, what are these characteristics? Research is objective; consequently, it is independent of the observer. Two or more people observing the same situation, using the same procedures, should arrive at the same conclusions. Research is also systematic, and the information must be collected according to a set of standards. These standards allow the user of information to determine how the results of the research can be interpreted and applied. Finally, research data must be seen as public and verifiable.

GOALS OF RESEARCH

Research attempts to do two things. First, it seeks to describe a phenomenon. For example, it is believed that as people reach old age their powers of reasoning decline. This belief gets support from observations we have all made at some time or other of an elderly person being mentally confused or having difficulty understanding. However, when this belief is investigated using research techniques, we find this common perception is not justified. Some elderly people have powers of reasoning as good as they have been at any time of their lives. Some aspects of memory become more acute for elderly people; some elderly seem to lose confidence in their ability to reason. If confidence is not lost, then reasoning continues to be maintained (Salthouse, 1982).

A second thing that research attempts to do is explain cause-and-effect relationships. We commonly observe in everyday life an association of events such that a result is preceded by a particular prior event. When we ask, "What happened?"

we assume that the outcome was caused by the prior event. In the human services we can observe an increase in the number of people turning to welfare agencies for financial assistance, clothing, or food. We know from government statistics that unemployment is increasing, and so we connect the two observations and deduce that the increase in unemployment has caused more people to seek relief. If you think about this problem, you can see that there might be alternative explanations as the cause. It is by using research methods that we can see which of the alternatives is the correct one.

So what is research? It is a method of collecting information, commonly referred to as *data,* that allows us to both describe and then explain the information we have gathered. It is systematic and, because it must follow certain procedures, is able to be replicated and verified or rejected by others using the same procedures.

Every day we have experiences that influence our perception of the world. The way we view our environment is colored by a variety of circumstances, including our culture, our state of mind, and even our capacity to use language. Notwithstanding these factors, this information is still important to us, and we carry it as part of our storehouse of knowledge. Many people might carry the same or similar perceptions of information. For example, consider how widespread are certain stereotypes. Nevertheless, the information has not been gained by scientific means, and until it is "tested" it might be biased and flawed. However, such observations are often the starting points for research, but until they are "proven" they remain personal viewpoints and are described as "anecdotal."

WHY DO RESEARCH?

It is not always easy to convince the human service student of the necessity for research. Naturally enough, many human service professionals believe their time is best spent by providing services to those people in need rather than answering another questionnaire from a federal agency or being interviewed by another researcher. Clearly, then, there have to be good reasons for diverting human service workers from their primary goal.

Perhaps one of the most compelling reasons for human service workers to engage in research is the ever-present threat of funding cutbacks. Increasingly, funding authorities—both governmental and nongovernmental—expect human service agencies to be more accountable for the funds they receive. There are several aspects of accountability. For example, agencies may need to demonstrate to the funding authority that every dollar has been spent within the original guidelines given to the agency. Another aspect of accountability is for the agency to show that an appropriate number of clients are receiving the services at a predetermined level of quality. This type of accountability is referred to as *program evaluation.*

Program evaluation requires an agency to demonstrate the effectiveness of a particular program or to show the extent to which the program is achieving its stated goals. To be able to do this, the program director needs to be familiar with the different research designs used in the social sciences and their limitations when applied to program evaluation. Any agency that makes claims about the effectiveness of its program that cannot be substantiated is likely to be critically reviewed by the funding authority.

At the other end of the continuum, agencies are often required to undertake a needs analysis within their communities to determine the extent to which a particular service may be required. As with evaluation studies, needs analysis surveys are dependent on research design logic. If, for example, you want to know how many people over the age of 50 are suffering from diabetes in your county, then you may have to draw on the sampling procedures used in social science research.

If you need to identify social trends such as the increased number of women in the work force, the increasing number of high school dropouts, or the growing number of people with literacy problems, then you need a sound understanding of the principles of research design. Planning of future human services is essentially based on statistical analyses of data gathered according to the principles of research methodology. Of course, any human service planning is always guided by the values of society.

It is possible for research to have a significant impact on the development of human service policies. Often, it is the researcher who brings to the attention of the policy maker the existence of particular problems in the community. For example, in a recent study of emergency accommodation services it was found that more than 70 percent of workers reported having to deal frequently with young people suffering from mental illness (Underwood, Lee, and Jackson, 1991). Further, the investigation revealed that the accommodation workers had received very little training in coping with behaviorally disturbed adolescents. The workers stated that they experienced significant difficulties in eliciting assistance from appropriate agencies. The study clearly showed that the policies applicable to emergency accommodation services required an urgent review.

Apart from the very pragmatic reasons for becoming a skilled researcher, the human service worker is inherently interested in understanding the dynamics of the community in which he or she operates. Unfortunately, social theory has not yet developed to the stage where it can provide an in-depth analysis of any community. For example, you may believe that the increased crime rate has been the outcome of increased unemployment. On the other hand, the rate of domestic violence may be directly related to increased violence being shown on television. These are the sorts of questions that influence human service workers and the programs they offer. Accurate conclusions must be based on well-conducted, sophisticated social research.

RESEARCH STRATEGIES

There is no one research strategy that is best for investigating all issues in the human services. The variety and diversity of research questions reflect several features of this area. Different disciplines contribute to human services. Psychology, sociology, political science, and economics are all important contributors to research method, but they have different techniques as well as differing types of information regarded as important.

Some methods of research have a long history. When Francis Bacon first wrote on the scientific method some four hundred years ago, he emphasized "cause and effect." This put great importance on experimental procedures. In very recent times, feminist writers have questioned the mainstream methods and called for fresh approaches to research technique and writing (Squire, 1989). These methods would recognize the importance of individual perceptions, feelings, and judgments as basic research data.

The Experimental Approach

The experimental paradigm is the most powerful means of determining whether a causal relationship exists between a particular intervention strategy or treatment and the outcomes. In its most rigorous form, the experimental paradigm is characterized by the random allocation of participants to experimental and control groups. Provided that those other features of experimental investigation such as validity and reliability of the measurements are sustained, the researcher is in the position of drawing sound conclusions regarding the relationship between the independent and dependent variables. The investigator is also able to determine the magnitude of the treatment effects on the outcomes.

According to Elliot (1980), the experimental approach to social research involves the following sequence:

1. The causal model or theoretical paradigm, which identifies a set of variables (attributes, relationships, or circumstances) connected by some logical process to social behavior.
2. The identification of a set of program activities or interventions that are designed to manipulate these causal variables.
3. The implementation of the program with these manipulations operationalized as program objectives.
4. Information feedback during operation to determine if the program activities are, in fact, occurring and the objectives are being met.
5. Feedback to determine if the realization of these program objectives is having the theoretically expected effect on the participants.
6. The modification of the theoretical paradigm and/or the program activities and objectives as suggested by the analysis, in order to increase the program's effectiveness (p. 509).

The Sherman and Berk (1984) study of the efficacy of different treatment strategies of police management of domestic violence incidents exemplifies the application of the experimental approach. The investigators examined the likelihood of repeat offenses occurring as a function of arrest or nonarrest interventions by the police. In a subsequent review of their study, Berk and Sherman (1985) conclude that

> we are increasingly convinced that until there is a compelling body of social science theory with which to properly specify causal models, true experimental or strong quasi-experimental designs are essential for sound impact assessments (p. 46).

The utility of the experimental approach depends on the degree to which the results of a study can be generalized to other situations. The decision maker needs to determine whether the outcomes of a particular study carried out in another place at another time, with different participants, are likely to be replicated if he or she implements a similar program. A number of factors militate against generalizing the results in many studies. There may be problems in defining the population from which the sample has been drawn for the study. This is particularly the case when the population is defined in terms of psychological or sociological characteristics such as psychopathy or delinquency. The methods used to select the participants for the study will influence the degree to which the findings can be generalized. Participants can be randomly selected from a population, they may be volunteers for the study, or they may be induced to participate in a program. Thus, the selection method used may determine the way in which the characteristics of the sample generalize to other groups. The conceptualization and measurement of variables, such as drug dependency or recidivism, suffer from a lack of universal agreement. Hence, the human service administrator who is implementing programs on the basis of other studies should be cautious and recognize the limitations of those studies.

Social research studies undertaken in the 1960s and 1970s typically sought to employ the experimental approach. Increasingly, this mode of research has been criticized by practitioners. Cook and Shadish (1986, p. 226) argue that "early experience suggested that they [that is, randomized experiments] were fundamentally flawed as models." The experimental approach came under attack from researchers for the following reasons:

1. It is not applicable to those situations in which possible causal factors cannot be manipulated, such as economic circumstances. Such situations tend to be the norm in the human services.
2. The random allocation of participants in a study to different treatment groups or to a control group is fraught with difficulties. Not the least of these difficulties are the ethical and moral concerns raised in those studies where efficacious treatment is withheld from participants in the interests of science. In the United States, laws have been passed that specifically prohibit the use of randomized experimentation in certain circumstances (Empey, 1980).
3. A critical assumption of the experimental paradigm is the equivalence of the treatment and nontreat-

ment groups. However, the very fact that the treatment conditions are differentially effective will significantly influence the rate of attrition. For example, the rate of attendance of alcoholics assigned to different therapeutic milieus will vary, among other reasons, according to the nature of the treatment. Hence the rigor of the paradigm is seriously weakened. The difficulties associated with establishing comparable treatment groups are well described by Davidson, Koch, Lewis, and Wresinski (1981) in their study of youth service programs in the United States.

4. Members of a cohort, particularly in an institutional environment, who are assigned to different treatment conditions may lack commitment to the program if they sense they are being put in the role of "guinea pigs." This may lead to deliberate sabotage of the program or to the demoralization of the participants (Cook and Campbell, 1979).

5. The experimental paradigm may well identify the impact of a particular program, but the processes associated with achieving the effect are not always revealed. There is a tendency to assume the "black box" situation exists: that is, that the conditions under which the program is conducted remain constant and relatively impervious to influences of the total system. Such an assumption is clearly fallacious.

Quasi-Experimental Research Models

A great deal of social research does not meet all the criteria necessary to be called a "true experimental design." These studies often involve the investigation of important matters in human services. Consider the question, "Are antismoking health campaigns effective in reducing the number of people who smoke?" It would be extremely difficult to investigate this question using a true experimental design where it would be necessary to randomly assign smokers to an experimental group and a control group. That is, the experimental group would be exposed to the information presented in the public health campaign, such as television advertisements. The control group of smokers would not receive the information. Immediately, we are confronted with an ethical dilemma. Do researchers have the right to withhold from people information that may be

of potential benefit to them, even though we are attempting to establish the efficacy of such health campaigns? It may be that such campaigns have no effect on reducing the prevalence of smokers in the community and that the money could be spent on much more effective approaches to the problem.

Campbell and Stanley (1963) use the term "quasi-experimental" to describe the broad category of research designs which, while attempting to be rigorous, are employed to seek answers to questions that cannot be addressed using an experimental design. The limitation of the quasi-experimental research design is that it does not permit the investigator to ascribe a causal relationship between the independent and dependent variables of a study. For example, a social scientist may be interested to learn whether people who attend church are less likely to get divorced than those who do not attend church. Obviously this is a question that cannot be investigated using an experimental design. We cannot ask some married couples to attend church and other couples not to attend so that we can answer the question. However, we may gather information about married couples who do or do not attend church. We may find that one in five married couples who attend church eventually get divorced, compared with one in three couples who do not attend. We may be tempted to conclude that the divorce rate, that is, the dependent variable, is determined by church attendance, that is, the independent variable. However, it may turn out that some factor other than church attendance accounts for the different rates of divorce. For example, it may be the case that married couples who attend church regularly have a higher level of income than nonattendees. Perhaps economic security leads to marital stability.

Correlation Studies   As human service professionals, we are continually looking for relationships between different variables. Do daughters of alcoholic parents tend to select partners predisposed toward alcoholism? Is crime rate related to the level of unemployment in a community? Are males who have vasectomies more likely to get cancer of the prostate in later years? We are looking to see if there is a correlation between these variables.

Knowing that two variables are correlated does not permit us to assume that a causal relationship exists, as discussed in the preceding section. Let us examine another example. We have known for many years that young people who play sports regularly are less likely to engage in delinquent behavior than their nonsporting counterparts. In fact, national youth policies of a number of countries have been based on this premise. So what have social scientists learned about the relationship between sports and delinquency? In their recent review of the literature on this issue, Mason and Wilson (1988) uncovered the following facts:

1. Those boys who participate in sporting activities are delinquent in lesser numbers than those who do not participate in sports.

2. Although sporting male youths commit less crime than their nonsporting counterparts, they are also involved to an even lesser degree in the more serious offenses.

3. Boys participating in major sports (e.g., football and baseball) tend to be more delinquent than those engaged in minor sports (e.g., badminton and volleyball).

4. Some sports of an aggressive nature may even have adverse effects on participants, and a highly aggressive sport, such as ice hockey, has been seen to have a greater number of male participants who are involved in delinquent acts than comparable nonathletes.

Unfortunately, no amount of research has been able to demonstrate a causal link between playing sports and not indulging in antisocial behavior. The fundamental question remains unanswered. That is, are young people well behaved because they play sports, or are well-behaved young people more likely to play sports? Only if the former statement is true does it make sense for governments to invest millions of dollars in recreational programs for the nation's youth.

Survey studies will often yield correlational information. We know that a relationship exists between years of education and level of income, between regular exercise and the probability of a heart attack, and between the age of a mother and the likelihood of giving birth to a child with Down syndrome. Although we may not be able to say that a causal relationship exists between these variables, nevertheless knowledge of the correlation is valuable for two reasons. First, the identification of a correlation between variables provides researchers with clues as to where they should direct their resources in seeking to understand the world in which we live. Second, the fact that variables are correlated permits us to make certain predictions. For example, we can predict that a high achiever in high school is likely to succeed at a university or that people who are abused as children may become abusing parents. Again, this type of information assists us in the allocation of resources for intervention programs.

Time-Series Design   The quasi-experimental model that deserves greater attention in social science research is the time-series design. Where it is not possible to implement an experimental design to determine a cause-and-effect relationship between two variables, the time-series design may be the best alternative. For example, the time-series design might be used to determine the impact of legislation requiring people in automobiles to wear seat belts. The important feature of the time-series design is that it requires more than one pre- and postintervention measurement. Essentially, the researcher is looking at trends over a period of time and changes in the direction of the trends that can be attributed to a particular intervention. In the seat belt example, the researcher will be interested in the number of automobile fatalities occurring at least three years prior and subsequent to the introduction of the legislation. By taking a series of measurements over a period of time, the effects of random fluctuations are ameliorated.

The time-series design is an important option for program evaluation. It is particularly applicable where the program affects everyone and where, therefore, a proper control group cannot be constituted. Campbell (1979) believes that if comparison group data are available, the time-series approach ranks as the strongest of all quasi-experimental designs.

Janus (1982) used the time-series design to evaluate the impact of organizational changes in federal correctional institutions. Other applications of the time-series design include a study of the effect of removing restrictions on the sale of pornography on the incidence of sex crimes in Denmark (Kutchinsky, 1973), measuring the impact of restrictive abortion laws on birth rates in Romania (David and Wright, 1971), and assessing the effects of the introduction of breath analyzer testing in the United Kingdom on traffic casualties (Ross, 1973). McCleary and Riggs (1982) used time-series analysis to assess the impact of the 1975 Australian Family Law Act on divorce rates. The time-series analysis can be used to strengthen a traditional study or to evaluate human service programs in which it has not been possible to create a control or comparison group. In the latter case, the experimental group can serve as its own control under certain conditions. According to Grizzle and Witte (1980),

> Time-series analysis produces strongest evaluations when good, consistent time series data are available, program implementation is relatively abrupt, and the nature of program effects are relatively well understood (p. 290).

The greatest threat to the validity of time series is the possibility of "historical factors influencing the outcome" (Cook, Cook, and Mark, 1977). In the case of the McCleary and Riggs (1982) study, for example, the investigators would need to establish that the increased rate of divorce that occurred after the introduction of the Family Law Act was not influenced by events such as economic recession or the impact of the Vietnam War on marital stability.

Single-Subject Design   In many human service settings the researcher is interested in the effect of an intervention strategy on the behavior of an individual. For example, an aged person living alone at home may be encouraged to prepare a daily meal by being positively reinforced for doing so by the home care worker. Or, the disruptive behavior of a school-aged child may be reduced by using a time-out strategy. In these cases it is not possible for the researcher to establish experimental and control groups to determine the efficacy of the proposed intervention strategy. Indeed, in some situations the withholding of potentially useful treatment or intervention strategy—which applies to those people who form the control group in any formal experimental study—may be unethical behavior.

In the single-subject design, there are usually at least three phases. In the first phase, the researcher will observe the number of times the target behavior occurs prior to the introduction of the intervention strategy. This process is called establishing the baseline rate of behavior. Thus, the home care worker may observe that the aged person prepares a meal on only three days a week over a period of three weeks. The second phase of the single-subject design refers to the period when the treatment or intervention strategy is introduced. For example, the home care worker might provide positive verbal reinforcement whenever the aged person prepares a meal. If the reinforcement strategy is successful, then the worker may observe that the aged person is preparing up to five daily meals per week over a period of three weeks. The third phase is a return to the baseline conditions for a short period of time. That is, the worker may withhold positive reinforcement for meal preparation for a period of one to two weeks. If the rate of meal preparation declines, then it is reasonable to infer that the rate is influenced by the intervention strategy. Reintroducing the reinforcement schedule, which ideally will provide confirming evidence, constitutes the fourth phase of the design. The sequence of baseline-treatment-baseline-treatment is normally referred to as an A-B-A-B design.

The above description of the A-B-A-B design is a very elementary type of single-subject study. The procedures for this type of research can become quite complex. However, regardless of the complexity of the study, the single-subject design is always limited by the extent to which the results of a study can be generalized to a particular population. No human service researcher would recommend, on the basis of a single study, that the dietary problems of aged persons can be solved by having home care workers provide positive reinforcement at appropriate times. If the study is replicated on several occasions then, of course, increasing confidence can be placed in the strategy.

Field Research

For the purposes of the present discussion, the term *field research* will be used to refer to that research that is conducted in a naturalistic setting, which must account for most of the human service research. The term *ethnographic research,* which you will come across from time to time, can be taken as synonymous with *field research.*

In essence, the field research approach requires the researcher to gather information by observation and interview about naturally occurring social phenomena in a predetermined environment. The eminent anthropologist Bronislaw Malinowski is recognized as having developed the research strategy with his study of the Trobriand Islanders in the early part of the twentieth century (Holy, 1984). Since that time the approach has been used extensively by sociologists to study communities (Kornblum, 1974), religious groups (Festinger, Reicken, and Schacter, 1956), and occupational groups (Miller, 1986). Educational researchers have undertaken field research studies in the classroom (Schultz and Florio, 1979).

Clearly, the field research approach can make a significant contribution toward our understanding the needs of the community. Human service researchers have used field research strategies to study mental illness in homeless people (Herrman et al., 1988), people in asylums (Goffman, 1961), and people in poverty (Lewis, 1966). By using this approach, researchers are able to provide insights into the human condition not normally accessible to other research strategies.

The field research approach requires the researcher to collect information across a number of variables over an extended period of time. For example, if the researcher is conducting a study of a community facility for aged persons, then he or she would be interested to learn about such matters as the perceived quality of care provided by the staff, the degree of independence accorded to the aged persons, and the opportunities for leisure and recreational activities, to name but a few variables. To gather sufficient data, the investigator is committed to conducting formal and informal interviews with the aged residents as well as recording systematic observations about activities occurring in the facilities that are relevant to the study.

In most field studies the researcher gathers information by becoming a participant-observer. That is, the researcher seeks to become a member of the community being studied. Researchers have carried out the role of participant-observer to varying degrees. In some cases, the community has been completely unaware of the fact that the researcher is anybody other than a bona fide member of the group (Pryce, 1979). Researchers who take on the role of the complete participant believe that by doing so they are able to come much closer to the perspective of the community on those issues pertinent to the study. Clearly, there are serious ethical problems associated with this approach. By becoming a complete participant, the researcher engages in an act of deception. For this reason most ethnographic researchers will declare the purpose of their presence in a community. It has been found that adopting a strategy of openness does not adversely affect the outcome of the study (Coffield, Robinson, and Sarsby, 1981).

There are a number of methodological issues to be considered by the researcher when conducting field research. It is essential that the researcher have a clear understanding of the purpose of the study. This approach involves more than a person recording vast amounts of information about a group of people in the hope of being able to yield interesting insights about their behavior. The competent researcher will have at least tentative hypotheses to be tested by the study. Hence, the variables to be observed will be clearly defined. For example, in a study of the quality of life experienced by deinstitutionalized mental patients, there are a number of variables requiring careful definition for the purposes of observation. In making these observations, the researcher will have established a predetermined method of recording the data to be sure that samples of the target behaviors are representative of the total occurrence of those behaviors. The researcher will also need to be able to demonstrate that steps have been taken to reduce possible bias in the observations. In a review of ethnographic research, Gay (1990, p. 212) cautions us that "as more and more people have gotten into the ethnography act, some with little or no related training, there has been an increase in the number of poorly conducted, allegedly ethnographic studies." The same observation applies to field research.

The Case Study

In the human services, the case study may be used as a means of conducting an in-depth investigation of one or more individuals, an institution, or an exemplar community project. To ascertain the effectiveness of a drug rehabilitation program, for example, the researcher may conduct a case study of several participants. As well as undertaking to conduct extended in-depth interviews with each of the selected participants, the researcher may also seek information from family members, friends, workmates, and others. By this means of building a comprehensive picture, the investigator is seeking to understand how the processes of the rehabilitation program affect the individual.

Is there a difference between field research studies and case studies? Yes. The case study will tend to focus on only one individual or a very limited number of individuals, whereas a field study will include data obtained from a sufficient number of individuals to allow the researcher to talk in terms of the behavior of a group of people. In the study of a human service agency, the field research approach will be focused on the individual clients, whereas the case study not only will deal with a number of individuals but also will have a much broader frame of reference, including, for example, a cost analysis.

Case studies have been carried out on institutions for a variety of purposes. A recent study by Cocks (1989) has documented the process of an institution for mentally retarded persons moving its clients into community-based residential units in accordance with current policies of deinstitutionalization. The primary purpose of the study was to identify those issues of concern to management, staff, and clients as they progressively moved into the residential units. The outcomes of the study showed where management needed to allocate its resources for maximum effectiveness, the training needs of staff, and those events likely to cause distress to the clients.

Often the case study approach is used in state- or federally funded programs. By undertaking an in-depth analysis of, for example, a youth employment project, the researchers are able to gain insights into those factors likely to contribute to the success or failure of the program. Such an analysis may reveal which youth should be targeted by the program (e.g., long-term unemployed, high school dropouts, or homeless youth), and the types of training programs that are most successful (e.g., relatively unskilled activities such as farm laboring, courses in automotive mechanics, computer programming, and so on).

The primary purpose of a case study is to identify the range of variables and the relationships among the variables that account for the project outcomes. The experimental design is best used to determine the impact of an intervention strategy. For example, by using the experimental approach one may be able to show that the crime rate in a particular community has dropped by 20 percent since the introduction of Neighborhood Watch. However, it is by using the case study that we are able to understand why the crime rate has diminished. It may be simply that people are reporting suspicious incidents more frequently to the police, who in turn are making more arrests. Hence, the crime rate has dropped because all the burglars are behind bars. On the other hand, it may turn out that the police have made no more arrests than is normally the case. However, the investigator learns that there has been a concomitant increase in crime rate in the adjacent community that has yet to introduce the Neighborhood Watch scheme. That is, the burglars are just as busy as ever—they have merely shifted to new ground.

A major problem with case studies is possible observer bias. That is, the observer sees what he or she wants to see. For example, the husband who has been attending marriage counseling sessions for an extended period of time now appears to be much more content in his relationship. It may be a case of the husband learning to behave in a socially acceptable manner in the public eye, while at night he is busy in the garage sharpening his chain saw. To reduce the possibility of observer bias, it is always desirable to have more than one person collecting information in a case study.

The case study approach is limited by the fact that it is not possible to generalize the findings. That is, the fact that one individual has been successfully weaned off heroin by participating in a particular methadone program does not mean that the program is going to be universally successful. The insights gained by the investigator in one case may not apply to any other case, for a variety of reasons. Case studies can, however, suggest hypotheses that can be tested using another method of research.

Participatory Research

The research endeavors of social scientists in the 1960s and 1970s were dominated by the application of the experimental paradigm. However, there was a growing awareness, particularly in the field of community development, that social scientists are not the repository of all wisdom. Those issues deemed to have a high priority by social researchers were not always accorded the same status by members of the community. The solutions proposed by the "experts" were not always put forward with a full understanding of the social dynamics of the community. As a consequence, the outcomes of community development programs were sometimes less than satisfactory. At the same time, community development personnel recognized that any program had a far greater chance of success if the participants developed a sense of ownership through involvement in its planning and implementation. Leviton and Hughes (1981) cite a substantial number of studies that demonstrate the importance of stakeholder involvement in social research.

Deutscher (1976) foreshadowed the application of the participatory paradigm to research by advocating the concept of "negotiating a scenario." He argued that is was possible to identify realistic program goals through a process of negotiation that actively involved all stakeholders.

According to the International Council for Adult Education (1982), the participatory paradigm is characterized by three processes, which will be discussed below.

1. Collective investigation of problems and issues with the active participation of the constituency in the entire process.

The participatory approach to community development grew out of a reaction to problems caused by bureaucratic domination of the social agenda. For example, it was found that the imposition of ideas and perceived needs from "outside" researchers can lead to a diminution of the status of community leaders that in turn is likely to militate against the success of the program.

The participatory approach should be distinguished from field research. In field research, or observational research, the investigator is essentially recording observations according to some predetermined criteria and seeking to explain the collected data in terms of relevant theories. In participatory research the agenda is determined by the participants, with the investigator taking more of an advisory role in the process.

2. Collective analysis, in which the constituency develops a better understanding not only of the problem at hand but also of the underlying structural causes (socioeconomic, political, cultural) of the problem.

The researcher working in communities defined by such characteristics as ethnic composition or geographical isolation becomes as much a facilitator as an investigator. Healy (1985) provides some useful insights into the methodological difficulties arising from attempting to gather data from a socially powerless constituency such as women who are the victims of domestic violence. These difficulties not only include the very real problems of locating the women after they have left the refuge and ensuring respondent confidentiality but also involve the extremely negative attitudes that some women have developed toward society, including those endeavoring to provide support.

3. Collective action by the constituency is aimed at long-term as well as short-term solutions to identified problems.

It has been suggested that because the participants have a commitment to the well-being of their community and are not constrained by the whims of voters, as are politicians, they will forgo the "quick fix" in preference to the achievement of more substantive goals.

In addition, the process of participatory research does not concern itself with the issue of generalizing findings to other programs or projects (Cook and Shadish, 1986). Rather, the emphasis of this approach is to account for the success or failures of a program within a particular community setting.

The participatory approach has had only limited application in human service areas such as health, education, and the criminal justice system. However, the model is seen to have particular relevance to areas such as crime prevention and services to victims of crime. According to Maguire (1986), for example, there are more than 300 voluntary organizations in the United Kingdom that provide support services to victims. The creation of these organizations has been a community response to a perceived shortcoming of statutory authorities in meeting the needs of victims. Programs such as Neighborhood Watch and the Safe Houses project clearly depend on active community support for continued success. Healy (1985) advocates using the participatory model to evaluate women's shelters:

> . . . the women's movement, and the shelter movement generally, have always argued that the women users should be able to participate in running their own services, for example, be on the management committees of women's shelters. Therefore the push for more consumer planning and evaluation should strike a responsive chord (p. 231).

The participatory approach puts the researcher in a very different role. The issues of concern are determined by the participants in any program. Questions such as whether the program had an effect on the participants, to what extent the program achieved the initial objectives, or how the program can be improved are addressed from the point of view of the constituents. If the program has been implemented to the full extent—that is, the goals have been set by the participants and the process has been guided by the participants—then the researcher takes on the role of an educator. The researcher shares with the participants his or her knowledge regarding social research. Essentially, the research is undertaken by the participants.

The participatory model is structured on the assumption that it will be necessary to collect different information to serve the needs of different audiences including community members, funding authorities, other researchers, and the general public. An inherent component of the research process is the imparting of knowledge and skills to the participants to enable them to take ultimate responsibility for the program. At the outset of the process, consideration is given to the clarification of goals, identification of the data required to measure progress toward those goals, the decision-making processes, and utilitarian skills such as record-keeping and budgeting.

The initial stage of the research process is characterized by actively soliciting feedback from members of the community, reviewing the relationship between the funding authorities and the program, as well as considering modifications. In addition to assessing the progress made toward achieving the objectives of the program during the summative stage of the process, attention is also given to the lessons learned by the participants and identifying future directions.

Cook and Shadish (1986) make the point that the participatory paradigm is not without its critics:

> It is argued that social problem solving is dependent upon a stakeholder seeking a solution to a given problem under this approach. Thus, there are concerns that issues of significance may not be addressed. Also, the trade-offs between the accuracy, timeliness, and comprehensiveness of results are not yet well known, but adherents of the stakeholders service approach run the risk of providing timely information that is wrong in its claims or is misleading because of its incompleteness (p. 288).

Other problems associated with the participatory model of research are highlighted by Brown and Ringma (1989). They make the point that the role of the participant may be seen as that of a commentator, a representative, a lobbyist, a partner, or a controller of services. The contribution that participants make toward program research will depend largely on their role in any program. In addition, Brown and Ringma claim that there is evidence to indicate that participants "have difficulty in finding a language with which to talk about and to evaluate services" (p. 37).

SECONDARY DATA ANALYSIS

So far, our discussion of different research paradigms has been based on the premise that the research data have been gathered directly by the investigator for the purposes of a particular study. That is, the investigator or his or her assistants have conducted interviews and recorded observations and client responses to answer a specified research question. However, in the secondary data analysis approach the researcher undertakes an analysis of data previously collected for other purposes. For example, the Current Population Survey, a monthly survey conducted by the Census Bureau, may be used by the human service researcher to identify the need for social programs for unemployed persons in a particular region.

There are significant advantages to using secondary data for research purposes. Clearly, the tasks of the researcher are reduced significantly if he or she has access to archival information that is relevant to the topic of investigation. In some cases, the information may be more extensive than the researcher would be able to gather as an individual. It may be, for example, that an organization has conducted a particular survey over a period of years and is able to provide the investigator with valuable longitudinal data for a project.

A variety of agencies hold large data banks of information that may be of interest to the social scientist. For example, the Census Bureau is a repository for vast amounts of social data. In addition to the ten yearly censuses of the population, the Bureau conducts other activities such as the American Housing Survey and the Consumer Expenditure Survey. The Interuniversity Consortium for Political and Social Research (ICPSR) at the University of Michigan will provide data to social scientists from its extensive archives. The ICPSR is part of an international network of similar agencies in countries throughout the world. Other sources of secondary data that may be of interest to the human service researcher include the Roper Center at the University of Connecticut, the Federal Bureau of Investigation, state agencies, and hospital and school records.

Frankfort-Nachmias and Nachmias (1992) have identified three problems in secondary data analysis. First, the data may not fit precisely with what the researcher requires. For example, the sampling method used to collect the secondary data may not have been entirely appropriate for the particular investigation currently being undertaken. Definitions of the same social variables can differ from one study to the next. For example, in one study the "recidivism rate" may be measured by the number of released prisoners who are charged by the police within twelve months of being paroled, whereas a second study may define the same variable as the number of prisoners returned to prison within two years of release. Even more problematic is the notion of a universal definition for concepts such as "delinquency," "homelessness," "learning difficulty," or "promiscuity."

Second, it may not be easy for the researcher to access the various archives for relevant information. Agencies are always concerned about the confidentiality of the information they have about their clients. It may be expensive in terms of staff time for agencies that do not normally provide data for research purposes to provide the information that has been requested.

Third, it is not always possible for the researcher to determine the quality of the data stored in archival form. There may well be sampling problems that have biased the data, problems of reliability, and data of questionable validity. Some organizations, such as ICPSR, are attempting to address these issues by grading their data by different criteria. However, this is a long way from being the case with most sources of secondary data.

META-ANALYSIS

The traditional method of scientific research involves looking at a problem, attempting to control for extraneous factors, and showing links, either correlational or causal, between the variables. As research on a topic continues to receive attention, more and more studies are conducted. Sometimes these studies will attempt to replicate the earlier studies, others will look to investigate variations that lead to improved understanding, and some will seek to disprove the theories or explanations that have been proposed.

However, this increasing body of literature is not always consistent in its findings. Rosenthal (1991) believes that the existence of many studies with differing conclusions leads to confusion and eventually pessimism on the part of those who use research to guide their decisions. Glass (1976, 1977) describes a procedure called "meta-analysis," which enables the disparate findings of different studies of the same topic to be integrated.

What, then, is a meta-analysis? The principle is relatively easy to describe but does not reflect the complexity of the procedure. First, the researcher identifies as many studies as can be found on the topic of interest from a variety of sources, including journals, technical reports, and unpublished dissertations. The primary criterion for selection is that the study has used an experimental and control group. By a complex statistical process, the researcher then is able to calculate an "effect size," which is a measure of the difference between the experimental and control groups in each study. It is then possible to calculate a mean (average) effect size for all studies as well as other statistical properties. The meta-analysis enables the researcher to determine when an overall effect size exists or whether the treatment has no significant effect on the dependent variable.

Let us consider a meta-analysis of studies on the efficacy of perceptual-motor training by Kavale and Mattson (1983). Perceptual-motor training is a procedure widely used in the treatment of children with learning disabilities. In all, 180 studies on the topic were reviewed by the investigators, who report that the results of thirty-four studies support the use of perceptual-motor training, whereas seventeen studies were found to be negative or neutral about the same procedures. Using meta-analytic procedures, Kavale and Mattson were able to show that perceptual-motor training is not effective in ameliorating the condition of children with learning disabilities.

Meta-analytic studies have been used to compare the effects of psychotherapy to the effects of placebo treatments (Rosenthal, 1983), to investigate sex differences in conformity research (Cooper, 1979), and the effects of teacher expectancies on academic achievement (Dusek and Joseph, 1983). There is no doubt that the human services will see many more meta-analytic studies being conducted in the future.

COST ANALYSIS

In essence, the information provided by much social research is used by decision makers to determine the extent to which a program is achieving its goals or to determine ways in which the delivery of services may be improved. However, this is only part of the total picture. On the basis of information yielded, programs will be maintained, enhanced, expanded, cut back, or discontinued. Decisions regarding the future directions of a program generally cannot be made without consideration being given to the costs associated with the derived benefits.

The allocation of resources to one program inevitably means fewer resources will be available to pursue other social objectives. Cost analysis, then, is a tool used by policy makers and administrators to arrive at decisions pertaining to the distribution of limited resources. A variety of cost-analysis models have been developed that take into account the nature of the issues about which decisions are required and the form of information available to the investigator. Two of the most widely used models in social research will be examined, namely, cost effectiveness and cost-benefit analysis.

Cost Effectiveness

The cost-effectiveness model was originally developed by the Pentagon to evaluate the effectiveness of different weapon systems in achieving certain defense objectives. The model is distinguished from the cost-benefit approach in that the outcomes of the program are not expressed in monetary terms. Rather, the model simply yields the cost of achieving a given objective per unit of outcome and provides a basis for selecting between alternative means that might be used to reach that objective.

A study by Knapp and Robertson (1986) illustrates the application of the cost-effectiveness model to the justice system. The investigators compared the cost per sentence for youths committed to a detention center with that for youths given intermediate treatment such as a community service order. Not surprisingly, it was found that the intermediate treatment was a cost-effective alternative to custody for juvenile offenders. However, as the researchers point out, this conclusion is based on the assumption that effects on the juvenile offenders are the same for both forms of sanctions.

A further application of cost-effectiveness analysis is to compare the unit cost for the same service delivered in different circumstances. For example, Raine (1986) compared the costs of different judicial court services in different counties throughout the United Kingdom. He found that the "amount devoted to staffing costs was calculated to vary from just over $25 per case in

Liverpool to over $60 in Cornwall" (p. 54). Obviously, this information alone is not sufficient to justify either increasing the budget of the court's services in Liverpool or reducing the funds allocated to their southern counterparts. It may be that differences in the quality of services provided account for the cost differential between the two counties.

The underlying assumption in the application of the cost-effective model to the comparison of services is that of equivalence. The uncritical acceptance of this assumption may lead to counterproductive decisions being taken by administrators. As suggested above, similar services or the same service delivered in different environments may differ on various dimensions. Not only may there be a difference in the quality of the service provided, but significant differences may also occur in the characteristics of the target populations, the experience of the staff delivering the service, the length of time the services have been operational, or the geographical locations of the service operations. Any comparison of services on a cost-effective basis must take these factors into consideration.

A major limitation to the cost-effectiveness model is the quality of the cost-accounting operations in many human service areas (Grizzle and Witte, 1980; Grabosky, 1988). In reviewing the application of the cost-effectiveness model to evaluating the impact of victimless crime legislation, Geis (1980) cautions,

> *In short, judiciousness would probably dictate that costs are best handled as longitudinal data indicating a real rise or decrease in the amounts involved in particular activities and the implications to be drawn from such information—rather than as very firm bases for policy-relevant conclusions (p. 411).*

Cost-Benefit Analysis

The cost-benefit analysis model used primarily by economists guides decision makers in choosing the public policy option that will yield the greatest benefits for the community. For example,

the issue of crime prevention might be tackled by increasing the size of the police force, by allocating funds to an urban renewal project, or by implementing an employment program for young people. In carrying out a cost-benefit analysis, the evaluator is required to quantify all the costs and benefits associated with each option in monetary terms. The preferred option should be that which provides the greatest benefit-for-cost ratio.

The cost of increasing the size of the police force by 10 percent can be readily calculated. However, it must be assumed that there will be a concomitant increase in the number of arrests and convictions. Thus, the attendant increase in courts and prison costs must be taken into account. Of course, assuming that the level of productivity remains constant, more lawyers will need to be trained, more parole officers appointed, and so on. Economists have developed techniques for measuring these reverberations, such as the general equilibrium analysis (see, e.g., Rothenberg, 1975). To complicate the cost side of the equation even more, it is necessary to introduce the concept of opportunity costs. The allocation of financial resources to the justice system will be at the expense of other social programs. Hence, the cost of fewer employment opportunities for young people, for example, would need to be considered.

Quantifying, in monetary terms, the benefits arising from the implementation of a particular social policy, such as increasing the size of the police force, is even more complex than estimating the costs. In the case of our example, the measurement of crime prevention is a fundamental issue. The notion that the increased number of arrests and convictions that have occurred as a result of recruiting more police can be taken as an indicator of the number of crimes prevented is problematic at best. Another strategy might be to calculate the economic cost of burglaries over a given period of time, both before and after the policy has been implemented. But how does one determine the monetary value of corporate crimes not committed or the number of incest incidents that have not occurred? Just as intangible is attempting to cost the reduced level of fear of crime within the community that ideally will be an outcome of the policy decision.

A strength of the cost-benefit analysis approach is that it provides the policy maker with information that makes it possible to choose between very different options or solutions to problems in the field of human services. The major limitation of the model is the quality of the data available from the field. As Rothenberg (1975) states,

> . . . regardless of its methodological claims, its practical usefulness will be most decisively at the mercy of the availability of data. Very serious inadequacy of relevant data exists in almost every area for which cost-benefit analyses have been undertaken (p. 88).

A second limitation is the costs involved in undertaking such an analysis. However, as Grizzle and Witte (1980) point out, it is possible to apply the methodology effectively in a more limited form. A modest application of the model, for example, would be to calculate the costs incurred and benefits derived from the introduction of the legislation requiring seat belts to be worn in motor vehicles. Any agency would find it useful to document all the costs and benefits associated with a particular policy or program.

Short (1980) points out that although cost-benefit evaluation studies are important to the development of public policy, such studies do not contribute significantly to our theoretical understanding of the issues involved. Cho (1980) has taken a different approach to analyzing public policy. Using a multiple regression model, Cho has been able to measure the impact of different public policies on crime rates in major U.S. cities. Cho reports that service policies, such as expenditure for education and for parks and recreation, affect crime rates more often than control policies, such as employing more police or reducing prison crowdedness. Although not directly addressing the criticisms of Short, the correla-

tional model developed by Cho can point the way for undertaking future impact studies.

ROLE OF THE HUMAN SERVICE WORKER IN RESEARCH

As a human service worker, you are likely to become involved in research in a variety of ways. Perhaps the most common involvement occurs when your agency is being evaluated by the funding authorities. It is important that you have a clear understanding of the purpose of such an evaluation study. If the funding authority is interested in the effectiveness of the program, for example, the evaluator will be seeking different information as compared with an investigation concerned with determining the efficiency of the program. In the first case, the researcher is interested primarily in the extent to which people benefit from the services provided by the agency. If you are working in a drug rehabilitation center, the obvious question is, How many people remain off drugs once they have been discharged? An efficiency study, on the other hand, is essentially concerned with the costs of the program. Here the investigator is dealing with questions such as which is the better of two programs: Program A, which successfully rehabilitates twenty drug addicts per month at a cost of $5,000 per person, or Program B, which rehabilitates only ten addicts per month at a cost of $2,000 per person. In these types of studies your role as a human service worker may be focused on the provision of information. It may sound trite to say that it is essential that you provide accurate and reliable information. However, any social scientist is constantly concerned about the quality of information obtained from participants.

Another research scenario often includes the human service worker as a member of the investigation team. You may become involved in a study examining the effects of a recently released drug on the behavior of mentally disturbed adolescents. As a member of the investigation team, you will be concerned about the implementation and maintenance of the program. Again, it is critical that you understand the purpose of the study. If the investigation is looking at the effects of different schedules of reinforcement on the rate at which an autistic child engages in disruptive behavior, then you should have an understanding of the rationale for the research.

In other circumstances, as a human service worker you may be the sole researcher. You may have applied for and received a grant from the federal government to develop a program aimed at reducing the amount of domestic violence that occurs behind the closed doors of suburban middle America. You will want to demonstrate that your program is more effective than any other program currently operating. You will have to design and implement a research project that will convince the funding authorities that they should continue to support your program. In this situation, you will need to demonstrate that your cautious but convincing claims for success are soundly based on data that are both valid and reliable.

As a professional human service worker, you will be a consumer of research findings. This means you will be required to keep abreast of relevant research developments occurring in your particular sphere of interest. You will need to be able to critically review published research findings and synthesize the results of those studies with the outcomes of earlier related investigations. For example, should current research into the applications of primal scream therapy indicate that this technique is particularly effective in dealing with the neuroses of anal-retentive bank managers, you would want to reflect on the potential usefulness of this therapeutic approach in dealing with the problems of people with whom you work. Here, of course, you need to think about the critical issue of generalizing the results of research studies. Only after you are convinced that the evidence suggests that you are likely to achieve more effective results with primal scream therapy than, say, your current neurolinguistic programming approach, would you implement the change. This is where you will exercise your professional judgment. You may be concerned with developing social policy statements on the basis of empirical research findings. For example, the latest research may indicate that adolescents who play sports do not engage in delinquent behavior to the same extent as adolescents who do not play sports. Hence, your policy for reducing the rate of antisocial behavior is to introduce a comprehensive sports program for young people. Your social policy is based on the assumption that young people will not engage in undesirable behavior if they are busy playing football, baseball, and basketball. That is, you have inferred that a causal relationship exists between the two variables of sport and delinquent behavior. As discussed earlier, it is interesting to note that although national youth policies have been based on the assumption that such a relationship exists, social scientists have never been able to demonstrate that such is the case. The moral of the story, of course, is that you cannot accept uncritically the findings of contemporary social research.

REFERENCES

Berk, R. A., and L. W. Sherman (1985). "Data Collection Strategies in the Minneapolis Domestic Violence Experiment," 35–48 in Leigh Burstein, Howard E. Freeman, and Peter H. Russi, eds. *Collecting Evaluation Data: Problems and Solutions*. Beverly Hills, CA: Sage.

Campbell, D. T. (1979). "Assessing the Impact of Social Change." *Evaluation and Program Planning, 2,* 67–90.

Campbell, D. T., and J. C. Stanley (1963). *Experimental and quasi-experimental designs for research*. Boston: Houghton Mifflin.

Cho, Y. H. (1980). "A Multiple Regression Model for the Measurement of the Public Policy Impact on Big City Crime." In D. Nachmias, ed., *The Practice of Policy Evaluation.* New York: St. Martin's Press.

Cocks, E. (1989). "Working Together with Your Community." *National Council on Intellectual Disability: Interaction, 3,* 39–48.

Coffield, F., P. Robinson, and J. Sarsby (1981). *A Cycle of Deprivation? A Case Study of Four Families.* London: Heinemann.

Cook, T. D., and D. T. Campbell (1979). *Quasi-Experimentation: Design and Analysis Issues for Field Settings.* Skokie, IL: Rand McNally.

Cook, T. D., F. L. Cook, and M. M. Mark (1977). "Randomized and Quasi-Experimental Designs in Evaluation Research: An Introduction." In L. Rutman, ed., *Evaluation Research Methods: A Basic Guide.* London: Sage Publications.

Cook, T. D., and W. R. Shadish (1986). "Program Evaluation: The Worldly Science." *Annual Review of Psychology, 37,* 193–232.

Cooper, H. M. (1979). "Statistically Combining Independent Studies: A Meta-Analysis of Sex Differences in Conformity Research." *Journal of Personality and Social Psychology, 37,* 131–146.

David, H. P., and N. H. Wright (1971). "Abortion Legislation: The Romanian Experience Studies." *Family Planning, 2,* 205–210.

Davidson, W. S., J. R. Koch, R. G. Lewis, and M. D. Wresinski (1981). *Evaluation Strategies in Criminal Justice.* New York: Pergamon Press.

Deutscher, I. (1976). "Toward Avoiding the Goal-Trap in Evaluation Research." In C. G. Abt, ed., *The Evaluation of Social Programs.* London: Sage Publications.

Dusek, J. B., and G. Joseph (1983). "The Bases of Teacher Experiences: A Meta-Analysis." *Journal of Educational Psychology, 75,* 327–346.

Empey, L. T. (1980). "Field Experimentation in Criminal Justice: Rationale and Design." In M. W. Klein and T. S. Teilman, eds., *Handbook of Criminal Justice Evaluation.* London: Sage Publications.

Festinger, L., H. Reicken, and S. Schacter (1956). *When Prophecy Fails.* New York: Harper & Row.

Frankfort-Nachmias, C., and D. Nachmias (1992). *Research Methods in the Social Sciences,* 4th ed. London: Hodder & Stoughton.

Gay, L. R. (1990). *Educational Research: Competencies for Analysis and Application,* 3rd ed. New York: Merrill Publishing Co.

Geis, G. (1980). "Evaluation Issues and Victimless Crimes." In M. W. Klein and T. S. Teilman, eds., *Handbook of Criminal Justice Evaluation.* London: Sage Publications.

Glass, G. V. (1976). "Primary, Secondary and Meta-Analysis of Research." *Educational Researcher, 5,* 3–8.

Glass, G. V. (1977). "Integrating Findings: The Meta-Analysis of Research." *Review of Research in Education, 5,* 351–379.

Goffman, E. (1961). *Asylums.* New York: Doubleday.

Grabosky, P. (1988). "Efficiency and Effectiveness in Australian Policing: A Citizen's Guide to Police Services." In J. Vernon and D. Bracey, eds., *Police Resources and Effectiveness.* Seminar Proceedings No. 16, Australian Institute of Criminology, Canberra.

Grizzle, G. A., and A. D. Witte (1980). "Criminal Justice Evaluation Techniques: Methods Other Than Random Assignment." In M. W. Klein and T. S. Teilman, eds., *Handbook of Criminal Justice Evaluation.* London: Sage Publications.

Healy, J. (1985). "After the Refuge: Methodological Issues in Follow-Up Surveys." In S. E. Hatty, ed., *National Conference on Domestic Violence.* Seminar Proceedings No. 12, Australian Institute of Criminology, Canberra.

Herrman, H., P. McGorry, P. Bennett, R. Van Riel, P. Wellington, D. McKenzie, and B. Singh (1988). *Homeless People with Severe Mental Disorders in Inner Melbourne.* Victoria, Melbourne: Council to Homeless Persons.

Holy, L. (1984). "Theory, Methodology and the Research Process." In R. F. Ellen, ed., *Ethnographic Research: A Guide to General Conduct.* London: Academic Press.

Janus, M. (1982). "Functional Unit Management: Organizational Effectiveness in the Federal Prison System." In G. A. Forehand, ed., *Applications of Time-Series Analysis to Evaluation.* San Francisco: Jossey-Bass.

International Council for Adult Education (1982). *Participatory Research: An Introduction.* New Delhi: Society for Participatory Research in Asia.

Kavale, K., and P. D. Mattson (1983). "One jumped off the balance beam." Meta-analysis of perceptual-motor training. *Journal of Learning Disabilities, 16,* 165–173.

Knapp, M., and E. Robertson (1986). "Has Intermediate Treatment Proved Cost-Effective?" In A. Harrison and J. Gretton, eds., *Crime U.K. 1986: An Economic, Social and Policy Audit.* Newbury, Berkshire: Policy Journals.

Kornblum, W. (1974). *Blue-Collar Community.* Chicago: University of Chicago Press.

Kutchinsky, B. (1973). "The Effects of Easy Availability of Pornography on the Incidence of Sex Crimes: The Danish Experience." *Journal of Social Issues, 29,* 163–181.

Leviton, L. C., and E. F. X. Hughes (1981). "Research on the Utilization of Evaluations: A Review and Synthesis." *Evaluation Review, 5*(4), 525–548.

Lewis, O. (1966). *La Vida: A Puerto Rican Family in the Culture of Poverty.* New York: Random House.

Maguire, M. (1986). "Victims' Rights: Slowly Redressing the Balance." In A. Harrison and J. Gretton, eds., *Crime U.K. 1986: An Economic, Social and Policy Audit.* Newbury, Berkshire: Policy Journals.

Mason, G., and P. Wilson (1988). *Sport and Juvenile Crime.* Canberra: Australian Institute of Criminology.

McCleary, R., and J. E. Riggs (1982). "The 1975 Australian Law Act: A Model for Assessing Legal Impacts." In G. A. Forehand, ed., *Applications of Time Series Analysis to Evaluation.* San Francisco: Jossey-Bass.

Miller, E. (1986). *Street Woman.* Philadelphia: Temple University Press.

Pryce, K. (1979). *Endless Pressure.* Harmondsworth, England: Penguin.

Raine, J. (1986). "Do Magistrates' Courts Give Value for Money?" In A. Harrison and J. Gretton, eds.,

Crime U.K.: An Economic, Social and Policy Audit. Newbury, Berkshire: Policy Journals.

Rosenthal, R. (1983). "Improving Meta-Analytic Procedures for Assessing the Effects of Psychotherapy vs. Placebo." *The Behavioral and Brain Sciences, 6,* 298–299.

Rosenthal, R. (1991). *Meta-Analytic Procedures for Social Research.* Newbury Park, CA: Sage Publications.

Ross, H. L. (1973). "Law, Science, and Accidents: The British Road Safety Act of 1967." *Journal of Legal Studies, 2,* 1–75.

Rothenberg, J. (1975). "Cost-Benefit Analysis: A Methodological Exposition." In M. Guttentag and E. L. Streuning, eds., *Handbook of Evaluation Research,* vol. 2. London: Sage Publications.

Salthouse, T. A. (1982). *Adult Cognition: An Experimental Psychology of Human Aging.* New York: Springer-Verlag.

Schultz, J., and S. Florio (1979). "Stop and Freeze: The Negotiation of Social and Physical Space in a Kindergarten/First Grade Classroom." *Anthropology & Education Quarterly, 10,* 166–181.

Sherman, L. W., and R. A. Berk (1984). "The Specific Deterrent Effects of Arrest for Domestic Assault." *American Sociological Review, 49,* 261–272.

Short, J. F. (1980). "Evaluation as Knowledge Building—and Vice Versa." In M. W. Klein and T. S. Teilman, eds., *Handbook of Criminal Justice Evaluation.* London: Sage Publications.

Squire, C. (1989). *Significant Differences—Feminism in Psychology.* London: Routledge.

Underwood, R., M. Lee, and R. Jackson (1991). "Community Support Services for Mentally Ill Young People." Paper presented at the Australian Sociological Association annual conference, Perth.

KEY TERMS FOR PART SEVEN

After studying Chapters 26, 27, 28, and 29, you should have a command of the following key terms, major concepts, and principal topical references:

cultural diversity
United States Census Bureau
interpersonal racial and ethnic conflict
American values
optimal life
differences in cultural perspectives
dominant or mainstream culture
cross-cultural helping
transcultural caring
differing ideas of caring
healer
community relief of suffering

role of computers
information technology
surfing
Internet
supply and demand
website
link
computer technology
technological
techno-babble
telecommuting
effect on social relations
information-processing model
Service-Learning program
experiential learning

experimental approach
correlation studies
time-series design
single-subject design
field research
case study
participatory research
secondary data analysis
meta-analysis
cost analysis
cost effectiveness
cost-benefit analysis

PIVOTAL ISSUES FOR DISCUSSION OF PART SEVEN

1. Identify three agencies or programs in your community that specifically advocate for ethnic or cultural minorities. How are these agencies integrated with other traditional human service agencies? How do these agencies support their consumer population?

2. What are three ways human service workers can better relate and respond to diversity in their client populations?

3. Design a basic human service research project utilizing one of the various designs described in the Underwood and Lee article on human service research. Outline your results and conclusions and present them in class for discussion.

4. As a community leader, you are committed to maximizing prevention techniques in the delivery of community human services. Describe how you would develop "prevention/promotion" programs throughout your city or town. How would these programs be used in schools, in agencies, in hospitals and clinics, in housing, in police and public safety, and so on?

5. Visit a community-based group residence program. Interview the manager of the program and record the description of the program, the clients served, funding, and the problems and barriers encountered in administering the program. Be sure to include how to become a staff member and what is required in this work.

6. Pick a topic relevant to human services and research it on the Internet. Then download the information and present your findings in class.

7. Does your college/university have a Service-Learning program? If so, what types of settings are students placed in? How do students feel about their experiences? If no program exists, how might your institution start a Service-Learning program? Who is the college official that you would need to contact?

SUGGESTED READINGS FOR PART SEVEN_____

1. Dillard, J. M. (1987). *Multicultural Counseling.* Chicago: Nelson-Hall.

2. Pedersen, P. (1990). "The Constructs of Complexity and Balance in Multicultural Counseling." *Journal of Counseling and Development, 68*(5), 550–554.

3. Atkinson, D., G. Morten, and D. Sue (1993). *Counseling American Minorities.* Madison, WI: Brown and Benchmark.

4. Banks, J. (1991). *Teaching Strategies for Ethnic Studies.* Needham Heights, MA: Allyn and Bacon.

5. Banks, J., and C. M. Banks (1993). *Multicultural Education.* Needham Heights, MA: Allyn and Bacon.

6. Baruth, L., and M. Manning (1992). *Multicultural Education.* Needham Heights, MA: Allyn and Bacon.

7. Dana, R. (1993). *Multicultural Assessment Perspectives for Professional Psychology.* Needham Heights, MA: Allyn and Bacon.

8. Ivey, A., M. Ivey, and L. Simek-Morgan (1993). *Counseling and Psychotherapy: A Multicultural Perspective.* Needham Heights, MA: Allyn and Bacon.

9. LeVine, E., and A. Padilla (1980). *Cross Cultures in Therapy: Pluralistic Counseling for the Hispanic.* Monterey, CA: Brooks/Cole.

10. Tiedt, P., and I. Tiedt (1990). *Multicultural Teaching.* Needham Heights, MA: Allyn and Bacon.

Mid-Term Interview: Observer Rating Form

Name of Interviewer Being Rated _____

Initials of Observer Doing Rating _____   Date _____

INSTRUCTIONS: Please use a rating from 1 to 5 or NO (i.e., Not Observed), with 5 being the highest rating.

                                                              COMMENTS

1. Beginning the Interview   _____   _____

2. Attending Skills   _____   _____
   a. Visual/eye contact (e.g.,
      looking at interviewee)   _____   _____
   b. Vocal tone and rate (e.g.,
      not speaking too fast)   _____   _____
   c. Verbal tracking (e.g.,
      not changing topic)   _____   _____
   d. Body language (e.g.,
      avoiding distracting
      mannerisms)   _____   _____

3. Questioning Skills   _____   _____
   a. Open-ended questions   _____   _____
   b. Closed-ended questions   _____   _____

4. Encouraging Skills   _____   _____
   a. Nonverbal
      (e.g., head nodding)   _____   _____
   b. Verbal/key word   _____   _____

5. Listening Skills   _____   _____
   a. Reflecting content
      (i.e., paraphrasing)   _____   _____
   b. Reflecting explicit
      feelings   _____   _____

   c. Reflecting implicit
      feelings   _____   _____

   d. Summarization   _____   _____

6. Ending of interview   _____   _____

OTHER COMMENTS OR GENERAL OBSERVATIONS
(Use space below and on other side of page, if necessary.)

Mid-Term Interview: Self-Evaluation Paper

The purpose of this self-evaluation paper is to allow you to demonstrate your knowledge of the skills required of effective interviewers, as well as your ability to judge your own effectiveness in an interview, and to assess your growth so far.

PART 1: SESSION SUMMARY (5 POINTS)

Please provide the name of your interviewee and a summary of the presenting issue.

PART 2: TRANSCRIPTION AND ANALYSIS (40 POINTS)

Using your videotape, provide a verbatim transcription of at least five (5) minutes of your interview. Be sure to note the interviewee's behavior (if noteworthy), as well as the duration of any significant silences (more than 3 seconds). Use the following classification codes for your interventions.

G = greeting (opening)	RC = reflection of content (paraphrase)
OQ = open-ended question	REF = reflection of explicit feelings
CQ = closed-ended question	RIF = reflection of implied feelings
*E = encourager	S = summarization
KW = key word	**F = feedback (about interviewee's behavior)
O = other (advice, reassurance, interviewer's opinion and self-disclosure, etc.)	

Examples of Classification Codes:

*Encourager statement: "I'm interested in hearing more about your family."

**Feedback involves remarking on the person's behavior: "I notice that every time you mention your boss, you grimace."

Format: Start with your greeting, (if you are transcribing the first five minutes of the interview), or your last intervention of the interview as the five minutes of your interview that you select to transcribe.

NUMBER	INTERVENTION/ RESPONSE	TRANSCRIPTION	INTENTION/ASSESSMENT/ ALTERNATIVE
1a	Intervention (G/OQ)	"Hello, How are you?	My intent was ___ however, I was surprised by the client's response. I wish I had said (alternative intervention)
1b	Response	"Crappy!"	

NUMBER	INTERVENTION/ RESPONSE	TRANSCRIPTION	INTENTION/ASSESSMENT/ ALTERNATIVE
2a	Intervention (Classify)	Write your exact verbatim description.	
2b	Response	Write the essence of what the interviewee says.	

For Each Intervention, Answer the Following Questions:

— **Intention:** What was your intention or purpose in making this intervention?

— **Assessment of Intervention:** Did it work? If not, why not (i.e., was the type of intervention not well matched with your intention, or was the intervention poorly worded or timed?)

— **Alternative Intervention:** Write an alternative for this intervention if it meets *any* of the following criteria: (*If you choose not to write an alternative, indicate that none is needed. Do not just leave this space blank, as I will assume you forgot.*)

  — Your original intervention did not capture the main point, and you went off on a tangent.
  — Your original intervention didn't work, even though it addressed the main point (e.g., it addressed content when addressing feelings would have worked better).
  — Your original intervention worked, but only because you got lucky and the interviewee was kind (e.g., you asked a CQ and got an elaborate answer).
  — Your original intervention was the appropriate type of intervention and it worked, but it was poorly or unclearly worded.

PART 3. NARRATIVE EVALUATION (30 POINTS)

Watch the tape of your initial (baseline) interview, then compare your mid-term interview with the baseline. To maximize your learning, please compare the coding of your baseline interview with your coding for your mid-term interview. You do not have to provide a transcription and analysis of your baseline interview. *Please comment on any growth in specific interviewing skills from the first interview until now.* Then, in narrative format, discuss the mid-term interview, *what you believe you did well, and what you might have done differently. Focus particularly on the skills you wish to practice and perfect before the final interview.* That is, your goal in the final interview should be to improve on your performance in the mid-term interview by demonstrating improvement in *specific skills.* Examples might be: "I noticed that I asked a lot of questions. I plan to work on asking fewer questions and using more reflective statements." Or, "I had a hard time knowing what to say next, and concentrated more on my own next response than on the interviewee's statements. I plan to work on concentrating better on the interviewee." Remember, *it is important to acknowledge your strengths* as well as your weaknesses. Your paper should demonstrate that you have reviewed and carefully considered the feedback and suggestions received from your peers and the instructor, and that you understand the concepts and techniques discussed in the text and demonstrated in the course.

ABOUT THE EDITORS

Howard S. Harris, prior to his passing, chaired the Social Sciences Department at Bronx Community College for more than twenty years and taught psychology for more than thirty years. He was Vice President for Publications for the Council for Standards in Human Service Education and was a founder and president of the Metropolitan New York Association of Human Services Education. He was the 1997 recipient of the National Organization for Human Service Education Lenore McNeer award for outstanding contributions to the Human Services Profession. He was a trustee and president of the Yonkers School Board during the initial phase of the federal court order desegregation plan and assumed a wide range of leadership roles in faculty organizations, in the Professional Staff Congress/CUNY, and in education, community service, and environmental advocacy organizations. Additionally, he directed projects funded by the National Endowment for the Humanities, the New York State Council for the Humanities, and the National Institutes of Health, which had funded his most recent research in collaboration with Suzanne Yates: "Values and Attributions in Caregiver Effectiveness." Also, he played four-wall handball at a championship level.

    David C. Maloney, Ed.D., is Professor of Psychology and Human Services and past coordinator of the Human Service Program at Fitchburg State College, Fitchburg, Massachusetts. He is a past President of the National Organization for Human Service Education and is a recipient of the Lenore McNeer and the Miriam Clubok Awards for leadership and professional contributions to both regional and national professional organizations. Dr. Maloney has worked for more than 30 years in the Human Service Education field and has an active clinical practice as a licensed psychologist in Massachusetts. His professional interests are in psychological testing, clinical supervision, and in court-related consultation. He is an avid and cruising sailor, enjoys playing piano, and loves spending time at his home in the seaside village of Wexford in southeast Ireland.

    Franklyn M. Rother is a Professor of Psychology at Brookdale Community College, Lincroft, New Jersey. He serves as the Social Sciences Division Chair, providing the academic leadership for nine disciplines in four departments. He is a former President, Vice President, and Treasurer of the National Organization for Human Service Education and past president of the Mid-Atlantic Consortium for Human Services. He has served as the founding President of the New Jersey Higher Education Consortia for Alcohol and Other Drug Abuse Prevention and Education and serves as the Director for the Center for Addictions Studies at Brookdale Community College. He is the Treasurer for The Center in Asbury Park, a grassroots interfaith organization supporting the needs of people living with HIV and AIDS. His first position in the human service field coincided with the first monies spent on the War on Poverty in 1964.

Naydean Blair, LPC, LDC, SW, NCAC II, department head for mental health programs at Houston Community College since 1986, has completed most graduate work in curriculum development. Specialty areas include Substance Abuse, Counselor Training, Multicultural Interviewing Techniques and Human Service Ethics. She is the Vice President for program approval for the Council for Standards in Human Service Education.

Paul F. Cimmino, Ph.D., MSW, is the founder and director of the Parent Emotional Awareness Training Institute (PEAT) and is a human service–mental health program/ professional development consultant in Billings, Montana. Cimmino's doctorate is in counseling psychology, and he is a licensed clinical social worker/psychotherapist. He is a former professor and coordinator of the Human Services Program at Montana State University–Billings, former chief of the psychiatric social services division of the department of psychiatry at UCLA, Olive View Medical Center, and assistant clinical professor at the UCLA School of Medicine/San Fernando Valley Psychiatry Training Program.

Peter Clark has worked as an Assistant Attorney General in the Massachusetts Medicaid Fraud Control Unit since 1994. He has specialized in prosecutions and investigations of complex criminal violations by physicians and corporate health care providers. Some current cases include prosecutions of physicians who are illegally prescribing drugs to addicts, and kickback schemes involving referrals between physicians and psychologists. Before joining the Medicaid Fraud Control Unit, Clark was the Director of Enforcement of the Massachusetts Board of Registration in Medicine, an Assistant District Attorney in Middlesex County, Massachusetts, and a staff lawyer for the Massachusetts Departments of Mental Health and Social Services. A graduate of University of Illinois at Champaign-Urbana and Yale Law School, Clark served in the United States Army from 1965 through 1968, including a tour as an infantryman in Vietnam in 1966 and 1967. He lives in Massachusetts with his wife Brenda and daughter Natalie; another daughter, Jessica, is in graduate school at Princeton University.

Miriam Clubok, MSW, has provided significant leadership throughout the development of the human service movement. Ms. Clubok was a founding member of NOHSE and served as its president from 1982 to 1985. She has worked on many task forces sponsored by NIMH and SREB to develop competencies, curriculum, certification, and other issues important to the field. She was Director of Ohio University's Mental Health Technology program for thirteen years.

Audrey Cohen, founder and president of the College (1964) that bears her name, devoted her career to reinventing education for the information and service-based global society. Her Purpose-Centered System of Education®, first developed at the college, has been adopted by public schools throughout the country. Ms. Cohen also led the creation in the 1960s of ten new human service professional positions, including the first teacher, social worker, and legal assistants. In 1974, she founded the first national organization for human service professionals, the American Council for Human Service, Inc.

Shirley Jean Conyard, MSW, MPA, DSW, is an educator, consultant, and clinical social worker. She has worked as a research technologist for the Downstate Medical Center in Brooklyn, New York; supervisor of community services for the Angel Guardian

Home in Brooklyn; researcher and psychotherapist for Brooklyn Jewish and Medical Center. The following positions were held at Audrey Cohen College from 1981 to present: professor, assistant dean for internships, associate dean and dean, School for Human Services, and research fellow at Metropolitan College of New York (formerly Audrey Cohen College). She is an adjunct professor at several other New York area colleges and serves on many human service agencies throughout the region.

Walter de Oliveira, M.D. (Psychiatry), Ph.D., is an Assistant Professor and the Director of the Institute of Youth Leaders at the University of Northern Iowa. His extensive work in the field of Youth Development and Human Services includes teaching, field-based research, articles, and conference presentations. He is internationally recognized for his work with street children and street youth workers. He is an advisor for the Center of the Theater of Liberation and has published on the role of the arts, especially drama, in education.

Eugene M. DeRobertis, Ph.D., is a psychology instructor at Brookdale Community College in Lincroft, New Jersey. In the clinical arena, Dr. DeRobertis worked as an individual and group psychotherapist. The majority of his work was spent in the area of addictions counseling prior to making a full commitment to higher education. In 1996 he published *Phenomenological Psychology: A Text for Beginners,* and in 2001 he acted as a contributing literary editor for his mentor's text, *The Quest for Personality Integration: Reimaginizing our Lives,* by Edward L. Murray. In 2002, he published an article entitled "The Impact of Technology-Induced Anonymity on Communications and Ethics: New Challenges for IT Pedagogy" in *The Journal of Information Technology Impact.* This last publication was co-written with Robert Saldarini. Dr. DeRobertis specializes in humanistic-existential perspectives on human development.

Madelyn DeWoody is associate director for program development with the Massachusetts Society for the Prevention of Cruelty to Children. Formerly, she was legal counsel and director of program development for the Child Welfare League of America in Washington, DC. Ms. DeWoody is an attorney with an LLM from Georgetown University Law Center; a social worker with an MSW from Louisiana State University; and a public health practitioner with an MPH from the University of North Carolina at Chapel Hill. She has worked as a front-line child welfare worker and supervisor in CWLA agencies. Her work most recently has focused on child welfare issues, particularly the health, mental health, and developmental needs of children, the financing of health care and social services for children, and legal issues that affect children. Her recent books, *Medicaid and SSI: Options and Strategies for Child Welfare Agencies; Confronting Homelessness among American Families: Federal Strategies and Programs;* and *Making Sense of Federal Dollars,* published by CWLA, explore a range of financing strategies for child welfare and housing services.

Joel F. Diambra, Ed.D., is Assistant Professor and Field Coordinator, Human Service Education, Educational Psychology and Counseling, at the University of Tennessee. He is also a Licensed Professional Counselor and Nationally Certified Counselor.

Mary Di Giovanni, RN, BS, MS, is a professor and coordinator of the Human Service programs in Mental Health Technology, Community Residence Manager Certificate Program, and the Alcohol Drug Abuse Counseling Certificate Program at Northern Essex Community College. Ms. Di Giovanni is a founding member of the New England Organization for Human Service Education (NEOHSE), and served as a member of the Southern Regional

Education Board (SREB) Credentialing National Task Force in the late 1970s. She is president of the Council for Standards in Human Service Education (CSHSE).

Maureen E. Doyle, MSW, CSW, is Assistant Professor of Human Services at LaGuardia Community College in Long Island City, NY. She has been a volunteer in service projects in Roxbury, MA, Northern Ireland, and Belize, and is a member of the Mayor's Increase the Peace Corps in New York City. She is a graduate of the Columbia University School of Social Work, has served as director of a family service center and a senior center, and has coordinated a city-wide wellness program. She and her husband, Gerry, live in Connecticut.

Marcel A. Duclos, M.Th., M.Ed., CCMC, NCC, CADAC, LCPC, has been an educator and counselor for more than thirty years. He received an award for his pioneering work in human services in New England, has served on the board of the Council for Standards in Human Service Education, and is a presenter at regional and national conferences. He currently specializes in substance abuse counselor education and supervision, maintains a private practice in Jungian Psychotherapy, and is a professor of psychology and alcohol and drug abuse counseling at the New Hampshire Technical Institute. He is an approved clinical supervisor by the Academy of Clinical Mental Health Councils.

Christopher R. Edginton is Professor and Director of the School of Health, Physical Education, and Leisure Services at the University of Northern Iowa. He has been identified as a leading proponent of the application of contemporary management concepts in the park and recreation field, where he has held direct leadership, supervisory, and administrative positions. Active in professional organizations, in editorial roles for their publications, and in other positions, he is, for example, Past President of the American Association for Leisure and Recreation. He is internationally recognized through his work, which includes authorship of more than 150 articles, coauthor of more than half a dozen textbooks, numerous professional presentations made throughout the world, and as founder of the *Camp Adventure* Youth Services Program, which serves children in about twenty countries. He has directed over $14.0 million in grants and, in addition, has received many awards and honors such as being named a Distinguished Professor by the Guangzhou Institute of Physical Education, the People's Republic of China, and as the recipient of the J. B. Nash Scholar award for 1998.

Margaret J. French has, since 1970, served as Department Chair of the Human Services Technology Program at Pitt Community College in Greenville, North Carolina. She is the South Regional Director of the Council for Standards in Human Service Education and is active in leadership positions in a variety of human service organizations. Initially trained as a Rehabilitation Counselor, she has developed a wide range of expertise within the field of human services and teaches courses in many areas. She is a frequent guest speaker, trainer, facilitator, workshop leader, and presenter at professional conferences and meetings. She has received recognition and awards for her service and for teaching, most recently as recipient of the 1996 Excellence in Teaching Award from the North Carolina State Board of Community College/First Union Foundation.

Marianne Gfroerer, MA, NCC, is a psychotherapist/consultant in private practice, and an Adjunct Professor at the New Hampshire Technical Institute. In addition, she directs service programs for homeless children and families and at-risk youth.

Janet Hagen, Ph.D., is an Associate Professor at the University of Wisconsin at Oshkosh in the College of Education and Human Services, Department of Human Services and Professional Leadership. She is the Midwest/North Central Regional Director of the Council for Standards in Human Services Education. She has researched and published in the area of coping and adaptation. Her current research interest is in the area of Mediation and Domestic Violence. She is active with the United Cerebral Palsy of Winnebagoland, where she assumes leadership roles.

John M. Hancock, Ph.D., is an Associate Professor and has been the Chair of the Behavioral Sciences Department at Fitchburg State College since 1995. He teaches both in the undergraduate human service program and the graduate counseling program. His primary teaching responsibilities in both the human service program and graduate counseling program are competence-based learning courses. At the undergraduate level he teaches Interviewing Techniques, Group Work, Crisis Intervention, and Professional Issues in Human Services. He is the immediate past president of the New England Organization of Human Service Education (NEOHSE) and has served as the NEOHSE regional representative to the National Organization for Human Service Education (NOHSE) for a number of years.

Michael Lee has recently been appointed Associate Dean, Faculty of Health and Human Sciences at Edith Cowan University, Perth, Australia. He was formerly the Head of the School of Community Studies at Edith Cowan University in Perth, Australia. Dean Lee has been active in community organizations in the aged care and disability fields. This, combined with research into such areas as values in child care and employer attitudes, has provided him with a diversity of experience in human services.

David S. Liederman, BS, MA, MSW, is the Executive Director of the Child Welfare League of America, Inc. Mr. Liederman is national co-chair of Generations United, a coalition of more than one hundred national organizations established to promote cooperation between the generations. He also chairs the National Collaboration for Youth, a coalition of sixteen national youth-serving organizations.

Lorence A. Long, MSW, ACSW, is Professor of Human Services at LaGuardia Community College in Long Island City, NY. He has written training manuals on working with homeless people for the National Institute of Mental Health and is author of the interactive computer course Human Services Worker. He is a graduate of the Adelphi University School of Social Work. He has been a social worker in an emergency room and a crisis unit and has directed a mental health clinic. He and his wife Marjorie live in Long Island City.

James Edell Lopez hold a Ph.D. in Anthropology from Columbia University and an MSW from the Hunter College School of Social Work. He currently works as Deputy Director and Research Scientist at the Administration for Children's Services in New York City. He has worked in child welfare for over sixteen years, specializing in issues of foster care, teen pregnancy, and child maltreatment.

Linda Mass is the Director of Experiential Learning at Brookdale Community College in Lincroft, New Jersey. Ms. Mass has extensive experience in developing and administering experiential programs, such as Service-Learning, Cooperative Education, and Internships. She is a member of The New Jersey Higher Education Service-Learning Consortium, and she continues to work for the expansion and development of Service-Learning programs both at Brookdale and around the state. Ms. Mass serves as board member and trainer for the Coalition for Service-Learning, an organization whose purpose is to promote and assist in the development of school-based service-learning programs in the K–12 curriculum. Linda is active on the executive boards of Monmouth County DOVIA (Directors of Volunteers In Agencies), New Jersey Cooperative Education Association, and is currently the President of the Board of the Volunteer Center of Monmouth County.

Wm. Lynn McKinney, Ph.D., is Professor of Education and Director of the bachelor's degree program in human science and services at the University of Rhode Island. He served as Interim Director of Rhode Island Project AIDS in the mid-1980s and continues to volunteer both his time and his money to caring for people with HIV and AIDS and for AIDS research.

Harold L. McPheeters, MD, is a psychiatrist who graduated from the University of Louisville School of Medicine and took his psychiatric training there. Much of his career was spent in administrative mental health work. He served as Assistant Commissioner and then as Commissioner of the Kentucky Department of Mental Health from 1955–1964 and then as Deputy Commissioner of the New York Department of Mental Hygiene. He served as Director of Health and Human Services Programs at the Southern Regional Education Board (SREB), an interstate compact organization of the fifteen southern states, from 1965 to his retirement in 1987. During the period of his work at SREB, he was project director for several projects, funded by grants from the National Institute of Mental Health, to develop and implement educational programs for human services workers in the South and across the nation. He lives in Atlanta, Georgia.

Joseph Mehr, Ph.D., is currently Chief of Inpatient Planning and Program Development for the Division of Mental Health, State of Illinois. He has been associated with the human service field since the mid-1960s, first as principal investigator on a NIMH Hospital Improvement Grant, a NIMH New Careers Grant, and a Fund for the Improvement of Post-Secondary Education Grant. All three sequential grants were focused on developing and implementing curricula for human service workers and developing human service worker career ladders. He has taught human service courses at the associate's, bachelor's, and master's level. Dr. Mehr has written a broadly accepted college text, *Human Services: Concepts and Intervention Strategies,* first published by Allyn and Bacon in 1980 and available in its seventh revised edition in 1998.

Rafael Mendez was first introduced to the community mental health movement as a student at Bronx Community College, where he enrolled after being honorably discharged from the United States Air Force. He served in the Vietnam War at Bien Thuy air base in Mekong Delta. After completing the doctoral program at Boston University, he returned to New York, where he was a founding member of the Institute for Social Therapy (a network of community mental health centers) and the Community Literacy Research Program, where he developed innovative youth programs such as the All-Stars Talent Show Network and Pregnant Productions. He teaches psychology at Bronx Community College.

Maria Munoz-Kantha, MSW, also has a Ph.D. from the NYU Graduate School of Social Work. She is currently a part-time Assistant Professor at the Columbia University School of Social Work. She was a child abuse trainer and provider for the Westchester County Department of Community Mental Health and a training consultant for the Fordham University Center for Training and Research in Child Abuse and Family Violence.

Kathleen J. Niccum, BA, MS, Ed.D., Ph.D., is currently the Patient Services Coordinator for Tri-State Renal Network, Inc., and part-time instructor at the University of Indianapolis and Indiana University. Ms. Niccum has a master's level Gerontology Certificate from Florida State University. She developed the first social services in long-term care training course in the state of Indiana. Further, she developed a noncredit, continuing education course for Indiana University on Motivating the Nursing Home Resident. Ms. Niccum is a past board member for NOHSE and the Midwest/North Central Organization for Human Service Education.

Anthony W. Pellicane is an Assistant Professor of Criminal Justice at Brookdale Community College in Monmouth County, New Jersey. He served as Director of Corrections and Youth Services in Middlesex and Monmouth Counties from 1972 to 1999. He administered and supervised staff at facilities holding 1,000 to 1,500 adult inmates and more than 100 juvenile offenders. He received his bachelor's degree at Monmouth University and completed his master's degree at Rider University.

R. Donna Petrie, Ph.D., NCC, is an associate professor and coordinator of the four-year undergraduate human service major at St. John's University, Jamaica, NY, and she works part-time as a psychotherapist in a Brooklyn, NY, community mental health center.

Frances Fox Piven is Distinguished Professor of Political Science and Sociology at the Graduate School and University Center of the City University of New York. She is co-author with Richard Cloward of *Regulating the Poor* (updated edition, 1993), *Poor People's Movements* (1997), and most recently, *The Breaking of the American Social Compact* (1997).

Stan Rosenzweig is president of Office Technology Consulting, Inc., and Phone-guru.com, providing computer telephone integration advice to major corporations and government. He writes more than two dozen articles each year and lectures extensively on office technology subjects. He never works for free, except perhaps just this once.

Robert A. Saldarini is a tenured full Professor in the Division of Business, Math, and Social Sciences at Bergen Community College in Paramus, New Jersey. He holds an MBA from Fairleigh Dickinson University. Saldarini has published his textbook, *Analysis and Design of Business Information Systems* (1989) and subsequently contributed to the *Technology and Teaching* anthology (L. Lloyd, Ed., 1997). In 2002, he published an article entitled "The Impact of Technology-Induced Anonymity on Communications and Ethics: New Challenges for IT Pedagogy" in *The Journal of Information Technology Impact.* This last publication was co-written with Dr. DeRobertis.

Lynne Schmelter-Davis is an Assistant Professor in the Psychology Department at Brookdale Community College, Lincroft, New Jersey. She currently serves as the Psychology Department Chair. She is a Clinical Nurse Specialist in Adult Psychiatric Mental Health and maintains a small private practice in Monmouth County, New Jersey.

Michael Seliger, Ph.D., is Associate Director of the State University of New York Educational Opportunity Center of the Bronx where he is responsible for program development, research, and systems development. His experience has been with Head Start, VISTA, the Peace Corps, Community Action Programs, health institutions, employment, welfare reform, and welfare-to-work strategies.

Christine Lewis Shane, M.S., is a human resource management and education consultant for both public and private organizations in the United States and Canada. She has designed and implemented major workforce initiatives on state and national levels, including the National Institute on Mental Health and in the Commonwealth of Massachusetts. Ms. Shane specializes in grant and program evaluation, education programs for students with special needs, and labor policy and disability. She lectures at colleges and universities throughout the United States and in Great Britain. She is an adjunct faculty member at Fitchburg State College in Massachusetts.

Barbara Somerville, CSW, MSW, is an Assistant Professor of Social Sciences at Bronx Community College and is a Human Service Fieldwork Coordinator. She was formerly the coordinator of the Marymount College BSW program, then part of the Westchester Social Work Education Consortium. Ms. Somerville was a Social Worker for many years both in New York City and Sydney, Australia.

Lee Stuart has worked as the lead organizer of broad-based organizations affiliated with the Industrial Areas Foundation in the South Bronx and Yonkers, New York, since 1991. Prior to that, she was a founder of the nationwide food assistance program, SHARE (Self-Help and Resource Exchange) and helped establish SHARE in San Diego, California, and southwest Virginia before coming to the South Bronx in 1985 to establish SHARE–New York on what was to have been a temporary leave of absence from an academic career. She holds a Ph.D. in ecology from the University of California–Davis and San Diego State University and was a specialist in arctic ecology before encountering the South Bronx and making a radical career change.

H. Frederick Sweitzer, Ed.D., is the director of the human service program in the College of Education, Nursing, and Health Professions at the University of Hartford, where he has taught for the past nine years. Before coming to the University of Hartford, Mr. Sweitzer taught in the human service program at the University of Massachusetts and served as clinical director of the Maple Valley School, a residential treatment center for emotionally disturbed adolescents. He is also Chairperson of the Division of Education. He has served on the Board of Directors for both the National and New England Organizations for Human Service Education and is currently the editor of *The LINK,* the newsletter for NOHSE. Mr. Sweitzer has published several articles on human service education and practice and is on the editorial board of the journal *Human Service Education.* His professional and consulting interests include human relations, group dynamics, support groups, and experiential education.

Megan C. Sylvester, BA, MA, MSW, is currently a social worker for the Baltimore County Department of Social Services, working in the Families NOW program. She formally coordinated special projects and field training at the Child Welfare League of America. She has been a case manager for persons with chronic and acute mental illness. Ms. Sylvester is a Nationally Certified Counselor.

Rod Underwood was appointed to the first chair in human services in Australia in 1991. Currently, he is Dean of the Faculty of Health and Human Sciences at Edith Cowan University in Perth, Western Australia. Dean Underwood's recent research activities have included a study of the needs of people with intellectual disabilities who are in the criminal justice system, the mental health problems of people in rural communities, and legal issues confronting young people. He has been responsible for the development of human service courses at baccalaureate, master's, and doctoral levels over the past ten years.

David Whelan is Assistant Professor in the Department of Law and Justice Studies at Rowan University in Glassboro, New Jersey. He is the former chair of the master's program in Criminal Justice at Fitchburg State College. Mr. Whelan has ten years of urban law enforcement experience, which included criminal investigation, juvenile affairs, and administration. He is active in community affairs and has worked with several youth groups.

A-B-A-B design, 394
AARP, 240
Abortion, 291
Abuse, 134. *See also* Child
    maltreatment and abuse;
    Domestic violence
Accessibility to client information,
    305
Accountability, 309–310,
    319–320, 388
ACT, 281–282
ACT UP, 209
Action, 271–273
Active listening, 83
Activity theory, 186
ADA, 293
Adaptive Child ego state, 343
Addams, Jane, 24, 171
ADEA, 240, 242
Administrative law, 260
Administrative rule making,
    260
Adolescent pregnancy prevention
    and parenting services, 142
Adolescents. *See* Youth
Adoption Assistance and Child
    Welfare Act (P.L. 96–272),
    148–149
Adoption services, 144
ADR, 106–110
Adult ego state, 343
Advertising, 319
Advocacy, 116
Advocacy/social policy orientation
    to youth work, 177
AFDC, 149
Age discrimination, 242–244
Age Discrimination in
    Employment Act (ADEA),
    240, 242
Ageism, 242
Agency survival, 318
Agency-related knowledge, 71–72
Aging. *See* Older adults

Aid to Families with Dependent
    Children (AFDC), 149
AIDS Care of RI, 205, 206
AIDS Coalition to Unleash Power
    (ACT UP), 209
AIDS cocktail, 204
AIDS service organization (ASO),
    204, 206–207
AIDS/HIV, 197–210
    AIDS agencies, 206–207
    blaming the victim, 209–210
    current issues, 208–210
    deciding whether to be tested,
        208
    employment, 206
    epidemiology, 200–201
    health insurance, 208–209
    housing, 205
    income assistance, 204–205
    mandatory HIV antibody
        testing, 208
    mandatory reporting of sex
        partners, 208
    medical issues, 198–201
    medical/dental needs, 204
    new medications, 209
    pediatric AID/HIV infection,
        144–145
    prevention/education issues,
        202–203
    self-help groups, 207
    social issues, 201–206
    social services, 206
    special needs/skills of workers,
        207
    transmission of HIV, 199–200
    volunteers, 207
    who is most at risk?, 201–202
Alcohol abuse. *See* Substance
    abuse
ALI rule, 313
Alinsky, Saul, 269
Alternative dispute resolution
    (ADR), 106–110

Alzheimer's disease, 240
American Association of Retired
    Persons (AARP), 240
American Humanics, 169
Americans with Disabilities Act
    (ADA), 293
Amish community, 380
And the Band Played On (Shilts),
    198
Anthony, William, 282
APSSW, 25
Arbitration, 106–107
Aronson, Sidney H., 369
ASO, 204, 206–207
Assertive community treatment
    (ACT), 281–282
Assessment, 113–114
Association of Professional
    Schools of Social Work
    (APSSW), 25
Audrey Cohen College, 41–57
Authoritarian style of leadership,
    101
Authors. *See* Contributors
Autogenic training, 364

Bacon, Francis, 389
Baird, Bill, 291
*Basic Attending Skills and Basic
    Listening Sequence,* 79
Battered child syndrome, 156
Battered woman, 134. *See also*
    Domestic violence
Battering, 134
Beers, Clifford, 25
Behavior changer, 8
Behaviorism, 26, 379
Belongingness and love, 10
Benefit-for-cost ratio, 401
Berkowitz, Alan, 234
Best interests of the child,
    308–309
Biographies. *See* Contributors,
    Editors

Blair, Naydean, 317, 414
Blues Net/Cable, 236
Boarder babies, 144
Born to Win (James/Jongeward), 343
Bounty hunting, 319
Brauner rule, 313
Breaking the Ice: A Guide to Understanding People from Other Cultures (Kabagarama), 326
Broad-based community organizing, 269–273. *See also* Community organizing
Brookdale's service learning program, 384, 385
Buckley Amendment, 304
Buckley, Robert, 304
Buddy programs, 207
Burnout, 339–353
  causes, 341
  clients, 348–350
  co-workers, 351–352
  dysfunctional patterns, 345, 347
  fears about oneself, 344
  interpersonal stress, 348–352
  intrapersonal stress, 342–348
  irrational beliefs, 347
  journal, 344–345, 348
  needs you bring, 342
  prevention, 341
  situation analysis technique, 345, 346–347
  supervisors, 350–351
  unfinished business, 342–344
  warning signals, 340
Burnout prevention, 341
Bush, George H. W., 33, 275
Butler, Robert, 242

Caplan, Gerald, 11
Capsule biographies. *See* Contributors, Editors
CAPTA, 148
Career entry/mobility, 337–338
Career tips, 333–335
CASA, 251
Case manager, 216

Case process, 310
Case study, 395–396
Cause-and-effect relationship, 387
Character-building orientation to youth work, 176
Cherniss, Carey, 340
Child abuse, 325
Child Abuse Prevention and Treatment Act (CAPTA), 148, 154
Child-custody mediation, 107–108
Child day care, 142
Child maltreatment and abuse, 153–166
  consequences of maltreatment, 155–156
  ecological model, 162
  emotional maltreatment, 158–159, 160
  environmental theories, 161–162
  extent of problem, 154
  learning theories, 161
  mandated reporting, 162, 164
  physical abuse, 156–157
  physical neglect, 157–158
  psychodynamic theories, 161
  sexual abuse, 159–161
Child placement review program, 251
Child protective services (CPS), 142–143
Child protective services (CPS) agencies, 147–148
Child Protective Services Act, 162
Child Welfare League of America (CWLA), 150–151
Child welfare services, 141–157
  adoption services, 144
  core services, 141
  CPS agencies, 147–148
  cultural competence, 145–147
  CWLA, 150–151
  incarcerated parents, 145
  institutional systems, 147–148
  legislation, 148–150
  Native American children, 148
  out-of-home care services, 143–144

  pediatric AIDS/HIV infection, 144–145
  protective services, 142–143
  public policy, 150
  substance abuse, 147
  support services, 141–142
Children's Bureau, 24
Cimmino, Paul F., 5, 414
Civic agencies, 268
Civil case, 106
Civil commitment, 312
Civil law, 106
Civil mediation, 107
Civil Rights Act of 1964, 291
Civil rights movement, 290–291
Clark, Peter, 301
Client interviews. *See* Interviewing
Client-related stress, 348–350
Client systems, 12
Clients' rights, 302–309, 323–325
  care and treatment, 324
  confidentiality, 306–307, 323, 324–325
  right to consent, 305, 324
  right to privacy, 303–305
  right to refuse treatment, 308
  right to treatment, 307
Clinton, Bill, 33, 36, 275
Closed-ended group, 100
Closed-ended questions, 82–83
Clubok, Miriam, 333, 414
CMHCA, 26, 276
Co-workers and stress, 351–352
Cognitive psychology, 379
Cohen, Audrey, 41, 414
Collective leadership, 270
College students, binge drinking, 233–238
Communication, 113
Community and service networking, 114
Community-based corrections, 251–252
Community living skills and supports, 115
Community Mental Health Centers Act (CMHCA), 26, 276

Community mental health movement, 277
Community organizing, 267–274
  example of actions, 271–273
  focus, 269
  leadership, 270
  membership, 270
  mode of actions, 271
  money, 270–271
  purpose, 269
Community planner, 8
Community policing, 249
Community service, 251
Community support skill standards. *See* CSSS competencies
Community Support Workers Skill Standards Project, 309
Competence-based learning methods, 77
Competency categories, 112–119
  advocacy, 116
  assessment, 113–114
  communication, 113
  community and service networking, 114
  community living skills and supports, 115
  crisis intervention, 116–117
  documentation, 117
  education, training, self-development, 115–116
  facilitation of services, 114–115
  future skill requirements, 119–122 (*See also* Future skill requirements)
  organizational participation, 117
  participant empowerment, 113
  vocational/educational supports, 116
Competency to stand trial, 313
Computer-mediated communication, 379–380
Computer technology. *See* Technology
Confidentiality, 306–307, 323, 324–325

Conflict resolution, 105–110
  ADR, 106–110
  arbitration, 106–107
  formal dispute resolution, 106–110
  informal dispute resolution, 105–106
  legal system, 106
  mediation, 107–110
Congregationally based organizing, 267
Consent, 305, 324
Constitution, U.S., 302
Construction action, 45–46, 53–56
Constructive feedback, 80–81
Contributors, 414–420
  Blair, Naydean, 317, 414
  Cimmino, Paul F., 5, 414
  Clark, Peter, 301
  Clubok, Miriam, 333, 414
  Cohen, Audrey, 41, 414
  Conyard, Shirley Jean, 49, 414
  De Oliveira, Walter, 167, 414
  DeRoberts, Eugene M., 375, 415
  Dewoody, Madelyn, 141, 415
  Diambra, Joel F., 23, 415
  Doyle, Maureen E., 67, 415
  Duclos, Marcel A., 225, 415–416
  Edginton, Christopher R., 167, 416
  French, Margaret J., 63, 416
  Gfroerer, Marianne, 225, 416
  Giovanni, Mary Di, 111, 415
  Hancock, John M., 77, 416–417
  Lee, Michael, 387, 417
  Liederman, David S., 141, 417
  Long, Lorence A., 67, 211, 417
  Maloney, David C., 111, 301, 413
  Mass, Linda, 383, 417
  McKinney, Wm. Lynn, 197, 417
  McPheeters, Harold L., 259, 417–418
  Mehr, Joseph, 275, 418
  Mendez, Rafael, 181, 418

  Munoz-Kantha, Maria, 131, 418
  Niccum, Kathleen J., 239, 418
  Pellicane, Anthony W., 253, 418–419
  Petrie, R. Donna, 359, 419
  Piven, Frances Fox, 33, 419
  Rosenzweig, Stan, 367, 419
  Rother, Franklyn M., 111, 233, 413, 419
  Saldarini, Robert A., 375, 419
  Schmelter-Davis, Lynne, 87, 419
  Shane, Christine Lewis, 287, 419–420
  Somerville, Barbara, 89, 420
  Stuart, Lee, 267, 420
  Sweitzer, H. Frederick, 339, 420
  Sylvester, Megan C., 141, 420
  Whelan, David C., 249, 420
Conyard construction action tool for learning scale, 53
Conyard, Shirley Jean, 49, 414
Corrections, 251–252
Correlation studies, 391–392
Cost analysis, 398–400
Cost-benefit analysis, 401–402
Cost-effectiveness model, 400–401
Council for Standards in Human Service Education (CSHSE), 31–32, 126, 318
Court system, 106
Court-appointed special advocate (CASA), 251
Courts, 250–251
CPS, 142–143
CPS agencies, 147–148
Credentialing, 309
Criminal justice system, 249–252
  corrections, 251–252
  courts, 250–251
  direct supervision management (DSM), 253–254
  police, 249–250
Criminal law, 106
Crisis intervention, 11, 116–117
Crisis intervention theory, 11

Critical Parent ego state, 343
Critical thinking, 336
Crosswalk, 112, 118, 121
Crusher, 345
Crystallized intelligence, 240
CSHSE, 31–32, 126, 318
CSSS competencies, 111–122
    competency categories,
        112–119. *See also*
        Competency categories
    crosswalk, 112, 118
    CSHSE standards, 118
    educational levels, 119
    future skill requirements,
        119–122. *See also* Future
        skill requirements
    historical overview, 111–112
Cultural competence, 145–147,
    326, 364–365
Cultural diversity, 359–366
    future population trends,
        359–360
    human service workers,
        364–365
    kinds of caring, 362–364
    types of programs, 363–364
    values, 360–362, 363
Cultural-performatory approach,
    190
CWLA, 150–151
Cybersex, 378

Data, 388
Data manager, 8
Davis, Jesse, 27
De Oliveira, Walter, 167, 414
Decision-making groups, 92
Deinstitutionalization, 277
Delivery of services, 310–311
Democratic style of leadership,
    101
DeRoberts, Eugene M., 235, 375,
    415
DeSoto, Robert L., 66
Destructive acts, 134
Detached youth work, 172
Dewey, John, 171
Dewoody, Madelyn, 141, 415
Diagnosis/assessment, 310–311

Diambra, Joel F., 23, 415
Direct civic action, 271
Direct supervision management
    (DSM), 253–254
Disabilities, persons with,
    287–296
    ADA, 293–295
    civil rights, 291
    historical images, 288
    historical overview, 287–289
    human service workers, 295
    increased numbers, 290
    Rehabilitation Act, section 504,
        291–292
    technological advances, 290
    timeline, 288–289
Disability rights movement, 289
Dispute resolution. *See* Conflict
    resolution
Distance learning, 377
Diversion programs, 251
Divorce mediation, 107
Dix, Dorothea, 289
Documentation, 117
Domestic violence, 131–139.
    See also Child maltreatment
        and abuse
    available services, 137
    cycle of battering, 135–136
    defined, 134
    emotional abuse, 134
    emotional acts, 134
    extent of problem, 132
    physical abuse, 133–134
    sexual abuse, 134
    shelters, 136–138
    sources of problem, 132–133
Doyle, Maureen E., 67, 415
Drucker Foundation, 169
Drug abuse. *See* Substance abuse
Drug courts, 251
DSM, 253–254
Dual relationships, 311
Duclos, Marcel A., 225, 415–416
Due process, 308
Durham rule, 313
Duty to warn and protect,
    324–325
Dysfunctional patterns, 345, 347

E-mail, 379–380
East Brooklyn Congregations,
    272–273
Ecological model, 162
Economic Opportunity Act, 29
Edginton, Christopher R., 167, 416
Edison, Thomas, 369
Editors, 413
    Harris, Howard S., 413
    Maloney, David C., 111, 301, 413
    Rother, Franklyn M., 111, 413
Education for All Handicapped
    Children Act, 289
Educational groups, 92
Ego states, 343
Eight tips (ETs), 335–337
Elderly persons. *See* Older adults
Electronic mail (e-mail), 379–380
Elizabethan Poor Laws, 6
Ellis, Albert, 347
Ellis, Tony, 318
EMILY's (Early Money Is Like
    Yeast) List, 262
Emoticons, 380
Emotional abuse, 134
Emotional intelligence (EQ), 377
Emotional maltreatment, 158–159,
    160
Empowerment, 41–58
Empowerment chart, 47–48
Environmental theories, 161–162
EQ, 377
Erikson, Erik, 168
Essential Interviewing (Evans
    et al.), 79
Esteem needs, 10
Ethical standards of human
    service professionals, 30
Ethics
    accountability, 319–320
    advertising, 319
    bounty hunting, 319
    case studies, 321–322
    defined, 318
    fraudulent billing, 320
    sexual impropriety, 311–312, 320
    standards for human service
        workers, 329–332
    tips/suggestions, 326

Ethnographic research, 394
Ethnotherapy, 363
ETs, 335–337
Eviction prevention services, 213
Experiential learning, 383
Experimental approach to social research, 389–391
Express consent, 305

Facilitation of services, 114–115
Family AIDS Center for Treatment and Support (FACTS), 205
Family foster care, 144
Family mediation, 108
Family Preservation and Family Support Program, 149
Family psychoeducational interventions, 283
Family sharing, 363
Family therapy and couples groups, 92
Family violence, 132. *See also* Child maltreatment and abuse; Domestic violence
Family-centered crisis services, 142
Federal Privacy Act (P.L. 93–579), 303
Feinstein, Ron, 259
Field experience, 65
Field research, 394–395
Fieldwork, 77
Fines, 251
Flaming, 380
Fluid intelligence, 240
Fontana, V. J., 154
Formal dispute resolution, 106–110
Frankl, Viktor E., 376
Fraudulent billing, 320
French, Margaret J., 63, 416
Freud, Sigmund, 25
Friedan, Betty, 291
Functionalists, 25
Funding cutbacks, 388
Future skill requirements, 119–122
    curriculum goals/objectives, 119–120

curriculum to match competency outcomes, 120
faculty requirements, 119
monitoring of internships, 121
supervision of students, 120–121
support/resources to promote CSSS, 122
technical assistance to training institutions, 121–122

Gay-related immune deficiency (GRID), 198
GBMI, 313–314
Generalist concept, 14
Generic human services concept, 14
Gfroerer, Marianne, 225, 416
Giovanni, Mary Di, 111, 415
Goleman, Daniel, 377
Gramm, Phil, 34
Graying of America, 239. *See also* Older adults
Group formation phase, 94
Group functioning/maintenance phase, 96
Group leadership, 101
Group norms, 102
Group residential care, 144
Groups, 89–104
    closed-ended vs. open-ended, 100
    defined, 90–91
    factors to consider, 99–101
    formation phase, 94–95
    integration, disintegration, reinterpretation, 95
    leadership, 101–103
    long-term *vs.* short-term, 100–101
    maintenance phase, 96–97
    norms, 102
    pregroup phases, 93–94
    programming, 101
    selecting membership, 102
    stages of development, 93–99
    termination phases, 97
    types, 92
Guardian ad litem, 148, 308

Guilty but mentally ill (GBMI), 313–314
Gulick, Luther H., 171

Halfway houses, 252
Hall, G. Stanley, 25, 171, 173
Hancock, John M., 77, 416–417
Handicap. *See* Disabilities, persons with
Hansell's motivation theory, 10
Harris, Howard S., 413
Hartford, Margaret, 93
Health Insurance Portability and Accountability Act (HIPAA), 304–305
Hierarchy of needs, 10
HIP grants, 277
HIPAA, 304–305
History of the Peloponnesian War (Thucydides), 273
HIV. *See* AIDS/HIV
HIV-1, 198
Homeless people, 211–223
    built-in deterrents, 221
    clothing services, 219
    denial of services, 222
    "doing for," 221
    education services for children, 217
    eviction prevention services, 213
    food programs, 214
    health care, 214–215
    housing, 218–219, 221–222
    job-related services, 217
    legal services, 217–218
    mail drops/addresses, 219
    mental health services, 216
    personal sanitation services, 219
    personal storage facilities, 219
    self-help, 220
    shelters, 214
    social services, 216–217
    staff resentment, 222
    substance abuse programs, 215
    thumbnail sketches, 212
    travel support, 220
House meetings, 271

Housing services, 142
Hull House, 24
Human service activity, 6
Human service ideology of the
   individual, 9–11
Human service intervention, 7, 9
Human service model, 7
Human Service Worker, The, 327
Human service workers. *See also*
   Human services
   burnout, 339–353 (*See also*
      Burnout)
   career entry/mobility, 337–338
   career tips, 333–335
   community-based settings,
      in, 124
   competency categories,
      112–119 (*See also*
      Competency categories)
   credentialing, 309
   cultural competence, 145–147,
      326, 364–365
   defined, 123
   delivery of services, 310–311
   duty to warn and product,
      324–325
   employment prospects,
      124–125
   ethical standards, 329–332 (*See
      also* Ethics)
   ETs, 335–337
   generic competencies, 67–68,
      123–124
   interviewing skills, 77–86 (*See
      also* Interviewing)
   keeping up-to-date, 76
   knowledge requirements, 71–73
   occupational titles, 125–126
   professional accountability,
      309–310
   professional identity, 29–31
   professional licensing law, 309
   professionalism, 23–24
   relationship issues, 311–312
   residential settings, in, 124
   roles, 8
   salary ranges, 125
   self-awareness/self-
      management, 74–75
      self-improvement, 75–76
      sexual misconduct, 311–312,
         320
      skills, 68–70
      social service agencies, in, 124
      stress, 342–352
      values, 73–74
Human services. *See also* Human
   service workers
   defined, 6, 23
   future skill requirements,
      119–122 (*See also* Future
      skill requirements)
   professional organizations,
      31–32, 126
   psychology/mental health roots,
      25–27
   self-regulation, 310
   social ideology, 8–9
   social service roots, 24–25
   vocational/school counseling
      roots, 27–28
Human services curricula, 64–65
Human services training
   movement, 317
Humanitarian ethos, 302
Humphrey, Hubert, 302

IAF, 269
ICM, 280
ICPSR, 399
Implied consent, 305
In re Gault, 309
Incarcerated parents, children
   of, 145
Independent Living Initiative Title
   IV-E of the Social Security
   Act, 149
Indian Child Welfare Act, 148
Individual relational meetings,
   271
Individuals with Disabilities
   Education Act, 289
Industrial Areas Foundation (IAF),
   269
Influencing legislation, 263–265
Informal dispute resolution, 105–106
Informal/professional helping,
   contrasted, 70–71

Information-processing (IP) model
   of thinking, 379
Informed consent, 305
Insanity defense, 313
Insurance, 325–326
Integrative paradigm, 174
Intensive case management (ICM),
   280
Internet, 370–372
Interpersonal stress, 348–352
Interuniversity Consortium of
   Political and Social Research
   (ICPSR), 399
Interviewing, 77–86
   attending skills, 82
   constructive feedback, 80–81
   encouraging skills, 83
   evaluating skill development,
      84–85
   greeting client/beginning the
      interview, 82
   instructor's role, 78–79
   listening skills, 83–84
   mid-term interview (observer
      rating form), 408–409
   mid-term interview self-
      evaluation paper,
      410–411
   mid-term reflection paper, 85
   observing skills, 82
   preparing, 81–82
   questioning skills, 82–83
   resources/instructional
      methods, 79–81
   simulated interviews, 80
   students' role, 79
   summarization/ending the
      interview, 84
*Interviewing in Action: Process
   and Practice,* 79
Intrapersonal stress, 342–348
IP model of thinking, 379
Irrational beliefs, 347
*Issues and Ethics in the Helping
   Professions* (Corey et al.),
   318, 347

James, William, 25
Johnson, Lyndon B., 36

Joint Commission on Mental Illness and Health, 276
Journal, 344–345, 348
Kabagarama, Daisy, 326
Kassenbaum, Nancy, 304
Kempe, C. H., 153
Kendall, Jane C., 384
Kennedy, John F., 36, 302
Kennedy, Robert, 302
Kennedy, Ted, 304
King, Jim, 63
King, Martin Luther, 290, 302
Kinship care, 144
"Know It!", 233–238

Laissez-faire style of leadership, 101
Lathrop, Julia, 24
Law of Settlement, 6
Leadership style, 101–102
Learner/mentor relationship, 189
Learning contracts, 121
Learning theories, 161
Lee, Joseph, 171
Lee, Michael, 387, 417
Legal issues, 301–315
    accessibility to client information, 305
    best interests of the child, 308–309
    clients' rights, 302–309
    due process, 308
    malpractice (delivery of services), 310–311
    mandated reporting, 314
    mental health, 312–314
    negligence, 311
    privileged communication, 306
Legal system, 106
Leininger, Madeleine M., 362
Leisure orientation to youth work, 176
Lewin, Kurt, 101
Liberman, Robert Paul, 282
Liederman, David S., 141, 417
Life Goes On, 288
Lippitt, R., 101
Listening, 83
Lobbying, 262–265

Lonely Crowd, The (Riesman et al.), 376
Long, Lorence A., 67, 211, 417
Long-term group, 100

Macropractice, 13
Macrosocial systems, 13
Malinowski, Bronislaw, 394
Maloney, David C., 30, 111, 301, 413
Malpractice (delivery of services), 310–311
Managed health care, 326
Mandated reporting, 314
Mandatory HIV antibody testing, 208
Marcel, Gabriel, 379
Maslach, Christine, 340
Maslow's hierarchy of needs, 10
Maslow, Abraham, 10
Mass, Linda, 383, 417
May, Rollo, 376, 380
McLuhan, Marshall, 368
McKinney, Wm. Lynn, 197, 30, 417
McNaughton rule, 313
McPheeters, Harold L., 4, 14, 15, 28, 29, 63
    capsule biography, 417–418
    letter to Paul Cimmino, 19–21
    selection (Policy and Politics), 259–265
Mediation, 107–110
Medical model, 7
Mehr, Joseph, 275, 418
Mendez, Rafael, 181, 418
Mental health, 275–285
    assertive community treatment (ACT), 281–282
    civil commitment, 312
    family psychoeducational interventions, 283
    future directions, 284
    general principles, 280
    historical overview, 276–279
    insanity defense, 313–314
    legal issues, 312–314
    psychosocial rehabilitation, 282–283

Mental Health Study Act, 26
MEPA, 149–150
Meta-analysis, 399–400
Micropractice, 13
Microsocial systems, 13
Mid-term reflection paper, 85
Mobilizer, 8
Modem, 370
Modern Times, 376
Moore, Gordon, 370
Moore's law, 370
Moral education, 172
Morals, 318. *See also* Ethics
Moratorium, 168
Motivation theory (Hansell), 10
Movements, 268
Multiethnic Placement Act (P.L. 103–82), 149
Munoz-Kantha, Maria, 131, 418
Murray, Charles, 34

National Association of Alcoholism and Drug Abuse Counselors (NAADAC), 228
National Committee for the Prevention of Child Abuse (NCPCA), 154–155
National Defense Education Act (NDEA), 28
National Institute of Mental Health (NIMH), 276
National Organization for Human Service Education (NOHSE), 31, 126
Native American child welfare matters, 148
Natural Child ego state, 343
"Nature of Morality, The" (Ellis), 318
NCPCA, 154–155
NDEA, 28
Needs analysis, 388
Negligence, 311
Nehemiah Program, 272–273
Niccum, Kathleen J., 239, 418
NIMH, 276
NIMH Hospital Improvement Program (HIP) grants, 277
No Pity (Shapiro), 288

NOHSE, 31, 126
Non-alcoholic happy hours, 236–237
Nursing homes, 242
Nurturing Parent ego state, 343

Oates, Kim, 138
OBRA, 149
Of Mice and Men, 287
Older adults, 239–247
  ADEA, 240, 242
  age discrimination, 242–244
  Alzheimer's disease, 240
  cultural aspects of aging, 241–242
  economic aspects of aging, 241
  human service workers, 243–244, 246
  job opportunities for human service workers, 246
  nursing homes, 242
  physical aspects of aging, 239–240
  programming techniques, 244–246
  psychological aspects of aging, 240–241
Omnibus Budget Reconciliation Act (P.L. 103–66), 149
Omnibus Victim and Protection Act, 106
Open-ended group, 100
Open-ended questions, 83
Opportunity to work, 65–66
Organizational participation, 117
Organized money, 270
Orton, William, 369
Out-of-home care services, 143–144
Outreach worker, 8

P.L. 93–579, 303
P.L. 96–272, 148–149
P.L. 103–66, 149
P.L. 103–82, 149
P.L. 104–193, 149
PAC, 262
Paraphrasing, 83–84
Parens patriae, 308, 309

Parent-teen mediation, 108
Parole, 252
Parsons, Frank, 27
Participant empowerment, 113
Participatory research, 396–398
Pediatric AIDS/HIV infection, 144–145
Peer reviews, 310
Pellicane, Anthony W., 253, 418–419
Performance, 183, 187–189
Performing, 187
Perkins, Wesley, 234, 237
Personal growth, 65
Personal Responsibility and Work Opportunity Reconciliation Act (P.L. 104–193), 149
Persons living with AIDS (PWAs). *See* AIDS/HIV
Persons with disabilities. *See* Disabilities, persons with
Petrie, R. Donna, 359, 419
PHI, 305
Philosophical analysis, 387
Physical abuse, 133–134, 156–157
Physical neglect, 157–158
Physiological needs, 10
Piven, Frances Fox, 33, 419
Police, 249–250
Political action committee (PAC), 262
Politics, 261–265
Post-traumatic stress disorder (PTSD), 87–88
Power, 269
Pregroup convening phase, 93
Pregroup private phase, 93
Pregroup public phase, 93
President's Commission on Law Enforcement (1968), 250
Pretrial release programs, 251
Privacy, 303–305
Privacy Act, 326
Privacy Protection Study Commission, 304
Privileged communication, 306
Proactive human services, 9
Probation, 251
Problem-solving groups, 92

Problem-solving policing, 249
Product test (insanity plea), 313
Professional accountability, 309–310, 319–320
Professional identity, 29–31
Professional/informal helping, contrasted, 70–71
Professional journals, 76
Professional licensing law, 309
Professional organizations, 31–32, 126
Professionalism, 335
Program evaluation, 388
Projection, 344
Prosocial paradigm, 173–174
Protected health information (PHI), 305
Protective services, 142–143
Psychodynamic theories, 161
Psychoeducational model, 283
Psychology/mental health roots, 25–27
Psychosocial rehabilitation, 282–283
Psychotherapy groups, 92
PTSD, 87–88
Public health (social welfare) model, 7
Public policy, 260–261
PWAs. *See* AIDS/HIV

Quasi-experimental research models, 391–394

Reagan, Ronald, 275
Reasonable accommodation, 292
Recreation groups, 92
Reed, Annai, 27
Reflection of content, 83–84
Reflection of feelings, 84
Regulation writing, 260
Rehabilitation Act, section 504, 291–292
Religious orientation to youth work, 177
Remedial paradigm, 173
Research, 387–405
  case study, 395–396
  cost analysis, 400–402

experimental approach, 389–391

field research, 394–395

goals, 387–388

human service workers, 402–403

meta-analysis, 399–400

participatory approach, 396–398

quasi-experimental models, 391–394

secondary data analysis, 398–399

single-subject design, 393–394

time-series design, 392–393

what is it?, 387

why done?, 388–390

Restitution, 251

Richards, Lysander S., 27

Right to consent, 305, 324

Right to Education for All Handicapped Children Act, 291

Right to privacy, 303–305

Right to refuse treatment, 308

Right to treatment, 307

Rights of human service clients. *See* Clients' rights

Riis, Jacob, 171

Roberts, Ed, 291

Roe v. Wade, 291

Rogers, Carl, 84

Roosevelt, Franklin D., 36

Rosenzweig, Stan, 367, 419

Rother, Franklyn M., 30, 111, 233, 413, 419

Safety needs, 10

Saldarini, Robert A., 375, 419

Schmelter-Davis, Lynne, 87, 419

Schneuer Sub-professional Career Act, 29

Scientific method, 387

Search engines, 371

Secondary data analysis, 398–399

Section 504 of Rehabilitation Act, 291–292

Self-actualization, 10

Self-awareness/self-management, 74–75

Self-development, 65

Self-healing methods, 363–364

Self-help, 220

Self-help groups, 92

Self-talk, 336

Seliger, Michael, 37, 419

Senior citizens. *See* Older adults

Service agencies, 268

Service delivery, 310–311

Service learning, 383–385

Settlement house movement, 24

Sexual abuse, 134, 159–161

Sexual impropriety (human service workers), 311–312, 320

Shane, Christine Lewis, 287, 419–420

Shapiro, Joseph, 288

Short-term group, 100

Simulated interviews, 80

Single-subject design, 393–394

Situation analysis technique, 345, 346–347

Skill-building recreation groups, 92

Skilled Helper, The (Egan), 79

Skinner, B. F., 26

Sling Blade, 287

Sobering News, The, 235

Social health generalist, 14

Social ideology of human services, 8–9

Social norms project for college students, 233–238

Social pedagogy orientation to youth work, 177

Social service agencies, 268

Social service orientation to youth work, 176

Social service roots, 24–25

Social trends, 389

Socialization groups, 92

Sociotherapy, 363

Solomon, Harry C., 276

Somerville, Barbara, 89, 420

South Bronx Churches, 271–272

Southern Regional Education Board (SREB), 8, 30, 277, 317

Sports/fitness orientation to youth work, 176

Sputnik, 27

SREB, 8, 30, 277, 317

SSDI, 205

SSI, 149

Starr, Ellen Gates, 24

Steinberg, Lisa, 154

Steinem, Gloria, 291

Stress, 342–352. *See also* Burnout

Stuart, Lee, 267, 420

Student drinking, 233–238

Substance abuse, 225–232

challenges for human service workers, 225–227

child welfare, 147

drug education programs, 227

homelessness, 215

in-hospital treatment program, 228

outpatient services, 229

prevention, 227–228

required skills/training for social workers, 229–230

residential treatment center, 228–229

social norms approach for college students, 233–238

treatment, 228–229

Summarization, 84

Supervisors and stress, 350–351

Supplemental security disability income (SSDI), 205

Supplementary security income (SSI), 149

Survey studies, 392

Sweitzer, H. Frederick, 339, 420

Sylvester, Megan C., 141, 420

TA, 343

TANF, 149

Task-oriented groups, 92

Teacher-educator, 8

Technology, 367–381

Amish community, 380

computer-mediated communications, 379–380

e-mail, 379–380

education, 377–378

(continued)
   ...et uses, 370
   loneliness/alienation, 376–378
   personal development, 371
   professional development, 371
   sample Internet search,
     371–372
   search engines, 371
   telecommuting, 378
   therapeutic services, 378–379
   websites for further reference,
     373
   work environment, 378
Technology-induced alienation,
   376–378
Teen pregnancy, 181–192
Teens. *See* Youth
Telecommuting, 378
Temporary Assistance to Needy
   Families (TANF), 149
Testimentio, 364
Therapeutic relationship, 311
Therapeutic State, 313
Therapy groups, 92
Therapy/treatment, 311
Thorndike, Edward, 26
Thucydides, 273
Ticket to Work and Work
   Incentives Improvement Act,
   294–295
Time-series design, 392–393

Torts, 106
Transactional analysis (TA), 343
Truthfulness, 74

U.S. Constitution, 302
Umbreit, Mark, 108
Unfinished business, 342–344

Values, 73–74
Victim-offender mediation,
   108–109
Virtual reality (VR) gaming, 377
Vocational Rehabilitation Act, 27
Vocational/career orientation to
   youth work, 177
Vocational/educational supports,
   116
Vocational/school counseling
   roots, 27–28
Vocophy (Richards), 27
VR gaming, 377
Vygotsky, Lev, 182

Wadsworth, Benjamin, 131
Walk for Life, 206
Walker, Lenore, 135
War on Poverty, 317
Watson, John, 26
Weaver, Eli, 27
Weinstein, Gerald, 345
Welfare reform, 33–40

Wellman, Bob, 85
Whelan, David C., 249, 420
White, Evelyn, 134
White, R. K., 101
Widow's pension, 24
Women's movement, 290–291
Wundt, Wilhelm, 25

Youth, 167–180. *See also* Child
   maltreatment and abuse
   future directions, 178
   general principles, 178–179
   historical overview, 170–171
   integrative paradigm, 174
   orientations to youth work,
     175–178
   Pregnant Productions
     (Vygotsky-inspired
     approach), 181–192
   prosocial paradigm, 173–174
   remedial paradigm, 173
   terminology, 172
Youth development, 172
Youth leaders, 172
Youth services, 172
Youth studies, 172
Youth work, 172
Youth work orientations, 175–178

Zone of proximal development
   (ZPD), 182